World Class Supply Management^{SM}

The Key to Supply Chain Management

World Class Supply Management^{SM}

The Key to Supply Chain Management

Seventh Edition

David N. Burt
University of San Diego

Donald W. Dobler
Colorado State University Emeritus

Stephen L. Starling
University of San Diego

McGraw-Hill
Irwin

Boston   Burr Ridge, IL   Dubuque, IA   Madison, WI   New York
San Francisco   St. Louis   Bangkok   Bogotá   Caracas   Kuala Lumpur
Lisbon   London   Madrid   Mexico City   Milan   Montreal   New Delhi
Santiago   Seoul   Singapore   Sydney   Taipei   Toronto

McGraw-Hill Higher Education

*A Division of The **McGraw-Hill** Companies*

WORLD CLASS SUPPLY MANAGEMENT:
THE KEY TO SUPPLY CHAIN MANAGEMENT^{SM}
Published by McGraw-Hill/Irwin, a business unit of The McGraw-Hill Companies, Inc., 1221
Avenue of the Americas, New York, NY, 10020. Copyright © 2003, 1996, 1990, 1984, 1977,
1971, 1965 by The McGraw-Hill Companies, Inc. All rights reserved. No part of this publication
may be reproduced or distributed in any form or by any means, or stored in a database or
retrieval system, without the prior written consent of The McGraw-Hill Companies, Inc.,
including, but not limited to, in any network or other electronic storage or transmission, or
broadcast for distance learning.
Some ancillaries, including electronic and print components, may not be available to customers
outside the United States.

This book is printed on acid-free paper.

domestic   1 2 3 4 5 6 7 8 9 0 DOC/DOC 0 9 8 7 6 5 4 3 2
international   1 2 3 4 5 6 7 8 9 0 DOC/DOC 0 9 8 7 6 5 4 3 2

ISBN   0-07-229070-6

Publisher: *John E. Biernat*
Sponsoring editor: *Andy Winston*
Editorial assistant: *Tammy Higham*
Marketing manager: *Lisa Nicks*
Project manager: *Natalie J. Ruffatto*
Production supervisor: *Gina Hangos*
Coordinator freelance design: *Mary L. Christianson*
Producer, Media technology: *Melissa Kansa*
Lead supplement producer: *Cathy L. Tepper*
Senior digital content specialist: *Brian Nacik*
Photo research coordinator: *Jeremy Cheshareck*
Photo researcher: *Catherine Nance*
Cover photograph: © PhotoDisc
Typeface: *10/12 Times New Roman*
Compositor: *Carlisle Communications, Ltd.*
Printer: *R. R. Donnelley*

Library of Congress Cataloging-in-Publication Data

Burt, David N.
    World class supply management: The key to supply chain management/David N. Burt,
Donald W. Dobler, Stephen L. Starling.—7th ed.
        p. cm.
    Rev. ed. of: Purchasing and supply management/Donald W. Dobler.
    Includes index.
    ISBN 0-07-229070-6 (alk. paper) — ISBN 0-07-112310-5 (international: alk. paper)
    1. Industrial procurement. 2. Purchasing. 3. Materials management. I. Dobler, Donald W.
Purchasing and supply management. II. Starling, Stephen L. III. Title.
HD39.5 .B875 2003
658.7—dc21

                                                                      2002021920
INTERNATIONAL EDITION ISBN 0-07-112310-5
Copyright © 2003. Exclusive rights by The McGraw-Hill Companies, Inc. for manufacture and
export. This book cannot be re-exported from the country to which it is sold by McGraw-Hill.
The International Edition is not available in North America.

www.mhhe.com

ABOUT THE AUTHORS

David N. Burt   is Distinguished Professor of Supply Chain Management and Director of the University of San Diego's undergraduate and graduate programs in supply chain management. He is founder and director of USD's Supply Chain Management Institute and of the Strategic Supply Management Forum, an annual meeting of innovative supply management professionals from North America, Europe, and Australia. Under Dr. Burt's leadership, the University of San Diego initiated two graduate hybrid residence/Internet programs in 2002. These programs transfer cutting-edge knowledge and practices, minimize time away from the participant's workplace, develop leaders in supply chain management, develop agents of change, and provide immediate payback to sponsoring firms. Dr. Burt is an active member of the Institute for Supply Management™ and the Purchasing Council of the American Management Association. Dr. Burt's articles have appeared in *Harvard Business Review, Sloan Management Review, California Management Review, The Journal of Purchasing and Materials Management,* and *Thexis.* In 1991, Dr. Burt was appointed the National Association of Purchasing Management Professor of Management. He has consulted with firms including IBM, Motorola, Lockheed, Avery Dennison, Southern California Edison, and Gateway with the objective of upgrading their procurement operations to world-class status. Dr. Burt received his B.A. in Economics at the University of Colorado, M.S.I.A at the University of Michigan, and Ph.D. in Logistics from Stanford University.

Donald Dobler   is a former Corporate Vice President for the National Association of Purchasing Management (NAPM), where he was responsible for its certification and education programs. He is also Dean Emeritus of the College of Business of Colorado State University. Earlier in his career he worked as an engineer for Westinghouse Electric Corporation, and later as a manager of Purchasing and Materials for FMC Corporation at one of its industrial chemical operations. Throughout his career, Don Dobler has been active as a consultant to manufacturing and service organizations in both the operations and the educational/training areas. For 17 years he served as editor of the *International Journal of Purchasing and Materials Management* (now *Supply Chain Management*), the scholarly publication in the field. Dr. Dobler has published widely and has been co-editor of the *Purchasing Handbook* and the *CPM Study Guide.* In 1987, he received NAPM's Shipman Gold Medal for distinguished service to the profession. He earned his Ph.D. degree in Management from Stanford University.

Stephen L. Starling   is an Associate Professor of Supply Chain Management (SCM) at the University of San Diego. He has worked with the faculty and staff in the Supply Chain Management Institute (SCMI) to develop world-class hybrid residence/Internet graduate SCM education programs and to bolster USD's 20-year tradition of excellence in SCM. Perhaps most important to Stephen is his love of working with students on campus in the Supply Chain Management Association (SCMA), which is quickly becoming one of the strongest student organizations in the United States. SCMA sponsors or co-sponsors about 70 events per year at USD, with a focus on creating agents of change who will enter the workforce armed with cutting-edge, but practical, knowledge. Stephen served in officer positions in two Institute for Supply Management™ (ISM) chapters in the San Francisco Bay Area, including President of the Diablo Valley Chapter in 2000–2001. He earned his Ph.D. from the University of Pittsburgh in 1998. His first position in academia was with California State University, Hayward, where he initiated a new MBA program in SCM and taught in MBA programs in Hong Kong, Beijing, and Singapore. He has taught 17 different courses and 13 different continuing education seminars, all focused on Supply Chain Management. He has published 16 research papers and proceedings, given 23 professional seminars, and conducted 18 research and consulting projects with industry. He also initiated the Supply Chain Management research track for The Western Decision Sciences Institute. His research is focused on supply management within the context of supply chain management.

BRIEF CONTENTS

CONTENTS

x

Chapter **3**

Supply Management: An Organization Spanning Activity   35

Chapter **4**

Supply Management: Implementor of Three of the Firm's Social Responsibilities   52

PART 2
Enabling Concepts   75

PART 3
The Requirements Process   207

PART 5
Strategic Cost Management   393

Chapter **17**
Pricing   395

Chapter **22**

Supplier Development   511

PART 7
Institutional and Government Procurement   575

PART 8
World Class Supply Chain Management 617

FOREWORD

THE EVOLUTION OF PURCHASING TO SUPPLY CHAIN MANAGEMENT[*]

Richard L. Pinkerton, Ph.D., C.P.M.[†]

We include this article because it provides a good introduction to how purchasing has gone from procurement of supplies to managing the supply chain. It provides a context for many of the ideas introduced in this text and an overview of what supply chain management is all about. Finally, it includes more than 30 references, many of which may be useful to you in learning more about the current and future directions of supply management. Earlier versions of the article have been published in the following:

1. Dieter Hahn and Lutz Kaufmann, eds., *Handbuch Industrielles Beschaffungs Management: Internationale Konzepte—Innovative Instrumente—Aktvelle Praxisbeispiele.* Betriebswirtschaftlicher Verlag Dr. Th. Gabler GmBH, Wiesbaden, Germany, 1999, pp. 399–414.

2. *World Markets Series Business Briefing: European Purchasing and Logistics Strategies.* Published by World Markets Research Centre, London, July 1999, pp. 16–28.

3. *Contract Management,* vol. 40, no. 2, February 2000, pp. 19–26. The Magazine of The National Contract Management Association, Vienna, VA.

4. John A. Woods and the National Association of Purchasing Management, eds., *The Purchasing and Supply Yearbook, 2000 Edition.* McGraw-Hill, New York, pp. 3–16.

INTRODUCTION, DEFINITION AND OUTLINE

The term "supply chain management" has become a popular buzzword, probably first used by consultants in the late 1980s and then analyzed by the academic community in the 1990s. If one wants a simple definition, supply chain management links all the supply interacting organizations in an integrated two-way communication system to manage high

---

[*]Revised in 2001.

[†]Richard L. Pinkerton has been a Professor of Marketing and Logistics (now Professor Emeritus) at the Sid Craig School of Business at California State University, Fresno, since 1986. In 1996, he was elected Chair of the department and designated Professor Emeritus in 2000. His industrial experience includes several years as Senior Marketing Research Analyst for the Harris Corporation of Melbourne, Florida, and Manager of the Sales Department at the Webb-Triax Company of Cleveland, Ohio. He is a specialist in price-cost analysis within the field of supply management. He has served as Chair of the Academic Planning Committee of the National Association of Purchasing Management (NAPM) and chaired the NAPM Research Symposium in 1992. Professor Pinkerton received his Ph.D. in marketing from the University of Wisconsin.

quality inventory in the most effective and efficient manner. This concept can be rather abstract and vague because it embraces a multitude of policies, procedures, and organizational structures. As one supply chain expert states, "you cannot telephone, fax or e-mail the chain." In very plain terms it means the buyer of tungsten for laser lamp manufacturing must have a long-term relationship with the tungsten processor and also ensure that the processor has a strategic plan to procure the raw tungsten; i.e., monitor the supplier of each supplier to some manageable number of levels. Why all the focus on supplies and the purchasing activities? The average manufacturing organization spends about 53.2 percent of every sales dollar on raw materials, components, and maintenance repair operating (MRO) purchases.

How and why did this concept develop; what are its prerequisites; and how does an organization implement what can be a very vague philosophy? It is the purpose of this article first to trace the evolution and the development from a passive-reactive purchasing function focused on paper trails and inward orientation to the proactive strategic supply chain concept which integrates the supply functions over an entire channel of distribution. We must learn the history to appreciate and understand the enormous change from purchasing as a cost center to supply management as a "value adder."

The analysis then moves to the necessary prerequisites for establishing both the philosophy and practice of an integrated supply system as part of the firm's strategic planning as against a purely tactical orientation. It is the author's experience that, while the term "supply chain management" is in vogue, only the *Fortune* 500–level firms (and not all of them at that) have, or are actually implementing, this concept. Certainly, the typical purchasing manager is still internally focused and rather reactive as he/she tries to implement the concept while operating under reactive organizational structures, policies, and procedures. To state that one embraces supply chain management is one thing; to actually do it is quite another.

Finally, a blueprint for change will be addressed that, hopefully, will give direction to those organizations which are serious about making what is a drastic change in procurement thinking and action. Indeed, many large firms have had to bring in an entirely new management team to effect this massive reorientation and execution. The author primarily uses professional books as they are longer lasting, they have more impact on practitioners, and they usually advocate creative change. There is no attempt to reference all the major contributors as this is an impossible task. The key people cited by the author are those studied by the author. Finally, this is a conceptual paper and not the usual survey.

EVOLUTION: FROM PAPER TO PROFITS

The first really new broader view of purchasing was the materials management concept. Undoubtedly, this movement was accelerated by the Second World War (WWII), the rapid growth of aerospace firms, and the influence of military logistics. The military always embraced a broad view of "supply" and the large manufacturing firms of WWII were influenced by, and clearly in many cases directed by, the War Department (and later by the Defense Department) to organize their defense contracting activities to reassemble their military customers. By the mid-1950s, articles were appearing on materials management and the first textbook on the subject of this broader view of supply appeared in 1962.[1]

It is also thought that the rapid post–WWII expansion of the marketing concept, which also grouped similar activities together, stimulated a similar addition in other functional areas. For example, by 1974, traffic and transportation activities gradually expanded into a definition using the term "logistics" defined as a combination of materials management and physical distribution management.[2] The reader should be warned that both movements encountered serious opposition as both advocates were viewed as taking over "my authority and responsibility." Marketing directors felt that finished goods distribution was their responsibility and production managers felt that production control and in-plant materials movement was their function. More will be written on this conflict later in the paper, as the dispute continues.

Although there are many different definitions of materials management, most experts seem to include the following subfunctions.[3]

1. Inventory control, or "how many" parts, pieces, components, raw material and finished goods.

2. Production control, or "when" including shop floor control–scheduling along with the materials handling, storage, and movements necessary to reach work-assembly stations. As any production manager knows, this is the key to his or her control over operations and few want to give up this activity for obvious reasons.

3. Subcontracting, or "what systems do we buy?"—this is a very misused word but in its purest form, it is a type of make/buy/outsourcing decision-making based on a prime contract held by the manufacturer. The best original examples are from defense contractors who could not possibly possess all the technology, time, ability, or capacity to produce all the subsystems of a final weapons system such as an aircraft, tank or warship. This concept is even more popular today as the emphasis to concentrate on core competencies continues, a focus which began in a major way during WWII. The key distinction here is buying a system of multiple assembled parts as against one component at a time.

4. Stores, or "work station storage and supporting or indirect materials."

5. Purchasing-procurement, or "buying" pieces, pounds, gallons, tons of raw material and maintenance, repair and operating supplies. In a few firms, this included capital equipment but purchases of this magnitude were (and still are) seldom the decision-making responsibility of purchasing.

6. Transportation, or "incoming and finished goods freight movement."

7. Salvage, or "disposing of surplus and scrap."

The advent of materials management and computer tools that came with it as Materials Requirement Planning (MRP) and Material Resource Planning (MRP II), pioneered by Oliver Wight, forced the organization—for the first time—to look at the entire flow of both incoming materials and the outgoing finished goods as a system.[4] This integration greatly improved internal production communication but did not bring about much improvement in external communication with suppliers or internal communication on the determination of specifications. Curiously, it accepted rather poor quality levels and did not involve suppliers at the design stage as the design engineers were still designing in isolation.

It also forced trade-off analysis. In theory, and in practice for many firms, one materials vice president or director and their staff would now look at the "big picture" and resolve the inherent conflict among accounting-finance, production, and marketing managers. For example, accounting-finance wants zero inventory, production wants lots of safety stock "just-in-case," and marketing wants warehouses filled with finished products to satisfy the unrealistic due dates they promised customers. Purchasing was caught in the middle with constantly changing delivery dates and/or quantities ordered from suppliers who have shaky quality and little, if any, long-range knowledge of the buyer's requirements. Again, design engineering continued to act on its own initiatives with little input from operations and suppliers.

D. S. Ammer was the first academic, and Victor H. Pooler, Jr., was the first practitioner, to write books and articles stressing the need to view purchasing as a potential profit center.[5] Both authors used the materials management concept to demonstrate that material savings directly improve profits as a higher leverage factor than merely increasing sales. However, Pooler still emphasized that purchasing could accomplish the same result on its own and he was the first to coin the term "proactive procurement."[6]

Materials management had a large following in the period from 1960 to 1985. During these years, the well-known, ever-intensifying competition from Japan with its growing reputation for high quality products and a different management style, started to panic U.S. executives at huge firms. They started to lose market share and, in some cases, total markets. Included in the analysis of Japanese methods, aside from the well-known Total Quality Management (TQM) process, was a growing awareness that they had also a totally different supply management chain system. One of the first, if not *the* first, observer of this change in procurement operation was D. N. Burt who in 1984, introduced the Integrated Procurement Systems or "IPS" as he called it. Burt defines IPS:

> The procurement of material and services is a process that cuts across organizational boundaries. The process includes activities in marketing, engineering, operations, production, planning, quality assurance, inventory control, purchasing, and finance. Integration of the procurement activities performed by these departments results in a synergism, a situation where the whole is greater than the sum of its parts.[7]

Thus Burt recognized and developed the cross-functional team approach which builds on the synergy advantages of materials management but expands it to include suppliers at the planning and design stage in a partnership atmosphere. He emphasized total ownership costs and the fact that component material price is merely one, and usually not the key, cost driver as is poor quality, improper specifications, late delivery, rework, and other critical cost drivers identified by the Japanese. Burt's 1984 book represents a major bridge from materials management to supply chain management. Although little read, this first major work by Burt deserves to be a procurement classic.

Another important author and an outstanding production manager/analyst at IBM is Witt. In 1986, Witt wrote a small trade book which may have triggered the "chain" aspect of a total logistics process.[8] He may be the first production manager to analyze the entire channel of distribution including the identification of total inventory in the pipeline from raw materials to finished goods. Like Burt's book, Witt's was little read but it was another big step in the march to supply chain management. Perhaps we should call him the father of Logistics Early Involvement or "LEI."

Building on the ideas and writings of Burt and Witt, although never quoting either, Leenders and Blenkhorn who, in 1988, wrote a trade book with a fascinating title, *Reverse Marketing*.[9] The principal contribution of this book is the 11-step process purchasing can use proactively to approach suppliers. In other words, purchasing takes the initiative to obtain supplier support and involvement in a variety of projects to reduce procurement cost and improve performance. This concept is a form of purchasing research, a subject developed by Harold E. Fearon, a key academic leader in purchasing circles.[10] The significant value of the work by Leenders and Blenkhorn is that the book sold well, thereby helping to promote the ideas and concepts of Ammer, Burt, Witt, Fearon and others who pioneered the movement to supply chain management.

During the period from 1984 to 1997, we see a proliferation of books and articles with slightly different versions, more examples, and clever titles but all focused on proactive strategic procurement, supply chain management based on a number of prerequisites which will be developed in the next section. However, a few key developments and works of this period must be cited.

As American industry continued its fascination with Japanese manufacturing systems and management with particular focus on just-in-time (JIT) production and supply, a method only made possible by TQM, the improvement of transportation networks and cycle time reduction became mandatory. With suppliers far more dispersed than in Japan, any JIT system to decrease inventory required a new emphasis to reduce time to produce, ship, and use. Deregulation of the transportation industry and the development of ever lower cost microprocessing computers and special software programs would promote integrated logistics, the first real "chain" concept. LaLonde, Grabner, and Robeson might be the first academics to promote integrated distribution systems in 1970.[11]

One of the logistics pioneers is William C. Copacino, a managing partner at Andersen Consulting and former consultant at Arthur D. Little, Inc. Copacino is a frequent writer for *Transportation Management* magazine and, from 1986 to the present, wrote extensively on integrated logistics and the supply chain management concept. His 1986 definition is a good start at understanding how the word "chain" is used to link all the related activities first identified by Ammer's materials management concept.[12]

Copacino writes:

> The total cost concept of logistics is based on the interrelationship of supply, manufacturing, and distribution costs. Put in another way, ordering, inventory, transportation, production set-up, warehousing, customer service, and other logistics costs are interdependent.

Copacino reinforces the concept of trade-offs which are only possible when inventory, supply, production, and transportation decisions are analyzed simultaneously. This helps to avoid cost reductions of, say, 10 percent in one area, which in reality inflate costs by 15 percent in another. This is the same theme argued by Burt in his 1984 book, that is, the IPS system, and Witt in his 1986 book. As Copacino observes, "For example, this full system view will quickly identify the cost, service, and velocity impact of any poorly conceived practices such as the tendency among buyers to procure large order quantities and generate bloated inventories because they are measured solely on the purchase price."[13]

The early General Motors (GM) experiment with JIT and TQM and supply chain management at the Buick plant in Flint, Michigan, was only a partial success as the auto giant learned that "Buick City," as it was called, was far more complicated than imagined.[14] One does not make such massive changes overnight even with gigantic resources. However, Buick City provided GM with many important chain management lessons, including how to make high quality cars before being scheduled to close by the end of 1999.[15]

Other logistics "chain" pioneers include A. J. Martin and R. L. Harmon. Martin's book, *Distribution Resource Planning,* talks about "total marketing channel integration" and how the term "logistics" is replacing the term "distribution." Martin develops his version of Quick Response/Continuous Replenishment (QR/CR) which is an adaptation of MRP and MRPII.[16]

Harmon talks about "links" and "demand update chain" and, like Martin, stresses the need to eliminate the middleman with what he calls strategy No. 1. "The first step [in establishing a networkwide system] is for the company to implement the system in its own distribution and production facilities, with linkage to the first tier vendors a second priority. Later phases would add additional supply network tiers to the already operational system."[17] The ultimate goal is to have inventory continuously moving in a pipeline and never in storage.

Martin, Harmon, Copacino, Bowersox, Lambert, Stock, and other logistics visionaries seem to concentrate (understandably) their analysis on the huge retail channel systems to "link" or integrate the supply chain from raw material to the producer to the retail outlet to the final customer.[18] The heart of this integration is the real-time computer data systems which share rather long-term demand schedules and release dates with all members of the channel. Such systems obviously require long-term partnerships—contracts with the trust so necessary to the sharing of sensitive information. In addition, the actual shipment orders are perpetually released, usually on a daily basis by electronic means.

Many of the manufacturers of consumer goods are now using "third party" service providers, such as integrated logistics firms, to run the continuous pipeline. The other requirements include the very latest material handling and bar coding equipment.[19] All these developments have promoted the rapid growth of distribution centers and the concept of "cross docking" or incoming shipments from the suppliers being immediately transferred to outbound trucks, i.e., boxes in and boxes out in a continuous operation being controlled by bar coding computer information systems. Thus, the goal of modern logistics is a network chain of continuous replenishment flow with zero, or minimum, storage at any distribution stage.

The best example of an integrated supply chain is Wal-Mart. A recent *Fortune* article summarizes the Wal-Mart supply chain story well.[20]

> Part of the genius of Wal-Mart's ecosystem was also its unprecedented involvement and entanglement in the affairs of its suppliers. By 1984, Wal-Mart, which had become a very powerful channel to customers, began exerting heavy pressure on their suppliers like P&G to keep their prices down. Moreover, Wal-Mart compelled its customers to set up cross company information systems to attain maximum manufacturing and distribution efficiency. For example, Wal-Mart and P&G reached an unprecedented partnership that involved extensive electronic ordering and information between the companies.

Quite clearly these developments drastically changed the way purchasing had traditionally operated with suppliers. The focus is now on a long-term relationship with fewer suppliers based on trust or "win-win" negotiation philosophy and the sharing of confidential information. Purchasing would have to be proactive and strategic and move from "exchange" thinking (purchase order to purchase order) to a long-term relationship. Most purchasing personnel still have real difficulty with this change given their paranoia and fascination with extensive legal (usually one-way) protection. If one needs a 100-page contract filled with penalty clauses, the two parties obviously do not have a partnership. This is not to suggest that tough negotiation is inappropriate, but it does indicate that straight competitive bidding, with its focus on price versus cost, is obsolete for strategic sourcing. Perhaps Harmon summarizes the evolution very well when he writes:

> Purchase, customer, and factory orders will become obsolete for use with repetitive demand items and will be replaced by electronic interchange of schedules between customer and supplier. Thus, all suppliers in the distribution network will have a time-phased schedule of all their customers' actual orders and future forecasts. Hence they will be better able to plan future operations based on the most timely and accurate information available.[21]

J. A. Carlisle and R. C. Parker made very important contributions in the area of buyer/seller relationship and trust development.[22] Their writings and consulting activities directed at changing the historic adversarial relationship between buyers and sellers are to be admired. The mutual suspicions are very ingrained on both sides even in the fairly young. Buyers are convinced they are not getting the best price (they still have trouble understanding total cost) and suppliers, with historical justification, feel buyers will dump them for the first competitor who offers even a slightly lower price. Buyers still tell professors and consultants that top management and even some engineers only understand unit price and focus on short-term savings "to look good and inflate dividends." There is truth in both arguments but, until both sides change their thinking, supply chain management will never be successful for the average organization. We can only hope more executives read *Zero Base Pricing* by D. N. Burt, W. E. Norquist, and J. Anklesaria, with its emphasis on total cost of ownership or what the authors called "All-In Costs."[23]

Jordan D. Lewis also deserves a mention. His observations on alliances, partnerships, and relationships are very astute. As Lewis writes:

> A senior executive of a major American auto company compared an experience of his firm with that of a Japanese rival. Yet the Americans gained only 4 percent of the reduction obtained by the Japanese. The main reason, says this executive, was the Japanese firms had long-term relationships with their suppliers. They were willing to take more risks; the firms had helped each other in the past and knew that they could count on each other in the future.[24]

Another important contribution was made by D. N. Burt and M. P. Doyle in their 1993 book.[25] This fine work actually blueprints how to move from reactive purchasing to strategic supply chain management and what they call "value chain management." Burt's co-author, Michael F. Doyle, a former Ford procurement executive also teamed with Robert C. Parker, another ex-Ford executive, as a consulting and speaking team extolling the virtues of supply chain management. They may be the first (along with Burt) to talk about tier one to tier N suppliers and the extended enterprise, i.e., managing raw materials from Mother Earth to disposal.[26] E. E. Scheuing's book on partnering in 1994 is another important contribution.[27]

In yet another and very recent book, D. N. Burt and R. L. Pinkerton take the purchasing responsibilities in supply chain management and blueprint the actual philosophy, strategy, tactics, policies, and procedures to ensure proactive procurement.[28] Burt and Pinkerton revise and update Burt's earlier 1984 IPS and document the savings achieved in actual case histories. Their focus, on the new product–service development process, is rather unique within procurement literature.

Finally, it is interesting to examine how the leading textbook in the field of purchasing defines supply chain management. D. W. Dobler and D. N. Burt define the supply chain in this way:

> This chain is the upstream of the organization's value chain and is responsible for ensuring that the right materials, services, and technology are purchased from the right source, at the right time, in the right quality. The value chain is a series of organizations extending all the way back to firms which extract materials from Mother Earth, perform a series of value-adding activities, and fabricate the finished good or service purchased by the ultimate customer.[29]

The textbook definition along with purchasing professionals in general seem to underplay the importance of transportation logistics and overplay the role of purchasing. They would be well advised to spend more thought, time, and effort on the entire field of channels of distribution–logistics and thereby grasp the bigger picture of the entire system and how they interact with other players as advocated by R. L. Pinkerton and E. J. Marien.[30] D. J. Bowersox and D. J. Closs as logistics writers do have the bigger picture but also underplay the role of purchasing and critical tasks of sourcing, negotiating, and contracting.[31] Perhaps someday, production, engineering, purchasing, materials and logistics people will really talk to each other as opposed to themselves and their own empires.

Supply chain management requires a balanced emphasis. This total systems view is extremely difficult to translate into actual operation. As Burt and a few others cited in this article have so long argued, tear down these departmental, functional walls and think macro. Plan strategically, then act locally with the proper integrated tactics.

PREREQUISITES FOR SUPPLY CHAIN MANAGEMENT

The short history above reveals, at least in my opinion, how the building blocks created this age of system "chain" channel integration. The materials management concepts started the synergistic management awareness, the American development of micro computers and software facilitated it, and the competition from the Japanese forced it.[32] Top management must (some do) realize that a supply chain is much bigger than procurement and logistics: it is an entirely new way of thinking and organizing the total life-cycle from raw materials to use of a final product or service by an ultimate user.

There is no chance of implementing the chain concept unless the following is in place or at least detailed plans set out to accomplish the following:

* *Top management understanding and commitment*—while this may be an old cliché for all new programs, chain management starts at the top, the bottom layers will never force it.
* *The quest for excellence*—the only organizations which will make this change are those which will provide at all levels the desire and ability to embrace lifelong continuous improvement in quality, service, and personal effort.

- *Effective and efficient communications*—real-time electronic communications with shared information at all levels is an absolute must. Firms must do a much better job of forecasting, which requires a mix of math modelling and industry experience–judgment. The entire chain operation starts with demand forecasting and, if marketing managers really understand their role, they must dramatically improve their forecasting ability and accuracy. B2B electronic Internet commerce systems can be of enormous value as buyers can now source the world and send enormous amounts of data. However, the use of reverse auctions and consortiums focus on price, *not* relationships. If misused, B2B e-commerce systems will have a negative effect on supply chain management.

- *Relationship instead of exchanges*—most people understand that partnerships, whether in marriage or business, require trust and long-term commitment.

   Purchasing personnel have a long history of being risk averse because they were seldom rewarded (no one knows how to do it) for creative efforts and severely punished for mistakes. The price buyer is so well known it hardly needs any explanation. Many negotiation seminars still preach intimidation and almost childish tricks. The legal seminars are still extremely popular in purchasing circles. The heart of any good relationship is open communication and trust, not a legal document.

   Conversely, the production, engineering, and logistics personnel must understand that sourcing is not the simple process they assume it is. Finding the right source and having fewer sources in long-term contracts make sourcing even more critical. The Internet provides a list of possible candidates and what they make; it does not evaluate a potential partner for a long-term relationship nor can it possibly iron out the details of the performance requirements. While you can buy generic products by computer, would you select a mate that way?

- *Cross-functional teams*—while most of us have been on a wide variety of teams—athletic, military, and some business projects—most business members carry over to the team all the bad habits of committees, which are merely temporary collections of people representing some other department or function. We all know most committee meetings are terribly dysfunctional, i.e., they either represent a speech forum for the boss or an opportunity for the members to protect vested interests. Team formation, training, operation, and rewards require enormous maturity, patience, and interpersonal skills. Ask any coach; many people simply cannot function on teams and that is why there are so few really great teams, even though many teams have a number of great individual performers.

- *The special philosophy-reality of teams, partnerships, and alliances*—this may seem repetitive of previous comments but this prerequisite actually builds on earlier observations. Few teams/partnerships and especially alliances start based on complete harmony and trust; they must grow into this relationship based on experience, revisions, and constant practice.

   Top management must provide constant support, guidance, and training to resolve the expected conflict. Impatience and the wrong kind of pressure have caused many a coach and their team or partnership to fail. WWII and Gulf War allied forces were marked by contentious behavior, yet both were magnificently successful with world issues at stake.[33] Unfortunately, many organizations have formed teams, partnerships, and alliances based on lip service with no real commitment evident on either side.

Long-term relationships, partnerships, and alliances can only be achieved by reducing the number of suppliers; i.e., an organization does not need, nor does it have the time and money to manage a large number of relationships. The analogy to personal friendships is the same; one does not have the time to sustain a large number of close friends. This means purchases must be consolidated, standardized, and simplified in order to increase the value or importance of the relationship.

HOW DOES ONE START TO LINK THE CHAIN?

A rather detailed plan must be completed as opposed to the traditional audit. The traditional management audits, so popular with the giant firms from 1945 to 1985, were, for the most part, merely verifications that the corporate policies and procedures were being followed. As one might expect, they were, and still are, control programs heavily, if not totally, run by the accounting departments. Audits almost always guarantee a continuation of the *status quo;* after all, the corporate manual is law.[34]

Thus, the good old-fashioned planning process must be followed. It includes four formal stages: the situation phase; the objective phase; and the creative or new action steps (the new plan or original plan in most cases); and the final phase, the implementation or execution phase. There are a number of good cookbooks that provide step-by-step operations to develop supply chain value-added programs. E. Banfield[35]; and C. Long and G. Meyer[36] are good examples.

THE SITUATION PHASE

The situation phase (sometimes called the diagnostic) is actually the fact-finding activity to determine where the firm is at any given time. It documents the actual activities and results of all the relevant players. The best place to start is with an analysis of the contracting record of key suppliers and then work backward. The organization is spending the big bucks with the critical suppliers, who, if there is failure or inefficiency, could shut down or damage corporate performance. With modern computer material data banks, the task is not very difficult. Count the number of requisitions and purchase orders per supplier, which usually reveals far too much repetitive paperwork with far too many suppliers. These data will start to reveal the supply links in the chain and the costs to operate it.

THE OBJECTIVE PHASE

This is where we want to go or be in the future in order to be more efficient and effective. We could call it the strategy phase. If we assume that the key managers understand the huge benefits of good supply management, then what we should do is a natural progression from "where we are." This assumes that the firm has or will have all the prerequisites. Failure to have, or want to have, these foundations will almost certainly produce inaction and failure. Benchmarking is often used to establish the standards or "the bar." Just be careful not to blindly copy another organization that has resources unavailable to the copying firm.

THE CREATIVE OR NEW PLAN

This phase takes the objectives, mission, and vision developed and agreed upon in the second stage into the action steps, or "how," "when," "who," and "where" of accomplishing the mission goal. The why part has been articulated in the situation and objective phases. The third stage is the operational time-phased marching orders, i.e., the flight plan to reach our destination. It is the failure to translate strategy into tactics and planning based on the wrong assumptions that produces analysis paralysis. At this stage, any hesitation on the part of top management is deadly as any organization has some people desperately trying to avoid change. These are the managers who find reasons not to take action and they are usually protecting their own subcorporate empires.

At this or a prior stage, the organization must issue a policy statement endorsing the new plan and it must be in writing and given to all the workers, not just the managers. It should be announced in a series of corporate meetings by the president who blesses the plan.

Training, training, training—the three important activities prior to implementation. People cannot simply read the new policy or procedures. They have questions that need answering and they need confidence-building skill preparation such as is implicit in the objective: "how to be a productive team member." Teams need team building and negotiation training and lots of it.

THE EXECUTION PHASE

The implementation act is the execution phase and we must monitor this mission progression. Anticipate the need for revision and/or restart; have contingency plans. Retraining is absolutely mandatory. We so often hear "we did that last year," as if everybody learned it, did it right, or even remembered it. Can anyone imagine getting on an airliner knowing the crew never practised a form of continuous improvement? Almost nothing is ever learned well in one step and yet I have heard executives say that a good afternoon session on TQM is enough. Who is kidding whom?

CONCLUSION AND OUTLOOK FOR THE 21ST CENTURY

The case to adopt supply chain management is well made with many documented success stories. The aphorism that it "takes money to make money" is still appropriate, so an organization must be willing to go through what will usually be a two/three year conversion period. How do you stop an operation long enough to change into a new one? With difficulty is the answer. If your people are already overburdened, even with nonvalue activities, like checking requisitions as just one minor example, an added team will probably be needed to extract them from one process while they change to another. After the planning, it is the actual starting with all its unknowns and anticipated problems that can grind a new plan to a halt. A companywide task force, including consultants, is one answer but whatever you choose, the payoff of supply chain management is enormous.

It must be remembered that the supply chain concept is a product of recent evolution. The full adoption and implementation will take place in the 21st century as world markets become even more dominated by multinational corporations operating in the three great trading areas: the European Union (EU), the North American Free Trade Association (NAFTA), and the Asian Informal Alliance.

Finally, B2B electronic–Internet schemes are not substitutes for personal negotiations and cross-functional teams. We must always remember that price is just a component of cost.

NOTES

1. D. S. Ammer, *Materials Management and Purchasing,* 4th ed. (Homewood, IL: Richard D. Irwin, Inc. 1980; 1st ed. 1962). See also L. J. De Rose, "The Role of Purchasing in Materials Management," *Purchasing Magazine,* March 1956, p. 115.

2. D. J. Bowersox, *Logistical Management: A Systems Integration of Physical Distribution, Materials Management and Logistical Co-ordination* (New York: Macmillan, 1974), pp. 14–25.

3. G. J. Zenz, "Materials Management and Purchasing: Projections for the 1980s," *Journal of Purchasing and Materials Management,* vol. 17, no. 1, Spring 1981, p. 18.

4. O. Wight, *Manufacturing Resource Planning: MPII: Unlocking America's Productivity Potential* (Essex Junction, VT: Oliver Wight Publications, 1984).

5. D. S. Ammer, "Materials Management as a Profit Center," *Harvard Business Review,* vol. 47, no. 1, January–February 1969, pp. 72–82; and Victor H. Pooler, Jr., *The Purchasing Man and His Job,* (New York: The American Management Association, 1964), pp. 19–22.

6. Pooler, Jr., op. cit., pp. 239–246; and for the "Proactive" citation, see Victor H. Pooler, Jr., and D. J. Porter, "Purchasing's Elusive Conceptual Home," *Journal of Purchasing and Materials Management,* Summer 1981, p. 16.

7. D. N. Burt, *Proactive Procurement: The Key to Increased Profits, Productivity and Quality* (Englewood Cliffs, NJ: Prentice Hall, 1984) p. ix.

8. P. R. Witt, *Cost Competitive Products: Managing Product Concept to Marketplace Reality* (Reston, VA: Reston Publishing, 1986).

9. M. R. Leenders and D. L. Blenkhorn, *Reverse Marketing: The New Buyer-Supplier Relationship* (New York: Free Press, 1988), pp. 36–73.

10. H. E. Fearon, *Purchasing Research: Concepts and Current Practices* (New York: The American Management Association, 1976).

11. B. J. LaLonde, J. R. Grabner, and J. F. Robeson, "Integrated Distribution Systems: A Management Perspective," *International Journal of Physical Distribution,* October 1970, pp. 43–49.

12. W. C. Copacino, *Supply Chain Management: The Basics and Beyond* (Boca Raton, FL: St. Lucie Press/APICS on Resource Management, 1997), p. 8, quoting from his December 1986 article in *Transportation Management.*

13. Ibid., p. 13. From his 1986 article in *Transportation Management.*

14. D. D. Buss, "GM Gears Up Buick City in Its Biggest Effort to Cut Costs, Boost Efficiency at Older Site," *The Wall Street Journal,* February 21, 1985, p. 4. Also see Kevin R. Fitzgerald, "Buick City Heralds a New Era in Auto Making," *Modern Materials Handling,* November 1985, pp. 59–62; and R. L. Pinkerton, "Buick City: The History and Analysis of the General Motors Corporation's Just-in-Time Manufacturing System in Flint, Michigan," California State University, Fresno, The Sid Craig School of Business, University Business Center, working paper series, no. 101, 1991.

15. G. Gardner, "Buick City's Demise," *Ward's Auto World,* June 1997, pp. 23–29.

16. A. J. Martin, *Distribution Resource Planning: The Gateway to True Quick Response and Continuous Replenishment,* 2nd ed. (Essex Junction, VT: Oliver Wight Publications, 1993).

17. R. L. Harmon, *Reinventing the Warehouse: World Class Distribution Logistics,* foreword by William C. Copacino (New York: Free Press, 1993) p. 18. Another good reference is John W. Schorr, *Purchasing in the 21st Century* (Essex Junction, VT: Oliver Wight Publications, 1992).

18. D. M. Lambert and J. R. Stock, *Strategic Logistics Management,* 3rd ed. (Homewood, IL: Irwin, 1993).

19. P. Quinn, "Tale of a Tiger: Tiger Accessories Earns Its EDI Stripes with Bar Coding Order Processing," *ID Systems,* August 1997, pp. 24–30.

20. J. Moore, "The Death of Competition," *Fortune,* April 15, 1996, p. 144.

21. Harmon, op. cit., p. 157.

22. J. A. Carlisle and R. C. Parker, *Beyond Negotiation: Redeeming Customer-Supplier Relationships* (New York: John Wiley & Sons, 1989).

23. D. N. Burt, W. E. Norquist, and J. Anklesaria, *Zero Base Pricing: Achieving World Class Competitiveness through Reduced All-In Costs* (Chicago: Probus, 1990).

24. J. D. Lewis, *Partnerships for Profit: Structuring and Managing Strategic Alliances* (New York: Free Press, 1990) p. 19.

25. D. N. Burt and M. P. Doyle, *The American Keiretsu: A Strategic Weapon for Global Competitiveness* (Homewood, IL: Business One Irwin, 1993).

26. R. C. Parker and M. F. Doyle, "The Future of Supply-Chain Management," *81st Annual International Purchasing Conference Proceedings,* 1996, pp. 181–186, published by the National Association of Purchasing Management.

27. E. E. Scheuing, "The Power of Strategic Partnering," *Great Management Ideas,* vol. 3 (Portland, OR: Productivity Press, 1994).

28. D. N. Burt and R. L. Pinkerton, *A Purchasing Manager's Guide to Strategic Proactive Procurement* (New York: Amacom Division of the American Management Association, 1996).

29. D. W. Dobler and D. N. Burt, *Purchasing and Supply Management: Text and Cases,* 6th ed. (New York: McGraw-Hill, 1996) p. 13.

30. R. L. Pinkerton and E. J. Marien, "The Fundamentals of Inbound Transportation," *NAPM InfoEdge*, vol. 2, no. 8, April 1997, The National Association of Purchasing Management, Tempe, AZ.

31. D. J. Bowersox and D. J. Closs, *Logistical Management: The Integrated Supply Chain Process* (New York: McGraw-Hill, 1996).

32. See the books and articles by R. J. Schonberger on the theme of Japanese management methods and philosophies. For example, one of his early works is "Just-in-Time Purchasing: A Challenge for U.S. Industry," with J. P. Gilbert, *California Management Review*, vol. 26, no. 1, Fall 1983, pp. 54–68. Also consult the classic works of W. Edwards Deming, J. M. Juran, Philip B. Crosby, and the other quality pioneers.

33. L. R. Clayton, "Trust Should Grow over Time," *Purchasing Today*, May 1997, p. 29. Also see "Trust Should Be Immediate," by Blaine Vortman on p. 28 of the same issue.

34. R. L. Pinkerton and K. A. Pettis, "From Reactive to Proactive Procurement: A Case Study," *The 82nd Annual International Purchasing Conference Proceedings*, 1997, pp. 169–172, published by the National Association of Purchasing Management.

35. E. Banfield, *Harnessing Value in the Supply Chain* (New York: John Wiley & Sons, 1999).

36. C. Long and G. Meyer, *Sacred Cows Make the Best Barbecue: Supply Chain Management: A Revolutionary 26-Week Action Plan* (Seal Beach, CA: Vision Press, 1998).

PREFACE

Welcome to the exciting, wonderful world of supply management! This decade, more changes are taking place in the areas of supply management, supply chain management, supply network management, buyer/supplier alliances, and virtual corporations than in the history of humankind.

Dynamic collaborative and trusting alliance relationships and networks are the keys to survival and success in the 21st century. These relationships are best established and nurtured by supply management professionals. Information technology, engineering, marketing, operations, quality, and finance all play critical, enabling roles in our quest for value-add relationships.

The transformation from clerical and mechanical purchasing through proactive procurement and on to World Class Supply Management^{SM} parallels the evolution of mankind from caves to visiting the moon. In some ways, this transformation has been mirrored by at least one of the leading supply management professional organizations. Where we once had the National Association of Purchasing Agents, and then the National Association of Purchasing Management, today we have the Institute for Supply Management^{TM}.

What is the primary reason for the shift from tactical purchasing roles to strategic supply management roles? Supply management has major impact on the organization's bottom line. It can facilitate or destroy marketing's efforts to increase sales. Supply management has always been a part of the "front-line" defense to contain costs. Now World Class Supply Managment^{SM} is also the "front-line" offense to improve the bottom line through reduced costs. And supply management has as much or more impact on the organization's return on assets than does any other business function.

The term "supply chain management" came into vogue during the 1990s. Many information technologists, logisticians, management scientists, and industrial engineers have argued that their individual function should be the drivers of the chain. But informed practitioners and academics alike recognize that carefully developed cross-functional supply management teams are the key to successful supply chains and supply networks. All functional areas must collaborate with relevant suppliers to realize the greatest opportunity for success.

Many executives have been brainwashed by aggressive software vendors into believing that e-commerce will eliminate the need for supply professionals. Wrong. Dead wrong! E-commerce must be viewed for what it is and what it contributes: e-commerce and the Internet are wonderful, powerful enablers. They are slaves, not masters!

The thinking underlying this seventh edition of our text began in the 1950s when I enjoyed my first appointment as a Chief Procurement Officer. My evolving philosophy first saw the power of the press in 1984 with the publication of "Proactive Procurement: The Key to Increased Profits, Productivity, and Quality." In 1984, I was privileged to join Lamar Lee, Jr., my former Professor of Purchasing during my days at Stanford and his co-author, Donald W. Dobler, as the junior co-author of the Fourth edition of *Purchasing and Materials Management.* Many wonderful people and several events have contributed to my knowledge and evolving philosophy during the years subsequent to 1984. Serious work on the current seventh edition began some four years ago.

In 2000, I had the good fortune to meet Stephen Starling, Assistant Professor of Operations Management at California State University, Hayward. Dr. Starling and I share philosophies and a missionary zeal for bringing procurement into the 21st century. In 2001, Stephen joined me as co-author of the seventh edition and as a colleague at the University of San Diego, where he is an Associate Professor of Supply Chain Management. Dr. Starling developed two totally new chapters and has contributed countless upgrades to many of the other chapters in this edition. Perhaps of greatest importance to our many adopters, Professor Starling is responsible for both the content of the Instructor's Manual and for taking it online.

Our new edition has benefited enormously from the invaluable contributions of countless colleagues. Rommy Los (my former student and currently Corporate Purchasing Manager at Henkel KGaA) developed the important material addressing supply management's role in protecting Mother Earth. Stephen Rodgers of Procter and Gamble contributed an important section on supply management's responsibilities in ensuring that workplace issues are addressed when sourcing with the global marketplace. Tom Oleson of Nationwide Insurance assisted with the services chapter. Robert Porter Lynch has contributed to my insight on buyer/supplier alliances. Ray Hummell took my preliminary work on the total cost of ownership and carried it forward as a key cornerstone of World Class Supply Management^{SM}. Ray also provided invaluable assistance in upgrading and updating our material on price and cost. Bill Richardson provided deep insight into Deere & Company's approach to supplier development. Professor Craig Barkacs brought our work on legal and ethical issues into the 21st century. Chuck Noland of the QP Group and former VP Supply Chain Management at Kaiser-Permanente Healthcare helped us reintroduce an updated chapter on institutional procurement. Cathy Eldridge of Raytheon and the National Contract Management Association provided invaluable assistance in updating and enhancing our chapter on government procurement. Jim Reeds provided much thoughtful input throughout the book's evolution. Dick Pinkerton was an invaluable sounding board and facilitator during the development of many of our ideas. R. David (Dave) Nelson, Chairman of the Institute of Supply Chain Management^{TM} and formerly employed as VP of Worldwide Supply Management at Deere & Company; Bob Kemp (former President of NAPM); Emiko Banfield, VP, Shared Services at Southern California Edison; Teresa Metty, VP Motorola; Dr. Dave Lehmann, VP Operations, Solar (ret.); Merle Roberts, Founder and President of Perpetual Frontiers; and Professor Scott Kunkel of USD, all played important contributing roles in the development of our final chapter: "Implementing World Class Supply Chain Management^{SM}."

I express my appreciation to Curtis Cook, Dean of the School of Business of the University of San Diego, for his assistance and support in bringing Professor Starling to our campus. We made a wonderful choice, Curtis, thank you!

It is with a combination of pleasure and pain that we say adieu and bon voyage to co-author Donald W. Dobler. Don has played a key role in the success of the previous six editions of our text. Don's contributions to the fields of purchasing and materials resulted in his selection as a Shipman Medalist by the National Association of Purchasing Management. Don, Sharon and I wish you and Elaine many years of happiness!

Kerry Kilber, Karen Kukta, and Kelly van der Dussen were the glue that held this project together. Their professionalism, patience, and tolerance of my humanness were, and are, appreciated beyond my ability to express in words. Steven Staninger, Business Librarian, Copley Library at the University of San Diego, was an invaluable resource! Thanks Steve!

My wife, Professor Sharon Burt, and Stephen's wife, Pam, have been the unsung heroes who put up with Stephen's and my obsession with making this seventh edition the best that it can be. We express our appreciation and our commitment to make it up to both of you.

David N. Burt
Cardiff by the Sea, California
May 1, 2002

PART 1

The Foundation

The World Class Supply Management^{SM} philosophy reflects those actions and values responsible for the continuous improvement of the design, development, and management processes of an organization's supply system, with the objective of improving its profitability and ensuring its survival, as well as the profitability and survival of its customers and suppliers.

Laying Bricks, Maryland *(Credit: Corbis)*

A firm's supply system includes all internal functions plus external suppliers involved in the identification and fulfillment of needs for materials, equipment, and services in an optimized fashion. Supply management lays the foundation for, and is the key to, successful supply chain management.

Supply management can positively impact the firm's bottom line more than any other business function. In this book, we present World Class Supply Management^{SM} as the philosophy and approach of choice for such improvements. World Class Supply Management^{SM} (WCSM) greatly contributes to increases in profitable sales by enhancing the quality of the firm's products, ensuring on-time performance, reducing time to market, enabling the inflow of technologies which are the basis of successful new products, and providing sales and marketing the freedom to maximize the firm's net revenue through the application of pricing elasticity. WCSM's focus on the total cost of ownership (defined as the summation of the costs of acquiring and owning or converting an item of material, piece of equipment, or service and post-ownership costs) plays the major role in reducing the firm's expenditures. Through its impact on both profitable sales and reduced expenditures, WCSM also has a major impact on the firm's return on investment and return on assets.

Supply management consists of four principle phases: the generation of requirements, sourcing, pricing, and post-award activities. These phases are interdependent. They are most successfully accomplished by cross-functional teams representing the key functions involved in the required processes. The generation of requirements is the most crucial of these four essential phases of supply management. Approximately 85 percent of the cost of purchased material, services, and equipment is "designed in" during this phase. One of life's interesting paradoxes is that supply management is a contributor to, not the "owner" of, this crucial phase. Supply management assumes a greater leadership role in the three remaining phases of sourcing, pricing, and post-award activities.

The Internet and B2B e-commerce are accelerating the transformation of supply management to status as a core competency. The key to optimizing the power of the Internet as an enabler of WCSM is to systematically analyze each critical supply management process and then to reengineer the process while incorporating the power of the Internet. Technological integration of processes that span the supply chain requires collaboration among the chain's members. As firms' supply management systems progress to world class status, they develop information technology (IT) systems which facilitate strategic planning of this critical process.

As presented in Chapter 1, World Class Supply Management^{SM} must focus on the following 10 strategic activities:

- Monitoring the firm's supply environment.
- Developing and managing the firm's supply strategy as an integrated whole.
- Developing and updating sound commodity supply strategies.
- Collaborating with the organization's IT function to develop a data management system which facilitates strategic supply planning.
- Joining marketing and operations as the key players developing the corporation's strategic plans.
- Designing and managing the firm's supply base in line with its strategic objectives.

■ Identifying the advantages of specific potential supply alliances and then developing and managing them.

■ Developing and managing the firm's supply chains or supply networks.

■ Developing and implementing programs which protect the environment; which facilitate the inclusion of diversity, women-owned, and small businesses in our economy; and which promote values in the workplace.

■ Studying and understanding the industries which provide key materials, equipment, and services; their cost structures, technologies, competitive nature, and their culture.

In Chapter 2, we see how purchasing has evolved to supply management, an activity which is recognized as a core competency at world-class firms. Four major developments are facilitating the transformation of purchasing into *supply management:*

■ *Supply networks.* The development and management of the organization's supply chains or supply networks is crucial. These chains or networks consist of a series or grouping of organizations extending all the way back to firms which extract materials from Mother Earth. All members of the chain perform a series of value-adding activities to create the finished good or service purchased by the ultimate customer.

■ *Strategic alliances.* Alliances are not legal entities, but rather mutually beneficial and open relationships wherein the needs of both parties are satisfied.

■ *Strategic sourcing.* This overused and misunderstood term calls for the planning, development, and management of the organization's supply base to support its strategic objectives. In effect, strategic sourcing applies the principles and processes described in this book in an effort to integrate suppliers into the organization's long-term business processes.

■ *E-procurement.* No longer are supply managers responsible for non-value-adding activities and paperwork processing. The internal end user of an item or service, whether for a direct or indirect requirement, is now empowered to place orders through the Internet directly to the supplier. (These suppliers have been carefully selected by sourcing teams which also establish delivery terms and prices.) The release of this tactical responsibility allows supply professionals to focus on value-adding activities, including:

■ Early involvement in the development of requirements.

■ Strategic sourcing or supply base management.

■ Pricing.

■ Post-award activities.

■ The strategic activities described above.

■ Cross-functional teams. Cross-functional teams are being used to proactively address a myriad of issues from design to salvage. The teams are composed of both internal and external members, reflecting the new interdependencies in today's competitive environment.

In Chapter 3, we will discuss how World Class Supply Management^{SM} spans functional boundaries and company borders. At a tactical level, supply management is responsible for the acquisition of required materials, services, and equipment. The supply management department is the hub of a large part of a company's business activity. By its very nature, supply management has continuing relationships with all other departments in the firm, as well as with the firm's suppliers. Supply management operations cut across virtually all departmental lines.

Supply management has as much impact on the success of nonmanufacturing organizations as it does on the success of manufacturing firms. The timely availability of reliable equipment, supplies, and services at the right total cost of ownership affects the ability of such organizations to provide timely quality services at a profit or, in the case of nonprofit institutions, while minimizing expenditures.

Supply management has a major impact on the efficient and effective use of our tax dollars at all levels of government. Not surprisingly, many of the advances in the art and science of supply management originated in the federal government. Virtually all of the problems present in manufacturing organizations are present in government procurement.

Supply managers are responsible for protecting their firms from unexpected threats or shocks from their supply world in the form of price increases or supply disruptions. These threats include material shortages which affect one or more industries that supply the firm. Shortages will affect both the price and availability of purchased materials and supplies. The firm should take actions to minimize the impact of such shortages by monitoring changes in the supply environment.

Chapter 4 addresses supply management's responsibility for implementing three social responsibilities: enabling diversity suppliers, protecting our physical environment, and addressing the challenge of an array of social, legal, and ethical issues in the firm's global supply world. And now, on to World Class Supply Management^{SM}. ∎

World Class Supply Management^{SM1}

The World Class Supply Management^{SM} philosophy reflects those actions and values responsible for the continuous improvement of the design, development, and management processes of an organization's supply system, with the objective of improving its profitability and ensuring its survival, as well as the profitability and survival of its customers and suppliers.

KEY CONCEPTS

---

[1]The Strategic Supply Management Institute, Ltd. of Reno, Nevada, holds a system mark on the term "World Class Supply Management^{SM}." The term is used with the permission of the Institute. For further information, please visit the Institute's website at www.supplysystems.com.

Case

In 1988, Xenia was the leading producer of transducers worldwide. The company took pride in its marketing, product innovation, and assembly excellence. By 1992, Xenia's Asian competitor was selling its transducers for what it cost Xenia to produce comparable units. At that time, Xenia engineers designed virtually all of Xenia's components that were then purchased from one or more of the firm's 4,000 suppliers. Widespread competition was used to obtain the best price. The selected supplier built to Xenia drawings and specifications.

Management at Xenia responded to the competitive threat. The corporation's strategy shifted to a new set of core competencies: marketing, product innovation, assembly, and supply management. Over a period of three years, Xenia reduced its supply base from 4,000 to 400 suppliers. Xenia worked with these suppliers to bring them to world-class status. These suppliers became involved in the development of Xenia's new transducers.

The result? Cost of goods sold was reduced 50 percent. Incoming quality problems virtually disappeared. The time required to move a new product from concept to customer was reduced 45 percent. Production lead times were reduced 65 percent. All of these results were achieved in only three years!

World Class Supply Management^{SM}

The World Class Supply Management^{SM} philosophy reflects those actions and values responsible for continuous improvement of the design, development, and management processes of an organization's supply system, with the objective of improving its profitability and ensuring its survival, as well as the profitability and survival of its customers and suppliers. The term "world class" recognizes that companies compete in an existing or impending global environment. As a philosophy, World Class Supply Management^{SM} spans functional boundaries and company borders. The philosophy of World Class Supply Management^{SM} requires change driven by upper management to shift decision-making processes from an internal department or single company focus toward optimization of the supply chain. Through continuous improvement, World Class Supply Management^{SM} is an ever-moving target that focuses on supply chain process improvement. World Class Supply Management^{SM} requires the development and management of institutional trust.[2] World Class Supply Management^{SM} involves purchasing, but is far more strategic. A world-class supply manager is not departmentally or internally focused, but concentrates on proactively improving processes with the long-term goal of upgrading the competitive capability of the firm and the firm's supply chain.

[2]For more on the critical issue of institutional trust, please see the appendix to Chapter 5.

Implementing World Class Supply Management^SM

In order to bring their supply management systems to world-class status, senior management must recognize supply management's critical nature and support the required transformation. One of the most visible ways of demonstrating its support of this transformation is the appointment of the Chief Supply Officer at an organizational level equal to that of marketing, engineering, and operations. The transformation must be carefully planned and executed. Getting top management's commitment and everyone's involvement are keys to success.

Firms must know where they are in relation to where they want to be. Benchmarking best-in-class practices and developing metrics enable firms to establish their progress toward World Class Supply Management^SM. Appropriate action plans and metrics allow them to focus on their vision and continuously improve their contribution to the bottom line. Figure 1.1 provides a road map for implementing World Class Supply Management^SM.

Supply Chains and Networks

The supply chain extends from the ultimate customer back to Mother Earth (see Figure 1.2). "The chain is viewed as a whole, a single entity rather than fragmented groups, each performing its own function."[3] Money enters the supply chain only when the ultimate customer buys a product or service. Transactions within the supply chain simply allocate the ultimate customer's money among the members of the chain. A firm's supply system includes all internal functions plus external suppliers involved in the identification and fulfillment of needs for materials, equipment, and services in an optimized fashion. This supply system plays a key role in helping the firm satisfy its role in its supply chain.

"Supply chain management is topping boardroom agendas in the United States and abroad as a vital part of the "race day" capabilities required for successful mergers, acquisitions, and alliances."[4] Professor Charles H. Fine of M.I.T. writes that "supply chain design is the meta-core competency for organizations."[5]

The Internet allows supply chain managers to manage their supply chains collaboratively and to synchronize their operations. The results: reduced cost, better time management, improved competitiveness, and profitability for all members of the chain. Lisa Henriott, Director of Product Strategy and Marketing at Manugistics' e-Chain Technologies business unit, writes: "In the future, an organization's success will be driven by its ability to compete effectively as a contributing member of dynamically connected supply chain communities, not as an isolated enterprise. The ability to interact quickly

---

[3]Gentry, J. J., "The Role of Carriers in Buyer-Supplier Strategic Partnerships: A Supply Chain Management Approach," *Journal of Business Logistics* 17(2) (1996), pp. 35–53, cited in Amelia S. Carr and Larry Smeltzer, "The Relationship of Strategic Purchasing to Supply Chain Management," *European Journal of Purchasing and Supply Management* 5 (1999) p. 44.

[4]Jorge Benitez and Bruce Gordon, "The Race Is On for Supply Chain Success," Andersen Consulting White Paper (date unknown).

[5]Charles H. Fine, *Clockspeed: Winning Industry Control in the Age of Temporary Advantage*. (Reading, MA: Perseus Books, 1998), p. 220.

The Progression to World Class Supply Management[SM]

World Class
- Supply management a core competence
- Strategic sourcing
- Monitor supply environment
- Develop and implement commodity strategies
- Commodity teams
- Supply base by design
- Develop and manage alliances and networks
- Time-based competition
- Virtually defect free materials and services
- Leverage supplier technology
- Integrated supply strategy
- Manage risk
- Emphasis: Total cost
- Relationships: Transactional, collaborative, and alliance
- Bottom-line impact: Increase shareholder value
- Reporting: Member, executive group
- Data: Facilitates strategic planning
- Understand key supply industries
- e-Commerce II

Proactive
- Coordinate Procurement System
- Develop Suppliers
- Long-term Contracts
- Involved in development of requirements
- Plan for recurring requirements
- Procurement adds value
- Active in source selection
- Near defect-free materials and services
- Emphasis: Cost, quality, timeliness
- Relationships: Transactional and Collaborative
- Bottom-line impact: Profit contributor
- Reporting: Upper management
- Data: Facilitates sourcing and pricing
- Fulfill social responsibilities
- e-Commerce

Mechanical
- Transactional focus
- React to requisitions
- Not involved in key source selections
- Emphasis: Purchase price
- Relationships: Transactional/ adversarial
- Bottom-line impact: Revenue neutral
- Reporting: Low level
- Data: Used to expedite
- Computers process paperwork

Clerical
- Process paperwork
- Confirm actions of others
- Emphasis: Convenience
- Relationships: Personal
- Bottom-line impact: Overhead
- Reporting: Very low level
- Data: Not available

1	2	3	4	5	6	7	8	9	10

Where Are You?

Figure 1.1 I The Progression to World Class Supply Management[SM]
(Adapted from the American Keiretsu by David N. Burt and Michael F. Doyle, BusinessOne-Irwin, Homewood, 21, 1993.)

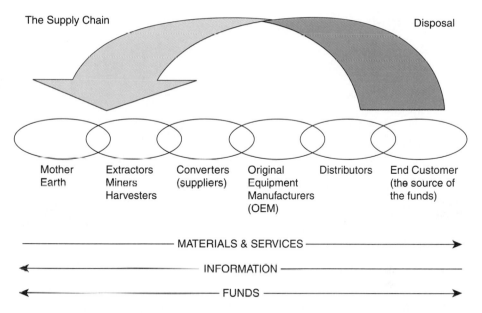

The Supply Chain   Disposal

| Mother Earth | Extractors Miners Harvesters | Converters (suppliers) | Original Equipment Manufacturers (OEM) | Distributors | End Customer (the source of the funds) |

MATERIALS & SERVICES ⟶

⟵ INFORMATION ⟶

⟵ FUNDS ⟶

Figure 1.2 I A firm's supply chain includes all internal functions plus external suppliers involved in the identification and fulfillment of needs for materials, equipment, and services in an optimized fashion. The supply system plays a key role in helping the firm satisfy its role in its supply chain.

with customers, suppliers, and other partners is already critical to survival. Tomorrow, a tightly connected e-chain will become a necessity."[6]

Supply chains are relatively easy to describe and visualize, but the terminology of a chain is already dated. "Traditionally, companies have connected with one another in simple, linear chains, running from raw material producers to distributors to retailers."[7] But the reality of the situation is that most firms already are or soon will be members of supply networks as portrayed in Figure 1.3. "Networks are flexible virtual systems linked together by communication systems and alliances. They optimize the flow of materials and services, information and money. Networks focus on the ultimate customer. They are designed and managed so that one member does not benefit at the expense of another. World-class networks are highly adaptive; they focus on speed; they are innovative; and they are tightly integrated."[8] Robert A. Novack, in his chapter in *The Purchasing Handbook,* 6th ed., writes, "Organizational boundaries between firms within a supply chain will become even more blurred as each firm becomes specialized in its contribution to the supply chain and its investment in the success of the supply chain increases."[9]

[6]Lisa L. Henriott, "Transforming Supply Chains into e-Chains," *Supply Chain Management Review Global Supplement,* Spring 1999, p. 16.

[7]Kevin Werbach, "Syndication: The Emerging model for Business in the Internet Era," *Harvard Business Review,* May–June 2000, pp. 85–93.

[8]Robert Porter Lynch, personal interview, April 4, 2001.

[9]Robert A. Novack, "Introduction to Supply Chain Management," in *The Purchasing Handbook,* 6th ed. (New York: McGraw-Hill, 2000), p. 165.

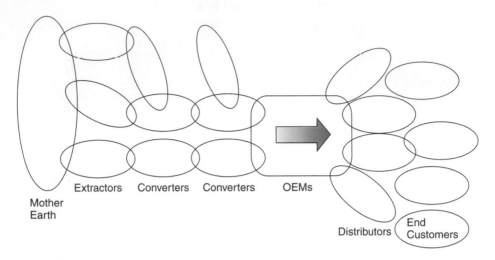

Figure 1.3 | Supply networks.

Rich Sherman, Senior Vice President, Visioneering, EXE Technologies, participating in a round table of eleven e-commerce visionaries in late 1999, observed, "The link and the chain are gone. They are already obsolete. What we're looking at is much more of an atomic model with no straight line whatsoever. It looks more like DNA. It's all about nodes, communications, and seamless information transfer."[10]

The Extended Enterprise

Jeffrey Dyer carries the concept of supply networks one step further. Based on eight years of study of the automotive industry, Dyer observes that when a group or network of firms collaborate in partnership (alliance) fashion, this is sometimes referred to as a *strategic network, virtual corporation,* or *extended enterprise.*[11] "When the group of firms view each other as partners (members of a supply alliance) and collaborate effectively for the good of the larger group, then they leave established an extended enterprise characterized by virtual integration."[12]

Supply Management and the Bottom Line

Supply management must be a core competency based on its overwhelming impact on the firm's bottom line. Supply management directly affects the two factors which control the bottom line: total costs and sales. Supply management also affects the investment in assets. Accordingly, supply management has a major impact on a firm's return on investment (please see Figure 1.4).

---

[10]Cited in *Modern Materials Handling,* Dec. 31, 1999.

[11]Jeffrey H. Dyer, *Collaborative Advantage: Winning through Extended Enterprise Supplier Networks* (Oxford: Oxford University Press, 2000), p. 27.

[12]Ibid., p. 32.

Net Income

Increased Sales:
- Faster to Market
- Improved Quality
- Pricing Flexibility
- Innovation
- Enhanced Customer Satisfaction
- Customer Fulfillment Flexibility
- Shorter Cycle and Lead Times

Lower Total Cost:
- Better Product Designs
- Acquisition Cost
- Processing Cost
- Better Asset Utilization
- Quality Cost
- Downtime Cost
- Risk Cost
- Cycle Time Cost
- Conversion Cost
- Non-Value Added Cost
- Supply Chain Cost
- Post Ownership Cost

Figure 1.4 I A Graphic Representation of Supply Managements' Impact on the Bottom Line

World Class Supply Management^{SM} enables us to maximize our bottom line in an ethical manner. Figure 1.4 shows how supply management can drive sales up and costs down. This impact on the firm's net income has a major impact on shareholder value.

Increased Sales

Supply management has a significant impact on the firm's sales, principally in the following seven areas.

Faster to Market or Time-Based Competition   Thirty years of marketing research have demonstrated the importance of being early to market. In many cases, the first firm to introduce a successful new product or service will hold 40–60 percent of the market after competition enters the picture. This research also demonstrates that the profit margins enjoyed by the first firm to introduce a new product tend to be twice those of its competitor, as first reported in the PIMS approach.[13] Firms which have embraced World Class Supply Management^{SM} have reduced their new product development cycles by an average of 30 percent as a direct result of a cross-functional

---

[13]Robert D. Buzzell and Bradley T. Gaze, *The PIMS Principles: Linking Strategy to Performance* (New York: The Free Press, 1987), pp. 183–84.

approach to product development (also known as concurrent engineering).[14] Purchasing and carefully selected suppliers are key members of these cross-functional teams. (This topic is addressed in greater detail in Chapter 6.)

Time-based competition also includes the firm's ability to meet unexpected surges in demand for its products. In many cases, a firm's ability to ramp up production is constrained by its suppliers' abilities to meet such surges in demand. The development and management of a competent, responsive supply base plays a critical role in the firm's ability to meet unexpected demand.

Improved Quality   We are all sensitive to the quality of the products and services we purchase. An automobile with a reputation for transmission problems will drive potential customers to its competitors. Conversely, a firm whose products or lines of products have a reputation for quality gains market share over its competitors and frequently is able to command premium prices.

Some 75 percent of many manufacturers' quality problems can be traced back to defects in purchased materials. (The percentage of quality problems that can be attributed to defective incoming materials for a services provider is usually less, but still significant.) Thus, if a manufacturer or service provider is able to reduce defects in incoming materials, it can improve the quality of its products in the marketplace. Firms that embrace World Class Supply Management[SM] work with their suppliers to design quality into the suppliers' products and maintain quality during production. The result is virtually defect-free incoming materials, improved quality in the marketplace, more sales, and improved profit margins.

Pricing Flexibility   Research conducted by the University of San Diego indicates that a world-class approach to supply management will reduce the total cost of ownership[15] associated with purchasing and owning or leasing materials, equipment, and services an average of 25 percent. When the cost of producing an item or service is reduced, marketing is given the gift of pricing elasticity. Through the application of sound economic principles, marketing can estimate whether net income will increase more by (1) holding selling price and sales volume constant and increasing net profit per unit, or (2) reducing the sales price, thereby increasing sales volume.

Innovation   The University of San Diego research study cited above indicated that of 240 firms surveyed, approximately 35 percent of all successful new products were the result of technology gained from their supply base.[16] This leveraging of supplier technology is a major source of income for these firms. Collaborative and alliance relationships with the firm's supply base play a key role in ensuring and enhancing this technology flow. The development and management of these supplier relationships is a key responsibility of supply management. (This important topic is addressed in Chapter 5.)

---

[14]For one of the classic works concerning cycle time reduction see Kim B. Clark and Takahiro Fujimoto, *Product Development Performance: Strategy, Organization, and Management in the World Auto Industry* (Boston: Harvard Business School Press, 1991), pp. 67–95 and 136–46.

[15]Total cost of ownership is addressed in Chapter 9.

[16]This research was reported at the 8th International Annual IPSERA Conference, London, U.K., March 1998.

Enhanced Customer Satisfaction   World Class Supply Management^{SM} helps achieve shorter fulfillment lead times, consistent on-time delivery, high fill rates, complete orders, quicker response to customers' requirements and the ability to meet unique or special requests.[17]

The Supplier of Choice   By providing the best value (a combination of quality, service and price), the firm becomes the supplier of choice, whether to another channel member or to the end customer.

Customer Fulfillment Flexibility   World Class Supply Management^{SM} provides the supply support which allows the firm to be responsive to customer desires for flexible lead time and changes in product configurations.

Lower Total Cost of Ownership

The total cost of ownership shown in Figure 1.4 is the summation of the costs of acquiring and owning or converting an item of material, piece of equipment, or service and post-ownership costs (the disposal of hazardous and other manufacturing waste and the cost of lost sales resulting from poor product quality reputation caused by defective materials or purchased services becoming incorporated in the end product or service).

Better Product Designs   We estimate the 70%–80% of the total cost of ownership is built into a requirement—whether for production materials, equipment, services or MRO—during the requirements development process. Early supply management and supplier involvement can significantly reduce costs during this critical stage.

Acquisition Cost   The acquisition cost or price paid for an item or service is normally a major component of the total cost of ownership. As will be seen in many of the following chapters, numerous actions may be taken to reduce acquisition cost. A few such activities are specification of the most cost-effective material or item of equipment, use of the appropriate specification, standardization, good sourcing, and pricing practices.

Processing Cost   The investment in developing, sourcing, and pricing requirements and then ensuring that they arrive on time in the quality specified can be reduced significantly through the application of efficient supply management processes and techniques.

Better Asset Utilization   Collaborative and alliance relationships allow buyer/supplier dyads to share critical assets. The smoother, more timely inflow of materials results in less waiting time, resulting in improved asset utilization.

Quality Cost   Costs are incurred in ensuring that the buying firm receives the optimal level of quality. These costs may be reduced through the application of progressive quality techniques, such as the design of experiments and statistical process control. Selection of suppliers capable of producing the desired level of quality and then certifying

---

[17]Fawcett, Stanley E. and Gregory M. Magnan, "Achieving World-Class Supply Chain Alignment: Benefits, Barriers, and Bridges: Center for Advanced Purchasing Studies, Tempe, AZ, 2001.

their design and manufacturing systems can improve incoming quality while reducing administrative quality costs.

Downtime Cost Downtime frequently is the largest component of the total cost of ownership for many items of production and operating equipment. One minute of downtime in a production line may cost $26,000.[18] At this rate, an hour can cost $1,560,000. Thus, when purchasing equipment, the sourcing team must place as much—or more—emphasis on downtime as on purchase price.

Risk Cost Firms spend millions of dollars in efforts to minimize risk. These firms maintain inventories and/or dual or even triple sources to ensure continuity of supply. Carefully developed and managed relationships with appropriate suppliers can eliminate the need for inventory and/or dual sources.

Cycle Time Cost While difficult to quantify, the shorter the cycle time for virtually all activities, the lower the cost. The shorter the cycle time to bring new products to market, to develop a statement of work, or to select a new source, the lower the total cost.

Conversion Cost Machine time, manpower, process yield lost, scrap, and rework are examples of conversion costs. These costs are every bit as real as the purchase price of an item entering the production process. A pound of brass may cost twice as much as a pound of steel; but the higher acquisition price for the brass may more than be offset by savings in machine and manpower costs during conversion of the brass to a component or end product.

Non-Value Added Costs A careful analysis of all of the costs involved in bringing an item or service to market frequently reveals that 40–60 percent of the costs involved no value added! Robert Handfield indicates that estimates of the amount of time spent on non-value activities can be as high as 80 to 90 percent of the total time required to complete a cycle.[19] James P. Womack and Daniel T. Jones, in their book *Lean Thinking,* indicate that "it takes an average of 11 months for the can of cola in a domestic refrigerator to actually get there. . . . During that 11 months, the time that the material is actually being converted as opposed to simply waiting is a mere three hours!"[20] All members of the supply management system (e.g., design, manufacturing; and quality engineering; manufacturing; and supply management) must be on the lookout for non-value added activities at any and all stages of the system.

Supply Chain Cost The development and management of supply chains and supply networks require a significant investment, primarily in the form of human resources. The proper selection, training, and education of the individuals involved in these activities together with the application of software systems can reduce the necessary investments.[21]

---

[18]Dave R., Nelson, Patricia E. Moody, and Jonathan Stegner, *The Purchasing Machine* (New York: The Free Press, 2001).

[19]Robert Handfield, *Reengineering for Time-Based Competition* (Westport, CT: Quorum Press, 1995).

[20]From a book review by David Jessop, *European Journal of Purchasing and Supply Management,* December 1997, p. 241.

[21]For an excellent collection of cost reduction articles, see *Articles for C.P.M. Exam Preparation* (Tempe, AZ: National Association of Purchasing Management, 2000), pp. 225–49.

Post-Ownership Cost Such costs frequently are overlooked but must be considered when addressing the total cost of ownership. They include the disposal of scrap and other waste, customer service, warranty costs, and the cost of lost sales resulting from customer dissatisfaction with the product.

Supply Management and Return on Investment (ROI)

Investors and other sources of funds frequently evaluate top management's performance by calculating the return on the total capital invested in the business. Look at Figure 1.5, which depicts the relationships of basic elements that influence return on investment. The figures in parentheses reflect a 5 percent reduction in the cost of materials for a manufacturing firm. Notice how, in our example, a 5 percent reduction in material cost increases ROI from 10 to 13 percent, a 30 percent increase!

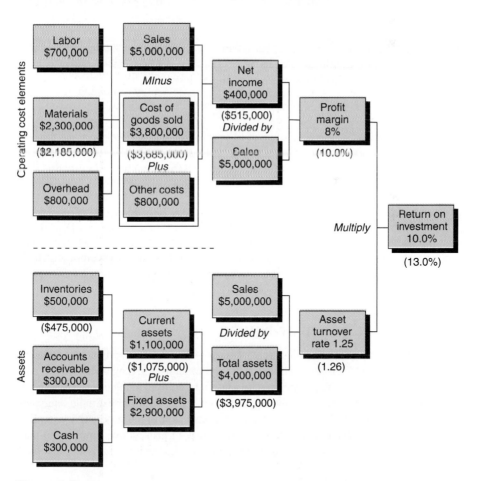

Figure 1.5 | A graphic view of the relationships of basic elements which influence return on investment. The figures in parentheses reflect a 5 percent reduction in the cost of materials

The Four Phases of Supply Management

The four phases of supply management all require many perspectives and inputs best obtained through a cross-functional approach. These four phases of supply management are as follows.

Generation of Requirements

The generation of requirements is a critical activity that results in the identification of the optimal materials and services to purchase, together with the development of specifications and statements of work describing these requirements. Approximately 85 percent of the cost of purchased material, services, and equipment is "designed in" during this phase.[22] Thus, supply management should be involved up-front during the generation of requirements to ensure that all commercial issues such as cost, availability, substitutes, and so on, receive appropriate consideration.

Sourcing

The objective of sourcing is the identification and selection of the supplier whose costs, qualities, technologies, timeliness, dependability, and service best meet the firm's needs. The development of supply alliances is a sourcing activity.

Pricing

The objective of pricing is the development of prices that appropriately reward the supplier for its efforts and which result in the lowest total costs of ownership for the customer firm. While negotiations occur throughout the supply management process, their most significant role normally is during the pricing phase.

Post-Award Activities

This important activity ensures that the firm receives what was ordered on time and at the price and quality specified. Post-award activities include supplier development, technical assistance, troubleshooting, and the management of the contract and the resulting relationships.

Supply Management Systems

Virtually all firms have supply management systems—even though many do not appear to be aware of this truth. A cross-functional approach to supply management allows each functional area affected by the procurement of materials, equipment, and services to be involved at a point where it may contribute to the lowest total cost. For example, engineering has expertise in technology and design; operations has it in the productivity implications of different materials; quality addresses the ability of prospective suppliers to meet quality requirements; and supply management addresses the commercial issues involved.

---

[22]D. Whitney, "Manufacturing by Design," *Harvard Business Review,* July–August 1988, pp. 83–91.

Functions that should be included up-front (but seldom are under traditional approaches) are more likely to be involved so that they may contribute their insight. Customer service and maintenance are examples of functions with valuable information that should be considered early in a product's development. Unfortunately, such activities normally do not participate early enough to voice their concerns and needs. This may result in the purchase of equipment that is difficult to maintain, which may result in unavoidable downtime.

Early in the development stage for new products or services (normally, after the objectives have been established and agreed to), one or more carefully selected suppliers is invited to join the in-house cross-functional team. Such action reduces the development and operation cycle and total costs.

Business-to-Business (B2B) E-Commerce and Supply Management

"The 21st century corporation must adapt itself to management via the Web. It must be predicated on constant change, not stability, organized around networks, not rigid hierarchies, built on shifting partnerships and alliances, not self-sufficiency, and constructed on technological advances, not bricks and mortar. . . . True 21st century corporations will also learn to manage an elaborate network of external relationships. That far-reaching ecosystem of suppliers, partners, and contractors will allow them to focus on what they do best and farm everything else out."[23]

B2B e-commerce is accelerating the transformation of supply management to status as a core competency. In order to obtain optimal benefits from the Internet, buying firms should use the practices involved in supply base management to separate their commodity classes, equipment, and service requirements into logical groups. Some groups of requirements will lend themselves to sourcing through reverse auctions conducted over the Internet. Other requirements will be obtained through electronic exchanges. B2B marketplaces or exchanges allow buyers and sellers powerful means of reducing transaction costs while enhancing the sellers' sales and distribution processes. In October 2000, Juniper Research predicted that B2B e-commerce will grow to $6.3 trillion in 2005 and that 80 percent of business-to-business transactions will be conducted online in six to eight years.[24] Anecdotal evidence indicates purchase price savings of 10 percent and more through the use of electronic exchanges in the procurement of indirect supplies and equipment. Many requirements will continue to be obtained through collaborative or alliance relationships. The Internet facilitates and expedites procurement of all these groups of requirements; however, firms must plan in advance in order to use the appropriate electronic technique. Such advanced planning minimizes administrative time when sourcing.

B2B e-commerce allows buying firms to consolidate requirements. Increased volume results in lower unit prices. Reverse auctioning and the use of electronic exchanges

---

[23]"The 21st Century Corporation," *BusinessWeek,* Aug 28, 2000, pp. 86 and 94.

[24]Larry Greenemeir, "B-to-B Commerce Credited to Reach $6.3 Trillion in 2005," *Information Week Daily!,* October 3, 2000.

result in wider and more aggressive competition and lower prices. B2B e-commerce also has a significant impact on inventory throughout a supply chain. During the period from June to September 2000, Dell "reinvented its procurement and manufacturing processes, and can now complete 90 percent of its purchases online—up from virtually zero just a few months earlier." As a result, Dell maintains only two hours of inventory for most parts. Suppliers who maintain parts and subassemblers in warehouses near Dell factories are told what to deliver electronically so that Dell can build the next two hours of computers. Dell virtually eliminates its inventory of parts, and suppliers are able to reduce their inventories by up to 70 percent. PCs are loaded onto trucks for shipment just 15 hours after receipt of an electronic order from a customer.[25]

The number of people involved in supply management and accounts payable is decreasing. The vast majority of tactical work is being eliminated. The staffs in both areas are being reduced. The remaining supply management staff is responsible for value-added strategic activities.

The requirements determination process is being compressed. Electronic meetings of all relevant players (including appropriate suppliers) significantly reduce delays in scheduling and conducting meetings. Technical communication (over the Internet) between suppliers and the firm's engineers compresses new product development. Similar time compression occurs in the development of requirements for equipment and services. "Electronic commerce technology will support electronic efficiency efforts . . . a very powerful communication integration is under way matching future improvements in the web with adoption of enterprise-based systems. This trend is being driven by the need for speed in both decision making and product and service fulfillment."[26]

Post-award activities also benefit from the use of the Internet. Information flow is greatly facilitated. Real-time information assists the buying firm in gaining timely receipt of the right quality of material, equipment, and services.

Michael Porter of Harvard writes, "We need to move away from the rhetoric of 'Internet industries,' 'e-business strategies,' and a 'new economy' and see the Internet for what it is: an enabling technology—a powerful set of tools that can be used, wisely or unwisely, in almost any industry and as part of almost any strategy."[27] The topic of B2B e-commerce is addressed in greater detail in Chapter 9.

Strategic Supply Management Activities

Supply management must focus on ten strategic activities:

1. Environment Monitoring. Supply management must understand supply markets and monitor the supply environment to identify threats and opportunities. These threats and opportunities include material shortages that affect one or more industries that supply the firm. Shortages will affect both the price and availability of purchased materials

---

[25]David Rocks, "Streamlining Dell's Second Web Revolution," *BusinessWeek,* September 18, 2000.

[26]P. L. Carter, J. R. Carter, R. M. Monczka, T. H. Slaight, and A. J. Swan, "The Future of Purchasing and Supply: A Ten-Year Forecast," *The Journal of Supply Chain Management,* Winter 2000, pp. 14–26.

[27]Michael E. Porter, "Strategy and the Internet," Harvard Business Review, March 2001, p. 64.

and supplies. The firm should take actions to minimize the impact of such shortages by monitoring changes in the supply environment:

■ *Changes in legislation* that affect the workplace. Such changes can affect both price and availability. An example is a new Environmental Protection Agency regulation on toxic wastes, which affects one or more suppliers.

■ *Wars and other conflicts,* which may disrupt the availability of materials the firm or its suppliers require. Firms that proactively monitor the environment take defensive action in anticipation of the resulting material shortages and price increases.

■ *A consolidation among suppliers.* The extreme case is consolidation to the point of monopoly. Such changes may require a change in the firm's supply strategy.

The Institute for Supply Management™ (formerly the National Association of Purchasing Management) publishes its *Report on Business*® each month in an effort to make economic data available to its members and government economists who treat much of the data as leading economic indicators. The report is reviewed in New York, Tokyo, London, Frankfurt, and many other international financial centers and undoubtedly has an impact on stock markets. It is cited in *The Wall Street Journal,* the *New York Times,* and the *Financial Times.* The report provides invaluable insight into near term changes in prices and availability of both manufactured goods and services.

   2.   Integrated Supply Strategy. Supply management must develop and manage the firm's supply strategy as an integrated whole instead of a series of unrelated strategies. The corporation's strategy is the key driver of the supply strategy. The technology, marketing, and production strategies are all inputs to the supply strategy. Conversely, the supply strategy is an input to the technology, marketing, and production strategies.

   3.   Commodity Strategies. Supply management must develop and update sound commodity supply strategies. The following activities must be performed in order to ensure the effectiveness of the firm's commodity strategies:

■ *Strategy updating.* Commodity teams must identify materials, items of equipment, and services that are or will be strategic and develop strategic plans for obtaining them. When environmental monitoring activities identify changes in threats and/or opportunities in the supply environment, the firm must react quickly by updating its commodity strategies and take appropriate actions.

■ *Technology access and control.* World Class Supply Management^{SM} organizations develop and update technology road maps, which list critical current and future technologies to be pursued. Many of these technologies can and must be obtained from the firm's supply base. Additionally, the firm must identify critical or strategic technologies developed by suppliers with the firm's funds. Action must be taken to protect the technologies that yield a competitive advantage and ensure they are not transferred to competitors.

■ *Supply management organization.* The internal supply management organization must be by design, not by accident or history. The organization of the supply management system must enhance the effectiveness and efficiency of the system in meeting its primary objective, which is maximizing the bottom line.

■ *Risk management.* The firm must take action to minimize the possibility of supply disruptions and price increases.

4. Data Management. Supply management, accounting, and information technology must cooperate in the collection and application of supply data with the objective of facilitating strategic supply planning. Strategic supply planning requires data that provide information for processes that span over functional and company boundaries. The responsibility for planning, collection, and compilation of supply data should not be placed on supply management alone. Rather, it should be an interfunctional activity where the leaders are supply management and information technology personnel. Suppliers should also be included in the planning of data collection and application after careful internal consideration and analysis of each supplier relationship.

5. Corporate Strategic Plans. Supply management must join marketing and operations as the key players in the development of each of the firm's corporate strategic plans. Supply management provides input to the strategic planning process on threats and opportunities in the supply world. Threats may be potential key material shortages or price increases. Opportunities may be in the form of likely new technologies, materials, and equipment that may lower the firm's cost of operations. Production and marketing are vitally involved.

Supply management provides input on constraints that may affect strategic initiatives. Supply management's knowledge of the firm's supply world may be a source of vital input during the strategic planning process.

Supply management must receive timely input on future needs that may drive changes in the firm's supply base. Early information on likely changes in the firm's markets, services, and products and likely changes in technological direction allow supply management adequate lead time to locate or develop the necessary suppliers.

6. Strategic Sourcing. The firm must design and manage its supply base in line with the firm's strategic objectives. Several actions must be taken in the area of supply base management or strategic sourcing:

■ *Periodically review the firm's base of active suppliers* to ensure that it is adequate to meet present and likely future needs. Such a systematic review helps the firm avoid supply disruptions. The technology road map is the key input to the process of determining the firm's likely future supply requirements.

■ *Identify the appropriate type of relationship* (transactional, collaborative or alliance) for each commodity class. These classes of relationships are described in Chapter 5.

■ *Optimize the supply base.* Several forces combine to increase the importance of the firm's supply bases:

Firms have discovered that they "need to stick to their knitting" . . . to do what they do best and leave the rest to others . . . to outsource.

Reductions in product life cycles force firms to develop and acquire technology quickly. The supply base is the source of the technology underlying 35–50 percent of all successful new products at many firms.

The cost pressure resulting from global competition requires companies to search for efficient, cost effective solutions. Frequently, these solutions are in the form of outside suppliers.

The periodic review of the firm's base of active suppliers has two divergent drivers: (1) The firm wants to have leverage or "clout" with its suppliers and wants a supply base small enough to allow members of the supply management system time to apply sound management practices to each relationship. (2) The firm wants a base large enough to help it avoid supply disruptions and to remain technologically competitive.

7. Strategic Supply Alliances. The development and management of supply alliances frequently are two of the most crucial and most strategic activities undertaken by any firm. Institutional trust is a key prerequisite to supply alliances.[28] The rapid growth of the American Society of Alliance Professionals gives testimony to industry's recognition of the importance of these activities.

8. Supply Chain/Supply Networks. The development and management of a firm's supply chain or supply network parallels the development and management of supply alliances, but is infinitely more complex. Information technology and relationship skills are essential prerequisites for personnel assigned to this task.

Charles Fine in his book *Clockspeed* writes, "The farther you look upstream in your technology supply chain, the more volatility you see. Customers are foolish if they don't spend any time or resources thinking about the health, survival, and possible independence of their core technology suppliers."[29]

9. Social Responsibilities. Supply management must develop and implement programs which protect the environment, which facilitate the inclusion of minority-owned, woman-owned, and small businesses in our economy, and which promote values in the workplace.

10. Understand Key Supply Industries. Supply management's impact is directly proportional to its knowledge of the industries in which it buys. Supply professionals study and understand the industries which provide key materials, equipment, and services, their cost structures, technologies, competitive nature, and culture.

We see that supply management has both strategic and tactical responsibilities. When both are executed efficiently and effectively, supply management becomes a key to the organization's survival and success.

Concluding Remarks

Supply management must be a core competency based on its impact on the bottom line. The philosophy of World Class Supply Management^{SM} requires change driven by upper management. The decision-making process must shift from an internal department or single company focus toward optimization of the supply chain. World-class supply managers proactively improve the supply processes with the long-term goal of improving the competitive capability of the firm and the firm's supply chain.

Endnote

Dave Nelson and Jonathan Stegner, formerly of Deere and Company, have joined the gifted writer Patricia Moody to produce the book *The Purchasing Machine*.[30] The book describes how 10 top companies use best practices to manage their supply chains.

---

[28]The issue of institutional trust is addressed in the appendix to Chapter 5.

[29]Fine, *Clockspeed,* p. 95.

[30]The Free Press, New York, 2001.

2 CHAPTER

Purchasing Becomes Supply Management

What Is a Profession?
A calling requiring specialized knowledge and often long and intensive preparation including instruction in skills and methods as well as in the scientific, historical, or scholarly principles underlying such skills and methods, maintaining by force of organization or concerted opinion high standards of achievement and conduct, and committing its members to continued study and to a kind of work which has for its prime purpose the rendering of a public service.
Webster's Third International Dictionary

Purchasing: A Dynamic Profession

Is purchasing a profession? Emphatically yes! Professional purchasing/procurement/ supply management[1] personnel contribute at least as much to the success of their organizations as other professionals in areas such as marketing, finance and accounting, engineering, and operations. Specialized knowledge in scientific principles of commercial, technical, and relationship management is essential. In no other profession are the opportunities to contribute greater. Intensive preparation—both in the classroom and through on-the-job experience—is required. The skills and methods required combine scientific principles with the art of developing and maintaining relationships.

Do the required skills have a historic foundation? Professor Harry Page (emeritus, George Washington University) in his draft manuscript on the evolution of purchasing writes:

> Inscribed clay tablets from the 13th Century BC days of the Phoenician traders refer to persons serving as "purchasing agents." The Holy Bible, in the Book of Deuteronomy, provides instruction for buyers in the honest use of weights and measures. Ancient purchase orders, written on parchment scrolls in the days of Julius Caesar, call for delivery of amphoras of wine, honey and oil.[2]

As is true of all modern business functions, many of the scholarly principles on which supply management is built are taken from economics. Just as supply/demand and marginal analysis form the backbone of economics, the principles of determining the organization's requirements, selecting the optimal source, establishing a fair and reasonable price, and establishing and maintaining mutually beneficial relationships with the most desirable supplier provide the conceptual backbone of the supply function. Numerous textbooks and articles in professional publications, including the *California Management Review, European Journal of Purchasing and Supply Management, Harvard Business Review, Journal of Supply Chain Management, Journal of Marketing Research, Sloan Management Review,* and the German language *Thexis,* provide an increasing flow of scholarly information on the supply profession.

The evolutionary nature of management in this field is such that continued study and self-improvement are necessary. A number of professional organizations, including the Institute for Supply Management™ (formerly know as the National Association of Purchasing Management), the American Production and Inventory Control Society,[3] the National Contract Management Association, the National Institute of Governmental Purchasing, the Purchasing Management Association of Canada, the Chartered Institute of Purchasing and

---

[1]The terms "purchasing" and "procurement" are used interchangeably, although somewhat imprecisely, in many business organizations. The term "supply management" is used increasingly today to encompass the purchasing department, the procurement process and more. Precise operational and strategic definitions of these terms are developed in Chapter 3. Throughout the book, however, the term "supply management" is used to describe the composite business function.

[2]Letter from Harry Robert Page dated May 12, 1994.

[3]The American Production and Inventory Control Society officially changed its name to the Educational Society for Resource Management; however the name change did not receive widespread adoption by its constituents.

Supply (U.K.), and the International Federation of Purchasing and Materials Management, are dedicated to the continuing training and upgrading of their members. Today, over 40 colleges and universities in the United States and Canada offer degree-granting programs in the areas of purchasing, procurement, and supply management. Similar programs exist in Europe, Australia, Asia, Africa, and the rest of the Americas.

Does the supply management profession render a *public service? Undeniably, it does!* The impact of supply professionals on the quality, cost, and productivity of their organizations is one of the keys to a nation's competitiveness in the global marketplace. And such competitiveness is the basis of value-adding employment.

Is the profession undergoing changes? Yes—and and at an exponential rate! For example, several management years ago, one of the authors was a speaker at the Tennant Company's annual manufacturing conference in Minneapolis. At a dinner for the speakers, we asked a member of the Japanese Management Association, "You treat supply management as a strategic weapon, don't you?" The response was, "Ah, you're very perceptive!" More recently, we visited the head of supply management at a highly successful multinational firm. This firm had just spent some $7 million studying supply management practices in Europe and Japan. When asked to share the insight gained, the director of supply management responded that since this knowledge would give his firm a strategic, global competitive advantage, he was unable to honor our request. Even more recently, a marketing colleague returned from a visit to a major Japanese transplant in the Midwest. His bemused reaction to the visit was, "You're right. Supply runs the transplant!"

At organization after organization—whether manufacturing, service, institution, or government—one sees examples of what might be called proactive procurement[4] (stage 3) or strategic supply management[5] (stage 4) as depicted in Figure 1.1 (see Chapter 1). Yet, based on self ratings, the majority of organizations appear to be somewhere else on the continuum shown in Figure 1.1.

The next 20 years will be the most exciting and challenging in the history of supply management as organizations progress to a "10" in Figure 1.1 *and beyond.* "Kaizen" (continuous improvement) is the word of the day—and all tomorrows! Supply management is becoming recognized as a function equal in corporate importance to design, conversion, marketing, and finance. In 1996, A. T. Kearney studied the practices of 26 North American companies with reputations for excellence in supply management. Lawrence Kohn, a vice president in Kearney's strategic-sourcing division, observed that "procurement professionals are prized partly because they are so rare." Kohn predicted that "people who make procurement their profession will come to be highly rewarded, both financially and in terms of career mobility."[6] Today, compensation of procurement (supply management) professionals is on a par with other professionals in leading-edge organizations. Supply management is becoming (or has become) a critical participant in the

---

[4]See David N. Burt, *Proactive Procurement: The Key to Increased Profits, Productivity and Quality* (Englewood Cliffs, N.J.: Prentice-Hall, 1984).

[5]See David N. Burt and Michael F. Doyle, *The American Keiretsu* (Homewood, IL: Business One-Irwin, 1993).

[6]Katherine J. Sweetman, "Procurement: A New Strategic Frontier," *Harvard Business Review,* November—December 1996, p. 12.

organization's strategic planning function. But before we spend more time on the tremendous changes taking place, let's develop a historic perspective of the origins and roots of purchasing.

Origins of Purchasing and Supply Management

Purchasing has long been considered one of the basic functions common to all organizations. Curiously, only during the past two centuries has purchasing been addressed in trade books and textbooks. For example, in 1832, Charles Babbage addressed the topic in his book, *On the Economy of Machinery and Manufacturing.*[7] One of the early books focusing on purchasing was written by H. B. Twyford of the Otis Elevator Company only some 90 years ago. Mr. Twyford was prophetic when he wrote:

> A (purchasing) staff which is entirely unsympathetic with the particular needs of the users of the material will fail to grasp what is one of the most essential things for their department. They will be dealing with papers and accounts instead of with men and things.[8]

It is believed that the first college textbook that focused on purchasing was authored by Howard T. Lewis of Harvard University in 1933.[9] Harvard University has long recognized the importance of supply management. Its first course was offered in the 1917–1918 academic year. Today, the *Harvard Business Review* continues Harvard's tradition by publishing numerous timely articles on the subject.

Unfortunately, since senior management's interests historically have focused on marketing, R&D, finance, and operations, purchasing was, all too frequently, subordinate to these familiar functions. With many notable exceptions, personnel historically assigned to purchasing had neither the skill nor the aptitude to lead this function to making its full contribution to the success of the organization. Ironically, during this period, purchasing was responsible for a significant portion of the cost of goods sold. Purchased materials were the source of a large share of the firm's quality problems. In many cases, purchasing had more impact on the bottom line than did any other function.[10]

During the 1960s and 1970s, purchasing and materials management frequently used manual "kardex" systems to manage inventory. The buyer's major focuses were *purchase price* and the *prevention of line shutdowns.* A tertiary issue was the management of inventory. The typical department had a series of senior and junior buyers, clerks, one or more expediters, a purchasing manager, and perhaps several purchasing supervisors, depending on the size of the firm. Then the world changed.

By the end of the decade of the 1970s, the marketplace had become more international, from both a marketing and a supply point of view. Computers began to help in the

---

[7]Charles Knight Publishers, London, 1832, pp. 202, 216.

[8]H. B. Twyford, *Purchasing: Its Economic Aspects and Proper Methods,* (New York: D. Van Nostrand Co. 1915), p. 56.

[9]Howard T. Lewis, *Industrial Purchasing* (New York: Prentice-Hall, 1933).

[10]David N. Burt, *Proactive Procurement: The Key to Increased Profits, Productivity, and Quality* (Englewood Cliffs, N. J.: Prentice Hall, 1984).

management of inventory. Also, the cost of material had become a more important topic as oil embargoes and inflation drove unit costs up. Concurrently, the amount of automation in the production process increased, thus promoting specialization and driving the unit cost of production down. Senior managers realized that it frequently was less costly to purchase from outside specialized suppliers than to make an item or perform a service internally. All of these forces resulted in material costs increasing as a percentage of the cost of goods sold.

These transitions brought about significant changes in purchasing's responsibilities. Purchasing and materials management began taking on a more important role within manufacturing, institutions, service firms, and government. Increased emphasis was placed on the control of inventory. During the early 1980s, many organizations became profitable largely through much more careful management of their inventories. These organizations had discovered that carrying inventories cost 25 to 35 percent of the value of the items carried, depending on the cost of capital. Computer-generated material requirements plans (MRP) and improved supplier discipline—including just-in-time inventory[11] allowed customers to reduce their inventories significantly. New people who were educated in materials, logistics, and computers were recruited into the materials and purchasing function. Purchasing stopped accepting people who could no longer make a *value-added contribution.* "Kardex cards" disappeared, and MRP action reports surfaced. The buyer became a person who was handling higher part loads because of the "efficiency" of materials management systems. There was no role change to the organization other than a recognition that purchasing and materials management were counted on to make a contribution to the financial success of the organization. Up until this point, when engineering assistance was required to interface with a supplier, manufacturing or design engineering would become involved, obviating the need for engineering expertise by the buyer.

Transition to Supply Management

By the late 1980s material costs made up approximately 60 percent of the cost of goods sold in the United States. The impact of purchasing and materials management on company assets became very significant and very visible. The U.S. manufacturing industry (and many service firms) emulated everything Japanese: kanban, quality circles, just-in-time, and kaizen (continuous improvement). These changes, coupled with electronic purchasing systems and growing recognition by senior management of the crucial role that must be played by purchasing and supply management, provided the stimulus for more change. Purchasing and supply managers began to see the need for two types of resources in their organizations: (1) a team of people who manage the operational and tactical activities of purchasing and materials management (materials coordinators) and (2) supply managers who are involved in the development of broader strategic aspects of the function.

---

[11]With just-in-time inventory, the required materials arrive just at the moment they are needed for incorporation into the item being assembled.

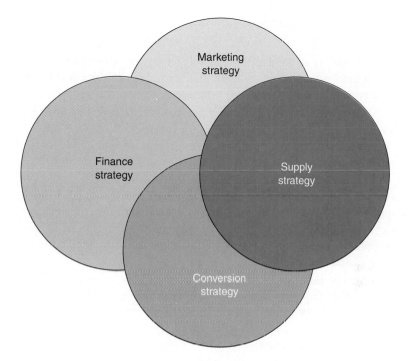

Figure 2.1 I The elements making up the strategic business plan.

Materials coordinators are responsible for placing orders against purchase agreements, keeping the production lines running, and minimizing inventories.[12] Supply managers participate in new product development and are involved in selecting sources, managing costs, developing and nurturing supplier partnerships and strategic alliances, and issuing and managing long-term agreements with carefully selected suppliers.

At proactive organizations, supply managers also are active participants in the organization's strategic planning process. An organization's supply strategy is becoming recognized as a strategic weapon equal in importance to the firm's marketing, conversion, and finance strategies.[13] These four strategies, when properly integrated, become the organization's strategic business plan, as shown in Figure 2.1.

Value-Adding Benefits

Historically, the performance of many purchasing managers and their organizations was measured and evaluated on changes in the purchase price of materials, their ability to keep the production line running, and the cost of their department's operation. Today,

---

[12]Purchase agreements identify approved sources of supply, prices, and delivery criteria for carefully defined materials and services.

[13]Burt and Doyle, *The American Keiretsu,* p. 5.

world-class organizations expect their supply management function to focus on the following five value-adding outputs of proactive procurement or supply management:

- *Quality.* The quality of purchased materials and services should be virtually defect-free.[14] (At most manufacturing and services firms, over 75 percent of all quality defects can be traced back to purchased materials.)

- *Cost.* The supply management function must focus on strategic cost management: the process of reducing the *total* cost of acquiring, moving, holding, converting, and supporting products containing purchased materials and services throughout the supply chain.

- *Time.* The supply management function and its outside suppliers must play active roles in reducing the time required to bring new products to market. Professionals in supply, design, and manufacturing estimate that the time required to bring a new product to market can be reduced by 20 to 40 percent through the establishment and implementation of a World Class Supply Management[SM] system (a "10" in Figure 1.1—see Chapter 1).

- *Technology.* The supply management function has two key responsibilities in the area of technology: (1) It must ensure that the firm's supply base provides appropriate technology in a timely manner. (2) It must ensure that technology which affects the firm's core competencies (the "things" that give the firm its unique reason for being) is carefully controlled when dealing with outside suppliers.

- *Continuity of supply.* The supply management function must monitor supply trends, develop appropriate supplier relationships, and take such other actions as are required to reduce the risk of supply disruptions.

Strategic Focus

As has been discussed, purchasing's historical focus was on purchase price and continuity of supply. In Chapter 1, we saw that supply management adds the following strategic activities and considerations:

- *Integration.* The firm's supply strategy must be integrated with the organization's marketing, conversion, and finance strategies and that of the corporation or strategic business unit.

- *Business environment.* Supply management must identify threats and opportunities in the firm's supply environment.

- *Technology.* Supply management must address issues of technology access and control. The firm wants to gain access to technology in its supply base while being careful not to create competitors through outsourcing activities.

- *Component and commodity strategies.* Supply management must develop formalized market-driven supply plans for critical purchased materials and services.

---

[14]In some cases, 10 or fewer defective parts per million (PPM).

- *Supply information system.* Supply management must ensure that a timely, cost-effective, and comprehensive information system is in place to provide data required to make optimal supply decisions.

- *Supply base strategy.* Suppliers and the resulting supply base must be carefully developed and managed to ensure that the supply chain to which the firm belongs is successful in an increasingly competitive marketplace.

- *Reporting responsibility.* The vice president of supply management (frequently referred to as the Chief Supply Officer) reports to the chief of the strategic business unit, or to the CEO.

- *Relationship management.* World-class firms assign senior supply professionals the responsibility of managing one or more key supply relationships or alliances.

- *Number of professional personnel.* There will be fewer, but far more *professional* and *strategic,* personnel assigned to purchasing/procurement/supply management.

Five Major Developments

Cross-Functional Teams

A number of years ago, one of the authors was in charge of a seven-person procurement office responsible for purchasing $20 million in goods and services. The biggest challenge was in dealings with the plant engineer. Virtually all the plans and specifications developed by this organization contained ambiguities which, if not corrected, could result in delays, contract disputes, and possible litigation. In order to reduce the time wasted in reviewing and requiring the revision of the plans and specifications, the members of the purchasing team offered to become involved earlier in the design process. The plant engineer summarily rejected this offer. He did not want outsiders "sticking their noses" in his operation.

Not surprisingly, when the plant engineer expressed a desire to become actively involved in the source selection process, he was politely notified to "go play in his own sandbox." Needless to say, such functional biases did *not* reduce cycle time (concept to customer), nor did they reduce costs.

Fortunately, this myopic approach to conducting operations is being replaced by a focus on what's in the best interest of the customer! Perhaps the most effective approach today which overcomes the negatives of specialization and departmental walls is the use of cross-functional teams. Such teams tend to be ad hoc organizations brought together to meet specific stated objectives such as the development of a new product or the negotiation of all terms and conditions of a purchase agreement. Others, such as commodity teams, may be ongoing.

In a 1990s study, members of the National Association of Purchasing Management were surveyed to study the current and future approach (individual or team) to the following activities:

1. Material requirements review
2. Specifications development
3. Make-or-buy analysis

4. Materials standardization
5. Determination of inventory levels
6. Quality requirements determination
7. Negotiation of price and terms
8. Supplier selection
9. Joint problem solving with suppliers
10. Supplier monitoring and analysis
11. Communication of specification changes
12. Productivity/cost improvements
13. Development of sourcing strategy
14. Market analysis
15. Price forecasting
16. Long-range purchasing planning
17. Determination of purchasing policy
18. Value analysis

The study indicated that a transformation from individual to team responsibility was taking place for all 18 activities.[15]

A new product development team normally will be chaired by a design engineer or a marketing professional. Other members may come from supply management, manufacturing engineering, operations, quality, and one or more customer and supplier organizations. A negotiating team for a $10 million piece of hospital equipment may be chaired by supply, with cardiology, plant maintenance, and finance playing active roles. A standardization committee may be chaired by configuration management, with supply management, design, and manufacturing engineering and operations represented.

Normally, membership on a cross-functional team is a part-time assignment or is full time for a specified duration. This approach ensures that the functional experts retain their identification with their functional areas and that they are kept up to date and are able to share what they have learned with their functional colleagues. This approach also helps ensure the required support by the functional area for decisions made by the cross-functional team(s).

The most important implication of being part of a cross-functional team is that members will have to possess (or develop) excellent team behavioral and leadership skills. In supply management, the days of John Wayne and the Lone Ranger are over. Cross-functional teams appear to be the way of the present and the future. This important topic is discussed in greater detail in Chapter 6.

Supply Chains and Supply Networks

Perhaps the most interesting and challenging aspect of supply management is the development and management of the organization's *supply chain* or *supply network.* As was seen in Figure 1.2 in Chapter 1, the supply chain is a series of organizations extending

---

[15]Lisa M. Ellram and John N. Pearson, "The Role of the Purchasing Function: Toward Team Participation," *International Journal of Purchasing and Materials Management,* Summer 1993, pp. 3–9.

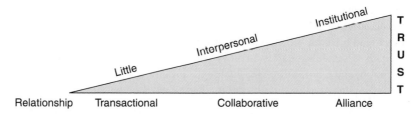

Figure 2.2 | Supply relationships and institutional trust. Institutional trust is the key element that differentiates supply alliances from collaborative relationships. This important concept is addressed in Chapter 5.

all the way back to firms which extract materials from Mother Earth. All members of the chain perform a series of value-adding activities and fabricate the finished good or service purchased by the ultimate customer.

The development and management of supply chains and supply networks is one of the most challenging and exciting aspects of supply management. Edith Kelly-Green, Vice President of Strategic Sourcing and Supply for Federal Express Corporation, observes, "Technology is the real key to supply chain management—allowing exponential cost reductions in internal processes through quick implementation and accelerated action."[16]

Once a service, commodity, or commodity class has been identified as being critical to the organization's operations, a strategic supply plan must be developed. This strategy must consider the organization's technology road map (which maps out where the organization is headed technologically); its supply base; a list of world class suppliers for the item(s); plans for selecting and, possibly, upgrading the supplier; objectives for the relationship; and plans for managing and nurturing the relationship. Frequently, a cross-functional team, under the leadership of a supply professional, will be involved in the selection of the desired supplier, negotiation of applicable terms and conditions, and ongoing management of the relationship. This supply professional must be both technically and commercially competent.

Supply Alliances

Another exciting and challenging change is progressing in parallel with the development of supply chains and networks: the development of supply alliances. These alliances *are not* legal entities, but, rather, mutually beneficial and open relationships wherein the needs of both parties are satisfied.

As shown in Figure 2.2, a customer organization may have three different types of supply relationships in support of its operations. Historically, the vast majority of buyer-seller relationships have been conducted in an arm's-length or transactional mode. In some cases, these relationships were adversarial wherein both buyer and seller believed that the only way to "get a good deal" was at the other's expense. Accordingly, much time and effort were involved in zero-sum games.[17]

---

[16]Interview by Marilyn Lester, *The Journal of Supply Chain Management,* Spring 2000, p. 3.

[17]A zero-sum game is where one of more participants gain or win while the other participant or participants lose.

Supply management personnel must identify the appropriate type of relationship. When a collaborative or alliance relationship is appropriate, supply management personnel must lead the appropriate team in the development and maintenance of the relationship. Such leadership requires a combination of technical expertise and leadership, communication, and team skills. The challenges are great; the rewards in both job satisfaction and compensation are equally great. (The issue of buyer-supplier relationships is discussed in greater detail in Chapter 5.)

Strategic Sourcing

Several years ago, the term "strategic sourcing" became popular. Strategic sourcing embraces several World Class Supply Management^{SM} concepts and greatly facilitates progression to world-class status. As Jon Ricker writes, strategic sourcing is a systematic process that directs "supply managers to plan, manage, and develop the supply base in line with a firm's strategic objectives. Strategic sourcing, seen another way, is the application of current best practices to achieve the full potential of integrating suppliers into the long-term business process. To understand its relationship to supply chain management, most advocates of strategic sourcing explain it as a core process within the larger function of supply chain management."[18] Strategic sourcing identifies new materials and technologies and the activities of competitors.

> Strategic sourcing is understanding the markets you're purchasing from inside and out and learning from your own organization and your suppliers' organizational processes, working as a mediator between suppliers and your organization, and capturing information and using it to improve relationships. Strategic sourcing requires two-way continuous improvement process work from each organization.[19]
>
> Strategic sourcing is a disciplined approach that improves the value we receive from suppliers. There are four principles that set it apart from traditional or tactical purchasing: (1) define the total value of the relationship between purchaser and supplier, (2) develop solutions based on a deep understanding of the supplier's economics and business dynamics, (3) use differentiated purchasing tactics in order to optimize the economic relationship for both purchaser and suppliers, and (4) imbed the required changes in the organization so the purchaser achieves not only a near-term measurable performance improvement but also the ability to continuously improve.[20]

During development of a strategic sourcing project, the appropriate cross-functional team follows a four-step process of implementation:

■ *Research* the industry economics and dynamics of the team's assigned commodity.

■ *Evaluate* sourcing strategies and suppliers' capabilities.

■ *Structure* the supply relationship jointly with suppliers and develop action plans to build the required infrastructure.

■ *Implement* the plan and organize for continuous improvement.[21]

---

[18]Jon Ricker, C.P.M., CPIM, "The Synergy of Strategic Sourcing," *Purchasing Today*, May 1997.

[19]Nancy Rurkowski, quoted in Ricker, "The Synergy of Strategic Sourcing."

[20]Thom Ray, quoted in Ricker, "The Synergy of Strategic Sourcing."

[21]Ricker, "The Synergy of Strategic Sourcing."

E-procurement

Without question, e-procurement is one of the most exciting developments in supply management in recent years. No longer are buyers responsible for non-value-adding activities and paperwork processing. The internal end user of an item or service, whether for a direct or indirect requirement, is now empowered to place orders through the Internet directly to the supplier. (These suppliers have been carefully selected by sourcing teams which also establish delivery terms and prices.)

The release of this tactical responsibility allows supply professionals to focus on value-adding activities, including:

- *Early involvement in the development of requirements,* whether for production materials, indirect supplies, equipment, or services. Design is the most critical phase of the procurement cycle with some 85 percent of the cost "designed in" during this activity.
- *Strategic sourcing or supply base management.* The periodic supply base review (discussed in Chapter 1) establishes the appropriate class of buyer-supplier relationship and determines if the existing supply base is optional. If not, supply management professionals lead cross-functional sourcing teams in selecting (or developing) a new source.
- *Pricing.* Supply management has many pricing techniques available to aid in the establishment of the right price, including competitive bidding, cost analysis negotiation, reverse auctions conducted over the Internet, cost models, target pricing, and various compensation methods (firm fixed price, fixed price incentive, award fee, and so on). These issues are discussed in Part V.)
- *Post-award activities.* These activities include all actions required to ensure timely delivery of materials or timely completion of services in the quality specified.
- The strategic activities introduced in Chapter 1.

The Future of Supply Management

Industry, institutions, and government will continue to have a supply management function—one which grows in importance. Many of the manual tasks previously performed by purchasing personnel are being automated or reassigned so that supply professionals focus on producing high value added, not paperwork. Supply management professionals are technically proficient so that they can work with technical customers and suppliers. They truly are becoming managers of the organization's outside production!

These individuals must possess a sound grounding in all the commercial aspects of supply management. As William L. Michaels, Chief Executive of ADR North American, recently stated, "Buyers of the future will focus on activities one and even five years out. They will understand the entire supply chain, all innovation trends, all technology trends, and global capacity. They will develop suppliers worldwide, who will meet their needs, and they will segment and articulate where their suppliers fall within their portfolios."[22] They will begin work as buyers, not as supply managers. Through application and hard work they will progress to become supply managers— one of the organization's most important professionals! And, as Tom Stallkamp, former President of Chrysler, and Richard Wagoner, G.M.'s President of North American Car Operations in 1996, have demonstrated, supply management can be a foundation for executive-level assignments.

---

[22]William L. Michaels, quoted in Cherish Karoway Whyte, "Channeling Your Purchasing Department's Expertise into Distinct Units Can Improve Its Flow of Revenues," *Purchasing Today,* November 1998.

CHAPTER 3

Supply Management: An Organization Spanning Activity℠

As a philosophy, World Class Supply Management℠ spans functional boundaries and company borders.

KEY CONCEPTS

Case

It is Saturday afternoon, September 6. Ted Jones, supply manager for the Eagle Manufacturing Company, is in his office reviewing his life at Eagle. Since becoming the head of supply management, Ted has been struggling with one crisis after another while trying to placate operations, plant maintenance, and seemingly half the management team (and their assistants). Although only 35, Ted feels like 60. Eagle is expecting a large return on the salary it is paying Ted.

In the two years since taking over the department, Ted has put together a great team of buyers, expediters, and support staff. Their work is tops. They are all professionals. But morale has started to be a problem. On Friday, Bill Wilson, Ted's senior buyer, submitted his resignation. Bill decided to take a job with a handsome salary increase at Cable Manufacturers of America. He said, "If I'm going to get ulcers, I might as well be paid for them!"

Ted looks at the August performance data for the office: 743 transactions, 98 percent with delivery dates on or before specified, 87 percent of supplies and material purchases at or within 5 percent of target price, 9 percent late deliveries, and a 5 percent rejection rate of materials and supplies received. When compared with the months previous to August, the trends look good, but there is still room for improvement. Ted feels that his department can have a much greater impact on the firm's profitability if he can generate more cooperation with the other departments. He also realizes that a better training program will bring along some of his own people a bit faster.

Ted thought about some of the "big ones" that had happened in August. The maintenance department had submitted a purchase request for a new robot on August 29. The machine, according to the estimates supplied, would cost $5.5 million. The machine was to be delivered and operational in seven months. Only one source of supply had been able to meet the delivery date. Ted wondered how much extra money the lack of lead time had cost on that one.

Tim Raines, vice president of operations, had held Ted's feet to the coals in the weekly staff meeting on August 7. Operations had run out of parts that week. The vice president of marketing, Ron Hankins, had helped to apply the coals on that one. In retrospect, Ted was puzzled over the hopscotch communication patterns among operations, material control, marketing, and his own office.

Tim confronted Ted on August 14, again during the staff meeting, saying that quality on the incoming parts was causing major production problems. Ted tried to explain the greater attrition rate inherent in new production processes, but Tim was not convinced.

In fairness, not all his problems were with operations, Ted thought during this Saturday afternoon reverie. The president's secretary had called twice to say that the janitorial services contractor had not washed the windows properly. Ted mentioned that poorly described, unenforceable specifications were part of the problem. But the secretary was just trying to do her job in seeing that somebody else's job was done right. She didn't know about the "contractual provisions."

Mary Jacobs, head of administration, had been complaining to Ted on a daily basis about the new brand of reproduction paper. Mary believed the quality of reproduction was down and the paper was constantly jamming the machine. Machine downtime was reducing productivity and increasing frustration with her people. Ted pointed out that finance had reduced funds available for supplies by 20 percent and that the reduction consequently forced some sacrifice in quality.

Yesterday, John McCauly, an experienced supply manager and normally as cool as a cucumber, had exploded when Ted asked how everything was going. John had replied, "Those blankety-blank estimators. This morning, I was negotiating with Fenwick Electronics for that robot. The maintenance department's estimate was $5.5 million. Fenwick proposed $7.2 million. You know that because of time, they were already a 'sole-source' position. Imagine my reaction when I learned that our $5.5 million 'estimate' was not an estimate at all but merely the amount budgeted for that machine last year! I had no basis for developing a realistic negotiating objective. I literally had to throw myself on the mercy of Fenwick's marketing manager." Bringing his thoughts back to the present, Ted decided there just had to be a better way.

Supply Management's Role in Business

What is the role of supply management in business? Why is it important? To answer these questions, the supply management function will be observed from three points of view: first, as a function of business; second, as one of the basic elements required to accomplish productive work; and third, as the key department responsible for outside manufacturing and services.

Six Key Business Functions

Supply is one of the basic functions common to all types of business enterprise. These functions are basic because no business can operate without them. All businesses are managed by coordinating and integrating these six functions:

1. *Creation,* the idea or design function, frequently based on research and development.
2. *Finance,* the capital acquisition, financial planning and control function.
3. *Personnel,* the human resources and labor relations function.
4. *Supply,* the acquisition of required materials, services, and equipment.
5. *Conversion,* the transformation of materials into economic goods and services.
6. *Distribution,* the marketing and selling of goods and services produced.

The research and design engineering departments, the finance or controller's department, the human resources department, the supply management department, the production department, and the sales or marketing department are the common titles of the organizational units responsible for performing these six functions in an industrial setting. In institutional and nonindustrial enterprises, the same basic functions must be performed, but they may be identified by different names.

Depending on a company's size, these basic functions may be supervised by a single manager or by individual managers for each function. Regardless of how they are supervised, someone performs them in every business. Some small firms, for example, do not have a supply management department; nevertheless, the supply function must still be performed. Sometimes the president performs the supply function. At other times an executive who administers several basic functions, including supply management, performs the supply function.

By its very nature, supply management is a basic and integral part of business management. Why is this fact important? For a business to be successful, all its individual parts must be successful. A successful supply activity is required for any organization to achieve its full potential. In the long run, the success of a business enterprise depends every bit as much on the supply management executive as it does on the executives who administer the firm's other functions. This is not to imply that all supply management departments are of equal importance to the success of their companies. They are not; their importance varies widely.

The importance of any individual business function within a specific organization depends on a number of factors. Among these factors are the type of business, its goals, its economic circumstances, and the way the enterprise operates to achieve these goals. In some situations, supply management can function in a perfunctory manner without jeopardizing a company's profit. These situations, however, are exceptions. Similar exceptions can be found in marketing, finance, or any other function of business. For example, in a firm that makes and sells a unique advanced technical product, the marketing department usually does not have weighty responsibilities. Engineering excellence and product performance do more than creative marketing to sell the product. On the other hand, marketing a highly competitive standard product requires ability of the highest order. In such companies, the marketing department has a position of major importance.

The basic functions of business vary in importance within a given firm, over time, as the firm passes through its life cycle. For example, in the early life of Hewlett-Packard (originally a highly successful producer of precision electronic instruments), design engineering was the dominant function of the company. The company's products were so far advanced technically, and demand for them was so great, that their cost was relatively unimportant. The firm's products literally were self-selling. Under such circumstances, neither supply management nor marketing was a critical function within the company.

With the passage of time, however, conditions changed. Competent competitors entered the market. Consequently, Hewlett-Packard products could no longer be sold at any price, because the insatiable market for its products had disappeared. As a result of these changes, the company had to reevaluate and reorganize both its marketing and its supply management functions. As a consequence, marketing and supply both became functions of major importance.

Increasing Importance of Purchased Materials

The basic goal of any industrial activity is the development and manufacture of products and providing of services that can be marketed at a profit. This goal is accomplished by the appropriate blending of what management authorities historically have called the five Ms: machines, manpower, materials, money, and management. Materials are the lifeblood of industry. Materials of the appropriate quality must be available at the right time, in the proper quantity, at the needed location, and at an acceptable total cost. Failure to fulfill any of these responsibilities concerning materials adds to company costs and decreases company profit just as surely as do outmoded production methods, inefficient personnel, and ineffective marketing activities. Increasingly, services ranging from landscaping and janitorial services to manufacturing and information technology are being outsourced—that is, provided by external suppliers. In many firms, the procurement of such services is as (or more) important as the procurement of production materials.

Materials have not always been so vital. Throughout the nation's industrial development, the relative importance of the five Ms has continually shifted. In the management sense, materials became important around 1900. Before then they were rightfully taken for granted. They were simple, readily available, and cheap. The role of the supply function in business can be seen more clearly after exploring the reasons that caused the shift in the relative importance of the five Ms.

During the first 100 years of the United States' industrial system, productivity increased very little. The availability of manpower and horsepower exceeded machine power almost a fiftyfold. This relationship started to change around 1850. Between 1850 and 1950 an unbelievable increase in productivity took place. In 1850, productive power was divided as shown in Figure 3.1: 2 percent machine power and 98 percent horsepower and manpower. By 1900, this division of power became approximately equal. In 1950, the 1850 power relationship was reversed: 98 percent machine power and 2 percent horsepower and manpower.

Because manpower was the first source of productive power, the initial industrial emphasis was on the human element; labor costs represented the major operating expense. As machines and technology began to develop, management emphasis shifted toward them. As new products, specialized labor, and materials distribution became more complex, emphasis shifted toward scientific management. Still later, as both the complexity

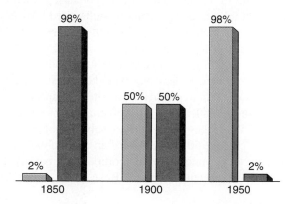

Figure 3.1 I Power source relationships, 1850 to 1950. The tan columns represent machine power, and the gray columns represent horsepower and human labor.

of materials and the volume of production skyrocketed, materials became an increasingly important element of cost. Consequently, emphasis naturally shifted toward this element of the five Ms.

The introduction of better machines, coupled with progressive management to develop and utilize more sophisticated man-machine systems, made emergence of the factory system possible. This, in turn, sparked many industrial changes—inventions such as the steam turbine, the electric motor, and automatic controls changed the entire complex of manufacturing. Gradually, materials became more complex, mechanization increased, automation emerged, and labor became more specialized. These changes inevitably led to specialization in manufacturing and the continuing need for more sophisticated and specialized materials.

As these trends accelerated and the volume of production increased, labor costs *per unit* decreased. The reduction of unit labor costs increased the relative cost and importance of materials in the manufacturing process. *Percentagewise, labor costs went down while materials costs went up.* This change in the value of materials relative to total production costs continues to this day. For example, in 1945 materials represented approximately 40 percent of the manufacturer's total cost to produce an airplane. In 1955 the materials proportion of total cost increased to around 50 percent. By 2000 the figure was slightly over 65 percent.

Supply Management and Outside Manufacturing

The materials that go into a typical company's products can originate from either of two sources. The company's production department is the first source; this department converts purchased materials into processed parts. The company's supply management department, often referred to as purchasing or procurement, is the second source. The supply management department not only purchases raw materials, which the production department converts into processed parts, but also purchases finished parts and components. The parts made by the production department are combined in assembly with the items bought by the supply management department to make the company's final products.[1]

The percentage of industrial components being purchased externally is constantly increasing compared with the percentage being manufactured internally. The trend toward specialization within our factory system inherently creates such a situation. The increasing specialization of technology and labor, the increasing complexity of new materials, and the increasing cost of high-volume specialty machines all tend to cause most industrial firms to buy more and make less. Not even the largest manufacturing concerns have sufficiently high volume requirements to compete with specialty manufacturers in all fields. For example, the so-called auto "manufacturers" more accurately should be called auto "assemblers." While they may make key subassemblies such as engines, suppliers to the "assembler" produce 50–80 percent of an automobile. Such purchasing action is taken not because they cannot make the components, but because they can buy them less expensively from specialty suppliers. Researchers Hamel and Prahalad say

---

[1]The Du Pont Company was among the first to recognize the importance of whether a company should make something itself or let its purchasing department buy it. See Ernest Dale, *The Great Organizers,* (New York: McGraw-Hill, 1960), p. 53.

that most successful firms identify, cultivate, and exploit their core competencies—they do the things they know how to do the best.[2]

The trend in manufacturing is toward the development of three distinct types of factories. The first type does not make finished end products; it is equipped with costly high-volume specialty machines and produces machined and fabricated parts in large quantities at low unit cost. These parts are sold to numerous factories of the second and third types. The second type of factory, like the first type, does not make finished end products; it makes subassemblies. The required parts for the subassemblies come from factories of the first type, or from the parts it makes, or from a combination of both. The third type of factory assembles finished end products. As economic circumstances dictate, this type of factory assembles the finished product from a combination of the parts it makes (usually parts that are unique to its product) and the standard parts or subassemblies it buys from factories of the first and second types. In recent years, several firms are outsourcing the entire manufacture and assembly of the products they sell. Firms such as Cisco, Hewlett-Packard, and IBM purchase several of the products they sell under their brand name.

In the multiple-type factory system of today, most firms generally use two distinct sources of supply: *inside* manufacture and *outside* manufacture. The production department is responsible for inside manufacture, including the authority to schedule production in economical quantities. Production schedules with specified quantities are greatly dependent on lead times for incoming materials; therefore, the schedules are usually set far enough in advance to have materials available when needed.

In world-class firms, supply management plays a key role in selecting outside suppliers, establishing prices for the materials and services, and managing relations with these suppliers. Supply management executives have the same managerial interests concerning outside production as production executives have concerning their internal production. Production executives are interested in low unit costs and high quality. Supply management executives are interested in keeping their suppliers' costs and prices down. In addition, they are interested in maintaining good working relationships that ensure timely deliveries of good quality.

Supply Management's Relations with Other Departments

A supply management department is the hub of a large part of a company's business activity. By its very nature, supply management has continuing relationships with all other departments in the firm, as well as with the firm's suppliers. Supply management operations cut across all departmental lines. Figure 3.2 provides a graphic illustration of supply management's many interfaces within the organization.

Supply Management and Engineering

Design engineers play key roles throughout the supply chain management process from their roles as new product development team leaders to members of off-spec (incoming materials which deviate from the relevant specifications) review teams. Many design

---

[2]C. K. Prahalad, "Core Competence Revisited," *Enterprise,* October 1993, p. 20.

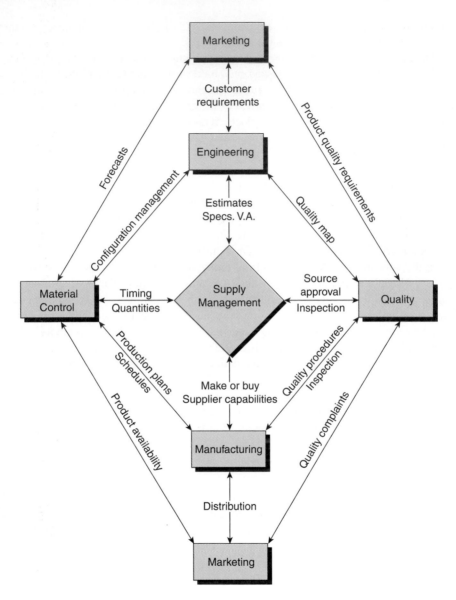

Figure 3.2 I The many internal interfaces of the supply management function.[3]

engineers have parlayed the experience gained in supply management assignments into promotions to supply management and general management.

Supply management, engineering, and operations have many mutual problems. Design engineering greatly influences the amount of time supply management has to handle

---

[3]David N. Burt, *Proactive Procurement: The Key to Increased Profits, Productivity and Quality,* (Englewood Cliffs, NJ: Prentice-Hall, 1984), p. 4.

a procurement assignment. Engineering has the initial responsibility for preparing the technical specifications for a company's products and the materials that go into them. To exercise this responsibility effectively, engineering should have the assistance of supply management and operations. A number of firms have initiated early supply management and early supplier involvement programs to ensure that supply management and suppliers contribute to the development of new products.[4] The product costs associated with quality, material, fabrication and production are inextricably related to the design specifications. Similarly, specifications can be written in a manner that reduces or enlarges the number of firms willing to supply specific items. If profit is to be maximized, the materials specified by engineering must be economical to purchase and fabricate. Materials should normally be available from more than one efficient, low-cost producer and the material's quality must satisfy operations and the ultimate customer.

Supply management and engineering occasionally differ in their concepts of materials problems. The differing views are understandable. Engineers naturally tend to design conservatively; hence, their specifications may provide amply for quality, safety, and performance. By training, the engineer may be inclined to seek the "ideal" design, material, or equipment without complete regard for cost or availability. A supply professional is more concerned with commercial issues such as cost and availability. Several situation-specific questions by supply management to engineering usually can help to clarify cost and availability needs. For example, Is it possible to reduce the designer's performance goals and safety margins and to work closer to actual performance requirements? Is an expensive design with a high safety factor necessary if a less costly design with a lower, but acceptable, safety factor will do the job? Why use costly chrome plate if brushed aluminum is adequate? Clearly, such conflicting functional interests cannot always be resolved easily. The answers to such problems are seldom clear-cut. Mutual understanding and a willingness to give and take are required from both sides if mutually satisfactory solutions are to be reached.

Supply Management and Manufacturing

The supply management–manufacturing relationship begins during new product development and intensifies when manufacturing transmits its manufacturing schedule or materials requisitions to materials control, which translates these documents into a procurement schedule. Purchase timing is often a cardinal difficulty in making this translation. When the user does not allow supply management sufficient time to purchase wisely, many needless expenses inevitably creep into the final costs of a company's products. When supply management has inadequate time to properly qualify suppliers, to develop competition, or to negotiate properly, premium prices are likely to be paid for materials. Costly special production runs and premium transportation costs are two additional factors that frequently result from inadequate purchasing lead time.[5]

---

[4]Since early supply involvement and early supplier involvement have identical acronyms, we will coin the expression E.S.I.[2] when referring to the two terms simultaneously.

[5]Supply management has the responsibility to keep users informed concerning supply lead times for all categories of production materials.

A production shutdown is the most serious problem stemming from insufficient procurement lead time. In most process types of operations (chemicals, cement, paint, flour, etc.), either equipment runs at nearly full capacity or it does not run at all. Consequently, material shortages in these industries can be catastrophic, resulting in complete production stoppage. Losses resulting from material shortages in nonprocess industries are not always so disastrous or apparent. A production shutdown in a metal fabricating shop, for example, can be piecemeal. The indirect costs of such shortages, consequently, are often hidden in production costs. One or two machines from a large battery of 50 can be shut down as a routine occurrence. Conventional accounting records fail to reveal the financial impact of this kind of slow profit-draining inefficiency.

Coordination between supply management and manufacturing pays off in many ways. For example, a more expensive alternative material that will save the company money can, on occasion, be selected. This may sound like a paradox. "Pay more and save more"—how can this happen? Savings in manufacturing and assembling costs often can exceed the increased purchase costs. In the normal manufacturing operations of casting, forging, machining, grinding, stamping, and so on, some materials are much more economical to work with than others. For example, government suppliers have saved thousands of dollars by using bronze instead of steel extrusions in aircraft elevator and rudder counterweights. Bronze costs more than steel, but savings in machining time more than offset the increase in material cost. In this case, not only is the direct cost reduced, but as an added benefit, skilled machinists and expensive machine tools are freed to do other high-priority work. See Table 3.1 for a comparison of these costs.[6]

Going beyond these day-to-day operational interfaces, supply management and manufacturing must coordinate effectively to achieve some of a firm's key strategic goals. For example, manufacturing management strives to achieve faster "time to market" performance and to reduce the time required for product changeovers and tool and line setup work. Supply management must be able to assist in these efforts by obtaining

Table 3.1 | Effect of different materials on productivity and cost.

		Costs Totals (steel)		Costs Totals (bronze)
Sales		$100		$100
Costs of goods sold	Man-Hours	Costs	Man-Hours	Costs
Raw material cost		5		10
Direct labor (machining)	2	30	1	15
Variable overhead		6		3
Fixed overhead		50		50
Total cost		$91		$78
Operating income		$9		$22

Note 1: Productivity improvement: |(.5 − 1.0)/.5| = 100% improvement.
Note 2: Profit Improvement: |(9 −22)/9| = 144% improvement.

[6]David N. Burt and Richard L. Pinkerton, A Purchasing Manager's Guide to Strategic Proactive Procurement, AMACOM, New York, 1996. p. 9.

faster responses from suppliers, working with suppliers to improve their capabilities, and so on. In these types of activities, it is imperative that manufacturing and supply management work together closely.

Information technology is greatly simplifying the relationship between supply management and manufacturing. Computers and sophisticated software allow the firm's MRP (materials resource planning) system to communicate seamlessly with the counterpart systems at the firm's suppliers. With this approach, supply management is not involved in the day-to-day tactical activity of placing orders.

Supply Management and Quality

Quality professionals should be involved in supply management from the development of new products, to involvement in sourcing, and on through supplier development with the objective of minimizing quality problems thoughout the supply chain.

Supply Management and Marketing

Supply management *should* be marketing's best friend! As presented in Chapter 1, supply management has a major impact on the firm's sales. The quality of the firm's products, its ability to introduce new products in a timely manner, new products based on technology obtained from the firm's supply base, and pricing flexibility resulting from reductions in the cost of goods sold combine to have an incredible impact on marketing's success in generating sales. Many companies recognize the direct relationship between marketing excellence and profitability. In their enthusiasm to increase sales, however, many companies overlook the leaks in profit that can occur when the sales activity is not properly meshed with the supply and production activities. The sales/supply/production cycle has its genesis in a sales forecast. The forecast is the basis for the production schedule, which in turn is the basis for the materials schedule. The sales forecast also influences a firm's capital equipment budget, as well as its advertising campaigns and other sales activities.

Prompt communication to manufacturing and supply management of changes in the sales forecast (and better yet, actual demand) permits these departments to modify their schedules as painlessly and economically as possible. Likewise, changes in the production schedules should be communicated immediately to sales representatives. This action permits marketing to alter its distribution schedule in a manner that will not alienate customers. Supply management must immediately transmit to marketing, as well as to other management groups, information concerning increases in material prices. The information permits marketing to evaluate the effect of rises in price estimates given for future sales quotations, on current selling prices, and on plans for future product lines.

Supply management and marketing must wisely blend their interests in the delicate area of reciprocity (buying from customers). If satisfactory legal reciprocal transactions are to be developed, they must be pursued with an understanding of the true costs of reciprocity. Buying from friends can be good business, but not when it is done at the expense of product quality or higher prices for purchased materials or services. In a zest for increased sales, a company can lose sight of the fact that increased sales do not always result in increased profit. Increased sales may result in decreased profit if they simultaneously require an increase in purchase prices.

A supply management department can be of major help to its marketing or sales department by serving as its practical sales laboratory. A firm's supply management department is the target for many manufacturers' sales operations. Supply management's files are replete with sales literature, policies, and promotional approaches of a broad range of manufacturers and distributors. Supply management professionals are aware of the personal selling methods sales representatives have used most effectively on them. They are equally aware of sales practices that fail or irritate them. Therefore, a company's supply professionals can be an excellent source of information for developing and refining the company's sales policies and procedures.

Many marketing departments spend considerable amounts of money on advertising and promotion. In many cases, the focus of these expenditures is the impact of the advertising, not its cost. Several years ago Warren Norquist, former Vice President of World Wide Purchasing and Materials Management of Polaroid, demonstrated that the application of sound supply management practices to the purchase of advertising resulted in an average savings of 24 percent.[7]

Supply Management and Finance

The finance department is charged with two principle responsibilities: obtaining funds and overseeing their use. Poor financial planning and execution is *the* major cause of business failure. Supply chain management is responsible for as much as 80 percent of many firms' financial resources. Thus the CFO (Chief Financial Officer) and his or her key subordinates have a vested interest in a cost-efficient Supply Chain Management system. Finance professionals should be involved in large capital projects—whether for equipment or facilities.

Regardless of the price advantage available, the right time to buy from the standpoint of business conditions is not always the right time to buy from the standpoint of the company's treasury. If the supply management department makes commitments to take advantage of unusually low prices without consulting the finance department, the company could find itself paying for these purchases with funds needed for other purposes. On the other hand, if the finance department does not strive diligently to make funds available for such favorable buying opportunities, the company may have to pay higher prices later for the same material.

Finances' willingness to reimburse suppliers in a timely manner affects both supply managements' ability to obtain low prices and to forge and maintain collaborative relationships. During the 1970s, for example, Timex had a policy of paying its suppliers the day the supplier's invoice and the receiving report arrived in the accounts payable office. Thus, Timex became a preferred customer of many of its suppliers. During two material shortage periods of the 1970s, Timex's preferred customer status allowed it to avoid the shortage problems experienced by most firms. As a result of enlightened supply management practices, Timex never missed a beat! Hence, a cooperative relationship between purchasing and finance clearly can impact the development of good supplier relations.

As presented in Chapter 1, supply management has a major impact on 10 major components of the firm's costs. An efficient and effective supply management function

---

[7]Personal discussions with Mr. Norquist, 1989.

significantly reduces the funds required to operate the firm. The timing of purchasing expenditures can be of significant importance to a finance department that is working diligently to protect the firm's financial ratios and solvency. Supply management and finance should coordinate on expenditures that may have significant impact on the firm's cash position. Finance should be represented on cross-functional teams that are purchasing major equipment or construction services because of the magnitude of the expenditures involved.

Investors are properly concerned with the firm's return on investment (ROI). As shown in Figure 3.3 (which repeats Figure 1.5), supply management has a major impact on this key indicator. Notice how a 5 percent reduction in a hypothetical firm's expenditures increases its ROI by 30 percent!

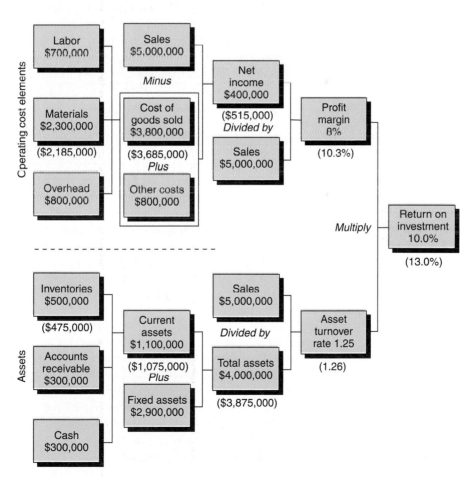

Figure 3.3 I A graphic view of the relationships of basic elements which influence return on investment. The figures in parentheses reflect a 5 percent reduction in the cost of materials.

Supply Management and Information Technology (IT)

Supply management and IT have an increasing number of interdependencies. In some cases, IT is outsourced. The director of IT and a supply management professional must work closely to develop the appropriate statement of work and the sourcing and pricing processes and to manage the resulting contract and relationship.

Many firms are purchasing B2B e-commerce buy-side software systems from firms such as Ariba, Commerce One, and People Soft. Such software systems have a major impact on the firm's procurement processes for indirect materials and equipment. End users are being empowered to purchase directly from the firm's or its approved supplier's electronic catalogs. The transition from a paper-based system of requisitions, manual approval, manual citation of budgetary authorization, requests for proposals, purchase orders, receiving reports, and payment checks to electronic purchasing must be carefully planned and implemented.

Electronic communication for production materials—whether over the Internet or through electronic data interchange (EDI)—requires coordination and cooperation between supply management, IT, and manufacturing or material control.

Another example of the interdependency between purchasing and IT is the development of a database which provides timely and accurate input to supply management for strategic planning and tactical activities. Relatively few firms have developed such an information system.

Supply Management and Logistics

When one of the authors was enrolled in the Ph.D. program at Stanford, purchasing was a component of the logistics program. At that time, both logistics and purchasing were relatively tactical. During the intervening years, both have progressed to being recognized as critical functions. Today, logistics spends approximately 10 percent of a manufacturer's income. Purchasing (supply management) spends some 60 percent.

Logistics is concerned with the movement of goods. In many cases, logistics is responsible for both incoming goods and the distribution of goods to the next member of the supply chain and frequently to the end customer itself. In virtually all cases, logistics professionals design and manage the firm's distribution system, consisting of warehouses, distribution points, and freight carriers.

The relationship between supply management and logistics tends to vary from firm to firm. In some cases, supply management plays a dominant role in sourcing and pricing logistics services. In other cases, the logistics department performs these services with little or no supply management involvement. The critical issue should not be one of jurisdiction. Rather, it should be one of professionalism and excellence. It should not matter whether supply management or logistics plays the key (or dominant) role. What does matter is that professional supply management practices are employed!

Supply Management and Accounts Payable

The introduction of corporate purchasing cards has had a major impact on both supply management and accounts payable. The use of such purchasing cards has had several beneficial effects: (1) It empowers end users of standard and low-value requirements to purchase directly from distributors, (2) it reduces tactical, non-value-adding purchases by the supply management department, and (3) it significantly reduces accounts payable activities.

Supply management and accounts payable frequently have conflicting interests and drivers in the area of timely payment to suppliers. Accounts payable commonly reports to the Chief Financial Officer. As we have seen, finance is responsible for obtaining funds and their productive use. Finance professionals frequently take considerable pride in seeing their "idle" funds invested at returns of 6–12 percent. This logical thinking causes many finance professionals to keep the money entrusted to their safe-keeping as long as possible. One means of achieving this apparently laudable objective is to delay paying suppliers as long as possible. For example, many suppliers to hospitals must wait for six months to be reimbursed for materials, equipment, or services provided.

Ignoring the ethical implications of such unilateral action for the moment, it is in conflict with supply management objectives. The sophisticated supplier who has experienced such delays in payment simply increases its selling price to such customers. Nobody wins. (We assume that the accounts payable/finance people must feel good that they have earned investment income on the backs of helpless suppliers.) But of greater importance, such nonresponsive payment often conflicts with supply management's efforts to become a preferred customer or to develop collaborative and even alliance relationships. Quite obviously, such conflicts can and must be overcome through open discussions between supply management and finance professionals.

Supply Management and Lawyers

Legal professionals are frequently actively involved in contract negotiations and contract formation. In other cases, their role is one of review and approval of contracts developed by supply management professionals. Value-adding attorneys who are involved in supply management issues normally must embrace a collaborative approach to dealing with the firms' suppliers.

Supply Management in Nonmanufacturing Organizations

Supply management has as much—and sometimes more—impact on the success of non-manufacturing organizations as it does on manufacturing firms. The timely availability of reliable equipment, supplies, and services at the right total cost of ownership affects the ability of such organizations to provide timely quality services at a profit.

In a manufacturing setting, design and manufacturing engineering professionals normally lead the new product development effort and the development of the appropriate specifications describing what is to be purchased. In a nonmanufacturing setting, supply management often must lead or facilitate the requirements process on account of the absence of engineering or other qualified requirements professionals. Thus a supply professional may need to assume the responsibility for leading a cross-functional team that is identifying or describing a requirement to be purchased.

While the total costs of purchases compared with net income or budget authorizations may be proportionately less than for a manufacturer, such expenditures still are very significant. Supply management's impact on sales can be every bit as significant as in manufacturing. Quality implications, time-to-market, pricing elasticity (based on reductions in the cost of goods sold), technology inflow, and continuity of supply combine to have a major impact on a nonmanufacturing firm's sales. Thus, we see that supply management also has a major impact on a nonmanufacturing firm's bottom line!

Supply Management in Government

Supply management (frequently called "procurement" in government circles) has a major impact on the efficient and effective use of our tax dollars at all levels of government. Not surprisingly, many of the advances in the art and science of supply management originated in the federal government. Virtually all of the problems present in manufacturing organizations are present in government procurement. This topic is addressed in more detail in Chapter 26.

Supply Management and the External Environment

Business Relationships

All phases of supply management involve relations with external suppliers: early supplier involvement in the development of requirements, strategic sourcing, pricing (including cost analysis and negotiations), and post-award activities. These interfaces are explained in detail throughout the book.

Monitoring the Supply Environment

Supply managers are responsible for protecting their firms from unexpected threats or shocks from their supply world in the form of price increases or supply disruptions. These threats include material shortages which affect one or more industries that supply the firm. Shortages will affect both the price and availability of purchased materials and supplies. The firm should take actions to minimize the impact of such shortages by monitoring changes in the supply environment such as the following:

- Changes in legislation that may affect the workplace. Such changes can impact both price and availability. An example is a new Environmental Protection Agency regulation on toxic wastes that affects one or more suppliers.
- Wars and other conflicts, which may disrupt the availability of materials the firm or its supplier require. Firms that proactively monitor the environment take defensive action in anticipation of the resulting material shortages and price increases.
- A consolidation among suppliers. The extreme case is consolidation to the point of monopoly. Such changes may require a change in the firm's supply strategy.

Supply managers should have early information that will allow them to take advantage of favorable market conditions. Opportunities result both from additional capacity coming on-line and from reductions in demand for required materials, equipment, or services.[8]

---

[8]The Institute for Supply Management™ (formerly the National Association of Purchasing Management) publishes a comprehensive report on business in *Purchasing Today* each month. The report shows macro trends in both manufacturing and nonmanufacturing sectors and featured reports on select industries.

The responsibilities of protecting their firms from unexpected threats or shocks motivate supply professionals to develop supply monitoring systems. One of the challenges confronting today's supply professional in monitoring is the abundance of data. "Today purchasers are literally inundated with bits of data concerning their suppliers, the markets in which those suppliers participate, and the functioning of the economy as a whole. Turning such data into meaningful, useful information—supply market knowledge—is one part of the supply professional's tasks, but so is leveraging supply information into knowledge that increases the competitive advantage of the firm. Before attempting to understand the supply market, supply professionals must first possess a clear understanding of what is meaningful to their own organizations."[9]

Monitoring supply markets is a fascinating and challenging activity. In the late 1980s, Warren Norquist, former Vice President of World Wide Purchasing at Polaroid, assigned three researchers the responsibility of monitoring Polaroid's supply environment and then advising Polaroid buyers of potential threats and opportunities in their supply world. Frank Haluch, writing in the August 2000 issue of *Purchasing Today,* outlines a six-step environment monitoring strategy:

■ Determine the cost, supply, and technology drivers of the materials and services that a supply manager is watching.

■ Identify the major suppliers and customers of the materials and services.

■ Determine the sources of information for those drivers.

■ Build a model that predicts the material (or service) behavior.

■ Monitor the model to determine its accuracy.

■ Continuously make improvements as new relationships are understood and additional data becomes available.[10]

Supply environment monitoring coupled with timely reaction to the threats and opportunities that are identified is a key strategic activity, which has significant impact on the firm's success and survival.

Concluding Remarks

The purchasing process is one that spans internal organizational boundaries. As the process evolves to supply management, both the complexity and strategic importance of the process increase dramatically. Supply management is critical to virtually all organizations: manufacturing, services, commercial, not-for-profit institutions, and government.

Supply management assumes three critical social responsibilities: implementing management's objectives of purchasing from suppliers representing the diversity of the population, protecting our physical environment so as to leave the world a healthier place for our children, and improving working conditions in supplier operations. In the next chapter, we turn our focus to these important topics.

---

[9]Richard R. Young, "Knowledge of Supply Markets," in *The Purchasing Handbook,* 6th ed. (New York: McGraw-Hill, 2000). For more on this report, see Ralph G. Kauffman, "Indicator Qualities of the NAPM Report on Business," *The Journal of Supply Chain Management,* Spring 1999.

[10]Frank Haluch, "Taking the Market's Pulse," *Purchasing Today,* August 2000, p. 6.

4

CHAPTER

Supply Management: Implementor of Three of the Firm's Social Responsibilities

World Class Supply Management^{SM} extends beyond financial goals to include social responsibilities toward diversity suppliers, the environment, and workplace values.

Case

Pete Varma is owner of a diversity supplier of equipment and spares for utilities, high tech firms, and government. Pete is very concerned with two threats to his business: cor porate America's rush to the Internet and its obsession with downsizing. Pete's research has shown that one nationwide equipment and spares supplier invested $25 million to put its business "on the net." Pete is very concerned with his business prospects. How can he avoid being disenfranchised by technology?

Supply management has three major social responsibilities: (1) the development and employment of diversity suppliers, (2) the protection our physical environment, and (3) the implementation of a program of values in the workplace.

Diversity Suppliers

Many enlightened supply management organizations have developed and implemented diversity programs whose objectives are to ensure that diversity suppliers receive a "fair" share of the buying firms' expenditures.

Who is a *diversity supplier?* To some, the term applies to most or all of the following: African-American, Asian/Indian, Asian Pacific, Hispanic, Mixed Minority, and Native Americans. Others include women-owned businesses. The State of California and others include disabled veterans. In general, the term "diversity" applies to individuals and businesses that have challenges in becoming successfully established and gaining economic representation proportional with their demographic representation.

Several forces may motivate businesses to establish a diversity program:

■ *Corporate social responsibility.* As the Director of American Express's diversity program recently told a supply management class: "A diversity program is the ethical thing to do!"[1]

■ *Supply base broadening.* Broadening the supply base to include diversity suppliers who mirror the buying firm's customer base. The minority business enterprises (MBE) coordinator of one electronics manufacturer stated, "Management has come to realize that, if our company can help minorities, particularly our suppliers, MBEs will employ more people and ultimately buy more of our products."[2]

■ *Government compliance.* The federal and many state and local governments may require their suppliers to spend a stated percent of their income from a government contract with diversity suppliers. "Governments around the world are using supply base diversity as a mechanism to increase the participation of underrepresented members of their economies. For example, Germany requires participation from firms that employ the handicapped. Canada requires Native Canadian Indian participation."[3]

---

[1]Presentation by Terry Applegate, Director of Diversity Programs, American Express, University of San Diego, October 11, 2000.

[2]Craig R. Carter, Richard J. Auskalnis, and Carol L. Ketchum, "Purchasing from Minority Business Enterprises: Key Success Factors," *Journal of Supply Chain Management,* Winter 1999, p. 28.

[3]Scott Beth (V.P. Procurement, Agilent Technologies), personal interview April 9, 2001.

■ *Governmental contract requirements.* Governmental entities frequently require the firms under their control (for example, government suppliers and public utilities) to spend targeted percentages of all purchases with diversity suppliers.

■ *Fear of economic boycotts.* Groups of diversity suppliers who feel that they are being treated unfairly may organize boycotts against targeted purchasers. Or, as in the case of a major bottling firm, they may join with employees who feel that they have been discriminated against to gain economic leverage against the targeted corporation.

■ *Pass down provisions.* Many second and lower tiered suppliers must comply with diversity requirements contained in contracts with higher tiered customers.

■ *Increased competition.* The realization that diversity "suppliers provide products and services that are competitive" with those of non-diversity suppliers.[4]

Well-run diversity programs have several characteristics in common:

■ *Top management support.* "Researchers, consultants, and management experts have long promoted top management support as being a key driver." Such support should be by example and "could include direct communication with suppliers and attendance at prominent conferences and meetings."[5]

■ *Goals.* Ideally, senior management, including the Chief Supply Officer, establishes diversity spending goals which are feasible, but which stretch those involved.

■ *Monitoring.* Establishing diversity goals is an essential first step. Measuring success (and failure) is of equal or greater importance.

■ *Training.* "Employee training not only allows personnel to more efficiently pursue the Diversity goals which have been established, but shows a commitment by management."[6] Suppliers also must be educated and trained.

■ *Support.* Buying organizations must be willing to invest resources such as management support, technical support, cash flow, contractual commitments for use as collateral, and even equity funds.

■ *Contracts.* Appropriate diversity objectives and controls should be included in Requests for Proposals, IFBs, etc.; supplier proposals; and the resulting contracts.

■ *Feedback.* Recognition is a powerful motivator. Those involved in successful projects should be recognized publicly.

■ *Diversity coordinators.* While company size is a limiting factor, a dedicated professional manages the majority of successful diversity programs.

■ *Evaluation.* An evaluation system that rewards supply management personnel for developing and sourcing from diversity suppliers.[7]

■ *Corporate Culture.* A corporate culture in which diversity development and sourcing is an ingrained way of doing business.

---

[4]Carter et al., "Purchasing from Minority Business Enterprises," p. 36.

[5]Ibid., p. 29.

[6]Ibid., p. 29.

[7]Ibid., p. 30.

When an organization establishes a diversity program, we recommend that diversity suppliers be selected on their own merits. The buying organization must accept the responsibility of going the extra mile to assist such suppliers. Tough competition requires excellent suppliers who are cost, quality, and time competitive. The sponsoring organization must be willing to assist promising diversity suppliers to become "World Class." When qualified diversity suppliers are not available, we encourage the selection of potential suppliers who can be mentored and developed into efficient cost-effective contributing members of a firm's supply base.

The Internet: Friend or Foe to Diversity Suppliers?

Supplier base consolidation and e-procurement are significant threats to diversity and other small business suppliers. As of 2001, the vast majority of diversity suppliers struggle with e-commerce and downsizing initiatives that are becoming increasingly prevalent in mid-size to large companies.

A few diversity firms such as mwSupplier of Burlingame, California, have formed alliances with B2B sell-side e-commerce software providers to provide a quick and effective way to aggregate diversity suppliers into a sell-side exchange. The sell-side exchange allows diversity suppliers to reach large buyers in a cost-effective manner without losing their brand identity. Large suppliers invest millions of dollars developing the infrastructure required to sell to their industrial customers via the Internet. Exchanges such as mwSupplier's MIWOVE.com aggregate and host diversity suppliers in an e-hub customized storefront environment, enabling buyer connectivity through buyer-specific e-procurement packages, portals, or buying communities at reasonable costs. Such exchanges level the supply-side playing field by empowering the diversity supplier to compete in the new era.

Three Benchmark Programs

Agilent Technologies has a very aggressive diversity program. Under the enlightened leadership of CSO Scott Beth and Director of Supplier Diversity Darlene Jones, Agilent received the Northern California Supplier Development Council (NCSDC) recognition as "Corporation of the Year" in March 2001. Agilent is on the forefront of supplier diversity. Recognizing the dynamic nature of 21st century business, Agilent has created a versatile program which it calls its "Supplier Diversification Process." In a personal interview with one of the authors, Ms. Jones pointed out,

> Our markets are customer driven. To capture new and emerging markets, paradigm ways of thinking need to be encouraged. Out-of-the-box thinking and risk taking must be a commitment driven from the CEO into the organization. Agilent's process drives this commitment throughout the organization with ongoing communication and success stories. All members of our organization are accountable for driving success. Clear expectations and measured goals clearly define our process.
>
> The majority of opportunities are not found, but created. With every product from its inception to end of life support we are given opportunities for small business development. Each product goes through several stages of changes, i.e., design, packaging, material, delivery, support. With each change a new business opportunity is created. Agilent's Supplier Diversification

Process seeks innovative suppliers with new ways of thinking: suppliers who are hungry, suppliers who are ready to do business, suppliers who are driven by unsurpassed methods to match their goals and align themselves with Agilent's future processes. This, in turn, leads to a strong foundation supported by fresh ideas and a concrete strategic foundation.

It is very important to provide the environment which encourages growth in innovation. By providing the opportunity, matching it with a small business partner who is aligned with the strategy, and furnishing the necessary support, we foster growth of our diversity suppliers. This opportunity is driven by measured goals and tracked for success. This creates the wheel of ever-changing opportunities . . . which in turn creates success and ownership by all.

Success is achieved when corporations commit to "carving out" opportunities for small business entrepreneurs which will allow direct opportunities and the ability to compete from a tier one level. Agilent's commitment is focused on supplier development from a tier one level. This allows direct business growth and supports the value of social responsibilities. Without this methodology we risk dilution of small business growth through nonmonitored subcontracting opportunities and defeat exactly what we are trying to accomplish.[8]

Deere and Company's Supplier Diversity Team makes the case for smaller and diversity suppliers as Deere business partners with Deere's four equipment divisions and corporate headquarters. An August 1999 meeting of these parties is representative of the teams' efforts. The objective of the meeting "was to focus on process gaps that get in the way of increased small, diverse supplier involvement and to find ways to improve Deere's use of those suppliers."[9]

Lucent Technologies is a benchmark of successful diversity programs. Under the enlightened championship of CEO Richard A. McGinn and CSO Daryl I. Skaar, Lucent awarded over $1 billion in business to minority- and women-owned business enterprises in 1999. These efforts resulted in both incremental sales and cost reductions for Lucent.[10]

Protecting Our Physical Environment[11]

Economic growth and environmental care: two conflicting goals? If we take on the responsibility to leave future generations with a world that is healthy, productive, and genetically diverse, we have to understand that environmental care and economic growth are not mutually exclusive goals.[12] Times change and so do the driving forces of today's business environment. From mass production to total quality management and time-based competition, we have finally reached the latest and perhaps most important force driving our society: environmental protection. With the rapid depletion of our global stocks of resources, the growing fragility of our ecosystem, the loss of biodiversity and clean, healthy air, and increasing marine pollution, environmental protection is emerg-

---

[8]Darlene Jones, personal interviews, week of April 9, 2001.

[9]*Linkages: A Newsletter,* from John Deere, Summer 2000.

[10]*Supplier Diversity, A Bridge Connecting Customers and Solutions,* Lucent Technologies, 2000.

[11]Appreciation is expressed to the senior author's former graduate assistant Rommy Los for his significant contributions in developing this section. Mr. Los currently is a Corporate Purchasing Manager at Henkel KGaA in Dusseldorf, Germany.

[12]"Profits One," *Business Week,* January 3, 1992, p. 88.

ing as an important process which affects our quality of life, while simultaneously increasing our employer's success in the marketplace.

The main objective of environment protection is not to promote recycling or reusing, but to focus on the prevention of any kind of pollution[13] in the first place. In other words, the objective of the program is zero pollution generation.

Three main groups are the driving forces of "environmentally friendly" products, packaging, and production processes. The key stakeholders of the first group are environmental activists and the general public. The second group consists of firms that respond to the political activism of the first group. The third group consists of firms that have to respond to their consumers' demands. Each of these groups has developed its own unique agenda, strategies, and goals to achieve a cleaner environment, enact environment protection regulations, or satisfy consumers' needs.[14]

Background   In order to understand the current state of environmental activity we have to go back into the history of the "Green Movement." Citizens all over the world have been shocked by the sight of oil spills contaminating our shores, radioactive accidents such as at Chernobyl, and daily reports of a growing ozone "hole" in our atmosphere. Incidents such as the infamous waste barge that left New York Island with no place to unload its garbage is yet another demonstration of the limits of our global ecosystem. The ecology movement's criticism of industry and technology was and is aimed mainly at their destructive impacts on the environment.

The fear of depleting limited resources in a finite world as described in the Economic Reports of Rome during the 1970s has become an additional force. Once the Green Movement became a fashionable media topic, television and newspaper journalists pushed it to its next level. Public concern turned into an environmental outcry, loud enough to attract government's full attention. Having reached this degree of national awareness, government was forced to analyze the different accusations, identify the variety of environmental issues involved, and develop and implement environment protection regulations.

Legislation   In addition to environmental protection acts such as the Clean Water Act of 1972 (1977) and the Clean Air Act of 1970 (1990), Congress reacted to growing environmental concerns by enacting the Superfund Law—formally known as the Comprehensive Environmental Response Compensation and Liability Act (CLERCA). With the passage of CLERCA, the liability for particular environmental issues has changed in important ways. Individuals, never before personally liable for hazardous substance cleanups, have become statutorily liable.

In addition, the responsibility for waste disposal and cleanup has become substantially more expensive than in the past. CLERCA defines several categories of parties that are responsible for hazardous substance release to the environment. Within these categories, the terms as defined implicate not only the owners of facilities who dispose of, generate, and transport hazardous polluting materials, but also, under particular circumstances, corporate

---

[13]Pollution: the act of contaminating, fouling, or making unclean.

[14]Arthur D. Little, Inc., *Packaging for the Environment, A Partnership for Progress* (American Management Association, 1991), p. 16.

parents, subsidiaries, and other affiliated entities; employees, directors, officers, individual shareholders; subsequent purchasers, corporate successors; and lenders. Under CLERCA, liability is strict and defenses are very difficult.[15]

CLERCA not only impacts the traditional "midnight dumper," but also the transportation of hazardous waste between two affiliated facilities. Without a Resource Conservation and Recovery Act (RCRA) permit, such transport can be a violation of the Superfund statute. Therefore, it is crucial to the above categories to be familiar with the current environmental legislation and statutes. "Lack of knowledge of specific environmental laws does not insulate purchasers and their companies from potential criminal liability for violations. Although Federal environmental law specifies that a company must 'knowingly' violate a provision, proving your company's innocence can be expensive and time consuming."[16] It is management's and the individual's obligation to monitor and control every form of hazardous waste activity.

The ecology trend is certainly not only of U.S. origin. The European Community (EC) environmental policy dates back to 1972. EC environmental policy has since grown through "Environmental Action Programs" similar to those in the United States The EC has taken policy initiatives across a variety of environmental issues such as those concerning water, air, wildlife, and so on. The EC's declared policy is to develop the communities' environmental standards to the highest of the levels existing among its member states. To realize the similarity to the developments in the United States and Europe, the EC's 1982 Seveso Directive (inspired by the Dioxin Disaster in Seveso, Italy) soon became the model of the Superfund Amendment and Authorization Act (SARA) in the United States.[17]

Economic Drivers   With the expansion of the Federal government's effort to prosecute environmental violations, today's companies have to comply with the growing range of environmental statutes. But simple acceptance of the new laws alone will not be enough. Similar to the concept of Total Quality Management (TQM), wherein one has to *live* the ideals, environmental protection must be actively internalized.

Management's challenge is to develop and implement an environmentally sound strategy that complies with the new environmental legislation, meeting the demands of environmentally conscious consumers while preserving the firm's competitive position. Senior management has to recognize that much of industry has already addressed a multitude of environmental issues. While some companies have done so because of legislative pressure to control pollution and waste, others have recognized the commercial opportunities inherent in this new direction.[18] Pollution prevention can save money; therefore, it is good for both profits and for the environment. Management has to understand that environmental care and economic growth are neither mutually exclusive nor antagonistic goals.[19] Companies with the most efficient environmental strategies today are among the most competitive, profitable, and secure in their industries.

[15]Timothy A. Weaver, *Attorney's Guide to Environmental Liability in Transactions* (IICLE, 1991), pp. 2–4.

[16]Jeff Marcus, "Trends, Purchasing and the Environment," *NAPM Insights,* April, 1994, p. 28.

[17]Arthur D. Little, Inc. *Packaging for the Environment,* p. 116.

[18]Australian Department of Administrative Services, *The Better Buying, Better World Strategy,* (Australian Government Publishing Service, June 1992), p. 17.

[19]"Profits One," p. 87.

In order to get the most out of embracing environmentalism, a firm has to find ways of benefiting economically. The first method to economic gain is through cost reduction and the second is through increased sales and profit.

Costs can be reduced through pollution avoidance. Maintaining global economic growth without compromising the environment means developing processes that generate less pollution per unit of product. Greater process efficiency can result not only in less pollution, but also in creating more output per unit of raw material consumed.[20] For example, when Henry Ford began making automobiles, he bought pallets for hauling materials and components and then used the wood from the pallets as floorboards for his cars. Ford wasn't merely being cheap; he was of a time when thrift and preservation were prized—values we somehow lost in post-war abundance.[21]

Marketing The second strategy to benefit from the new environmental awareness is to promote the "green" advantages of the firm's product (and packaging) in the marketplace. Companies already face pressure from their consumers to provide environmentally friendly products and packaging. Today, the consumer believes him or herself to be environmentally conscious. Many consumers are willing to switch brands or change their purchase behavior to help protect the environment.[22] The consumer will switch brands if quality and price are the same but the environmental impact is less destructive. Consumers' willingness to switch brands should not be seen as a threat but rather as a new economic opportunity.

Reduce, Reuse, Reallocate, Recycle (the 4 Rs)

The U.S. Environmental Protection Agency has defined a process-based hierarchy of integrated waste[23] management systems.

1. Source reduction, including reuse.
2. Recycling, including composting.
3. Waste combustion with energy recovery.
4. Landfilling.[24]

Waste disposal is inevitable. However, in reviewing and identifying opportunities for waste diversion, it should be understood that there are four basic methods that need to be considered:

■ **Reduce** in the generation of waste.
■ **Reuse** and **Reallocate** materials as much as possible.
■ As a last choice, **Recycle** as much and as energy efficiently as possible.

[20]Ibid., p. 86.

[21]R. Jerry Baker, "The Environment: Playing Our Part," *NAPM Insights,* April 1994, p. 2.

[22]Arthur D. Little, Inc., *Packaging for the Environment,* p. 17.

[23]Waste in this chapter's context is defined as something which is returned to Mother Earth. Waste normally, but not always, pollutes the environment.

[24]Arthur D. Little, Inc., *Packaging for the Environment,* p. 89.

The traditional environmental business posture has been reactive, with companies acting mainly on the impetus of legislative pressure or public opinion. Based on their goals of remaining profitable, companies have favored solutions that pander to common perceptions (usually those involving minimum effort required to ensure compliance). However, the risks involved in this approach include unpredicted cost, loss of market share, and acceptance of a follower role. Forward-looking companies accept the environmental imperative and willingly assume the mantle of environmental leadership. Such companies support voluntary product and process redesign, as well as the avoidance of pollution and waste in the short as well as in the long run. In addition, forward-looking companies take the long-term view and address environmental problems by attacking their root causes.

Management must develop and implement a corporate strategy that allows economic growth and environmental consciousness to go together synergistically. For example, the synergistic integration of product packaging development and environmental sensitivity is essential to ensure both political and economic sustainability.[25] Before developing a company-specific environmental strategy, management needs to fully understand the complexity and implications of the different environmental issues. As a result of the efforts of many different interest groups, there is a great deal of public confusion over what is environmentally sound, as witness such common ideas as "plastic is bad" or "biodegradability is good." For example, very few consumers know that virtually nothing decomposes in today's air and watertight landfills.

Reduce　While reducing the generation of solid waste, source reduction also slows the depletion of our natural resources and often results in less expensive products.[26] Source reduction is a continuous materials and energy conservation process to minimize postconsumer solid waste by developing and adapting a variety of systems and techniques that minimize the use of materials and energy resources.[27] Source reduction is simply a response to the ongoing search for materials that are either completely superfluous or unnecessary in the present quantities without loss of function.[28]

Reuse　Reuse mainly refers to the salvageability of items such as equipment and packaging material. Opportunities for reuse should be evaluated while ensuring that the design reduces the volume of solid waste without incurring a net increase in economic or environmental costs, thereby compromising the health and safety of consumers or increasing the risk of product damage. First priority should be given to the use of components that are reusable for their original purpose without remanufacturing (for example, pallets). For this type of reuse to be viable, it is necessary to have suitable collection, return, and reuse programs established. The materials should be capable of being reusable

---

[25]*The Global Partnership for Environment and Development* (United Nations, June 1992), p. 17.

[26]*Environmental Design Guidelines for IBM Packaging Engineers* (The IBM Competence Center for Packaging Engineering, September 28, 1990), p. 46.

[27]Arthur D. Little, Inc., *Packaging for the Environment,* p. 26.

[28]*Handbook for Environmentally Responsible Packaging in the Electronics Industry* (Institute of Packaging Professionals, 1992), p. 4-1.

or refillable safely at least five times if reuse is anticipated. All efforts should be made to achieve this goal, which should not be considered an absolute.[29] Honda of America Manufacturing protects the environment through its reusable container program—and saves over a half million dollars a year in the process.

Reallocation   Reallocation is an extended variation of reuse. Whereas reuse often focuses on a business unit's internal process, reallocation includes other S.B.U.s and entities outside the organization as customers for the unit's used materials.

Recycling   Recycling includes more than the simple reprocessing of salvageable materials. Recycling is a technology that involves collection, separation, preparation (e.g., baling), sale to intermediate or final users, reprocess, and eventual resale and reuse of the recycled material. Recycling typically reduces the volume of solid waste material in two ways:

- Recycling materials otherwise sent to landfill.
- Reducing the amount of waste material generated from manufacturing processes that utilize raw materials.[30]

Recycling of packaging material is of particular importance. There is a hierarchy for such recycling. "Primary or closed loop recycling calls for packaging material to be recycled into its original material or container form. It is a viable option, provided that all health and other regulatory requirements are fully met. Recycling into some other package form—secondary recycling—is also a desirable option. Recycling into a product other than a package or a packaging material—tertiary recycling—may be the only available option for some materials."[31]

Recycling currently is the most promoted and most popular waste management option. State and city governments establish curbside pickup programs and provide drop-off recycling centers for a large number of recyclable materials. Recycling, as an important and necessary method within the EPA hierarchy of integrated waste management systems, refers to the process of end-of-the-line activity. The recycling process itself redirects salvageable materials that otherwise would be waste and which would end up in landfills. Recycling also reduces the usage of raw materials from Mother Earth, and, therefore, is a key component of resource management. Some companies may be satisfied knowing that the majority of their potential waste material will not directly end up in any landfills. Others might even determine that recycling is the perfect way to avoid disposal fees.

No doubt, recycling is better than dumping, but is it the best alternative? Like quality control, recycling is an end-of-the-line concept. Just as quality control does not prevent the production of defects, *neither does recycling prevent the generation of potentially polluting materials.* With recycling, the company focuses on ensuring that not all waste materials end up in the landfills; however, this is done through waste control, not waste avoidance.

---

[29]Ibid., p. 2–4.

[30]*Environmental Design Guidelines for IBM,* p. 29.

[31]*Handbook for Environmentally Responsible Packaging,* p. 2-3.

Supply Chain Pollution Avoidance (SCPA)

SCPA is the broadest and most logical approach to protecting the environment. Through this approach, we go back to the beginning of the supply chain, attempting to reduce the initial generation of waste throughout the chain. SCPA focuses on processes that prevent or minimize pollution from being created throughout the chain. While traditional end-of-the-line approaches represent an add-on expense (collection, separation, transportation, etc.), the avoidance option is based on increased process efficiency at all stages, from Mother Earth to the end user. Michael Porter and Claas van der Linde observe, "Avoiding pollution entirely or, second best, mitigating it early in the value chain is almost always less costly than late-stage remediation or cleanup."[32] Companies committed to waste prevention will often apply statistical procedures to collect data to monitor the process along the value chain (similar to quality assurance), with the focus of minimizing the impact of the different process variables. Waste avoidance, like quality assurance, is a systematic approach to optimizing the efficiency of a given process.

To believe that the company pays only for its own waste is a costly misconception. The company also pays for its suppliers' waste by purchasing their outputs at a higher price, a price which includes the costs of the supplier's and its suppliers' waste. Indirectly, the company even pays for the generation of post-consumer waste. A company's broad image also is dependent on the brands of the participants in its supply chain. Whom you buy from will have profound effects on your broad image (e.g., suppliers who use child labor).[33]

The cost of waste is positively correlated to the type of material entering the waste stream. For example, if the waste is hazardous, the company has to provide a higher level of safety with the collection, sorting, storing, labeling, and transportation of the material. In addition, the company pays a substantially higher amount of money for the final disposal of more hazardous materials. Therefore, to determine the total costs of waste, management has to have the composition of the firm's waste analyzed. The organization must identify the different types and quantities of waste and the amount of money (for collecting, sorting, and so on) that is spent on each type. This systematic approach enables the company to allocate individual cost elements to a single waste material or waste material group. The establishment of an effective waste control monitoring and documentation system is crucial for the efficiency of continuous pollution prevention.

However, because of the importance of both supplier- and consumer-generated waste, the company also has to integrate these sides of the supply chain into the analysis of the total waste stream composition. Surveys can and should be used to collect supplier and customer data regarding the different types and quantities of waste that the party generates. Both sides are elements of the supply chain and both sides have, therefore, the potential to reduce total waste generation. Customers, like suppliers, are

---

[32]Michael E. Porter and Claas van der Linde, "Innovation-Friendly Regulation," *Harvard Business Review*, September–October 1995, p. 124.

[33]Scott Beth, personal interview.

important information sources that cannot be ignored by any company concerned with pollution avoidance. A firm that does not integrate both parties in the development of any kind of total value chain concept will never reach its total potential for protecting the environment. One of the greatest challenges is to maximize value and minimize costs (including environmental costs) throughout the supply chain. This challenge requires that manufacturers and firms in process and service industries, their suppliers, their distributors, and their customers focus their collective efforts on reducing the total cost of pollution within their supply chain.[34]

The composition of the total waste throughout the supply chain is a combination of many different materials. Waste documentation allows the supply chain leader (normally, the key processor or manufacturer) to identify the most costly and environmentally destructive waste materials throughout the chain. Such cost is based on the quantity, the degree of risk involved, or customer perception of the waste. In order to establish a list with the most critical materials, management should rank each material based on the Pareto concept. Typically, a Pareto list can reveal that approximately 20 percent of the waste materials cause nearly 80 percent of the total waste cost. Pareto analysis helps the company obtain an overview of the actual cost impact of an individual waste material. The final Pareto listing can also identify those materials that should be addressed first.

Supply Chain Pollution Avoidance usually requires the application of statistical process control (SPC), monitoring procedures, involvement of employees at firms along the supply chain, and involvement of the customer. SCPA includes all aspects of a company's business, from marketing (representing the customer's voice) to supply management (representing the supplier's voice). The system requires the analysis of the entire supply chain from Mother Earth, through suppliers, through the company itself, to the ultimate customer, and, possibly, back to Mother Earth.

Implementation of a Supply Chain Pollution Avoidance (SCPA) Program

Like every other strategy in a business, the implementation of SCPA requires a detailed plan of action that delineates the different steps to be followed, including a basic time frame for implementation. The plan must be complete, so that everyone in every member organization of the supply chain understands what is expected and when it must be done. The implementation plan detailed below describes the common activities a company is likely to encounter.[35]

Each organization in the supply chain should include in its mission statement a long-term vision and direction of what the organization is trying to become—a unique goal that differentiates the organization from competitors. It is important to realize that the need for a mission statement is not the stated purpose itself. The mission statement

---

[34]David N. Burt and Michael F. Doyle, *The American Keiretsu* (Homewood, IL: Business One Irwin, 1993), p. 109.

[35]Sanders Quality Association, Inc., *How to Qualify for ISO 9000* (American Management Association, 1993), p. 179.

provides direction and significance to all members of the organization.[36] A mission statement of an SCPA firm could include the following:

> Our company wants to protect the environment and natural resources related to all of our operations including the responsible sourcing and management of partners in our supply chain. We will exercise excellence in environmental control and will strive to design products that contribute to environmental responsibility.

Responsibility   A company will benefit from a wide variety of ideas and suggestions from its employees, with the empowerment of its employees and the establishment of challenging incentive programs. However, this alone will not be enough to integrate an effective waste prevention strategy. The company needs a systematic approach to evaluate the impact of its different operations on the environment. Many functions within the firm must be involved in pollution avoidance. Senior management should develop cross-functional pollution avoidance teams consisting of design, supply management, process and quality engineers, distribution, marketing, finance, and the firm's customers and suppliers. Small teams at each link of the supply chain actually carry out the step-by-step approach and report back to the top management of their company and the super ordinate team consisting of representatives of all members of the supply chain.

Pollution Generation   In order to develop ideas of how to minimize waste throughout the supply chain, one has to know where waste is generated in the first place. If we look at the overall value chain (supplier-company-customer), we can find five main locations:

1. The first source of polluting waste is the specification imposed by a customer firm as we move up the supply chain to Mother Earth.
2. The second potential source of waste includes quality requirements, which may force the supplier to produce the material in a nonstandard way. This nonstandard specification may make it impossible for the supplier to manufacture with its highest degree of efficiency, thereby generating waste.
3. The third type of waste generation is the interface waste that results from the geographic distance and the different process or quality requirements between supplier and customer. Geographic distance forces the supplier to transport the material while preserving the integrity of the product. This means the supplier has to use some form of packaging material that generally ends up in the waste stream, because it is not requested and therefore not needed by its customer, nor considered salvageable by the customer.
4. The fourth main location of waste generation is the company's internal processing of purchased materials. Internal waste typically originates from three main sources:

   First, *surpluses from internal production processes* are inevitable. Not all production materials are wholly consumed in most manufacturing processes. Frequently, a residue is left. This excess is called scrap, and must be disposed of as surplus. Surplus also results from wasteful production processes, or

---

[36]J. Paul Peter and James H. Donnelly, Jr., *Marketing Management,* 3rd ed. (Homewood, IL: Richard D. Irwin, 1992), p. 11.

inefficiencies in general. This type of surplus can be either salvageable or waste. Either way, it remains unusable material for the original application.

The second source of internal waste that often ends up in the external waste stream is from *obsolete or damaged stocks*. Any warehouse operation, regardless of how efficiently it is controlled, also accumulates some salvageable or waste material from breakage, deterioration, and errors in record keeping. And finally, changes occur constantly in the designs and specifications of fast-moving technological products. As a consequence, obsolete labels, packaging materials, and the products and parts themselves constitute a continuing source of surplus (salvageable or waste) materials. A just-in-time approach to distribution greatly reduces such waste.

The third main internal source of waste is the *interface between the company and its customer.* This waste is largely composed of packaging materials. Today, packaging materials have evolved into a highly sophisticated medium which allows manufacturers to deliver their products to consumers many times over great distances with a minimum of damage, spoilage, or deterioration. In order to meet this goal, packaging performs a number of important functions during transportation, storage, and use:

- Containment of the product to ensure its integrity and safety.
- Protection of the product from physical damage, spoilage, etc.
- Convenience of use and consumer acceptance.
- Compliance with legal and regulatory requirements.
- Conveyance of information/data.[37]

5. The final source of pollution is post consumption waste, basically the portion of the product itself (including packaging) that is not consumed by the end customer. Packaging is the largest, fastest-growing, and most complex component of municipal solid waste (that is, municipal waste generated by homes and businesses, as opposed to industrial and agricultural waste).

Once the specific waste generation locations are identified, the next step is to determine the waste composition of the combined sources. These five sources of waste within the supply chain are shown in Figure 4.1.

Economics of Environmental Responsibility

Doing what should be done, rather than what has to be done, means that economic objectives should be broadened to include intangible benefits such as corporate reputation and employee morale. An "SCPA" goal should encourage technical innovations to prevent pollution at the source, through the methods of product reformulation, process modification, equipment redesign, and source recovery, while simultaneously ensuring the consideration of the environmental factors for the entire life cycle of the product.[38]

---

[37] *Handbook for Environmentally Responsible Packaging,* p. 2-2.

[38] Arthur D. Little, Inc. *Packaging for the Environment,* p. 173.

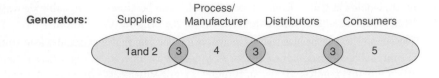

Sources of Waste: (1) Production of waste based on customer specification
(2) Production of nonstandard items
(3) Packaging due to geographic separation of parties
(4) Internal generation of waste by processing firm/manufacturer
(5) Unconsumed portion of product (including packaging)

Figure 4.1 | The pollution supply chain.

SCPA is not a mechanical system that, once implemented, runs automatically. SCPA is like Continuous Quality Improvement (CQI), a philosophy that lives with and within the members of the organization. A successful pollution avoidance program requires the involvement and visible commitment by top management to the waste-prevention philosophy by all members of the value chain. SCPA needs executive sponsorship to enhance the importance of the policy to employees at all levels. Positive environmental awareness can be created through internal management speeches and publications, employee briefings, company slogans, publicly proclaimed emission reduction goals, and incentive programs that reward initiative and innovation in meeting or exceeding environmental objectives.[39] Top management has to prepare the organization for a new way.

One very effective and inexpensive way of promoting the implementation of a sound environmental agenda within an organization is to incorporate environmental thinking into current programs, rather than creating new programs from scratch. The TQM concept is emerging in several organizations as an ideal vehicle for environmentally based quality programs. TQM encourages the emergence of ideas in the organization from the bottom up (empowerment of the individual employee), and it also provides a logical framework for environmental objectives.[40]

Further Analysis Once the decision is made and management has agreed on those materials that are the first to be addressed, the cross-functional pollution avoidance team has to answer the following three questions:

1. Where is this waste material generated?
2. At what stage was it planned into the supply chain?
3. Why was it built into the supply chain?

Each of the waste materials accumulates at some point in the supply chain. The team has to follow the physical waste stream from the customer and distribution system, over the

---

[39]"Profits One," p. 95.

[40]Arthur D. Little, Inc. *Packaging for the Environment,* p. 248.

internal supply chain links of the company, through the supplier(s) to Mother Earth. End-of-the-pipe solutions are not the goals of SCPA. The team has to determine the location at which the waste material is produced in the first place. Focusing on the internal process, this could be in the internal warehouse and logistic arrangements, the production process, or purchasing requirements. Once the physical location of generation is identified, the team has to go one step further. It has to analyze the remaining portions of the supply chain in order to find the chain link that caused this material to end up in the waste stream. At which level was this material initially integrated into the supply chain? During the investigation phase of the new product, the development phase, the procurement plans, the production process, the warehouse stage, or the logistic phase? Once this second question is answered, the team can move along to address the third question: Why was it built into the supply chain?

To meet the challenge of sustainable development, production must become more resource efficient, adding more value while using less energy and raw materials and generating less pollution. This requires the redesign of both products and production processes, and it requires manufacturers to consider the entire life cycles of their products.[41] To realize this goal, the justification of the existence of each waste material has to be questioned. With Supply Chain Pollution Avoidance (SCPA), the cross-functional pollution avoidance team has to question the justification of why the material(s) were initially built into the supply chain. Questioning each detail might "mean redesigning processes, upgrading cleaning practices and material handling, reevaluating product design and choice of raw materials and solvents, and modifying product packaging, loading, and transportation."[42]

The specific manner in which an environment and cost based value analysis is performed cannot be standardized. The different members of a team possess unique analytical abilities and employ unique patterns of thought. However, management should require analysts to follow several general steps that are designed to stimulate and organize their efforts. Those commonly used are (1) the value analysis checklist, (2) the functional environment and cost approach, (3) the use of brainstorming, and (4) the use of suppliers and customers. The checklist consists of a number of general questions followed by several highly specialized questions for particular company characteristics. During the functional environment and cost approach, the question would be, Do particular functions performed by a single part justify its environmental impact and costs?[43] The use of brainstorming stimulates creative problem solutions. Depending on personal preference, step (4) can either be an isolated step by itself or, as we recommend, should be integrated into the first three steps. Value analysis possesses tremendous potential. However, if its potential is to be realized, those responsible for administration of the value analysis program must adopt a broadly based management point of view. This is important, because the purpose of value analysis should be to optimize the total value chain efficiency. (See chapter 21 for more on value analysis.)

---

[41]"Profits One," p. 87.

[42]Ibid., p. 91.

[43]Dobler and Burt, *Purchasing and Supply Management,* p. 563.

After evaluating the current system, the team members must reach a consensus on the parts of the systems (including other members of the supply chain) that must be changed and exactly how and when they should be changed. Once a general course of action has been agreed upon, a detailed plan can be developed. This plan will define all the process improvements the company and the members of its supply chain must make in order to achieve an efficient SCPA system. In addition, the plan must also establish a realistic timeframe for implementation and delineate the person or persons responsible for overseeing each improvement. As is true with TQM, complete and accurate documentation is the key to achieving the full potential of SCPA. All of the elements, requirements, and provisions adopted by the company for its SCPA system must be documented in a systematic and orderly manner in the form of written policies and procedures.[44]

How Is Supply Management Affected? Companies that adopt SCPA as the guideline for their environmental commitment put supply management right in the middle of corporate environmental management, coupling value for money and environmental issues. Environmental impact is a threshold issue in supply. Where appropriate, relevant environmental criteria are to be included in specifications, requests for offers, and evaluations of potential suppliers.

For example, it may be appropriate to specify recycled products or to require energy efficient office accommodation. Potential suppliers should be required to provide information relating to the nominated environmental criteria just as they provide information on their financial situation, project management skills, and quality processes. Compliance with these criteria could be determined during evaluation and offers not meeting them rejected, just as noncompliance with other aspects of the specification or request for offers may lead to rejection.[45]

Selecting strategic suppliers is based on the development of specific measurement criteria for the sourcing of critical components. Supply management and, let us hope, other members of the sourcing team should carefully review the potential supplier's pollution avoidance capabilities against the established criteria. With the implementation of SCPA, having an environmentally sound management strategy should be the next criterion to be added to the list. The supply management department is the closest link to the supplier. When integrating particular suppliers into the processor/manufacturer's cross-functional pollution avoidance team, supply management should be the one introducing the individual supplier(s). Supply management plays an important role within SCPA, but it does not have to play the leading one.

An Example Theory is wonderful, but an example is even better! Recently, Henkel KGaA (Germany) integrated two of the four "Rs" (reduce and recycle) in an environmentally sensitive manner.

In the early 1990s, Henkel received the World Star Award from the International World Packaging Organization for developing the so-called "Sleeve Pack." The concept

---

[44]Sanders Quality Association, Inc., *How to Qualify for ISO 9000,* p. 180.

[45]Australian Department of Administrative Services, *The Better Buying Better World Strategy,* p. 9.

is so powerful that even Church & Dwight (Arm & Hammer in the United States) licensed the patent from Henkel in order to market its own products in similar sleeve pack bottles.

The original idea and goal was to develop a product that would meet the demands of both the present and the future:

- Reduced raw material usage.
- Easy separation of different recyclable materials, complete recyclability.
- No quality loss when recycling the synthetic bottle material, Handelskonforme Losung (Direct Product Profitability).
- Brand name suitable decoration possibilities.
- Manufacturability using existing equipment and production lines.
- Waste volume reduction, based on easy to fold up characteristics.

The result was the Sleeve Pack: a synthetic bottle supported by a card sleeve. The card sleeve is made from unbleached and long fiber type cardboard and heavy metal-free colored printing ink. This material combination allows 100 percent recyclability, because the fiber type used in the cardboard is in strong demand in the paper industry. The choice of fiber type was based on the demands and needs of the potential user of the recycled card sleeve. Many fiber types would have done the job, but only a few are of particular interest to the paper industry, the potential user of the recycled card sleeve. Therefore, it was crucial to involve both the supplier base and the potential consumers of the recycled sleeve in the early stage of product development.

The design of the bottle reduced the usage of the raw material by approximately 50 percent. Only with the know-how of the supplier base was it possible to develop a synthetic bottle whose sides were so thin that the stability as well as a 50 percent reduction in material could be realized. The cross-functional new product team at Henkel decided on noncolored synthetic material for both the bottle and the cap. As a result, the synthetic material can be recycled and reused to produce new bottles.

It was important to find an approach that minimized the required investment and allowed the usage of the existing production lines. It was also important to develop a bottle concept that ensured an active marketing promotion: The bottle must represent an image of brand name quality. And finally, the material choice had to be discussed with the purchasing side, in order to meet quality, timeliness, and cost objectives.

And last, but most important, was the customer orientation. The shape of the bottle had to be "Handelskonforme" (Direct Product Profitability). The two different materials of synthetics and cardboard had to be easily separated and foldable. The final product had to convey the image of being environmentally sound, while simultaneously representing a high-quality brand name product. And, of course, the price level had to be acceptable to both Henkel and the end consumer.

With the development of the Sleeve Pack, Henkel showed the possibility of involving the supplier as well as customers in the early stage of product development. This is one example of how beneficial it can be to consider the company's supply chain, including the supplier's supplier and the customer's customer.

A Call for Action The goal for the future should be the development of concepts that do not push waste or costs from one side of the supply chain to the other, but that reduce the total sum of produced waste and cost throughout the entire supply chain. Surprisingly, the International Organization for Standardization publication ISO 14000 mentions the role of suppliers in avoiding pollution only once. We hope to see a forthcoming version of ISO 14000 adopt procedures for the entire supply chain. Uniform SCPA standards would allow for third-party audits to be conducted with the goal of certifying a company's pollution avoidance improvement efforts. SCPA does not have a predetermined goal, which once reached, translates into the successful completion of the program. There are few processes that could not be improved. The ultimate goal should be zero waste generation. Recognizing the boundaries of physics, chemistry, and economics, we propose a legitimate goal of reducing the level of pollution 50 percent every two years until it is negligible.[46]

Values in the Workplace[47]

As the world economy has become more global and companies have expanded their business to locate in many countries and seek customers across national borders, it has become increasingly evident that the cultural, legal, political and even basic business practices vary significantly across the world. What is legal in one country is not legal in another. What is the norm in one culture is not so in another. Key social issues in one part of the world are seen as unimportant and replaced by other issues in another part of the world. Companies are at times faced with a bewildering array of conflicting expectations and regulations spanning a wide range of issues.

Examples abound. Diversity in the United States is a concept that emerged from the Civil Rights and Women's Liberation movements in the latter half of the 20th century. Diversity in other parts of the world can be far less race and gender focused and, instead, focus on religious, ethnic, and national heritage first. Witness the ethnic and religious issues in the Balkans, Northern Ireland, the Middle East, and on the Indian/Pakistani border. Similarly, bribery—strictly forbidden in many parts of the world—is a normal and expected part of business in some parts of the world. Human rights policies, viewed as part of a country's independent prerogative a century or two ago, are key political issues that impact trade and how a company must conduct itself today. They are no longer seen as something that can be ignored across borders. For years China's human rights and intellectual property practices hindered its attempts to enter the World Trade Organization. Minimum wage laws and workplace safety regulations are widely different across the world. Some third world countries view environmental efforts, worker safety, and high minimum wages as attempts to control their most salable resource, cheap labor, by a developed world that rose at a time when such issues were not carefully regulated. On the

---

[46]For more insight into the issue of supply management's role in protecting our physical environment, see "Environmental Purchasing: A Framework for Theory Development" by George A. Zsidisen and Sue P. Siferd, *European Journal of Purchasing & Supply Management* 7 (2001) 61–73.

[47]This section was developed by Stephen C. Rogers, Director, Purchases Technology of Procter and Gamble and was presented to the 16th Strategic Supply Management Forum, University of San Diego, Nov. 7, 2001.

other hand, the developed world sees these as basic needs that must be met if society is to continue to progress.

Two questions quickly emerge. First, how does a company deal with situations in which what is legal and expected in one culture is illegal and/or viewed as inappropriate in another culture? Second, why is this an issue for supply management? The answer to the first question is that companies must create and communicate to their employees across the world a set of principles and values that will govern how they operate regardless of location. Often these principles are founded on those of the culture from which a company emerged—American companies conduct business subject to U.S. international trade law and domestic legal and regulatory requirements, as well as many American cultural values about workplace conditions. In addition, a number of international conventions have emerged on issues such as child labor and forced labor. These conventions provide a set of broadly recognized ground rules across the world.

As for the second question (Why is this an issue for supply management?), this is an emerging reality. For many years these kinds of issues were seen as things a company managed within its own business—its plants were safe, it had a diversity plan, no children worked in the plants or offices. However, in recent years companies are being held accountable for the actions of their suppliers in the eyes of their customers, governments, special interest groups, and the media—witness high-profile media stories in recent years, including Wal-Mart "Made in the USA" clothes made by foreign suppliers, Kathy Lee Gifford apparel made by suppliers running sweatshops, and so on. The list is extensive. Buyers are expected to penetrate their suppliers and hold them accountable to meeting the same standards as their internal operations. The use of suppliers half a world away is no excuse for violations. Public opinion of customers and consumers is a powerful business driver that translates into one of supply management's social responsibilities.

Principle-Based Approach

Given this wide range of potential social issues, where does a company begin to create a set of principles to manage these areas? One answer to these questions was addressed by the pastor of a Philadelphia church, Reverend Leon Sullivan, who in the 1970s became a leader in the worldwide effort to change the apartheid policy of South Africa. In doing this, Sullivan, who was also an outside Director of General Motors for more than 20 years, developed a set of eight principles as a code of conduct for companies operating in South Africa. These principles have become a good guide for any corporation's social responsibility policies as it expands across the globe. The Global Sullivan Principles, as they would be espoused by a corporation, are:

- Express support for universal human rights and, particularly, those of our employees, the communities within which we operate, and parties with whom we do business.
- Promote equal opportunity for our employees at all levels of the company with respect to issues such as color, race, gender, age, ethnicity, or religious beliefs, and operate without unacceptable worker treatment such as the exploitation of children, physical punishment, female abuse, involuntary servitude, or other forms of abuse.
- Respect our employees' voluntary freedom of association.

■ Compensate our employees to enable them to meet at least their basic needs and provide the opportunity to improve their skill and capability in order to raise their social and economic opportunities.

■ Provide a safe and healthy workplace; protect human health and the environment; and promote sustainable development.

■ Promote fair competition, including respect for intellectual and other property rights, and not offer, pay, or accept bribes.

■ Work with governments and communities in which we do business to improve the quality of life in those communities—their educational, cultural, economic, and social well-being—and seek to provide training and opportunities for workers from disadvantaged backgrounds.

■ Promote the application of these principles by those with whom we do business.

Each company needs to translate these principles into a set of values its employees can follow. They must understand whether their actions are the right thing to do, would withstand public scrutiny, and protect the company's reputation as an ethical organization.

Supply Management Practices

Once such a set of principles is in place, the supply management organization bears the task of implementing them in a way that protects corporate integrity, recognizes and assigns responsibility to the supply base to manage their own operations, and performs this task in the most cost effective way possible. In the execution of this responsibility Supply Management must take three key steps.

1. *Set clear expectations.* Supply management, as owner of the commercial relationship with the supply base, needs to translate corporate principles into a set of expectations that suppliers understand is a condition of doing business with the firm. Suppliers must understand their role in the supply chain for their customer's products and that their performance on social responsibility priorities as part of this chain reflects on the reputation of their customers—represented by the supply management organization. Importantly, the supplier must understand specifically what is expected, not just some generalities. Expectations of performance on management areas such as child labor, forced labor, aid in counterfeiting its customer's products, and allowing dangerous working conditions need to be spelled out during any negotiation and award of business. These expectations can be incorporated in contractual agreements or as necessary criteria prior to any request for proposal.

2. *Assign supplier responsibility.* Perhaps one of the toughest challenges for supply management is to recognize that suppliers must take responsibility for their own operations. No customer can fully know everything that goes on in its suppliers' operations. Therefore, part of the task of ensuring successful delivery of socially responsible business practices is to understand the policies and systems of its key suppliers with regard to social responsibility issues. Suppliers must run their businesses in a way that meets the legal and moral requirements of their customers. If this is not a clear value of the organization, no amount of inspection or supply management involvement in supplier operations can guarantee compliance when the supplier's normal management approach has not embedded these values into routine operation.

3. *Enforce consequences for lack of performance.* The buying company must back up any expectations set with the supply base with commercial actions that enforce them. Supply management observations of any violations or risks within a supplier's plants need to be communicated internally. More important, clear plans must be put in place to remedy the situation. Urgency is a success criterion for the supplier's improvement plan. When a pattern of continued violation occurs, the buying company must be prepared to terminate the business relationship. Its track record of taking action when social responsibility questions arise is what creates supply management's credibility with the supply base. Even when the supplier's culture and local legal system do not match the buying firm's expectations, these criteria need to be viewed as a condition of doing business.

Supply management has a critical role in protecting the reputation and integrity of its company. The implications of ignoring these issues can be devastating to a firm's business, especially when its customers become aware of a violation. In addition to special interest groups and media coverage, upholding the ethical standards of the company and meeting the spirit as well as the letter of the law in these areas is an important responsibility.

Concluding Remarks

Supply management plays a key role in implementing three of the corporation's social and ethical responsibilities: ensuring that diversity suppliers receive a fair share of the firm's expenditures, protecting our environment, and addressing social, legal, political, and ethical issues in our diverse global economy.

Endnotes

For more insight into supply management's role in protecting our environment, see:

1. Steve V. Walton, Robert B. Handfield, and Steven A. Melnyk, "The Green Supply Chain: Integrating Suppliers into Environmental Management Processes," *International Journal of Purchasing and Materials Management,* Spring 1998.

2. George A. Zsidisin and Sue P. Siferd, "Environmental Purchasing: A Framework for Theory Development," *European Journal of Purchasing and Supply Management,* July 2000.

For more on values in the workplace, see, "The Global Sullivan Principles," published by the International Foundation for Education and Self Help, 5040 East Shea Blvd, Suite 280, Phoenix, AZ 85254.

PART 2

Enabling Concepts

Computer Screen showing a graph *(#1) Tommy Ewasko/Image Bank/Getty Images #2) Thierry Dosogne/Image Bank/Getty Images)*

In this section of the book, we describe and discuss five key concepts which both enable and facilitate World Class Supply Management[SM]. These concepts underlie and enable two or more phases of the supply management process.

Chapter 5 describes the three fundamental types of relationships which exist between professional buyers and suppliers: transactional, collaborative, and alliance. Although these relationship types are implicitly straightforward, supply managers often have varying definitions of them. The result? A term such as "partnership" has been misinterpreted so frequently, we have chosen to purge it from this book. Many of us have heard the story of the sales manager who charged his sales force to "establish partnerships . . . whatever that means." The salespeople, in turn, informed their customers that they wanted to establish partnerships, with little or no understanding of the implications to both parties.

World-class supply managers recognize that there is a time and a place for transactional, collaborative, and alliance buyer-supplier relationships. They know the strengths and weaknesses of each type of relationship and design their "relationship strategy" so as to maximize the return on the available investment in human resources. There is no question that well-developed and well-managed alliances deliver the optimum in the areas of cost, quality, time to market, technology flow, and continuity of supply. But such relationships require a significant investment in human resources. Based on anecdotal evidence, we recommend that buyer-supplier relationships evolve through a collaborative phase before blooming into alliances. Unfortunately, most alliances appear to be doomed to failure *unless* the strategic objectives of the two firms are properly aligned; there is a compatibility of corporate cultures; and institutional trust is developed and maintained.

Supply management is the most interdisciplinary of all functions. It cuts across department lines and requires the involvement of many disciplines. Thus, it is essential that the professional supply manager possess or develop cross-functional team participation and leadership skills. Chapter 6 introduces several key teaming concepts which will assist all members of an organization's supply management system to maximize the system's contribution to the firm's bottom line. These concepts apply equally within the firm and with interfirm teams. Careful application of these concepts and practices will help all members of the supply management system to properly balance their personal workload between functional and cross-functional activities.

It is our belief that no other functional area or system has more impact on the quality of the organization's products and services than does supply management. Experience indicates that some 75 percent of field failures can be traced back to defects in purchased materials. Chapter 7, Quality Management, demonstrates that there are many approaches to proactively mitigating quality problems. The chapter describes several philosophies, approaches, tools, and methodologies that supply management may perform in order to eliminate or minimize defects throughout its supply chains. The focus of the chapter is on developing quality design and prevention systems rather than reactive detection systems.

Some 40 years ago, the U.S. Air Force introduced the concept of life cycle costing. Instead of addressing operating characteristics and flyaway costs only, we analyzed the cost of owning and operating a weapon system over its expected life. The private sector has learned much from the Department of Defense in what has come to be known as the Total Cost of Ownership. We believe that every supply manager, every program manager, every design engineer—in fact, every decision maker—must be familiar with and support the principles described in Chapter 8, Total Cost of Ownership.

The last chapter of this section is entitled "e-Commerce II." Much as MRP laid the foundation for MRPII, we believe that e-Commerce, with its focus on impersonal electronic systems, must evolve to a more realistic approach: e-Commerce II. e-Commerce II goes beyond the transactional capabilities of electronic commerce to fulfill strategic goals across supply chains. It is our belief that electronic commerce is adapting to facilitate long-term collaborative relationships and provide synergistic rewards that could not be obtained through e-Commerce I. As will be presented in this chapter, two key missing ingredients in e-Commerce I were trust and the human element in buyer-supplier relationships. World Class Supply Management^{SM} calls for trust to be developed between supply chain members. Trust as presented by WCSM is developed between individuals who can have an open dialog on real issues and possible solutions. Only then can e-Commerce II succeed in providing open sharing of information across company boundaries to enable the potential for optimization of the supply chain. As seen throughout this book, e-Commerce II is an enabler, not a replacement, of the essential human aspect of buyer-supplier relationships.

5 CHAPTER

Buyer-Supplier Relationships

Systematically selected supply alliances built on institutional trust help organizations complete their evolution to World Class Supply Management^{SM}.

Case

The Microprocessor Manufacturing Co. is a major supplier to the automotive industry. Ten years ago, MMC supplied 50 percent of all microprocessors used by automotive manufacturers in the Americas and Europe. Today, over 200 microprocessors are required for the average automobile. A new product, scheduled for release 14 months ago, has just been introduced. In an emotional and finger-pointing review of the causes of the delay, it has become apparent that the nine-month delay in receipt of required equipment was a key culprit. The VPs of supply, engineering, manufacturing, and finance have been charged with determining why equipment is not available when it is required. The committee's findings are as follows:

- Three firms supply all of MMC's critical equipment.
- MMC engineers have resisted working with the suppliers as the engineers develop new microprocessors, stating their fear of technology transfusion through the suppliers to MMC's competitors.
- Although relations exist with each of the three equipment suppliers, the procurement of each item of equipment requires lengthy and detailed technical and commercial discussions. The supply relations are transactional; that is, they are arm's-length (in other words, a nontrusting, noninteractive, not cocreational relationship). Each procurement is a new transaction, never building upon the unique value the supplier may provide through a collaborative relationship.
- Similar items of equipment are delivered to MMC's competitors 9 12 months earlier than to MMC.
- MMC does not share its technology or volume forecast with its suppliers.

What action should MMC take *first* in an effort to eliminate the competitive disadvantage of late equipment availability?

A Transformation in Relationships

The transformation from reactive and mechanical purchasing to proactive procurement and on to World Class Supply Management^{SM} parallels a similar transformation in relationships between buyers and suppliers. During the dark days of reactive purchasing, relations between salespersons representing suppliers and their counterparts in purchasing were reasonably cordial, but frequently adversarial. A gain for one resulted in a loss for the other, which is often called a win-lose outcome. The interaction between vendor and purchasing was often characterized by highly manipulative tactics by both parties designed to maneuver the other side into a position where one's gain would be the other's loss. As purchasing became more professional, buyers and suppliers began to see benefits of more collaborative relationships, where the outcome can result in a win-win relationship for both parties.

During the late 1980s and early 1990s, suppliers saw many advantages in developing "partnerships" with customer firms. Sales managers charged their salespeople with becoming "partners" with their key customers. However, based on a lack of clarity from management, many of the salespeople did not understand the implications of the term "partner." Additionally, the legal implications of the term "partner" raised concerns. For example, is a buyer "partner" free to solicit prices from competing suppliers? Is a supplier "partner" required to give all of its "partners" the same price and services?

While the term "partnership" is still relatively common, we avoid use of the term, preferring the terms "collaborative relationship" and "strategic alliance." These terms and their advantages and disadvantages will be addressed shortly.

Three Types of Buyer-Supplier Relationships

Figure 5.1 portrays the three principle classes of relationships and activities and attributes common to each.

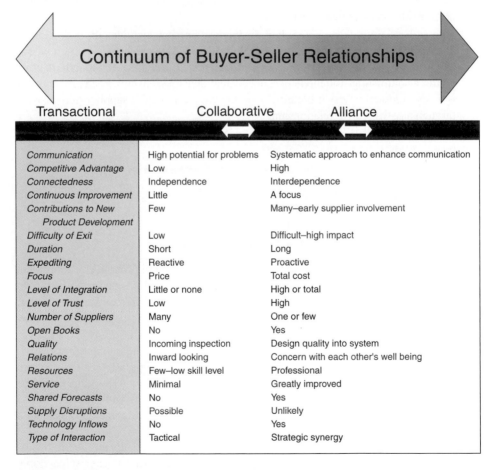

	Transactional	Alliance
Communication	High potential for problems	Systematic approach to enhance communication
Competitive Advantage	Low	High
Connectedness	Independence	Interdependence
Continuous Improvement	Little	A focus
Contributions to New Product Development	Few	Many–early supplier involvement
Difficulty of Exit	Low	Difficult–high impact
Duration	Short	Long
Expediting	Reactive	Proactive
Focus	Price	Total cost
Level of Integration	Little or none	High or total
Level of Trust	Low	High
Number of Suppliers	Many	One or few
Open Books	No	Yes
Quality	Incoming inspection	Design quality into system
Relations	Inward looking	Concern with each other's well being
Resources	Few–low skill level	Professional
Service	Minimal	Greatly improved
Shared Forecasts	No	Yes
Supply Disruptions	Possible	Unlikely
Technology Inflows	No	Yes
Type of Interaction	Tactical	Strategic synergy

Figure 5.1 | Characteristics of Three Types of Relationships.

Transactional Relationships

We call the most common and most basic type of relationship "transactional."[1] Such a relationship is neither good nor bad. Transactional simply describes an arm's-length relationship wherein neither party is especially concerned with the well-being of the other. Virtually all buying firms will have transactional relationships. Most will have collaborative ones and some will have strategic alliances.

Transactional Relationships Have Several Characteristics:

- An absence of concern by both parties about the other party's well-being. With transactional relationships, there is little or no concern about the other party's well-being. What one party wins, the other loses.
- One of a series of independent deals. Each transaction is entered into on its own merits. Little or no basis exists for collaboration and learning.
- Costs, data and forecasts are not shared. Arm's-length transactions, not openness, are characteristics of transactional relationships.
- Price is the focus of the relationship. Getting the best price is the focus of the transaction. Ideally total cost analysis, as described later in this book, precedes any procurement transaction. Since there is little or no concern for the other's well-being, neither buyer nor supplier will rush to the other's assistance in bad times or when problems arise.
- A minimum of purchasing time and energy is required to establish prices. Market forces normally establish prices in transactional relationships. Thus, little purchasing time and energy are required to establish prices.
- Transactional purchases lend themselves to e-procurement and, in some cases, reverse auctions.

The Advantages of Transactional Relationships Include:

- Relatively less purchasing time and effort are required to establish price. As we have noted, the market forces of supply and demand establish the price with transactional procurements. Therefore, little purchasing time and effort are required to establish price.
- Lower skill levels of procurement personnel are required. Much less judgment and managerial expertise are required with the vast majority of transactional procurements.

The Disadvantages of Transactional Relationships Include:

- The potential for communication difficulties is much greater with transactional relationships than with collaborative or alliance ones.
- Considerable investment in expediting and the monitoring of incoming quality is required to ensure timely delivery of the right quality.

---

[1]We reserve the term "vendor" for those wonderful people at ballparks who sell frankfurters and, more important, beer.

■ Transactional relationships are inflexible when flexibility may be required. Changing technology and changing market conditions can require flexibility in buyer/supplier relationships.

■ Transactional procurements tend to result in more delivery problems than do collaborative and strategic alliance ones. Friends look out for friends, not opportunistic buyers or suppliers.

■ Quality with transactional relations will be only as good as required. Far more incentive and opportunity exists to improve quality in a collaborative or alliance relationship.

■ Transactional suppliers tend to provide the minimum service required.

■ Buyers tend to experience less effective performance by their transactional suppliers than do those employing collaborative or strategic relationships. Transactional suppliers have much less to lose from a dissatisfied customer than do collaborative and strategic relationship suppliers.

■ Transactional customers are subject to more supply disruptions than are collaborative or alliance ones. Buyers who maintain continuing, collaborative relations with their suppliers are much less subject to supply shortages than are opportunistic ones.

■ Since the supplier recognizes the transactional and price nature of the relationship, it is not motivated to invest time and energy in the development of the potential buyer's products.

Collaborative and Alliance Relationships

"Collaboration is the new imperative," declares Michael Dell, founder and CEO of Dell Computer and *Industry Week*'s CEO of the Year for 1998.[2] Collaborative and alliance relationships for the procurement of noncommodity[3] items and services tend to result in lower total costs than do transactional relationships for several reasons. Process improvements and the adoption of technical innovations require a high level of certainty and continuity of demand. The risks and uncertainties present with transactional relationships reduce the likelihood of investments in R&D and training as well as the procurement of new, more efficient equipment focused on the customer firm's needs. Thus, major opportunities for cost reduction within supplying organizations may be lost with transactional relationships.

Cost reductions resulting from value engineering and value analysis (VE/VA) are much more likely with collaborative and alliance relationships.[4] Suppliers are more likely to take the initiative to reduce costs through VE/VA when they are involved in long-term relations than with short-term transactional ones.

---

[2]John L. Mariotti, "Collaboration Is the Way to Go," *Supply Chain Management Review,* Spring 1999, p. 75.

[3]Commodity items/services are those which are highly interchangeable with another supplier's offering. School writing tablets and noncritical fasteners (nuts, bolts, rivets, etc.) are examples of commodities.

[4]Value engineering is addressed in Chapter 10.

Longer-term performance agreements allow suppliers an opportunity to reduce their costs. The extended learning curve effect[5] with both production and services allows collaborative and alliance suppliers to reduce their costs and share these savings with customers.

Collaborative and alliance relations replace the market forces employed by transactional procurement with controlled competition, benchmarking, and advanced supply management pricing practices. The results are lower total costs, higher quality, reduced time to market, and reduced risk of supply disruptions.

Researchers Stanley and Pearson found that the three most important factors in a successful buyer-supplier relationship are (1) two-way communication, (2) the supplier's responsiveness to supply management's needs, and (3) clear product specifications.[6] Both collaborative and alliance relationships require a quality of management not common in the 1990s.[7]

Collaborative Relationships

An awareness of the interdependence and necessity of cooperation is the key difference between collaborative relationships and transactional ones. "The focus on relationship management will require that all elements of relationship management, including trust building, communications, joint efforts, and planning and fostering interdependency, will be increasingly studied and managed to achieve competitive advantage."[8] Recognition of interdependency and need of cooperation provides many benefits to both parties to the relationship. Both parties are aware that money enters their supply chain (or supply network) only if the chain's end products are cost competitive. Recognizing the need for interdependence and cooperation, the customer's firm enjoys the benefits of early supplier involvement (ESI). Improvements in cost, quality, time to market, and the leveraging of supplier technology result.

Continuous improvement is far easier to implement and manage with recognized interdependence and cooperation. The end objective with continuous improvement is a reduction in total costs. Improved quality and timeliness also result.

The likelihood of supply disruptions is greatly reduced. Collaborative suppliers look out for their friends, not their opportunistic customers. Collaborative relationships help cushion bad times. Both customers and suppliers who value each other, based on long-term relations and respect, are more likely to come to each other's aid during times of adversity.

Lower total costs are the common result of collaborative and alliance relationships. The relative level of certainty and continuity of demand in collaborative and alliance

---

[5]For more on the effects of the learning curve, see Chapter 18.

[6]Linda L. Stanley and John N. Pearson, "Buyer-Supplier Strategies and Their Impact on Purchasing Performance: A Study of the Electronics Industry," Conference 2000, Richard Ivey School of Business, University of Western Ontario, London, May 24–27, 2000.

[7]P. L. Carter, J. R. Carter, R. M. Monczka, T. H. Slaight, and A. J. Swan, "The future of Purchasing and Supply: A Ten-Year Forecast," *The Journal of Supply Chain Management,* Winter 2000, pp. 14–26.

[8]Ibid.

relationships increases the likelihood of investments in R&D, training, and the procurement of new, more efficient equipment focused on the customer firm's needs. Cost reductions resulting from value engineering and value analysis are enhanced, and the extended learning curve effect with both production and services activities allows collaborative and alliance suppliers to reduce their costs and share these savings with their customers.[9]

The major disadvantage of collaborative and alliance relationships is the amount of human resources, time, and energy required to develop and manage the relationships. However, firms such as Honda and Deere & Co. have demonstrated that the required investments provide very attractive returns.

Supply Alliances

The fundamental difference between collaborative relationships and supply alliances is the presence of institutional trust[10] in alliances. The failure to develop and manage institutional trust is the principle reason that so many supply alliances fail.

Supply alliances reap incredible benefits as a result of physical asset specialization and human specialization. Dyer defines *physical asset specialization* as "relationship-specific capital investments (e.g., in customized machinery, tools, information systems, delivery processes, and so forth) that allow for faster throughput and greater product customization. Physical asset specialization allows for product differentiation and may improve overall quality by increasing product integrity. *Human specialization* refers to relationship-specific know-how accumulated by individuals through long-standing relationships. In other words, individuals across companies have substantial experience working together and have accumulated specialized information and language that allows them to communicate and coordinate effectively with each other. They are less likely to have communication breakdowns that result in errors; this, in turn, results in higher quality, faster development times, and lower costs."[11]

The Primary Benefits of Supply Alliances Include:

■ *Lower total costs.* Synergies can be created in alliances that cannot happen in transactional or even collaborative relationships. The synergies result in reductions of direct and indirect costs associated with labor, machinery, materials, and overhead.

■ *Reduced time to market.* Reducing the time to design, develop, and distribute products and services is a key driver that leads to improved market share and better profit margins.

---

[9]See Chapter 18 for insight into the learning curve.

[10]Institutional trust: The term "trust" has such a wide variety of meanings and interpretations that we have chosen to coin the term "institutional trust." Institutional trust is the key element that differentiates supply alliances from collaborative relationships. With institutional trust, the parties have access to each other's strategic plans in the area(s) of the interface. Relevant cost information and forecasts are shared. Risks and rewards are addressed openly. Informal agreements are as good as written ones. Institutional trust is measured and managed. The issue of institutional trust is addressed in greater detail in the appendix to this chapter.

[11]Jeffrey H. Dyer, *Collaborative Advantage,* N.Y., N.Y. Oxford University Press, 2000, pp. 42–3.

- *Improved quality.* The use of both the design of experiments[12] and supplier certification[13] are the norm with supply alliances. These two activities design and manufacture quality in rather than inspecting for errors. The result is improved quality at lower total cost.

- *Improved technology flow from suppliers.* Openness and institutional trust enhance the inflow of technology from alliance partners that leads to many successful new products. In 1999, Dell and IBM formed an alliance worth some $16 billion over 10 years. In effect, Dell is harnessing IBM's vast research, development, and production abilities. Dell is purchasing storage devices, custom logic chips, static random-access memory and other components. The two companies are cross-licensing patents—that is, they are sharing relevant technologies.[14]

- *Improved continuity of supply.* Alliance customers are the least likely group to experience supply disruptions.

Alliances Share Several Attributes:

- The focus of most supplier alliances is achieving the simultaneous objectives of continuous improvements along with squeezing cost out.

- A high level of recognized interdependence and commitment is present.

- An atmosphere of cooperation exists. Potential conflicts are addressed and resolved openly. When problems occur, the focus is a search for the root cause, not the assignment of blame.

- The alliance is controlled through a complex web of formal and informal interpersonal connections, information systems, and internal infrastructures that enhance learning.

- Openness exists in all areas of the relationship including, cost, long-term objectives, technology, and the supply chain itself.

- The alliance is a living system that progressively evolves with the objective of creating new benefits for both parties.

- The alliance partners share a vision of the future in the area of the interface.

- Ethics take precedence over expediency.

- The relationship is adaptable in the face of changing economics, competition, technology, and environmental issues.

- The design of experiments and supplier certification are the norm with supply alliances. These two activities design and manufacture quality in. The result is improved quality at a lower total cost.

---

[12]The design of experiments is a quantitative approach of analyzing deviations from desired outcomes during the design process. Identifying deviations during this stage—before progressing to production—has a powerful positive effect on an item's quality.

[13]Supplier certification requires the customer to carefully review a supplier's manufacturing operation to ensure that it has the necessary processes in place to meet the customer's quality requirements. Items produced by a supplier whose system has been certified for the specific item can flow directly into the customer's production without being inspected. This issue is discussed in greater detail in Chapter 7.

[14]"Dell to Buy $16 billion in IBM Parts," *Los Angeles Times,* March 5, 1999, p. C-1.

■   Negotiations and renegotiations occur in a win-win manner.

■   Executive level commitment and alliance champions protect the alliance from incursions by nonbelievers.

If supply alliances are so attractive, why aren't they the way to conduct all business? Alliances are a very resource-intense approach to supply management and tend to be reserved for the most critical relationships. In 1999, Honda of America had over 400 procurement professionals developing and managing some 400 alliances. Unfortunately, few firms are as enlightened.

During the 1990s, Chrysler became a fascinating example of the power of alliance relationships. In 1989, Chrysler had some 2,500 suppliers in its production supply base. Chrysler was rated as the least desirable customer of the big three U.S. auto assemblers. With a surprising amount of assistance from Honda of America Manufacturing, Chrysler transitioned itself from a transaction-based buyer to a collaborative one. Results? Time to market was reduced 30 percent. Profit margins per vehicle increased an average of 750 percent.

Chrysler employed many of the principles introduced in this text: cross-functional teams, early supplier involvement, target costing, value analysis (with incentives in the form of additional profits or additional sales aid to suppliers), improved communications through techniques such as colocation of supplier engineers at Chrysler design centers, and a supplier advisory board.[15]

Which Relationship Is Appropriate?

How does a supply management executive determine whether a relationship should be transactional, collaborative, or a strategic alliance? Several key questions should be asked to determine the "strategic" elements of a relationship:

1.   Are there many relatively undifferentiated suppliers providing what amounts to interchangeable commodities? If so, a collaborative alliance or relationship would not be appropriate: Try a transactional relationship instead.

2.   Does the potential supplier possess economic power which it is willing to employ over its customers? A transactional or very carefully developed and managed collaborative relationship is usually appropriate.

3.   If there is recognition by both parties of the potential benefits of an alliance, but adequate qualified human resources are not available at one or both firms, a collaborative relationship is usually appropriate.

4.   A collaborative relationship frequently is an appropriate first step on the road to a strategic alliance.

5.   Is one supplier head and shoulders above the rest in terms of the value it provides, including price, innovation, ability to adapt to changing situations, capacity to work

---

[15]For more detailed insight into Chrysler's transition, please see Jeff Dyer, "How Chrysler Created an American Keiretsu," *Harvard Business Review,* July/Aug 1996, pp. 42–53.

with your team, task joint risks, and so on? If so, an alliance may be in order, assuming that the supplier is willing to enter into an interdependent, trusting relationship.

6.   Are some suppliers "strategic" to your business? In other words, do they have a major impact on your competitive advantage in the marketplace? Are you highly reliant on them to provide a unique product, technology, or service? If so, an alliance may be vital.

7.   Would your company benefit greatly if the supplier were more "integrally connected" with your company, perhaps with their engineers working side by side with yours, or colocating their manufacturing facilities adjacent or within yours? If yes, consider an alliance.

8.   Do your customers require high degrees of flexibility and speed of responsiveness, causing you to demand the same performance from your suppliers? This is a classic alliance driver.

Trust is another key factor differentiating the three classes of relationships. The simplest definition of trust is "being confident that the other party will do what it says it will do." Some level of trust must be present in all three of our types of relationships. But the level of trust increases with collaborative relationships and becomes an essential characteristic with strategic alliances.

Few of these relationships are pure: A transactional relationship may have one or more collaborative characteristics while a collaborative relationship may have one or more transactional as well as some alliance characteristics.

The Supplier's Perspective

The competition for world-class suppliers is well under way. As a result, the most attractive supplier may decide that a collaborative or alliance relationship with the potential customer firm is not in its best interest. In effect, the supplier may possess economic power which it desires to exercise in an effort to maximize its net income. Or, the preferred supplier may be unavailable since the buying firm's key competitor may have already established an exclusive relationship. World-class suppliers are careful in their selection of customer firms. The supplier will be very concerned with the potential customer firm's finances, especially as they affect its ability to pay. The customer firm's finances also provide insight into prospects for a long-term relationship and continuing demand for the supplier's product(s) or service(s). Quality suppliers want customers who have good growth prospects.

The potential customer's demand pattern for the supplier's product is of great interest, especially in the areas of stability and fit. World-class suppliers want to ensure that potential customers' quality requirements are within their capabilities. The supplying firm is also very concerned with the buying firm's approach to problems. Does it discipline suppliers who encounter problems, or does it help solve problems together in a mutually beneficial way, deriving critical learning along the way, thus making the problem a "learning foundation" from which to improve? Suppliers are attracted to customers who have a reputation for working collaboratively with suppliers who experience a problem to identify and correct the root cause of the problem.

Suppliers want "good" customers. Several issues affect a customer firm's rating as a "good" customer including:

■ Does the customer have a reputation for timely payment? Cash flow is a major concern of all suppliers.

■ Is the customer secretive? Suppliers prefer customers who are open and approachable.

■ Are the customer's supply management personnel responsive? Suppliers prefer customers that are available (e.g., supplier hours are 11:30–1:00, Monday–Friday).

■ Are the customers known as professionals? World-class suppliers conduct themselves professionally, and expect to be treated professionally.

For suppliers and buyers who comprehend the value of shifting from tactical, transactional-based relationships to strategic value-based alliance relationships, it will be essential to engage the multidimensional assessment of the elements of Total Cost of Ownership (see Chapter 8) to determine exactly where cost can be reduced, value enhanced, and substantial competitive advantage created.

Questions to Be Addressed before Proceeding

While strategic supplier alliances receive a great deal of media coverage and discussion within the supply management community, are they for everyone? Will the benefits of an alliance outweigh the effort, risk, and resources required? For those supply management professionals and organizations that are investigating the possibility of strategic supplier alliances, it can be helpful to ponder the following questions:

■ Is there a danger that the supplier may act in an opportunistic manner over time?

■ Do electronic systems at the purchasing and supplier organizations allow for optimum communication and sharing of information?

■ Is the potential strategic alliance supplier well equipped, in terms of knowledge, expertise, and resources, to stay current in the industry?

■ Are both the purchasing and supplier organizations willing to keep attention focused on the joint customer, in order to establish supply chain objectives and goals?

■ Are there other suppliers in the marketplace, perhaps now more accessible because of e-procurement, who are worth investigating before committing to a strategic alliance?

■ Has the supply manager been thoroughly trained in managing an alliance relationship?

■ Is the purchasing organization proud to be aligned and associated with the supplier organization, as they present a joint marketing front for the links further downstream in the supply chain?

■ Is the purchasing organization comfortable with the level of risk associated with reducing the supply base?[16]

■ Are both supplier and buyer aligned in what their ultimate customer considers to be valuable?

---

[16]Roberta J. Duffy with input from Dr. Joseph L. Cavinato, "Align to Be Strategic," *Purchasing Today,* September 2000, p. 40.

- If there is substantial risk for the supplier to develop new technologies, sub-systems, products, processes, or service support, is the buying firm willing to share or reduce the risks?
- Are both supplier and buyer aligned in their respective visions to be able to make long-term commitments to each other?
- If an alliance is in order, are there sufficient operational points of interaction where the supplier can engage with the buying firm, such as joint development programs, just-in-time inventory, electronic communication, or colocation of service personnel?

Developing and Managing Collaborative and Alliance Relationships

The development and management of collaborative and alliance relationships are fascinating and challenging activities that are addressed in Chapter 23.

Situations wherein Alliances May Not Be Appropriate

Quite obviously, alliances are not always appropriate. Professor Ralph Kauffman has identified 14 such situations and has developed them into 5 major categories:

1. **Stability** of the prices, market, and buyer's demand.
   - **Price Volatility.** Commodities traded on open markets that have significant price volatility. The problem for a partnership/alliance is how to share risks and bene fits that may result from price volatility. Some arrangements can be made to mitigate this problem including price adjustment mechanisms based on costs or indexes and, for some commodities, hedging in futures markets.
   - **Demand Volatility:** Materials or services that have significant volatility in individual buyer demand. If the buying firm's needs are not predictable, the supplier must deal with the likelihood of overstock or stockout or erratic productions schedules. To do this may generate additional costs for the supplier that must be built into the price that the buyer pays.
   - **High Switching Likelihood with High Switching Costs:** Situations with high switching costs that also have a high likelihood of switching being desirable. Purchases that involve changing technology or critical quality or other characteristics where there are at the same time no strong suppliers may indicate a high likelihood of needing to switch in spite of high switching costs. In such cases, maximum flexibility is desirable.
2. **Capability** of potential suppliers.
   - **No Partnership/Alliance–Capable Supplier for the Item:** Items for which there is no full-service, world-class supplier capable of a partnership/alliance relationship. The lack of a capable supplier would dictate some other form of supply relationship. No partnership or alliance would be preferable to one with an inept supplier.

- **No Partnership/Alliance–Capable Supplier in the Geographic Area:** Areas of the world where there is no full-service, world-class supplier capable of a partnership/alliance relationship. Depending on the material or service required, there may be regions where a partnership or alliance is not possible on account of lack of a competent supplier in that region.
- **Rapid Technological Change:** Situations of rapid industrywide technological change where the buyer would be disadvantaged if locked into one supplier. The buyer must have assurance that technology (either that which is being purchased, or that which the supplier uses in its production, or both) is maintained at the state of the art required by the buyer's industry. Not all suppliers have the capability to remain technologically competitive.
- **Mismatch of Clock Speed:** Mismatch of, or rapidly changing, clock speed between supplier and buyer (Fine, 1998). If the buying firm's industry is changing and developing more rapidly than that of the supplier's industry it may be difficult to arrive at a partnership or alliance that is fully beneficial to the buyer.

3. **Competition** in the supply market.
   - **Noncompetitive Market:** Noncompetitive markets where the supplier partner may be in a position to take advantage of the buying firm. Generally a partnership or strategic alliance will reinforce the supplier's power relative to the buying firm.
   - **Supplier Dependency Creation:** Situations where extreme dependency on a particular supplier would be created by a partnership or strategic alliance. If the buying company is relatively small compared to the selling company and the buyer's business is not vital to the seller, the buyer may be at risk of future supply. For example, a buyer becomes totally dependent on a seller through a partnership or alliance for a material vital to the supplier and for which there are few, if any, alternative suppliers. If the supplier determines at a future time that the business is not compatible with its business objectives, it may terminate the agreement and cause supply difficulty for the buyer.
   - **Neglected Areas:** Situations where purchases have been mismanaged or not managed for years, e.g., many types of indirect purchases. Kapoor and Gupta (1997) indicate that for these types of purchases, in order to obtain the lowest total cost, a relationship that leverages the free market should be used. They advocate partnerships for such situations only if there are few supply alternatives available and/or if there are high supplier switching costs.
   - **Suppliers Seeking to Reduce Competition:** Situations where suppliers appear to be using partnerships/alliances as a marketing ploy to eliminate competition and reduce industry capacity. These may save cost in the short run but, if the supplier's strategy truly is to reduce capacity and competition, costs may increase in the long run. Being locked into such a supplier would not be desirable.

4. **Benefits** to the buying firm from the relationship.
   - **No Leverage from Partnership:** Situations where there is nothing to leverage with a partnership/alliance. Typically, a partnership or alliance will leverage some aspect of the exchange involved. Leveraged items include volume, total cost,

process or procedural cost, inventory, or innovation. If there are no leverage possibilities, there may not be a justification for the work involved in establishing and maintaining a partnership or alliance.

- **No Hard Savings from Partnership:** Situations where hard savings are not present as a result of a partnership/alliance. Soft savings such as nonquantifiable quality improvements and partial-person staff reductions are nice but, unless they result in some other cost avoidance, they never show up on the bottom line. To justify the work involved in establishing and maintaining partnerships and alliance, there must be some hard savings.

5. **Internal Buy-In** to partnership.
   - **No Internal Customer Buy-In:** Situations where the internal customers of the buying organization do not have joint ownership with supply management of the partnership/alliance arrangement. Most purchasing organizations use a team approach to develop, implement, and maintain partnership and alliance agreements. If that is not done, or if the internal customer members of the team do not agree with all the terms of the agreement, the partnership or alliance will be likely to fail.

The Role of Power

Recent books and articles on supply management have largely ignored the impact and role of power. Thus, unfortunately, relatively little is known about the role of power in collaborative or alliance relationships. At the Third Annual North American Research Symposium on Purchasing and Supply Chain Management hosted by the Richard Ivey School of Business, University of Western Ontario, in May 2000, two professors from the Netherlands observed: "Power has an ideological tinge and produces negative associations." Pfeffer (1981) recognized that power is a topic that makes people uncomfortable. Andrew Cox argues, "Power is at the heart of all business to business relationships."[17] Using power is often seen as unethical. However, power, influence, and dependence do exist. Ignoring them will not make them less important for understanding buyer-seller relationships. Power obviously is not always being used, although it can still influence decisions and strategies, simply because it is recognized by both trading partners. There is always a threat of (mis)use of power to which parties respond in advance. Studying networks, Thorelli (1986:38) argued that power is the central concept in networks analysis, because its mere existence can condition others.[18] Thus, it is highly likely that the use and role of power in supply chain management will be the subject of research over the coming years.

Power plays a key role in two important subclasses of buyer-supplier relationships: the captive buyer and the captive supplier. In a captive buyer relationship, "the buyer is

[17]Andrew Cox, "Understanding Buyer and Supplier Power: A Framework for Procurement and Supply Competence," *The Journal of Supply Chain Management,* Spring 2001.

[18] H. B. Thorelli, "Networks: Between Markets and Hierarchies," *Strategic Management* Journal (1986) pp. 37–51.

held hostage by a supplier free to switch to another customer."[19] The captive supplier makes investments in order to secure a portion of the buyer's business, with no assurance of sufficient business to recoup the investment. Cooperation and some level of recognized interdependence suggest that these two classes of relationships are subsets of the broad heading of collaborative relationships.[20]

A Portfolio Approach

No single approach to relationship management is inherently superior. "Successful supply chain management requires the effective and efficient management of a portfolio of relationships."[21] The portfolio approach has its roots in 1950s financial investment theory. One of the most useful approaches to selection of the appropriate relationships is advanced by Bensaou, who proposes three environmental factors to consider: (1) the product exchanged and its technology, (2) the competitive conditions in the upstream market, and (3) the capabilities of the suppliers available.[22]

New Skills and Attitudes Required

Developing and managing collaborative and alliance relationships requires skilled professionals who recognize the benefits of collaboration. These individuals must be able to identify and obtain necessary data and use the data to exploit and enhance relationships. As Smith and Tracey point out, these professionals must "learn to work in and adjacent to chaos, unpredictability, and uncertainty. They must be agile, flexible, and highly adaptive."[23]

Smith and Tracey support the use of role playing, sensitivity training, diversity training, and live cases to develop the professionals who work in this area. These researchers go beyond individual development to advocate the creation of a learning organization, as introduced by Peter Senge. The learning organization is one "where people continually expand their capacity to create results they truly desire, where new and expansive patterns of thinking are nurtured, where collective aspiration is set free, and where people are continually learning how to learn together. A learning organization excels at advanced, systematic, and intentional collective learning and is effective, productive, adaptive, and very good at setting and achieving goals."[24]

---

[19]M. Bensaou, "Portfolios of Buyer-Supplier Relationships," *Sloan Management Review* 40 (4) (Summer), pp. 35–44.

[20]The Spring 2001 issue of *The Journal of Supply Chain Management* addresses power in buyer-supplier relationships. The devoted student of supply management is encouraged to read the thought-provoking articles authored by Andrew Cox, Joe Sanderson, Chris Lousdale, and Glyn Watson.

[21]Bensaou, "Portfolios," p. 37.

[22]Bensaou, "Portfolios," p. 42.

[23]Kimberly A. Smith-Doerflein and Michael Tracey, "Training as a Component of Supply Chain Management," The Third Annual North American Research Symposium on Purchasing and Supply Chain Management, Richard Ivey School of Business, University of Western Ontario, May 24–27, 2000.

[24]Smith-Doerflein and Tracey, ibid

E-Commerce and the "Right" Type of Relationship

We are frequently asked: How does B2B e-commerce affect our selection of the "right" type of relationship? Selection of the "right" type of relationship must be a function of the requirement, not of the Internet! B2B e-commerce is an enabler that is most effective when adopted by firms that embrace World Class Supply Management^{SM}. It is unfortunate that some software sales personnel and some members of customer firms mistakenly assume that B2B e-commerce will eliminate the need for professional supply management. B2B e-commerce must be seen for what it is: a powerful enabler! In the last few years, there has been an evolution from paper-driven transactions to electronic transactions with a transition to integrated supply management processes. Now, the Internet offerings will prompt even more transaction reduction initiatives and a greater transformation from paper to electronic tools. But tools are not strategies. The supply professional of the future will be, first and foremost, a strategic thinker and a creator of competitive advantage.

Unfolding before us is a massive array of new opportunities that will forever redefine the role of supply in the corporation, facilitated by a new set of tools ranging from the worlds of computer software, electronic commerce, and the Internet. However, these tools are simultaneously alluring and deceiving.

The allure comes from the multitude of new possibilities created by e-commerce and all of its siblings, including e-procurement, e-bidding, e-payment, and e-business. But these tools can also be deceptively attractive to the uncritical eye and used inappropriately with little thought given to the solution and the net effect. Therefore, three traps must be steadfastly avoided.

First, we must avoid the trap of "guilding the pig," by which we take an archaic, cumbersome procurement process and "webbize" it—the process remains ugly and inefficient, despite its newfound digital disguise.

Second is the temptation to seek the holy grail of the "magic pill," the one solution that can be used to solve every procurement situation, thus circumventing design of a more thoughtful strategy and solution tailored to fit specific goals and needs.

Third is the trap of "supplier equality." Equality may be the law in civil rights, but it makes for poor procurement. Some suppliers are simply commodity vendors and should be treated in a tactical, transactionary manner, squeezed on price, and handled through e-bidding auctions. Other suppliers are far more strategic to a corporation's business and should be treated as close alliance partners, integrated into a company's business processes, and challenged to create powerful value streams, such as product and process innovations and fast time to market. Alliance partners are a company's assets in creating competitive advantage for the ultimate customer. The world of procurement is rapidly splitting into vendor-based and alliance-based relationships, and procurement professionals must know how to differentiate between the two.

As discussed in Chapter 2, while B2B e-commerce may eliminate the day-to-day sourcing and pricing aspects of supply management when a transactional relationship is appropriate, cross-functional development and sourcing teams still have many vital responsibilities with such procurements.

The Internet greatly facilitates communication and, when properly employed, will enhance the development and maintenance of collaborative and alliance relationships. However, the Internet does not terminate the need for personal relationships based on face-to-face contact. Michael Dell states, "The real potential lies in its [the Internet's] ability to transform relationships within the traditional supplier-vendor-customer chain and to create value that can be shared across organizational boundaries. The companies that position themselves to build 'information partnerships' with suppliers and customers and make the Internet an integral part of their strategy—not just an add-on—have the potential to fundamentally change the face of global competition."[25]

The new world of electronic commerce holds the promise of a bold, new, and enticing future by focusing on speed, connectivity, and innovation. But foremost, we must understand and differentiate our supply base to understand what suppliers bring to the corporate table. The evolutionary integration of electronic commerce requires a new set of strategies and tools that will help to make supply professionals treasured assets in the corporation. The evolution will continue to require a new type of thinking, a new set of rewards and measures, and a new set of skills. Let us not forget that it will be a challenging time, designed for those who are willing to learn, adapt, change, and take a leadership role. We must seize the Internet opportunities being offered and take risks in the electronic commerce arenas, understanding that it is acceptable to make a mistake, and that it is often from trial and error that we learn. As leaders, we must continue to challenge "it won't work here" and "this too shall pass" attitudes that have prevailed in the past.

Continuous learning and capability building will be the norm, not the exception. The two functions will need to be more cross-functionally oriented and work together more to select and implement the optimum buying process tools. Supply management thinking, now more than ever, needs to encompass the whole supply process, the end-to-end "need it, design it, buy it, receive it, transform it, deliver it, service it" process.

Greater focus is needed to have supply professionals become change leaders and problem resolvers rather than followers and problem identifiers. Supply personnel, who over the years have been tagged as non-value-added paper pushers having a "green eyeshade" mentality, will need to overcome this stigma and change their focus to become value-added creators and analysts to support the supply strategy.

What's more, supply professionals will need to shift to a new level of understanding: They have a strategic role in the corporation. They must each keep a business focus in the forefront, understanding that long-term competitive advantage, speed to market, supplier management for cash conservation, and profit maximization are far more critical to long-term success than the historic role of squeezing suppliers for lower prices and concessions.

Relationships of the Future

The terms used today—supply chain, tiers, and channels—all imply a static, rigid set of links that do not change position relative to one another. In these models, information, materials, and money flow sequentially, one link at a time, and only between adjacent

---

[25]*Industry Week,* November 16, 1998.

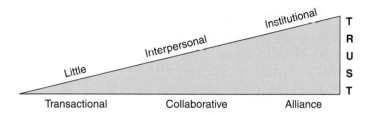

Figure 5.2 | Spectrum of supply relationships and institutional trust.[26]

links. This environment creates friction, inertia, and inflexibility. Every exchange increases the risk of error and multiplies cycle times. Incompatibility within and between supply chain member IT applications prevents fluid information flow. Compounding these problems is the fact that most companies are part of multiple supply chains. The resulting uncertainty creates mistrust among partners and leads to withholding of critical information. High inventories, uncoordinated schedules, and dissatisfied customers are the result.

As the corporate world develops more Internet competence, there may be an uncomfortable convergence of professionals from supply management, accounts payable, information systems, and e-commerce. For the uninitiated, these professionals will interact with a set of traditions oftentimes filled with conflicting points of view. Instead, professionals from each functional area will need to reinvent the way they have traditionally interacted. Supply management will need to enter the information age in a powerful, proactive, and innovative manner. Accounts payable will need to design and link its paying processes to the buying processes in a creative way. Information systems will need to be more functionally adept and user friendly. E-commerce will need to intensify its focus on totally integrated supply process solutions instead of promoting the latest electronic solution searching for a problem or a need.

If the 1990s reengineered the internal business processes of corporations, the next decade will be the era of reengineering entire value chains—from the initiation of the purchase request through design, manufacturing, logistics, and service to the final customer. The winners in the future marketplace will be those linked companies who can combine their internal advantages into a powerful value chain that is faster, more efficient, more agile and innovative, and ultimately more profitable than other competing supply chains. The wise supply executive will recognize this shift early, knowing that supply chain reengineering may well determine the fate of the corporation.

---

[26]Institutional trust: As noted on footnote 10 earlier, the term "trust" has such a wide variety of meanings and interpretations that we have chosen to coin the term "institutional trust." Institutional trust is the key element that differentiates supply alliances from collaborative relationships. With institutional trust, the parties have access to each other's strategic plans in the area(s) of the interface. Relevant cost information and forecasts are shared. Risks and rewards are addressed openly. Informal agreements are as good as written ones. Institutional trust is measured and managed.

APPENDIX A: INSTITUTIONAL TRUST

Research, including personnel interviews, and much of the current literature demonstrate the importance of trust between alliance partners.[27] Dyer points out, "Trust is critical for partner success because without it suppliers and customers will spend considerable resources negotiating, monitoring, and enforcing inflexible contracts.[28] As previously noted, when institutional trust is present the parties have access to each other's strategic plans in the areas of the interface between the companies and their respective cross-functional teams. Relevant cost information and forecasts are shared. Risks and rewards are addressed openly. Informal agreements are as good as written ones. Institutional trust is measured and managed.

Traditional organizations that memorialize their supply agreements with detailed legal contracts often overlook the value of trust. In an ever-changing world that is moving faster and faster, trust creates a major competitive advantage in that fast decision-making can be done only in an environment of trust. Further, in an ever-changing, highly uncertain business world, trust based on integrity, commitment, and common values is the only thing that remains stable, while everything else—strategy, technology, people—move. An ever-changing world requires frequent renegotiations between alliance partners. If there is no trust, the renegotiations are likely to be degenerative, antagonistic, and often result in a win-lose relationship, at which point the alliance dies.

In addition, shared innovation between buyer and supplier is typically a major strategic driver, and one of the most powerful elements of competitiveness. Cocreated innovation is stymied when distrust is rampant. People communicate better in a trusting environment, and cross-functional coordination is more facile. What's more, distrust causes companies to engage in additional non-value-added work, such as time wasted in legal contracts, burdensome paperwork, redundancy, and so forth. Thus trust translates directly to more profit.

Trust in alliances is not at all "blind trust," but rather a "prudent trust" that is carefully designed, planned, and mutually agreed upon. Initially, as alliances are first formed, this trust is typically established interpersonally, usually between the alliance champions and senior executives that create the entity.

This interpersonal trust, based on the vision and values of the founders, is critical at the inception of the alliance. When problems occur (and inevitably they will), the trust will be the foundation for the problem resolution. Similarly, as strategic or technological conditions change, as will occur in fast-moving environments, trust will be a critical ingredient in renegotiating and strategically repositioning the alliance.

However, for the alliance to survive in the long term, and for supplier networks to evolve, interpersonal trust is not enough—institutional trust, a higher order of trust, must prevail. The following list is the result of six years of research on the issue of institutional trust by faculty and students at the University of San Diego.

---

[27]Nirmalya Kumar, "The Power of Trust in Manufacturing–Retailers Relationships," *Harvard Business Review,* November–December 1996, pp. 92–106 and R. M. Monczka, K. J. Peterson, R. B. Hanfield, and Gary L. Ragatz, "Success Factors in Strategic Supplier Alliances: The Buying Company Perspective," *Decision Science* 29 (3) (Summer 1998), pp. 553–75.

[28]Dyer, *Collaborative Advantage,* p. 38.

Attributes of Institutional Trust Include:

■ Institutional trust is developed over time—part of a process.

■ Internal trust is developed before external trust.

■ Institutional trust is based on individual and institutional integrity.

■ Institutional trust is greater than individual trust.

■ Trust and the relationship are viewed as worthwhile investments.

■ The partners have access to each other's strategic plans in the area(s) of the interface.

■ Relevant cost information and forecasts are shared.

■ When key individuals leave, fingerprints are left behind that hold the relationships together.

■ Trust is visible—something for others to see, feel, and emulate.

■ Informal agreements are as good as written contracts.

■ Both parties are sensitive to changes which might affect the cultural bridge between the two firms.

■ The relationship is adaptable in the face of changing needs by either party.

■ Personnel at both firms recognize the interdependent nature of the relationship.

■ Personnel at both firms consider the sharing of information to be a means of developing trust in the relationship.

■ Conflict in the relationship is openly addressed and resolved.

■ Both parties consider the rights, desires, and opinions of their partners during the internal discussions.

■ The firms have mutual goals in the area of the interface.

■ Firms build a bank account of trust based on many deposits.

■ Trust has different meanings in different cultures.

Antecedents of Trust

In 2001 Fawcett and Magnon reported on a comprehensive study addressing Supply Chain Management. The study was based on both a literature review and 52 in-depth interviews with representatives of leading companies at each stage of the supply chain.

The authors observed that "trust has numerous antecedents including open and honest information sharing, commitment, clear expectations, and follow through. The passage of time, high levels of actual performance, and the fulfillment of promises also precede trust. Finally, real trust exists only when both sides agree that it does. Relationships that one party describes as trust-based are often viewed as less friendly and less mutually advantageous by the other side.

Actions Which Are Taken to Develop and Manage Trust Include:

■ Both CEOs make a personal investment.

■ Appropriate senior managers from both firms commit to nurturing the relationship.

■ Either party may bring up ethical issues without fear of retribution.

■ A problem resolution mechanism is established and maintained.

■ An ombudsman is assigned at both firms.

- An interfirm team consisting of representatives of relevant functional areas is appointed to develop and manage the relationship.
- Discussions between the two firms' personnel are conducted in an atmosphere of respect.
- The interfirm team receives guidance and training in the implementation of practices which facilitate the development of strategic alliances before addressing specific project details.
- Listening, understanding, time, and energy are invested to develop and maintain trust.
- Senior leaders at both firms act as a champion to teams.
- Members of the interfirm team share in the development of the communication system between the firms.
- Members of the interfirm team take specific actions to develop, measure, and manage trust in the relationship.
- Risks and rewards are addressed openly.
- Negotiation is used as a trust-building opportunity.
- Within the parameters of the relationship, appropriate members of both firms work together on technology plans for the future.
- Confidentiality agreements are used to protect proprietary technologies and processes.
- Technical personnel from both firms visit their partners to learn and observe how the others' products are developed, manufactured, and utilized.
- Contractual relations are designed to enhance trust (and lawyers who engage in the contractual negotiations must be acutely tuned to the necessity of building trust into their legal interactions).
- Contractual relations focus on continuous improvement.
- Team and relationship skills are developed early.
- Both company leaders create a formal relationship agreement—an agreement that memorializes a commitment to work well together.
- A contracting philosophy and a legal infrastructure are designed to enhance buyer-supplier relationships rather than the legal mechanism (t's and c's) to protect each firm.
- Formal written guidelines are established.

Supply management is one of the keys to Toyota's incredible success. Toyota has perfected the art and the science of supplier relationships, with trust playing a key role. Jeffrey Dyer points out, "Toyota's ability to develop trust with suppliers is not based primarily on personal relationships between Toyota and its suppliers. Nor is it based primarily on the stock ownership it holds in its keiretsu suppliers. Rather, this trust is linked to the perceived fairness and predictability of Toyota's routines for managing external relationships."[29]

---

[29]Dyer, *Collaborative Advantage,* pp. 15–16.

APPENDIX B: SUPPLY MANAGEMENT IN ACTION

A Supplier Alliance at Quaker Oats[30]

This section describes how Quaker Oats Company of Chicago, Illinois, formed an alliance with Graham Packaging of York, Pennsylvania. Graham is a leading global manufacturer of custom blow-molded plastic containers. Plastic bottles are the largest single quantity and cost item purchased by Quaker Oats. Topics to be discussed in this section include how to select an alliance partner, how to negotiate a massive joint building construction and equipment project, and what kind of contract facilitates a "win-win" relationship based on trust and sharing of cost information. This alliance actually became a joint venture with Quaker building an addition for the plastic bottle plant and Graham investing in the equipment and people required to operate the plant at the Quaker Gatorade facilities in Atlanta, Georgia.

Introduction Founded in 1901, Quaker Oats had sales of $4.6 billion in 1998 produced by 11,860 employees. One of Quaker's successful brands, Gatorade, had $1.7 billion in worldwide sales and is far and away the number one brand in the sports beverage category with 82 percent share of market in the United States. Other well-known brands include Cap'n Crunch cereal, Life cereal, Chewy Granola Bars, Quaker Fruit and Oatmeal breakfast bars, Rice-A-Roni, Near East, and Aunt Jemima syrups and pancake mixes.

Plastic Bottles Plastic bottles are big business at Quaker Oats. Quaker is one of the world's largest purchasers of plastic bottles for sports drinks, with Gatorade as one of the great global brands. Total U.S. case volume is roughly 100,000,000 cases purchased mostly from April through September. The incumbent bottle supplier had been supplying Quaker since 1986. Demand had grown from 100 million to over 1,400 million bottles by 1998. Because the initial emphasis had been on bottle supply and performance, the supplier had negotiated a price based on new investment and defined quantities. Over the 12-year period negotiations had taken place, but the supplier had managed to increase/retain its high start-up margins. The incumbent supplier did offer various means of cost reduction. These were deemed not to be sufficient.

Quaker after Snapple and Supply Chain Management By 1997, new purchasing management was engaged to find supply chain cost efficiencies. The bottle was a logical first place to look (i.e., the low hanging fruit). A quick analysis indicated that the material cost was less than 40 percent of the bottle price to Quaker, a ratio that indicated there was tremendous opportunity for price reductions. After paying what the company thought was a reasonable price for many years, it was now apparent to Quaker that the bottle price was too high.

A cross-functional team from accounting, engineering, technical, and the purchasing staff was formed to model the bottle's manufacturing cost. After numerous trips to plants and discussions with consultants, an independent cost model confirmed Quaker's

---

[30]By Richard L. Pinkerton, Ph.D., C.P.M., Former Chair and Professor Emeritus of Marketing and Logistics, The Sid Craig School of Business, California State University, Fresno, and Richard G. Reider, Director, Packaging Purchasing, Quaker Oats Company. Published in the Proceedings of the 85th Annual International Purchasing Conference, April 30 to May 3, 2000.

initial belief that bottle prices could be reduced substantially. The current supplier was not willing to reduce the price even though Quaker demonstrated the profit was excessive. Competition for Quaker's business would be the strategy.

The Alliance Options   Several options were examined to meet the requirement to reduce cost and improve quality and service:

1. Merchant supplies the total product.
2. Self-manufacture with key raw material suppliers.
3. In-house plant operated by a supplier. This option would require an alliance due to: long-term commitment needed, ongoing cost containment, contractual issues regarding having another company operate on Quaker's premises.

Merchant supply was rejected due to:

1. Absence of lower cost alternative merchant supply (freight cost hurdle).
2. No known way to gain effective cost understanding/cultural improvement with arm's length relationship (lack of both parties' commitment).

Self-manufacture was rejected due to:

1. Not a core competency.
2. Supplier's cost of capital was generally lower than Quaker's—best to use their money.

In-house plant was chosen because:

1. Best cost–no freight, direct feeding of filling line eliminated palletizing, fresher materials.
2. Best opportunity to institutionalize continuous improvement. Alliance relationship comes from the open book need to drive improvement. Quaker and Graham (the selected supplier) agreed to act as one company on each other's behalf.

Negotiating an Alliance   The Quaker Negotiation Team included:

■ The Director of Packaging Purchasing
■ Senior Manager of Purchasing
■ Supervisor of Finance
■ Industrial Engineer
■ Manager, Supply Chain Planning

The Graham Packaging Company team included:

■ Senior Vice-President and General Manager, Food & Beverage Business Unit
■ Director of Sales, Beverage and Business Unit
■ Director of Finance, Beverage Business Unit

Quaker visited eight bottle companies, two consulting companies, one practitioner of in-plant molding, two machinery suppliers, and two resin manufacturers. This effort took approximately one year and involved many, many sessions. In addition, Quaker refined the performance "should cost" model with the cross-functional team. Finally, trust-building sessions were held with two potential suppliers (the finalists). These sessions included senior management dinners, use of an outside consultant as a facilitator on part-nering, and frequent visits to each other.

In the survey to understand the market, it was determined that Graham Packaging of York, Pennsylvania, had the capability to meet Quaker's needs because of its focus on Quaker's type of bottle and its proven record with customers. A key to begin developing an alliance was to build trust by disclosing bottle costs.

Graham and Quaker held a series of meetings to define what each company wanted from a potential business relationship. It was determined that both were aligned on views of how to jointly create value. Quaker discussed Graham's target ROI needs and Graham acknowledged and understood Quaker's needs for low-cost bottles. A key Quaker issue was how to find a supplier who would manage the risk of unused bottle-making capac-ity after the substantial Gatorade seasonal peak and do it to Quaker's benefit. Graham agreed early in the discussions to price the bottle on a highly utilized machine basis in spite of Quaker's inability to commit to fill the equipment 100 percent of the year. If needed, Graham would find other customers to keep the plant running and to maintain the full economic benefit for both companies.

Although the basis for the agreement ended up to be partnering, it did not start that way. As both parties discussed how to work to manage cost and find efficiencies, the only apparent way was to create an open-book accounting relationship based on trust.

At the core of supply chain management, the reason why trust fails to develop between buyer and supplier, and why maximum value in the relationship is not created, is because parties hide information from each other. The largest source of hidden information is cost. Opening the books is the best way to eliminate distrust and truly find a better relationship that would warrant any company's investment in developing a relationship.

The Contract Without divulging confidential information, the arrangement is not long term if Graham does not perform adequately. The incentive for the relationship to be constantly renewed has been built in through periodic "rewarding" of the business based on performance. While those close to the relationship know this is not needed, the board of directors required these safeguards.

Construction of the in-plant facility at the Gatorade plant in Atlanta, Georgia, has been completed. Quaker spent $10 million in plant expansion; Graham spent $28 mil-lion on equipment and will own and operate the plant and be responsible to meet certain quality and efficiency standards. If Graham fails to meet these standards, it will bear the cost of nonperformance.

Type of contract:

1. Evergreen from one fixed period to another.

2. Completely open book—Quaker pays all expenses and a fixed return on invested capital (which was mutually costed).

3. Cancelable for failure to perform.

4. Volume sensitive: Quaker will compensate for volume shortfalls. However, Gatorade has not failed to grow at least 9 percent per year over the last 18 years. Never bet against your own business.

How Is the Alliance Working? What about Future Alliances?   The bottles produced in the in-house plant are the lowest-cost bottles in the Quaker system. The alliance has produced much better (more accurate) forecasting that helps lower costs by schedule stabilization. While this is not the only cost reduction benefit in the endeavor, it demonstrates the need to capture and analyze total cost of ownership. The few start-up quality issues were resolved very quickly, and as one would expect, the delivery and other service aspects are "perfect." Joint quality improvement initiatives enabled by the alliance are generating impressive results on the Quaker Oats filling lines as improved quality translated to increased productivity, reduced scrap, and lower costs. Joint cost savings initiatives and the "open book" approach are also already delivering bottle cost savings to Quaker that exceed ingoing project objectives by over $1 million annually.

As to other alliance possibilities, Quaker would like more such alliances in other packaging materials. Unfortunately, the packaging industry is very "old school" and adversarial. Consolidations result in frequent management changes which negate building long-term relationships. In the field of packaging, costs are driven by machinery utilization. Thus, huge volumes are required for economies of scale. This is especially true for flexible film and folding cartons. Perhaps Quaker can partner with other noncompetitors to consolidate and achieve such volume's . . . but that's another story.

CHAPTER 6

Cross-Functional Teams

A world-class supply manager is not departmentally or internally focused, but concentrates on proactively improving processes with the long-term goal of upgrading the competitive capability of the firm's supply chain.

Taken from the definition of WCSM^{SM} in Chapter 1.

KEY CONCEPTS

Case

You are a privileged fly: You are allowed to be on the wall of a corporate boardroom during a high-powered discussion. The corporation is an engineering firm whose sales total approximately $280 million a year. Up to now, things appear to have been going well. Production does an efficient job, and inventories have been reduced. But danger signs are cropping up. Although no orders have been lost as yet, several shipments have missed their deadlines. Customers are beginning to complain. In addition, transportation costs on incoming and outbound freight shipments are mushrooming. It is 9 A.M., and several people are nervously sitting at the conference table. A stern-looking individual enters.

The Cast

■   *Production manager:* Heinrich Holtz, former blue-collar worker. Loves his machines and hates to see them idle. But beneath his "good of the corporation" exterior lies the soul of a power maniac who seeks control over traffic and purchasing.

■   *Marketing manager:* Harold Levi, a stereotype. Is afraid of losing sales because of late deliveries. Generally, echoes presidential statements. Appears ready to support Heinrich Holtz's power play.

■   *President:* Joe Gish, old-line type. Extremely successful. Has just attended a National Industrial Conference Board (NICB) seminar and is throwing a lot of new buzz words and thoughts around. From his subordinates' point of view, he is dangerous.

■   *Traffic manager:* Harold Tracks, another old-liner, but much less successful. Not good at verbalizing, except to quote percentage increases. His freight bills are going up, and he is being made to look bad by comparison.

■   *Purchasing and materials manager:* Joan Glass, much younger than her associates. Does her best. Understands president Gish's words and tries to put some of them into action. Extremely inventory conscious.

■   *Director of finance:* Sol Stein, dedicated to cost reduction.

Action

(This is what the privileged fly observes and hears.)

President Gish brings the meeting to order. "Look at these air freight bills! Here's one for $955—more than the damn part is worth! I know, I checked! These things are murdering us. You must realize that in our business today, transportation has great cost-cutting potential!"

Traffic manager Tracks responds, "I know that freight bills have risen 30 percent in the last six months, but what can I do? Miss Glass here is cutting inventories so hard that she never has anything in stock. Her short lead times force me to use air freight. And the way she spreads small orders, I almost never find a way to consolidate them to get volume rates. And I'm having the same problems on outgoing shipments. I'm caught in a two-bladed buzz saw!"

Purchasing and materials manager Joan Glass interrupts to say, "Harold, we're operating on low inventories because we save money doing it. Many times air freight is the only way I can be sure of getting what I need on time."

Production manager Holtz comments, "And when I need something, I need it. Take spares. This 'downtime' is an awfully expensive proposition, and we all know it. Further, by the time Miss Glass here gets me needed production materials, we are so late that the only way to meet delivery dates is with overtime and the use of air freight."

Marketing manager Levi joins in, "Whatever the trouble, it seems there must be a way to get an efficient pipeline. If Heinrich is late, then I'm late. We're losing our image as a reliable supplier. Soon, we'll be losing sales!"

Traffic manager Tracks defends himself by saying, "I don't want to seem bitter, but it looks like I'm getting the short end of the stick."

President Gish interrupts to say, "No more excuses. I want action! Costs must come down."

Purchasing and materials manager Glass defends herself by saying, "The lead-time problem goes right back through production and eventually to Harold's sales forecasts. I need earlier information."

Marketing manager Levi says, "I have to promise prompt delivery. We all know that the problem is at the other end."

Production manager Holtz suggests, "Like I've been saying for a long time, we should combine supply, materials and traffic and get them closer to production."

At this point, purchasing and materials manager Glass sounds frustrated when she says, "Heinrich, we're right back where we started. We need lower freight costs, but at the same time we must keep inventory down."

Director of finance Stein says, "Inventory carrying cost is over 25 percent a year. I think that Joan has done a great job. But I do agree with Mr. Gish that transportation costs are way over budget."

President Gish concludes the meeting by saying, "Heinrich's idea is a possibility. We could create a materials management setup. I understand it's the coming thing. I'll give each of you one week to put all your ideas on paper. Be prepared to deliver your reports at our next meeting. I want us out of this fix . . . and soon!"

Introduction

The third conceptual foundation underlying modern supply management is the involvement of cross-functional teams. These teams, on an as-required basis, are composed of professionals from supply management; design, manufacturing, quality and plant engineering; customer services; finance; information technology; and, when appropriate, carefully prequalified suppliers. One of the early examples of a cross-functional approach to procurement and supply management is the integrated procurement system described in the 1984 book *Proactive Procurement.*[1]

Teams have become increasingly important as a means of implementing World Class Supply Management[SM]. "Chrysler's reorganization into cross-functional teams was a critical first step . . . " to the success it enjoyed in the 1990s.[2]

Cross-Functional Teams and Supply Management Activities

Cross-functional teams have become a common approach to addressing many supply management related activities, including new product development,[3] value analysis and value engineering, standardization and simplification, engineering change management, the development of statements of work describing services requirements, commodity teams, the acquisition of capital and operating equipment, make/buy and outsourcing analysis, source selection,[4] potential supplier field reviews, negotiation, post-award management and problem solving, supplier development, and the development of strategic alliances. Since cross-functional teams require a significant investment in human resources, their use is commonly limited to time-critical and high monetary value activities.

Benefits Resulting From Cross-Functional Teams[5]

Synergy

The many activities identified above have one thing in common: They all benefit from a variety of functional inputs. For example, during the new product development process, marketing has information on customers' wants and needs, their willingness to purchase at different prices, and present and potential competition. Design engineering has

---

[1]David N. Burt, *Proactive Procurement: The Key to Increased Profits, Productivity and Quality,* (Englewood Cliffs, NJ: Prentice-Hall, 1984).

[2]Jeffrey H. Dyer, "How Chrysler Created an American Keiretsu," *Harvard Business Review,* July–August 1996, p. 119.

[3]Laura M. Birou, Stanley E. Fawcett, and Gregory M. Magnam in their study, "The Product Life Cycle: A Tool for Functional Strategic Alignment," found that ". . . companies are striving to break down functional barriers that inhibit effective product and process design." *International Journal of Purchasing and Materials Management,* Spring 1998.

[4]"Chrysler used a team approach and chose suppliers before the parts were even designed, which meant virtually eliminating traditional supplier bidding." James Bennet, "Detroit Struggles to Learn Another Lesson From Japan," *New York Times,* June 19, 1994, p. F5.

[5]Many of the ideas contained in this section were first introduced by one of the authors' mentors, Professor Norman Maier of the University of Michigan during the mid-1960s.

knowledge of current and future design processes and constraints. Manufacturing engineering has information on the firm's (and its suppliers') manufacturing processes and their limitations. Supply management provides a window to the supply world and its capabilities and limitations and the likely cost and availability of various materials and services under consideration. Customer service, quality, finance, IT, and carefully selected suppliers all have many additional contributions to make during the new product development process. When these professionals come together under the leadership of a capable team leader, the result is normally a synergy that, in turn, results in a far more profitable new product, far quicker than would have occurred with the traditional sequential approach to new product development.

Input from All Affected Functions

The cross-functional approach greatly increases the likelihood that all issues that should be considered are addressed. For example, customer support and service frequently were overlooked in the traditional sequential approach to new product development. Standardization efforts, which are conducted or controlled by one functional area such as manufacturing engineering, frequently overlook the supply, manufacturing, and marketing implications of implementing new standards. The result? Surplus purchased materials, manufacturing bottlenecks, or products that do not compete in the marketplace.

Time Compression

A hypothetical example may help in understanding the traditional sequential or functional approach to many of the above activities. Marketing at Alpha Corporation has identified a need for a new, complex transducer. Marketing describes this need to design engineering, which designs the transducer. On completion of the design, the resulting specifications and drawings are forwarded to manufacturing engineering, the function responsible for translating design engineering's specifications into production plans. Manufacturing engineering determines that certain tolerances cannot be met by the firm's production equipment. Design engineering is requested to revise the specifications. Design engineering contacts marketing to determine what impact the revised tolerances (ones which the firm's equipment can meet) will have on sales. If the impact is significant, manufacturing, and possibly plant engineering, may become involved. They may decide that new equipment is required. (Such a decision will initiate the procurement of an item of operating equipment, described in Chapter 13.) This process continues on through the quality assurance function. Quality assurance reviews the specifications and production plans to ensure that the required level of quality will be obtainable. The customer service function then reviews the specifications and manufacturing plans so that it may develop plans to support the transducers in the field. Obviously each function along the sequential path leading to production of the desired transducer may question (or even challenge) the design specifications and manufacturing plans. This back-and-forth process ultimately leads to a product that is late to market and overpriced. (See Figure 6.1.)

Now, let's take a moment and observe procurement's involvement with the sequential approach to obtaining widgets, a component of the firm's new product. After

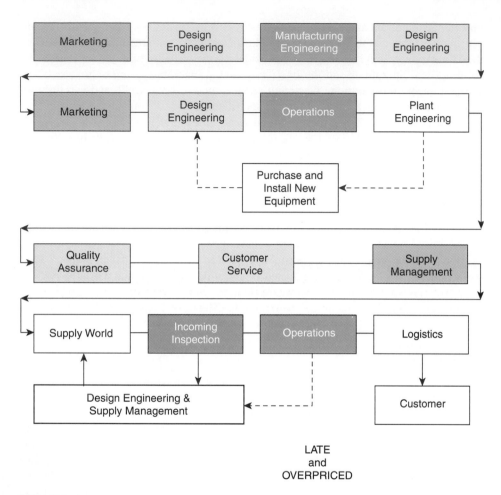

Figure 6.1 I Sequential, functional approach to new product development.

marketing, design engineering, manufacturing engineering, production, quality assurance, and customer service have each completed their duties, a purchase requisition for the widgets with specifications and drawings is submitted to the supply management department. A greatly simplified and compressed description of activities indicates that supply management solicits proposals from the supply world. Oops! No proposals. Inquiries to two or three potential suppliers: "We can't meet your specifications!" Or *worse:* A potential supplier submits a reasonably acceptable proposal. Negotiations result in an acceptable agreement. The first shipment arrives. None of the items meet specifications. Ah, the joys of the sequential, functional approach! (See again Figure 6.1.)

Contrast this sequential functional approach with a cross-functional one: Marketing, design engineering, manufacturing engineering, production, quality, customer service, supply management, and carefully prequalified suppliers are involved, at appropriate points, of the design process (see Figure 6.2). Design time is compressed. Cost is

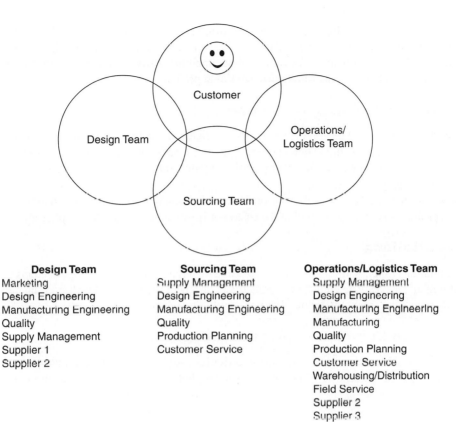

Design Team	Sourcing Team	Operations/Logistics Team
Marketing	Supply Management	Supply Management
Design Engineering	Design Engineering	Design Engineering
Manufacturing Engineering	Manufacturing Engineering	Manufacturing Engineering
Quality	Quality	Manufacturing
Supply Management	Production Planning	Quality
Supplier 1	Customer Service	Production Planning
Supplier 2		Customer Service
		Warehousing/Distribution
		Field Service
		Supplier 2
		Supplier 3

Figure 6.2 I Cross-functional team approach to new product development.

reduced. Quality is enhanced.[6] Delivery schedules are met. Market opportunities are exploited. Clearly, the cross-functional approach becomes an imperative with the ever-increasing emphasis on compressing all activities in order to bring new products to market quickly, meet customer demands quickly, maintain minimal inventories, and provide high quality.[7]

Overcoming Organizational Resistance

With the cross-functional approach, all functional areas are involved up front, which helps to reduce organizational resistance to decisions that will affect specific functional areas. In contrast, decisions that impact multiple functional areas, which are made without representation of those areas, are likely to meet resistance. The representatives of each of the functional areas involved on the team constructively provide their input and

[6]The design of new products is described in detail in Chapter 10.

[7]For more insight, see Robert M. Monczka and Robert J. Trent, "Cross-Functional Teams Reduce New Product Development Cycle Times," *NAPM Insights,* February 1994, pp. 64–66.

are involved in the resulting agreement. In turn, each representative is responsible for ensuring acceptance by his or her functional area of the team's decisions. Experience indicates that once a team makes a decision, implementation of the resulting plan is much easier and faster than with the sequential approach.

Enhanced Problem Resolution

The cross-functional team approach is far more efficient and effective at solving problems than the traditional functional one. For example, if a supplier, in spite of its best efforts, is unable to meet the contract schedule or quality requirements, a cross-functional team representing supply management, manufacturing engineering, and quality may be formed to work with the supplier to resolve the problem. (The solution to a surprising number of such problems is found to be within the customer firm's control—not the supplier's!)

Negotiations

Negotiations for critical or large monetary value materials, services, supplies, or items of equipment are conducted much more effectively by a well-prepared and well-coordinated cross-functional team than by the finest of supply professionals alone.

Improved Communication and Cooperation

The traditional functional approach to the activities listed in the opening paragraph normally results in efficiency within each department, but this approach inhibits communication and cooperation among the departments involved in the activities.

Some 40 years ago, one of the authors was the Chief Supply Officer (CSO) of a relatively small business unit. The organization's plant engineering department designed specifications for construction projects. These specifications served as the basis of Invitations for Bids (IFB) and the resulting contracts. Numerous questions and problems were encountered with potential suppliers during the bidding process and, in turn, with the successful bidder. The specifications were ambiguous and, in several cases, contained inconsistencies.

The CSO met with the plant engineer and offered to become involved in the development and review of the specifications. The plant engineer rejected the offer, stating: "Development of specifications is my responsibility. Butt out!" Interestingly enough, the plant engineer subsequently expressed his desire to become involved in the sourcing process. Guess what happened?

Challenges and Problems with the Cross-Functional Approach

There are several challenges and problems inherent in a cross-functional approach.

Additional Investment in Scarce Resources

A single professional normally requires far fewer labor hours to accomplish a task than does a team. For example, a single supply management professional can accomplish the many actions involved in selecting a critical supplier in considerably fewer labor hours than can a cross-functional sourcing team. But a team consisting of a design engineer, a manufacturing engineer, and a quality engineer together with a supply professional will do a far more thorough job of selecting the right source.

Role Conflict

Normally, cross-functional team assignments are additional duties for many or all of the individuals involved. In many cases, the team member's functional manager expects the individual to perform his or her normal functional responsibilities. Such responsibilities require about 40 hours per week. At the same time, the individual is expected to satisfy his or her team responsibilities. A number of years ago, one of the authors directed thesis research at the Graduate Logistics Division of the Air Force Institute of Technology. The research focused on minimizing role conflict between functional and team assignments. The subjects were assigned to cross-functional teams developing the B-1 bomber. The researchers focused on a multi-matrix approach to project management as a means of avoiding or minimizing the inherent role conflict. While promising, the research results were inconclusive. Some 25 years later, management is still attempting to cope with the issue of role conflict resulting from part-time assignment of individuals to cross-functional teams. Despite these issues, the benefits of teams usually outweigh the resulting problems.

Overload for Key Team Members

Overload is an obvious result of the role conflict inherent in the additional duty assignment of key team members. Paradoxically, the most attractive team members are those individuals who are key contributors to their functional organizations. Management must be sensitive to the danger of such an overload in an effort to avoid burnout and the possible loss of such individuals.

Continuity

Quite obviously, once team members have been trained and developed and have learned to work together in a synergistic manner, continuity of membership becomes critical. Retirement, departure to become employed at another firm, promotion, and layoffs can all have a negative impact on the team's operation. Careful selection and assignment of team members can reduce, but not eliminate, such problems.

Rewards

By now, it should be apparent that individuals who are assigned to cross-functional teams as an additional duty should be rewarded appropriately. The greatest reward is the satisfaction associated with "making a difference" in the team's success. Senior professional managers ensure that functional managers (i.e., the Chief Supply Officer, Director of R&D, Director of Manufacturing, etc.) recognize each individual's contributions to both their functional organizations and to their cross-functional team.

A few enlightened organizations have demonstrated success with team incentives. These incentives range from team dinners, to a team vacation in Hawaii, to the award of stock options. In some cases, the team will receive a bundle of rewards (e.g., 1,000 stock options). The team members then allocate the options according to a consensus of the members on the relative contribution of each member. More information on this subject may be found in *Rewarding Teams: Lessons from the Trenches.*[8]

Prerequisites to Successful Cross-Functional Teams

While there are many such prerequisites, we will focus on four especially critical ones.

Executive Sponsorship

An absolute prerequisite for successful cross-functional teams is the support of an executive sponsor. "Top management team support and political factors may be even more critical to the success of cross-functional teams than the internal team processes."[9] The individual sponsor should either have all of the functional areas involved reporting to him or her, or have the informal ability to secure the cooperation and support of colleagues in obtaining the assignment of the appropriate human resources to the project. Additionally, the executive sponsor must track the cross-functional team's progress, run interference, and obtain additional resources as appropriate.[10]

Effective Team Leaders

Without skilled leadership, teams frequently become lost, flounder, get off course, lose sight of their goal, lose confidence, become mired in interpersonal conflicts, stop short of their goal, and never contribute their full potential. Surveys of highly effective teams have shown that their team members rated their leaders as highly skilled. Lower-performing teams rated their leaders as being much less effective.

Ideally, a team leader has people skills, communication skills, technical knowledge, enthusiasm, and experience working with the people who will be on the team. The new role of the team leader is to build a team with vision, authority, accountability, information, skills, and commitment to assume more and better operational control of the team's work. The new leader expands the capabilities of the team members and the team itself. As a result, the team can perform some of the leader's traditional work roles, such as budgeting, scheduling, setting performance goals, and providing training. The team gradually assumes the day-to-day operations, thereby allowing the leader to manage resources, ideas, technologies, and the work processes. The most challenging aspect of

---

[8]Glen Parket, Jerry McAdams, and David Zielinski, *Rewarding Teams: Lessons from the Trenches* (New York.: Jossey-Bass, 2000).

[9]Michael A. Hitt, "Corporate Entrepreneurship and Cross-Functional Fertilization: Activation, Process and Disintegration of a New Product Design Team," *Entrepreneurship: Theory and Practice,* Spring 1999, p. 145.

[10]For additional insight, see David N. Burt and Richard Pinkerton, *Strategic Proactive Procurement* (New York: AMACOM, 1996), p. 33; and James W. Dean, Jr., and Gerald I. Susman, "Organizing For Manufacturing Design," *Harvard Business Review,* January–February 1989, pp. 28–36.

this new role is that the leader must give up a part of his or her former more authoritarian role. Such a shift of roles allows the leader more time to take on strategic roles. The result of the shift is that the team is able to contribute more, and with greater speed.

Team leaders must assume a number of roles. They must understand people so they can influence them. They should encourage and maintain open communication and help the team develop and follow team norms. The team leader needs to step back from his or her management role of directing employees and assume a more collaborative role as a facilitator. The leader should help guide the team and allow the team to identify problems, develop solutions, and then implement the solutions. The team members must be free to express themselves as long as such expression is not destructive. The team leader should support the expression of conflicting points of view. "Team synergy begs for a conflict of ideas. Conflict can bring into being the creative tension where paradigm-shifting ideas are born."[11] While the team leader may need to retain some of the final decision-making in the early stages, it should be the leader's goal to develop the team so that it can assume responsibility for the decision-making entirely.

The team leader helps the team focus on the task and removes obstacles that stand in the way of the team's performance. Helping the team to focus will ensure that the team progresses through productive stages of team development and will reduce the tendency for it to revert back to one of the less productive stages. Effective team leaders help minimize turf issues and keep the team focused on the good of the organization. Additionally, the leader needs to make sure that the team members have all the resources that they may need so that they don't become distracted. And the team leader should remove any obstacles to the team's success.

Additionally, team leaders help establish a vision, create change, and unleash talent. The leader helps the team establish a mission statement and define its goals. Leaders create change within both the organization and the team. They force people to think outside the box and help develop creative solutions to problems. Leaders need to have good people skills in order to identify and draw out hidden talents of the team members.

Former American League relief pitcher David Baldwin, writing in the *Harvard Business Review,* addresses the issue of "blame." He focuses on how managers in Major League Baseball employ blame. Baldwin contends that blame plays an important role in shaping an organization's culture. He proposes five important rules of blame, which we believe apply to most or all team leaders:

1. Know when to blame—and when not to.
2. Blame in private and praise in public.
3. Realize that the absence of blame can be far worse than its presence.
4. Manage misguided blame.
5. Be aware that confidence is the first casualty of blame.[12]

---

[11]Tom Schulte, quoted in "Conflict Resolution, A Required Skill for Engineering Team Managers," IOMA's Report on Managing Design Engineering, January 2000, p. 2.

[12]David G. Baldwin, "How to Win the Blame Game," *Harvard Business Review,* July–August 2001, p. 57.

Lippincott's book, *Meetings: Do's, Don'ts, and Donuts* (Lighthouse Point Press, 1994), offers the following suggestions to team leaders:

- Decide whether a meeting is the best way to accomplish this. Consider circulating routine information via e-mail. If a meeting is required, distribute an agenda at least two days in advance.
- State in one or two sentences what you would like your meeting to accomplish.
- Set ground rules to maintain focus, respect, and order during the meeting.
- Take responsibility for the outcome of the meeting. For example, help keep the meeting on track and help resolve conflicts.
- If your meeting isn't working, try other tools, such as brainstorming techniques or computer software that helps you create the agenda.[13]

Qualified Team Members

Experience indicates that the most critical variable influencing one's ability to be a "high" contributor is a willingness and desire to contribute. Baxter Health Care of Paramatta, New South Wales, Australia, ensures that team members are "willing" participants by announcing forthcoming team projects to all employees. Individuals are encouraged to volunteer for the additional assignments as team members representing their functional areas. In many cases, competition for a team position is intense. Thus the team leader is in the enviable position of being able to select members from a pool of volunteers. Obviously, team membership has the potential for satisfaction and tangible rewards at Baxter.

The Wisconsin Department of Revenue has identified the following communication skills as being significant to employee success. (If an individual is deficient in one or more areas, he or she can obtain training offered by the department, attend management development programs, pursue self-study, or obtain a mentor.)

Listening (the ability to understand, organize, and analyze what we hear)
- Actively attend to and convey understanding of the comments and questions of others.
- Identify and test the inferences and assumptions we make.
- Overcome barriers to effective listening (semantic, psychological, physical).
- Summarize and reorganize a message for recall.
- Keep the speaker's intent, content, and process separate.
- Withhold judgment that can bias responses to the message.

Giving Clear Information
- Assess a situation, determine objectives, and give information that will best meet the objective.

[13]Cited in: "Relationship-Building Skills" by David J. O'Shea, *NAPM InfoEdge,* September 1998, p. 9. Used with permission of the National Association of Purchasing Management.

- Construct and deliver clear, concise, complete, well-organized, convincing messages.
- Keep on target—avoid digressions and irrelevancies, and meet the aim of the communication.
- Determine how to use persuasion effectively.
- Maintain a climate of mutual benefit, trust, rapport, and a win-win outcome.

Getting Unbiased Information (minimize the filtering and editing that takes place when information is transmitted from person to person)

- Use direct, nondirect, and reflective questions.
- Identify forces that may bias the information.
- Confirm understanding and obtain agreement and closure.

Foster Open Communication

- Create an atmosphere in which timely, high-quality information flows smoothly between self and others.
- Encourage open expression of ideas and opinions.[14]

Team Development and Training

Each team will develop its own personality. But the key objective of all teams must be a willingness to subordinate personal and functional interests to the team's goals. Having a competent leader and well-qualified team members are two critical first steps. The third step is team development and training. Team development and training call for investments that should pay a high return. For example, Southern California Edison (SCE) has used team development and training to create one of the best supply management systems in the utility industry. Under the leadership of Emiko Banfield, 24 cross-functional supply management teams have been established to manage supply issues. Each SCE team receives three days of team development and training as a foundation for its activities. As a result, SCE has taken over $350 million out of a spend of approximately $1 billion during the past six years.

The Supply Chain Management Institute at the University of San Diego is pioneering an alternative approach to team development. Four-person, cross-functional teams from client firms undergo interactive training on selected supply management topics. A one-hour workshop is conducted after each one-hour training module. During the workshop, each team conducts a gap analysis comparing one of its processes with the world-class processes presented in the previous training module. The team then develops a preliminary action plan to close the gap. The plan identifies key actions, a time line, and an estimate of the bottom-line impact of the team's proposed plan. Preliminary findings indicate that cohesive teams evolve with this approach to training and organizational transformation. Although the findings are preliminary, this approach to team development appears to be very cost effective.

---

[14]O'Shea, "Relationship-Building Skills," p. 7.

Adequate Time

Unrealistic deadlines are major problems that block the success of many cross-functional teams. As Burt and Pinkerton wrote, "Too much pressure for results too soon will almost always force a team to premature and less effective decisions."[15] The tendency for management to act now rather than allowing time for good analysis is an old habit in the United States. Many of America's global competitors have the patience to allow time to nurture participative management. The results of nurturing participative management are well known. Just ask American automotive manufacturers about the cost of quick reactions without fostering participation.[16]

Interfirm Teams

When buying and supplying organizations recognize the interdependence and the benefits to both parties of a collaborative or alliance relationship, development of an interfirm team should be considered. In effect, a superordinate cross-functional team will result. Dan Mohr, Director of Supplier Relations for GTE, observes: "Relationship teams are the building blocks upon which the relationship prospers. Team meetings provide a forum to jointly discuss new ways to reduce process costs, improve service to our customers, and enhance time to market, which ultimately expands market share for both organizations."[17] As with cross-functional teams within each firm, assignment of the "right" individuals and team training are essential prerequisites for success. One significant difference is that two executive sponsors will be required, one at each firm. The interfirm's first task, after receiving appropriate training, is the development of a customized effective and efficient communication system.

As we saw in the previous chapter on relationships, many progressive organizations are working with selected collaborative suppliers to develop and manage supply alliances. One of the keys to success with such efforts is the development and use of interfirm teams. Experience indicates that the basis of such interfirm teams must be the existence of cross-functional teams at both the buying and the supplying organizations. The development and use of interfirm teams is more challenging than are in-house cross-functional teams. But the benefits are even greater!

Supply Management's Roles on Cross-Functional Teams

Timothy M. Laseter, vice president, Booz-Allen & Hamilton Inc. in New York, identifies four principle roles for supply management professionals who are members of cross-functional teams:

■ Provide the process expertise of supply management in areas such as supply base research, supplier cost modeling, or (more typically) negotiation.

---

[15]Burt and Pinkerton, *Strategic Proactive Procurement,* p. 195.

[16]Diane Brown, "Supplier Management Teams," *NAPM Insights,* August 1994, p. 33.

[17]Mary Crews, "Relationship Management Yields Results," *Purchasing Today,* June 2000, pp. 8–9.

■ Provide content knowledge of a specific supply market or commodity area that the supply management individual directs.

■ Serve as the liaison with the supply management organization to ensure project needs obtain priorities among other staff in the corporate organization.

■ Represent the supply management point of view in considering trade-offs, setting priorities, and making decisions affecting policy.[18]

Concluding Remarks

In 210 B.C., Arbiter Petronius of the Greek Navy wrote, "We trained hard . . . but it seemed that every time we were beginning to form up into teams we would be reorganized, and I was to learn later in life that we tend to meet any new situation by reorganizing.[19] Fortunately, great progress has been made in the design and use of teams, especially in the areas of new product development, project management, source selection, and negotiation.

Endnotes

While many variables have an impact on the success or failure of a cross-functional team, none is more critical than the team leader. Professor Robert Trent of Lehigh University has conducted extensive research on the role of cross-functional teams in supply management. Professor Trent defines an effective team leader as "one who is capable of satisfying a set of essential operating responsibilities and requirements while still promoting the creativity, leadership ability, and innovativeness of individual team members."

Professor Trent identifies 10 requirements for effective team leadership:

■ Work with the team to establish and commit to performance goals.

■ Secure individual member involvement and commitment.

■ Manage internal team conflict.

■ Help maintain team focus and direction.

■ Secure required organizational resources.

■ Prevent team domination by a member or faction.

■ Deal with internal and external obstacles confronting the team.

■ Coordinate multiple tasks and manage the status of team assignments.

■ Clarify and help define each member's role.

■ Provide performance feedback to members.[20]

---

[18]As quoted by Marilyn Lester, "Purchasing and Supply, Meet Project Management," *Purchasing Today,* December 1998, p. 17.

[19]Cited in David M. Moore and Peter B. Antill, "Integrated Project Teams: The Way Forward for UK Defence Procurement," *European Journal of Purchasing & Supply Management,* September 2001, p. 57.

[20]Robert J. Trent, "Understanding and Evaluating Cross-Functional Sourcing Team Leadership," *International Journal of Purchasing and Materials Management,* Fall 1996.

The interested reader is encouraged to read both Professor Trent's full article and the 1994 book, *Leading Teams: Mastering the New Role.*[21]

In the spring of 1999, Michael A. Hitt reported on a longitudinal case study of a cross-functional new product development team that became dysfunctional and obtained suboptimal results. Hitt's research supports the following important conclusions:

- Top management support of the cross-functional team is essential to the success of critical projects.
- Management leadership of the cross-functional team is critical.
- Functional activities, suppliers, and key customers who have significant input should be involved throughout the project's life.
- Geographically dispersed teams are difficult to manage.[22]

---

[21]John Zenger et al., *Leading Teams: Mastering the New Role,* (Homewood, IL: Irwin, 1994).

[22]Michael A. Hitt, "Corporate Entrepreneurship and Cross-Functional Fertilization: Activation, Process, and Disintegration of a New Product Design Team," *Entrepreneurship: Theory and Practice* 23(3) (Spring 1999), pp. 145–68.

CHAPTER 7

Quality Management

Supply professionals who plan to guide their organization and their supply chains to World Class Supply Management[SM] must understand how to evaluate the management of quality both within their own facilities and those of their suppliers. Evaluation of the underlying philosophy, management system, facilitating tools, and methodologies of a supplier is the first step; however, World Class Supply Management[SM] calls for going beyond mere evaluation to aiding in the development and improvement of supplier quality.

KEY CONCEPTS:

Case

The Quality Walk

Beth Stuart noticed that employees tended to disappear into their offices and down connecting aisles as she walked through the supplier's facility with her escort Michael Spade. Michael Spade, the youngest Vice President of Manufacturing in the supplier's history, had agreed to meet with Beth to show her the facility in North Carolina where the parts would be produced.

Beth had set up the meeting to personally evaluate the supplier's facility before her company, Epic Communications, entered into a long-term contract for a rough demand of 1,200,000 high-speed communications printed circuit boards in 2001. Follow-on contracts would be negotiated each year thereafter, if the relationship worked out to the benefit of both parties. On paper, the potential supplier, PushTel Technology, appeared to be a viable supplier. PushTel's marketing department had provided Beth and Epic with information about its high quality standards, activity based costing system, and satisfied customers. Further, PushTel appeared to be a company on the rise based on the company's financial reports.

Reflecting on Michael's employees avoiding him, Beth recalled the last supplier facility she had visited, where as she walked through the plant the quality manager who had given her the tour greeted workers by name. The workers there actually had gone out of their way to say hello. Employees now did the complete opposite with Michael.

Moving from the office area into the production facility, Beth could not help but notice area rugs and posters on the walls that had slogans encouraging workers to produce high-quality products. The rug at the entrance stated "Zero Defects" with a smiling cartoon character holding a wrench. Two posters near the entrance stated "Think" and "Quality is Job One." Beth asked the question, "Michael, did you or some of your upper managers go through Crosby philosophy training?" Michael replied, "We sure did, about eight years ago, why do you ask Beth?" "Whenever I see rugs and posters with exhortations and goals, it is an indication to me that Crosby's teachings influenced the organization. Deming was adamantly against such practice. So you tend to not see such practice in Deming-influenced facilities."

Suddenly, a loud spraying noise could be heard about twenty feet away. A high-pressure hose had come off of a machine and fluid was pouring out onto the factory floor. Beth watched in amazement as the operator of the machine quickly reattached the hose and proceeded to clean the floor—as if the breakdown was business as usual. Embarrassed and angry, Michael went straight over to the operator and criticized him for his ineptness.

As he walked back over to Beth, he quickly changed his composure to appear as if nothing of significance had happened. "Beth, breakdowns like that rarely happen here. We are ISO 9001:2001 registered, after all," said Michael in defense of his plant. Beth replied, "Yes, I know that sometimes we can't control everything, but could I see documentation on the maintenance of your production line?" A little shocked, Michael said, "Sure, let's go over to the supervisor's desk for the information." Sure enough, Michael was able to retrieve the maintenance schedule and records; however, the records for preventive maintenance were mixed in with the records for repairs. Beth asked, "Michael, how are you able to discriminate between preventive maintenance and repairs?" Michael replied, "I am sure that the supervisors know how to tell the difference." Beth then observed, "Also, just glancing over the report, I notice that about six weeks of data are missing." Looking at the supervisor's desk she noticed similar looking data sheets placed under one leg of the supervisor's desk in order to balance the desk. "Is that the data?" she asked. Overhearing the conversation, the supervisor quickly grabbed the data from under the leg and handed it to Beth. "Sorry," he said, "the desk was a bit wobbly and I forgot about the data being there." Visibly angry with the supervisor, Michael said to Beth, "Let's continue with the tour."

Walking through the facility Beth noticed as many employees conducting what appeared to be testing and inspection as were actually producing the products. In addition, she noticed parts that had been pulled from the line to be reworked or scrapped sitting to the sides of the production lines. She thought to herself, "Lots of inspection, rework, scrap, and work-in-progress—all indications of processes that are either incapable or out of control." Pointing to a rack of printed circuit boards, she asked, "Michael, can I see the scrap records for these parts?" "I don't think all of the parts are scrap, some may be reworks," Michael replied. He continued, "Let's go to the QC (quality control) department and have those records pulled for you."

As they walked to the QC department, Beth saw out of the corner of her eye an employee drop a printed circuit board, instinctively catch it by crushing it with his elbow against a conveyor belt casing, and then place the board back on the production line as if nothing had happened. She decided not to bring the event to Michael's attention after his reaction to the machine breakdown earlier.

After asking several QC employees who was responsible for the scrap records, Michael traced the records to Martha Ryder, a QC employee located in a cramped little room about 40 yards away from the QC offices. Martha managed the quality records in a small, enclosed area of the factory with no windows. Tagged parts were strewn throughout the room. Martha was able to retrieve the scrap records for the process in question very quickly. She handed the manila folder for the last month to Beth.

Looking through the records, Beth noticed that, on average, the scrap forms were dated about three weeks after the part was pulled from the production line. Scanning down the forms she expected to find bogus causes for the scrap listed. Sure enough, the causes were written in the shortest form possible with "operator error" listed most of the time. Beth knew that there was no way the company could possibly trace the causes and improve the processes with the data sheets. She thanked Martha for her time. Michael and Beth then left and resumed the tour.

Curious, she asked Michael, "Can I see descriptions of the processes for how you handle scrap?" Michael replied, "Sure, I can give you that information, but it will take me a couple of days to get it together. I will e-mail it to you." She recalled another of her visits to a supplier in San Jose who was able to pull up specific process information in an instant with an online ISO 9001:2000 documentation system.

Finally, they reached the end of the production and assembly lines, where quality control conducted final inspection. Michael stated with a hint of pride, "We maintain high inspection levels, usually 100 percent, to assure that you as the customer get the highest quality possible."

Beth left the facility thankful that she had taken the time to visit. "The irony," she thought, "is my new manager has plans to reduce the number of facility visits because, according to him, 'The cost of visiting suppliers is really eating into my budget'!"[1]

Evolution of Quality Management

Firms have taken many different pathways to world-class quality management, but the end destination has been very much the same. A frequently overheard statement is "same wine, different bottles." The wine in this case is quality. The different bottles are the different approaches and pathways. The fact that new bottles continue to sell is proof that quality is still and will always be critically important.

In historically understanding the evolution of the quality management movement over the last 50 years, it is useful to reflect on the multiple pathways that companies have taken to achieve competitive capability on a quality basis. The beginning of almost all pathways can be traced to a relatively small number of individuals who essentially "preached" quality when very few companies recognized quality as a source of competitive advantage. Instead many companies, such as General Motors, did not initially heed the call of the "preachers" and waited until quality was required for survival. Some com-

---

[1] The case is based on a combination of real events observed independently at two supplier facilities by one of the authors while conducting research. Unfortunately, the telecommunications company (the buying firm) did not actually visit the supplier's plant, but it did enter into a "partnership" with the supplier. The result? Catastrophic costs due to poor quality and missed deadlines. Results of the contract were observed at the telecommunications company two years after research at the supplier's facility. Dates, company names, and individuals presented in the case are fictional. It is doubtful that all of the events in the case would have been discovered by one visit, but one thing is for sure—the telecommunications company would have been far better off if it had invested the time and money to take "the quality walk."

panies, such as American Motors Company, never heeded the call and simply went out of business. For companies that decided to survive, the chief executive officer administered one or more management approaches that adhered to the philosophical understanding or the "religion" he or she had accepted. The management approach then drove which methodologies and tools the companies used to implement, improve, and maintain quality. The remainder of this chapter follows the pattern of influence by presenting philosophers, approaches, methodologies and tools.

Philosophies of the Gurus

Quality management has been blessed with many visionaries who have helped to develop the field to its current importance within companies. These visionaries are often referred to as gurus or preachers. The reason for this reverence is rooted in the fact that quality management investment in the past was often decided upon within companies on the basis of belief or "gut feelings" and not hard costs. (The issue of costs of quality is addressed later in the chapter.)

The influences of gurus such as Deming, Crosby, Juran, Taguchi, and Imai are still evident in corporate cultures. As noted in "the quality walk" given in the opening case, a supply manager can identify which guru influenced any given company the most by simply listening to managers and observing their processes. From a supply management perspective, understanding the influence of one or more guru on a supplier aids in evaluating, selecting, understanding, and helping the supplier. Although their teachings were directed at managers who were trying to improve their own internal quality, most of the guru's concepts are general enough to apply across supply chains.

W. Edwards Deming

W. Edwards Deming was perhaps the most influential quality guru of the last century. Ironically, his message was ignored by Western countries until the 1980s. Prior to that time he spent most of his career in Japan as a consultant, helping the Japanese to rebuild their industries after World War II. Deming is best known for his 14 points summarizing the philosophy of quality management that he developed over time in Japan.[2] The 14 points are general enough that they are still very applicable today and many of the concepts are directly transferable to modern supply management. A discussion of Deming's 14 points is provided for the reader on this book's web site.

Statistical Methods   In his seminars on the 14 points, Deming always stressed the use of statistical methods in order to identify when a process is becoming unstable or unpredictable in order to identify the problem and prevent the process from actually producing defects. This important topic is discussed later in this chapter under Statistical Process Control (SPC). Showing that he was far ahead of his time in supply management

---

[2]N. Logothetis, *Managing for Total Quality—From Deming to Taguchi to SPC,* The Manufacturing Practitioner Series (United Kingdom: Prentice Hall International, 1992). The authors of *World Class Supply Management*[SM] highly recommend this book on the basis of its conciseness, straightforward clarity, and global view.

(called purchasing back then), Deming advocated the use of SPC at supplier's facilities as well as at the buying firm's facilities.

Causes of Defects   Deming contended that the vast majority of defective or poor products produced in processes are directly traceable to poor quality input materials, parts, and components. These, according to Deming, are often the result of poorly coordinated design specifications and then poorly managed processes after the design is in production. From a supply management perspective, this means that better coordination with our suppliers in specifications development and usage will improve quality and decrease costs. In addition, developing our suppliers to use statistical techniques like SPC can help reduce costs and maintain high quality after the design stage.

Philip Crosby

Philip Crosby is another American quality guru who rose to international fame as a management consultant. Before he became a consultant, he had worked his way up from line inspector to corporate vice president and quality director of ITT. Crosby authored several seminal books. Among the best known are *Quality Is Free* and *Quality without Tears*.[3]

Zero Defects   Crosby is best known, and misunderstood, for championing the zero defects standard and popularizing many slogans, such as "Do it right the first time." The focus of the zero defects standard is on defining quality from the customer's perspective as conformance to requirements and then improving processes through prevention activities to meet the requirements. Crosby pushed the idea of measuring the costs of quality to support efforts toward zero defects, which culminated in his zero defects management approach (presented later in this chapter).

Crosby intended the zero defects approach to be a management performance standard, not a motivational program. Despite his intentions, it was treated as a motivational program in many companies that eventually gave up on the program because they could never reach perfection. Deming believed the zero defects standard created anxiety, fear, frustration, and mistrust of management when it was not accompanied by the means to actually achieve the standard.

Masaaki Imai

Like Deming and Crosby, Masaaki Imai became one of the world's leading management consultants. Imai introduced the world to continuous improvement through his book *Kaizen: The Key to Japan's Competitive Success*.[4] In a working environment, kaizen means continuous process improvement involving everybody.

Kaizen and Supply Management   Kaizen calls for everyone in an organization to work for constant and gradual improvement in every process. Since processes span supply chains, we believe that Kaizen should be extended to calling for everyone in the chain to

---

[3]Logothetis, *Managing For Total Quality.*
[4]M. Imai, *Kaizen: The Key to Japan's Competitive Success* (New York: Random House, 1986).

work for constant and gradual improvement in every process. When a new standard is achieved, management should make certain it is maintained and conditions are present to ensure the attainment of even higher standards. Kaizen improvement is, by Imai's definition, a long-term and long-lasting improvement resulting from team efforts focused on processes. Since it draws from existing employees, it usually requires less investment compared to other management approaches, but great internal effort to maintain.[5]

Genechi Taguchi

Genechi Taguchi served as the director of the Japanese Academy of Quality and is a four-time recipient of the Deming Prize. Taguchi believed the goalpost philosophy (discussed later in the section on Loss to Society) is incorrect. Taguchi notes that, as the level of conformance moves out toward the upper and lower limits, there is a quadratic increase in costs. Taguchi referred to this as the "quadratic loss function." Hence, the goalpost philosophy underestimates the costs of poor quality.[6]

Taguchi advocates identifying target values for design parameters and producing robust designs using statistical experimentation. The approach focuses on consistency in hitting the target values rather than being within a band of tolerance. Taguchi's "loss to society" model is presented in greater detail in the tools and methods section of this chapter.

Joseph Juran

Joseph Juran is perhaps best known for his *Quality Control Handbook*. First published in 1951, the book is still periodically revised to remain relevant. Like Deming and Crosby, Juran is an American consultant with international fame. Also, like Deming, Juran worked in post–World War II Japan, conducting seminars for top and middle-level executives.

The main principles of Juran's message are to focus on planning, organizational issues, creating beneficial change (breakthrough), preventing adverse change (control), and management's responsibility.[7] He recommends a formula for results which comprises four important stages, as follows:

1. **Establish specific goals to be reached**—identify what needs to be done, the specific projects that need to be tackled.
2. **Establish plans for reaching goals**—provide a structured process.
3. **Assign clear responsibility**—make clear who is responsible for meeting the goals.
4. **Base the rewards on results achieved**—feed results information back and utilize the lessons learned and experience gained.

Planning for quality is seen by Juran as an indispensable part of what he calls the quality trilogy, which consists of quality planning, quality control, and quality improvement.

---

[5]Logothetis, *Managing for Total Quality,* p. 90.
[6]Neil Fuller, "Taguchi Quality Control," *Supply Management,* September 24, 1998.
[7]Logothetis, *Managing For Total Quality,* p. 62.

He believes that objectives should be set yearly for increased performance and decreased costs. To develop the habit of always striving for these yearly goals, a company needs quality planning and a quality structure. Juran believes the development of the goals, plans, and structure are the responsibilities of top management.

Juran countered Crosby's approach by stating that simplistic slogans and exhortations do not constitute a structure. According to Juran, "There are no shortcuts to quality." The emphasis should be put on the results and the experience gained from those results, not on the quality campaign itself. Juran insists, "the recipe for action should consist of 90 percent substance and 10 percent exhortation, not the reverse!"[8]

Juran's approach to quality received widespread acceptance due to the clear setting of responsibility and detailed focus on planning. Juran's approach is especially popular with managers who feel the teachings of Deming and Crosby are vague and difficult to evaluate.

Management Approaches

Six Sigma, Total Quality Management (TQM), continuous improvement, zero defects, Quality Management System (QMS), and just-in-time (JIT) are all management systems that continue to make large contributions to the improvement and maintenance of quality internally in companies and across supply chains. As presented earlier, which system a company or chain chooses is greatly dependent upon the philosophical views of upper management as influenced either directly or indirectly by the gurus. It should be noted that the type of production or service a company provides also influences which system is chosen. In addition, companies may implement several approaches sequentially or simultaneously. In the automobile industry, for example, continuous improvement in a just-in-time framework coupled with Total Quality Management is fairly common. In companies that bought into the zero defects movement many now use the similar "set an ambitious goal" approach of Six Sigma. All of the systems may be used in manufacturing or service environments, but service operations are less likely to have a comprehensive quality management system because of the lack of physical outputs.

Management usually believes it needs a new approach to "rally the troops" much in the same way that psychologists discovered that painting the walls of a factory temporarily increases productivity. New quality management systems will always be appearing in corporations. In most cases, the latest approach will incorporate lessons learned from past systems, so new initiatives should not be ignored. For example, Six Sigma incorporates the best tools and methodologies of the other approaches, such as cause and effect analysis and statistical process control, while advancing several newer tools and methodologies, like balanced scorecards and project charters (discussed in chapters 21 and 22, respectively). The most recent incarnation of a quality system is the Quality Management System (QMS) as defined by the International Organization for Standardization.

---

[8]Ibid., p. 64.

Role of Supply Management   So how does a supply professional fit into a comprehensive system such as TQM or Six Sigma? In most cases, supply managers play a critical role in making the entire program work effectively. Most quality experts now agree that poor quality of incoming materials causes approximately 75 percent of the problems and related costs associated with final product quality.[9] It is very clear that quality consultant Joseph Juran is correct when he writes: "The assurance (for good quality) must come from placing the responsibility on the supplier to make the product right and supply proof that it is right."[10] Consequently, supply management becomes the "point" player or "the playmaker" in a firm's quality program.

Total Quality Management

Total Quality Management (TQM) received enormous recognition and adaptation in the 1980s in answer to the increasing need for firms to compete on a quality basis. By the late 1980s and early 1990s publications were touting the reasons why TQM had succeeded and failed in many organizations. The reviews were mixed, but generally in favor of a comprehensive quality management system. Most quality experts agree that the reasons for failure of TQM are usually poor management execution of the system.

By the late 1990s, TQM essentially had matured and management needed "new bottles for its wine." Six Sigma appears to be the latest "new bottle" or management system. Although Motorola popularized Six Sigma in the 1980s, the management approach did not gain widespread recognition until the late 1990s. Six Sigma is discussed later in this section of the chapter. Although the terminology of TQM will eventually pass, the management approach will never die since quality management in everything a company does is a requirement to compete today and in the future. In fact, this entire chapter is essentially about TQM if one goes by the vague definitions that once were in vogue. For example, the International Organization for Standardization offered the following definition of TQM:[11] *A management approach to an organization centered on quality, based on the participation of all its members, and aiming at long-term success through customer satisfaction and benefits to the members of the organization and to society.* A generalized TQM model is presented in Figure 7.1.[12]

---

[9]While a majority of a firm's quality problems commonly can be attributed to purchased materials and subassemblies, the root cause of most of these problems is in the design and resulting specifications of the items and their production processes. Supply management professionals have two areas of responsibility in the design/quality issue: (1) They and invited suppliers must work cooperatively with the firm's design engineers to design appropriate quality characteristics into the materials to be purchased, and (2) this same group must ensure that suppliers design variability out of their production processes to the extent that is practical.

[10]As quoted by Paul Moffat in "Quality Assurance," in *The Purchasing Handbook* (New York: McGraw-Hill, 1992), p. 421.

[11]As quoted by Greg Hutchins, *ISO 9000* (Essex Juntion, VT: Oliver Wight-Publications, 1993), p. 4.

[12]James F. Cali, *TQM for Purchasing Management* (New York: McGraw-Hill, 1993), p. 36.

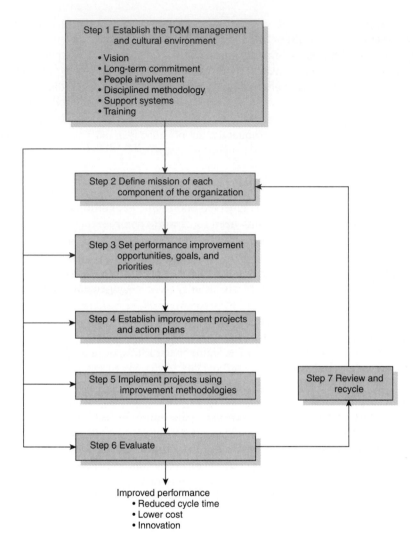

Figure 7.1 I A generalized total quality management model

Continuous Improvement

The concept of continuous improvement was introduced in an earlier section on Imai, the champion of kaizen. Kaizen is synonymous with continuous improvement. Although Imai brought continuous improvement to the world through his books, Taiichi Ohno, the pioneer of the kanban system at Toyota, developed continuous improvement into a viable, tangible management approach. In this section, continuous improvement is presented within the just-in-time (JIT) framework. Continuous improvement is a concept independent from JIT. It can be implemented without JIT, but it has received its most publicized adopters in companies that run JIT systems.

Just-in-Time   Two major tenets form the basis for just-in-time as practiced at Toyota: respect for people and elimination of waste. Ohno is credited with identifying categories of waste which are avoidable: waste of overproduction, waste of unneeded motion and transportation, waste in needless processing and machine time, waste in holding excessive inventory, and waste resulting from defects.[13] In taking "the quality walk" as given in the opening case of this chapter, a supply manager with a solid grasp of these wastes can quickly see them openly on a factory floor of a supplier. Often managers working in the supplier's facilities have become complacent as regards their systems and their inherent wastes such that they no longer see them. A knowledgeable supply manager needs to be able to see what the managers of the facilities cannot.

Ohno demonstrated that most of the above-mentioned waste can be eliminated if a kanban system is coupled with continuous improvement. A kanban system can also be called a "pull" system. In a pull system, units needed by an upstream stage of production are transported to that stage only when needed and in the exact amount needed. This is in contrast to traditional "push" production systems in which units are transported to the next stage as soon as they have completed the previous stage. Using the kanban system, the operator of each stage has the responsibility for the collection of the units from the previous stage, hence the operator "pulls" the material through the system. A kanban (signpost) is attached to the box of parts as they go to the assembly line, and the same kanban is returned when the parts are all used, to serve as an order for more and as a record of work done.

Supply managers must understand that JIT can be extended to subcontractors and external suppliers. Extending JIT across a supply chain requires supply professionals and suppliers to work in collaboration so that only enough units to meet demand (that is, small lots) are produced and moved from one stage to another. The supply chain members should work together to assure that the need for speculative, just-in-case production is eliminated.

Elimination of Waste   In eliminating waste within a continuous improvement methodology, a company may choose to use the following steps: First, form a small group team that will go through kaizen training using the tools and methods discussed later in this chapter. The people in the group are usually factory floor workers, hence the tenet of respect for people. Second, the team will gather data on existing systems to discover where waste is and what the wasteful activity is costing the company. Many managers do not believe in assigning cost to waste because they believe it does not matter—waste is waste no matter how small or large, and it should be eliminated. Juran and Crosby would argue that we need to know the cost of the waste to prioritize projects to eliminate the waste. Third, once a project for eliminating a waste is identified, then the Plan, Do, Check, Act(P-D-C-A) cycle is often used, as described in chapter 22. After the P-D-C-A substeps are completed, the group then returns to step two again (data gathering) and selects a new project.

---

[13]Logothetis, *Managing For Total Quality.*

Sigma	Corresponding Yield	DPMO
1	30.9%	690,000
2	69.2	308,000
3	93.3	66,800
4	99.4	6,210
5	99.98	320
6	99.9997	3.4

Figure 7.2 | Sigma quality levels and corresponding yields

Six Sigma

In the book, *The Six Sigma Way,* Six Sigma is defined as a broad and comprehensive system for building and sustaining business performance, success, and leadership.[14] The key focus of Six Sigma is on processes, but with measurement of both processes and products. With Six Sigma, companies strive to achieve the statistical six sigma goal of near-perfection as measured at 3.4 defects per million opportunities (DPMO). The corresponding yield from six sigma process is 99.9997%, as shown in Figure 7.2. The lofty goal, very reminiscent of the Zero Defects management philosophy, is used by Six Sigma advocates as a driver of organizational change.

Six Sigma was developed at Motorola in the late 1980s, as a way of accelerating the company's rate of improvement, providing a clear and objective goal for improvement, and creating a stronger focus on the customer. The success of the six sigma measure as a mantra for change led Motorola to institutionalize the goal into a comprehensive management system. While the objective of statistical "six sigma" is the overarching goal, Six Sigma as a management system shifts the attention to the rate of improvement in processes and products. According to supporters of the Six Sigma management approach, there are some clear measurement benefits.

1. *Six Sigma starts with the customer.* Measures demand a clear definition of customers' requirements.
2. *Six Sigma provides a consistent metric.* Once you've defined the requirement clearly, you can define a "defect" and measure almost any type of business activity or process. For example, some measures from a supply management perspective could be late deliveries, incomplete shipments, and parts shortages.
3. *Six Sigma links the effort to an ambitious goal.* Having an entire organization focused on a performance objective of 3.4 defects per million opportunities can create significant momentum for improvement.[15]

DMAIC Cycle   Similar to the P-D-C-A cycle discussed later in chapter 22, Six Sigma offers a cyclical improvement model called DMAIC that focuses on improving processes. DMAIC stands for Define, Measure, Analyze, Improve, and Control.[16] The

---

[14]Peter S. Pande, Robert P. Neuman, and Roland R. Cavanagh, *The Six Sigma Way* (New York: McGraw-Hill, 2000), p. 77.

[15]Ibid., p. 29.

[16]Ibid., p. 37.

Six Sigma model has elements of both continuous and discontinuous (reengineering) improvement. Six Sigma's focus on processes is evident from the combination of process improvement and design (including redesign), "incorporating them as essential, complementary strategies for sustained success." The process design approach is reminiscent of reengineering, where the objective in Six Sigma is not to fix but rather to replace a process (or a piece of a process) with a new one. Six Sigma also calls for addressing product and service design through what the approach calls "Six Sigma Design." Six Sigma Design principles are intended to link the creation of new goods and services to customer needs and validate the linkage by data and testing.[17]

Six Sigma Blackbelts A differentiator of the Six Sigma management system versus other quality management approaches is the designation of levels of understanding of Six Sigma into belts: green, black, and master. The excitement that the belts cause is very real and, to put it bluntly, shrewd marketing. Taking the term from the martial arts, a color of belt is a level attained through intensive training and experience. Although no solid definition of the levels exists, a master blackbelt is essentially an individual who has attained the highest level of understanding of Six Sigma and is capable of training others and working as an internal consultant in a corporation. Blackbelts become the primary drivers of Six Sigma improvements within companies by essentially managing specific projects. A greenbelt is a training level that is encouraged by Six Sigma advocates for all workers.

At G.E., blackbelts receive three weeks of training, with follow-up exams and continued learning through conference and other forums. A greenbelt at G.E. is the lowest commitment, which is training for a minimum of two weeks in Six Sigma. At G.E., every management employee is required to become at least a greenbelt in Six Sigma.[18]

Six Sigma Themes In the book, *The Six Sigma Way,* the authors present six themes (or principles) of Six Sigma, summarized as follows:

- **Theme One: Genuine Focus on the Customer.** In Six Sigma, customer focus becomes the top priority. For example, the measures of Six Sigma performance begin with the customer. Six Sigma improvements are defined by their impact on customer satisfaction and value.

- **Theme Two: Data- and Fact-Driven Management.** Six Sigma discipline begins by clarifying *what* measures are key to gauging business performance; then it applies data and analysis so as to build an understanding of key variables and optimize results. Six Sigma helps managers answer two essential questions to support fact-driven decisions and solutions. What data/information do I really need? How do we use that data or information to maximum benefit?

- **Theme Three: Process Focus, Management, and Improvement.** Whether designing products and services, measuring performance, improving efficiency and customer satisfaction—or even running the business—Six Sigma positions the process as the key vehicle of success.

---

[17]Ibid., p. 33.
[18]Ibid.

■ **Theme Four: Proactive Management.** Proactive management means making habits out of what are, too often, neglected business practices: defining ambitious goals and reviewing them frequently; setting clear priorities; focusing on problem prevention versus firefighting; questioning why we do things instead of blindly defending them as "how we do things here."

■ **Theme Five: Boundaryless Collaboration.** The opportunities available through improved collaboration within companies and with their suppliers and customers are huge. Billions of dollars are left on the table (or on the floor) every day, because of disconnects and outright competition between groups that should be working for a common cause: providing value to customers.

■ **Theme Six: Drive for Perfection; Tolerance for Failure.** No company will get anywhere close to Six Sigma without launching new ideas and approaches—which always involve some risk. If people who see a possible path to better service, lower costs, new capabilities, etc. (i.e., ways to be closer-to-perfect), are too afraid of the consequences of mistakes, they'll never try.

Successes with Six Sigma are being published in a variety of industries. One of the most outspoken advocates of Six Sigma is former G.E. Chairman John F. Welch. According to Welch, "Six Sigma has forever changed G.E. Everyone—from the Six Sigma zealots emerging from their Black Belt tours, to the engineers, the auditors, and the scientists, to the senior leadership that will take this company into the new millennium—is a true believer in Six Sigma, the way this company now works."[19] At G.E., the best Six Sigma projects begin ". . . not inside the business but outside it, focused on answering the question—how can we make the customer more competitive? What is critical to the customer's success? . . . One thing we have discovered with certainty is that anything we do that makes the customer more successful inevitably results in a financial return for us."[20]

Quality Management System

The International Organization of Standardization (ISO) released its ISO 9000:2000 standards with radical revisions that justify the inclusion in this section of what ISO calls a Quality Management System (QMS). The principles are intended for use as a framework to guide organizations toward improved performance. According to ISO, the principles are derived from the collective experience and knowledge of international experts. Although discussion of the standards that drive the QMS is given later in this chapter, it is appropriate to present the principles that drove the change in the ISO standards. The principles form the foundation of a QMS approach to managing quality. The principles are as follows:[21]

■ **Principle 1 Customer Focus:** Organizations depend on their customers and therefore should understand current and future customer needs, should meet customer requirements, and strive to exceed customer expectations.

---

[19] Address to General Electric Company Annual Meeting, Cleveland, OH, April 21, 1999.

[20] General Electric Company Annual Meeting, Charlotte, NC, April 23, 1997.

[21] www.iso.ch, website for the International Organization of Standardization, January 2002.

- **Principle 2 Leadership:**   Leaders establish unity of purpose and direction of the organization. They should create and maintain the internal environment in which people can become fully involved in achieving the organization's objectives.

- **Principle 3 Involvement of People:**   People at all levels are the essence of an organization and their full involvement enables their abilities to be used for the organization's benefit.

- **Principle 4 Process Approach:**   A desired result is achieved more efficiently when activities and related resources are managed as a process.

- **Principle 5 System Approach to Management:**   Identifying, understanding, and managing interrelated processes as a system contributes to the organization's effectiveness and efficiency in achieving its objectives.

- **Principle 6 Continual Improvement:**   Continual improvement of the organization's overall performance should be a permanent objective of the organization.

- **Principle 7 Factual Approach to Decision Making:**   Effective decisions are based on the analysis of data and information. Applying the principle of factual approach to decision making typically leads to ensuring that data and information are sufficiently accurate, reliable, and accessible.

- **Principle 8 Mutually Beneficial Supplier Relationships:**   An organization and its suppliers are interdependent, and a mutually beneficial relationship enhances the ability of both to create value.

Tools and Methodologies

The quality movement, whether embraced through TQM, continuous improvement, Six Sigma, or some other management approach, is accomplished in the "trenches" on the floors of factories, warehouses, offices, and wherever business is accomplished. To accomplish quality, a plethora of tools and methodologies have been developed that are used whenever needed by middle management and the general workforce. Improvement-focused tools and methodologies all contributed and continue to contribute to quality improvement.

Terminology and Usage   The term "tool" emerged from the use of the methodologies in small group improvement efforts, such as quality circles, wherein the group would focus on solving a problem by using a mix of the methodologies. Some of the methodologies would be used in the same problem-solving session, rather like a screwdriver being used for many phases of a construction project. Some of the tools are better used to discover where focus should be placed. For example, a cost of quality analysis helps clarify what areas of investment may require attention. If downtime resulting from breakdowns exists, perhaps increasing investment in maintenance or training is warranted. We can view these "tools" as available in our "quality toolbox" for use when appropriate to help us achieve quality. Not all tools will be used on every project. Some may never be used.

Implications for Supply Management   Why should a supply professional need to be aware of the tools and methodologies of quality management? Some companies talk a great deal about quality at the upper-management level, but real improvements in quality occur in the trenches where the tools and methodologies are used. Physically seeing that these activities are occurring is reassurance that the company is investing in its quality system and the people running the system. When a supply manager does "the quality walk" through a supplier's facility, he or she often will discover meeting rooms or factory walls pasted with diagrams, charts, and lists that are outputs of using these tools and methodologies. Depending on whom you talk to that championed quality at his or her company, the list of tools and methodologies will be different.

During a recent visit to a Pacific Bell logistics facility in Los Angeles, one of the authors observed a quality improvement team's output of poster-size paper taped to the walls of the facility showing the aftermath of a very productive small group meeting focused on quality improvement. The team used run charts, Pareto charts, cause-and-effect diagrams, flowcharts, and brainstorming lists.

Common Tools

The most commonly used tools of quality are Pareto charts, cause-and-effect diagrams, process flowcharts, run plots, frequency histograms, correlation plots, and control charts. These are often called the "seven tools of quality."

1. *Pareto Charts* are used to distinguish between critical and trivial problems. For example, a company could use Pareto charts with checklists to identify the number of occurrences or quality costs for each variable that cause their products to be scrapped. The variables themselves could be identified using cause-and-effect diagrams.

2. *Cause-and-Effect Diagrams* show possible causes of a problem. Also called a fishbone diagram, the cause-and-effect diagram is an aid to brainstorming and hypothesis generation. For example, the causes of defects, causing product to be scrapped, could be identified using this method. Always try to find the underlying causes of causes. Ask, "Why is this a cause?" several times, until the true underlying cause is discovered.

3. *Process Flow Charts* are useful for showing linkages among parts of a process. This is a good tool for identifying bottlenecks and non-value-added activities in processes. Simulation is a natural extension of flow and run charting to increase knowledge about the flows of a process.

4. *Run Plots* graph samples over time of some variable that is thought to be important. A run plot can be examined to see whether the process is subject to change or behaves consistently over time. Noting when changes occur may suggest hypotheses about their cause.

5. *Frequency Histograms* show the distribution of some variable that is thought to be important. Frequency histograms are useful for hypothesis testing. For example, how do the distributions of process times for manufacturing processes compare with ones you would expect?

6. *Scatter Diagrams* show correlations between two variables, typically a problem and a potential cause. To examine interactions between more than two variables, multiple regression should be used. For example, a negative correlation between increased quality and increased total costs could be investigated using a simple scatter diagram.

7. *Control Charts* are similar to run plots, but they are used for operational control. Control charts show the upper and lower allowable limits for a process variable. When the process exceeds those limits or shows a recognizable pattern, action should be taken to adjust the process. Once set up, control charts are effective tools for day-to-day monitoring and management of a process. They are discussed in greater detail later in this chapter.

Example Using the Tools Consider a supplier who has recently installed a new production process and assigned several operators to a team to manage improvement projects. The team decides to map the process stages using a flowchart in order to identify where data should be gathered. The decision is to gather data at each of the inspection points to start. After data are gathered on where failures are occurring and estimating the costs of the failures (costs of quality), a Pareto chart may be used to identify which problem is generating the greatest failure costs. A cause-and-effect diagram could then be used to help identify the root causes of the highest cost failure. Through the cause-and-effect analysis and brainstorming, the team determines that higher levels of maintenance of the tools used in the production process are needed. To prevent the problem from occurring in the future, the team decides to implement statistical process control to measure the process outputs and identify when the process is in need of additional maintenance before new defects are produced. Data is accumulated on the new solution and a decision is made at a later date as to whether the project has been a success or not. If it has been a success, the team moves on to the next highest-priority project. If the project has not been a success, then the team restarts the improvement process. Regardless of the success or failure of the project, the team maintains detailed documentation of the effort, so that the gains can be maintained, lessons can be learned, and the information can be disseminated to other production processes within the company.

The successful use of the seven tools has partly been the result of the simplicity and ease of use they facilitate, while revealing much about a process. They are designed so that little training is required. Still, they do require commitment on the part of management to provide time and resources for small-group members to utilize them properly.

Costs of Quality

Since the introduction of the traditional quality cost model in the 1950s, managers have been urged to base quality-related decisions on the hypothesized trade-off between the costs of prevention and appraisal and the costs of internal and external failure.[22,23] From a supply management standpoint, understanding the costs associated with quality decision making enables better understanding of both the total cost of ownership and how suppliers make decisions in their production facilities. (Please see the chapter on the Total Cost of Ownership.)

According to the traditional costs of quality (COQ) model, a company producing poor quality products can reduce nonconformance or failure costs by investing in

---

[22]A. V. Feigenbaum, "The Challenge of Total Quality Control," *Industrial Quality Control,* May 1957, pp. 17–23.

[23]J. M. Juran, *Quality Control Handbook* (New York: McGraw-Hill, 1951).

prevention and appraisal activities. The model resolves a hypothesized trade-off by specifying a nonzero optimal level of defects at the point where the marginal cost of increased prevention and appraisal activities equals the marginal benefit from failure cost reductions. An important note here is needed with respect to the optimum point. Within many progressive quality systems, the optimal levels of defects are very close to zero.[24] A six-sigma process, for example, should have 3.4 defects per million op-portunities. The cost categories in the COQ model are as follows:[25]

- *Prevention costs* are costs of all activities specifically designed to prevent poor quality in products or services. Examples are the costs of maintaining equipment and supplies, new product reviews, quality planning, supplier capacity surveys, process capability evaluations, quality improvement team meetings, quality improvement projects, quality education, and training.

- *Appraisal costs* are costs associated with measuring, evaluating, and auditing products or services to assure conformance to quality standards and performance requirements. These include the costs of incoming and source inspections, tests of purchased material, in-process and final inspection, product, process, or service audits, calibration of measuring and test equipment, and the cost of associated materials and supplies.

- *Failure costs* are costs resulting from products or services not conforming to requirements or customer or user needs. Two categories of failure costs exist: internal and external. Internal failure costs are costs occurring prior to delivery or shipment of the product, or the furnishing of a service, to the customer. Examples are the costs of scrap, disposing of scrap, rework, redoing inspection, redoing testing, material review, and downgrading. External failure costs are costs occurring after delivery or shipment of the product, and during or after furnishing a service to the customer. Examples are the costs of processing customer complaints, customer returns, warranty claims, and product recalls. Opportunity costs of lost customers due to poor quality are sometimes included as an external failure cost, but are extremely difficult to estimate.

Loss to Society

In continuing the COQ discussion, Taguchi teaches that a traditional "conformance to specifications" definition of costs underestimates failure costs. The conventional conformance to specification definition assumes that no loss occurs as long as output lies within upper and lower specification limits. The view has also been referred to as the "Goalpost Philosophy."

Tolerance Stacking   One problem with the goalpost philosophy is "tolerance stacking." When two or more parts are to be fit together, the size of their tolerances often determines how well they will match. This is tolerance stacking. Should one part fall at a lower limit of its specification, and a matching part at its upper limit, a good fit is unlikely.

---

[24]Many textbooks present figures for the COQ showing a plot where the optimum point is plotted somewhere midway between 0% and 100% good; this has confused many students over the years in believing that the optimal point is somewhere around 50% good.

[25]Jack Campanella, ed., *Principles of Quality Costs* 2nd ed. (ASQC Quality Press, 1990).

Taguchi developed a way to confront the stacked tolerances conformance problem. Taguchi begins with the idea of "the loss function," a measure of losses from the time a product is shipped. The theoretical notion is that "losses to society" occur whenever output deviates from its target value.[26] In more tangible terms, these losses include warranty costs, nonrepeating customers, and other problems resulting from performance failure. Taguchi then compares such losses to two alternative approaches to quality. The first approach is simple conformance to specifications. The second approach is a measure of the degree to which parts or products diverge from the ideal target or center. Taguchi demonstrates that tolerance stacking will be worse when the dimensions of parts are more distant from the ideal target of a specification than when they cluster around it, even if some parts fall outside the tolerance band entirely. Knowing that the problem of stacked variances exists and understanding Taguchi's loss function causes managers to focus on reducing the variances of parts and processes.

Process Capability Analysis

No operations activity can produce identical results time after time. This is true even for machine-based production processes. Every process possesses some natural variability on account of such things as machine part clearances, bearing wear, lubrication, variations in operator technique, and so on. In the language of statisticians, these are "chance" or "common" causes that produce *random variations* in the output. Over time, this natural variability in the output of a process will produce a distribution of outputs around the mean quality level. In many cases this distribution approximates the normal bell-shaped curve. The difference between the two extremes of the curve, the high and low values, is defined as the *natural tolerance range* of the process. As long as the process is properly adjusted and is not affected by any outside nonrandom forces—as long as the process is "in control"—the distribution it produces is predictable, as shown in Figure 7.3.

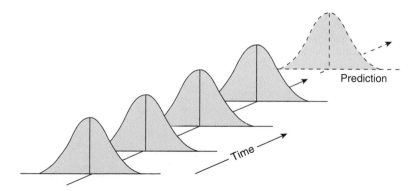

Prediction

Time

Figure 7.3 | The output distribution of a process that is "in control"

---

[26]G. Taguchi and D. Clausing, "Robust Quality," *Harvard Business Review,* January–February 1990, pp. 65–75.

If a buying firm's desired range of quality for a given purchased part is compatible with the natural tolerance range of a potential supplier's production process, the supplier should have little difficulty in providing the buying firm with parts that meet specifications. On the other hand, when the buying firm's required quality range is narrower than the natural capability range of the process, the supplier is bound to produce some unacceptable parts.

Implications for Supply Management   Alert supply managers recognize the direct economic relationship between their specified quality requirements and the producer's ability to perform consistently at the specified level. In the case of a nonstandard item, the capable supply manager, before selecting a supplier, must determine (1) whether the potential supplier in fact knows what the natural capability range for its production process is; (2) if so, whether the buying firm's *desired* range of quality is compatible with the supplier's natural capability range; and (3) if so, how the supplier plans to monitor the process to ensure that it stays in control so that it will consistently produce satisfactory output. The following examples should clarify this concept.

In Figure 7.4*a,* assume that a supply manager wants to purchase 100,000 metal shafts that are 1 inch in diameter with a tolerance of $\pm$ 0.005 inch. Assume further that the supplier has studied its process, stabilized it, and knows its natural capability for this type of job to be 1 inch $\pm$ 0.004. Examining Figure 7.4*a,* the supply manager sees that as long as the supplier's process operates normally and remains centered on 1.0 inch, every piece produced will fall within the acceptable range of quality. In this example, then, if the supplier is able to keep the process in control, this situation appears to represent a sound purchase for the buying firm from a quality point of view. In this case, the supplier's process is said to be "capable."

Assume now that the supply manager wants to purchase 100,000 shafts that are 1 inch in diameter with a tolerance of $\pm$ 0.003 inch. Examination of Figure 7.4*b* reveals that, dealing with the same supplier under normal operating conditions, the production

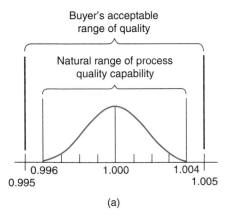

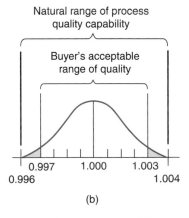

(a)   (b)

Figure 7.4 | An illustrative comparison of quality requirements with process capability (process frequency distribution curves for shafts are shown)

process cannot entirely satisfy the buying firm's requirement. Some shafts will be produced with diameters less than 0.997 inch and some with diameters larger than 1.003 inches. It is important for the supply manager to understand this type of situation. Unusable shafts, whether reworked or scrapped, create cost that must eventually be recovered by the supplier. In the long run, it will be the buying firm who pays. Assuming that the buying firm's requirements cannot be compromised, the supply manager is faced with two alternatives:

1. Negotiate with the supplier to determine whether the natural range of process capability can be narrowed economically to a point nearer the buying firm's requirements.
2. Seek another supplier whose process can meet the requirements more economically.

Process Capability Index Another way of expressing a process's capability relative to a buying firm's specific design requirement is by means of a *process capability index (Cp)*. This index is defined as

$$Cp = \frac{\text{Buying firm's absolute design tolerance}}{\text{Natural capability range of the process}^{27}}$$

A *Cp* value of 1 indicates that the capability range of the process matches *exactly* the quality range required by the buying firm. From a practical point of view, this is a very marginal fit for the buying firm. A value of more than 1 reveals excess process quality capability, while a value of less than 1 indicates insufficient process capability. Consider the examples in Figure 7.4.

$$Cp(\text{a}) = \frac{1.005 - 0.995}{1.004 - 0.996} = \frac{0.01}{0.008} = 1.25$$

$$Cp(\text{b}) = \frac{1.003 - 0.997}{1.004 - 0.996} = \frac{0.006}{0.008} = 0.75$$

In case (a), the $Cp = 1.25$, indicating that the quality capability of the process, if it stays centered and stable, exceeds the buying firm's requirement. In case (b), the $Cp = 0.75$, showing clearly that the process is not capable of satisfying the buying firm's quality requirement. In case (a), the process is "capable," whereas in case (b), the process is "incapable."

The preceding discussion makes the important assumptions that the manufacturer's process is stable and the average can be adjusted to line up with the center point (the target value) of the buying firm's specification (as is the case in Figure 7.4). In some operating situations this is not always possible. Suppose, in the situation discussed in Figure 7.4a, that after a great deal of experimentation the best process average the supplier was

---

[27]In practice, the natural capability range of the process frequently is *estimated* by taking the mean output quality value ± 3 standard deviations of the output values. In the case of normally distributed output values, this means that the process capability range includes 99.7 percent of the expected population values. In other words, there are 3 chances in 1,000 that the process output will fall outside the estimated process capability range. Some firms with high precision requirements estimate the natural capability range of a process by using the mean output value ± 4, ± 5, or ± 6 standard deviations.

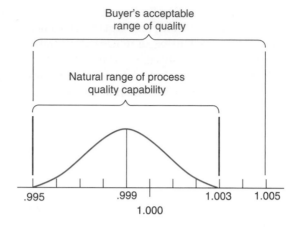

Figure 7.5 I An illustrative comparison of quality requirements with process capability when the process mean is not centered

able to achieve was 0.999 inch. This condition is depicted in Figure 7.5. One can see by inspection of the sketch that there is adequate excess quality capability at the upper end of the scale (1.005 − 1.003), but at the lower end there is no excess (0.995 − 0.995). Any movement of the process distribution to the left will produce out-of-specification shafts.

So we see that one additional factor is important in making a process capability analysis—the location of the process average relative to the buying firm's target specification value. That means that the previously calculated capability index *(Cp)* must be adjusted for the off-center location of the process average. The adjusted *Cp* is called the *process capability/location index (Cpk)*. It can be calculated as follows:

$$Cpk = Cp(1 - k)$$

where $k = \dfrac{\text{Buying firm's target value } - \text{ process mean}}{\text{Buying firm's absolute design tolerance divided by 2}}$

For the situation in Figure 7.6, the location index is:

$$k = \frac{1.000 - 0.999}{(1.005 - 0.995)/2} = \frac{0.001}{0.005} = 0.2$$

$$Cpk = 1.25(1 - 0.2) = 1.25 \times 0.8 = 1.0$$

The *Cpk* value is interpreted just like the *Cp* value; less than 1 indicates an incapable process, and a value greater than 1 indicates a capable process. In this case the fit is marginal because of the absence of any leeway on the lower end of the distribution.

Statistical Process Control

The preceding discussion about the natural process capability range was based on the premise that the supplier could keep the process operating in a stable manner—that is, "in control."

At this point in the discussion, it is necessary to point out that in addition to the random variations that occur naturally in any process, during the course of operation some *nonrandom* variations caused by external factors also occur. At times a machine goes out of adjustment, cutting tools become dull, the hardness or workability of the material varies, human errors become excessive, and so on. When these things happen, they usually take the process "out of control." What really happens is that *the quality capability of the process changes because of these unplanned events.* The process output distribution changes. It may spread out, increasing the range; it may shift up or down, altering the mean and the extreme values; or a combination of these things may occur. The end result is that the characteristics of the distribution no longer can be predicted—statistically, *the process is out of control.*

The statistical process control technique has the ability to detect these process shifts due to outside forces, or assignable causes, as they occur. When such changes are detected, the process is stopped and an investigation is initiated to find the cause of the problem. An operator who is familiar with the process and the equipment typically can locate the problem fairly quickly. This technique thus enables the operator to detect the problem, make necessary corrections, and continue operation, with the production of few, if any, defective products.

After a supply manager locates a potential supplier whose process capability matches his or her needs as discussed in the previous section, the final step for the supply manager is to persuade the supplier to use an SPC system that will keep the process in control and ensure the consistency of the process's output quality.

The following paragraphs discuss the basics of SPC theory and application.

Control Charts Several different types of control charts are used for different kinds of applications. The most common, however, are the $\overline{X}$ and R control charts for variables. These typically are applied in situations in which the quality variable to be controlled is a dimension, a weight, or another measurable characteristic. Operationally, the two charts are used together. The $\overline{X}$ chart monitors the absolute value, or the location, of the process average; and the R chart monitors the spread (range) of the output distribution, that is, the piece-to-piece variability.

Figure 7.6 illustrates an $\overline{X}$ and an R chart in simplified form. Before the charts are constructed for operating use, *the process must be studied carefully to determine that it is, in fact, stable*—that it is in statistical control. This is usually done by quality assurance and maintenance specialists and often is a time-consuming experimental task. Once the process has been stabilized—that is, its operation is influenced only by natural, random variations—its natural capability range can be determined and process control limits can be calculated.

At this point, the operating procedures are established. Usually the operator will inspect a small sample of output units every 15 minutes or so. Sample size typically runs between 3 and 5 units. The idea is to sample sequentially produced units in a manner that tends to minimize the quality variation within a given sample subgroup, and to maximize variation between the periodic sample subgroups.

The measurements are recorded as they are taken in the upper portion of the table shown below the R chart. (For illustrative purposes, hypothetical shaft dimension data

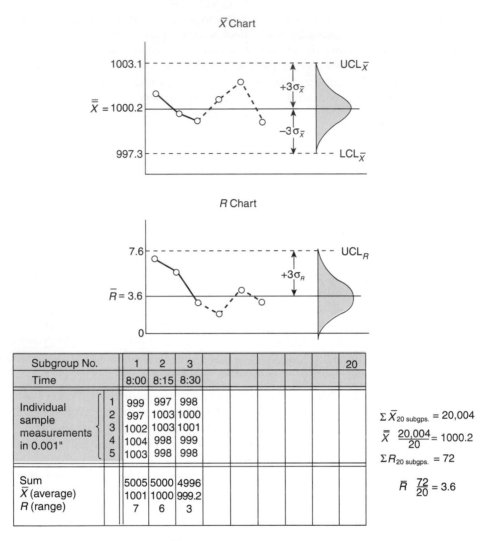

Figure 7.6 | An illustration of $\bar{X}$ and R charts in simplified form

from the example in Figure 7.6 are included in the first three subgroup columns.) The measurements for the *subgroup sample* are then summed and the average, $\bar{X}$, is computed. The range for the subgroup is also determined and entered in the table. After 20 to 25 subgroups have been inspected, enough data are available to provide good estimates of the process average and spread. At this point, an average of the subgroup $\bar{X}$ values is computed as $\bar{\bar{X}}$ (the average of the averages), and an average of the subgroup R values is computed *as* $\bar{R}$. The $\bar{\bar{X}}$ value represents the mean value of the average shaft diameter sizes determined in each subgroup; *this is the value used as the process average on the $\bar{X}$ chart*. The $\bar{R}$ value represents the mean value of the range of the shaft diameter sizes found in each subgroup; *this is the value used as the average range on the R chart*.

In most applications, $\overline{X}$ *control chart limits are set at* $\overline{\overline{X}} \pm 3$ standard deviations of the $\overline{X}$ values (3 sigma limits). Parenthetically, the reader should note that the frequency distributions used in constructing control charts are distributions of averages, not distributions of the individually measured values produced by the process. This fact ensures the existence of a normal distribution of control chart values when the process is in control.[28] Thus, the 6 sigma range (± 3 sigma limits) of the chart encompasses 99.7 percent of the $\overline{X}$ values that will result from the process operation as long as only natural random process variations are occurring.

The 3 sigma control chart limits can be determined by calculating the standard deviation of the $\overline{X}$ values, multiplying by 3, and subtracting and adding to $\overline{\overline{X}}$. In practice, however, this calculation has been simplified by the construction of a table of constant factors (for various sample sizes) that can be applied to $\overline{R}$ (and $\overline{X}$) to obtain the control limit values directly. This can be done quickly and easily.

The same rationale and procedure apply to the construction of R chart control limits. In this case, however, it should be noted that only the upper control limit is of practical significance in operation.

After the control charts are constructed, *as the operation continues data are plotted and the charts are interpreted.* As shown in Figure 7.6, the operator plots both the $\overline{X}$ value and the R value on their respective charts following his or her inspection and computations for each subgroup sample.

In the majority of cases, interpretation of the charts is a relatively simple matter. Any points falling outside the control limits usually indicate the existence of nonrandom variation. (If the process were actually in control, this would happen only 3 times in every 1,000 subgroup inspections.) The appearance of other nonrandom patterns may also be observed. For example, an unusually large number of points in sequence on the same side of the average line may indicate a shift in the process average or an expansion of the spread. As a rule of thumb, a run of seven points usually indicates an out-of-control situation. Clear-cut trends of points in one direction may indicate a tool wear or adjustment problem. As noted previously, when the operator suspects an out-of-control situation, he or she stops the process and investigates the potential problem.

Quality Movement Support

Support for the quality movement over the last several decades has been gained from three sources: organizations, standards, and awards. Organizations such as the American Society for Quality (ASQ) have helped support the quality management movement through seminars, local meetings, conferences, certifications, and research. Standards institutions such as the International Organization for Standardization, American National Standards Institute (ANSI), and the British Standards Institute (BSI) have helped support the quality management movement through development of common standards and registration bodies for certifying the quality of company systems. Awards such as the Deming Prize, Malcolm Baldrige National Quality

---

[28]The statistical central limit theorem states that the *means of small samples* tend to be normally distributed regardless of the type of distribution from which the individual sample values are taken.

Awards, and the European Quality Awards all support the quality management movement through documentation and recognition of companies achieving world-class status. These awards serve to motivate others and disseminate the best practices of the companies to society.

Organizations

The world has many organizations that support quality initiatives and education. In Europe, the European Organization for Quality and the European Foundation for Quality Management (EFQM) are two excellent sources. The main quality-focused organization in the United States is the American Society for Quality (ASQ).

Most supply professionals receive quality training, education, and networking through the Institute for Supply Management,[29] which integrates almost everything discussed in this chapter into its teachings. The Educational Society for Resource Management, more commonly referred to as APICS,[30] is another source.

Standards

Standards in quality management referred to in this section are process-based standards or norms that do not deal with technical specifications of the products and materials, but with how they are made. Globally, there are quite a few standards-developing institutes and organizations. The International Organization for Standardization's ISO 9000 system is currently the most dominant standards system used for quality control.[31]

International Organization for Standardization   The International Organization for Standardization (ISO), headquartered in Geneva, Switzerland, is an international body composed of members representing standards organizations.[32] The objective of the organization is to promote the development of standards, testing, and certification in order to encourage the international trade of goods and services.[33] The global emphasis on economic competitiveness, the unification of the European market, and a broad array of different quality standards among countries led to concentrated ISO work in the quality area over the last 20 years. The main product of this work was the issuance in 1987 of the ISO 9000 series of *quality system* standards, which are periodically revised to maintain their relevancy. As of 2002, ISO reports that its standards have resulted in certification of around 400,000 organizations worldwide.[34]

---

[29]Formerly the National Association of Purchasing Management.

[30]APICS stood for the American Production and Inventory Control Society. After the society changed its name it decided to continue using its well-known acronym APICS.

[31]Steven Casper and Bob Hancke, *Global Quality Norms within National Production Regimes: ISO 9000 Standards in French and German Car Industries, Organization Studies* (Berlin: Walter De Gruyter and Company, 1999).

[32]The American National Standards Institute (ANSI) is the U.S. member of the International Organization for Standardization.

[33]Hutchins, *ISO 9000,* p. 3.

[34]www.iso.ch, website for the International Organization for Standardization.

Prior to the last major revision of the standards in 1994, the ISO 9000 series consisted of five separate standards: ISO 9000, 9001, 9002, 9003, and 9004. A firm that adopted one or more of the standards was required to document what its quality management procedures were for each element in the standards. The firm was then required to be able to prove to an ISO auditor that the procedures were in fact followed in practice.

The main problem with the 1994 standards was that it was possible for a manufacturer to comply with the standards but still produce a mediocre product. The new standards have reportedly resolved the problem. The new standards are given below.[35]

- **ISO 9000:2000, Quality management systems—Fundamentals and vocabulary:** Establishes a starting point for understanding the standards and defines the fundamental terms and definitions used in the ISO 9000 family.

- **ISO 9001:2000, Quality management systems—Requirements:** ISO 9001, ISO 9002, and ISO 9003 in the old standards were integrated into ISO 9001:2000. The ISO 9000:2000 standard is used to assess a firm's ability to meet customer and applicable regulatory requirements and thereby address customer satisfaction. It is now the only standard in the ISO 9000 family against which third-party certification can be carried.

- **ISO 9004:2000, Quality management systems—Guidelines for performance improvements:** The standard provides guidance for continual improvement of a firm's quality management system to benefit all parties through sustained customer satisfaction. The new emphasis is important to supply managers since it creates greater focus on the supply chain than in the previous ISO 9000 series.

Recall the underlying eight principles of the ISO 9000:2000 series presented earlier in this chapter in the section on the Quality Management System. ISO 9001:2000 requires that one plan and manage the processes necessary for the continual improvement of one's quality management system. Continual improvement as defined by the International Organization for Standardization is "a process of increasing the effectiveness of your organization to fulfill your quality policy and your quality objectives." ISO 9004:2000 even goes beyond ISO 9001:2000 to improving the efficiency of an operation. ISO 9001:2000's focus on continual improvement of the quality management system is a major departure from the past reputation of the ISO 9000 series about which a commonly heard joke was, "As long as you document it and make it as your documentation says you make it—you can make cement life preservers and still get ISO 9000 certified!" The new standards do not allow companies to pass registration without showing tangible efforts to improve processes.

Impact on Supply Managers   Since their inception in 1987, the ISO 9000 standards have had implications for supply professionals—but the revisions to ISO 9000:2000 create even greater focus on supply management.

- The new standards promote the adoption of a process approach compared to the procedural approach described in the 1994 versions. This is important to supply man-

---

[35]Ibid.

agement since processes are what span supply chain boundaries and are, as a result, a responsibility for supply professionals.

■ Changes have also occurred in terminology. The most important changes concern the use of the term "organization" instead of "supplier," and the use of the term "supplier" instead of "subcontractor." According to ISO, these changes respond to the need of being more consistent and friendly with the normal use and meaning of the words.

■ The number of requirements for documented procedures has been reduced in ISO 9001:2000, and the emphasis placed on the organization demonstrating effective operation. This reduces the barriers to suppliers in achieving ISO 9000 registration and brings greater relevancy to the outcomes.

■ The standards have become a competitive weapon in global business. Consequently, if a firm wants to do business in the global marketplace, the chances are good that it will have to be ISO 9000:2000 registered.

■ While the standards do not require that a registered firm's suppliers also be registered, the revisions make it clear that registration of supply chain members is preferable.

■ The implications of the "continual improvement" emphasis in the standards includes suppliers, which places greater importance on supply management's role in meeting the ISO 9000:2000 series challenge whether suppliers are registered or not.

Awards

Malcolm Baldrige Award   In 1987, President Ronald Reagan signed into law the Malcolm Baldrige National Quality Act. The act called for establishment of a national quality award that would provide a comprehensive framework of guidelines an organization could use to evaluate its quality program and its quality improvement efforts. Additionally, the award was designed to provide recognition for U.S. organizations that had demonstrated excellence in the attainment and management of quality. Each year firms compete for this recognition in three categories where up to two firms per year can be recognized in each category:

1. Large manufacturing companies or subsidiaries.
2. Large service companies.
3. Small manufacturing or service companies.

On balance, the program has been extremely popular and has certainly elevated the interest of American businesspeople in quality and their awareness of the importance of quality. Most managers recognize that quality improvement is a developmental process that takes time and that there are seldom any quick fixes. But, clearly, the Baldrige Award format provides a helpful road map. Part of the significance of the Baldrige Award has been in how companies have used it to audit their company to see where they stood and to target the weak areas uncovered.[36] Additionally, previous award winners are required to share their success stories with other interested firms.

---

[36]Cole, "Learning From the Quality Movement," p. 67.

European Quality Award Following the trend of establishing geopolitically driven awards, the European Foundation for Quality Management (EFQM) in partnership with the European Commission and the European Organization for Quality announced the creation of the European Quality Award in 1991. The award consists of two parts: The European Quality Prize and the European Quality Award. The prize is given to companies that demonstrate excellence in quality management practice by meeting the award criteria. The award goes to the most successful applicant. The award recognizes criteria very similar to the Malcolm Baldrige criteria, with the addition of results criteria that address "people satisfaction" and impact on society.

Deming Prize In appreciation for Dr. W. Edwards Deming's contributions to Japanese industry, in 1951 the Japanese technical community established this prestigious award that bears Dr. Deming's name. The Deming Prize is designed to recognize both individual and organizational achievements in the field of quality, with a unique emphasis on the use of statistical techniques. Any firm that meets the requirements is eligible to receive the award, including individuals and firms outside Japan. Past recipient companies include Nissan, Toyota, Hitachi, and Nippon Steel, and Florida Power and Light.[37]

Supply Management Issues

In the previous edition of this book, we stated ". . . one of the most important responsibilities of a supply manager is to ensure that suppliers have the *ability,* the *motivation,* and *adequate information* to produce materials and components of the specified quality in a cost-effective manner. In fulfilling this responsibility, a supply manager can, to a great extent, control the quality and related costs of incoming material." The responsibility of the supply manager has remained the same, except for one discrepancy—the term "control" is no longer appropriate. Supply managers trying to make their efforts more proactive came to realize in the late 1990s that working with suppliers to improve their quality management systems yielded greater benefits than trying to control an existing system fraught with waste. Control is certainly still needed, but it should not be emphsized today as much as in the past. Collaborative quality management will enable supply chains to gain competitive advantage over other chains. Supply management is central to such collaboration.

Generally speaking, four factors determine the long-run quality level of a firm's purchased materials:

1. Creation of complete and appropriate specifications for quality requirements (see the chapter on specifications and standards later in this book).
2. Selection of suppliers having the technical and production capabilities to do the desired quality/cost job (see the chapter on sourcing given later in this book).
3. Development of a realistic understanding with suppliers of quality requirements and creation of the motivation to perform accordingly.
4. Monitoring of suppliers' quality/cost performance—and exercise of appropriate control.

---

[37]Logothetis, *Managing for Total Quality,* p. 28.

Supply management is directly responsible for factors 2 and 3, and it should play a strong cooperative role in factors 1 and 4.

Requirements Development

At the beginning of a quality management seminar given by one of the coauthors of this book to supply managers pursuing their Certificates in Purchasing Management, participants wrote their definition of quality on notebook paper and passed it to the front. As expected, none of the definitions were identical since the perspective of each individual defines quality.

Quality can be defined in three ways:

1. In absolute terms.
2. Relative to a perceived need.
3. As conformance with stated requirements.

In *absolute terms,* quality is a function of excellence, intrinsic value, or grade, as determined over time by society generally or by designated bodies in specialized fields. Hence, most people consider gold to be a high-quality precious metal. In a more utilitarian sense, "prime" beef is generally considered to be among the highest-quality meats in the meat market. While few absolutes endure the test of the ages, for a given period of time in a given culture, most people hold views about the absolute quality of many things.

In business and industrial activities, generally quality is first defined in terms of *relationship to a need* or a function. In these cases the important thing is not the absolute quality of an item, but the suitability of the item in satisfying the particular need at hand. Thus, design engineers, users, and supply managers attempt to develop a material specification in which the quality characteristics of the specified material match closely with the quality characteristics needed to satisfactorily fulfill the functional requirements of the job. Consequently, in the *development* of product or material specifications, quality is defined relative to the need.

Once the specifications have been finalized, the specific requirements have been set for those who subsequently work with the specifications. For these people, especially supply management personnel and suppliers, quality is defined very simply—*conformance with the stated requirements.* A supply manager's responsibility, and a supplier's job, is to deliver material whose quality conforms satisfactorily to specification requirements.

The last two definitions are the ones with which supply managers regularly contend. As supply management works with users and suppliers in the development of material specifications, it is concerned with quality relative to a functional need. In dealing with suppliers' output quality levels, supply management is concerned with quality in the sense of its conformance to requirements.

A sound material specification represents a blend of four different considerations: (1) design requirements, (2) production factors, (3) commercial supply management considerations, and, frequently, (4) marketing factors. When dealing with the commercial considerations, supply management personnel should make the following investigations with respect to quality:

■ Study the quality requirements.

■ Ensure that quality requirements are completely and unambiguously stated in the specifications.

■ Investigate their reasonableness, relative to cost.

■ Ensure that specifications are written in a manner that permits competition among potential suppliers.

■ Determine whether existing suppliers can build the desired quality into the material.

■ Ensure the feasibility of the inspections and tests required to assure quality.

For some materials and components, such investigations are relatively simple. For others, they are extremely complex, involving highly technical considerations. Some firms, for example, include reliability or quality engineers on the supply management staff to assist with analysis of the more complex problems. When technical quality problems arise, a reliability engineer and supply manager jointly review the specifications to determine the appropriateness of the quality requirements. Working in a coordinating capacity, they make their recommendations to the design engineer, directing to his or her attention the potential quality problems arising from commercial considerations.

As discussed in the cross-functional teams chapter, many firms utilize a cross functional product development team in the overall design process. This approach is ideal for integrating the views of supply management, as well as the other appropriate functions, in the specification development process. In some cases it is desirable to involve appropriate designers or application engineers from the supplier's organization in the specifications development process before the specifications are finalized. Early cooperative involvement of these individuals frequently provides technical and manufacturing input from the supplier's perspective that is useful in reducing costs or in avoiding subsequent processing and quality problems in the supplier's operation. This type of cooperative activity is becoming more common in progressive buying organizations today. Clearly, supply management is responsible for planning and coordinating this type of supplier involvement.

Supplier Quality Analysis

Most firms can minimize their material quality problems simply by selecting competent and cooperative suppliers in the first place. The following paragraphs briefly discuss some of the methods used to achieve this objective.

Product Testing   One practical approach used in determining potential suppliers' quality capabilities is to test their products before purchasing them. The quality of most purchased materials can be determined by *engineering tests* or by *use tests*. Usually such tests can be conducted by the buying firm; when this is not practical, commercial testing agencies can be employed.

The object of product testing is twofold: (1) to determine that a potential supplier's quality level is commensurate with the buying firm's quality needs, and (2) where feasible, to compare quality levels of several different suppliers. This permits the development of a list of qualified suppliers that the supply manager can compare on the basis of the quality/cost relationship.

Supply managers frequently utilize their own operating departments for the performance of use tests. It is not uncommon, for example, for a manager to test several brands of tires on his or her firm's vehicles during the course of regular operations. Although still feasible, use testing of most *production* parts and components is more difficult because tests often cannot be conducted until the buying firm's finished product is placed in service. In many cases, though, the buying firm's sales force is able to obtain feedback data on operating performance from customers. In such cases, various kinds of use tests can be conducted to compare the performance of different suppliers' components. Regardless of the method used, supply management usually needs the cooperation of other departments in setting up and conducting the tests. Consequently, the supply manager typically functions as an organizer and an administrator in coordinating the efforts of others.

A word of caution is appropriate, however, for the practitioner unskilled in experimental testing. Test results for products being compared must be obtained through well-designed experiments that permit *valid* comparisons. For example, mileage data on two sets of tires, each taken from a different truck, are not comparable if the two trucks were operated under significantly different conditions. The variables in the testing situation must be controlled to the extent that the results are truly comparable. A "comparison of apples with oranges" is of little value in the decision-making process.

Unfortunately, in conducting use tests without the benefit of controlled laboratory conditions, it may be difficult to generate truly comparable test data. Consequently, experience and judgment play an important role in determining the extent to which test results are comparable and, hence, useful. At times, interpretation of test data may also require a basic knowledge of statistical inference. While many supply managers have this background, it is essential to recognize when the help of an experienced statistician is required.

In firms that have testing laboratories for their engineering and research work, the supply management department has an additional resource to support its quality management activity. Such laboratories can take much of the experimental and interpretive burden off supply management's shoulders. In addition, they are usually equipped to conduct more precise and sophisticated tests with greater speed and ease than use testing allows. An example will illustrate the point. One of IBM's computer-manufacturing plants has an electronic testing laboratory used primarily for research and development work. The laboratory, however, also serves the supply management department. Before new electronic components are purchased for assembly into IBM products, a sample of each new component is subjected to rigorous tests in this laboratory to determine whether its performance characteristics meet the company's quality specifications.

Firms without testing laboratories frequently use one of the many commercial testing laboratories located throughout the country. A directory of these laboratories, indicating their locations and their types of services, is published annually by the U.S. Department of Commerce.

Proposal Analysis   A second point at which supply management can assess a potential supplier's quality capabilities is in the proposal analysis. Firms indicate in their proposals, either directly or indirectly, how they intend to comply with the quality requirements of the purchase. The supply manager must be especially alert in detecting areas of misinterpretation or possible areas of overemphasis by the prospective supplier that could result in excessive costs. In purchases with critical quality requirements, the trend today is to *require* potential suppliers to state *explicitly* how they plan to achieve the specified quality level with consistency.

For those potential suppliers whose written proposals survive the supply manager's analysis, the next step in evaluating quality capabilities is an on-site capability survey. Because of the time and expense involved, most companies conduct this survey only for their more important purchases and for government contracts requiring it. In inspecting a prospective supplier's facilities and records, and in talking with management and operating personnel, the buying firm's investigating team attempts to answer questions such as these:

■ What is the firm's basic policy with respect to product quality and quality control?

■ What is the general attitude of operators and supervisors toward quality? Does the firm utilize a specific quality program that focuses attention on the attitudes of people toward quality and responsibilities assumed by each individual for high-quality work?[38]

■ Does the prospective supplier use statistical methods to reduce process variation?

■ What is the prospective supplier's engineering/production experience and ability with respect to this specific type of work?

■ Is the production equipment capable of consistently producing the quality of work required?

■ Exactly how is the firm organized to control quality and to what extent does quality receive management support?

■ What specific quality measurement techniques and test equipment does the prospective supplier employ? Is statistical process control utilized effectively?

These questions make it clear that a supply manager alone usually cannot conduct an effective survey; rather, the endeavor must be a *team effort.* Specialists from design and process engineering, quality assurance, and sometimes maintenance are needed to give professional interpretation to the facts the survey uncovers. The supply manager's major responsibility in such an endeavor is to organize and coordinate the efforts of these specialists and to make a composite evaluation of the potential supplier, considering the findings of all team members.

Inspection Dependence

Even with the continuing improvement of quality systems to prevent defects, most firms maintain a traditional inspection department. In addition, some selected operations in both the buying firm's and the supplying firm's plants may still require either 100 percent or sampling inspection. This is particularly true in some cases following certain

---

[38]For two classic discussions about the individual's responsibility for quality, see William Ouchi, "The Q-C Circle," *Theory Z* (Reading, MA: Addison-Wesley, 1981), pp. 261–68; and Robert M. Smith, "Zero-Defects and You," *Management Services,* January–February 1966, pp. 35–38.

types of assembly or final assembly operations. In any case, to some extent inspection activities are still part of a supply manager's world—and for this reason, the topic is discussed briefly in the next few paragraphs.

Receiving and Inspection Procedure   If a shipment is coming from a certified or a JIT supplier, it may go directly to the point of use, bypassing the traditional receiving and inspection operations. In a majority of cases, however, when a purchase order is issued, the receiving and inspection departments both receive electronic or paper copies of the order, which specifies the inspection the material is to receive. When a shipment arrives, receiving personnel check the material against the supplier's packing slip and against the purchase order to ensure that the firm has actually received the material ordered. This is the basis for subsequent invoice/payment approvals. The receiving clerk then visually inspects the material (looking for shipping damage and so on) to determine its general condition. Finally, a receiving report is prepared on which the results of the investigation are noted. In some cases, no further inspection is required. In the case of more complex materials, a copy of the receiving report is forwarded to the inspection department, advising it that material on a given order has been placed in the "pending inspection" area and is ready for technical inspection.

The inspection department performs the specified technical inspection on a sample or on the entire lot, as appropriate, and prepares an inspection report indicating the results of the inspection. If the material fails to meet specifications, a more detailed report is usually completed describing the reasons for rejection. Rejected material, in some cases, is clearly useless to the buying firm, and the supply management department immediately arranges with the supplier for its disposition. In other situations, the most desirable course of action is less clear-cut. The buying firm often has three alternative courses of action:

1. Return the material to the supplier.
2. Keep some of the more acceptable material and return the rest.
3. Keep all the material and rework it to the point where it is acceptable. (From a strategic point of view, this is not a good alternative. It says to the supplier that it is permissible to ship off-spec material, and it can be interpreted as an invitation to do it again.)

Cases involving rework may be sent to a materials review board for study and decision. A typical board is composed primarily of personnel from production, production control, quality, and supply management. After the board reaches its decision, the appropriate papers are sent to the supply manager, who concludes final cost negotiations with the supplier.

Technical Inspection   Before a contract or a purchase order is issued, quality control personnel, in conjunction with engineering and supply management, should decide what type of inspection the incoming material will require to ensure that it meets specification requirements. If the supplier is certified, perhaps no inspection will be required. If the supplier is using SPC in the item's production, it may be sufficient simply to review the supplier's control charts for selected processing operations to determine if further inspection is required. In other cases sampling inspection may be desirable,[39] and in still other situations 100 percent inspection may be required.[40]

The most common sampling methods are single, double, and sequential. Single sampling is the most common approach. With single sampling, one sample is taken from a production lot and the lot is rejected or accepted based on a metric such as percentage of good units. In double sampling, if the first sample taken fails, then a second sample is taken to assure that the lot should be rejected. Sequential sampling requires a range between acceptable and unacceptable levels of failures be established. If the first sample falls between these levels then another sample is taken and the cumulative results are calculated. If the cumulative results lie between the acceptable and unacceptable limits, then another sample is taken. Samples continue to be taken until the cumulative results of all samples exceeds a limit, at which point the lot is accepted or rejected. The primary reason companies prefer to use double or sequential sampling is that smaller sample sizes can be taken initially, thereby reducing sampling cost.

In all cases, quality personnel should prepare a technical inspection plan. Key information from the plan should then be communicated to the supplier on the purchase order or a related contractual document. In this way, appropriate people in both organizations are fully aware of the procedures to be followed and can work together toward that end.

Defect Detection Systems   To control the quality of production materials entering a manufacturing or assembly operation, companies have historically utilized defect detection systems using inspection. That is, after a batch of items has been produced at one step in the process, the items are inspected to identify the ones that do not meet the design specification. Those that do not are reworked or scrapped, and the good items pass on to the next processing operation. Frequently, though not always, a similar inspection activity is also conducted after this operation, and so on through the entire manufacturing process until a finished product is produced.

Three basic problems are inherent in the defect detection type of operation. First, there tends to be some duplication of inspection activity, both within the supplier's manufacturing operation and between the buying firm's and the supplier's operations. Second, a very large number of items are inspected. Third, *and most important*, defective items are found only after they are finished (or semifinished)—after the mistakes have been made and after substantial processing costs have been incurred.

---

[39]Industry uses a wide variety of statistical sampling plans. Two of the more commonly used sources are Dodge and Romig, *Sampling Inspection Tables-Single and Double Sampling* (New York: John Wiley & Sons,); and Freeman, Friedman, Mosteller, and Wallis, *Sampling Inspection* (New York: McGraw-Hill,). The Dodge and Romig tables are designed specifically to minimize total sampling. Sampling inspection, by Freeman et al., contains plans which are particularly useful in inspecting material coming from statistically controlled production processes. These plans tend to minimize the "consumer's risk" of accepting off-spec material.

[40]In many types of inspection activities involving human operation or judgment, experience indicates that 100 percent inspection may detect only 80 to 95 percent of the defects present. Consequently, when quality is extremely critical, a second inspection operation may be required.

Defect detection systems are inefficient and expensive. Because they require time and resources to execute, there is a tendency to cut back on inspection and to reduce the standards, resulting in the acceptance of some off-spec items. Cutbacks usually occur in the interest of cost control and maintenance of production schedules. The bottom line is that in many firms using this system, quality levels tend to be inconsistent and perhaps lower than originally planned.

In Deming's 14 Points given earlier in this chapter, one of the points is to cease dependence on inspection. To alleviate the problems inherent in most defect detection systems, Deming proposed the use of a *defect prevention* system. The idea is to identify operating (process) problems that may produce defective items, preferably before any defective products are produced. This approach monitors the output of a process as it occurs and identifies unacceptable process changes soon after they occur. When an unsatisfactory situation is identified, the process is stopped and the operating cause (tool wear, machine adjustment, operator error, and so on) is determined. Appropriate corrective action on the operating system is then taken to prevent the production of more defectives. The specific technique Deming suggested to use to detect such process changes was *SPC*. A defect prevention system utilizing SPC is shown in simplified graphic form in Figure 7.7.[41]

Another approach to preventing defects and reducing the need for inspection in a repetitive manufacturing environment is to implement jidoka, championed by Ohno while he was with Toyota. Jidoka uses an automatic mechanism to stop the entire production system whenever a defective part is found along the process line. Appropriate adjustments then take place so that major problems are prevented from arising in the future. This concept, apart from adhering to the principle of prevention rather than cure, can substantially save on work allocation times, since the worker needs to attend to the machine only when it stops because of a problem. Jidoka forces resolution of the cause of a problem at the source when it happens and is still traceable. The fact that Jidoka can shut down a production line highlights the importance of resolving the cause of the discrepancy, whereas defects discovered through traditional inspection are frequently not traced to the cause. As a result, traditional inspection procedures rarely reduce the need for the same inspection in the future.

Jidoka is usually coupled with the use of poka-yoke, which could be called another form of inspection; however, most poka-yoke methods do not delay the product flow in the way that traditional inspection does since poka-yoke builds the inspection into the process. In the early 1960s Shingo developed the concept of poka-yoke (or defect = 0), meaning mistake-proofing: source inspection is employed actively to identify process errors before they become defects; when an identification takes place, the process is stopped until the cause is determined and eliminated. Monitoring potential error sources takes place at every stage of the process, so that errors (leading to defects) are detected as soon as possible and corrected at the source, rather than at a later stage.

---

[41]Figure 7.7 was developed from material in Gordon K. Constable, "Statistical Process Control and Purchasing," *Freedom of Choice* (Tempe, AZ: National Association of Purchasing Management, 1987), p. 15.

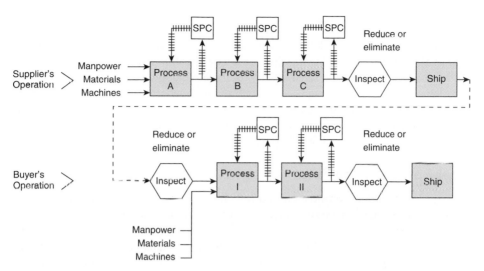

Figure 7.7 I Defect prevention concept

Needless to say, Ohno's and Shingo's techniques can be effective only if a certain (high) level of quality has already been built into the process as early as possible. This can be achieved through the use of appropriate statistical tools by the workers who should be allowed the initiative to eliminate bottlenecks and interruptions; also through proper cooperation with the suppliers of the process components. Otherwise, jidoka or poka-yoke will cause a prohibitively large number of stoppages, and cost-efficient production will never materialize.[42]

Critique   In summary, it is important that a buying organization develop some type of system that monitors a supplier's quality performance. Historically, defect detection systems have been widely used, but they are expensive and results frequently are not as effective as desired. In his classic book *Quality Is Free,* Philip Crosby summarizes the attitudes in American industry well in the following statement:[43]

> A prudent company makes certain that its products and services are delivered to the customer by a management system that does not condone rework, repair, waste, or nonconformance of any sort. These are expensive problems. They must not only be detected and resolved at the earliest moment, they must be prevented from occurring at all.

Once a defect prevention system is in place, benefits of improved quality control capability and reduced costs of quality flow to both the buying and supplying firms. Properly implemented, it should be a win-win situation that tends to improve cooperation and set the stage for a continuing relationship that is mutually beneficial.

---

[42]Logothetis, *Managing for Total Quality,* pp. 97–98.

[43]Philip B. Crosby, *Quality Is Free* (New York: Mentor New American Library, 1979), p. 106.

Supplier Development

A *cooperatively* developed defect prevention system, including appropriate training of suppliers' personnel by the buying firm, creates a situation that should enhance a supplier's motivation to perform satisfactorily for the buying firm. The anticipated prospect of follow-on business in a longer-term continuing collaborative relationship normally provides a significant incentive for the supplier to perform well in the quality area. We mention supplier development here in order to stress its importance and to refer the reader to the chapter in this book dedicated to supplier development.

Supplier Certification

The concept of supplier certification has been practiced by a number of progressive firms for years. However, the increased emphasis on quality in last two decades has sharpened the focus on the real values of a certification program. The certification concept recognizes the fact that a supplying firm's and a buying firm's quality systems are two parts of a larger quality system, and that through integration of the two the total costs associated with quality can be reduced.

Certification agreements take many forms, ranging from a simple supplier's guarantee of quality to a formally negotiated document that specifies the responsibilities of both parties for specifications, process design inspection procedures, SPC applications and training, reporting and correction procedures, and so forth. Although certification programs vary widely from firm to firm, the general approach to supplier certification involves three steps:

1. Qualification
2. Education
3. The certification performance process

Qualification   Because of the mutual trust and dependence that exists in a certification relationship, a supplier is not considered for certification until the buying organization has had a fairly lengthy positive experience with the firm. In addition to quality and reliability performance, the supply manager again verifies the broader supplier characteristics that are important to the relationship—management philosophy, financial stability, R&D capability, shop organization and management, manufacturing support capabilities including supply management, and so on.

The technical qualification requirements for certification typically are rigorous. They start with product and process design, tightened process capability studies, and a stringent quality capability survey to ensure mutual agreement on the quality system the supplier will employ. Applications for potential design of experiments and statistical process control are identified and the procedures are detailed. At this point in the process, the supply manager's quality personnel work with their counterparts in the supplier's organization to fine-tune the system and develop the procedures to be used in final inspection, but with the goal to eventually eliminate the need for final inspection.

Education   Two types of supplier education typically are required: The first deals with the buying organization's structure, people, mode of operation, and the resulting expectations for a certified supplier's performance; the second focuses on specific quality concepts and techniques that may be new to the supplier but that are needed for successful operation—such as various applications of SPC, unique inspection measurement techniques, the philosophy of Six Sigma or TQM, and so forth.

The extent to which education is required obviously varies from supplier to supplier. The important point, however, is that the buying firm must assume responsibility for ensuring that the education function is accomplished. In some cases, this education must continue upward through the supply chain to the supplier's suppliers.

The Certification Performance Process   To use an old operations expression, this is where "the rubber meets the road." The supplier must now demonstrate that it can meet the buying firm's requirements for certification.

After the manufacturing and assembly processes are stabilized and the quality assurance system is in place, the supplier's test period is begun. Initially both parties subject the supplier's output to 100 percent inspection. This process facilitates the identification and correction of unanticipated problems. When the predetermined quality level has been maintained for a specified period of time, full inspection is replaced by sampling inspection of declining severity as quality levels are maintained. At some point in the process, the supplier provides key evidence of implementing proactive quality management methods, such as SPC control charts, to the buying firm for continued analysis. And periodically the buying firm's quality expert visits the supplier's plant to ensure that control tests are being conducted appropriately. This process is continued for a period of perhaps six months to several years, depending on the specifics of a given operation, until the predetermined quality performance requirements have been fulfilled.

Once a supplier has gained certification, the buying firm's goal is to do very little, if any, inspection of incoming materials. When possible, material is delivered directly to the point of use after the required receiving activities. Periodically, however, the buying organization checks supplier performance in one of several ways: (1) by reviewing the supplier's critical manufacturing operations through their control charts and other statistical outputs, (2) by using a minimal sampling inspection program, (3) by reviewing test reports from the buying firm's laboratories, and (4) by periodic visits to the supplier's plant.

The concept of supplier certification fits very logically with supplier quality and collaborative arrangements, but there are potential problems:[44]

■ Once a process has been "certified," it tends to be perceived as "unchangeable."
■ The process of documentation and then certification can be long and resource consuming, such that once documentation does exist, companies don't want to commit the additional resources to improve it.
■ Quite a few organizations have a team of full-time staff dedicated to maintaining certification documents and conducting internal compliance audits—but have fewer or no people focused on actually improving the processes.
■ Some companies do use their certification efforts to improve their processes, but such instances are relatively rare.

[44]Pande et al., *The Six Sigma Way,* p. 63.

Despite these potential problems, firms that have used certification programs generally have experienced favorable results. Inspection costs typically are reduced while quality levels usually remain high. Most suppliers take pride in being included on a customer's certification list. They are also aware that good performance places them in a favored position to receive additional business.

Concluding Remarks

Quality management is a major component of supply management's supplier performance management responsibility. Quality failures lead directly to costly difficulties that reduce productivity, profit, and often market share. To preclude such losses, supply management should participate creatively in the corporate quality management program and in the firm's critical supplier quality efforts.

To contribute most effectively to the organizational effort, supply management's role in the program should include (1) participation in the development of specifications; (2) participation in the selection of appropriate quality control, inspection, and test requirements; (3) active involvement in analysis and development of proactive prevention measures at the supplier's facility; (4) the selection and motivation of qualified suppliers; and (5) the subsequent monitoring and nurturing of the ongoing relationships between the buying and supplying firms.

Beth's experience in "the quality walk" at the beginning of the chapter emphasizes the importance of assessing quality management prior to entering into critical contracts with suppliers. All supply managers should have at least a rudimentary understanding of quality systems, tools of quality, process capability analysis, and statistical process control (SPC) concepts. A World Class Supply Management[SM] firm views its quality system and the supplier's quality system as two parts of a single integrated system. The supply manager responsible for developing the relationship between the buying and selling firms is the "person in the middle" of this integrated system. He or she first must be able to cooperate with in-house quality people in designing and making operating decisions about the firm's quality system. Finally, because the supply manager is the key communication link with suppliers, he or she must be able to deal with them effectively on a wide variety of quality issues.

CHAPTER 8

Total Cost of Ownership (TCO)[1]

To achieve World Class Supply Management^{SM}, managers must shift their focus from price to total cost.

KEY CONCEPTS

[1]Appreciation is expressed to Ray Hummell of the University of San Diego for his assistance in writing this chapter.

Case

Purchase Price: Just *One* Component of Cost

Adam Smith, the supply manager of Invisible Hand Research (IHR), is in the market for a new copier. The current copier, a five-year-old Xero model PDS 10/10 (known by the staff as the Pretty Darn Slow 10 copies/10 minutes), is down again. It's 8:15 A.M. and the coffeemaker hasn't even finished filling the first pot. The service firm won't arrive until tomorrow morning and there is a backlog of customers' orders.

How should Adam proceed? One choice is to get a new copier as quickly as possible. Another is to find the least expensive copier designed to handle IHR's current monthly copy requirements. Perhaps the best choice is to spend some time and analyze the short- and long-run copier requirements with regard to purchase price, ownership costs, and post-ownership costs.

Purchase price alone is not a guarantee of meeting office copier needs. In this case, ownership *costs,* both quantitative and qualitative, should play a major role in selection of the new copier. These costs may include those related to per copy costs, reliability, copy quality, warranty, service response time, operator frustration, financing (e.g., leasing versus buying), upgradability, ease of use, and functionality. Post-ownership costs may include those related to trade-in or disposal value and environmental waste concerns. A generally accepted figure is that the purchase price makes up from 30 to 50 percent of the total cost of ownership of a capital purchase.[2]

Adam should minimize the total cost of ownership over the life of the copier. In some cases, a low purchase price may be only the beginning of inefficiency and frustration. Durable/capital goods purchases such as copiers, cars and trucks, production machinery, computers, furniture, and fixtures will usually benefit from a TCO analysis, as will direct materials (manufacturing), or even nondurable, personal purchases such as clothing. Actually, almost any purchase decision may benefit when one embraces the *philosophy* of TCO.[3]

The Importance of Total Cost of Ownership (TCO) in Supply Management

As Adam will learn, purchase price is only one component of the cost of purchasing material, a product, or a service. TCO should be a permanent concept in every supply management professional's mind whether in a service, retail, or manufacturing firm. Overemphasis on acquisition cost/purchase price frequently results in a failure to address other significant ownership and post-ownership costs. Total cost of ownership is a

---

[2]Lisa M. Ellram, "A Structured Method for Applying Purchasing Cost Management Tools," *International Journal of Purchasing and Materials Management,* Winter 1996.

[3]Ibid. According to Lisa Ellram, "[A TCO analysis] tends to be fairly time consuming to complete. Thus, it generally is not worthwhile with low-value or low-impact items. However, if an organization has a fully automated approach to capturing costs, this technique can and should be applied to all major purchase decisions. This technique can also be a useful tool for continuous improvement when used as a strategic cost analysis technique."

philosophy for really understanding all supply chain–related costs of doing business with a particular supplier for a particular good or service.[4]

Some typical ownership costs include those associated with processing inventory (direct materials), repair, maintenance, warranty, training, operating, inventory carrying, contract administration, and downtime cost for operating equipment. Post-ownership costs may include those of disposal and environmental cleanup. The addition of risk and its associated costs adds yet another dimension. These costs and others must be estimated and included in a total cost analysis.

TCO is relevant not only for the firm that wants to reduce its cost of doing business, but also for the firm that aims to design products or services that provide the lowest total cost of ownership to end customers. For example, some automobile manufacturers have extended the tune-up interval on many models to 100,000 miles, thus reducing the vehicle operating cost for the car owner.

TCO analysis draws from a variety of disciplines such as finance (Net Present Value [NPV] analysis), accounting (product pricing and costing), operations management (reliability and quality), marketing (understanding and meeting customer wants), information technology (systems integration and e-commerce), logistics (material movement), and economics (minimum average total unit cost of production). The best and, perhaps, only way of addressing all relevant costs is to employ a cross-functional team representing the key stakeholders.

Supply management personnel can facilitate the TCO analysis by combining their broad-based analytical skills with those of other team members to ensure that all relevant costs are considered. A brief examination of each type of business together with supply management's vision and role in minimizing total costs is a good place to begin.

Service Providers

Service firms provide "intangible" products to satisfy human wants and needs. Service providers run the gamut from the accounting, legal, and medical professions to federal, state, and local governments to window washers, gardeners, and taxi drivers. Service providers procure capital equipment, products, and services as well as hire employees and provide employee benefits such as health and life insurance.

Like all businesses, service firms enhance profitability by increasing sales at a faster rate than costs, maintaining sales and reducing costs, or increasing sales and reducing costs, while maintaining the desired quality and timeliness. Understanding what drives the cost of overhead expenditures is crucial to any service business. Service revenue must cover the direct costs, material and labor, and overhead in order to generate a profit. Depreciation is a key element of overhead. We define depreciation as the systematic transfer of the cost of a capital expenditure (an asset on the balance sheet) to expense (the income statement). Another important cost element is the cost of maintaining capital and operating equipment. A TCO analysis of equipment purchases may help reduce the expenditures for maintenance and parts over the lives of the investments.

---

[4]Lisa M. Ellram, Seminar on Strategic Cost Management for Purchasing Professionals held at NAPM Convention, San Diego, CA, May 1999.

An important consideration in service businesses, as well as in retail and manufacturing, is the total cost of maintaining the employee base. Paying the lowest wage does not necessarily result in the best employee. The cost of getting a new and inexperienced employee "up to speed" can be high, and the learning curve (addressed in Chapter 18) may be long. Paying more for an experienced person with a short "ramp up" time may be the best long-run solution for a given position. A total cost/total benefit analysis of company-sponsored health insurance programs can reap rewards in terms of lower per person total costs, greater benefits for covered employees, and improved morale.

Retail

The considerations that apply to service businesses also apply to retailers. Retail businesses sell a product that often must be ordered, received, inventoried, sold, and perhaps, delivered to the customer. The choice of a system that facilitates the processes involved in inventory ordering and turnover will influence the total cost of inventory ownership. Many major retailers have empowered select suppliers to manage their product inventory for them,[5] thus reducing purchasing overhead and inventory carrying costs without necessarily increasing the product cost. Embracing the Just-in-Time (JIT) philosophy is another way to improve QCT (quality, cost, and time) while reducing TCO. Lowering the cost of goods sold and the overhead costs associated with procurement, inventory carrying costs, and sales improve the bottom line. It is often easier to lower costs than to increase sales in a competitive business environment.

A retail business may own a product for a short time, but may be responsible for after-sale adjustments, warranty claims, and maintaining general customer satisfaction for an indefinite period. If a retailer selects an item or product for sale solely based on price,[6] thus ignoring reliability and product liability issues, customer satisfaction and future sales may suffer. Further, the retailer may incur an increased risk of financial and/or moral liability. Retailers must know their customer base and tailor the products they sell to satisfy that base. Retailers must also consider the long-term effects of every purchase made for resale.

Manufacturing

Manufacturing businesses are concerned with the same TCO issues as are service and retail firms. In addition, they procure direct materials (raw materials, products, subassemblies, etc.) and incur overhead in the production of their finished goods inventory and other activities required to conduct business. Managerial accountants place emphasis on the variance between what something "should cost" or is expected to cost and what it actually costs. Price variance analyses are often misleading. For example, a favorable price variance (the material cost less than anticipated), when compared to an unfavorable quantity variance (more material was used than anticipated), may indicate

---

[5]The acronym for suppliers managing inventory at the buyer's site is VMI, which stands for vendor managed inventory.

[6]Usually, this reflects the reliability and quality of the product, i.e., "you get what you pay for."

that although the material was less expensive, it was of a lower quality and, therefore, more was used. If one compares this to an unfavorable labor efficiency variance (more labor was used to work with the material than anticipated), it becomes clear that a lower acquisition price may translate into higher production costs. Considering all costs simultaneously, supply management professionals and other members of the product development team can better determine the right specifications for the material and ensure that suppliers meet these guidelines.

The accurate allocation of manufacturing overhead is a major factor in calculating the true unit cost of a product. Using the wrong cost driver (the process or activity that creates the need for overhead) can make a product seem more or less expensive than it actually is. Activity Based Costing (ABC), although initially somewhat complicated and expensive to implement, can return long-run benefits by providing more accurate unit cost information that serves as the basis for better decisions. Careful budgeting and procurement of overhead items, from the purchase of capital equipment to lubricants used in production, and the implementation of systems to ensure the timely availability of accurate information are methods used in obtaining the lowest total cost of production.

Supply Chains/Supply Networks

A supply chain is a set of three or more entities (organizations or individuals) directly involved in the upstream and downstream flows of products, services, finances, and/or information from a source to a customer.[7] A supply network is a less linear, more flexible virtual system linked by advanced communication systems and enhanced supplier alliances. (See Figures 1-2, 1-3, and discussion in Chapter 1.) A supply management professional/organization can apply the philosophy and practice of TCO to the strategic optimization of costs within the chain or network. For example, an American company with the option of making a new product in Asia (potentially lower manufacturing costs) and shipping it to their customer base in the United States (higher transportation costs) or manufacturing it in the United States (potentially higher manufacturing costs) with minimal shipping (lower transportation costs) will have to determine the total cost of each alternative before making a decision. This TCO analysis should include[8] the study of:

- The manufacturability of the product (value engineering/value analysis).
- The manufacturing infrastructure requirements (the basic facilities, services, and installations needed for the optimal functioning of the manufacturing operation).
- Whether to outsource or self-manufacture.
- The abilities/location/responsiveness of potential tier two, three, . . . suppliers relative to the manufacturing operation.
- The structure of foreign and domestic tariffs/duties/taxes.
- The costs of transportation and the timeliness of delivery.
- Foreign business/labor/environmental regulations.

---

[7]John T. Mentzer et al., *Journal of Business Logistics* 22, no. 2, p. 4.

[8]The bulleted list provides some general considerations and is by no means exhaustive.

- Foreign political/economic stability.
- Foreign exchange risk.
- Language/communication requirements.
- Volatility of end-customer demand and the responsiveness of the network to changes in that demand.
- Inventory carrying costs (investment versus service levels).
- Inventory risk (relocation, damage, obsolescence, shrinkage).
- Quality costs.

Although much of this analysis is ultimately quantifiable in dollars, some elements will require a qualitative evaluation offering less certainty. In this example, Asia may seem, at first, the logical choice, but distance from the customer base and other international issues may guide the decision to domestic production.

The Three Components of Total Cost

Acquisition Costs

Acquisition costs are the initial costs associated with the purchase of materials, products, and services. They are not long-term costs of ownership, but rather represent an immediate cash outflow. Scrutinizing purchase price, planning costs, quality costs, taxes, and financing costs to determine the lowest total cost of ownership/usage may provide significant savings.

Purchase Price   The price paid for direct and indirect materials, a product, or a service is often a major component of the item's total cost. Acquisition costs may include the costs of freight and delivery, site preparation (capital purchases), initial training, installation, and testing. Supply management professionals can reduce acquisition costs by negotiating effectively, obtaining quantity discounts, standardizing specifications, and completing a value analysis. In addition, strategic cost analysis offers methods of analyzing and understanding suppliers' costs—allowing for more fruitful negotiations and enhancement of supplier relationships. The purchase of used materials and equipment of acceptable quality is another way to lower acquisition costs. A supply management professional must not compromise long-term ownership costs by focusing on purchase price alone.

Planning Costs   Costs incurred during the acquisition process include the costs of developing requirements and specifications, performing price and cost analysis, supplier selection/sourcing, contract determination, initial order processing, and monitoring. Increasing the spending in these areas while following World Class Supply Management^{SM} (WCSM) principles and processes can reduce future ownership/use costs. For example, during the development phase of a new product, time spent with engineering representatives and the supplier to replace custom parts with standardized ones will generally reduce the initial purchase price, as well as future repair, replacement, and inventory carrying costs.

Subscribing to e-procurement, B2B e-commerce, or electronic supply networks provides many businesses with a means to lower acquisition costs by reducing or eliminating overhead such as the time-consuming research and paperwork often associated with ordering the best product or service to satisfy specifications. The higher initial development and start-up costs are negated by the potential benefits of better communication, more information, reduced clerical overhead, and lower purchase costs.

Quality Costs The higher initial cost of engineered-in quality during the design phase generally lowers future ownership and post-ownership costs for both the purchaser and the customer. Selecting and certifying a supplier to obtain the optimal level of quality and monitoring the results using, for example, design of experiments and statistical process control ensures the achievement of the desired quality. In addition, the *quality* of the relationship established during this process can have long-run benefits. Long-term strategic relationships improve communications and may facilitate product innovation and cost reduction, especially in a cross-functional environment. Costs associated with quality are discussed in detail in Chapter 7.

Taxes According to Richard Janis, a partner with KPMG LLP, a firm that sources internationally must address the impact of taxes, both direct (e.g., duties, processing fees) and indirect (e.g., foreign fuel taxes, tolls, facility fees), on the cost of procured materials and products. "Companies spend endless hours haggling over freight rates, the cost of warehousing services, and the purchase price of goods. But they typically pay little attention to the hidden expenses that can inflate a supply chain's costs. And one of the most pervasive of these is taxes. Supply chain managers need to sit down with their tax colleagues to minimize the global impact of all taxes on supply chain operations."[9] Janis adds that when sourcing nationally, the firm must consider differences in state and local taxes. Experienced tax professionals must be included in the cross-functional team when taxes are a concern. Janis provides examples of solutions to reduce acquisition costs by minimizing taxes:

- **Customs duties and tariffs**—focus on compliance to eliminate penalties and on planning to ensure the proper tariff classifications with the lowest rates are applied.
- **Virtual warehouses**—in the EU, for example, information about goods can flow through a centralized virtual customs clearinghouse while goods would move unhindered from source to destination.
- **Regional trade agreements/free trade zones**—source and/or produce in free trade areas that reduce or eliminate duties on all or part of a product.
- **Income-base shifting**—use transfer pricing to legally shift income from high-tax areas to lower-tax areas.

The impact of taxes can be significant. The added cost of addressing domestic and international tax issues, up front, may have a significant effect in reducing the purchase price.

---

[9]Richard Janis, "Taxes: The Hidden Supply Chain Cost," *Supply Chain Management Review,* Winter 2000, pp. 72–77.

Financing Costs   Whether purchasing inventory and materials, opening new facilities, or investing in equipment, the acquisition team should consider the quantitative and qualitative costs of financing alternatives, which are considered ongoing acquisition costs. A business can finance an acquisition using surplus cash, debt financing (secured and unsecured term loans, mortgages, revolving lines of credit, capital leases, sale-leaseback arrangements, bonds, securitization of receivables, etc.), or equity financing (issue different classes of stock, form new partnerships and joint-ventures, etc.). Each form of financing has costs and benefits. The creditworthiness of the firm (cash flow, profitability, debt load, future sales) and the expected return on the investment are key variables in making this determination. The cost of money is normally not a supply management professional's concern, but must be considered by the firm.

Ownership Costs

Ownership costs are the costs, after the initial purchase, associated with the ongoing use of a purchased product, material, or item of equipment. Ownership costs are both quantitative and qualitative. Examples of costs that are quantifiable include energy usage, downtime, scheduled maintenance, repair, and financing. Qualitative costs, although difficult to quantify, remain important considerations when making purchases. Examples of qualitative costs include ease of use (is it a time saver?), aesthetic (psychologically pleasing to the eye), and ergonomic (maximize productivity, reduce fatigue). The sum of both types of costs may exceed the initial purchase price and have a significant bearing on cash flow, profitability, and even employee morale and productivity. Understanding and minimizing these costs can have strategic significance. The supply management professional considers the following additional cost categories before making a significant purchase decision.

Downtime Costs   Making a purchase decision based solely on purchase price may have long-term implications depending on the reason for the lower price. A seller may discount a premium item to move excess inventory and to increase sales. It may also want to dump a troublesome product on an unsuspecting purchaser. A new entrant in the market may discount an unproven product in an effort to increase market share. Often the selling price is representative of the quality of the product—presumably, the higher the price, the higher the quality. Whatever the reason, the long-run costs associated with a purchase may include non–value-added downtime. Costs associated with downtime include, for example:

■   Reduced production volume and idle resources in a manufacturing environment. Downtime is often caused by unreliable and/or inflexible equipment or direct materials that are substandard or misspecified in the design stage. Downtime for an automobile production line can run $27,000 per minute.[10]

■   Opportunity cost of lost sales due to lower production volume.

---

[10]Personal interview with R. David Nelson, former Senior VP of Purchasing of Honda America Manufacturing, October 14, 1998.

■ Goodwill costs due to undelivered or late orders, resulting in unhappy customers. Careful scrutiny of reliability and dependability problems can reduce the cost of downtime.

Risk Costs Weighing the risk of an inventory stock-out in a retail or manufacturing business against the opportunity cost of maintaining excess inventory is an important issue. Keeping extra inventory *just in case* can be a stopgap decision or a needlessly costly move. In just-in-time literature, just-in-case inventory is treated as a form of waste that a company should endeavor to reduce or eliminate. Some costs of excess inventory include those associated with financing, reduced cash flow, lost interest on cash flow, obsolescence, theft, and additional floor space.

Consider risk costs when purchasing from new suppliers (issue: dependability—risk avoidance maneuver: multiple sourcing); using new materials, processes, and equipment in manufacturing (issues: reliability, flexibility, suitability—risk avoidance maneuver: parallel processing); hiring new employees (issue: adaptability—risk avoidance maneuver: additional training and backup personnel), or choosing legal representation (issue: expertise—risk avoidance maneuver: multiple representation).

Careful investigation and the development of appropriate sources of supply will reduce the inherent risk associated with the unknown, untried, and unproven. The appropriate place to begin is in the planning or acquisition stage at which time a risk assessment study should be conducted. Spending up front to reduce risk is an investment in the long-run efficiency and profitability of any firm.

Cycle Time Costs Whether decreasing a new product's time-to-market or increasing the number of items produced in an hour (throughput), reducing cycle time can increase profitability and ROI via lower total costs. An organization that subscribes to the WCSM vision and philosophy will apply the principles discussed throughout this text to shorten the time to complete all relevant purchasing and production activities. Practices that a supply management professional can employ that may have significant impact include implementing JIT materials management, forming strategic alliances with key suppliers, and establishing cross-functional alliances within the organization. The higher initial cost of establishing and implementing these goals will provide long-run savings in the cost of direct material, direct labor, and manufacturing overhead. In addition, qualitative *savings* may accrue in the form of a smoother running, more *user-friendly* organization.

Conversion Costs Buying the wrong material whether in quality, form, or design can increase the cost of conversion (the application of direct labor and manufacturing overhead to direct materials to create a product or service). As discussed earlier, material not optimized for the production process can increase labor and overhead usage and thus, because throughput is decreased and the cost of maintaining the quality of the finished product is increased, the total cost of production. In addition, machine time, labor requirements, scrap, and rework may add to the unit cost. Spending too little time and money in the acquisition of materials may result in spending more time and money during production.

Other areas that affect conversion costs include production methods (assembly lines versus cells, labor-intensive versus automated production), employee training and working environment, and the methods of accounting for product costs, especially in the application of overhead costs to units of product. A well-informed and well-trained supply management professional may have the ability to influence decision-making in these areas when working in a cross-functional environment.

Non–Value-Added Costs   Non–value-added costs flourish in most businesses. It is estimated that some 40 percent of all costs add little or no value. Examples of non–value-added activities that add costs to a product or service include:

- Moving and stockpiling batches of direct materials and work-in-process inventory due to a poor factory layout, poor scheduling, and a variety of wastes that increase uncertainty in the outputs of the system.
- Maintaining cumbersome operating procedures that duplicate efforts and steps for no apparent reason.
- Routing daily service appointments in a random fashion rather than designing routes that minimize travel time.

Total Quality Management (TQM), continuous improvement, Activity Based Costing (ABC), and Activity Based Management (ABM) are incremental change approaches that help identify non–value-added activities. Process reengineering is a more radical approach to change that focuses on simplification and elimination of wasted effort.

Supply management professionals with a background in management, operations, manufacturing, finance, information technology, and logistics are qualified to make suggestions to suppliers (and suppliers' suppliers) that reduce non–value-added costs. A successful strategy, when possible and cost effective, is to visit a supplier's manufacturing site and observe how production takes place. Careful scrutiny may reveal a number of non–value-added costs that the supplier can reduce or eliminate, thus allowing for negotiations on lowering the supplier's price. Observing a service provider's processes, either on-site or at their place of operation, may reveal non–value-added costs that, when eliminated, will provide savings to both parties.

Supply Chain/Supply Network Costs   "If you process-map a supply chain and examine the material movement alone, such as the ins and outs of material flow from one organization to another, you will find many opportunities to eliminate waste."[11] Of course, waste adds unnecessary costs to purchased materials and services, as well as to logistics.

James E. Morehouse, a vice president for A. T. Kearney in Chicago, asserts that extended enterprises are beginning to develop and will hasten improved efficiency and cost reductions along the supply chain. He believes that "organizations will be outsourcing transportation, purchasing operations, manufacturing, warehousing, order entry, and customer service. As a result, organizations will be more integrated with their suppliers and customers in order to manage the total supply chain from raw materials to the ultimate customer, the only source of revenue."[12] A supply management professional should consider the following interrelated areas for developing better cost reduction strategies:

---

[11]Leroy Zimdars, C. P. M., former Director of Supply Chain Management for Harley-Davidson, quoted in John Yuva, "Reducing Costs through the Supply Chain," *Purchasing Today,* June 2000.
[12] Ibid.

- **Forecasting** — Improving customer demand forecasting and sharing the information downstream will allow more efficient scheduling and inventory management.
- **Administration** — Implementing EDI[13] within an organization and between members of the supply chain will facilitate communication, thus reducing purchasing time, paperwork, and errors.
- **Transportation** — Streamlining material movement through the chain will reduce supply chain cycle time.
- **Inventory** — Embracing a JIT-type philosophy will help reduce unnecessary stockpiling and movement of inventory; suppliers can share inventory type and level information.
- **Manufacturing** — Improving capital budgeting procedures and designing and developing manufacturing processes that provide quality, efficiency, and reliability will lower costs and improve quality.
- **Customer service** — Listening to the customer will help identify supply chain inefficiencies and blockages.
- **Supplier selection/supplier relationships** — Determining the appropriate source of supply and type of relationship (transactional, collaborative, or strategic alliance) with each supplier will minimize administrative overhead and focus on the lowest cost at the required quality.
- **Global sourcing** — Expanding sourcing internationally may provide cost savings and quality improvements by focusing on an international supplier's comparative advantage and utilizing EDI and available low-cost transportation.

Well-trained supply management professionals armed with this knowledge and the World Class Supply Management[SM] philosophy and vision can bring fresh insight to the table when developing TCO models and negotiating throughout the supply chain.

Post-Ownership Costs

In the past, salvage value and disposal costs were the major inputs required when estimating post-ownership costs of capital purchases. These costs could be estimated as cash inflows (such as the sale of used plant and equipment) or outflows (such as demolition of an obsolete facility). For many purchases, there was an established market that provided data to help estimate reasonable future values, for example, the Kelley Blue Book for used automobiles. An appraiser of industrial equipment could help estimate the future worth of plant and equipment. Often companies made investments claiming *absolute certainty* of future appreciation, although estimating actual appreciation required more information than was available (e.g., property in a major metropolitan area). Today, supply management professionals must address these issues. In addition, three other factors with potential long-term impact must be addressed when performing a TCO analysis on equipment, a plant, direct materials, a product, or a service: long-term environmental impact, unanticipated warranty and product liabilities, and the negative marketing implications of low customer satisfaction.

---

[13]EDI, or Electronic Data Interchange, is a very efficient means of transmitting large batches of data between customer and supplier firms.

Environmental Costs   Gasoline stations in California have faced the unplanned expenditure of replacing their underground gas storage tanks with more environmentally friendly models. They have also been required to sanitize the soil near the tank if leakage has occurred. This expenditure has cost many independent operators their businesses, devalued the property (if polluted and unsafe), and increased the margin required on each gallon of gas sold to help recover the expenditure. This type of post-ownership cost is becoming more common as environmental problems persist.

Warranty Costs   A poorly designed and produced product may have unanticipated warranty related costs. Tire tread difficulties that occurred between 1978 and 1980 and again in 2000 resulted in such a problem for Firestone. In 2000, General Electric, in cooperation with the Consumer Product Safety Commission, recalled selected dishwashers manufactured between April 1983 and January 1989 to rewire a defective slide switch (as an option, GE offered a rebate toward a new unit). After-sale costs such as replacements, returns, or allowances can accrue to service providers (e.g., a carpet cleaning company whose poorly trained employee inadvertently uses a cleaning solution that fades the carpet fibers) and retail companies (e.g., a department store that misrepresents a product's capabilities). A well-trained supply management professional participating in a cross-functional team in product or service design may point out potential warranty/recall costs early enough so that more emphasis is placed on designing and producing a defect-free and reliable product or service.

Product Liability Costs   Companies engaged in all types of business have faced unanticipated product liability costs because of poorly designed and/or produced products and services. Fuel tanks that explode on impact because of poor design; tire treads that separate because of poor design, inferior materials, and/or improper inflation by end users; faulty ignition switches that cause cars to stall at inopportune moments; ground beef with the *E.coli* bacillus from improper processing; lawyers and accountants who have not performed their services according to professional standards; retail outlets that sell defective merchandise—the list is long and the remedies usually require expenditures, often not covered by insurance reimbursement.

Customer Dissatisfaction Costs   Some 75 percent of field failures in consumer goods can be attributed to defects in purchased materials. Field failures lead to customer dissatisfaction. When a customer is dissatisfied with a product, he or she frequently shares this dissatisfaction with many friends and acquaintances, some of whom may be potential customers. This flow of negative publicity frequently results in lost sales or "customer dissatisfaction" costs.

TCO, Net Present Value Analysis (NPV), and Estimated Costs

One method of evaluating a potential capital investment is to analyze the present values of the initial expenditure (initial cash payment), the likely future revenue streams (cash receipts, or the reduction or elimination of expenses), and likely future expenditure streams (cash payments, or the reduction or elimination of revenues). Analysts discount the positive and negative streams using an interest rate usually referred to as the opportunity cost of holding capital—the minimum required rate of return a business expects to receive on its investment. The opportunity cost of capital is linked to the riskiness of the investment and the firms' capital structure.[14]

TCO and NPV analyses are very similar in philosophy. Both attempt to estimate and analyze the acquisition cost, operating costs, and post-ownership costs in terms of value likely to be received by the company—in addition, NPV analysis attempts to analyze revenues and other cash inflows. NPV uses the present value of a sum of future cash flows discounted by a required rate of return—the larger the positive net present value the more likely the investment will return more than required over its life. A net present value of zero (NPV = 0) is the point of indifference. An NPV greater than zero usually suggests that the investment should be accepted. A negative NPV indicates that the overall return will be less than the minimum rate of return required by the company for the investment. An example of an NPV analysis is presented in Table 8.1.

Table 8.1 provides an example that demonstrates, based on actual and *accurately* estimated cash inflows and outflows, that this machine would be an unattractive investment—the required rate of return is 20 percent and this investment returns 15.66 percent. Alternatively, the NPV is negative so the investment opportunity should be rejected. Other potential investments may be more attractive.[15] Qualitative considerations, which cannot be used in this calculation, may either support or not support this purchase. Obviously, poorly constructed estimates of future cash flows and discount rates may provide meaningless information.

TCO like NPV requires an analysis of the holding period of the asset. TCO focuses on estimating and analyzing the ownership and post-ownership costs. The following formula represents a simplified approach to TCO analysis:

$$\text{TCO} = A + P.V. \sum_{i=1}^{n} (T_i + O_i + M_i - S_n)$$

where:

$$\begin{aligned}
\text{TCO} &= \text{Total cost of ownership} \\
A &= \text{Acquisition cost} \\
P.V. &= \text{Present value} \\
T_i &= \text{Training costs in year } i \\
O_i &= \text{Operating cost in year } i \\
M_i &= \text{Maintenance cost in year } i \\
S_n &= \text{Salvage value in year } n
\end{aligned}$$

---

[14] In financial management literature the opportunity cost of capital is referred to as the "Weighted Average Cost of Capital" or WACC.

[15] This example does not consider the income tax on the revenue generated by the copier or the tax savings that accrue by depreciating the copier (known as the *depreciation tax shield*). Including the tax effects in this analysis will change the NPV results.

Table 8.1 | Net Present Value Analysis—*Copier*

Invisible Hand Research								
Required rate of return	**20.00%**							
Year	**NOW**	**1**	**2**	**3**	**4**	**5**	**6**	**Present Value**
Cost of machine including installation and testing (actual)	(120,000)							(120,000)
Manufacturer required overhaul (estimated)				(9,000)				(5,208)
Cash inflows generated by using machine (estimated)		40,000	40,000	40,000	40,000	40,000	40,000	133,020
Cash outflows incurred by using machine (estimated)		(7,000)	(7,000)	(7,000)	(7,000)	(7,000)	(7,000)	(23,279)
Salvage value (estimated)							7,500	2,512
Net present value of potential investment								(12,955)
(Alternative Method)								
Total of annual streams (from above)	(120,000)	33,000	33,000	24,000	33,000	33,000	40,500	
Required rate of return		20%	20%	20%	20%	20%	20%	
Sum of present value of annual streams equals net present value of potential investment	(120,000)	27,500	22,917	13,889	15,914	13,262	13,563	(12,955)
Internal rate of return	(120,000)	33,000	33,000	24,000	33,000	33,000	40,500	15.66%

Using the data presented in Table 8.1, the TCO calculation is shown in Table 8.2:

Table 8.2 | Sample TCO Calculation

Acquisition Cost = $120,000		*Present Value Formulas*
Present value of cash outflows for years 1–6 =	23,279	$7,000 [1/.20 - (1/.20(1 + .20)^6)]$ *
Present value of overhaul in year 3 =	5,208	$9,000/(1 + .20)^3$ †
Present value of salvage value in year 6 =	(2,512)	$7,500/(1 + .20)^6$ **
TCO =	$145,975	

*$PV_{\text{Annuity}} = CF[1/r - 1/r(1 + r)^t]$
CF = periodic cash inflow or outflow (must be the same each period)
r = discount rate per period (annual rate divided by the number of periods in one year)
t = total number of periods
†$PV = FV/(1+r)^t$
FV = future value of single cash inflow or outflow
r = discount rate per period (annual rate divided by the number of periods in one year)
t = total number of periods

(This type of analysis can be repeated on competing copiers—the copier with the lowest TCO should be the best choice, other considerations being equal.)

This analysis focuses on costs or cash outflows and not cash inflows. Additionally, it considers the present value of those outflows. Incorporating NPV analysis, when applicable, into a TCO analysis will provide additional input that will allow the analyst to make a sound recommendation between alternatives.

A note about estimated costs: Since TCO and NPV analyses require estimates of future costs of cash outflows, their reliability in providing useful information is only as good as the quality of the input data. A well-conceived analysis should rely on inputs provided by cross-functional representatives with specific knowledge of and interest in the subject of the analysis. The most interested team member might provide the estimate. For example, supply management provides data on purchase price; plant engineering provides an estimate of potential downtime; marketing provides an estimate of downtime and support costs; and manufacturing provides an estimate of productivity or efficiency costs, and so on. A good rule of thumb is to include relevant participants who want to be part of the process.

Another method of arriving at estimates is for the cross-functional team leader to propose a cost figure and submit it for discussion. Frequently, one or more team members will react by saying, "No, x is too much. It would be closer to y." Two other approaches of arriving at estimated costs include parametric (several variables which affect costs are addressed), and Delphi (the cross-functional team members reflect on and refine an initial guesstimate). Both approaches, when applied in a strict sense, tend to be needlessly costly.

Neither of these methods can quantify many intangible variables that may color a choice between alternatives or influence whether to proceed with an investment or not. For example, in choosing between a sports car and a sports utility vehicle, a cost analysis is often not enough. Many people use their vehicles to make a statement about themselves, so ego may hold more substance than cost in this instance. Similarly, a company may want to project an image that only an automobile with a higher TCO can provide. This image may or may not be quantifiable in terms of increased future sales or executive image. It can be difficult at times, if not impossible, to quantify cash inflows on purchases—in these instances a strict NPV analysis may be pointless.

Concluding Remarks

TCO is an analytical tool and a philosophy that supports management decision-making. A supply management professional can modify the TCO approach to support each major purchase decision, as well as integrate it into strategic cost analysis to support make or buy (outsourcing), pricing and costing, critical direct material purchases, and other decisions that require analysis of costs over time. TCO is also a powerful adjunct—for example, in evaluating employee benefit programs and aiding in analyses such as the total cost of implementing an integrated activity based costing system in a manufacturing business. Estimates are the basis of most ownership and post-ownership costs. The care with which a supply management professional, in a cross-functional team, estimates these costs will determine the effectiveness of the resulting analysis.

As a philosophy, TCO can become an active part of everyday decision-making. For example, TCO can help a family determine the total costs of maintaining a pet or choosing kitchen appliances. If the expression "There are no free lunches" is true, then everything we do has a tangible or intangible cost that can be analyzed if necessary.

SUPPLY MANAGEMENT IN ACTION

Implementing and Using TCO Principles at Scott Paper: Prepared by Robert Porter Lynch[16]

Prior to being acquired by Kimberly Clark several years ago, Scott Paper was one of the world's largest producers of paper, with 20 plants in nearly 20 countries.

The papermaking process requires that wet pulp slurry be deposited uniformly on a continuously moving fabric belt. The fabric belt (known as "fabric" in the industry) is approximately 12 feet wide and the belt is about 60 feet in circumference. Fabrics are woven to enable the water in the pulp to be drawn out through the fabric, so that when the pulp leaves the end of the belt, it is in a semi-solid, rather gelatinous form. Once leaving the fabric belt, the pulp goes onto other machines, which further dry and then press the pulp into paper. Fabrics cost approximately $25,000 each.

For years, each plant's procurement team had negotiated with fabric vendors. Knowing that the sales price was about $25,000 (a simple "component cost" to Scott), the procurement directors were always rewarded for driving costs down. Every buyer was trained in being a tough negotiator; they all knew that there was 5–10 percent that

---

[16]Case study contributed by Robert Porter Lynch, President, The Warren Company (http://www.warrenco.com).

should be driven out of the sales price. Each year the procurement group aimed to push prices down, thereby driving down the profit for the fabric manufacturers. At the end of the year, rewards were allocated to those buyers who got the most favorable pricing. Moreover, for years, Scott Paper's procurement department patted itself on the back for doing a wonderful job at keeping both the supplier's profits and Scott's prices low.

Scott Paper's profitability was among the lowest in the industry, making it ripe as a takeover target. Nevertheless, the purchasing managers were all confident that they were doing their part to get costs down to the lowest level possible.

In 1994, a new VP of Procurement, Ted Ramstad, arrived on the scene and began challenging traditional thinking. In an effort to understand the real cost of the fabric, Ted began conducting a reevaluation of cost. Internal data was gathered:

- While replacing fabrics, the paper machine must be shut down, at a cost of nearly $100,000/day to the paper company (because paper manufacturing requires a continuous process, and the machine is considered efficient only when it runs 24 hours a day).
- It takes about 8 hours to put fabric on a paper machine.
- Fabrics lasted an average of 40 days.
- Most fabrics broke on the machines.
- When a fabric broke, it normally had less than 10 percent wear.
- Seventeen companies supplied fabrics to Scott around the world. Each plant manager had a "favorite" supplier, but there was no compelling reason for using one supplier over another. Procurement assumed it could use the large number of suppliers in a competitive manner to keep the purchase prices low.
- Cost of Goods Sold (COGS) for most suppliers was about 35 percent and R&D was 3–5 percent.
- Most plants had 4–6 fabrics in inventory.

While most of the buyers were unconcerned about this information, Ramstad and his team, applying TCO thinking, began probing and asking more questions:

- How can we lengthen the time a fabric lasts on a machine?
- How long should a fabric last?
- Are we getting the *best* fabrics from our suppliers, or just the *cheapest?*
- What suppliers are providing the research and development to give us better performance from our fabrics?
- Would fewer suppliers give us volume-purchasing power?
- Could we build win-win incentives to get more value from our suppliers and their fabrics?
- Where is there significant "non–value-added" in the system?
- What benchmarks should we be using to be "best in class"?
- If the "absolute component cost" of a fabric is $25,000, what is the "Total Cost of Ownership," and how does this compare as a "relative competitive advantage (or disadvantage)"?

Armed with a new focus and an energetic spirit, Ramstad's team began a worldwide search for answers. Fabric suppliers were interviewed, and information was gathered regarding competitors, indicating:

■ The industry average fabric life span was 60 days.

■ The industry benchmark fabric life span for one paper producer was 470 days.

■ Only three suppliers were interested in helping Scott increase fabric longevity.

■ None of the suppliers believed their fabrics were at fault for Scott's low life span; all blamed either the operators or the machinery manufacturers.

A Crucial Juncture Now came the real test. In a "Simple Accounting, Component-Cost" world, fabrics clearly cost $25,000 apiece. However, Ramstad stuck his neck way out and maintained that this was only true in a narrow, "absolute" sense. In a broader, "relative advantage" perspective, the formulation of cost looked radically different. Ted decided to employ a variation of the traditional TCO methodology. He decided to look at the incremental cost of *not* purchasing the most intuitively attractive fabric (the one whose life is 470 days).

Here's what Ramstad's TCO calculations looked like:

■ *Fabric Cost:* If the highest standard benchmark life is 470 days and Scott's standard is only 40 days, the relative cost of the fabrics Scott was purchasing is really 470/40, or 11.75 times that of the highest-priced benchmarked competitor.

Therefore, $11.75 \times 25,000$ unit purchase cost = $293,750.

(To understand Relative Competitive Advantage, think of relative motion. Consider the analogy of driving down a highway at 40 miles per hour in the right-hand lane. The average competitors are in the middle lane, passing you at 60 mph. However, the Best-in-Class competitor flies by in the left lane at 470 mph. This is the Relative Competitive Advantage view of costing.)

■ *Downtime Cost:* Add an additional 8-hour portion of $100,000 per day to reflect the downtime for changing the fabric (8hrs/24hrs $\times$ $100,000 = $33,333). Relative to the best-in-class competitor, Scott has to make 11.75 changes of the fabric compared to the best-in-class competitor's one change.

Additional downtime relative cost to Scott is $11.75 \times 33,333 = 391,663$.

■ *Burdened Labor Costs:* It takes two men 8 hours to change a fabric. At a burdened labor rate of $45/hour, the labor costs are $2 \times 45 \times 8 = 720$. Relative to the best-in-class competitor, Scott has to make 11.75 changes to the best-in-class competitor's one change.

Additional relative labor cost to Scott is $11.75 \times 720 = 8,460$.

■ *Incremental Cost of Purchasing the Low-Price Fabric:* Adding these figures, the results are overwhelming. Relative to the best-in-class, Scott's "relative disadvantaged cost" is $693,873![17] Very different from what was thought by procurement to be a $25,000 belt.

---

[17] Fabric cost ($293,750) + downtime ($391,663) + labor ($8,460) = $693,873.

The procurement group had naively engaged in myopic thinking; it was playing the game "too small." Squeezing the supplier for a 5–10 percent discount made no sense when the stakes were really about how to gain an advantage of nearly $700,000. This is a "strategic systems" view of cost, versus a "component cost" view.

Ramstad did not stop there. He saw the relative disadvantage to be multiplied by the number of plants globally. Therefore, by multiplying the "relative single plant competitive disadvantaged cost" by the 20 plants throughout the world, there was nearly $14 million of advantage to be gained on this single line item alone. (Note: The standard accounting systems at Scott could not measure this factor, and therefore it was "invisible" to the Chief Financial Officer, who steadfastly called this accounting hocus-pocus.)

Undaunted, Ramstad pressed on. He advocated that the problem was even worse, since much of this inventory was actually scrapped due to product redesign before the inventory was utilized. What's more, he took the position that if Scott bothered to add the time-value of money for financing the inventory of belts (because of frequent breakage several extra belts had to be kept on hand), the extra inventory was tying up capital. Eventually Ramstad was able to eliminate $20 million in inventory.

And it didn't stop there. By selecting the best-in-class suppliers, thereby reducing the number of suppliers to two globally, and negotiating long-term contracts, Ramstad was able to convince suppliers that they no longer needed to make sales calls on Scott's procurement officers. Sales costs were 35 percent of the component price. Ramstad persuaded the remaining suppliers to lower their prices 25 percent since they would not need to make sales calls, increase their R&D budgets to provide better products, provide technical support, and work with the machinery companies to improve sensing and tuning devices. Because of the higher volumes for the remaining two suppliers, the supplier's actual profits were substantially higher under the new model than previously. In addition, by not handling a continuous stream of bidding and contracting, which previously accounted for 3–5 percent of the cost of ownership, Ramstad was able to reduce the procurement force as well.

9
CHAPTER

e-Commerce II

e-Commerce provides many opportunities for supply chains and individual chain members to improve their efficiency and effectiveness at both the tactical and strategic levels. However, such possibilities must be tempered with the knowledge that no e-Commerce solution will ever be capable of replacing the human element that is at the core of truly successful supply chains. As such, e-Commerce is not a replacement but an enabler of World Class Supply Management^{SM}.

Case

Reverse Auctions: A Lively Topic

Javier Urioste, global procurement director of Policy and International Operations at IBM, stepped away from the front of the room to much applause at the 16th Annual Supply Chain Management Forum, held in November 2001 in San Diego, California.[1] He had just completed outlining the evolution of IBM's strategic sourcing and Internet strategies. Many of IBM's initiatives focused on leveraging e-Commerce to help develop and work with suppliers in collaborative relationships rather than pitting buyer and supplier against one other.

Javier also commented on IBM's policy of not engaging in online auctions. "Online auctions," Mr. Urioste stated, "are not consistent with the strategy of long-term relationships. Initial price reductions (as outcomes of auctions) are not sustainable (in future auctions for the same items or services) because they drive suppliers beyond the point of profitable reinvestment."

The next speaker, Steve Ogg, director of Supply Chain Management at Raytheon Electronic Systems, stepped to the front of the room with a big smile on his face. His

---

[1] The University of San Diego sponsors two to three forums per year on Supply Chain Management topics. Each forum has a different focus. This particular forum always focuses on Supply Management issues within SCM. Contact the University of San Diego Supply Chain Management Institute at 619-260-4894 for details of future forums.

presentation was titled "eCommerce at Raytheon," but Steve knew it focused on Raytheon's positive experiences with reverse auctions.

When Steve put the first slide up describing how Raytheon uses reverse auctions to reduce costs, the audience roared with laughter[2] at the irony of the timing. Steve noted, "At Raytheon the true market price is determined through reverse auctions." He presented compelling evidence of commodity product and service acquisition reverse auction price savings. Statistics compiled for 233 reverse auctions showed Raytheon had price savings averaging 22 percent.

The reverse auctions at Raytheon were run using FreeMarkets, a Pittsburgh-based e-Commerce provider. During the auctions, both Raytheon and suppliers could see the reverse bids visually, "live" on computer screens at many locations. The suppliers' names were disguised, but the real-time feedback of the auctions' progress was revealed to everyone. Raytheon's feedback from suppliers indicated that they, too, liked the auctions since they learned more about where they stood against their competition than with a traditional closed bid process. Steve pointed out that preparation was a key to successful auctions. He praised FreeMarkets in particular for its value-added service in helping Raytheon find and select qualified suppliers to participate in the auctions.

The timing of the two presentations could not have been orchestrated better. Both companies presented compelling reasons for either engaging or not engaging in reverse auctions. Reverse auctions are certainly one of the hottest e-Commerce issues today.

e-Commerce and Supply Management

e-Commerce, according to Schneider and Perry, authors of one of the top-selling textbooks on e-Commerce, is defined broadly as "activities conducted using electronic data transmission via the Internet and the World Wide Web." These elements include:[3]

- Consumer shopping on the Web, called business-to-consumer (or B2C).
- Transactions conducted between businesses on the World Wide Web, called business-to-business (or B2B).
- The transactions and business processes that support selling and supply management activities on the World Wide Web (B2B and B2C).

The Internet is the key to making e-Commerce for supply chains less expensive, quick, and reliable. The Internet is a large system of interconnected computer networks that spans the globe. Figure 9.1 provides a visual representation of a segment of the Internet showing how organizations are linked via servers to the Internet's backbone. The backbone enables connection to other organizations throughout the world. Using the Internet, individuals and companies can communicate with other individuals or companies. The part of the Internet known as the World Wide Web, or, more simply, the Web, is a subset of the computers on the Internet that are connected to each other in a specific way that makes those computers and their contents easily accessible to each other.[4]

---

[2] Many of the people in the audience knew each other as friends and business associates. The laughter was not at Mr. Ogg, but at the situation.

[3] Schneider G. and Perry, J. *Electronic Commerce,* 2nd annual ed. (Boston: Thomsen Learning, 2001), p. 3.

[4] Ibid., pp. 14–15.

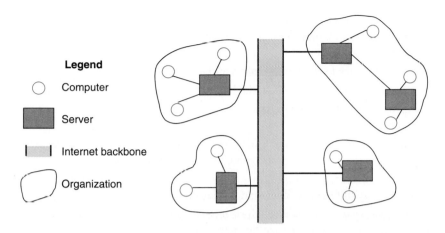

Figure 9.1 | Visual Representation of a Segment of the Internet

As presented in Chapter 1, "World Class Supply Management^{SM}," the Internet enables supply managers to manage their supply chains collaboratively and to synchronize their operations. The results are reduced cost, better time management, and improved competitiveness and profitability for all members of the chain. The Internet helps organizations compete effectively as contributing members of dynamically connected supply chain communities or networks, not as isolated enterprises.

Evolution to e-Commerce II

In reviewing the above definition and the advantages and disadvantages of e-Commerce in the subsequent sections, consider this question: "Does e-Commerce, as it was implemented in most supply chains in the 1990s, enable opportunities for synergistic collaboration built on trust between supply chain members?" The answer to the question by supply professionals is almost always a resounding "No!" We believe e-Commerce can and will be used to foster such opportunities; however, cultural and philosophical change must occur at the highest levels within firms to actuate such change. We define such an evolution in strategy of e-Commerce usage as e-Commerce II. e-Commerce II is presented in greater detail in the last section of this chapter.

Advantages for Supply Management

The following are advantages of using e-Commerce technologies in managing supply management activities:[5]

- Help share information about customer demand fluctuations.
- Help enable collaboration among supply chain members and functional areas on design of new products and services.

---

[5]Ibid., p. 347.

- Help speed notification of product design changes and adjustments. Specifications, drawings and process changes can be electronically dispersed, both efficiently and effectively.
- Enable companies to share information about quality problems.
- Identify new suppliers throughout the Internet-connected world.
- Compare potential suppliers quickly on a wide variety of criteria, such as quality, price, and delivery.
- Increase the speed and accuracy with which businesses can exchange information, thereby reducing costs and errors on both sides of transactions.
- Provide a wider range of choices than traditional commerce. The supply manager can consider many different products and services from a wider variety of sellers.
- Provide an easy way to customize the level of detail in the information obtained about both the prospective supplier and the purchase.
- Run 24/7 (24 hours a day, 7 days a week).
- Reduce the cost of the purchase order. The average cost of processing a purchase order ranges from $80 to $150. Automating the procurement process brings the cost of processing a purchase order down to about $20.[6]

Disadvantages for Supply Management

Today, most of the disadvantages of e-Commerce for the supply professional result from the relative newness and rapidly developing pace of the underlying technologies. The potential disadvantages of e-Commerce from a supply management perspective include:

- Costs and benefits are hard to quantify. This creates tremendous confusion in determining where supply managers should focus their efforts and resources.
- Usually, e-Commerce requires highly educated supply professionals who may be difficult to find, recruit, develop, and retain.
- Frequently requires integrating relatively incompatible existing databases, standards, data accumulation systems, and software.
- Exposes a company to a myriad of global issues. Currency conversions, tariffs, import and export restrictions, local business customs, and the laws of each country in which a supplier resides can make international e-Commerce difficult.
- The cost of entry into some e-Commerce reengineered supply chains may eliminate or limit small companies who otherwise could be very good suppliers. As discussed in Chapter 4, diversity firms may be financially incapable of investing in many e-Commerce initiatives, effectively eliminating them from competition.
- Resistance to change may be high. Employees, customers, and suppliers who are accustomed to conducting business using traditional methods, such as phone, fax and face-to-face meetings, may have difficulty with the required technology.

---

[6]Taken from an informal discussion with Dave Nelson, former VP of Worldwide Supply Management at Deere & Company, January 2002.

■ Success may translate into a call for a reduction in the supply management staff if personnel are perceived as transaction processors who have been replaced by e-Commerce applications.

e-Commerce as an Enabler

The significance of e-Commerce for supply management is readily understood when one considers the amount of purely administrative work involved in the procurement cycle at the average company. Literally thousands of requisitions, requests for quotation, purchase orders, change orders, status reports, receiving records, invoices, and other documents must be processed and recorded. These transactions take place across facilities and companies that are located throughout the world. Technologies available today in e-Commerce can make these transactions and their associated information flows relatively instantaneous. e-Commerce and computer-based systems free supply professionals from a vast amount of routine, non-value-added work. Generally speaking, the basic transactional supply activities that can be performed well by a computer-based system are the same in all cases. They include:

■ Maintenance of inventory records.
■ Computation of order quantities.
■ Preparation of purchase requisitions for inventory items.
■ Preparation of requests for quotation.
■ Preparation of purchase orders.
■ Maintenance of order status records.
■ Distribution of accounting charges.
■ Automatic preparation of follow-up memos.
■ Posting of delivery and quality records, by part and by supplier.
■ Preparation of numerous operating reports for management.
■ Provision of decision support system information.
■ Auditing of invoices and preparation of checks for payment.
■ Electronic data interchange (open and closed) communications.

e-Commerce enables supply managers to receive real-time data for use in making cost-effective, supply-related decisions. The Internet's speed allows a computer system to process virtually instantaneous reports which otherwise might take weeks to prepare and update. The timeliness of such reports enables supply professionals to manage by exception and do a more effective and profitable job of managing the flow of materials throughout the internal operations and supply chain. Despite all of the transactional benefits listed above, the systems are still dependent upon solid supply management practices to ensure that the information in the system is accurate.

Evolution to World Class Supply Management^{SM}

Despite the clear impact on improving transactions in supply management, the improvements listed in the previous section do not constitute strategic supply management. Firms that achieve automation of their transaction system may still be in the mechanical stage in their evolution to World Class Supply Management^{SM}. In the mechanical stage of WCSM, companies usually implement one or more of the following e-Commerce initiatives:

■   The company uses e-mail to aid in communicating with suppliers.

■   The Internet is used to help find new suppliers.

■   The company may also use reverse auctions and trading networks in a way that is not strategic—to simplify finding and creating short-term, price-focused contracts with suppliers that have not been researched by the firm itself.

Unfortunately, it is common that a transaction-based procurement system has been purchased, implemented, operated, and maintained with almost no input or participation from supply management. Such systems are ripe with fattened lead times, hidden expediting costs, quality problems, and high inventories. The transaction processing systems are justified in part by software vendor[7] statistics showing savings possible with an automated system. The statistics often show metrics such as order cost reductions of 60-90 percent and a numeric reduction in FTEs (full time employees). Both metrics are very seductive justifications for upper management to select the vendor's systems. Frequently, the reduction in FTEs occurs in the purchasing and accounts payable departments. The purging of FTEs in purchasing often does not discriminate between individuals performing tactical and strategic value-added activities. Such purging increases future problems the company will experience since few professionals are left to: contribute during the critical requirements development process, assess supplier capabilities, and work with suppliers as described in the chapter on supplier development later in this book.

In a proactive firm, full-time employees who were previously performing transactional tasks are retrained and refocused on strategic activities when possible. Purchasing personnel become supply managers. Who better qualified to advance the goals of the organization into the new age of e-Commerce than those who already understand the production processes and the existing supply chains? In the proactive and WCSM stages of e-Commerce and supply management integration, synergies between suppliers and buying firms that go beyond mere transactions are examined and acted upon.

■   Suppliers are actively involved in the development of requirements and specifications. The Internet enables this interaction to occur with the participants located anywhere in the world.

■   Supply managers work continuously with suppliers to update key system inputs such as lead times to reflect the most accurate information possible.

■   Forecasts and plans for meeting customer demand are actively shared with suppliers through intermittent face-to-face discussions if needed, phone conversations, online discussions, virtual meetings, and real-time online updates.

---

[7]We have digressed to using the term "vendor" in this situation due to our disagreement with a few software firms that sell their software by advertising great reductions in costs in one category, such as order transaction costs, while other areas of cost balloon. See Chapter 8, "Total Cost of Ownership," for an understanding of total cost versus only looking at a subset of total cost.

- When appropriate, buying firms work with suppliers to reveal opportunities for improvement at both the buying and supplying firms. Once again, the enabling features of the Internet can help achieve the required collaboration.

- Nonstrategic commodity and indirect requirements that are purchased through online reverse auctions are conducted only after supply management has completed appropriate research.

- Cost, quality, and timeliness are improved through collaboration in cross-functional teams composed of supplying and buying firm members who hold the meetings in both face-to-face and online venues.

- Reports are generated by the e-Commerce system(s) with metrics that expose opportunities to work with suppliers with the objective of improving collaboration.

e-Commerce enables supply managers to go beyond day-to-day transactions to collaborative commerce. Online exchanges facilitate the flow of business processes, data, designs, and ideas. In collaborative commerce, business partners exchange information rapidly, easily, and at low cost. Inventory data, for example, can be shared in a supply chain by simply posting it to a centralized website or data warehouse. Since the interface is usually built on web browser technology, collaborative commerce simplifies data interchange by eliminating the need for special client software at each customer's site. By using Web servers as hubs for collaborative commerce efforts, companies can exchange proprietary data, jointly manage projects, and cooperate on the design of new products.[8]

Electronic Data Interchange

Once a firm has an effective electronic supply management system in operation, a logical extension of that system is to link it, in one way or another, with the order-handling computer system of selected suppliers. The term generally given to this type of supply chain communications operation is electronic data interchange—EDI.

In its purest sense, EDI is the direct electronic transmission, computer to computer, of standard business forms, such as purchase orders, shipping notices, invoices, and the like, between two organizations. In a supply environment, documents are transmitted electronically, eliminating the need to generate hard copies and to distribute them manually. EDI increases the speed of information flow while simultaneously decreasing the potential for data errors.

Figure 9.2 presents the traditional approach without electronic transmission of standard business forms, such as purchase orders, shipping notices, invoices, and the like, between two organizations. Figure 9.3 presents the three electronic data interchange transmission alternatives: direct connection, value-added network, and open EDI using the Internet.

---

[8]Warren D. Raisch, *The E-Marketplace — Strategies for Success in B2B Commerce* (New York: McGraw-Hill, 2001), p. 133.

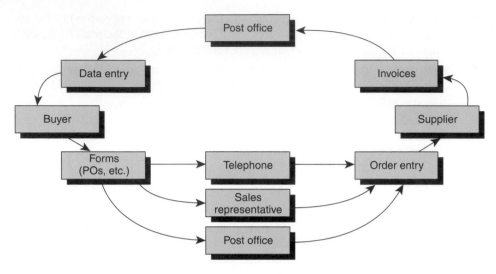

Figure 9.2 | Traditional Transmission of Standard Business Forms

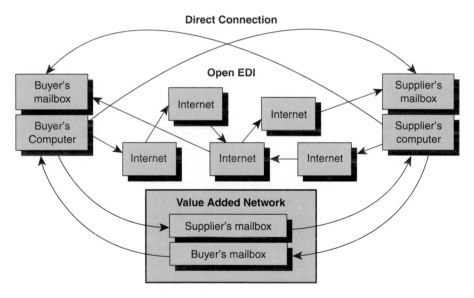

Figure 9.3 | Three Electronic Data Interchange Choices

Traditional EDI

Before the mid-1990s, the high cost of implementation was a major barrier faced by potential adopters. EDI required the purchase of expensive computer hardware and software, then either establishing direct network connections using leased telephone lines to connect supply chain members or subscribing to a value-added network (VAN) that provided the connection through a centralized location. A VAN is a third-party firm that offers connection and EDI transaction forwarding services to buying and selling firms. As a result of the high implementation cost, many small firms could not afford to participate in EDI. The Internet now provides the inexpensive communications channel that EDI lacked for so many years.[9]

Open EDI

EDI on the Internet is also called *open EDI* because the Internet is an open architecture network. Trading partners who had been using direct transmission or VAN EDI began to view the Internet as a potential replacement for the expensive leased lines and dial-up connections they had been using to support both direct and VAN-aided EDI. Companies that had been unable to afford EDI began to look at the Internet as an enabling technology that might get them back in the game of selling to large customers who demanded EDI capabilities of their suppliers.[10]

The major roadblocks to conducting EDI over the Internet initially were concerns about security and the Internet's inability to provide audit logs and third-party verification of message transmission and delivery. The lack of third-party verification continues to be an issue, since the Internet has no built-in facility for such information. Since EDI transactions are business contracts and often involve large amounts of money, the issue of nonrepudiation is significant. Nonrepudiation is the ability to establish that a particular transaction actually occurred. It prevents each party from repudiating, or denying, the transaction's validity or existence. In the past, the nonrepudiation function was provided either by a VAN's audit logs for indirect connection EDI or a comparison of the trading partners' message logs for direct connection EDI.

Wal-Mart's POS System Using EDI   Wal-Mart, the largest discount retailer in the world, built much of its core competency by leveraging point-of-sale (POS) technologies coupled with EDI. When a customer purchases an item at Wal-Mart, the item's bar code is scanned at the customer checkout station. The scanning serves the dual purposes of speeding movement of the customer through the checkout and gathering POS information on the items sold.[11] A computing system records the point-of-sale data into a database, aggregates the quantities, and electronically sends the information to a centralized information processing location that aggregates demands by location for the item and sends the information to the appropriate supply collaborator, such as Procter and Gamble or Clorox. If the relationship is truly evolved, the supplier is empowered to manage its own inventories, deliver the merchandise, and place it on Wal-Mart's shelves.

When inventory is managed by the supplier in this manner it is commonly referred to as *vendor managed inventory or VMI*. The terminology of "vendor" is giving way to

---

[9]Schneider and Perry, *Electronic Commerce,* p. 350.

[10]Ibid., p. 342.

[11]F. Kuglin and B. Rosenbaum, *The Supply Chain Network @ Internet Speed* (New York: Cap Gemini Ernst & Young U.S. LLC, 2001), p. 41.

the use of supplier, since "vendor" historically has many negative connotations associated with it. Use of the term "vendor" may prevent the relationship between the buying and supplying firms from improving to a state of collaboration. Already in many supply chains we are seeing the term *supplier managed inventory* being used. Regardless of the terminology, the supplier owns the inventory until it is used by the buying firm—or in the case of Wal-Mart when the merchandise is sold. When items are scanned, the software immediately sets up an electronic payable. The payable accesses the pricing and trade allowances information from a common database, and a check is issued or payment is made electronically.

Wal-Mart's POS system has improved customer service, decreased inventories throughout its supply chain, and improved the overall competitive capability of the company. EDI is the underlying technology that enables the system to work. The benefits to suppliers are numerous. Demand is visible. Obsolete stocks are minimized. Volume increases. Capacity planning is improved. The conclusion? Wal-Mart's networked supply-chain process has helped to change the way consumer-products companies and wholesaler distributors do business with retailers.

Figure 9.4 presents an example of a point-of-sales system integrated with an electronic data transmission capability. In the figure, the supplier is responsible for restocking the retail store's shelves.

Exchanges, Hubs, and Marketplaces

Business-to-business (B2B) exchanges are essentially websites on which member companies buy and sell their goods and exchange information.[12] Other names used for essentially the same type of activity are: trading networks, electronic marketplaces (e-marketplaces), hubs, and communities. A selling company usually needs an electronic catalog and both buyers and sellers often need to register with the market in order to participate in an exchange.

Exchange Variations

Exchanges also have several variations, among the most common: public versus private, buyer- versus seller-centric, consortium versus independent, and vertical versus horizontal.

■ **Public versus Private** A public exchange is open to all buyers and sellers. Usually public markets use auctions as a means of bringing buying and selling individuals or firms together. e-Bay is an example of a public exchange. In contrast, a private exchange is open to only selected, certified, or member buyers and sellers. Volkswagen, for example, operates its own private trading network with its suppliers.

---

[12]Michael Leenders, Harold Fearon, and Anna Flynn Fraser Johnson, *Purchasing and Supply Management,* 12th ed. (New York: McGraw-Hill Irwin, 2002).

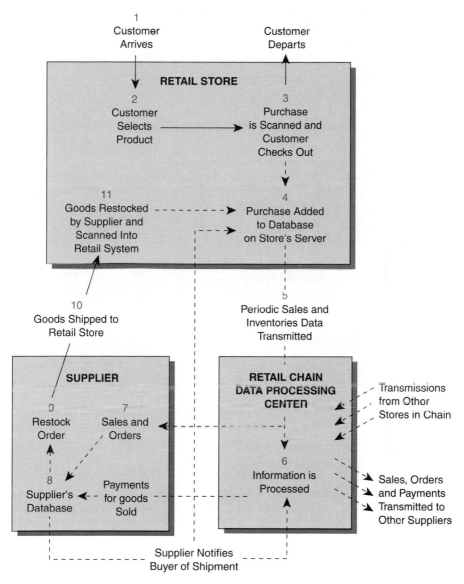

Figure 9.4 | Point-of-Sales System Integrated Using Electronic Transmission

■ **Buyer- versus Seller-Centric** A buyer-centric exchange is developed by one or more buying firms to consolidate requirements, create competition among a large number of suppliers, or gain one of the other many synergies that an electronic environment can provide over traditional buying. Conversely, a seller-centric market is developed by one or more sellers with the primary goal of creating more demand for products and services than would be created without the use of the market and/or disseminating information to buyers. Both buyer- and seller-centric markets are private.

- **Consortium versus Independent**   A consortium refers to several companies that come together to form one marketplace or exchange. The companies that form the exchange may or may not actually participate directly in it themselves as a buyer or seller. Usually the consortium consists of members in the same industry (which can raise concerns about violations of antitrust laws). For example, automobile manufacturers General Motors Company, Ford Motor Company, and Daimler-Chrysler initiated the Covisint eMarketplace in early 2000. Covisint has since expanded to include several other automobile manufacturers. Covisint provides a central source for automobile parts and related components that includes suppliers and dealerships.
- **Vertical versus Horizontal**   Vertical-focused exchanges are developed to support a specific industry or segment of a market. Covisint is an example of both a consortium and a vertical exchange. Horizontal exchanges serve several or all industries, such as office supplies markets. In general, as the number of buyers and sellers in a horizontal market grows, vertical markets are able to spin a "critical mass" off.

Success with Exchanges

IBM has developed its own trading network with selected suppliers. Utilizing the categories given above, IBM's network is private, buyer-centric, independent, and vertical. IBM's trading network is portrayed in Figure 9.5. Looking at the figure, one sees that the differentiating features of IBM's trading network design versus most trading networks are the focuses on communication and collaboration. Javier Urioste, former global procurement director of policy and international operations at IBM, observed, "The network accelerates IBM's ability to leverage opportunities provided by a web-linked supply network." IBM believes that the network must facilitate sharing of information with suppliers to create a collaborative "win-win" environment in its supply chain.[13]

In contrast to the private network of IBM, public exchanges must do the following to be successful:

- Be open to all buyers and sellers.
- Match the right buyers with the right sellers.
- Provide relevant content that accurately represents goods and services.
- Support various transaction types.
- Provide business services and practices that are flexible enough to adapt to the differing needs of customers and market segments.

[13]Javier Urioste, presentation at 16th Annual Supply Chain Management Forum, November 2001, San Diego, CA.

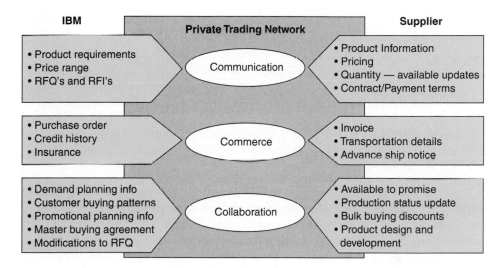

Figure 9.5 | IBM's Trading Network Showing Integration of Communication, Commerce, and Collaboration

Source: Javier Urioste, "Strategic Sourcing and the Internet," presentation given at The University of San Diego's Supply Chain Management Institute's 16th Annual Supply Chain Management Forum, November 2001.

■ Maintain a technological infrastructure that enables companies to seamlessly conduct business with anyone, anytime, anywhere.[14]

Future of Exchanges

In his book, *The E-Marketplace—Strategies for Success in B2B Commerce,*[15] Warren Raisch presents a four-phase evolution of e-Marketplaces (or exchanges) to what he calls Value Trust Networks (VTN). The four phases are useful to help supply managers understand the positioning of their e-Marketplace(s). According to Raisch, the four phases are as follows:

1. **Phase One: Commodity Exchanges and Marketplaces**   The focus is on buying, selling, and trading of commodity-type products and services.

2. **Phase Two: Value-Added e-Marketplaces**   These marketplaces provide value-added services to support their customers with transaction support, as well as to enable the customer-driven creation of customized products and services.

3. **Phase Three: Global Knowledge Exchanges/The Global Knowledge Network**   The Internet is emerging as the central point for communication and collaboration of knowledge workers around the world. The development and availability of

---

[14]Raisch, *The E-Marketplace,* p. 131.
[15]Ibid.

knowledge tools for knowledge workers creates the building blocks for global knowledge exchanges.

4. **Phase Four: Global Value Trust Networks**   e-Marketplaces provide an integration point for business process, people, and technology, as well as products and services. These new Value Trust Networks (VTNs) come together to support industry value chains. VTNs provide a combination of interoperability and trusted relationships that forge the foundation of new global innovation. VTNs weave enterprises, marketplaces, industries, and individuals together into empowered and productive digital workgroups. These Value Trust Networks, according to Raisch, will be the new business platform for the 21st century.

Kuglin and Rosenbaum, in their book *The Supply Chain Network @ Internet Speed,* state, "In the future, purchasing professionals will demand intelligent procurement processes that span multiple trading sites and portals. Suppliers will demand the ability to electronically present their goods and services, and those of their trading partners, to supply professionals. In addition, new product development designers will demand online, 24×7 design and development collaboration to optimally allocate scarce resources to the prioritized new products in their pipelines." Kuglin and Rosenbaum continue, "The next generation of trading exchanges will encompass decision support processes that evaluate multiple courses of action before arriving at a solution."[16]

Enterprise Resource Planning Systems

The basic idea of enterprise resource planning systems (ERP) is to put all of a company's data in a central repository where it can be matched, cross-matched, and shared across departments and with other trusted companies using Internet or EDI interfaces. Using ERP, a company can eliminate wasteful duplications and streamline operations to create, in effect, one efficient, enterprisewide application.[17]

Benefits of ERP

According to Thomas Davenport, there are several key business benefits of enterprise systems:[18]

1. **Cycle time reduction**   ERP can provide substantial benefits in terms of cost and time reduction in key business processes.

2. **Faster information transactions**   IBM's System Storage (disk drive) division achieved a reduction in the time to enter pricing information from five days minimum to five minutes.

---

[16]Kuglin and Rosenbaum, *Supply Chain Network@Internet Speed,* p. 188.

[17]Mathew Friedman and Marlene Blanshay, *Understanding B2B* (Chicago: Dearborn Trade, 2001), pp. 113–119.

[18]Thomas H. Davenport, *Mission Critical—Realizing the Promise of Enterprise Systems* (Boston: Harvard Business School Press, 2000), pp. 6–7.

3. **Better financial management**   One of the basic functions of ERP systems is managing financial information across the enterprise.

4. **Laying the groundwork for e-Commerce**   Centralized data in an ERP system facilitates linkage to e-Commerce systems.

5. **Making tacit process knowledge explicit**   Key processes, decision rules, and information structures are well understood and documented in an ERP system.

In the best of all ERP worlds, there is complete transparency throughout the enterprise and even across the supply chain, so every department and supply chain member knows exactly what every other department and supply chain member is doing. In addition, everyone knows what resources are available at any given time. Achieving such openness requires organizational and cultural change as well as hardware and software change. There is little point in implementing an ERP system if the data in each department will be secured to the point that it is not shared. In spite of this obvious conclusion, many companies buy expensive ERP systems and continue business as usual without ever drawing on the massive data sharing capability at their fingertips.

Criticisms of ERP

ERP systems have many critics. Criticisms are in five areas: long implementation periods, inflexibility, overly hierarchical organizations, antiquated technology, and high cost.[19] In the late 1990s, ERP implementations could take as long as three years.[20] Today, most ERP suppliers advertise that they can help a company implement a system in as little as six months.[21] Usually a fast implementation time requires a relatively "plain vanilla" implementation wherein the system has very little customization. As a result, companies often modify their processes to integrate with the "plain vanilla" defaults. The "plain vanilla" approach can create adoption resistance with actual users of the systems at the buying firms. Most users want the ERP system to reflect and improve their current processes, not create entirely new processes.

To answer many of the criticisms, in the late 1990s ERP providers reinvented themselves in two critical ways. The first was to become e-Commerce solution providers. All of the major ERP packages now support XML. Davenport states, "XML provides the interface to the Internet and heterogeneous commerce processes at the transaction front end, while the database interfaces provide integration with legacy data at the back end." The second way was acceptance of their role as "backbone" for best of the breed software. "Best of the breed" software is software developed to address specific problems or areas of interest. Peachtree Accounting and Microsoft Project are two examples of "best of the breed" solutions. Given the existence of best-of-breed packaged solutions in supply chain management (SCM), many ERP customers prefer to add on supply chain software developed by third-party suppliers.

---

[19]Ibid., pp. 16–19.

[20]Some ERP implementations have taken longer, depending upon how one defines the implementation start and end points.

[21]Often the ERP vendor does not directly assist in the implementation, but a third-party firm is employed that is qualified by the ERP vendor.

Enterprise resource planning systems can be an enormously complex, expensive technology. In a 1999 survey of 63 companies, the Mesa Group found that the total cost of ownership of ERP averaged a staggering $15 million.[22] The main reasons that ERP is so expensive are that ERP involves: reengineering and improvement of business processes, a philosophical shift in corporate culture, employee training and education, and migration of departmental data stores to centralized data warehouses. Scheer and Habermann estimate that the cost of implementation is typically five times the cost of the ERP product itself.[23] Still, many companies show cost savings that are far greater than the implementation and maintenance costs of the ERP system.

An ERP Success Story

Discovery Toys is a medium-size company that has recorded positive total cost of ownership savings from implementing an ERP system. Discovery Toys designs, distributes, and sells toys with educational value. The company outsources all manufacturing activities. Richard Newton, vice president of Operations, estimated that in the first year of operation of their ERP system, Discovery Toys saved approximately 10 million dollars.

The reasons for Discovery Toys' successes appear to be in the selection and implementation process. Richard Newton used six criteria for ERP supplier selection: risk, implementation, functionality, partnership, cost, and technology. *Risk* was assessed by how much the selected ERP system would interrupt business during implementation. (Many companies have had major problems with implementing ERP systems and he wanted Discovery Toys to avoid the problems.) *Implementation* referred to the speed and ease with which the software could be integrated into the company's working information technology. *Functionality* covered the issue of how closely the software actually met Discovery Toys' business needs. (Mr. Newton had noticed that many vendors provided "bells and whistles" that were unnecessary, but did add cost and complexity.) The fourth criteria, *partnership,* addressed the relationship the supplier provides, primarily in terms of support during and after the implementation. *Cost* addressed the total cost of ownership, which included estimating the hidden costs such as training, upgrades, and maintenance. The last criteria, *technology,* referred to an investigation into the software's compatibility with existing legacy hardware and software systems.

Discovery Toys implemented a J. D. Edwards ERP system. J. D. Edwards designed its software for small to medium-size companies like Discovery Toys, so the *cost* was low compared to that of other suppliers. The software did not have as many "bells and whistles," but it did meet the *functionality* requirements of Discovery Toys. In addition, Richard evaluated the system as quick to implement. In fact, *implementation* took Discovery Toys only about six months. One of the most important criteria to Richard was *partnering.* J. D. Edwards demonstrated to Richard through its actions during the proposal phase that it would provide Discovery Toys with strong support after the sale.

---

[22]Friedman and Blanshay, *Understanding B2B,* p. 113–120.

[23]August-Wilhelm Scheer and Frank Habermann, "Making ERP a Success," *Communications of the ACM* 43, no. 4, p. 57.

The results? After stabilization of the ERP system, the purchasing staff at Discovery Toys was reduced from nine to two full-time employees. The seven employees released or cross-trained into other areas had been performing clerical work prior to implementation of the ERP system. Similarly, the accounting staff was reduced even more dramatically from 21 to five full-time employees. The ERP system automated most transactions, thereby eliminating almost all of the paperwork and enabling instantaneous tracing of orders and transactions. The two retained purchasing professionals essentially became supply managers and are now able to focus on strategic decision-making. As a result, Richard pointed out that the qualifications for future employment of supply professionals at Discovery Toys had increased significantly, to the point where a college degree in supply management is now essential. Additional improvements were: customer service staff reduced, overall inventories reduced, and average lead time for processing orders dropped from five days to one day.[24]

Negotiation and Bidding

Online negotiation is one of the most controversial uses of e-Commerce. Debate has occurred at industry and academic conferences for several years as to whether "real" negotiation can even take place without face-to-face or voice-to-voice interaction.[25] Communications research shows that approximately 70 percent of all communication between individuals is nonverbal, meaning that facial reactions, movements, and other nonverbal reactions are part of the traditional negotiation process. In an online negotiation, nonverbal communication is completely removed. Supporters of online negotiation argue that by removing the nonverbal communication, the negotiation process can focus better on facts instead of emotional reactions.

Online Negotiation

Almost all companies that provide auction services online advertise that their software enables online negotiations during the auctioning process. In our investigation of several online auctioning services, we discovered that this claim was false. Anytime one starts a bidding process based upon a predefined set of criteria (lowest price, special delivery considerations, high quality, etc.), negotiation can no longer occur unless the process is a two-step bidding/negotiation. (In two-step bidding/negotiation, bidding is undertaken in the first step to select one supplier with whom the buying firm will negotiate to reach an agreement. If the negotiation is unsuccessful, the buying firm will usually negotiate with the second-lowest bidder.)

In regular bidding, the company that meets the specified criteria (usually price) is awarded the contract. This is also the way most online auctions are conducted. The main difference is that online bidding is dynamic, with multiple bids from the same firm possible. Although the dynamic nature of online bidding is a powerful way to speed the bidding process and reduce the supplier's profit margins, it is not a new form of negotiation.

---

[24]Richard Newton, personal interview, November 1999.

[25]Most companies that engage in online negotiations today do not use video or voice streaming.

Imagine an online reverse auction in which the criterion for winning is the lowest bid price. However, as with most traditional bidding processes, the suppliers qualified to bid must meet some minimum performance levels, such as quality, delivery, and volume. Midway through the auction one of the suppliers states that it can provide higher quality than the buying company asked for in its minimum specifications, but it cannot beat a competitor's price bid. If the buying firm believes it can benefit from the higher quality level and changes the criterion for awarding the contract, then the bidding process has indeed become a negotiation.

A fundamental problem exists in the previous scenario. If the buying firm gains a reputation for negotiating with the lowest bidders *after* bids are opened, then future bidders will tend *not* to offer their best prices initially, believing that they may do better in any subsequent negotiations. They will adopt a strategy of submitting a bid low enough to allow them to be included in any negotiations. Nevertheless, their initial bid will not be as low as when they are confident that the award will be made to the low bidder without further negotiation.[26] For more information on the issues between bidding and negotiation, please refer to our discussions in Chapter 15, "Sourcing," of this book. For a detailed presentation on both online and traditional negotiation, please refer to Chapter 20, "Negotiation."

Online Negotiation Example   The following example presents how auction service providers believe that a negotiation can be executed online. It is presented here to clarify the difference between a negotiation with a single company and a negotiation in which competitors are pitted against each other.

Suppose an automobile manufacturer needs to purchase 10,000 tires for delivery within two days. Perhaps an earthquake shut down the production process of its current supplier and required delivery dates will not be met. A quick search identifies eight potential suppliers. Since the company does not have the time to call each supplier individually in an effort to obtain quotes and does not want to award the contract to the lowest bidder automatically, an online, multistage, and multiparameter negotiation format is used for the selection process.

The eight suppliers are notified of the request by e-mail and directed to the company's e-Commerce website where the negotiation is to be conducted. The first stage of the negotiation involves delivery time, and the second stage of the negotiation is price and delivery package. In an environment similar to an online threaded discussion, the supply manager determines that only three suppliers can provide the tires in the requested period.

In the next stage, the three suppliers are asked to provide their prices. Further suppose that, as expected, there is wide variation in the initial price offerings. As a result, the supply manager has the option to begin negotiating with each supplier individually on a price-delivery package. The supply manager will determine, through negotiations,

---

[26]On occasion, a supply manager may intend to use the initial proposal solicitation process to identify firms with which he or she plans to conduct follow-on negotiations. In this case, professional ethics as well as good business judgment dictate that the initial solicitation clearly state that follow-on negotiations will be conducted.

which provides the greatest value. These negotiations are dynamically communicated online simultaneously, and typically, the suppliers are unaware of the details of the other suppliers' negotiations. These negotiations can also support third and fourth stages of negotiations depending on a buying or selling firm's business needs. At any point, the purchaser or seller can accept, reject, or counter an offer.

Reverse Auctions

In a reverse auction, the buying firm may specify a particular requirement and allow suppliers to bid on it. Typically, the lowest bid wins in a reverse auction; however, some auctions, such as FreeMarkets' reverse auction service, can support very complex auctions so that businesses can better align the auctions with their business practices. For example, sales terms may be determined by price, delivery, quality, service, or some combination of them all. The entire bid process can be controlled electronically.

In addition to defining which elements are cost critical, buying firms can also determine what information will be visible to the suppliers who choose to respond. The buying firm may choose to let suppliers see information such as the current bid. Multiple bids may be accepted right up to the closing moments of the bidding process. Supply managers may choose to have an open reverse auction, in which any supplier can respond, or a closed reverse auction, in which the bidders are limited to those who meet some predefined criteria. Either way, the appropriate suppliers are notified automatically, and they can choose to respond and submit their bids or not. Supply managers then review supplier responses online and make the award or allow additional rounds of bidding.[27]

FreeMarkets, for example, uses its software and hardware tools to coordinate private online auctions that allow businesses to solicit bids from suppliers. One satisfied repeat customer, Raytheon, reports FreeMarkets' reverse auction services resulted in average price reductions of 22 percent over historical prices.[28] Instead of undergoing the laborious process of sending out requests for proposal packages to many suppliers, Raytheon can list its requests for proposals with FreeMarkets. Online reverse auction services give firms a way of beginning to procure electronically without investing in their own integrated system. In effect, these services have moved the traditional first-price sealed-bid auction form onto the Internet.

Websites that offer auction search and price-monitoring services include Bidder's Edge, Price Watch, and PriceSCAN.[29] The Bidder's Edge site allows users to monitor bidding action on specific items or categories of items as it occurs on some of the more popular Web auction sites. Price Watch is an advertiser-supported site on which potential suppliers post their current selling prices for computer hardware, software, and consumer electronics items. Although this monitoring is a retail pricing service designed to help supply managers find the best price on new items, Web auction-goers find it can help them with their bidding strategies. PriceSCAN is a similar price-monitoring service that also

---

[27]Raisch, *The E-Marketplace,* pp. 136–137.

[28]Steve Ogg, "e-Commerce at Raytheon," presentation given at the 16th Annual Supply Chain Management Forum, University of San Diego, November 2001.

[29]Schneider and Perry, *ECommerce,* p. 373.

includes prices on books, movies, music, and sporting goods, in addition to the types of items monitored by Price Watch.

Forward Auctions

Sellers often use forward auctions to reduce or liquidate excess finished goods, parts, assemblies, and equipment. A forward auction has one seller and two or more potential buyers. A forward auction is usually referred to simply as an "auction." The auction usually starts with a low price that the buyers will bid up on until a set time has expired or no other buyer wishes to place a higher bid.

Three main online auction models are emerging: large company, small company, and consumer Web model.[30] In the large company model, the business creates its own auction site that sells excess inventory. In the small company model, a third-party Web auction site takes the place of the liquidation broker and auctions excess inventory listed on the site by a number of smaller sellers. The third online auction model resembles consumer Web auctions. In this model, a new business entity enters a market that lacked efficiency and creates a site at which buying and selling firms that have not historically done business with each other can participate.

Information Sharing

Information sharing through e-Commerce activities can create synergies between supply chain members resulting in increased efficiency and effectiveness. Information sharing systems presented earlier in this chapter include electronic data interchange, enterprise resource planning systems, trading exchanges, online communities, trading hubs, and electronic marketplaces. Most of these systems are used for purely tactical information sharing leading to transactions for the transfer of goods, services, payments, schedules, and inventory levels. Information sharing can be expanded to include strategic information, such as: reports, forecasts, demands, designs, specifications, tolerances, costs, processes, project updates, problems, performance measurements, inventory levels throughout the supply chain, and expansion plans. Essentially, almost all information relevant to decision-making can be shared.

Two issues must be addressed in order to make an electronic system capable of sharing tactical and strategic information: first, data must be in a form that is transferable and understandable and, second, the organizations involved must be willing to share critical and confidential information. Both of these requirements present problems in most supply chains. For data to be transferable, standards must be agreed upon between either the supply chain members or the key industry leaders. Extensible Markup Language (XML) appears to meet most of the needs of data transferability today and in the near future. While the standards issue appears to be nearing resolution, the issue that may be insurmountable in some supply chains is the willingness to share strategic information among members of the chain. XML is discussed in the next section followed by several methods that firms are using to share information, including intranets and extranets, data

---

[30]Ibid., p. 369.

warehouses, electronic supplier catalogs, electronically enabled project management, and intelligent agents.

Extensible Markup Language

In the 1960s, scientists developed the Generalized Markup Language (GML) to describe electronic documents and specify how they are formatted. In 1986, the International Organization for Standardization (ISO) adopted a particular version of the standard called Standard Generalized Markup Language (SGML). Hypertext Markup Language (HTML) was the next inception of the markup languages. HTML became the code that helped revolutionize the information age. Most Internet surfers are familiar with hypertext markup language, the technology used to build Web pages. HTML uses tags which define a Web page's format that is read and interpreted by a Web browser. Tags are invisible to the user, which means that no knowledge of HTML is needed to use HTML-based documents.

XML works in the same way as HTML except that, instead of defining the format of a Web page, XML's tags define the context and meaning of the text. For example, a purchase order might have the buying firm's name, such XYZ Corporation, indicated by a <buyer> tag and the quantity defined by <quant>. A schema, a kind of XML vocabulary, defines just what the tags mean and which ones are used. A specialized software program called an XML parser simply interprets the tags according to the schema indicated in the message header. Unlike EDI, which demands strict compliance with a predefined message length and field order, the information in an XML document can appear and be in whatever order or length the sender desires. The XML parser will still make sense of a purchase order if the name of the selling firm precedes the name of the buying firm and even if the order quantity appears in the first line and the catalog number in the last.

Intranets and Extranets

An intranet is a Web-based private network that hosts Internet applications on a local area network. Often an intranet facilitates dissemination of company information within the confines of the company and its suborganizations. Figure 9.6 presents an illustration of an intranet.

An extranet extends the intranet concept to provide a network that connects a company's network to the networks of its business partners, selected customers, or suppliers. While the facsimile, phone, electronic mail, and express carriers represent the way business has been conducted until now, the extranet is a likely candidate to displace these slow and expensive techniques. Extranets connect companies with suppliers or other business partners. An extranet can be any of the following types: a public network, a secure (private) network, or a vital private network (VPN). Each has the same capability of sharing information between companies. Information on extranets is secure to prevent security breaches from unauthorized users.[31] Figure 9.7 presents an illustration of an extranet.

---

[31]Ibid., pp. 65–66.

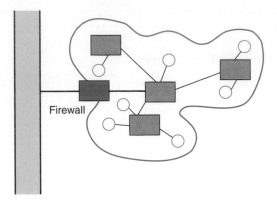

Figure 9.6 | Intranet

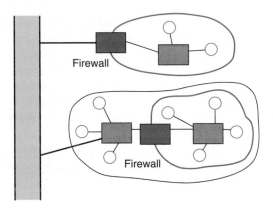

Figure 9.7 | Extranet

Data Warehousing

Data warehousing provides a way for companies and, more important, chains to centralize selected data electronically. For example, consider a university that has a data warehouse filled with student information. Suppose a professor needs to access grade information for all students within six months of graduation so he or she can plan a graduation party for seniors (in a perfect world). All the professor would have to do is query the data warehouse, after using a password to gain entry into the data warehouse interface. The whole process should take less than five minutes. Now consider a system in which the professor has to fill out a grade report form and use campus mail to send the request to the university's management information system (MIS) department. MIS receives the query the next day, then the request sits one day. Finally, the MIS employee goes into the department's database and prints off the information requested. The document is put back in the campus mail to the professor. The whole process takes four days minimum. Finally, imagine such inefficiencies when working with supply chain data and you should have a grasp of the way things used to be before data warehouses.

From the perspective of managing an enterprise's information assets, data warehousing and ERP have similar—and complementary—goals. Just as ERP traditionally promised great efficiencies and economies of scale by tying enterprise processes into a single application, data warehousing's principal value is the way an enterprise can leverage all of its information assets quickly and effectively.[32]

Electronic Supplier Catalogs

An electronic catalog is a digitized version of a supplier's catalog that allows buyers to view detailed information about the supplier's products and services through the buyer's own computer browser.[33] A catalog can contain a wide range of information. Simple catalogs may contain only basic information, such as products and prices. Detailed catalogs may contain complex information, such as design specifications and quality data.

e-Commerce systems can host electronic catalogs that feature all types of goods and services, including MRO, production, nonproduction, administrative, and capital goods. Registered suppliers can upload their catalog content to a hosting server, provided the supplier has become a registered member so it can be accessed by a number of buying firms. Today, one of the selling points of catalog hosts is that once a catalog is updated, price changes can occur dynamically, which means that the suppliers don't have to upload the entire catalog or re-create content just to change a price.

Some catalog hosting services will also register suppliers that do not have an electronic catalog. If an item or service a buyer requires is not listed in an electronic catalog, the buyer can search for a list of suppliers who are capable of offering the item or service. Supply managers can directly search these supplier "white pages" at any time to locate new sources for an individual item or an entire commodity.

Project Management

Although project management theory has been in existence since the 1950s, until recently many supply management professionals have not used project management techniques. Times certainly have changed. If one picks up a major city newspaper's classified advertisement section today and reads the description of skills needed for positions in supply management, he or she will usually discover that project management skills are listed.

The primary reason for the increased number of listings calling for project management skills is the proliferation of software solutions that can reduce the workload of a project manager while simultaneously improving the management of projects. Before improvements in software and computers, project management was difficult to implement, and poor information flow made inaccurate estimates of completion times and required resources. Early software versions did not enable a manager to model the real world.

---

[32]Friedman and Blanshay, *Understanding B2B,* p. 123.

[33]Leenders, Fearon, and Fraser Johnson, *Purchasing and Supply Management.*

More recently, the growth in project management usage has been accelerated by the centralization capability of projects using Internet servers. The use of the Internet has enabled real-time posting of project information to all resources in projects both internally and externally across supply networks. Off-the-shelf software has advanced to the point where rules can be selected by the project manager to manage and update key resources even in the absence of the project manager. Although use of project management by supply professionals is still in its infancy, there is little doubt among today's managers that the need for project management education will continue to grow for companies in order to reduce waste and gain competitive advantage.

Intelligent Agents

An agent, intelligent agent, or software agent is a program that performs functions such as information gathering, information filtering, or mediation running in the background on behalf of a person or entity. Truth be known, it may be many years before agents are functional in the real world, but it is intriguing to think about the future. Just a few very strong words of caution: Intelligent agents will remain "intelligent" only through continuous maintenance of the knowledge base by which their decision-making rules are driven. Even a very well-written supply management agent can become useless very quickly.

From a supply management perspective, imagine sending your personal Web agent out on the Internet to search for the best price and availability of 300 laser printers for your company. Such an agent, programmed with all the critical specifications one supplies, would first locate e-Commerce sites that sell what is wanted. Then, the agent would collect information about the price and characteristics of the equipment that the site sells from comparable selling agents that work on behalf of the commerce site. Loaded with similar information from other websites selling laser printers, the agent then performs its next critical task: determining from which of several printer selling agents one should purchase the equipment. Once the software agent identifies the best supplier, the agent then can proceed to negotiate any remaining terms of the transaction. Finally, the buying and selling software agents agree on purchase and delivery details.[34]

Software Solutions

Supply Chain Solutions

Supply chain management software includes demand forecasting tools and planning capabilities that allow supply chain members to coordinate their activities and continually adjust their production levels. Speaking generally, the packaged software currently available for supply chain management falls into four basic categories:[35]

- ■ Supply planning tools that help to align all the resources and activities required to get goods to market cost-effectively.

---

[34]Schneider and Perry, *Electronic Commerce,* pp. 109–110.

[35]Davenport, *Mission Critical,* pp. 245–246.

- Demand planning tools that help companies anticipate market demand for their products using sophisticated modeling and statistical analysis.
- Plant scheduling tools that translate overall supply requirements into day-to-day production plans.
- Logistics systems tools that support warehouse management, transportation, and order management.

Currently, the two most popular firms offering supply chain management software are i2 Technologies and Manugistics. The i2 Technologies product, RHYTHEM, includes components that manage demand planning, supply planning, and demand fulfillment. The demand-planning module includes proprietary algorithms customized for specific industry markets that examine customer's buying patterns and generate continuously updated forecasts. The supply planning module coordinates distribution logistics, inventory level forecasting, collaborative procurement, and supply allocations. The demand-fulfillment module handles the execution elements, including order management, customer verification, backlog control, and order fulfillment.

Manugistics, Inc. offers a suite of software, including tools for vendor-managed inventory; point-of-sale-driven demand; and collaborative planning, forecasting, and replenishment. Strung together, its products enable companies to analyze and manage the flow of products from demand, distribution, and manufacturing through to supply management, transportation, and logistics, not only across an enterprise but throughout the supply chain.[36] The Manugistics supply chain management product includes a constraint-based master planning module that controls the other elements of the system. These other elements include modules for transportation management, replenishment management, manufacturing planning, scheduling, supply management planning, and materials control.

Competitive pressure on companies such as i2 and Manugistics will increase as ERP suppliers continue to introduce their own supply management tools. It is likely that this competition will lead to even better and more comprehensive products to help manage the supply chain.

Maintenance, Repair, and Operating Suppliers

W. W. Grainger is one of the largest maintenance, repair, and operating (MRO) suppliers in the world. Its website offers over 220,000 products for sale. Grainger's Web store offers visitors a variety of ways to access information about and order Grainger products. A visitor can enter the online catalog, use the product search box at the top of the page, or search by clicking a hyperlink to one of the categories listed in the middle of the page.

Ariba is currently the leading choice for very large companies that want to automate routine supply management decisions. Ariba provides a way for companies to standardize purchase requisitions for office supplies. Ariba also provides firms with standardized access to MRO products and other routinely purchased items that are used throughout

---

[36]Ibid., p. 245.

their organizations. This type of software is called an operating resource management system (ORMS). Ariba defines operating resources as including information technology, telecommunications equipment, professional services, MRO supplies, travel and entertainment expenses, and office equipment.[37]

Ariba uses a Web browser interface that allows any employee to enter the system and complete an online requisition. The requisition is automatically routed to the appropriate person for electronic authorization and then sent directly to the supplier. Ariba automatically sends information about the purchase to the firm's accounting system. Ariba is written in java, so it works on most platforms. This is important in large companies that may be running a variety of operating systems. Ariba also includes programming interfaces to all major ERP software packages, which helps ensure that the accounting and logistics for each transaction are properly tracked. Ariba is a very expensive software product—a typical installation costs between $1 million and $3 million—but the large firms that use it find that they save tremendous amounts of money by lowering the cost of handling so many mundane transactions. The end of maverick buying (purchasing done by the organization's personnel who are outside the supply management department and who have little or no knowledge of sound purchasing techniques) has an equal or greater impact. Deere & Company, for example, claims to have saved more than its investment in four months.[38]

Expert Systems

Expert systems are computer programs that solve problems by emulating the problem-solving behavior of human experts. Knowledge engineers who conduct interviews with one or more experts to capture their knowledge and problem-solving logic regarding a specific problem, develop these systems. The engineers construct a computer model using an artificial intelligence programming language.

An expert system consists of a knowledge base and an "inference engine." The knowledge base contains program goals, facts generally agreed upon by the experts, and "rules of thumb" that an expert would use in making decisions. The inference engine represents the expert's problem-solving approach and uses the contents of the knowledge base to reach conclusions. Thus, an expert system uses information obtained from consultation with experts, the department's own database, and possibly external databases.

e-Commerce II

Some chain leaders, such as Dell and IBM, have done an excellent job of leveraging technology to improve their supply chains. The truth is that most supply chains do not have such leadership and most of the members are still very far behind in understanding how e-Commerce can improve supply chain coordination and collaboration. What really makes e-Commerce work for supply chains? The answer is knowledge: knowledge that

---

[37]Schneider and Perry, *Electronic Commerce,* p. 350.

[38]Dave Nelson, "Transformation, Integration and Collaboration: The John Deere Experience," presented to the National Association of Procurement Professionals, Marco Island, FL, January 21, 2002.

cannot be captured easily in computer-based systems; knowledge accumulated through the experience of the people developing, running, and maintaining the e-Commerce system. The "e" in e-Commerce should be called "experience." Experience is what creates the knowledge needed to move e-Commerce systems to the next level, what we call e-Commerce II.[39] Supply professionals need to become involved and help move companies to e-Commerce II. e-Commerce II is based on two critical human contributions, experience and interpersonal relations, enabled by the power of the Internet.

Collaboration Built on Trust

According to Harry B. DeMaio of Deloitte and Touche, "B2B is at its best when it is *not* a zero-sum game. It can be win-win, provided that all the players take cooperation seriously and come to the table prepared to play with shared goals and objectives. For many organizations, that's a new type of business experience, and it's not always comfortable." DeMaio continues, "Trust is the real essence of relationships in the e-universe. Security is a state. Control is a process. But trust is an ongoing interaction that establishes and maintains confidence between or among entities. Trust requires security and control but it goes beyond them. It depends on technology and protective mechanisms, but it also involves reputation, contracts, law, openness, familiarity, fair business practices and ethics, quality, timeliness, and a host of other relationship characteristics."[40]

e-Commerce II at Dell

The concepts that we are presenting are not completely new, although the terminology of e-Commerce II is. Essentially, Dell embodies many of the ideas underlying the e-Commerce II philosophy. The following excerpts are taken from the book *Direct from Dell,* by Michael Dell.[41]

- "Just as the Internet increases customer intimacy, it can also be used to enhance supplier intimacy. The idea is to connect with your suppliers in much the same way you connect with your customers."

- "We use our supplier connections to share inventory data, quality data, and technology plans; to give our partners immediate visibility to the field; and to serve as a central repository for information we all need—which we can access simultaneously, in real time."

- "By using the Internet to maintain a continuous flow of materials from our suppliers into our factories, our people spend less time placing orders or expediting parts and more time adding value."

---

[39]Our thanks to Dick Lyle who stated the term "e" in e-commerce should mean "experience" during a January 2002 presentation at the University of San Diego. Additional thanks to Bob Harrington, who helped us come up with the term e-Commerce II.

[40]Harry B. DeMaio, *B2B and Beyond—New Business Models Built on Trust,* John Wiley and Sons, Inc., New York, NY. pp. 3 and 21.

[41]Michael Dell, *Direct from DELL: Strategies that Revolutionized the Industry* (New York: HarperBusiness, 1999), pp. 190–192.

- "The other thing the Internet gives us is immediate transmission of quality data. We have data on product quality that come in every minute of the day. We'd like our suppliers to see the information in real time."

- "If we've given them a goal of 500 defects per million and they're at 750 or 1,000, we don't want to have to wait for a monthly meeting to report customer response. We want them to see it almost as soon as it happens."

- "If we can accelerate the availability of the data, our chances of encouraging suppliers to improve also will increase exponentially."

- "By providing real-time information on the day-to-day mix and volume, we can help our suppliers level-load their factories and minimize their level of inventory. By helping our suppliers do a better job of reducing their supply chain lead times and moving to a higher degree of flexibility within their supply base, we can reduce the total cycle time from when we place the order to when they fulfill it."

Concluding Remarks

During the past 25 years, we have witnessed the evolution of one of the most important trends in the history of organized society—the increasingly sophisticated use of computers and e-Commerce. Managers must not lose sight of the fact, however, that a computer is only as capable as the people who design the software and the systems in which it is used. Finally, it is essential to remember that the integrity of the output is no greater than the quality and integrity of the data the computer-based system is asked to process.

PART 3

The Requirements Process

Balance Sheet in the red *(Credit: David Gould/Image Bank/Getty images)*

In Chapter 1, we introduced the idea that there are four principle phases of supply management: the requirements process, strategic sourcing, strategic cost management, and relationship and contract management. In our minds, the first of these—the requirements process—is the most crucial. We rest our case on the observation that some 70–85 percent of a product's cost is built in during this phase.

In Chapter 10, we describe the process of developing a new product and describe the role which supply management must play. Historically, buyers, purchasing agents, and supply managers have been frustrated in their efforts to get themselves and their key suppliers involved in the new product development (NPD) process. While there are many reasons for this phenomenon, the best way to become involved is to bring value! Supply managers must understand the NPD process and possess or acquire knowledge of the supply world which contributes value. No managerial fiat can replace the charge: bring value!

Chapter 11 describes two of the values which supply managers can and must bring to the NPD process: a knowledge of the commercial implications of specifications and a knowledge of the savings to be achieved from, and the processes involved in standardization and simplification. Proper use of standardization can significantly reduce inventories, improve quality, reduce costs, and enable postponement.

The procurement of capital and operating equipment frequently has a far greater impact on the success of an organization than does the amount of money involved. Downtime costs can far exceed the purchase price of an item of equipment. The cost and flexibility of operations or manufacturing must be considered. OSHA issues and other environmental issues must be addressed. The frequently conflicting objectives of the program's budget and the total cost of ownership make the equipment procurement process challenging, to say the least. The question of lease versus buy frequently must be addressed. As we describe in Chapter 12, World Class Supply Management^{SM} advocates the proactive involvement of qualified supply professionals in order to compress the procurement cycle while minimizing the total cost of ownership of the purchased equipment.

Chapter 13 discusses the third type of requirement addressed in this book: services. With more and more money being spent purchasing services (including outsourcing at many firms) the procurement of services has gained increased prominence. The development of the specification describing the buying organization's requirement (frequently referred to as the Statement of Work) can be every bit as challenging as the development (or adoption) of specification for a material or a subassembly. Selecting the best source, obtaining the "right price," and management of the contract and the services relationship is more subjective and more challenging than when purchasing materials.∎

New Product Development

Case

An Opportunity at Elite Electronics?

Management at Elite Electronics is faced with a golden opportunity—or is it only fool's gold? Six months ago, marketing research indicated a potential market of 10,000 oscilloscopes per year, if Elite's selling price could be brought down to $1,000 per unit. (Elite's lowest-priced model, the EE201, currently sells for $1,485.)

   Engineering had been working day and night to develop a new model whose variable production cost would be no more than $700. Supply Management had been working with present and potential suppliers to lower the total cost of purchased material. Recently, supply management learned of the possibility of a breakthrough on material costs for the new oscilloscope. Gamma Conglomerates, working on the development of an analog-to-digital (ADC) module for three years, developed a revolutionary new process that allowed it to produce 1,000 modules a month. In order to guarantee the amortization of its research and development and setup costs, Gamma offered a price of $90 per unit F.O.B. if Elite would agree to purchase all of its ADCs for the new oscilloscope from Gamma for a period of five years. Full-scale production could begin in three months.

Incorporation of the new ADC would allow the elimination of four modules required in the present model EE201 oscilloscope with only a slight loss of resolution. This would result in a system whose variable production cost would be between $650 and $700, including $200 for assembly and testing. Allocations for fixed general, administrative, and marketing expenses would add approximately $200 per unit. Five prototype oscilloscopes incorporating the new ADC were built and tested. The new system was an engineering success!

Both engineering and marketing were very enthusiastic about the new system. Supply management, manufacturing, and quality control shared their enthusiasm, but with some reservations. Supply management was concerned that Gamma Conglomerates would be the sole source of supply for the ADC. Quality control, production and supply management shared another concern: the quality of incoming materials. The firm already had experienced unpleasant situations with new "state-of-the-art" materials. Many electronics items and the systems that incorporate them are extremely complex and interdependent. It is not always possible to detect defective items until they are incorporated into larger modules or even the complete system. This is an inherent aspect of the sophisticated state-of-the-art processes used to produce modern electronics components. Things go along fine for a while, and then for no apparent reason defects get completely out of control. It often takes 10 to 14 months to stabilize new production processes and eliminate the problems.

Great amounts of test and rework time may be required by Elite's production department to locate and correct this type of problem. For example, Elite currently is experiencing just such a situation on a new premium-quality oscilloscope. Test, rework, and assembly time is running at 400 percent of the work hours budgeted for the new oscilloscope. On the basis of his experience with previous state-of-the-art materials, Elite's production manager estimates that there are two chances in five of such a situation occurring with the new low-cost model if it incorporates Gamma's new ADC.

The high cost of such test and rework time can have disastrous implications for a firm like Elite. Items projected to make a profit contribution can wind up as losses. And, in some ways even more damaging to such a firm, promised delivery dates might not be met. As a result, current sales, customer goodwill, and future business all can suffer.

In many industries, the first firm to market a new product successfully is able to build and maintain a much stronger market position than firms that enter the market later. Elite believes that its likely market would be 10,000 units of the new low-priced oscilloscope for the first year of production and 6,000 per year for the following four years if it is the first firm to market such a low-priced oscilloscope. However, if the introduction is not successful (for quality or manufacturing reasons), the negative impact would reduce likely sales to 4,000 units for each of the five years. Production estimates that it would take approximately one year to clear up the problem. Accordingly, it appears realistic to assume that some 4,000 units would require excessive test, rework, and assembly time. The unit variable cost of the 4,000 units would be an estimated $1,275. Marketing believes that likely sales would be 6,000 units per year for four years if Elite were to wait for the ADC production process to stabilize or if a less risky approach became available in approximately 10 to 14 months.

Supply management is confident that alternatives to the ADC will be available at that time. These alternatives will use proven technology and cost approximately $45, lowering variable production costs to about $630 per unit. Management at Elite truly is in a predicament. Should it grab the new ADC and run for the pot of gold, or should it play things safe and wait for more proven technology and competitive sources?

Overview

This chapter addresses four key issues: (1) early supply management and supplier involvement; (2) the process of designing and developing new products, with emphasis on supply management's role in the process; (3) several approaches to increasing supply management's role in the new product development process; and (4) a description of supply management professionals who interface successfully with engineers during the new product development process.

World-class firms excel at a crucial triad of activities consisting of new product development, the design of the required production process, and development of the optimal supply chain. This chapter addresses the first member of this triad.

"Rapid changes in technology, the emergence of global industrial and consumer markets, increasing market fragmentation and product differentiation, and the increasing options for developing and producing products have increased the pressure on all firms to more effectively and efficiently develop new products."[1] In many progressive firms, the design of new products is conducted by a team representing a number of functional areas. Marketing, product planning, design engineering, reliability engineering, supply management, manufacturing engineering, quality, finance, field support, and, frequently, carefully selected suppliers and customers are involved, as appropriate.

Anecdotal evidence indicates that the development of new products by such cross-functional teams and the use of concurrent engineering[2] have the potential of significantly improving three key objectives: time to market, improved quality, and reduced total cost.[3] The turnaround of many troubled manufacturers during the recent decade was the result of replacing departmental walls with teamwork among those who should be part of the design process. Supply management professionals and carefully selected suppliers are moving to earlier involvement in the new product development process because of the im-

---

[1]Michael McGinnis and R. Vallopra, "Purchasing and Supplier Involvement: Issues and Insights Regarding New Product Success," *Journal of Supply Chain Management,* Summer 1999, pp. 4–15.

[2]Concurrent engineering is a process in which functional specialists execute their parts of the design as a team concurrently instead of in separate departments serially.

[3]Charles O'Neal, "Concurrent Engineering with Early Supplier Involvement: A Cross-Functional Challenge," *International Journal of Purchasing and Materials Management,* Spring 1993, pp. 3–9.

portant contributions they can make in the areas of quality, cost, and timely market availability. This early involvement commonly is referred to as *early supply management involvement* and *early supplier involvement* (ESI). Researchers Essig and Arnold of the University of Stuttgart conclude, "By involving supply management and suppliers in simultaneous (cross functional) engineering process teams at an early stage, R&D gets the chance to increase efficiency. . . . In fact, early supply management involvement helps to shorten engineering time and increase engineering quality.

The lack of effective, cooperative teamwork among the functions noted frequently has been accompanied by quality problems, cost overruns, forgone all-in-cost savings,[4] major scheduling problems, and new products which are late to enter the marketplace. Further, early recognition of problems is difficult or impossible in the absence of cooperative teamwork. Extensive redesign, rework, and retrofit operations are common when operating in the traditional functional mode. Ultimately, the absence of teamwork results in products which are a continuing burden to the firm's long-term competitiveness.

Cost overruns and forgone cost savings frequently result when the designers (or the design team) fail to consider the supply base's design, manufacturing, quality, and cost capabilities. For example, during the early 1980s, design engineers at GE's Jet Engine Division frequently designed materials to be purchased from outside suppliers under the mistaken belief that the outside suppliers had the same manufacturing and process capabilities as GE. In fact, this was not the case; outside suppliers frequently did not possess the same equipment, processes, and quality capabilities. The results were cost growth and schedule slippages as the suppliers, through a trial and error process, attempted to meet GE's specifications. Frequently, it became apparent that these specifications could not be met and a costly and time-consuming process of reengineering would be required.[5]

A similar example of costs resulting from the failure to consider supply implications during design involves IBM. In 1993, IBM's PC units' sales were just over $8 billion, with earnings of about $200 million (2.5 percent). By contrast, Compaq's profits were $462 million on sales of $7.2 billion (6.4 percent). According to *BusinessWeek,* "At least one reason . . . seems clear, IBM still does not use common parts across its product families." Another contributor to lower profits was IBM's failure to shift away from pricey Japanese components as the value of the yen rose.[6] It was noted that IBM recognized that its supply management system had been the source of significant cost overruns and forgone dollar savings. This recognition resulted in 1994 in the appointment of a new Chief Supply Officer: Mr. Gene Richter. Under Mr. Richter, three-time Purchasing Man of the Year, IBM Procurement has undergone an incredible transformation and is now approaching "World Class" status.

---

[4]"All-in-cost" is a summation of purchase price, incoming transportation, inspection and testing, storage, production, lost productivity, rework, process yield loss, scrap, warranty, service and field failure, and customer returns and lost sales associated with the purchased item. The term "all-in-cost" is similar to "total cost of ownership" and simply "cost." All recognize that the purchase price of an item is merely one component of the total cost of buying, owning, and using a purchased item.

[5]Personal interview with Gene Walz, Materials Manager, General Electric, Jet Engine Division, June 1983.

[6]Ira Sager, "IBM: There's Many a Slip . . .," *BusinessWeek,* June 27, 1994, pp. 26–27.

[7]"Apple Net May Fall Up to 30% in Quarter," *The Wall Street Journal,* September 21, 2000.

Scheduling problems frequently are the result of the late delivery of required parts. For example, earnings at Apple Computer fell nearly 30 percent in the third quarter of 1999, largely on account of supply shortages. Apple received only 45 percent of the G4 chips its supplier had originally promised. This, in turn, led to significant reductions in the sales of Apple's Power Mac G4 computers.[7] When supply considerations are not addressed during new product development, unique nonstandard components may be specified. Such components frequently require longer lead times than do standard items. The use of nonstandard items often results in the inability of the manufacturer to react quickly to changes in market demand, frequently resulting in lost sales. In order to reduce its reaction time to changes in demand, firms are now replacing unique components with standard "commodity" ones. In addition to being more readily available, such commodity components tend to be far less expensive than the unique items they replace.

The global marketplace and global competition coupled with advanced communication systems, computers, and sophisticated software have generated an environment in which "time to market" and first to market have significant competitive advantages. Clearly, the need to reduce development time has forced companies to look for new methods to compete. The use of supply professionals and suppliers earlier in the product development cycle is a key means to reducing time to market.

In the early 1990s, the Chrysler Viper went from concept to production in 36 months, against an industry norm of 60 months. Chrysler did not achieve this goal by itself. It got a lot of support from its suppliers. "They were as much a part of the Viper team as anyone . . . suppliers are an integral part of the team," said Dave Swietlik, the man in charge of procurement for the Viper program. "Their processes drive design."[8] (Unfortunately, Chrysler appears to have retreated to a more adversarial approach.)[9]

When a cross-functional team has the responsibility for the development of new products, a concurrent approach to the myriad of tasks involved is taken. This avoids the traditional (and time-consuming) passage of a project from concept development to design to manufacturing engineering to supply management to manufacturing to marketing to field support. Such a sequential approach requires even more time and personnel resources when changes have to be made in the product's design. The cross-functional team uses a concurrent approach wherein the team members work together and collaborate throughout the process. (See Figures 6.1 and 6.2 in Chapter 6.)

The Design Process[10]

Design is the progression of an abstract notion or idea to something having function and fixed form. The desired levels of quality and reliability must be "engineered in" during the design phase of the new product. "Suppliers must have access to product design as early as humanly possible in the design process to assure optimal use of any special skills

---

[8]Ernest Raia, "The Chrysler Viper: A Crash Course in Design," *Purchasing,* February 20, 1992, p. 48.

[9]"The Tight Squeeze at Chrysler," *BusinessWeek,* October 9, 2000, p. 54.

[10]Portions of this section are based on David N. Burt, *Proactive Procurement: The Key to Increased Profits, Productivity, and Quality* (Englewood Cliffs, NJ: Prentice Hall, 1984).

or processes they can contribute."[11] The design stage is also the optimum point at which the vast majority of the cost of making an item can be reduced or controlled. If costs are not minimized during the design stage, excessive cost may be built in permanently, resulting in expensive, possibly noncompetitive, products that fail to fully realize their profit potential.

The new product development process is a series of interdependent and frequently overlapping activities which transform an idea into a prototype and on to a marketable product. The process is much more fluid and flexible than is portrayed in the forthcoming flow diagrams. As the original idea progresses through the development process, it is refined and constantly evaluated for technical and commercial feasibility. Trade-offs between the various objectives (price, cost, performance, market availability, quality, and reliability) are made throughout the process. These days one hears a great deal about designing for manufacturability; however, invariably, the focus is the firm's internal manufacturing process. But when those responsible for design ignore the manufacturing process and technological capabilities of outside suppliers, problems with quality, time-to-market, configuration, control, and cost are the inevitable result. If optimal design performance is to be achieved, suppliers must be active from the beginning, when they can have a major impact on performance, time, cost, and quality. Selected suppliers should participate in feasibility studies; in value engineering; and in prototype, failure, and stress analysis, among other product development tasks.

There is a growing trend among manufacturers to develop an "envelope" of performance specifications for suppliers. For example, instead of determining the materials, manufacturing processes, and engineering drawings for a seat for one of its motorcycles, in the 1980s Kawasaki began specifying the environmental conditions and the maximum weight which the seat must withstand together with a drawing showing how the seat was to attach to the motorcycle frame. The suppliers' engineering and CAD/CAM[12] tools, not the buying firm's, were then dedicated to designing selected components. This approach allows engineers at the buying firm to focus on the development of more sophisticated core technologies and proprietary systems. The customer firm's engineers do not prepare engineering drawings for nonstrategic components. However, they review and approve the supplier's designs. Such action not only redirects critical engineering resources to higher-value activities, but places responsibility for manufacturability and quality with the supplier.

In order to involve suppliers effectively and early, manufacturing companies invite carefully selected suppliers' engineers into their own engineering departments. In a 1995 *Harvard Business Review* article, management guru Peter Drucker describes William Durant as the inventor of the keiretsu. Durant designed and built General Motors during the early 1900s. "Durant deliberately brought the parts and accessories makers into the design process of a new automobile model right from the start. Doing so allowed him to

---

[11]John A. Carlisle and Robert C. Parker, *Beyond Negotiation: Redeeming Customer-Supplier Relationships* (Chichester, U.K.: John Wiley & Sons, 1989), p. 127.

[12]Computer-assisted design/computer-assisted manufacturing.

manage the total cost of the finished car as one cost stream."[13] Manufacturers should allow key suppliers to review the design of the entire subassembly before committing to it. Not only does this tease out new ideas, but it also helps the supply partner understand the customer's real needs—and likely future needs.

Involving suppliers in the new product development process is more challenging than one might imagine. Hanfield and Ragatz observe, "Successful supplier integration initiatives result in a major change to the new product development process. Further, the new process must be formally adapted by multiple functions within the organization to be successful. One of the most important activities in the new development process is understanding the focal supplier's capabilities and design expertise, conducting a technology risk assessment, weighing the risks against the probability of success."[14]

The changing competitive environment forces much more planning, coordination, and review to take place during the design and development process than previously was the case. Complexity of product lines must be addressed. Lower levels of complexity result in higher schedule stability, a necessary prerequisite to just-in-time manufacturing. Feasibility studies, computer simulations, prototype analysis, failure analyses, stress analyses, and value engineering all must be conducted in an effort to develop producible, defect-free products quickly at the lowest possible total cost.

The new product development process has undergone a tremendous change during the past years. The process is described in Figures 10.1, 10.2, and 10.3 and is discussed below.[15]

The Investigation or Concept Formation Phase

There are several types of new product design. The first is that used for a totally new product. This is the least-used approach since completely new products are the exception. Most new product design is actually an adaptation or an expanded feature set for a previous design. Advancing technology, process improvements, and market expansion drive the majority of new product design activity. The process described is equally applicable to a totally new product or a "new improved" one.

Defining the New Product The design and development process begins with the investigation phase. First, the product is defined. This function is normally performed with considerable marketing involvement. Intel carries marketing to its logical extreme: It emphasizes design ethnography, which focuses on understanding the customer and the culture in which a product is to be used.[16] The design and development process has been

---

[13]Peter F. Drucker, "The Information Executives Truly Need," *Harvard Business Review,* January–February 1995, p. 56.

[14]Robert B. Hanfield and Gary L. Ragatz, "Involving Suppliers in New Product Development, " *California Management Review,* Fall 1999, p. 60.

[15]Some world-class firms prepare a report at the end of a new product development project to document the major lessons learned—ones which can be applied to future projects.

[16]Peter Tarasewich and Suresh K. Nair, "Designing for Quality," *Industrial Management,* July–August 1999, p. 18.

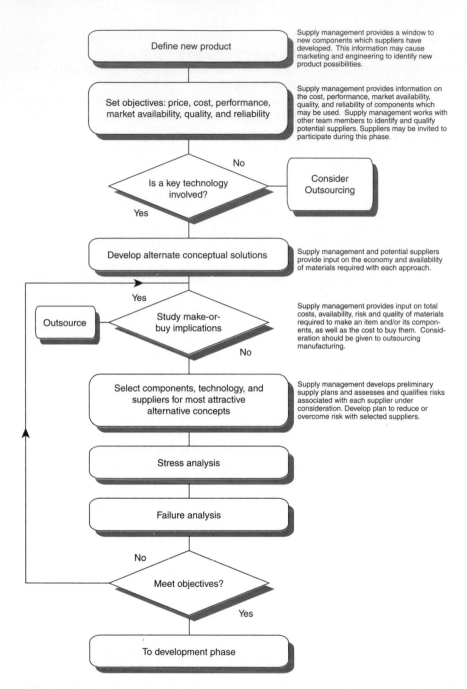

Figure 10.1 I Team and Supply Management Activities during New Product Development *Investigation Phase*

Source: Adapted from *Strategic Proactive Procurement* by David N. Burt and Richard L. Pinkerton, AMACOM, New York, 1996.

formally titled "customer focused product and process development" at some firms, or "quality function deployment" at others.[17] Marketing authority Regis McKenna is quoted as saying:

> Companies need to incorporate the customer into product design. That means getting more and more members of an organization in contact with the customer—manufacturing and design people, as well as sales and marketing staff. You can, for example, have customers sitting in on your internal committee meetings.[18]

Designers can make up for some of the shortcomings of consumer input, since they usually understand more about future technological possibilities and look at a longer time line. They are also in a better position to know what competitors might offer. For example, consumers may desire a "user-friendly" personal computer that is easy to get started with, but the designer realizes the computer should also meet longer-term needs. Therefore, designers should have the freedom to create innovative product designs that not only meet current user requirements but are also up to the demands of future consumer expectations. This give-and-take requires a delicate balance between designers and consumers since research has shown a high correlation between inadequate feedback from users and the failure of new products containing technical innovations.[19]

One of a supply management professional's key responsibilities is to acquire, assimilate, digest, and share information concerning new or forthcoming developments in the supply markets for which he or she is responsible. Interviews with present and potential suppliers, visits to suppliers (with emphasis on their research and development and production activities), attendance at trade shows, weekly reviews of relevant literature, and discussions with colleagues at local supply chain management organizations and American Production and Inventory Control Society meetings help the professional remain current. Through such activities, the supply management professional will become aware of new products and new technologies which may be of interest. This information may help product managers in marketing and senior design personnel responsible for identifying and developing new products. While being careful to screen out inappropriate information, the supply manager should share potentially attractive information with marketing and engineering.

Statement of Objectives Next, a statement of needs, desires, and objectives is developed. Needs are based on marketing's perception or knowledge of what customers want (or the customer's direct input if the customer is a member of the design team), balanced against the company's objectives and resources. Needs that are potentially compatible with the firm's objectives (profit potential, sales volume, and so on) and resources (personnel, machines, and management) are considered for development. Product objectives, including performance, price, quality, and market availability, are then established and become the criteria that guide subsequent design, planning, and decision making.

---

[17]The interested reader is referred to John R. Hauser and Don Clausing, "The House of Quality," *Harvard Business Review,* May–June 1988, pp. 63–67.

[18]Interview with Regis McKenna by Anne R. Field, "First Strike," *Success,* October 1989, p. 48.

[19]Tarasewich and Suresh K. Nair, "Designing for Quality," p. 18.

The well-informed procurement professional is the key source of information on the cost, performance, market availability, quality, and reliability of supplier-furnished components which may be used in the new product.

Establishing a realistic target cost at this stage of the new product development process is mandatory at world-class firms. (Target cost = Targeted market selling price − Targeted profit.)

Purchasing authority Lisa Ellram writes, "By establishing the target cost up front, purchasing, the supply base, designers, and marketing can all work toward a common goal in the value engineering, design for purchasing, and early supplier involvement processes."[20] The planned product life cycle typically includes not only the original product but several future products that will incorporate improvements in design, function, features, and so on. These new products are driven by advances in technology, design, and/or materials; competitive offerings; and customer expectations. These desired advances frequently are known at the time of the original product design, but they are not included in the design, since the technology does not exist, or requires additional development to be production-ready. This product feature design "wish list" is very important to the design engineer since he or she most closely understands the design trade-offs and compromises that were included in the original design. This "wish list" of technology requirements is extremely important. Unfortunately, most firms do not document these technical interests that eventually drive a subsequent iteration through their product development process. Not only should these data be documented, but they must become an important focus for a supply partner's R&D efforts. Quick development will drive new product offerings that add additional sales volume, frequently at premium prices, for both the manufacturer and supplier.

Key Technology   The development team should determine if a key technology is involved. If not, the team may decide to have an outside supplier develop both the technology and the product.

Development of Alternatives   Alternative ways of satisfying needs, desires, and objectives should be developed and then evaluated against the established criteria.

There is an unfortunate tendency to proceed with the first approach that appears to meet a need, although less obvious alternatives may yield more profitable solutions. Alternative approaches should be evaluated on the basis of suitability, producability, component availability, economy, and customer acceptability.

- *Suitability* refers to technical considerations such as strength, size, power consumption, capability, maintainability, and adaptability. Engineering has primary responsibility for these issues.
- *Producability* is the ease with which a firm can manufacture an item. In the past, designs needed to be changed to accommodate the firm's or its suppliers' ability to produce the item economically. Problems arose when the needed changes were im-

---

[20] Lisa Ellram, "Cost Reduction: Match the Tool to the Purchase," *Purchasing Today,* October 1998. For more insight into this process, see also Lisa M. Ellram, "Purchasing and Supply Management's Participation in the Target Cost Process," *Journal of Supply Chain Management,* Spring 2000, pp. 39–51.

plemented. Early manufacturing engineering involvement in the design is needed to ensure the producability of items made internally, while early supplier involvement helps ensure the producability of items furnished by suppliers.

■ *Component availability* is the time at which components are available, while component economy describes the cost of the item or service. Component availability and economy are the responsibility of supply management.

■ *Customer acceptability* is defined as the marketability of an item to potential customers.

The selection of components, technologies, and suppliers for the most attractive conceptual solutions is a complex process. At progressive firms such as GE, Hewlett-Packard, and Deere & Company, this selection process is a team effort, with design engineering providing the majority of the staffing and the team leadership.

Often, an engineer has a need that must be filled—a power transmission gear ratio, a structural component, a capacitance, a memory requirement. This need usually can be met in more than one way, and yet many times the engineer may not be aware of the options available. In such a case, a supply management professional may be able to offer suggestions. A gear, for example, might be machined of bronze or steel, die cast in aluminum or zinc, molded from plastic, or formed by powder metallurgy. All these options may meet engineering's constraints while offering a wide range of cost, availability, and reliability choices. Supply management and potential suppliers can provide information on the economy and availability of the materials and subassemblies to be purchased under each approach.

The Internet is playing an increasingly critical role in compressing development time. In 2000, Spin City began providing its customers a service which allowed customers to search electronically for current data sheets, pricing, and availability for more than one million components. Electronics parts suppliers were able to communicate product and service information directly to the engineer's desktop in real time, thereby reducing costs and development time.[21] Practiced by leading firms today, early supplier involvement (ESI) is a key contributor to the product development process.

With ESI, suppliers are carefully prequalified to ensure that they possess both the desired technology and the right management and manufacturing capability. Prior to inviting an outside supplier to participate in the development of a new product, the cross-functional development team will ask the following and related questions:

■ Will the supplier be able to meet our cost, quality, and product performance requirements?

■ Does the supplier possess the required engineering capability?

■ Will the supplier be able to meet our development and production needs?

■ Does it have the necessary physical process and quality capabilities required?

■ Does the supplier have both the resources for and the reputation of being able to overcome problems and obstacles as they arise?

---

[21] Personal interview with Pat Guerra, CEO, Spin City, October 10, 2000.

- Is the supplier financially viable?
- Are the supplier's short- and long-term business objectives compatible with ours?
- If a long-term relationship appears desirable, are the technology plans of the two firms compatible?
- If a long-term relationship appears desirable, is it likely that we can build a trusting relationship?

When a component or subsystem is to be developed by an outside supplier under an ESI program, normally two or three potential suppliers will be requested to design and develop the required item. Potential suppliers are given performance, cost, weight, and reliability objectives and are provided information on how and where the item will fit (interface) in the larger system. These potential suppliers must develop quality plans during the design of the item to ensure that the item will be producable in the quality specified. Selection of the "winning" supplier is a team effort, with supply management, design engineering, reliability engineering, product planning, quality, manufacturing, finance, and field support participating. Performance, quality, reliability, and cost are all considered during the selection process. When a carefully crafted strategic alliance for the item or the commodity class (e.g., fasteners, resistors, safety glass) exists, the alliance supplier alone will be invited to design and develop the required item.

Early supply management and supplier involvement can reduce the well-known start-up problems that occur when the design and the supplier's process capability are poorly matched. Ideally, supplier suggestions will be solicited and the matching of design and manufacturing process will take place during the investigative phase of the design process. The support suppliers provide in the early stages of design is a critical factor in squeezing the material costs out of a product, improving quality, and preventing costly delays.

Make-or-Buy and Outsourcing Analysis   The make-or-buy and outsourcing issues should be addressed for all new items which can be either purchased or produced in-house. Every job release and every purchase request implies a decision to make or to buy. Supply management plays a key role in the make-or-buy process by providing information on the cost, quality, and availability of items. (For more on this critical issue, see Chapter 14.)

Select Components, Technologies, and Supplies   Several options may meet engineering's constraints while offering a wide range of cost, availability, and reliability choices. Supply management professionals and selected suppliers provide information on the availability of the materials and subassemblies to be purchased under each approach. The Internet allows engineers to check for component capability and product attributes in real time. The early involvement of quality engineers allows advanced quality planning to commence in a timely manner. Quality standards are developed to ensure that components and products being designed can be produced at the quality specified.

The selection of required standard components is facilitated by the availability of a current internal catalog of standard items and sources which have been prequalified.[22] The use of such a catalog simplifies the design engineers' job while simultaneously supporting the efforts of standardization engineering or materials management to standardize the items used. The use of standard materials, production processes, and methods shortens the design time and lowers the cost of designing and producing an item. In addition, standardization reduces quality problems with incoming materials, inventories, administrative expenses, inspection, and handling expenses, while obtaining lower unit costs. For more on the critical issue of standardization, please see Chapter 11.

The selection of technologies is a complex issue because of inherent cost/benefit trade-offs and functional orientations. Engineers are eager to incorporate the latest technology. The marketplace often richly rewards those who are first to market with innovative products; therefore, there is a strong case for incorporating new technology or processes before they are perfected. But, as was seen at Elite Electronics at the beginning of the chapter, the cost of such a decision can be high. Not only does such an approach result in a proliferation of components to be purchased and stocked, but it frequently results in the use of items whose production processes have not yet stabilized; quality problems, production disruptions, and delays frequently result, all increasing project risk. Engineering, quality, supply management, and manufacturing personnel must ensure that both the costs and benefits of such advanced developments are properly considered. The design team should design new products to the requirements of the customer, not necessarily to the state of the art.

Stress Testing and Failure Analysis   Once candidate component and subsystem items have been identified, they are subjected to stress testing and failure analysis. Failures are caused by failure mechanisms which are built into the item and then activated by stresses. Studying the basic stresses and the failure mechanisms they activate is fundamental to the design of effective reliability tests. The correct design approach is to find and eliminate the fundamental causes of failure. This means that the most successful stress tests are ones that result in failures. Successful tests are also ones that are tailored to look for particular failure mechanisms efficiently, by selectively accelerating the tests.

Every failure has a cause and is a symptom of a failure mechanism waiting to be discovered. The tools of failure analysis are both statistical and physical; used together, they are a potent means for detecting the often unique fingerprint of the underlying source of the failure.

---

[22]This catalog is developed and maintained by the joint efforts of design engineering, reliability engineering, supply management, and manufacturing engineering. It reflects the technical and commercial implications of the items included. The catalog typically classifies components as low, medium, or high risk, in an effort to dissuade design engineers from using high-risk components in new products. The internal catalog is in contrast to a supplier's catalog, which, while simplifying the engineer's efforts to describe an item, places the firm in an unintentional sole-source posture.

The Development Phase

Rapid advances in computer technology and software have made the feasibility of large-scale, complex computer simulations possible. Manufacturers typically conduct extensive computer simulations to identify interferences, fit issues, functionality, algorithmic logic accuracy, and so forth, prior to the development of prototypes. As the technology continues to advance, computer modeling and simulation may replace prototype development.

Notwithstanding these technical advances, breadboard and/or hardware prototypes commonly are developed so that the design team may conduct tests on the integrated system to eliminate performance and quality problems. The selected approach is reviewed in detail for feasibility and likely risk. Efforts are taken to reduce risk to acceptable levels by developing and testing prototypes.

Prototypes   As shown in Figure 10.2, the first complete prototypes of the new product are designed, built, and tested. Documentation such as materials lists, drawings, and test procedures is created. It is not unusual to repeat this phase more than once, perhaps building the first prototype in the laboratory to test the design and the second prototype in manufacturing as a test of the documentation. The design should not exit this phase until a prototype has met all the design goals set for it, although it may not be possible to demonstrate the reliability goal because of the small number of prototypes available to test.

Design Reviews   The design review is the point at which the new design can be measured, compared with previously established objectives, and improved. Supply management participates in design reviews and provides information on the effect of specifications and the availability of items that are standard production for, or are inventoried by, suppliers. The supply professional must ensure that the specification or other purchase description is complete, is unambiguous, and provides necessary information on how items furnished under it are to be checked or tested. He or she should be satisfied that the purchase description is written in terms relevant to and understandable by potential suppliers.

Boeing provides an example of how computers impact on new product development. It can now design a commercial aircraft entirely by computer. It solves nearly all of its design issues through computer animation, avoiding the need to build physical prototypes. This approach reduces the cost of making design changes during production. The practice cut the time required to design the 777 by 50 percent.[23]

Qualification Testing   Qualification tests are conducted on the prototype equipment. There are two different types: (1) margin tests and (2) life tests. *Margin tests* are concerned with assuring that the threshold of failure—the combination of conditions at which the product just begins to malfunction—is outside the range of specified conditions for the product's use.

Life tests are intended to find patterns of failure which occur too infrequently to be detected by engineering tests on one or two prototypes. These tests differ from margin tests primarily in the number of units tested and the duration of the test.

---

[23] "The Economy," *Fortune,* October 2, 2000.

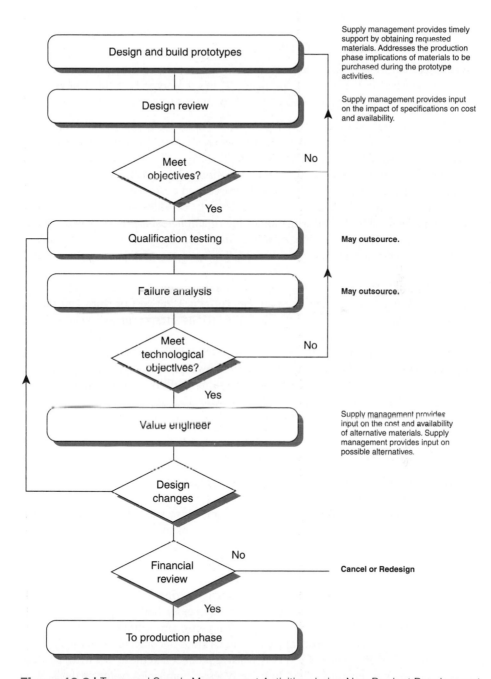

Figure 10.2 I Team and Supply Management Activities during New Product Development *Development Phase*

Adapted from *Strategic Proactive Procurement* by David N. Burt and Richard L. Pinkerton, AMACOM, New York, 1996.

Failure Analysis   The stress testing and failure analysis techniques described in the investigation phase are applied to the prototype.

Meet Objectives?   The design team determines whether the prototype meets the objectives established in the investigation phase. If the prototype fails this analysis, the project reenters the design process and a new or upgraded prototype is developed.

Value Engineering   During World War II many critical materials and components were difficult to obtain, and most manufacturers were required to incorporate numerous substitutions in their design and production activities. Harry Erlicher, then vice president of purchasing for the General Electric Company, observed that many of the substitutions required during this period resulted not only in reduced costs but also in product improvements. Consequently, Mr. Erlicher assigned to L. D. Miles the task of developing a systematic approach to the investigation of the function/cost aspect of existing material specifications. Larry Miles not only met this challenge successfully, but subsequently pioneered the scientific procurement concept General Electric called "value analysis."

In 1954 the U.S. Navy's Bureau of Ships adopted a modified version of General Electric's value analysis concept in an attempt to reduce the cost of ships and related equipment. In applying the concept, the Navy directed its efforts primarily at cost avoidance during the initial engineering design stage and called the program "value engineering" (VE), even though it embodied the same concepts and techniques as GE's value analysis (VA) program. In an operational sense, however, the two terms typically are used synonymously in industry today—only the timing differs. Hence, throughout this book when the term "value analysis" is used, it carries the same conceptual meaning as the term "value engineering," except for the practical matter of timing.

Value Engineering vis-à-vis Value Analysis

As practiced in U.S. firms for many years, value analysis techniques were most widely used in programs designed to engineer unnecessary costs out of existing products. Finally, the more progressive firms began to follow the Navy's lead by establishing what they too called "value engineering" programs—programs that applied the value analysis concept during the early stages of the new product design process. And, clearly, this is the first point at which it should be applied. This is where the greatest benefits are produced for both the firm and its customers.

What is the mix of value analysis and value engineering applications in American industry today? No one really knows. But the number of both programs has grown markedly in the last decade, with value engineering programs setting the pace.

The VE concept finds its most unique use in two kinds of companies—those that produce a limited number of units of a very expensive product and those that mass-produce products requiring expensive tooling. In these types of companies, value analysis of an item already in production is often impractical because it is then too late to incorporate changes in the product economically. In manufacturing certain electronic instruments used in defense systems, for example, the production run is often so short that it precludes the effective use of value analysis after production has been initiated. In fact, the Federal

Acquisition Regulations now stipulate that most major defense procurement contracts must be subjected to value engineering studies prior to initial production.[24]

A somewhat different situation that produces similar operating results is found in firms mass-producing automobiles. For example, in manufacturing the body panel for a car, once the design is fixed and the dies are purchased, it is usually too costly to change them, even though value analysis studies might subsequently disclose design inefficiencies.

Value engineering utilizes all the techniques of value analysis. In practice, it involves very close liaison work between the supply, production, and design engineering departments. This liaison is most frequently accomplished through the use of product design teams or various supply and production coordinators who spend considerable time in the engineering department studying and analyzing engineering drawings as they are initially produced. Once coordinators locate problem areas, value analysis techniques are employed to alleviate them.[25]

Value Engineering (VE) is a systematic study of every element of cost in a material, item of equipment, service, or construction project to ensure that the element fulfills a necessary function and at the lowest possible total cost. Ideally, the value engineering thought process is instilled in all members of the new product design team through appropriate training. (World-class firms provide 40–50 hours of VE training per year to those who would benefit!) The team members (including selected suppliers) apply VE as the product development project evolves. In some instances, Value Engineers are assigned to the development teams to ensure that these powerful tools are applied.

The inclusion of the value engineering step in Figure 10.2 is a safeguard: if VE thinking has been incorporated throughout the development process, a separate VE review may not be necessary. But experience indicates that a VE review at the indicated point will result in significant savings and improved quality and/or performance. Two tools aid those involved in the VE process:

- Design Analysis
- The VE Checklist

Design Analysis   Design analysis entails a methodical step-by-step study of all phases of the design of a given item in relation to the function it performs. The philosophy underlying this approach is not concerned with appraisal of any given part per se. Rather, the appraisal focuses on the function which the part, or the larger assembly containing the part, performs. This approach is designed to lead the analyst away from a traditional perspective which views a part as having certain accepted characteristics and configurations. Instead, it encourages the analyst to adopt a broader point of view and to consider whether the part performs the required function both as effectively and as efficiently as possible. Both quality and cost are objects of the analysis.

---

[24]For an interesting discussion of how the Department of Defense utilizes value engineering, see "DOD Honors ASD Value Engineering Program," *Skywriter,* August 1991, p. 7.

[25]For a complete discussion of this topic see D. W. Dobler, "How to Get Engineers and P.A.s Together," *Purchasing World,* November 1980, pp. 48–51; and D. N. Burt, *Proactive Procurement* (Englewood Cliffs, NJ: Prentice-Hall, 1984), chapter 2.

One technique many firms use in analyzing component parts of a subassembly is to dismantle, or "explode," the unit and then mount each part adjacent to its mating part on a pegboard or a table. The idea is to demonstrate visually the functional relationships of the various parts. Each component can thus be studied as it relates to the performance of the complete unit, rather than as an isolated element. Analysis of each component in this fashion attempts to answer four specific questions:

1. Can any part be *eliminated* without impairing the operation of the complete unit?
2. Can the design of the part be *simplified* to reduce its basic cost?
3. Can the design of the part be changed to permit the use of simplified or less costly *production methods?*
4. Can less expensive but equally satisfactory *materials* be used in the part?

Design simplifications frequently are more apparent than is possible under the original design conditions when viewed from the standpoint of the composite operation. (This in no way reflects unfavorably on the work done initially by the design engineer.) The discovery of such potential improvements is simply the product of an analysis with a substantially broader orientation than that possessed by the original designer. An organized VE study usually utilizes a number of individuals with different types of backgrounds, experience, and skills impossible to combine in the person of a single designer. Resulting design changes often permit the substitution of standardized production operations for more expensive operations requiring special setup work. In some cases, considering the volume of parts to be produced, an entirely different material or production process turns out to be more efficient than the one originally specified. Figure 10.3 shows the logic underlying a VE study.

The Value Engineering Checklist   Most companies develop some type of checklist to systematize the value engineering process. Literally hundreds of questions and key ideas appear on these lists. Some of the checklists are highly specialized for particular types of products. Illustrative of the more general questions is the following checklist:
First, determine the function of the item, then determine:

1. Can the item be eliminated?
2. If the item is not standard, can a standard item be used?
3. If it is a standard item, does it completely fit the application, or is it a misfit?
4. Does the item have greater capacity than required?
5. Can the weight be reduced?
6. Is there a similar item in inventory that could be substituted?
7. Are closer tolerances specified than are necessary?
8. Is unnecessary machining performed on the item?
9. Are unnecessarily fine finishes specified?
10. Is "commercial quality" specified? (Commercial quality is usually more economical.)
11. Can you make the item less expensively in your plant? If you are making it now, can you buy it for less?

Elements of the Study	Activities of the Study	

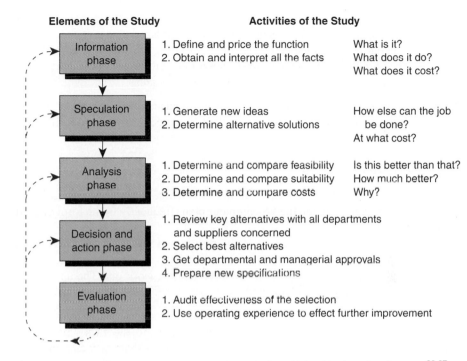

Information phase	1. Define and price the function 2. Obtain and interpret all the facts	What is it? What does it do? What does it cost?
Speculation phase	1. Generate new ideas 2. Determine alternative solutions	How else can the job be done? At what cost?
Analysis phase	1. Determine and compare feasibility 2. Determine and compare suitability 3. Determine and compare costs	Is this better than that? How much better? Why?
Decision and action phase	1. Review key alternatives with all departments and suppliers concerned 2. Select best alternatives 3. Get departmental and managerial approvals 4. Prepare new specifications	
Evaluation phase	1. Audit effectiveness of the selection 2. Use operating experience to effect further improvement	

Figure 10.3 I A Generalized Procedural Model of the Value Engineering Process[26,27]

12. Is the item properly classified for shipping purposes to obtain lowest transportation rates?

13. Can the cost of packaging be reduced?

14. Are suppliers contributing suggestions to reduce cost?[28]

---

[26]Most items perform more than one function—usually a basic function plus several supporting functions. Experience has shown that often the basic function constitutes 20 to 25 percent of the cost of the item and supporting functions account for the rest of the cost. Consequently, it is important to clearly identify these two types of functions. Use of the FAST (function analysis system technique) diagram approach provides an easy way to organize functions and subfunctions in their logical relationships. Details are available in (1) Carlos Fallon, *Value Analysis,* Wiley Inter-science Publishers, 1991; and (2) Gary Long, *VA/VE Workshop Workbook,* Society of American Value Engineers, September 24, 1993, Phase One and Phase Two.

[27]The development of alternative materials and processes is the most challenging, but perhaps the most stimulating, phase of value engineering. Creativity and brainstorming should be encouraged and supported. Professor Alvin Williams and his colleagues suggest a number of other techniques that readers may find helpful. For details see Alvin J. Williams, Steve Lacey, and William C. Smith, "Purchasing's Role in Value Analysis: Lessons from Creative Problem Solving," *The International Journal of Purchasing and Materials Management,* Spring 1992, pp. 37–41.

[28]*Basic Steps in Value Analysis,* a pamphlet prepared under the chairmanship of Martin S. Erb by the Value-Analysis-Standardization Committee, Reading Association, NAPM, Tempe, AZ, pp. 4–18.

In using this or similar checklists, those involved evaluate the component under investigation with respect to each item on the checklist. When a question is found to which the answer is not entirely satisfactory, this becomes a starting point for more detailed investigation. The checklist focuses the analyst's attention on those factors which past experience has proved to be potentially fruitful cost reduction areas.[29]

Viability   Prior to proceeding to production, a careful business analysis must be completed. In effect, the development team asks: "Will the product provide our firm's required return on its investment?"

The Production Phase

Manufacturing and Production Plans   In the production phase, as shown in Figure 10.4, the manufacturing plan and the procurement plan (frequently in the form of a bill of materials) are finalized.

As a result of its early involvement in the design and specification development process, supply management also should have been able to develop contingency plans that will satisfy the firm's needs if the first source doesn't work out. The appropriate plans are now formalized and implemented.

Knowledge Transfer   Manufacturing engineering applies experience from similar projects and new developments from other manufacturers to the firm's production process. Manufacturing engineers also work with suppliers to share new and improved production techniques.

Process Control   Contrary to popular opinion, the design is not finished when the transfer from development to production takes place—quite the contrary. Unfortunately, changes at this stage of product development are very costly and tend not to be evaluated with the same thoroughness as the original alternatives. Finding a quick fix typically is the order of the day, preferably a fix that does not require extensive retooling or scrap. Still, there are some legitimate reasons why changes in the design occur after release to production. For example, there may be phenomena that occur so infrequently that they are not discovered until a large number of products are manufactured. Another reason for changes at this point is the pressure to develop new products in a shorter time. This time compression frequently results in concurrent engineering. This means that a new manufacturing process is developed simultaneously with a new product using that process, rather than the more traditional sequential approach. This is a risky approach, but one that is gaining popularity because it saves time and results in earlier new product release.

When manufacturing problems arise, whether in the buying firm or the supplier's manufacturing operations, there is a tendency to look for a quick fix. One type of solution is to adjust the manufacturing process to minimize the problems, rather than to change the design. Perhaps this approach is taken because the process documentation is internal and

---

[29]For an interesting list of suggestions, see Dave A. Lugo, "Boost Your Creativity with Divergent Thinking and Checklists," *NAPM Insights,* May 1994, p. 12.

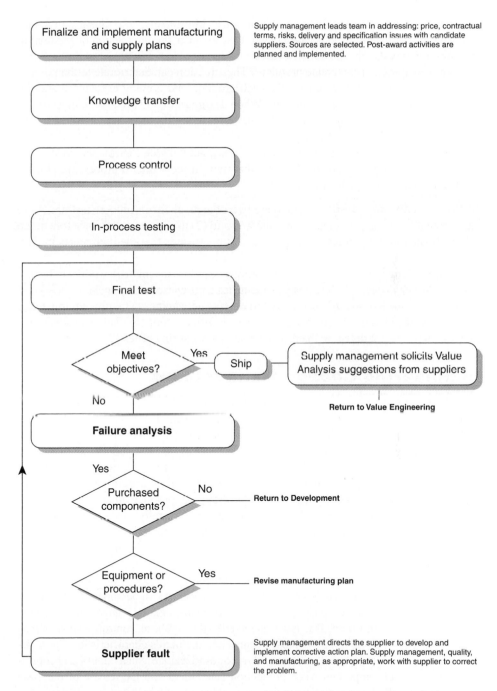

Figure 10.4 | Team and Supply Management Activities during New Product Development
Production Phase

Source: Adapted from *Strategic Proactive Procurement* by David N. Burt and Richard L. Pinkerton, AMACOM, New York, 1996.

not shipped to the customer along with the product. More likely, such changes in manufacturing processes are made because the process is under the jurisdiction of production and consequently the change does not require design engineering's approval.

Such an approach can create problems. The situation can deteriorate to the point at which there is a customized process for each product, and nothing is standard and the process is out of control most of the time. When design rules and process parameters are both being varied at the same time, the situation quickly becomes too complex to understand or control, and quality suffers.

The correct solution is to optimize the process, get it under control, and keep it that way. Then the designs can be modified so that they fit the standard process, producing stable and predictable yields day after day.

In-Process and Final Testing   There are two objectives for in-process testing: (1) to adjust or calibrate the performance in some way and (2) to eliminate defects before much value is added to the product. Final product testing ensures that the item meets its performance objectives.

Every failure has a cause and is a symptom of a failure mechanism waiting to be discovered. For example, if failure analysis identifies a purchased component as the source of the failure, further analysis is required to determine whether (1) faulty equipment or procedures are to blame or (2) the problem resides with the supplier. Failure analysis also may identify a latent defect in the product's design, requiring redesign.

Engineering Change Management

Any changes in components or the product itself may have profound effects on its cost, performance, appearance, and acceptability in the marketplace. Changes, especially at the component or subassembly level, can have a major impact on manufacturing. Unless changes in the configuration of an item or its components are controlled, manufacturers may find themselves in trouble. They may possess inventories of unusable raw materials or subassemblies. They may possess materials that require needlessly expensive rework to be adapted to a new configuration. Or they may produce an end item that will not meet the customer's needs. Uncontrolled changes generally mean that quality and reliability requirements have been compromised without appropriate retesting.

Engineering change management, a discipline which controls engineering changes, has been developed to avoid such problems.[30] How often engineering change management is required is a matter of managerial judgment. But for most modern technical items, engineering change management is a necessity. In some cases, it will be imposed on the manufacturer by its customer. Using engineering change management, changes are controlled and recorded. Marketing and all activities involved in the purchase, control, and use of purchased materials are told of any proposed changes to the item's characteristics. These organizations then comment on the effect of the proposed change. Such control and coordination is especially important when production scheduling and the release of purchase orders are controlled by a material requirements planning system.

---

[30]Engineering change management controls the changes to a product's design—specifically, its form, fit, and function.

There are many ways to organize an engineering change management group. Ideally, an engineering change management board is established with engineering, manufacturing, marketing, production planning, inventory management, and supply management represented. When a materials management organization exists in the firm, a senior representative of production planning and inventory control is a logical candidate to chair this board. It is crucial that supply management and the function responsible for materials control be involved in the review of proposed engineering changes for three reasons: (1) to provide input on the purchased materials implications of a proposed change, (2) to discuss the timing of proposed changes in order to minimize costs associated with unusable incoming materials, and (3) to be aware of forthcoming changes so that appropriate action can be taken with affected suppliers.

Adherence to this or a similar design process is key to the firm's success in the development of new products. Product quality, cost, and availability all must receive proper attention. Engineering, manufacturing, marketing, quality assurance, and supply management all have vital roles to play in the design process.

How to Expand Supply Management's Contributions

This chapter has described the design and development process. In too many firms, the design engineer attempts to address not only the technical and functional issues of design and development, but also manufacturing considerations, marketing implications, and the commercial considerations of economy and availability. Many of these individuals enjoy interacting with suppliers on both technical and commercial issues. And most believe they are serving their employer's best interests—even when making sourcing and specifications decisions that turn out to be suboptimal in the long run.

It is important to note that the effectiveness of early supplier involvement appears to be a function of the industry involved. Researchers McGinnis and Vallopra found that "supplier involvement is not a panacea for every new product development effort." They also found that the potential for supply management's "contribution to new product development is substantial. These potentials can be realized if the supply management staff has the abilities to successfully participate in (and lead) multi-functional teams; has the skills needed to identify, screen, and select suppliers to include in new product development; and the competence to manage, control, and coordinate supplier involvement in a multi-functional team environment."[31] Supply management professionals have their work cut out for them. They must develop and maintain cooperative relations with engineering that protect the profitability of the firm. Early supply management involvement is an essential ingredient of the program to maximize a firm's profitability.

Supply management professionals must understand the orientation and dedication of the typical design engineer. Obviously, an ability to speak the engineer's language (i.e., *engineeringese*) is very helpful. In a study conducted by one of the authors, it was

---

[31]Michael A. McGinnis, "New Product Development with and without Supplier Involvement: Factors Affecting Success in Manufacturing and Nonmanufacturing Organizations," *2000 Conference,* Richard Ivey School of Business, pp. 455–61. (London, Ontario, May 24–27)

found that supply management personnel who think in the same manner as engineers have a much higher success rate when dealing with engineers than do other individuals. Such thought processes can be identified through established testing procedures.

Whenever feasible, supply professionals should provide advice on the commercial implications of designs under consideration in a positive and constructive manner. They must learn to co-opt their engineering counterparts by providing value and service. Supply management then is seen as a partner who takes care of business problems, thereby allowing engineers to concentrate on technical issues. Several successful approaches to obtaining the desired level of supply management input during the design process now are described.

Design or Project Teams

When the importance of a project or program warrants it, a dedicated project team is the ideal means of ensuring early supply management involvement.

Materials Engineers

Individuals with an engineering background are good candidates for supply management positions whose responsibilities require involvement with design engineering. Some supply management organizations divide buying responsibilities into two specialties: (1) materials engineering and (2) the supply management activities of sourcing, pricing, and negotiating. The materials engineer is responsible for coordinating with design engineering, for prequalifying potential sources (usually with the assistance of quality assurance), and for participating in value management.

Co-Location

This approach calls for the placement of members of the supply management staff in locations where design engineering and development work is done. These individuals are available to collaborate with design engineers and others by obtaining required information from prospective suppliers and advising designers on the procurement implications of different materials and suppliers under consideration. When Harley-Davidson opened its product design center in 1997, it co-located design engineering, supply management, manufacturing, marketing and key supplier personnel. Cross-functional teams are the order of the day. The result? Faster to market, reduced total cost, and improved quality.[32]

Supply Management Professionals Who Interface Successfully with Engineers

The supply professional is the key to successful early supply management involvement in the new product development process. Management directives, policies, and procedures supporting early supply management involvement all help. But it is only when de-

---

[32]Personal interviews with Leroy Zimdars, former director of Product Purchasing, Harley-Davidson, 1997 and 1998.

sign engineers realize that the early involvement of a supply professional is a productive asset, and not a nuisance or an infringement on their territory, that early supply management involvement makes its full contribution.

The supply management professional who recognizes the importance of being involved early in the process must acquire the necessary skills and knowledge to be seen and accepted as a contributor. Courses in the development and interpretation of engineering drawings, as well as in a wide variety of technologies, can be taken via correspondence, night school, or a few degree-granting programs.[33] Sales personnel love to talk and will gladly help a willing listener gain technical insight into their products. Visits to suppliers' operations provide further insight and understanding.

Concluding Remarks

The design and development of new products is one of a manufacturing firm's most crucial activities. Profitability and even survival are affected. Supply management and the firm's suppliers have major contributions to make during this process. An increasing number of successful firms involve supply management and suppliers up front because of contributions they can make in the areas of quality, cost, and time to market.

Endnotes

In a recent article, Simon Croom of the Warwick Business School, Coventry, U.K., establishes the need for two types of competencies during product development: operational and relational. He defines operational competencies as those related to the design, manufacture, and delivery of a product. Relational competencies are involved in communication, interaction, problem resolution, and relationship development. Croom demonstrates the importance of relational competencies in achieving successful collaborative product development.[34]

European researchers Finn Wynstra, Bjorn Axelsson, and Arjan van Weele argue that authors in the fields of purchasing, procurement, and supply management have failed to identify many of supply management's activities in product development. These highly respected researchers identify 21 supply management activities related to product development. The interested reader is encouraged to review their provocative articles contained in the Summer 1999 and Autumn 2000 issues of the *European Journal of Purchasing and Supply Management.*

In a recent article, Handfield, Ragatz, Petersen, and Monczka address the complex issue of evaluating the capabilities of suppliers being considered for early involvement

---

[33]A small but growing number of universities now offer an integrated procurement and engineering management program.

[34]Simon R. Croom, "The Dyadic Capabilities Concept: Examining the Process of Key Supplier Involvement in Collaborative Product Development," *European Journal of Purchasing and Management* 7 (2001), pp. 29–37.

during new product development. The interested reader is encouraged to review this insightful article.[35]

Charles Fine, author of *Clockspeed,* advocates that firms design their supply chains strategically and concurrently with their products and production processes. "When firms do not explicitly acknowledge and manage supply chain design and engineering as a concurrent activity to product and process design and engineering, they often encounter problems late in product development, or with manufacturing launch, logistical support, quality control, and production costs. In addition, they run the risk of losing control of their business *destiny.*"[36] We agree with Dr. Fine.

---

[35]Robert B. Handfield, Gary L. Ragatz, Kenneth J. Petersen, and Robert M. Monczka, "Involving Suppliers in New Product Development," *California Management Review* 42, no. 1 (Fall 1999), pp. 59–82.

[36]Cited Ch1 Lt. Note 5 (May p. 5)

CHAPTER 11

Specifications and Standardization

World Class Supply Management^{SM} requires supply management professionals and suppliers to be actively involved in the tactical and strategic development of specifications and standards to proactively reduce total costs of products and services.

KEY CONCEPTS

■ Simplification   256
■ Developing a Standardization Program   256

Case

The Simple Sandwich

In a recent training session for Chili's restaurant chain, prospective employees were asked to write a description for making a peanut butter and jelly sandwich. One of the trainees was then summoned and asked to randomly select a description. The instructor asked the trainee to follow the description to make a sandwich strictly using the vast resources in the restaurant's kitchen.

What was the result? Complete chaos! The trainee could not even start, because the materials specified did not state whether the bread was wheat, white, rye, Texas toast, or hamburger bun. The author of the specifications assumed everyone knew that a peanut butter and jelly sandwich was made with white bread, creamy peanut butter, and grape jelly.

Even assuming the use of Rainbow brand white bread, Skippy creamy peanut butter, and Welch's grape jelly, the specifications still failed to state how the materials were to be assembled and with what tools. How much peanut butter? Should a spoon be used for spreading the jelly? Should one, two, or three pieces of bread be used?

The manager at Chili's had made her point. Don't assume specifications given by a customer to you or by you to the kitchen are readily understood. In an analogous way, don't assume that you, as a supply manager, understand all specifications given to you by an internal customer. In addition, do not assume that suppliers will understand your descriptions in a purchase order or contract.

Specifications and Standardization

Participation by both critical suppliers and supply management in the development of clear specifications and comprehensive standardization is required for an organization to evolve to World Class Supply Management^{SM}. Proactive development of specifications and standardization can aid an organization in reducing total costs of a product or service developed either in-house or externally. The importance of including supply management in the design process was established in our chapter on new product development.

In a manufacturing firm, when specifications for the tangible product are fixed, the final design of the product is also fixed. The final design of the product often dictates fixing ancillary costs such as packaging and required service for the product. Therefore, when the final design is fixed, the product's competitive stance and its profit potential are also fixed. As we stated in our new product development chapter, it is estimated that

75 to 85 percent of avoidable total costs are controllable at the design stage. Consequently, early involvement of supplier professionals is essential in the firm's effort to reduce total cost.[1]

Specifications and standardization are two related topics in the field of supply management. Specifications form what is called the purchase description. Standardized parts, components, and services may be included in the purchase description, but standardization goes beyond mere inclusion in a description. Standardization is treated in many companies and supply chains as a philosophy for creating competitive advantage. As will be discussed in this chapter, the development of specifications and standardization requires strategic action as well as tactical vigilance. This chapter first discusses specifications and then standardization.

Purposes of Specifications

The purchase specification forms the heart of the procurement. Whether or not a purchase order or contract will be performed to the satisfaction of the buying organization frequently is determined at the time the specification is selected or written. Purchase specifications serve a number of purposes, among them to:

- Communicate to professionals in the supply management department what to buy.
- Communicate to prospective suppliers what is required.
- Establish the tangible goods to be provided.
- Establish the intangible services to be provided, such as warranty, maintenance, and support.
- Establish the standards against which inspections, tests, and quality checks are made.
- Balance the specification goals of individual departments, relevant suppliers, desired product or service performance and cost.

Recognition that procurements should be made with the understanding of total cost of ownership (as discussed in the Total Cost of Ownership chapter) requires supply managers to consider specifications that go beyond the tangible good or primary service needed. For example, laptop specifications should include the desired warranty and support levels.

Collaborative Development

Development of specifications should be conducted as a collaborative process whenever economically justified. Through collaborative interactions of various departmental representatives and relevant suppliers, the specifications output can balance goals that often conflict with each other. Performance goals, such as quality and delivery, should be balanced against cost. Individual department goals should be balanced. Supplier goals should be considered. The balancing concept is illustrated in Figure 11.1. The balancing process is

---

[1]David N. Burt and Michael F. Doyle, *The American Keiretsu* (Homewood, IL: BusinessOne-Irwin, 1993), p. 158.

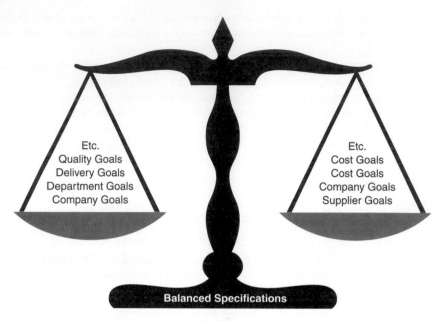

Figure 11.1 | Considerations in Developing Balanced Specifications

best done in an atmosphere of collaboration and mutual desire to develop specifications outcomes where "win-win" opportunities are maximized.

As suggested by Figure 11.1, multiple goals are balanced simultaneously. For example, in the design of a DVD player, high quality and timely delivery goals may conflict with cost containment goals. The objective in collaboratively developing the specifications would be to simultaneously achieve the quality, delivery, and cost goals. Perhaps a supplier suggests that a standard part that the buying firm was unaware of could be used where the original specification used a nonstandard part. The standard part would decrease production time, improve quality, and cost less than the nonstandard part. Unfortunately, many companies do not pursue balanced specifications through collaborative efforts.

Categories of Specifications

Purchase specifications can be classified into two broad categories—simple and complex—also referred to as low detail and high detail. The classification simple or complex is a reflection of the development of the specification itself and not the complexity of the product or service or the fulfillment of the specification. Both simple and complex specifications require a balancing of departmental differences, along with quality, delivery, and cost. However, in most cases, simple specifications require less balancing than complex specifications.

Complex or detailed specifications are used when a simple specification is not possible or preferable. A complex specification requires more resources and time to de-

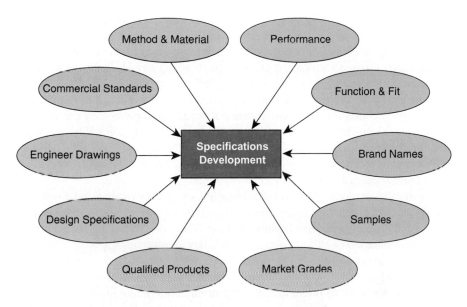

Figure 11.2 | Categories of Specifications

velop. We discuss simple specifications first, and then complex specifications. All categories of specifications are presented in the Figure 11.2, since combinations of the categories of specifications are possible.

Simple Specifications

Simple specifications require less resources and time to develop than complex specifications. In many cases, simple specifications are completed with one sentence and have little need for collaboration between functional areas or supply chain members. For example, the specification of an accounting department for supply management to purchase "12 Fujitsu Lifebook S Series model 4542 laptops with their default components package and warranty" is a complete, yet simple, specification. Nothing other than the brand name, model and package type, and warranty is needed. The astute reader will recognize that supply management could contribute to the specification by working with accounting to meet their needs with a lower-cost manufacturer or prequalified supplier. The six categories of simple specifications are desired performance, function and fit, brand or trade names, samples, market grades, and qualified products.

Performance Specifications A performance specification, in theory, is the perfect method of describing a requirement. Instead of describing an item in terms of its design characteristics, performance specifications describe in words, and quantitatively where possible, what the item is required to do. This type of description is used extensively in buying highly technical military and space products. For example, the product wanted could be a missile capable of being launched from a submarine with a designated speed, range, and accuracy. Potential suppliers are told only the performance that is required. Though performance is specified in precise detail, suppliers are not told how the product should be manufactured or what material should be used in its manufacture.

Performance specifications are not limited to such complex items as spacecraft. Electronics, aircraft, and automobile companies, for example, frequently use this method to buy such common materials as electrical wire, batteries, and radios. A performance specification for wire may require it to withstand a given temperature, have a designated resistance to abrasion, and have a given conductivity capability. No mention is made in the specifications of what materials are to be used or how the wire is to be manufactured or insulated to give it the required characteristics. Manufacturers are free to make these choices as they see fit.

Industry uses performance specifications extensively to buy expensive, complicated machines and machine tools. Today, more production machines are replaced because of technological obsolescence than because of wear. Therefore, in buying such a machine, a firm should make every effort to obtain the ultimate in technological advancement. Often this can be done best by using performance specifications. To reduce and control the expense associated with this approach to describing requirements, descriptions should be written as explicitly as possible. Also, the product being purchased should be sectionalized into the greatest practical number of distinct components, with potential sellers required to quote on each component. This practice helps solve the difficult problem of comparing sellers' prices by allowing comparison of individual components.

There are two primary advantages of describing quality by performance specifications: (1) ease of preparing the specifications and (2) assurance of obtaining the precise performance desired. For complex products, it is by far the easiest type of specification to write. It assures performance, and if the supplier is competent, it assures inclusion of all applicable new developments. The clarity of a performance specification also brings clarity into any legal or liability issue that may ensue if the supplier does not meet the specification as agreed. A potential disadvantage is when the performance specification is out of date given current technology. For example, a late model computer hard drive will often cost more than a current technology hard drive that stores more and has faster access rates and a lower price.

Proper supplier selection is essential when performance specifications are used. In fact, the ability to select capable and honest suppliers is prerequisite to the proper use of performance specifications. Because the supplier assumes the entire responsibility for designing and making the product, quality is entirely in its hands. If the supplier is not capable, it cannot apply the most advanced technical and manufacturing knowledge. If it is not honest, materials and workmanship may be inferior. When using performance specifications, supply managers must solicit competition among two or more capable sellers. Capable suppliers ensure quality; competition ensures reasonable prices.

Function and Fit Specifications   Such purchase descriptions are a variation of performance specifications and are used in *early supplier involvement (ESI)* programs. With this approach, the design team describes the function(s) to be performed and the way the item is to fit into the larger system (e.g., automobile, computer, etc.), together with several design objectives (cost, weight, and reliability).

Robert May supports the argument that ESI best meets the needs of companies by giving suppliers performance specifications. According to May, "The optimal use of suppliers' special skills and processes is experienced when suppliers are provided with a set of performance specifications."[2]

As ESI becomes more common, this approach to describing requirements undoubtedly will increase in popularity. With careful prequalification of suppliers, there are no significant disadvantages with this approach.

Brand or Trade Names When manufacturers develop and market a new product, they must decide whether or not to brand it. Branding or differentiating a product is generally done to develop a recognized reputation and thus gain repeat sales, protect the product against substitutes, maintain price stability, and simplify sales promotion.[3] The primary reason most manufacturers brand their products is to obtain repeat sales. Consumers develop a preference for brands. Therefore, branded products can generally be sold at higher prices than unbranded products of similar quality. A brand represents the manufacturer's pledge that the quality of the product will be consistent from one purchase to the next. A supply manager can be certain that a reputable manufacturer will strive to keep this pledge.

Brand name products are among the simplest to describe on a purchase order. Thus, they save time and reduce supply management expense. Inspection expense is also low for branded products. The only inspection required is sight verification of the brand labels. The brand is the quality ordered. The higher prices usually paid for name brands thus are offset to some extent by reduced description preparation and inspection costs.

A supplier's success in maintaining a consistent quality level is greatest in those situations in which production and quality control are under the supplier's own supervision. If a supplier buys an item from several manufacturers, the quality variation in all probability will be larger than if the supplier made the item or bought it from a single source. For this reason, it is important for supply managers to know who is responsible for the production and quality control of all branded products they buy. In situations in which tight quality control is essential, multiple sources of production should be avoided if possible.

It is often said that when a supply manager purchases by brand name he or she eliminates competition by limiting the purchase to a single source of supply. If a supply manager had to limit purchases to a single brand from a single source, this would represent a major disadvantage of purchasing by brand name. In fact, however, there are very few situations in which only one brand is acceptable for a given purpose. A profitable market for any item in a competitive enterprise economy attracts other manufacturers to make the item. Competition, therefore, is available by brands just as it is by other types

---

[2]Robert E. May, C.P.M., Sr. Consultant, Harris Consulting, Inc., "Top Ten Approaches to Cost Reduction," presentation at the 1998 NAPM International Purchasing Conference, May 1998. See napm.org for full transcript of the proceedings paper.

[3]Manufacturers also produce merchandise for wholesalers and retailers who market it under their own private brand labels. In such arrangements the manufacturer is relieved of marketing and promotional responsibilities.

of quality descriptions. In addition, the same branded product may be available from different wholesalers or jobbers who are willing to compete on price and service to get a buying company's order.

Making a specification of "brand A or equal" on the bid forms usually ensures competition among brands. What does "or equal" mean? This question generates many arguments. Realistically, it means materials that are of equal quality and are capable of performing the function intended. Equal quality means similar quality of materials and similar quality of workmanship. Comparing the quality of materials is relatively easy, but comparing the quality of workmanship is particularly difficult. Here such nebulous considerations as precision of production, fit and matching of adjacent parts, types of finish, and shades of color must be resolved. The key to the "or equal" consideration is, "Can the 'equal' perform the function for which the specified brand is desired?" If it cannot, it certainly is not equal; if it can, it is equal.

One practical way of resolving the "or equal" problem is to let the using department decide which products are equal before prices are solicited. Only companies whose products are accepted by using departments as equal are requested to submit prices. This technique helps avoid wounded feelings among potential suppliers. It also permits requisitioning departments to make more objective decisions.

In some situations, purchasing by brand name can be made more effective by including additional references or limitations in the purchasing description. For example, if the supply manager suspects that other materials can perform the desired function, reference in the description should give prospective suppliers the opportunity to offer such other materials for consideration. When limitations concerning physical, functional, and other characteristics of the materials to be purchased are essential to the buying company's needs, they should be set forth clearly in the brand name description. For example, in many purchases of equipment, interchangeability of repair parts is essential. When this is the case, the above limitation should be spelled out in the brand name description. The invitation for bids or requests for proposal should reserve the right to examine and test the proffered item should an "or equal" product be offered.

For small quantities, brand buying is excellent.[4] The primary disadvantage of purchasing by brands frequently is higher price. Many categories of branded items sell at notoriously high prices. Antiseptics and cleaning compounds are common examples of such items. For these, another type of purchase description is preferable. When they are purchased by detailed or performance specifications, savings often exceed 50 percent. In recent years, buying drugs by generic name rather than by brand has resulted in spectacular savings for many hospitals; savings up to 70 percent are not uncommon.

Samples   Samples have been called the lazy person's method of describing requirements. When samples are used, the supply manager does not have to look for an equal brand, pick a standard specification, or describe the performance wanted. Samples are neither the cheapest nor the most satisfactory method of purchase. Usually the money

---

[4]Brand buying is mandatory in some situations. Common examples are when a supplier's production process is secret, when its workmanship exceeds all competitors', or when testing competitive items is too costly.

spent on inspection costs substantially exceeds the money saved in description costs. It usually is difficult to determine by inspection that the product delivered is, in fact, the same as the sample. Quality of materials and quality of workmanship are generally exceedingly difficult to determine from routine inspection. Therefore, in many cases, acceptance or rejection becomes a matter of subjective judgment.

Samples generally should be used only if other methods of description are not feasible. Color and texture, printing, and grading are three broad areas in which other methods of description are not feasible. A precise shade of green, for example, is difficult to describe without a sample. Proposed lithographic work is best judged by the supplier's proofs. Establishing grades for commodities such as wheat, corn, and cotton by samples has proved to be the best method of describing these products.

Market Grades   *Grading* is a method of determining the quality of commodities. A grade is determined by comparing a specific commodity with standards previously agreed on. Grading is generally limited to natural products such as lumber, wheat, hides, cotton, tobacco, food products, and so on. The value of grades as a description of quality depends on the accuracy with which the grades can be established and the ease with which they can be recognized during inspection. There are, for example, 13 grades of cotton, each of which must be determined from an examination of individual samples. Trade associations, commodity exchanges, and government agencies all expend great effort in establishing and policing usable grades.

In buying graded commodities, industrial supply managers often use personal inspection as a part of their buying technique. Just as individuals select by inspecting the shoes, dresses, and shirts they buy, so industrial supply managers select by inspecting some of the commodities they buy in primary markets. There can be a significant difference between the upper and lower grade limits of many commodities. The difference is so great in some that materials near the lower limit of the grade may be unacceptable. Hence, inspection is critically important in buying many materials by market grade. Brewers and millers, for example, usually inspect all the grains they buy. Inspection is necessary if they are to obtain raw materials of the quality needed to produce a finished product of consistent quality.

Beef is an excellent illustration of the wide quality spread that can exist within a grade. Normally, 700-pound steers dressed and graded as "U.S. Prime" have a spread of roughly 40 pounds in fat content between the beef at the top of the grade and beef at the bottom of the grade. Such a wide spread may be a minor consideration to the purchaser of a one-pound steak. However, to the industrial food service manager buying millions of pounds of beef, the difference can be thousands or hundreds of thousands of dollars.

Qualified Products   In some situations, it is necessary to determine in advance of a purchase whether a product can meet specifications. These situations normally exist when (1) it takes too long[5] to conduct the normal post-purchase inspections and tests that are required to ensure quality compliance, (2) inspection to ensure compliance with the quality aspects of the specifications requires special testing equipment that is not commonly

---

[5]The federal government and some large industrial firms have defined "too long" as a period exceeding 30 days.

or immediately available, and (3) the purchase involves materials concerned with safety equipment, life survival equipment, research equipment, or materials described by performance specifications.

When advance qualification is indicated, suppliers are prequalified by a thorough review and test of the entire process by which they ensure compliance with their specifications. After qualification, the products of the approved suppliers are placed on what is called a *qualified products list (QPL)*. Trade name, model number, part number, place of manufacture, and similar identifying data describe approved products on the QPL.

Complex Specifications

Complex or detailed specifications are descriptions that tell the seller exactly what the buyer wants to purchase. A simple specification for buying ketchup might be "12-ounce plastic bottle of Heinz tomato ketchup." In contrast, ketchup specifications become complex if the actual recipe is given with ingredients and production procedures. A complex specification often goes beyond the design of a product, to include specifications regarding methodology, packaging, transport, delivery schedules, warranty, and service.

There are four principle types of complex specifications: commercial standards, design specifications (generally accompanied by engineering drawings), engineering drawings, and material and method-of-manufacture specifications.

Commercial Standards Recurring needs for the same materials have led industry and government to develop commercial standards for these materials. A commercial standard is nothing more than a complete description of the item standardized. The description includes the quality of materials and workmanship that should be used in manufacturing the item, along with dimensions, chemical composition, and so on. It also includes a method for testing both materials and workmanship. Commercial standards are a cornerstone of the mass production system; therefore, they are important to efficient supply management and to the standard of living in the United States.

All nuts, bolts, pipes, and electrical items that are made to standard specifications can be expected to fit all standard applications, regardless of who manufactured the item. Materials ordered by standardized specifications leave no doubt on the part of either the buyer or the seller as to what is required. Standard specifications have been prepared for many goods in commercial trade. National trade associations, standards associations, national engineering societies, the federal government, and national testing societies all contribute to the development of standard specifications and standard methods of testing. Commercial standards are applicable to raw materials, fabricated materials, individual parts and components, and subassemblies.

Purchasing by commercial standards is somewhat similar to purchasing by brand name. In both methods, the description of what is wanted can be set forth accurately and easily. Commercial standards are more complex because they require greater detail in the description. With the exception of proprietary products, most widely used items are standard in nature; hence, they are highly competitive and readily available at reasonable prices. There are many users of standard products; therefore, manufacturers who make them can safely schedule long, low-cost production runs for inventory. They do not need specific sales commitments before production. They know that materials will be ordered under these standard specifications when they are needed.

Inspection is only moderately expensive for materials purchased by commercial standards. Commercial standard products require periodic checking in addition to sight identification to assure firms that they are getting the quality specified.

Commercial standard items should be used whenever possible. They contribute greatly to the simplification of design, supply management procedures, inventory management, and cost reduction. Copies of standard specifications can be obtained from a number of government, trade association, and testing association sources. In fact, the easiest way to get a particular specification is to ask a manufacturer to provide a copy of the standard specification of the material or product that it recommends for the supply manager's intended need.

Design Specifications Not all items and materials used in industry are covered by standard specifications or brands. For many items, therefore, a large number of buying firms prepare their own specifications. By so doing, these firms broaden their field of competition. All manufacturers capable of making the item described in the firm's specifications are potential suppliers.

By preparing its own specifications, a company can often avoid the premium prices of brand name items and the sole source problems of patented, copyrighted, and proprietary products. When preparing its own specifications, a company should attempt to make them as close as possible to industry standards. If any special dimensions, tolerances, or features are required, every effort should be made to attain these "specials" by designing them as additions or alterations to standard parts. Doing so will save time and money.

Describing requirements with chemical or electronic specifications, or with physical specifications and accompanying engineering drawings, entails some risk. For example, if a buying company provides the exact chemical specifications of the paint desired, it assumes complete responsibility for the paint's performance. Should the paint fade in the first month, it is the buyer's responsibility. If a buying company specifies for a metal fabricator the exact dimensions wanted in a part, the buyer assumes all responsibility for the part's fitting and functioning. Should it happen that a part, to fit and function properly, must be 26.045 inches long, rather than 26.015 inches as specified in the purchase order, the responsibility for failure rests solely with the buying firm.

The very nature of the materials purchased under this method of description tends to require special inspection. The cost of such inspection to assure compliance with company prepared specifications can be high.

Engineering Drawings Engineering drawings and prints are occasionally used alone, but more typically in conjunction with other physical purchase descriptions. Engineering drawings may be part of design specifications described above. Where precise shapes, dimensions, and spatial relationships are required, drawings are the most accurate method of describing what is wanted. Despite their potential for accuracy, exceptional care must be exercised in using them. Ambiguity, sometimes present in this method of description, can produce costly repercussions. All dimensions, therefore, must be completely covered, and the descriptive instruction should be explicit.

Engineering drawings are used extensively in describing quality for construction projects, for foundry and machine shop work, and for myriads of special mechanical parts and components. There are four principle advantages in using drawings for description: (1) They are accurate and precise, (2) they are the most practical way of describing mechanical items requiring extremely close tolerances, (3) they permit wide competition (what is wanted can easily be communicated to a wide range of potential suppliers), and (4) they clearly establish the standards for inspection.

Material and Method-of-Manufacture These specifications are used most appropriately by technically sophisticated large companies or organizations dealing with small suppliers having limited research and development staffs. When this method is used, prospective suppliers are instructed precisely as to the specific materials to be used and how they are to be processed. The buying firm assumes full responsibility for product performance. It believes that its own organization has the latest knowledge concerning materials, techniques, and manufacturing methods for the item being purchased. In such a case, the purchaser sees no reason to pay another company for this knowledge.

A modified version of these specifications is sometimes used by industry. Large purchasers of paint, for example, frequently request manufacturers of a standard paint to add or delete certain chemicals when producing paint for them. Purchasers of large quantities of steel make the same type of request when purchasing special steels. Chemical and drug buyers, for reasons of health and safety, sometimes approach full use of the material and method-of-manufacture technique in describing quality. Usually, this technique is little used in industry because it puts such great responsibility on the buying firm. It can deny a company the latest advancements in both technical development and manufacturing processes. Specifications of this type are expensive to prepare. Inspection generally is very expensive. Material and method-of-manufacture specifications are used extensively by the armed services and the Department of Energy.

There are two important advantages of this method of description. First, the widest competition is possible, and thus good pricing is assured. Second, since the product is nonstandard, the provisions against discrimination in the Robinson-Patman Act pose no barrier to obtaining outstanding pricing and service.

Combination of Methods

Many products cannot adequately be described by a single method. In such cases, a combination of two or more methods of description should be used. For example, in describing the quality desired for a space vehicle, performance specifications could be used to describe numerous overall characteristics of the vehicle, such as its ability to withstand certain temperatures, to perform certain predetermined maneuvers in space at precise time sequences, and to stay in space for a specific period of time. Physical specifications could be used to describe the vehicle's configuration as well as the television cameras and other instruments it will carry. Commercial standards or brand names might be used to describe selected pieces of electrical or mechanical hardware used in the vehicle's support systems. A chemical specification could be used to describe the vehicle's paint. Finally, a sample could be used to show the color of this paint.

Few products are as complex as space vehicles; nevertheless, an increasing number of industrial products require two or more methods of quality descriptions. For instance, something as commonplace as office drapes could require chemical specifications to describe the cloth and fireproofing desired, physical specifications to describe the dimensions desired, and samples to describe the colors and texture desired.

Development of Specifications

Developing specifications can be a difficult task to manage because it involves many variables, including the problem of conflicting human sensitivities and orientations. Many departments are capable of contributing to specifications development; they are frequently thwarted from fully doing so, however, because of conflicting views. Before the optimum in design can be achieved, these major conflicting views must be reconciled.

Organizational Approaches

Several approaches to developing balanced specifications are used individually or jointly by most companies. The approaches in order of collaborative orientation from lowest to highest include informal approach, supply management coordinator approach, early supply management involvement (formerly EPI), early supplier involvement (ESI), consensus development, and cross-functional team approach.

Informal Approach   The informal approach emphasizes the concept of a supply manager's responsibility to "challenge" materials requests. At the same time, top management urges designers to request advice from supply managers and work with them on all items that may involve commercial considerations. Emphasis at all times is placed on person-to-person communication and cooperation between individual supply managers and designers. Using this approach, a company-oriented, cost-conscious attitude is developed at the grass-roots level throughout the organization.

Two potential problems exist with the informal approach. The most obvious is that the lack of formalization through corporate policy or organizational structure may render the supply manager powerless and make the approach completely ineffective. The second problem is that the supply manager may create animosity when it is appropriate to challenge a specification.

Supply Management Coordinator Approach   One or more positions are created in the supply department for individuals, frequently called *materials engineers,*[6] to serve in a liaison capacity with the design department. Typically, the materials engineer spends most of his or her time in the engineering department reviewing design work as it comes off the drawing boards. The materials engineer searches for potential supply

---

[6]The reader should not infer from this discussion any intention to disparage the work of the design engineer. Nothing of the sort is intended. Often, for reasons of policy, tradition, or expediency, the design engineer is required to make decisions alone that could be made more effectively in collaboration with others. Nevertheless, billions of dollars are lost annually through the adoption of unnecessarily stringent specifications at the design stage.

management problems in an attempt to mitigate them before the specifications are completed.

The supply management coordinator approach is highly structured, as well as expensive. It also is very effective. Therefore, it should be used whenever coordination problems stemming from the technical nature of a firm's product or from the magnitude of its cost justify such an investment.

Early Supply Management Involvement   As we discussed in the chapter on new product development, progressive firms increasingly are creating design policies to involve supply management in the early stages of new product development. Early supply management involvement was popularized in industry through the now dated term EPI,[7] which stands for early purchasing involvement.

Too often design engineers and production engineers resolve among themselves all four of the major departmental considerations of specifications preparation without consulting supply management. This is regrettable because professional engineers seldom have the commercial experience and the market information required to resolve the supply management considerations of specifications. In their attempts to do so, they frequently develop stringent specifications that do not provide sufficient latitude to encourage effective competition.

Early Supplier Involvement   Early supplier involvement, or ESI, is widely used in industry. To properly implement ESI, a buying company should first establish the policy of involving supply management in the design process. After such a policy is enacted, then ESI can be actively engaged. ESI coupled with early supply management involvement can improve product quality and reliability, while compressing development time and reducing total material cost.[8]

Consensus Development Approach   Consensus development calls for specifications to be agreed upon by the department managers. This collaborative approach falls short of developing a formal team. Although department managers disagree occasionally, compromise and consensus usually can be worked out when the various aspects of the problem are understood and the organizational mechanism for reaching consensus has been established. When specifications conflicts arise and consensus cannot be reached, final authority for the decision should rest with the department having responsibility for the product's performance.

Cross-Functional Team Approach   The cross-functional team (CFT) approach recognizes that a good specification is a compromise among basic objectives. A specifications CFT is established, with representatives (as appropriate) from design engineering, production engineering, supply management, marketing, operations (including produc-

---

[7]While we expect the acronym EPI to continue to be used over the next several years, we believe the term "purchasing" has become primarily associated with tactical activities. The involvement of supply management in the design process is clearly a strategic activity, thereby requiring the shift in terminology.

[8]Burt and Doyle, *American Keiretsu*, p. 116.

tion control), quality, and standards. As described in the chapter on new product development, members of the design team are involved, as appropriate, throughout the development of the product and its specifications. A common variation to the above approach is for the development of the specification to be delegated to an appropriate technical expert with the resulting specification being reviewed and approved by the CFT.

Supply Management Research

Once a need has been identified and functionally described, and when the size of the contemplated purchase warrants, supply management research and analysis should be conducted to investigate the availability of commercial products able to meet the need. This research and analysis also should provide information to aid in selecting a strategy appropriate to the situation. Supply management research and analysis involves obtaining the following information, as appropriate:

■ The availability of standard products suitable to meet the need (with or without modification).

■ The terms, conditions, and prices under which such products are sold.

■ Any applicable trade provisions or restrictions or controlling laws.

■ The performance characteristics and quality of available products, including quality control and test procedures followed by the manufacturers.

■ Information on the satisfaction of other users having similar needs.

■ Any costs or problems associated with integration of the item with those currently used.

■ Industry production practices, such as continuous, periodic, or batch production.

■ The distribution and support capabilities of potential suppliers.

Writing Specifications

After the design of a product is determined, the next step is to translate the individual part and materials specifications into written form. Optimal performance in all departments is contingent on good specifications. To meet the needs of all departments, a specification must satisfy many requirements:

■ Design and marketing requirements for functional characteristics, chemical properties, dimensions, appearance, and other features.

■ Manufacturing requirements for workability of materials and manufacturability.

■ Inspection's requirements to test materials for compliance with the specifications.

■ Stores' requirement to receive, store, and issue the material economically.

■ Supply management's requirement to procure material without difficulty and with adequate competition from reliable sources of supply.

■ Production control's and supply management's requirement to substitute materials when such action becomes necessary.

■ The total firm's requirements for suitable quality at the lowest overall cost.

■   The total firm's requirement to use commercial and industrial standard material when-
    ever possible and to establish company standards in all other cases in which nonstan-
    dard material is used repetitively.

Common Specifications Problems

Several problems that are caused by the specifications themselves commonly arise unnecessarily. These should be headed off beforehand and addressed in the specifications
development process, before the specifications have been completed. Three of these
common problems are given below.

Lack of Clarity   Lack of clarity can result in unpleasant surprises. Specifications
should be written in clear and unambiguous terms. Clarity in written expressions is not
always easy to achieve but the effort is worthwhile. One company recently lost $65,000
on a closed circuit television installation. Its written specifications misled the supplier
into believing that a more expensive installation was specified than the buyer really
wanted. The likelihood of such experiences can be reduced, if not altogether eliminated,
by writing specifications clearly.

Limiting Competition   Care must be exercised to ensure that specifications are not
written around a specific product, so as to limit competition. Several years ago, a fire
chief wrote into the specifications for a new fire truck the requirement that the supplier
of the truck manufacture the truck's 12-cylinder engine. This completely restricted competition, since only one supplier of fire engines manufactured 12-cylinder engines in its
own plant. Had the fire chief specified what was wanted in terms of performance characteristics, such as speed and acceleration, competition would have been plentiful. This
example typifies one of industry's most common forms of specifications abuse—
slanting specifications to one supplier's product, thus reducing or precluding competition. In this particular case, fortunately, the situation had a happy ending; the supply
management department challenged the specifications, and the fire chief agreed to
rewrite them in a form permitting maximum competition. A significant savings resulted
from this change *before* the specs were completed.

Unreasonable Tolerances   Specifying an unreasonable tolerance is another common
specification mistake. Unnecessary precision pyramids costs! It costs more to make materials to close tolerances, it costs more to inspect them, and more rejects typically result. The best method of avoiding such unnecessary costs is (1) to adhere to the most
economical method of manufacture while (2) using standard specifications wherever
possible. For example, in procuring 1,000 drive pulleys for use in vacuum motors, the
first decision would be to determine whether a casting process could manufacture the
pulleys satisfactorily. Although this method dictates the use of looser tolerances, in large
volumes its unit cost is considerably lower than that of the alternative, machining the
pulley from bar stock. The second decision would be to select an industrial standard for
the part, regardless of the method of manufacture used. This leads us directly to a consideration of standardization.

Unreasonable Tolerances Example   Ben Rogers, a Ph.D. student in Production Operations Management at The University of Pittsburgh, was excited to start gathering research data at a manufacturer of heavy construction equipment in Ohio. The goal of the research was to develop a model to forecast product costs based on specifications given in designs. Yesterday, he had met the managers in operations, design, and quality to decide what data to accumulate. Today he hoped to start the data accumulation process with a senior design engineer, Keith Sampson.

As Ben walked up to the engineering department, he heard a loud and angry argument ensuing between Keith and Gary Hamm, a production manager. In an agitated tone Gary said, "Keith, we are on the floor reworking another nonstandard bore from our supplier that once again did not meet the tolerances your group specified. For four years these tolerances have given us headaches. The tighter tolerances on the bores sure haven't reduced the complaints from customers about the road grader. Heck, there weren't any complaints that I can recall that were ever related to the old tolerances for this part anyway. I still don't understand why you never consulted our department on the change to begin with. One thing is for sure, the tighter tolerance has increased frustration on the factory floor, angered our supplier who we keep charging for the reworks, and screwed up my schedule so I continuously miss due dates. I am fed up. It's time you changed this tolerance back to the old standard!"

Keith replied in a tense voice, "Gary, you know that to compete we needed to improve quality continuously and that means tightening tolerances. There is no way I am going to change the design again! If your supplier is incapable of producing to our specifications, then dump the supplier. You are the operations manager—so start managing your operations and deal with it!"

Gary bumped Ben as he stormed out of Keith's office. Ben quietly walked on by, deciding that this was not the time to ask Keith for data. As Ben walked away, he wondered if he had just had a foretaste of the problems he would discover in the next six months.

This true story[9] illustrates what can happen when internal functions do not work together to develop specifications. The overspecification problem is a common one that has been discussed for the last 30 years but unfortunately still exists today in most companies. Regardless of the method(s) used to describe specifications, only the minimum quality needed for the product to perform the function intended should be specified. Overspecifying and including restrictive features in purchase descriptions causes delays and increases costs.

The importance of developing balanced specifications and standards through interfunctional and relevant chain member participation is paramount for companies that need to improve their competitive position. The balancing act is accomplished by meeting the needs of the functional areas while setting off performance measures, such as quality and delivery, against cost.

---

[9]The names of the individuals and company location involved in the story are changed. The story itself is true with respect to the actual events that occurred.

Standardization

A uniform identification that is agreed on is called a *standard*. In business practice, the concept of standardization is applied in either industrial or managerial standardization. *Industrial standardization* can be defined as "the process of establishing agreement on uniform identifications for definite characteristics of quality, design, performance, quantity, service, and so on." *Managerial standardization* deals with such things as operating practices, procedures, and systems.

History of Standardization

Eli Whitney contributed to the development of standardization in 1801, when he accepted a contract to furnish 10,000 muskets to the United States government. When it appeared that Whitney had fallen behind on his contract, he was summoned to Washington by Thomas Jefferson to explain his delay. Whitney took with him a box containing the parts of ten muskets. On a table before his congressional interrogators, he separated these parts into piles of stocks, barrels, triggers, firing hammers, and so on. He asked a congressman to pick a part from each pile. Whitney then assembled these parts into a finished musket, repeating the process until all ten muskets had been assembled. After his demonstration, it was easy for Whitney to explain his apparent delay. Rather than furnishing a proportional number of guns each month, as an artisan gunsmith would have done after individually making the parts for each gun and then assembling each gun in turn, Whitney had been working to design machine tools and dies with which he could mass produce parts which were interchangeable with each other. He had standardized the parts. When his machine tools were completed, he was able to produce all the muskets in a period of time in which an artisan gunsmith could have produced only a few muskets.

Whitney discovered that by standardizing parts, the skills of artisans could be transferred to machines that could be operated by less skilled labor. This, in turn, reduced the need for highly skilled labor, which, at the time, was in extremely short supply. Of greatest significance, it was this practice that introduced mass production and brought sizable industrial growth to the United States.

The burning to the ground of Baltimore's business district in 1904 clearly illustrated the need for standards in urban living. Like the battle that was lost for the lack of a horseshoe nail, Baltimore was lost for the lack of standard fire hose couplings. Washington, New York, and Philadelphia all responded to Baltimore's cry for help. When their pumping equipment arrived in Baltimore, however, the rescuers just stood by helplessly. There was no way to connect the different-sized hose couplings to Baltimore's fire hydrants.

Eli Whitney introduced mass production in the United States. Henry Ford made it universal. Ford, however, misinterpreted in one important aspect the relationship between standardization and mass production: He visualized mass production to mean a standard product produced on an assembly line. Ford thought he spoke correctly when he said, "The customer can have any color car he wants as long as it is black." Actually, he missed the full implication of mass production. Mass production is the production of many diverse products, assembled from standardized parts that have been mass-produced.

Today, standardization has become a way of creating competitive advantage through mass customization. Perhaps no company today exemplifies this more than Dell, the largest assembler and seller of personal computers in the world. Dell works with many suppliers to design and produce parts, components, and modules that can be used with multiple models. For example, several laptop models use the same DVD player module. A supply chain standard design was developed to allow interchangeability of several suppliers' modules and ease of installation and support.

Types and Sources of Standards

In industry, there are three basic types of materials standards: (1) international standards, (2) industry or national standards, and (3) company standards. If a designer or user cannot adapt a national or international standard for his or her purpose, the second choice is to use a company standard. If the required part is truly a nonrepetitive "special," then use of a standard is impossible.

Where can one get standard specifications? Specifications for items that have been standardized can be obtained from the organizations that have developed them, such as those listed below:

- International Organization for Standardization
- National Bureau of Standards
- American National Standards Institute
- American Society for Testing and Materials
- American Society for Quality
- Society of Automotive Engineers
- Society of Mechanical Engineers
- American Institute of Electrical Engineers
- Federal Bureau of Specifications
- National Lumber Manufacturers' Association

The European-based International Organization for Standardization (ISO) has several hundred specialized committees that develop a wide variety of standards that are promulgated by ISO and usually are accepted worldwide. Many of these standards are adaptations of standards from the American National Standards Institute, the German Institute for Standards, the British Standards Institute, and other national standards organizations around the world.

A catalog of United States standards, international recommendations, and other related information is published annually and distributed without charge by the American National Standards Institute.[10] The Institute is a federation of more than 100 nationally recognized organizations, trade associations, and technical societies, or groups of such organizations. Its members can gain ANSI assistance in developing any

---

[10] ANSI, 1430 Broadway, New York, NY 10018.

standard desired. Recommendations for establishing a standard can be made at any time. If, after appropriate research and debate, ANSI approves the recommended standard, it will be adopted as a U.S. standard.

Both the civilian and military departments of the U.S. government participate in standardization work that greatly assists industry. For example, the National Bureau of Standards (NBS), among other things, was established to serve "any firm, corporation, or individual in the United States engaged in manufacturing or other pursuits regarding the use of standards."

The need for international standards is fundamental; by eliminating technical trade barriers, international standards facilitate increased international trade and prosperity. The ISO 9000 series of quality standards, now used voluntarily worldwide, is a good illustration. The economic stakes associated with the development of international standards are so high in terms of increased international trade and prosperity that progress, albeit slow, is inevitable. Because private organizations, national and regional governments, and other international organizations are all involved in the adoption process, political infighting is inescapable.

Metric system measurements are among the important international standards. In December 1975, Congress passed the Metric Conversion Act, which provided for only voluntary action. The voluntary conversion appears to be working, but at a very slow pace. In many industries, America has already gone metric. The shutters of thousands of 8, 16, and 35-millimeter cameras daily click across America. Work is done daily in hundreds of repair shops on thousands of foreign automobiles manufactured to metric standards in foreign countries. U.S. pharmaceutical companies went metric over 20 years ago, and the electronics industry has used the metric system since 1954.

More recently, in 1996, the International Organization for Standardization adopted ISO 14000 to establish environmental performance standards. Conflicting environmental regulations across national borders have long been a problem for international supply management. Like the ISO 9000 series, ISO 14000 series focus on processes, not outcomes, and both involve audit by a third party.[11]

Benefits of Standardization

Standardization benefits an organization in a variety of ways: it enables mass production, enables customization, improves supplier coordination, improves quality, enables simplification, enables delayed differentiation and, as a result of many of the other benefits, lowers inventories.

■ **Enables mass production.** As Eli Whitney discovered, mass production becomes possible through the creation of interchangeable parts. Standardized parts and components enable management to stabilize production processes and focus on continuous improvement, thereby reducing costs.

---

[11]Frank Montabon, "ISO 14000: Assessing Its Perceived Impact on Corporate Performance," *Journal of Supply Chain Management,* National Association of Purchasing Management, Spring 2001.

- **Enables customization.** Standardized parts and modules enable manufacturers to make a wide variety of finished products from a relatively small number of parts. With standardization, the wide variety of finished products may be assembled when ordered, thereby reducing inventory carrying costs and increasing flexibility to meet specific consumer demands. Dell exemplifies this in its ability to customize computers for customers on the same the day the order is placed. Dell accomplishes customization largely through standard components and modules.

- **Improves supplier coordination.** Standardized parts and components provide a very clear specification for the supplier. The dimensions, characteristics and performance of a standard part or component improve the ability to communicate between the buying and selling companies.

- **Improves quality.** Standard parts and components are repetitively manufactured to the same design, enabling investment by the producing company in better machinery, training, and materials. The result is a significantly lower defect rate.

- **Enables simplification.** Once standard parts are identified, simplification can be used to identify redundant standard parts that can be eliminated. Simplification is discussed in the next section.

- **Enables delayed differentiation.** When customization of the product is accomplished as close to customer demand as possible, the differentiation of the product or service is delayed. For example, suppose a customer purchases a computer online with a customized configuration of standard parts and modules. The manufacturer has two possible ways to fill the order. The manufacturer can preassemble hundreds or even thousands of computer configurations that customers may want so they are ready to ship when the demand occurs. Or, using delayed differentiation the manufacturer stocks standard components and modules that can quickly be assembled into customized configurations. Delayed differentiation results in carrying much lower inventory levels.

- **Lowers inventories.** Lower inventories result from the number of distinct parts carried being reduced. There are several other reasons standardization lowers inventories. Better quality from greater use of standard parts and components reduces safety stock. Delayed differentiation reduces the need to carry as many finished goods in stock, thereby reducing overall inventory levels. Standard parts and modules usually have more certain and shorter supplier order lead times. Reduced uncertainty in production lead time reduces the need for additional inventories required for unreliable lead times. Shorter lead times directly translate into smaller order quantities.

The use of standards permits a firm to purchase fewer items, in larger quantities, and at lower prices. Thus, fewer items are processed and stocked. This reduces supply management, receiving, inspection, and payment costs. Stocking fewer items makes controlling inventories easier and less costly. The use of standardized approved items drastically reduces the number of defects in incoming materials. Consequently, the purchase of standardized materials reduces total costs in four ways: lower prices, lower processing costs, lower inventory carrying costs, and fewer quality problems. The benefits of standardization are presented in Figure 11.3.

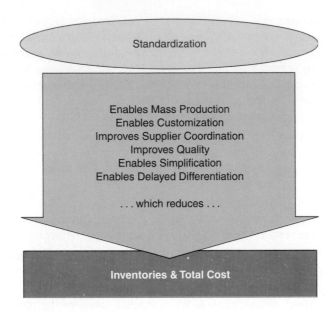

Figure 11.3 | Benefits of Standardization

Simplification

Simplification, a corollary of standardization, is another term for which recognized authorities have varying definitions. Most frequently, simplification means reducing the number of standard items a firm uses in its product design and carries in its inventory. For example, one company formerly used 27 different kinds of standard lubricating greases in the maintenance of its machinery. Analysis showed that in some cases the same grease could be used for several different applications and that a total of only 6 kinds of grease were needed. Hence, through simplification the number of standard greases used was reduced from 27 to 6. Similar analysis showed that the number of standard bearings and fasteners used in production could be reduced by about 50 percent. Reductions of this scope are commonplace. Simplification savings result primarily from reduced inventory investment, more competitive prices, greater quantity discounts (because of larger volume purchases and the use of blanket orders), and reduced clerical and handling costs (because fewer different items have to be handled and controlled).

Some authorities consider simplification an integral part of standardization, rather than a corollary of it. They visualize the simplification process as taking place primarily at the design level, rather than at the stocking level. They think in terms of simplifying (or reducing) the number of related items that are approved as standards in the first place.

Developing a Standardization Program

The benefits of standardization cannot be fully realized when solely developed internally by design engineers. The next level up is to involve cross-functional teams with internal members from supply management, marketing, quality and other relevant functional areas. However, to yield all of the benefits of standardization presented earlier, standardization should be addressed across the supply chain through cross-functional teams containing chain members.[12] A standardization program can be approached in various ways; but because so many departments and suppliers are affected by standards decisions, a team effort is the most appropriate approach.

Standards Team

A standards team typically consists of representatives from engineering, supply, operations, marketing, and transportation. Relevant suppliers should also be included in the team under the guidance of supply management. The standards team typically is charged with the responsibility of obtaining input from all user departments and relevant suppliers, reconciling differences between them, and making the final standards decisions.

Theoretically, a member from any department could serve as head of the team. Supply management is particularly well qualified to head the team in companies at which materials complying with national standards or maintenance, repair, and operating (MRO) items form a large portion of the company's total purchases. In companies that manufacture highly differentiated technical products assembled from parts made to company standards, engineering is well qualified to head the team.

Importance of Supply Management

Regardless of the organization employed, the supply management department occupies a focal point in the process. Only in supply management are duplicate requests for identical (or nearly identical) materials, overlapping requests, and "special buy" requests from all departments visible. Hence, no program for standardization can be optimally successful unless supply management is assigned a major role in the program.

Materials Catalog

Once the decision to implement a standardization program has been made, the most common approach is to work toward developing a comprehensive materials catalog. A current, easily accessible materials catalog or database of approved standard items is the logical output of a standardization program. The catalog greatly aids the firm's design efforts. Many benefits of developing a materials catalog exist, the most obvious of which are:

- ■ **Improved quality.** The documentation of materials is the first step toward accumulating data to determine which materials have quality problems. The availability of such a catalog virtually eliminates the possibility that designers will incorporate materials that previously caused problems.

---

[12]An assumption is made that standards exist at the industry, national, or international levels that a supply chain team can use in its standardization decisions. If no such standards exist, then the supply chain members should consider addressing the industry's reasons for not having industry standards and lead the development of such standards in conjunction with developing standards within their own supply chain.

- **Reduction in design time.** Access to a materials catalog provides designers with a resource that will shorten the materials selection process in the design stage, thereby reducing the total design time.

- **Reduction of nonstandard parts.** The exercise of developing a materials catalog facilitates the use of standard parts.

- **Reduction of standard parts.** Simplification is easier since the standard parts documentation is centrally maintained. See the discussion on simplification given earlier in this chapter.

- **Reduction of inventory.** Through standardization and simplification, two activities enabled by the development of a materials catalog, inventories are reduced. The reduction is primarily owing to the decrease in the variety of parts carried and the improved quality.

- **Benefits of centralization.** Development of a materials catalog for a company with several physically separated facilities provides the opportunity to take advantage of centralization benefits, including pricing leverage.

Electronic Materials Catalog

An emerging trend in companies is to move the materials catalog from a hardcopy form to an electronic one. A simple electronic materials database can be created in virtually any software package capable of organizing and maintaining data. The complexity of the software is directly related to the complexity of the data. Included in the term "data" are graphical images such as photos, drawings, and designs. The designs may be quite complex. For example, the rail industry (railroads) chose to include vector drawings in its electronic catalogs. Vector drawings are created with a computer-aided design software package that generates arcs and lines from mathematical formulas. The rail industry decided that converting from a vector drawing to an image resulted in a loss of the underlying intelligence.[13]

A simple database software package such as Microsoft Access is sufficient and allows for relatively sophisticated data maintenance, centralization, queries, and graphics. On the more complex end of the materials database continuum are enterprise resource planning (ERP) systems, which can centrally locate materials catalog information for access, updating, and utilization by all departments. Most ERP systems have already converted over to Web-based interfaces, allowing maximum access to centralized materials information in even the most remote regions of the world.

Benefits of Electronic Catalogs   Materials catalogs that are electronically maintained are superior to hardcopy versions since they can be centralized in one location, updated easily, electronically disseminated, and queried using search techniques, and since they provide links to activate ordering and obtain additional information. The increasing dissemination of information using technologies such as secured intranets and extranets,

---

[13]Dennis Smid and Jo-Anne Kane, "Another Link in the Chain—Electronics Parts Catalogs," *NAPM 81st Annual International Conference Proceedings,* 1996. For proceedings paper see napm.org.

data warehouses, and database-driven websites enable greater growth of electronic materials catalogs. As companies move much of their intellectual property to cyberspace, the use of electronic materials catalogs is on the rise.

Concluding Remarks

Both specifications and standardization play important roles in the search for the right quality and the right value. They also assist in resolving the design conflicts that exist between engineering, manufacturing, marketing, and supply management. As presented in this chapter, specifications serve as the heart of the resulting procurement. The strategic dimension of specification development cannot be ignored in today's globally competitive environment. Long-term planning through organizational change and philosophical transformation must occur in most companies so that balanced specifications contribute to the viability of the firm's supply chain.

Likewise, many firms still do not fully appreciate the concepts embraced in standardization and its corollary, simplification. Nevertheless, the philosophies underlying these concepts play an important role in creating competitive advantage. It seems highly probable that these same philosophies will continue to be important in the future. Aided by improved information technology and increased automation coupled with computer-aided design and computer-aided manufacturing systems, standardization is part of the answer to meet this decade's desire for customized products and services at low cost.[14] By further standardizing component parts, processes, and operations, companies can refine and streamline their systems. Such refinement should permit the production of low-cost, high-quality, differentiated products that will be competitive in the global marketplace.

---

[14]Recall the discussion in Chapter 1 describing the direct relationship between reductions in material costs and increases in profit margins and return on investment.

12 CHAPTER

The Procurement of Equipment

Case
The True Cost of Equipment

Keith Erickson, supply manager for Bath Straits Petroleum Company, sat in his office in Melbourne. Keith was studying a purchase requisition his equipment buyer, Mandalay Curry, had just brought him. Sixty safety valves for the refinery were to be purchased from BHP Valves. Keith: "But we just bought 60 valves nine months ago. I remember that I had a major blowup with Willy Woodrow, the plant engineer. As usual, Willy did us a favor and selected Queenbyan Valves since they were the lowest-priced ones available. Willy had to meet his budget! I'm going to call Milt Cottee, the maintenance manager, to see what's gone wrong."

Shortly thereafter, Keith and Milt were talking on the telephone. Keith: "Milt, what's with the requirement for 60 new safety valves? We just spent $100,000 to buy 60 Queenbyan valves."

Milt responded, "Those Queenbyan valves are a disaster! The seals leak and there is oil and diesel fuel everywhere. Last night, the shift foreman slipped on some oil and broke a vertebra. The refinery's been down 12 hours in the last six months because of these damn things. I need those BHP valves now!"

The acquisition of equipment has an impact far beyond the dollars involved: The capacity, longevity, profitability, productivity, and cost of operation and maintenance of the equipment usually are far more significant than the purchase price. Of even greater importance is the cost of unscheduled downtime: A defective pump can halt an entire refinery's operation or an automobile assembly line at a cost of hundreds of thousands of dollars.

The Nuances of Capital Equipment Procurement
Nonrecurring Purchases

The purchase of a particular piece of capital equipment typically occurs no more than once every three to five years or so. For example, one supply manager recently purchased a unique high-temperature electric furnace for use in her company's research and development laboratory. Since the furnace is used only periodically for experimental work, it is very unlikely that another purchase of this kind of equipment will be made in the foreseeable future.

On the other hand, a few industrial operations require the use of many identical machines in their production process. In petroleum and chemical processing plants, the product is transported by pipeline throughout most of the production operation. This requires dozens, at times hundreds, of similar pumps, which vary only in size and details of construction. To keep capital expenditures at a fairly uniform level from year to year and to minimize maintenance costs, pumps are often replaced on a continuing basis, rather than all at once. Although relatively uncommon, this type of operating equipment purchase assumes some of the characteristics of conventional production purchasing.

The lead-time requirement is a unique feature of most equipment purchases. While some types of equipment are standard off-the-shelf products, many are not. Much production machinery and prime moving equipment are built (at least in part) to operate under specific conditions peculiar to each purchaser's operation. Consequently, manufacturing lead time for potential suppliers is usually a matter of months or perhaps years. The production of a large steam turbine generating unit, for example, may require negotiating and expediting work substantially different from that normally required in production procurement.

Nature and Size of Expenditure

An expenditure of company funds for capital equipment is an investment. If purchased wisely and operated efficiently, equipment generates profits for its owner. Because it impacts on the costs of production, the selection of major capital equipment should be a matter of significant concern to top management.

The purchase of most major equipment involves the expenditure of a substantial sum of money. The purchase price for a piece of equipment, however, is frequently overshadowed by other elements of cost. Since a machine is often used for many years, the cost of operation and maintenance during its lifetime may far exceed its initial cost. For example, downtime costs easily may exceed the equipment's purchase price. An auto assembler estimates its production line downtime cost as $26,000 *per minute.* Hence, the *total life cost* of a machine, relative to its productivity, frequently is the cost factor of primary importance.[1] Although estimating operating and maintenance costs which will be incurred in future years is not easy, such costs will be incurred and must be addressed when comparing the total cost of ownership of two or more items of equipment which will satisfy the firm's needs.

The timing of many equipment purchases often presents a paradox. Typically, the general supply capabilities of equipment producers do not adjust quickly to changes in demand. Thus, because most firms' equipment purchases are made rather infrequently and can often be postponed, producers of industrial capital goods frequently find themselves in a "feast or famine" type of business. When a potential purchaser's business is good, it needs additional production equipment as quickly as possible to satisfy cus-

---

[1]This type of analysis is also called *life cycle costing.* The term and the concept were originally developed and refined in military procurement. Subsequently, industry adopted the concept and now it is widely used in most industries. This topic is discussed in more detail shortly. The terms *total life cost* and *life cycle cost* are virtually identical to *total cost of ownership* described in Chapter 8.

tomers' burgeoning demands. But because other purchasers are in the same situation, the buyer also may find equipment prices rising in a market of short supply. Conversely, when a buyer's business is down and additional production equipment is not needed, equipment is in plentiful supply, often at reduced prices.

Building the Foundation

Identify the Need for a Procurement

At least five functional areas may identify a need for the acquisition of equipment: the using department, marketing, process engineering, supply management, and plant engineering. (Please see Figure 12.1.) The using department may desire equipment which is more productive, that is, requires less equipment or operator time (or both) per unit of throughput. Marketing may identify new products whose production processes require new equipment. Process engineering (or operations) is concerned with the equipment's

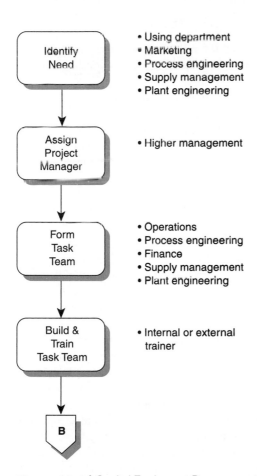

Figure 12.1 | Capital Equipment Procurement Phase I: Build the Foundation

ability to meet new and changing requirements. Supply management is responsible for monitoring threats and opportunities in the supply world. In the process, supply management may identify relevant new technology and new equipment. Additionally, supply management should be potential suppliers' primary point of contact. Supply management should be both a filter and a conduit for suppliers whose products may be of interest to other functions within the firm. Plant engineering may stimulate equipment procurement by identifying potential risks of downtime if an item of equipment is not replaced.

Project Management

If the equipment is critical, because of either cost or schedule, a project manager should be selected to drive the process. Ideally, such an individual will champion and oversee the project to success. Good people, communication, leadership, and project management skills should be a requirement for the person to fill this position.

Selection of an Equipment Sourcing Team

Depending on the criticality of the procurement, the following functional areas may be represented on the team responsible for obtaining the equipment: operations, process engineering, finance, supply management, and plant engineering.

Operations is responsible for identifying the required and desired operating characteristics of the equipment. (These characteristics are described in greater detail in the next section.) Process engineering — also know as manufacturing engineering — is concerned with the equipment's ability to meet current and likely future needs. The process engineer must balance two frequently conflicting forces: A very specialized piece of equipment may be the most productive one but may be incapable of being adapted to possible future production needs.

Finance's involvement is based on four primary interests in equipment purchases and leases. First, this department usually administers the firm's capital budget; it is therefore concerned with the allocation of funds for the proposed purchase. If the budget contains a provision for such equipment, all is well; if not, the team will need to secure a budget authorization. Second, the finance department has the responsibility of deciding how to finance such purchases. Is enough cash available internally? Can a long-term loan be arranged? Will it be necessary to raise the money through a bond issue? For large purchases, the answers to these questions bear heavily on the final equipment selection decision. Third, the finance department should be involved in the economic analysis of alternative machines. Finance typically chairs the lease versus buy analysis. In some firms, the finance department conducts the original analyses; in others, they are made by engineering or supply management. In any case, the finance department usually is involved in these activities in connection with its capital budgeting responsibility.

Supply management plays many roles: It is the primary point of contact with potential suppliers and a conduit for the flow of information. Supply management ensures that the statement of work or specification developed to describe the firm's needs is sufficiently specific to protect the firm's interests while being broad enough to ensure competition — assuming that competition is appropriate. Supply management guides the sourcing process and leads the negotiating team. And supply management is responsible for the post-award activities.

Plant engineering is concerned with both current and future issues. Immediate considerations include physical issues such as size, foundation, and power requirements. Future concerns include reliability, maintainability, service support, and the availability of replacement and spare parts.

Build and Train the Team

The careful selection of the "right" representatives of the appropriate functional areas is an essential task. Unless the representatives have recent, successful experience working as a team, an internal or external trainer should be called on to build and train the team. (Please see Chapter 6.)

Identify Objectives and Estimate Costs

Identifying Objectives

As is true with production requirements, some 80 percent of the costs associated with the procurement of equipment are built in during the requirements development stage! (Please see Figure 12.2.) Estimating the acquisition cost (purchase price, installation, spares, and training costs) and the total cost of ownership is always difficult. It is especially challenging at this early stage. However, it is strongly recommended that the team agree on both a target acquisition cost and a target total cost of ownership. Normally, the total cost of ownership is based on the present value (P.V.) of the anticipated stream of expenditures and downtime, minus the P.V. of the item's estimated salvage value. (See Chapter 8.)

The desired operating and engineering characteristics are by far the most influential factors in selecting the supplier for a particular item of equipment. The user and appropriate engineering personnel must clearly establish the function the equipment is to perform and its design and operating capabilities. Operating characteristics include the equipment's capacity, setup and run times, product yields, operator ease of use, and adaptability to meet unforeseen requirements.

Closely related to the equipment's operating characteristics are its engineering features. *Ideally these features will be compatible with the buying firm's existing equipment, process, and plant layout.* They also must comply with standards established by state and federal regulatory agencies such as the Occupational Safety and Health Administration (OSHA) and the Environmental Protection Agency (EPA). Some major engineering considerations are reliability (how long will it operate before requiring maintenance or replacement?), size and mounting dimensions, interface with other equipment, power and maintenance requirements, safety and OSHA requirements, and pollution and EPA requirements.

Used Equipment

A buying firm is by no means restricted to the purchase of new capital equipment. Purchases of used machinery, in fact, constitute an important percentage of total machinery sales.

Reasons for Purchasing Used Equipment   The firm may consider buying or leasing used equipment for several reasons. First, the cost of used machinery is substantially less than that of new equipment. Analysis of payback or return on investment may well reveal

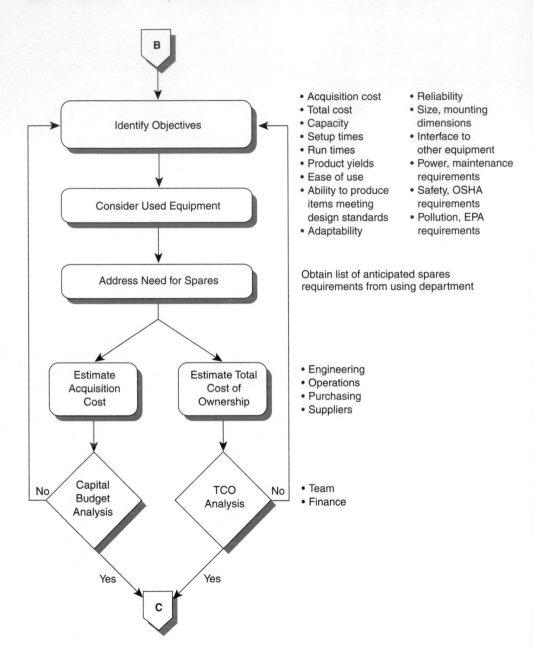

Figure 12.2 I Capital Equipment Procurement Phase II: Identify Objectives and Estimate Costs

that a piece of used equipment is a better buy than a new machine. Even if this is not the case, a firm's financial position may dictate the purchase or lease of a lower-priced used machine. Second, used equipment frequently is more readily available than new equipment. In some situations, availability may override all other considerations.

A third and very common reason for the purchase or lease of used equipment is that used equipment may adequately satisfy the purchasing firm's need, in which case there is no point in acquiring new equipment. In cases in which operating requirements are not severe, a used machine in sound condition frequently provides economical service for many years. In the event that equipment is needed for standby or peak-capacity operation, or for use on a short-lived project, more often than not used equipment can satisfy the need very well. The used equipment must not negatively affect the manufacturing process (i.e., the equipment is not a critical "technology" dependent item).

The Used Equipment Market   Used equipment becomes available for purchase for a number of legitimate reasons. When a firm buys a new machine, it frequently disposes of its old one. Although the old machine may be obsolete relative to the original owner's needs, it is often completely adequate for the needs of many potential buyers. If significant changes are made in the previous owner's product design or production process, it may be advantageous to the original owner to purchase or lease more specialized production equipment. Finally, some used equipment becomes available because the owner lost a particular contract or has discontinued operation altogether.

Whatever the reason, a great deal of used equipment is available and commonly is purchased from one of four sources: (1) used equipment dealers, (2) directly from the owner, (3) brokers, and (4) auctions. In recent years, the majority of these purchases have been made from used equipment dealers who specialize in buying, overhauling, and marketing certain types of equipment. Dealers are usually located in large industrial areas, and, as a rule, they periodically advertise the major equipment available.

Used Equipment Dealers   These dealers typically specialize in certain kinds of equipment and sell two types of machines—"reconditioned" machines and "rebuilt" machines. Generally speaking, a reconditioned machine carries a minimal dealer warranty and sells for approximately 40 to 50 percent of the price of a similar new machine. The machine usually has been cleaned and painted, broken and severely worn parts have been replaced, and the machine has been tested under power. A rebuilt machine typically carries a more inclusive dealer warranty and sells for perhaps 50 to 70 percent of a new machine's price. A rebuilt machine usually has been completely dismantled and built up from the base. All worn and broken parts have been replaced, wearing surfaces have been reground and realigned, the machine has been reassembled to hold original tolerances, and it has been tested under power.

Sale by Owner   Some owners prefer to sell their used equipment directly to the next user because they think they can realize a higher price than by selling to a dealer. Some buying firms also prefer this arrangement. It permits them to see the machine in operation and learn something about its usage history before making the purchasing decision.

Brokers   A broker is an intermediary who brings buyers and sellers together but generally does not take title to the equipment sold. Brokers sometimes liquidate large segments of the equipment of a complete plant. Occasionally, an industrial supply house or a manufacturer's agent will act as a broker for a good customer by helping the firm dispose of an odd piece of equipment which has a limited sales market.

Auctions   Auction sales represent still another source of used equipment. Several types of auction firms are in operation. Some actually function as traders, buying equipment and selling from their own inventory. More common, however, are the firms which simply provide the auction sale service. Their commission is usually somewhat less than a broker's commission. Generally speaking, buying at auction is somewhat more risky than the other supply sources because auctioned machines usually carry no warranty, and rarely is it possible to have the machine demonstrated. In some cases, however, machines can be purchased at auction via videotape or closed-circuit TV; this permits the buyer to see the machine operating in a distant plant.

Cautions in Purchasing Used Equipment   The age-old adage of caveat emptor—let the buyer beware—is particularly applicable when purchasing used equipment. It may be difficult to determine the true condition of a used machine and to estimate the type and length of service it will provide. For this reason it is wise to have one supply professional specialize in used equipment. Moreover, it is virtually essential to enlist the co-operation of an experienced production or maintenance specialist in appraising used equipment. It is always sound practice to check the reputation of a used equipment supplier and to shop around, inspecting several machines before making a purchase. Whenever possible, a machine should be observed under power through a complete operating cycle. Finally, a prospective buyer should determine the age of a machine. If not available in the seller's records, the age of a machine can be traced through the manufacturer simply by serial number identification. The combined knowledge of age and usage history is a key guide in predicting the future performance of a used machine.

In preparing a purchase order or contract for used capital equipment, care must be taken to include all essential data. In addition to an adequate description of the machine, an order should specify the accessories included, warranty provisions (if any), services to be performed before shipment, and financing as well as shipping arrangements. Generally speaking, sellers do not provide service for used equipment after the purchase. All transportation, handling, installation, and start-up costs, as well as risk, are usually borne by the purchaser.

Spares

When is the optimal time to obtain prices on spares and service agreements? Quite obviously, when competition is present! Wise supply professionals obtain a list of anticipated spare parts and service requirements from the prospective user of the equipment so that they can solicit prices for these items when soliciting the price of the equipment itself. Otherwise, excessive prices frequently become the norm when the need for the spare part or service arises.

Estimating Acquisition Costs and the Total Cost of Ownership (TCO)

After the desired operating and engineering objectives have been identified, the team should develop both acquisition cost and TCO cost estimates. If the item to be purchased is a standard one, supply management will obtain estimates of the purchase price from its files or from potential suppliers. If customized or nonstandard equipment is to be purchased, it is desirable for supply management to obtain informal estimates from potential suppliers. These estimates are compared with the budget authorization and are input to the total cost of ownership analysis. If these analyses indicate that either cost is likely to be excessive, the team must reexamine the list of desired objectives and make appropriate adjustments. Ideally these analyses and adjustments are made before proceeding to the development of the appropriate specifications.

Develop Specifications and Initiate Sourcing, Pricing, and TCO Analysis

Develop Specifications

Normally, a performance specification is developed by the team. As was seen in the chapter of this book addressing specifications, a performance specification describes the desired performance (160 units per minute, setup time of 5 minutes, specific tolerances of output, etc.) together with the required engineering features. If another type of specification is determined to be appropriate, one or more qualified potential suppliers may become involved in the process of developing the specification. (See Figure 12.3.)

One of the advantages of formally establishing a sourcing team is that more *cooperative* action usually is generated in attacking the procurement. This can be extremely useful in development of the equipment specifications. Quality/cost trade-offs are best addressed by a team. When specifications are nearing completion and requests for proposal are to be issued, a supply management professional should function in the role of an informal auditor. Although technical requirements predominate, the supply management professional should make every effort to see that specifications are written as functionally as possible. Most equipment users hold biases for and against specific types of equipment. Every effort should be made to exclude personal biases from the specifications. The nature of many equipment requirements limits the number of possible suppliers. This number should not be further reduced by arbitrarily excluding certain potential suppliers on the grounds of personal prejudice. After development of the appropriate specification, sourcing, pricing, and negotiations are next to be accomplished.

Sourcing

The sourcing of equipment suppliers involves the quantitative and qualitative analyses described in detail in Chapter 15. Briefly, the first step in equipment sourcing is the development of a request for proposal. Once proposals are received, they are evaluated for responsiveness. The supplier or suppliers that appear to be most attractive are identified. Some suppliers are more qualified in the "soft" or qualitative area than are others. The degree of qualification should be considered carefully by the team in deciding which machine to buy. The team must determine the level of a supplier's *technical, production, and commercial* capabilities. The team must assess the supplier's capability and willingness to provide any engineering service required during the installation and start-up of the new equipment. This is an extremely important financial consideration when complex, expensive equipment such as steam turbines and numerically controlled machine tools are involved. Closely related to this factor is the necessity of training op-

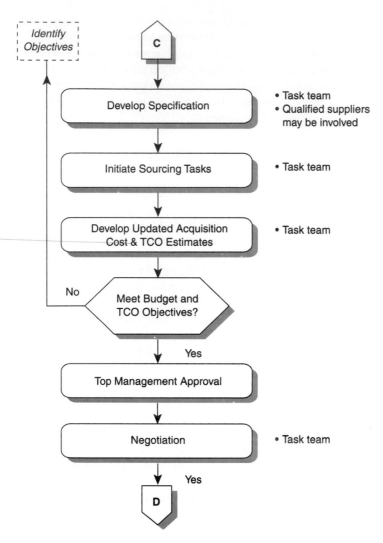

Figure 12.3 | Capital Equipment Procurement Phase III: Specifications, Sourcing, Pricing, and TCO Analysis

erators. What service is the supplier willing to provide in this area? The reliability of a supplier in standing behind its guarantees is another important consideration. A combination of the supplier's history of satisfactory performance and financial viability must be addressed. Once the equipment is installed, unexpected problems beyond the purchasing firm's control sometimes add significantly to the total cost of a machine. Finally, what is the supplier's policy on providing spares and replacement parts? When the purchased machine is superseded by a new model, what will be the availability of obsolete parts? The policy of one pump manufacturer, for example, is to produce a small stock of replacement parts for obsolete equipment once every six months. The semiannual production policy of this manufacturer, combined with its low inventory levels, forces some customers to carry unreasonably large stocks of major replacement parts. The other costly alternative for the customer is to risk occasional breakdowns, which might leave a machine out of service as long as three or four months, waiting for the next run of parts. In practice, unfortunately, such considerations frequently play a minor role in the initial selection of equipment suppliers, only to assume major proportions at a later date. It is the responsibility of the supply management department to evaluate potential suppliers in light of these qualitative factors and to bring significant considerations before the evaluating group.

Develop Updated Acquisition Cost and TCO Estimates

When proposals are received, a supply management professional tabulates them and makes the necessary calculations so they can be interpreted on a comparable basis by the team responsible for the final recommendation. Because administration and control of such activities are clearly related to the capital budgeting function, the finance department frequently assumes responsibility for conducting a total profitability study. The authors' view, however, is that once management has selected the types of analyses to be used, the supply management department might well perform the analyses more easily and effectively. Such analyses are a logical extension of the supply management department's proposal analysis activities. Clearly, the supply management professional is familiar with any proposal complications. Through his or her involvement in the preceding technical discussions, the supply management professional should also understand any technical problems involved in developing estimates for maintenance and operating costs. Consequently, an individual with a good understanding of the total cost situation may effectively prepare, interpret, and present the complete package of price, cost, and profitability data for the group's consideration.

The team now has considerable information to update its TCO estimate including all likely acquisition costs and data on actual operating characteristics. As a result, a reasonably accurate TCO estimate can be developed. One of the most challenging issues confronting the team responsible for the selection of an expensive item of equipment is the possible conflict between the budget authorization and the total cost of ownership. The budget focuses on "now" costs (purchase price, transportation, installation, training, and initial spares). The total cost of ownership addresses both now and likely future costs. Compare the total cost of ownership for items X and Y in Table 12.1. If the budget authorizes the expenditure of $1,000,000, the sourcing team will tend to acquire 'X', incurring a likely $500,000 excess cost, based on the total cost of ownership for the two alternatives.

Table 12.1 | Total Cost of Ownership for Items X and Y

	X	Y
Acquisition cost	$1,000,000	$1,200,000
Present value of future costs for spares, maintenance, operator labor, downtime, etc.	2,000,000	1,300,000
Total	$3,000,000	$2,500,000

Meet Budget and TCO Objectives?

The team now ensures that the updated acquisition and TCO estimates are at or below their objectives. If they exceed either objective, the project is returned to the objectives phase for revision. (See again Figure 12.2.)

Top Management Approval

If significant funds are involved, once the project satisfies budgetary and total cost considerations it should be forwarded for top management's review and approval.

Negotiation

Once appropriate approvals have been received, the team proceeds to negotiate all terms and conditions of a contract with the most attractive potential supplier as discussed in Chapter 20. During negotiations, the negotiating team may explore the advantages of leasing.

Leased Equipment

In addition to purchasing new or used equipment to satisfy a firm's requirements, an equipment customer has a third alternative—*leasing* the equipment. (See Figure 12.4.) In recent years, leasing has become big business. It is now a $190 billion industry whose volume of business has doubled in the last five years. Approximately 20 percent of the new office and industrial equipment used in American business today is leased. Generally accepted reasons underlying this trend appear to be the heavy demand for capital in most firms, the cost of capital, and the increased flexibility that can be negotiated in the contract.

Types of Leases

If one looks at leases in terms of the basic purposes for which they are used, most fall into one of two categories—operating leases and financial leases.

As the name implies, an *operating lease* is used by most firms as a vehicle to facilitate business operations. The focus typically is on operating convenience and flexibility. Frequently, a firm has a temporary need for equipment to be used in the office or on a special production or maintenance job. The firm requires the use of the asset but is not interested in owning it. In some cases, the need stretches beyond the temporary period, but the firm still is not interested in ownership and the risks and responsibilities that accompany it. Equipment obtained by means of an operating lease may fit such a firm's needs well. Most operating leases are *short term,* for a fixed period of time that's considerably less than the life of the equipment being leased. In many instances, an operating lease is used when the customer firm wants the freedom of being able to avail itself of new and unexpected technology.

A *financial lease,* in most cases, is used for a very different purpose. When operating equipment is obtained by means of a financial lease, the primary motivation is to ob-

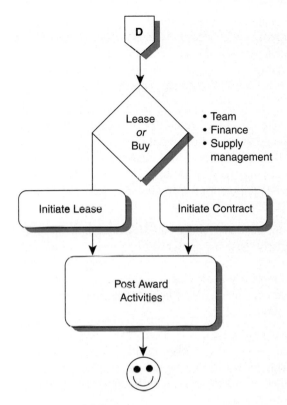

Figure 12.4 | Capital Equipment Procurement Phase IV: Sourcing, Lease/Buy Analysis, and Post Award Activities

tain financial leverage and related longer-term financial benefits.[2] Relatively speaking, a financial lease is a *long-term* lease that usually covers a time period just a bit shorter than the approximate life of the equipment being leased. Many financial leases are noncancelable. Several purists argue that such leases distort the firm's financial reports by reducing debt, which might otherwise be required to finance major purchases. Additionally, assets will be understated, resulting in a lower asset base when calculating the firm's return on assets.

Factors Favoring Leasing

Operating and Managerial Convenience   While there are different types of leasing organizations, most industrial leasing firms are called *full-service* lessors. This means that the leasing organization owns the equipment, has its own continuing source of financing,

---

[2]For the financial analysis of leases, see R. A. Brealey and S. C. Myers, *Principles of Corporate Finance,* 6th ed. (Burr Ridge, IL: Irwin/McGraw-Hill, 2000), chapter 25.

and is prepared to assume all the responsibilities of ownership for the lessee. Hence, the lessee has full use of the equipment and can concentrate on its regular business operations without having to worry about maintenance, special service, and other administrative tasks associated with equipment ownership. This can become a major benefit in the case of complex equipment requiring highly specialized technical support.

Operating Flexibility   With relatively short-term leases for selected pieces of operating equipment, a lessee is not locked into long-term commitments resulting from large capital investments. The lessee can maintain maximum flexibility in its operations to respond to changing business conditions and subsequent production requirements. It can use a leasing arrangement to meet temporary operating needs with relative ease, and in the same manner it can test new equipment prior to making a longer-term purchasing decision.

Obsolescence Protection   Leasing substantially reduces the risk of equipment obsolescence. In many businesses, particularly those using high-tech equipment, some machines become technologically obsolete in a very short time. When leasing such things as data processing equipment, for example, an arrangement usually can be made with the lessor to replace or upgrade the old equipment. This can be an extremely important consideration in a highly competitive industry.

Financial Leverage   A major advantage of leasing expensive equipment stems from the fact that a leasing decision typically replaces a large capital outlay with much smaller, regularly timed payments. This frees working capital for use in meeting expanded operating costs or for investment in other segments of the business operation. Leasing equipment reduces the up-front start-up cost for new businesses.

Viewing the lease strictly as a financing mechanism provides a cash flow advantage over a conventional bank loan financing arrangement. Most equipment leases can be stretched over a longer payment period, thus reducing the relative size of monthly payments.

In the United States, the Financial Accounting Standards Board (FASB) requires that all financial leases be capitalized. This means that the present value of all the lease payments must be shown as a part of the firm's debt.

Income Tax Considerations   If a lease fulfills the Internal Revenue Service requirements for a "true lease" from an accounting point of view, lease payments are recorded as operating expenses. As long as lease payments exceed the value of allowable depreciation (if the asset were owned), an additional tax shield is provided for the lessee. Comparatively speaking, the amount of taxable income is reduced by the difference between the lease expense payments and allowable depreciation expenses. So if a lessee plans on obtaining this tax benefit, it is important to compare the proposed lease payments with the corresponding allowable depreciation figures (if the asset were owned) over the life of the lease—to ensure that the anticipated positive relationship actually exists.

It is also important to bear in mind that the IRS has established rather stringent guidelines to distinguish between a true lease and a lease which is really intended to be a disguised conditional sales contract. Whenever it appears that the actual intent of the parties is simply to use the lease as a financing arrangement for a subsequent purchase of the equipment, no incremental tax benefit is allowed.

The Tax Reform Act of 1986 has had a significant influence on the lease/buy decision for some firms. The 1986 tax law eliminated the investment tax credit and modified the allowable depreciation preferences, forcing many firms into an alternative minimum tax position. The combined effect of these two provisions has made it more costly, from a tax perspective, for some capital-intensive firms to buy capital equipment. Although the situation is different for each firm, experience to date indicates that the 1986 law has made leasing a more attractive alternative for many firms.

Factors Weighing against Leasing

Cost   As a general rule, the primary disadvantage of leasing is its cost. "Margins" are typically higher on leases than interest rates are on direct loans. This is understandable, because in addition to covering financing charges, the lessor must also bear all the risks associated with ownership (including obsolescence and inflation risks). The typical financial lease runs for approximately three-quarters of the equipment's estimated useful life, and monthly fees total approximately 120 to 135 percent of the purchase price over the life of the lease contract.

Control   A second disadvantage is that the lessor retains control of the equipment. This often places restrictions on the manner in which the equipment can be operated; it also requires that the lessee allow the lessor access to the equipment for inspection and maintenance. There are usually times when such control by the lessor creates inconveniences for the lessee. Closely related is the possibility that the lessee may have its purchasing prerogatives constrained with respect to the purchase of operating supplies for the leased equipment. A lessor normally wants to have the equipment operated with its own supplies. In the event that use of other manufacturers' supplies could conceivably impair the machine's performance, the lessee usually agrees to such an arrangement. Frequently, higher prices are paid for such supplies than if they were purchased on the open market.

To Lease or to Buy?

Cost Comparison   It is imperative for the supply and/or finance professional to make a comparative analysis of the cost to lease and the cost to own. A discounted cash flow analysis of the two alternatives over the life of the lease is the most accurate and straightforward approach to use.

Procedurally, the same approach is used in this analysis as is used in making a life cycle cost analysis. Basically, all cost and savings factors for the lease alternative are identified and quantified—and then projected to appropriate future dates when they actually will be incurred. This produces a cost matrix over the life of the lease. All future costs are then discounted to their present values and subsequently summed to express the total cost in present value terms.[3] The same procedure is followed for the "buy" alternative. Total present value costs then can be compared directly to determine the additional true cost (or saving) associated with the leasing alternative.

---

[3]The cost of capital for evaluating lease cash flows is the firms' after-tax cost of debt. See Brealey and Myers, *Principles of Corporate Finance,* chapter 25.

The Decision   The lease-or-buy decision should be made just as any other sound purchasing decision is made. First, the merits of the alternative items of equipment must be assessed relative to the buying firm's functional needs. The total cost of each is then considered in light of the preceding functional analysis. To these factors are added the relevant qualitative considerations that may vary among suppliers, markets, economic conditions, and so on. A decision is then made on the basis of the relative cost/benefit assessments. In the case of a lease-or-buy decision, this process can be summarized in the following four steps:

1. Determine the *operating* (including financing considerations) advantages and disadvantages of leasing and of owning. Input from operations, finance, and supply management is required.

2. Compare the two alternatives and answer the question: From an operating point of view, is leasing the preferred alternative?

3. If leasing is preferable, calculate and compare the *present value costs* of the two alternatives.

4. Make the decision: Are the operating benefits of leasing worth the additional cost?

More often than not, the final decision will center on a determination of whether the extra cost entailed in leasing is justified by the avoidance of the major risks and responsibilities associated with ownership.

Initiate Lease or Contract

The purchase order, contract, or lease agreement should be written with care, specifying the responsibility of both the buying and supplying firms for equipment performance and post-sale activities. Acceptance testing and inspection methods, acceptance timing, machine specifications and performance standards, and guarantee conditions should be addressed during negotiations and in the resulting contract. In the aviation industry, it is common for penalties to be paid by the supplier if performance standards are not met. For example, International Aero Engines when selling its new engine (V2500) agreed that if the fuel consumption was above specifications, IAE would pay a penalty to the engine user. Similarly, supplier responsibility for post-sale services pertaining to installation, start-up, operator training, maintenance checks, and replacement parts should be spelled out clearly so there is no question about what is to be furnished and at what price.

In the event that the purchase or lease involves a lengthy manufacturing period, a special follow-up and expediting program should be developed. This may call for periodic plant visits and in-process inspection of the work. Responsibility for monitoring this activity normally rests with supply management.

Post-Award Activities

We strongly recommend that the key individuals from the buying and supplying firms who are concerned with timely delivery, installation, training, and delivery of spares meet to ensure total understanding of each firm's and each function's responsibilities.

Normally, supply management will assume responsibility for the day-to-day management of the contract and the relationship.

After a machine is purchased, the wise supply professional works closely with plant engineering in keeping and interpreting historical records (part by part) of machine performance. Data of this kind are valuable in making similar future analyses. (Such information may indicate that reimbursement under the warranty is appropriate.)

Concluding Remarks

In most firms, equipment is not purchased frequently. Equipment purchases can be major investments. Such purchases frequently represent important management decisions that lead to the manufacture of more competitive products or the delivery of more competitive services which increase sales in the marketplace and/or lead to improved productivity.

The role of supply management in this type of buying activity is distinctly different from its role in production buying. In the procurement of equipment, supply management personnel function in a creative capacity as facilitators, coordinators, contract administrators, and consultants to management. Specifications must be precise and complete, yet they must be written as functionally as possible. Economic analyses should utilize appropriate techniques, they must be thorough, and they must be based on data that is as accurate as possible. In many cases, supply management becomes the champion of total cost of ownership analysis. Supply management should be actively involved and, optimally, guide the team through the sourcing and negotiation activities. The contract must be precise and complete. There should be no doubt about installation and start-up responsibilities, performance requirements, test and inspection methods, related post sale responsibilities, spare part support, and warranties.

Endnote

For a comprehensive analysis of the lease/buy question, see William L. Ferrara, James B. Thies, and N. W. Dirsmith, *The Lease-Purchase Decision* (New York: The National Association of Accountants, 1979).

13 CHAPTER

Purchasing Services[1]

[1]Appreciation is expressed to Tom Oleson, Assistant Vice President–Purchasing, Nationwide Insurance for his assistance with this chapter.

Case

Lessons Learned

Al Carpenter, Materials manager at Captiva Conglomerate, has called a meeting with his Inventory and Spares manager Sam Sliderule and his Supply manager Aaron Blumen-cranz. Jason Patel, vice president of Operations, Monica Stein, vice president of Finance, and Jana Perry, director of Information Technology, are also in attendance. The topic: the contract with *Supply Operations Software* (SOS), developer/supplier of a custom inventory management and spare parts management system.

Al begins, "Here's our agenda: I. Status of the SOS contract; II. Development of a corrective action plan; III. Lessons learned. Any questions?"

"How did we get in such a mess?" asks Monica.

Al interrupts, "Let's save this for agenda Item III. Let's start with a status report. Sam, you're the user. Begin."

Sam answers, "We just completed a test of the spares management module. It's a disaster! It might be an O.K. system but it's four months behind schedule and my people can't use it."

"Well, I certainly can use it. I think it's great!" comments Jana.

"Yes, but you have an M.S. in Information Technology. My guys want to access the relevant data without all the hassle the system requires," continues Sam.

"How about the regional and centralized inventory management system?" asks Al.

"It's 10 months late," says Sam.

"Aaron, sounds like we should sue them," adds Al angrily.

Aaron replies, "Under the contract Gerry (Captiva's president) signed, we don't have a leg to stand on. The contract calls for 'best efforts,' 'whenever possible,' etc. Oh, and one additional small item: The project manager at SOS says that they've used up the $1 million called for in the contract. In fairness to the supplier, there have been 17 unpriced change orders."

Jason Patel (VP Operations) joins the discussion: "This system was supposed to provide me with better support. 'More uptime' were your words, Jana. And you said, 'We should be able to cut our inventory while providing the improved support.' Who wrote the specs for the software?"

"When we received the contract from Gerry, the specs looked like they were drafted by SOS. But Jana (IT Manager) had initialed each page," answers Aaron.

What do *you* think is *the main* cause of Captiva's problem?

Introduction

The procurement of services is an increasingly important activity. Expenditures on services by commercial firms, not-for-profit organizations, and government increase each year. In some cases, services procurements represent more than 25 percent of the organization's expenditures. Purchased services play key roles in the successful operation of these organizations. In many instances, the impact of the services themselves on the success of the organization's operation is far greater than the impact of the dollars spent. Services ranging from architectural engineering, promotion and advertising, and the development of software, to the maintenance and repair of production equipment are of critical importance to the operation of the organization. More mundane purchases such as cafeteria and janitorial operations impact the morale of all employees.

A tidal wave of "outsourcing" of services is taking place in America and abroad. At one level, services that are not at the core of the organization's competencies, such as management information systems, payroll, travel services, delivery services, even the procurement of MRO supplies and services, are being outsourced to service providers. These suppliers have the expertise and economies of scale to allow them to provide the services at the same or higher quality level than the purchasing firm and at a lower total cost. At another level, in economies that have traditionally been characterized by a high level of government participation in service delivery in the provision of health, transport, utilities, and municipal services, there has been large-scale outsourcing to private sector providers. This move to outsourcing adds a new dimension to procurement. Expenditures on such third-party service provision can reach 60 percent to 70 percent of total organizational expenditure and require higher-level supply management skills than hitherto imagined.

Obtaining services is one of supply management's most challenging responsibilities. In no other area is there a more complex interdependency between the purchase description (statement of work), method of compensation, source selection, contract administration, and a satisfied customer.[2] The purchasing of services frequently leads to relationships with suppliers that focus on trust rather than on the transaction and that can stretch supply professionals beyond their traditional zones of comfort and competence.

Hidden Opportunities

Warren Norquist, former vice president of International Materials Management at Polaroid, involved his staff in many of the following nontraditional procurements:

- Print ad production
- General consultants
- Computer consultants
- Computer network management
- Design of exterior of products
- Television ad production
- Outplacement agencies
- Training consultants
- Network TV time
- Financial auditors

---

[2]This material is based, in part, on David N. Burt, Warren E. Norquist, and J. Anklesaria, *Zero Base Pricing™: Achieving World Class Competitiveness through Reduced All-in-Cost* (Chicago: Probus, 1990).

- Training courses
- Per diem help
- Placement agencies
- Technical consultants
- Spot TV and radio time

- Telephone customer service
- Annual reports
- Logistics and inventory control
- Market research

Mr. Norquist's experience was that when qualified procurement personnel were involved in the planning and procurement of such services, savings of approximately 25 percent were enjoyed with equal or improved quality and service.[3] In addition, an increasing number of proactive supply management operations now purchase services such as utilities, disposal services, and insurance.

Stephen Sutton, Supply manager for Ok Tedi Mining Limited (OTML) in Papua New Guinea, talks of the increasing significance of services procurement in world-class organizations. OTML's spend on services now exceeds 50 percent of total expenditures. Mr. Sutton cites examples of outsourcing major areas of core on-site activity at OTML such as blasting (for which a contractor now delivers a total drilling, charging, and explosives detonation service) and major equipment maintenance, for which a contractor has total responsibility on site for activities that include buying and holding inventory and the provision of the associated maintenance labor requirements. Such examples clearly indicate the shift in the manner in which leading-edge organizations operate in their supply markets today.[4]

The Statement of Work

As is true in the purchase of production requirements and capital equipment, the most critical prerequisite to a successful procurement of services is the development and documentation of the requirement—the statement of work (S.O.W.). And as is true with production requirements and capital equipment, one of the keys to success is the involvement of qualified supply management personnel at this point in the procurement process. In fact, supply professionals know that many of their service customers lack training and experience in the development of service requirements or specifications. Accordingly, a supply professional can provide invaluable assistance during this phase of the procurement. In many instances, supply professionals invite two or three carefully prequalified potential contractors to aid in the development of the statement of work. Such early involvement aids the internal customer in fully understanding the organization's true needs. At the same time, the potential contractor gains insight into the nature and level of effort required.

The statement of work identifies what the contractor (supplier) is to accomplish. The clarity, accuracy, and completeness of the S.O.W and how the effectiveness of delivery will be measured will determine, to a large degree, whether the objectives of the contract will be achieved. The S.O.W. clearly identifies first the primary objective and

---

[3]Ibid., p. 177.
[4]Personal interview with Laurie LeFevre (consultant with OTML),October 14, 2000.

then the subordinate objectives, so that both the buyer and the seller know where and how to place their emphasis. Those responsible for developing the S.O.W. must ask themselves questions such as, Is timeliness, creativity, or artistic excellence the primary objective? And, How will customer satisfaction be measured?

One of the objectives of writing a statement of work is to gain understanding and an agreement with a contractor concerning the specific nature of the technical effort to be performed. Satisfactory performance under the contract is a direct function of the quality, clarity, and completeness of its statement of work and of the contractor's understanding of the outcome required.

The S.O.W. also affects the administration of the contract. It defines the scope of the effort, that is, what the contractor is to do and what the buyer is to receive and how satisfaction is to be measured. The manner in which the scope of work is defined governs the amount of direction that the supply professional can give during the contract's life.

A well-written statement of work enhances the contractor's performance in pursuit of S.O.W. objectives. Before writing it, those responsible must develop a thorough understanding of all the factors that will bear on the project and that are reflected in the S.O.W.

Four Formats for Statements of Work

The majority of formats fall into four basic types of statements of work, plus a combination of these four types, called a "hybrid" S.O.W.

- **Performance S.O.W.** details everything wanted by the buyer. This statement of work is broken down into tasks describing the required outcome performance of the task(s).
- **Functional S.O.W.** defines what the buyer is "trying to do," leaving the seller free to come up with the most efficient means to do it.
- **Design S.O.W.** is the most detailed type of statement of work, used mainly in the construction and manufacture of goods or equipment projects. Statements of work of this type require the inclusion of plans, blueprints, CAD designs, or specifications.
- **Level-of-Effort S.O.W.** is a specialized version of the performance statement of work, generally used on research and development, or studies contracts.[5]

Planning the Statement of Work

A statement of work is frequently described as a document that details a strategy for contractor and buyer accomplishment of the objectives of a project. But before any strategy can be developed, certain basic questions must be answered and understood:

- What are the objectives of the project?
- Where did the objectives come from, who originated them, and why were they originated?
- What is the current status of the effort?

---

[5]Janet Sickinger, "Writing a Complete and Effective Statement of Work," *InfoEdge,* November 1997, p. 3.

■ Given the current status, what are the risks associated with the achievement of the project objectives?

The planning phase of S.O.W. preparation is aimed at a thorough investigation of the why and what of the project. The following checklist will assist the program manager and the supply manager in this determination.

■ Identify the resource, schedule, and compensation constraints for the project.

■ Identify all customer and contractor participation needed for the project and define the extent and nature of their responsibilities. All customer support, such as customer-furnished equipment, materials, facilities, approvals, and so forth, should be specifically stated.

■ Challenge the tasks identified, including sequencing and interrelationships of all required tasks. For example, on a janitorial services contract, should the contractor be required to wash (versus completely erase) blackboards every evening or only once a week? On a landscape maintenance contract, should the contractor be required to furnish expendables such as fertilizer?

■ Identify contractor delivery requirements at specified points in time; include details about the type and quantity of any deliverables.

■ Identify specific technical data requirements such as plans, specifications, reports, and so on.

■ Identify realistic desired or required service levels.[6]

O'Reilly, Garrison, and Khalil provide the following list of typical elements that may be in a statement of work:

■ Description of the work
■ Schedule
■ Specifications and requirements
■ Quality requirements
■ Performance measurements
■ Deliverables
■ Delivery and performance schedule
■ Service levels
■ Changes and modifications
■ Bonds
■ Charges and costs
■ Project management
■ Reporting requirements
■ Safety
■ Supplier responsibilities

---

[6]A desired service level might call for response within three hours 97 percent of the time.

- Buyer responsibilities
- Work approvals
- Use of subcontractors
- Authorized personnel
- Exhibits, schedules, and attachments[7]

Writing the Statement of Work

As a result of a thorough planning effort, the individuals writing the S.O.W. should have determined the tasks and details that need to be included. These must now be documented.

Writing a quality statement of work is not an easy task. The S.O.W. must maintain a delicate balance between protecting the customer's interests and encouraging the supplier's (contractor's) creativity during both proposal preparation and contract performance. For example, when purchasing janitorial services, some well-intentioned firms specify the number of personnel the contractor must supply, in the rather questionable belief that this provision will guarantee satisfactory performance. But such action blocks the supplier's creativity and generally results in needlessly high prices. The use of a carefully developed S.O.W. which specifies the required performance and procedures for monitoring (inspecting) the contractor's performance allows the contractor to apply its experience and creativity—usually at a significant savings. To further complicate the task, those developing the S.O.W. must remember that it will be read and interpreted by customer and contractor personnel of widely varying experience and expertise.

The following issues deserve special attention on a case-by-case basis. Required provisions may be in either the S.O.W. or special terms and conditions included in the request for proposal and the resulting contract.

- *A performance plan.* The contractor is required to develop a nonsubjective, quantifiable blueprint for providing the services. Staffing, equipment, and supplies should all be identified. After developing the blueprint, the contractor must identify all required processes.
- *Quality monitoring system.* The contractor will be required to specify and implement fail-safe measures to minimize quality problems.
- *Personnel plan.* The contractor is required to develop and maintain recruiting and training programs acceptable to the customer.
- *Performance and payment bonds.* The contractor must provide performance and payment bonds equal to a specified percentage of the value of the contract amount.
- *Metrics.* When possible, performance objectives should be quantified.
- *Progress reviews.* If progress reviews appear to be appropriate, how, when, where, and by whom they should be conducted should be specified.[8]

---

[7]Peter O'Reilly, David H. Garrison, and Frediric Khalil, "Purchasing Professional Services," *InfoEdge,* May 2001, p. 8.

[8]Sickinger, "Writing a Complete and Effective Statement of Work," p. 2.

Artificial Intelligence

While executive director of Purchasing at Pacific Bell, colleague Joe Yacura began the development of artificial intelligence applications used to develop specifications for statements of work for both services and products. He carried this effort forward while SVP of Purchasing at American Express. His efforts have progressed to the point that an individual requiring a service to be purchased from an outside provider could get on a website which answers a number of detailed questions. The system algorithm and business rules then generate a statement of work together with a set of performance metrics and a total life cycle cost model.[9]

Tips on Writing an Effective S.O.W.

Experience indicates that a clause such as the following should be added to the bidder's instructions section of the RFP to ensure that the bidder's proposal will be responsive to the mandatory requirements:

> This RFP describes the minimum content and general format for responding to our RFP. Your reply shall be submitted on the forms and in the formats requested (or equivalent) with all questions answered in detail. Elaborate format and binders are neither necessary nor desired. Legibility, clarity, and coherence are more important. Your proposal should present information in the order requested in the RFP. It is mandatory that the Bidder use the same numbering format as used in this RFP so that responses correlate to the same paragraph in the RFP requirement. This will make your proposal more "evaluator friendly" to the evaluation team conducting the evaluation of the proposals.
>
> Whenever a question is asked in the RFP subparagraphs or a requirement stated by the use of the phrase "The Bidder Shall," the Bidder is expected to answer these as fully and completely as possible. Failure to do so may deem your proposal "nonresponsive" to that requirement.
>
> Responsiveness will be measured by the Bidder's response to the requirements in each paragraph of the RFP. Merely "parroting" back the RFP requirements statement in the Bidder's proposal may deem the response nonresponsive. The Bidder's response must demonstrate an understanding of the requirements. This might be done by providing what was asked for, or by citing how the Bidder has achieved the requirements in its normal business practices (such as submitting samples of procedures or award letters).[10]

To make sure that the S.O.W. accurately reflects what the contracting parties have agreed to, follow these suggestions:

- Be clear — use simple, direct language. Avoid ambiguity.
- Use active, not passive tenses. (The seller "shall conduct a test," as opposed to "a test should be conducted by the seller.") Active verbs assign responsibility more clearly than do passive verbs.
- Be precise — especially about task descriptions. The clarity of the S.O.W. affects the administration of the contract since it defines the scope of work to be performed. Work outside this scope will involve new procurement with probable increased costs.

---

[9]Mr. Yacura currently is CEO of Ridgewood Development Corporation of Ridgewood, N. J.

[10]Sickinger, "Writing a Complete and Effective Statement of Work," p. 9.

■ Spell out the buyer's obligations carefully. Don't just imply things or "back into" a work requirement.

■ Limit abbreviations to those in common usage and spell them out in the first usage with the abbreviation in parentheses. Provide a list of abbreviations and acronyms to be used at the beginning of the S.O.W.

■ Include procedures. When immediate decisions cannot be made, it may be possible to include a procedure for making them (for example, "as approved by the purchaser," or "the seller shall submit a report each time a category B failure occurs").

■ Do not overspecify or overstate. Depending upon the nature of the work and the type of contract the ideal situation may be to specify results required or end times to be delivered and let the contractor propose the best method.

■ Eliminate extraneous statements. If a statement has no practical value, it shouldn't be in the S.O.W.

■ Include all relevant reference documents.

■ Don't mix general/background information, guidance, and specific direction/requirements.

■ Don't sole-source the work statement unless competition isn't desired.

■ Describe requirements in sufficient detail to assure clarity, not only for legal reasons, but for practical application, such as in closing loopholes.

■ Be aware that contingent actions may have an impact on price as well as schedule.

■ Provide a ceiling on the extent of services, or work out a procedure that will ensure adequate control where appropriate (for example, a level of effort, pool of labor hours).

■ Avoid incorporating extraneous material and requirements which may add unnecessary cost. (Data requirements are common examples of problems in this area.)

■ Don't repeat detailed requirements or specifications which are already spelled out in applicable documents. Instead, incorporate them by reference.

■ Explain the interrelationship between tasks and how tasks are related to required results and deliverables.

■ Identify all constraints and limitations.

■ Include standards that will make performance measurement possible and meaningful.

■ Be clear about phase requirements, if applicable, and the timing used to gauge work phases.

■ Proofread for errors and omissions, as well as for format and information consistency.[11]

Selecting Service Contractors

Selecting the "right" source is much more of an art when purchasing services than when purchasing materials. Because of the complexity of many service procurements and the unexpected problems that tend to arise, it is usually prudent practice to select only es-

---

[11]Ibid., p. 11.

tablished, reputable firms. Exceptions may be made occasionally in cases involving promising new suppliers who have not yet established a reputation. Unless the potential supplier possesses some truly unique skill or reputation, competition typically is employed. In some service markets, however, experienced supply managers find that the competitive process is not completely effective because of the structure of the market. This issue is discussed later in the chapter.

When a large number of potential contractors is available and the dollars involved warrant the effort, the customer firm's sourcing team normally reduces this list to three to five firms. Ideally, a weighted scorecard should be developed to facilitate the process. The team interviews prospective contractors' management, talks with previous customers, and checks out employees through random interviews. The supply manager then invites proposals only from the potential suppliers with which the buying firm would be comfortable doing business.

During the evaluation process, emphasis should be placed on the total cost and total benefits to the purchasing organization. Assume, for example, that two architect-engineering (A-E) firms are under consideration for the development of plans and specifications for a new building estimated to cost approximately $10 million. Firm X has a reputation of designing functional buildings whose costs are relatively low. Firm Y, on the other hand, has a reputation of designing more elaborate and aesthetically more attractive buildings whose costs tend to run about 10 percent more than X's. For the sake of illustration, however, assume that firm X's professional fees tend to run about 12 percent more than Y's. Table 13.1 illustrates these cost differentials and shows the overriding influence of construction costs in the complete analysis. Hence, in this case, the contractor's design fee is a relatively minor item in the total cost package.

In addition to the traditional concerns about a prospective contractor's financial strength, management capability, experience, and reputation, the area of technical capabilities requires special analysis. An article in *Purchasing World* identifies the following issues that should be addressed when selecting a contractor for computer maintenance. This list of issues is introduced simply as an example of the depth of analysis required when selecting a contractor for this specialized service.

■ Will the contractor maintain all the equipment in your computer installation?

■ Can the contractor quickly correct the problem?

■ How close to your facilities is the contractor's field engineering office? Does the contractor specialize in your type of equipment?

■ Does the contractor have a prescribed schedule of service calls?

■ Does the contractor have troubleshooting escalation procedures, skilled field engineers, and ready availability of spare parts?

Table 13.1 | Total costs for the construction project

	Firm X	Firm Y
Construction cost	$10,000,000	$11,000,000
Design fee	739,200	660,000
Total cost	$10,739,200	$11,660,000

- If there is any possibility of having to move the computer equipment, does the contractor have proven successful experience moving computers?
- Does the contractor offer equipment brokerage?
- Does the contractor have the technical ability to make low-cost modifications to your equipment? If so, can the firm support the resulting system?
- Will the contractor service refurbished equipment?
- Does the contractor have high hiring standards, require appropriate training, and equip field service personnel with appropriate tools and equipment?
- Does the contractor supply maintenance documentation?
- Will the contractor develop custom products for your special needs?
- Is the contractor flexible in meeting your specific requirements?[12]

The selection of suppliers for repair services depends on the situation. The best way to cope with emergency services is to anticipate them. Vehicles, office machines, and plant equipment do break down. Sewer lines do get clogged. In many cases, it is possible, and certainly desirable, to establish the source and the price or dollar rates for such services before the emergency occurs. When purchasing transportation services, consistent on-time pickup and delivery, equipment availability, and service to particular locations typically are more important than price.[13]

Competitive prices should be solicited every two or three years for recurring services. Such action tends to avoid complacency and helps to maintain realistic pricing. More frequent changes in contractors often cause too many service disruptions.

Tips from a Professional

Barbara Stone-Newton, *Manager of Purchasing* for the State of North Carolina, provides the following tips:

- *Partner with users.* Be sure that you understand their needs, goals, and constraints. You will be the bridge between them and potential service providers. If users are not already familiar with your organization's procurement procedures (and possible options), use this time to go over them.
- *Learn from the past.* For ongoing services, review the prior specifications and any comments in the contract administration file. If there were questions during the previous procurement, try to incorporate answers into your new request for proposal (RFP) or invitation for bid (IFB).
- *Update specifications.* Service standards and environment often evolve over the contract term. Generic specs might leave out important features that users have come to expect and thus create problems. For example, the current contractor may price for today's level of service (assuming rightly or wrongly that you want that to continue)

---

[12]"How to Choose a Computer Maintenance Service," *Purchasing World*, August 1987, p. 73.

[13]James R. Stock and Paul H. Finszer, "The Industrial Purchase Division for Professional Services," *Journal of Business Research*, February 1987, p. 3.

while others submit costs for exactly what's in the specs. Be equally cautious about overspecifying, since that can increase costs or limit competition.

- *Minimize assumptions.* Be specific about deliverables, schedule, performance measures, and similar expectations. The "fudge factor' is a particular concern in service procurements.

- *Encourage questions.* Provide some mechanism for questions—a deadline for written inquiries, a site visit, or a preproposal conference. Issue a summary addendum formalizing substantive questions and answers so that all potential suppliers have the same information.

- *Facilitate comparison.* Make it easy for prospective suppliers to provide everything you need to evaluate responses. Include a checklist, outline, or similar section detailing what information is to be included in the responses. A "fill-in-the-blank" format is great for simple procurements.

- *Plan evaluation.* Outline the evaluation process and any weighting or scoring method to be used.

- *Reduce surprises.* Include contractual terms and conditions in the solicitation document. This counters the mind-set of "we'll fix it with the contract" and streamlines your award process.

- *Check yourself.* When you think the RFP or IFB is ready to go, put it aside (at least for a few hours), then take a fresh look. Read it from the suppliers' viewpoint. Does it contain everything they'll need to offer a competitive response? Finally look forward to contract administration. Are the deliverables, standards, and so on, defined clearly so that both parties can measure performance? If the answers are positive, you probably have a good solicitation document [14]

The Ideal Services Supplier

The ideal services supplier listens to what users complain about most and then designs service products that supply the market's missing ingredients. Satisfaction is built into service products rather than added as an afterthought. Employees of "ideal" services providers are given every conceivable form of automation to help them deliver a consistently satisfactory service product. The ideal services supplier invests to increase both employee productivity and customer satisfaction.

If such an "ideal" services supplier or contractor is not available, the purchasing firm should consider the development of a long-term relationship with a supplier willing and able to grow into an "ideal" provider.

Pricing Service Contracts

Procurement authority Louis J. DeRose writes, "the competitive process is not truly efficient in services markets. It is constrained by three forces and factors of supply.

---

[14]Barbara Stone-Newton, quoted in Julie Roberts, "Services Purchases in the Public Sector," *Purchasing Today,* February 2001, p. 57.

1.   "One of the strongest factors influencing competition and prices—a continuing or cumulative supply—is absent.
2.   "Interchangeable services generally are not available because of the personal effort and involvement of the supplier.
3.   "The supply of services is more easily restricted or restrained than is the supply of commodities or products."

For these reasons, DeRose writes, "buyers must negotiate service agreements."[15] Yet there are some situations in which competitive bidding is an effective method of determining both source and price. A janitorial services contract for which competition is intense is an example. Again, the supply professional's judgment plays a key role: Are all of the conditions required for the use of competitive bidding (as discussed in Chapter 15) satisfied? Are time and qualified resources available to prepare for and conduct negotiations? Are supply management's internal customers prepared to play a constructive role in professional negotiations? In most instances, negotiation often results in better pricing and the supply of a more satisfactory service.

Too frequently, the pricing of service contracts is not tailored to motivate the supplier to satisfy the organization's principal objective. Once the primary requirement (artistic excellence, timeliness, low cost, and so on) is identified, the supply professional must ensure that the resulting contract motivates the supplier to meet this need. When conditions require, the contract should reward good and penalize poor service. (See Chapter 19.)

Professional Services

Architect-engineering firms, lawyers, consultants, and educational specialists are representative of the individuals and firms that provide professional services. Supply professionals pay particular attention to the relationship between the price mechanism (e.g., firm fixed price, cost plus incentive fee, fixed price with award fee, and so on) and the contractor's motivation on critical professional services contracts. For example, fixed price contracts reward suppliers for their cost control. Every dollar that the supplier's costs are reduced results in a dollar of additional profit for the supplier.

Assume that you were selecting an individual or a firm to prepare a fairly complex personal income tax return for a gross income of $125,000. Firm C advertises that it will prepare any tax return, regardless of its difficulty, for a guaranteed maximum of $200. Firm D offers rates of $75 per hour. Discussion with a representative of firm D indicates that approximately five hours will be required to prepare your return. If forgone tax savings are considered as a cost, which firm is more likely to provide the service at the lowest total cost? The use of firm D will cost an estimated $375 ($75 × 5 hours), or $175 more than firm C. Assuming that C and D had similar hourly costs, it is likely that D would spend about two hours more preparing the tax return. Most individuals with a $125,000 income would pay the extra $175 in hope of offsetting the outlay with a larger tax saving.

---

[15]Louis J. DeRose, "Not by Bids Alone," *Purchasing World,* November 1985, p. 46.

Cost-type contracts should be considered when there is significant uncertainty concerning the amount of effort that will be required or when there is insufficient time to develop a realistic S.O.W. Obviously, the dollar amount involved must warrant the administrative cost and effort involved. For smaller dollar amounts, a time and materials or labor-hour contract should be considered to avoid contingency pricing. Such contracts require close monitoring to ensure that the specified labor skill is furnished and that the hours being billed are in fact required. (Please see Chapter 19 for more on the types of compensation.)

Administratively, it may be impractical to use anything other than a fixed price contract or an hourly rate price for relatively small professional services contracts. Even on larger dollar amounts, the supplier's reputation may allow the use of a fixed price contract. But supply managers should be aware of the potential effect of the pricing mechanism on the contractor's performance.

Technical Services

Technical services include such things as:

- Research and development
- Software development
- Machine repairs
- Printing services
- Payroll services
- Mailroom services maintenance
- Elevator maintenance services

- Pest control
- Energy management
- Accounting and bookkeeping services
- Advertising and promotion
- Heating and air-conditioning
- Copyroom and message

R&D services normally are purchased through one of two methods of compensation: a fixed price for a level of effort (e.g., 50 days) or a cost plus fixed or award fee. Software development lends itself to cost plus award fee contracts. This approach rewards excellent performance and punishes poor performance while ensuring the contractor that its costs will be reimbursed and at least a minimum fee will be received.

In a competitive market, once a good S.O.W. is available for services such as printing, promotional services, and the development of technical manuals, competition should be employed to select the source and determine the price, using a fixed price contract.

Operating Services

Janitorial, security, landscaping, and cafeteria operations are typical operating services. Experience has shown that obtaining effective performance of such services can be very challenging for contract administrators. Accordingly, the compensation scheme should reward the supplier for good and penalize it for poor service. (The use of a fixed price award fee scheme, as described in Chapter 19, may be appropriate.) Such an approach to pricing greatly aids in the administration of the contract and frequently results in a far higher level of customer satisfaction.

Insurance, plant and equipment maintenance, and anticipated emergency services should be sourced and priced through the use of competition of carefully prequalified suppliers. Unanticipated emergency repairs normally are purchased on a "not-to-exceed" time and materials basis (as described in Chapter 19).

Third-Party Contracts

Contracts for the provision of a service to a third party may result in a nonlinear supply chain, and create ambiguities in contract relationships, for instance, between the supplier and the end user. While a contract may exist between an organization and its customer, and between an organization and its supplier, it does not necessarily follow that a contract will exist between the supplier and the customer unless explicitly provided for in the contract.

An example is a nationwide automobile insurer that puts in place across all regions of the country arrangements with suppliers for the provision of windshields for its customers. The question of whether a contract exists between the windshield supplier and the customer of the insurance company probably will be incidental if the relationship between the insurance company and its supplier is well managed. But if this is not the case, the relationship between the insurer and the customer may be at risk.

So, Your Services Contract Is about to Expire

The requirement for many services continues beyond the duration of the service contract. If a collaborative, mutually beneficial relationship has been established, many members of the purchasing firm may want to extend the contract. An additional pressure to extend the contract is in the form of switching costs. We estimate that it may cost as much as 5 percent of the face value of some services contracts to switch to a new supplier.

But what should the price be for such an extension? If we enjoy an open book relationship, we could study the present supplier's costs and use this information as the basis of a contract extension. A more objective and more scientific basis for determing the price of a contract extension is to apply the "experience" or "learning curve" as discussed in Chapter 18. The supplier, its site management, and its direct labor should learn how to do things more efficiently the more times they do a task or activity. Supply management should work with the supplier to develop a realistic estimate of what performance "should cost" (based on past and future learning). While the mechanics of such an approach are beyond the scope of the present chapter, we emphasize that our readers need to be sensitive to some of the subtleties of extending services contracts.

Contract Administration

The four keys to successful service contract administration are (1) a sound S.O.W., (2) selection of the "right" source, (3) a fair and reasonable price, and (4) aggressive management of the contract. The administration of many service contracts can be a very challenging responsibility. The supply professional needs to monitor and have a realistic degree of control over the supplier's performance. Crucial to success in this area is the timely availability of accurate data, including the contractor's plan for performance and the contractor's actual progress. The supply professional must proactively manage the relationship to ensure success. Chapter 21 describes the actions required to ensure timely, high-quality performance.

Services Purchases and the Internet

Clearly, the Internet is becoming increasingly important in the purchase of services. Firms are employing electronic requests for proposals and the receipt of proposals. Electronic collaboration, both within a firm and with potential suppliers, is becoming increasingly common. The Internet will allow purchasing firms to obtain increased competition and lower prices for some services. When used properly, the Internet has the potential of reducing total cost of ownership, reducing order processing costs, compressing the sourcing cycle time, and improving the flow of information required to manage the resulting contract. Electronic marketplaces can provide a directory of services suppliers and frequently can provide the role of matchmaker.

Leading firms use the prospect of incorporating the Internet as a stimulus to optimize their services supply chains. Reengineering frequently is appropriate. One Fortune 500 company reengineered its temporary labor service process prior to going digital. The documented savings was in the millions of dollars. This and a host of similar experiences cause us to encourage firms to reengineer to optimize the process before developing (or acquiring) the enabling e-solution.

Construction Services

The purchase of new facilities is a commitment for the future. Quality, productivity of the new plant or office, the time required to effect the purchase, and cost all must be considered. Aesthetic requirements, time requirements, and the availability of highly qualified designers and builders all will tend to influence the selection of a purchase method.

There are five common methods of purchasing construction; however, it is unlikely that any one of the five methods will consistently be the proper choice for all building requirements. Figure 13.1 provides a graphic presentation of the various steps involved in each method, from start to completion of a construction project.

Conventional Method

This is the most frequently employed approach to buying building construction in the United States. With this approach, design of the required facility is performed by architects and engineers without the involvement of a builder. Design of the facility is completed before potential suppliers are requested to submit bids. Two separate organizations are responsible: one for the design work and one for the construction phase of the project.

Many architects are noted for not being cost-conscious. Nevertheless, the cost factor can be controlled in several ways. A common approach involves employment, on a consulting basis, of a "cost-control architect" who is concerned solely with cost reduction. Naturally, the general architect typically does not appreciate having his or her work reviewed or "second guessed." However, use of a consulting architect undeniably tends to make the primary architect more cost-conscious.

If a consulting architect is not used because of the general architect's sensitivity, alternative methods of cost control are available to the supply professional. For example, for major interior furnishings, the architect or interior decorator can be required to

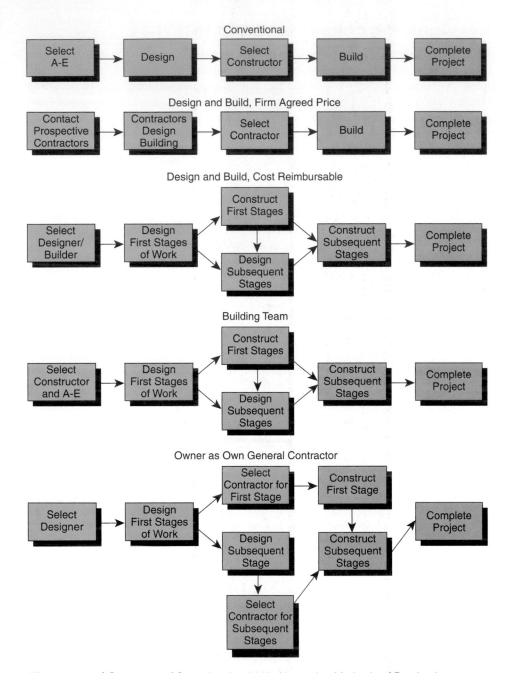

Figure 13.1 | Sequence of Steps Involved with Alternative Methods of Purchasing Construction

specify three manufacturers' products that can be purchased through competitive bids (any one of the specified products being satisfactory). The actual purchasing can be done by the customer's organization, the architect, or the interior decorator. The three-bid requirement itself ensures competitive pricing. As an added bonus, this practice helps eliminate conflicts of interest, unreasonable personal bias, and the specifying of low-volume, proprietary items.

Design and Build, Firm Agreed Price Method

This approach could be described as construction with gratuitous design. The owner determines the basic facility requirements, such as size, temperature, electrical, mechanical, and so on. These requirements become the basis of a performance specification. This specification is furnished to carefully prequalified builders who, with their prospective subcontractors, prepare a bid package consisting of a design and price proposal. The purchasing firm awards a fixed price contract for construction to the builder whose bid is most attractive.

Design and Build, Cost-Reimbursable Method

With this method, only one contract is awarded for both design and construction. Design is accomplished by architects and engineers employed by the general contractor. Thus, the builder has ample opportunity to influence the design of the required facility. With this approach, construction of a work element (excavation, structural work, and so on) proceeds when the design of the element has been completed. It is not necessary to await design of the total project since one firm is responsible for both the design and the construction phases. This approach is particularly useful when a structure is required within a very short time period and the design and build, firm agreed price method is not applicable.

Building Team

With this approach, the owner retains both a designer and a builder concurrently. In contrast to the conventional method, the builder is retained during the design phase and is expected to contribute information on costs, procedures, and time requirements to the designer. As the A-E completes the plans and specifications for a work element, the builder either accomplishes the work with its own crews or obtains prices from several specialists and awards the work to the qualified subcontractor making the best offer (price, time, and quality considered). As with the other methods, the general contractor oversees and integrates the efforts of the subcontractors.

The Owner as a Contractor

With this method, the owner contracts directly for the various work elements (including design) and performs the functions of integrating and controlling that would otherwise be accomplished by a general contractor. Since purchase orders and contracts are awarded on a work element basis, it is possible for construction to proceed prior to completion of the total design phase.

Table 13.2 | Purchase Price of a Hypothetical Building under Five Compensation Methods

Method	A&E Fee	Construction Contract(s)	Total	Time (months)
Conventional	$740,000	$12,300,000	$13,040,000	16
D&B (firm agreed price)	—	9,750,000	9,750,000	11.5
D&B (cost-reimbursable)	—	11,830,000	11,830,000	12
Building team	670,000	11,160,000	11,830,000	12
Owner as his own general	600,000	11,800,000	12,400,000	15.5

Findings: Research conducted by one of the authors on these five methods shows that the conventional method is, by far, the most costly approach to purchasing construction. Savings of approximately 25 percent were found to result when the design and build, firm agreed price method was used rather than the conventional method. Savings of 9 percent resulted when either the design and build, cost-reimbursable or the building team method was used in lieu of the conventional method. Savings of about 5 percent resulted when the owner acted as his or her own general contractor (see Table 13.2).

The amount of time from first contacting the designer or builder until completion of the facility frequently is as or more important than the price paid. Availability of the required facilities varies significantly with the methods used. On a typical 130,000-square-foot manufacturing plant, 16 months were required with the conventional method; 11.5 months with the design and build, firm agreed price method; 12 months with both the design and build, cost-reimbursable method and the building team method; and 15.5 months when the owner acted as the general contractor.

Supply professionals know that selection of the most appropriate method of purchasing plant facilities can significantly reduce the cost and time required to purchase new facilities. Their early involvement in such projects is a key to saving both time and money.

Construction Purchasing Entails Unique Problems

Construction purchasing is a highly specialized field. Of particular importance is the fact that proper financial, legal, and planning actions must be undertaken to prevent possible losses. For example, a purchasing organization sometimes discovers that after completion of a new building a mechanic's lien is filed against the firm. In such cases, the organization has typically paid the general contractor, but the general contractor has not paid its subcontractors. Under the law, if a "general" does not pay its "subs," the owner of the building is financially responsible.

The proper financial and legal steps that must be taken differ among states and municipalities; hence, the specific steps to be taken must be determined individually in each case. In general, though, the first step that must be taken when selecting the supplier is to carefully analyze the financial status of all prospective contractors. Next, the supply professional should consider the desirability of utilizing such protective devices as bid, performance, and payment bonds,[16] liquidated damages contract clauses, and the development of construction cost estimates by the organization's own engineering personnel

---

[16]Some organizations require performance bonds on all construction contracts, at times mistakenly believing that performance bonds per se assure quality performance.

(perhaps with the assistance of a specialized consultant). Finally, legal protection is achieved when the organization properly files all required completion and related reports, at the appropriate times, at the appropriate courthouses.

Construction Insurance   Because construction is a high-risk business, the insurance a purchasing organization requires the contractor to carry is very important. All construction contracts should stipulate specific insurance responsibilities. For example, a contract clause might require the contractor, at its expense, to maintain in effect during performance of the work certain types and minimum amounts of insurance coverage, with insurers satisfactory to the customer.

In addition, the contract should specify that prior to the performance of any work, the contractor must provide certificates of insurance as evidence that the required insurance is actually in force and that it cannot be canceled without 10 days' written notice to the customer organization. Failure to require any of the foregoing insurance provisions could be very costly.

Performance Contracting

There are many opportunities to correlate the design and construction fees to the "performance" of the resulting facility. Throughput and productivity are obvious examples. Energy conservation is an especially "hot" example today, although it has been around since the 1970s. An article in *Facilities Design and Management* cites an example of how performance contracting saves the facility owner money while reducing energy demands. When the owner of one of the largest high-rise office/retail complexes in the United States—comprising two 51-story buildings and an underground retail center for a total of 1.56 million square feet—undertook a major facilities upgrade to reduce operating costs and retain Class A tenants, it used a performance contract to execute the project. Not only did the performance contract provide turnkey delivery for design, construction, and maintenance, it also allowed the owner to finance the project off its balance sheet, secured against operations costs and installed equipment value, which would have been difficult to arrange under a traditional design/construction contract.

The project comprised design and installation of a direct digital-controlled energy management control system; variable frequency drives; variable air volume terminal units; fire- and life-safety control upgrades; utility control and monitoring systems; a fiber-optic Ethernet network with multiple workstations; and the development of custom software drivers to third-party terminal unit controllers. Following completion of the project, operating savings were 10 percent overall, more than double the owner's target.[17]

Concluding Remarks

The procurement of services is one of supply management's most interesting and challenging assignments. Large sums of money are involved. Of equal or greater importance, successful operation of the organization is affected by the effectiveness with which key services are purchased. Supply management frequently must assume a far more active role in all phases of a services procurement than when purchasing materials.

---

[17]Trevor Foster, "Performance Contracting Can Yield Significant Returns," *Facilities Design and Management,* January 2000, p. 34.

PART 4

Strategic Sourcing

Assembly-line Process *(Credit: selection #1) John Lund/Stone/Getty Images #2) Gregg Pease/Stone/Getty Images)*

S ourcing, in recent years, has become much more proactive than it once was. Today, professional supply managers work with the organization's engineers in an effort to ensure that the firm's supply base will support the firm's technology requirements now and in an uncertain future. The organization's information system allows supply managers to study the aggregation of its supply requirements. Professional supply managers then determine the most appropriate type of buyer-supplier relationship for each relevant commodity class, study their existing supplier base, and plan action to ensure that the base will meet the organization's needs efficiently and effectively. Those activities, frequently called "strategic sourcing" are key components of WCSM.

In Chapter 14, we address the incredibly complex issue of outsourcing. Its predecessor, the make-or-buy analysis, pales by comparison in both complexity and strategic implications. The make-or-buy issue is largely tactical. But the outsourcing of manufacturing and even product design has strategic long-term implications which, all too frequently, are ignored.

Sourcing, as discussed in Chapter 15, appears to be far less challenging. By and large, there is agreement on world-class sourcing practices. The most impactful aspect of sourcing is that of prequalifying suppliers who become involved in the new product development process. Extreme caution must be exercised.

The growth of the Internet and electronic commerce has forever changed global supply management. Today, there is virtually no way to avoid going global somewhere in your supply chain. Chapter 16, Global Supply Management, addresses several benefits of global sourcing, the use of intermediaries, problems and dangers which may be involved, and world-class processes required. Even though we have dedicated a chapter to the topic, global supply management is addressed throughout the book. Regardless of whether or not the firm's products are sold globally, world-class supply managers pursue global supplier relationships. These relationships must be based on fairness, honesty, and trust. ■

CHAPTER 14

Outsourcing: To Make or To Buy

Outsourcing has become a way to increase an organization's flexibility to meet rapidly changing market conditions, focus on core competencies, and develop competitive advantage. As a result, the need for World Class Supply Management^{SM} has intensified and positioned supply managers as agents of strategic change critical to supply chain success.

KEY CONCEPTS

When a firm considers which components, subsystems, or services it should make and which it should buy, it should analyze the issue at two levels: strategic and operational or tactical. The strategic, obviously, is the more important of the two as far as the future of the firm is concerned. So this initial analysis has a forward-looking, futuristic aura about it.

This chapter focuses initially on the strategic analysis and later on the tactical analysis. But first, let's look at a typical make-or-buy scenario.

Case

Making or Outsourcing Pump Housings

The Muenster Pump Company has manufactured high-quality agricultural pumps for over 40 years. The firm's only plant is located in the small midwestern city of Muenster. The company is Muenster's largest employer. Bob Dorf, president of the firm, is the grandson of Emil Dorf, the founder. Bob and his family, along with all key personnel, live in or near the city of Muenster. Cordial relations exist between the firm and the city officials.

Since its founding, the firm has always been as self-sufficient as possible. Shortly after setting up business, Emil Dorf established a foundry to cast pump housings and related items. Today, the foundry provides virtually all of the required pump housings.

Bob's cousin, Terry, is the purchasing manager for Muenster Pump. After graduating from State University, Terry worked as a buyer at a large appliance manufacturer in the southwestern corner of the state. But after two years of life in the big city, Terry returned to Muenster. Bob was delighted to have Terry back in town. He established the

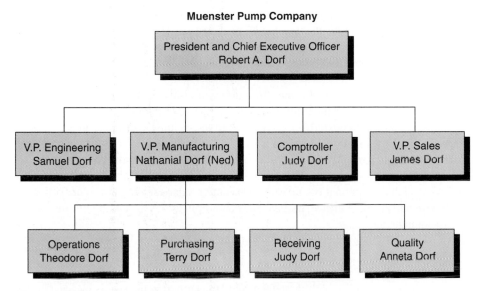

Muenster Pump Company

Figure 14.1 | The internal organization of the Muenster Pump Company.

position of purchasing manager by consolidating the buying functions previously performed by himself and other members of the firm. As seen in Figure 14.1, Terry reports to her Uncle Ned, who is the vice president of manufacturing.

Terry is an aggressive and conscientious professional. Materials costs have come down from 60 percent of the cost of sales to 50 percent in the two years since she assumed responsibility for purchasing.

Recently a representative of Union Foundry, a firm located in the southeastern part of the state, called on Terry. The rep was aware that Muenster Pump made its own cast pump housings. But he claimed that new developments in casting pouring allowed his firm to offer extremely attractive prices.

Terry requested a price on the L-1012 case housing, Muenster's most popular size. The L-1012 represents 60 percent of Muenster's demand for cast (or pump) housings. The pump that incorporated the L-1012 is sold to distributors for $500. Within a week of the meeting, a letter arrived from Union Foundry, quoting a price of $90 F.O.B. Muenster. Delivery was promised in 120 days after receipt of the first order. Thereafter, delivery would be made in 60 days after receipt of an order. Minimum orders were established as 100 units. Terry contacted two other foundries and obtained quotations for the L-1012 housing. The prices were $94 and $98 F.O.B. Muenster.

Terry met her Uncle Ned, discussed her findings with him, and asked how much it cost Muenster to produce the cast (or pump) housings internally in its own foundry.

Ned Dorf was not at all enthusiastic about Terry's efforts in this area of the business. He said, "Terry, I appreciate your interest and efforts at reducing cost, but a lot more is involved here than meets the eye. We produce a quality housing that is not equaled in the industry. It's one of the primary keys to our success! Furthermore, we can respond to requirements much quicker than those city boys."

Terry responded, "Ned, let's assume that all your doubts could be overcome. How much does it cost us to make the housings?" Ned replied, "Terry, there is something else involved. We have 16 men working in that foundry. If we stop making our own housings, we'll have to close down the foundry. And there's no other place in the firm where these men could work."

At this point, Terry thought that discretion would be the better part of valor. She thanked her Uncle Ned for the information and returned to her office.

Later that day, her cousin Bob stopped by. In the ensuing conversation, she learned that the L-1012 housing cost Muenster about $180. Total overhead at Muenster was calculated to be approximately 200 percent; hence, direct costs for material and labor for the housings would be about $60. Approximately 70 percent of the overhead was for fixed costs such as depreciation, taxes, and executive salaries. Terry sat in her office debating with herself the political, human, and cost implications of making or outsourcing the casting housing.

Outsourcing: A Growth Industry

The use of outsourcing by both manufacturing and service industries is increasing rapidly. An increasing number of business functions are being outsourced. In order to meet competitive challenges, corporations are outsourcing to highly specialized firms that can use their expertise to increase the efficiency of the outsourced function. The increase in outsourcing has resulted in lower staffing levels, reduced costs, and more flexibility. Outsourcing is more than a means of cutting costs; it provides the opportunity to achieve innovation. Managers are transforming from traditional roles into brokers or facilitators of outsourced activities. "The make/buy decision continues to be one of the key strategic issues and options confronting the purchasing function."[1]

Strategic Issues

The starting point most firms use in conducting the strategic outsourcing analysis is to identify the major strengths of the firm and then build on them. The supply manager needs to ask, "What is it we really do better than most firms?"

A firm's competitive advantage is often defined as cost leverage, product differentiation, or focus. It is important to perform a competitive analysis before initiating the outsourcing analysis. A competitive analysis will provide a report of the firm's strategic position relative to the market, industry, and competitors.

Core Competencies

Do our strengths lie in certain design skills, unique production skills and equipment, different types of people skills? A thorough investigation of these such questions is what many people today call identifying the firm's existing core competencies. The next step

---

[1]Lisa Ellram, Ph.D., and Arnold Maltz, Ph.D., "Outsourcing Supply Management," *The Journal of Supply Chain Management,* Spring 1999.

in the process is to look at the current and expected future environment in which the firm operates including the competition, the governmental regulatory climate, the changing characteristics of sales and supply markets, and so on. Subsequently, the bottom-line question management must answer is, "Precisely what business do we really want to be in to maximize the use of our core competencies as we proceed into the future?"

Once a clear answer to this question has been formulated, expected competency requirements necessary for future operations must be identified. Competency requirements are then compared with existing core competencies to determine which ones need to be refined and which ones need to be supplemented with related competencies that must be developed to create a competitive advantage. Two researchers place these ideas in sharp focus when they say, "Senior managers must conceive of their companies as a portfolio of core competencies rather than just as a portfolio of businesses and products."[2] The products and the nature of the business flow from the core competencies.

In considering what to make and what to buy, then, the decisions should cultivate and exploit the firm's core competencies. The items or services that should be made or conducted in-house are those that require capabilities that are closely linked with the core competencies and are mutually reinforcing, as opposed to those that can be separated. This is the fundamental strategic consideration that guides the original make-or-buy decisions that ultimately shape the character of the firm.[3]

Supplier Dominance

Chris Lonsdale at the Centre for Business Strategy and Procurement at the University of Birmingham in the United Kingdom observes that a majority of the problems outsourcing firms have experienced can be traced to suppliers who exploit the leverage they gain through the relationship. Lonsdale writes, "The significance of asset specificity for outsourcing is that if activities that require 'transaction-specific investments' are outsourced, the firm will find itself locked into its supplier, as it will not want to write off those investments by revisiting the market. This lock-in can then be exploited by the supplier, by renegotiating the terms of the contract or insisting on different terms next time around. This post-contractual lock-in (dependency) will cause the power relation between the two parties to change — the situation can become one of supplier dominance."[4] We share Lonsdale and his colleague Andrew Cox's concerns with the potential for suppliers to exercise the power they gain through such relationships. However, we believe that a carefully crafted and managed alliance will avoid such problems.

The Creation of Strategic Vulnerabilities

Michael E. Porter, author of the landmark book *Competitive Strategy,* inserts a timely cautionary note by observing, "when you outsource something, you tend to make it more

---

[2]C. K. Prahalad, "Core Competence Revisited," *Enterprise,* October 1993, p. 20.

[3]Hays and Pisano, Robert B. Hays and Gary Pisano, "Beyond World Class: The New Manufacturing Strategy," Harvard Business Review, January/February, 1994, vol. 72/1, pp. 77–87.

[4]Chris Lonsdale, "Locked In to Supplier Dominance: On the Dangers of Asset Specificity for the Outsourcing Decision," *The Journal of Supply Chain Management,* May 2001.

generic. You tend to lose control over it. You tend to pass a lot of the technology, particularly on the manufacturing or service delivery side, to your suppliers. That creates strategic vulnerabilities and also tends to commoditize your product. You're sourcing from people who also supply your competitors."[5]

The Dangers of Vertical Integration

On the other hand, if a decision to make or in-source results in vertical integration, the critical connection between output and rewards is broken. Cost and responsiveness both suffer. Vertical integration frequently results in a loss of flexibility and responsiveness.

Horizontal Integration

A general trend in competitive strategy is emerging that supports the outsourcing of all noncritical activities to achieve significant cost leverage. Known as critical dependencies, these activities are common to other businesses and are not a unique part of the firm's product. In order for this approach to be successful, the minimum resources and value-adding activities that are key to supporting the firm's core competencies must be defined. All other activities are decidedly noncore activities creating a dependency and making them potential candidates for outsourcing.

Companies are outsourcing a large range of services including customer service, warehousing, training, and travel. Horizontal integration, often referred to as a "virtual corporation," involves outsourcing nearly everything except a few core activities. Companies that separate intellectual activities from the resulting processes and then outsource the processes create virtual corporations. Cisco Systems is an ideal example of this type of organization. The company outsources most of its manufacturing, order fulfillment, and distribution. New product development is outsourced to the small companies frequently acquired by Cisco Systems. This company has developed a competitive advantage over competitors and established a standard for the virtual corporation. The company is able to provide its products faster and at a lower cost than its competitors due to its flexibility.

New Product Development and Outsourcing

The option to make or buy is first presented at the beginning of a product's life cycle, during new product development. The process of designing a new or modified product often presents new technologies, minimal information, and a high level of uncertainty. It is essential that supply managers conduct an analysis based on the availability of resources in terms of timeliness and optimal cost. Extensive supplier market research should be conducted on new technologies and innovations. The firm's technological core competencies must be identified and defined. Often suppliers will develop technology and new innovations that are beyond the reach of the firm's core competencies. In order to take advantage of new technology, many manufacturers will outsource development

---

[5]Michael E. Porter quoted in John A. Byrne, "Caught in the Net," *BusinessWeek,* August 27, 2001.

to suppliers. By utilizing suppliers during the development of new and modified products, manufacturers are gaining a competitive advantage and developing dependencies. To maintain a technological competitive advantage, manufacturers need suppliers to continue developing innovative designs.

A great deal of project planning is involved in the make-or-buy decision for new product development. Although outsourcing is considered a long-term activity, it can be considered in the context of finite projects. A project's strict deadlines may force a firm to make the decision to outsource. Coordination of the development activities of selected suppliers may be necessary depending on the number of suppliers involved and the type of development required. The supply manager will need to coordinate horizontal suppliers producing parts that will affect the product as a whole. Vertical coordination is necessary for suppliers interacting on different tiers when technological collaboration is required.[6]

Lean Manufacturing

If one steps back to assess the current situation in American industry, it is clear that the concept of "lean manufacturing" is widely embraced for competitive purposes. This means that "lean" firms increasingly buy more and make less. A rule of thumb used by some firms is to outsource subsystems and components unless they fall into one of the following three categories:

1. An item that is critical to the success of the product, including customer perceptions of important product attributes.

2. An item that requires specialized design and manufacturing skills or equipment and the number of capable and reliable suppliers is extremely limited.

3. An item that fits well within the firm's core competencies or within those the firm must develop to fulfill future plans.

Components or subsystems that fit into one of these categories are considered strategic and are produced in-house if possible. The analytical procedure used in making these decisions is straightforward and is shown in Figure 14.2.

If the analysis to this point indicates that a make decision is desirable from a strategic point of view, before the decision is made several additional factors must be analyzed. These practical considerations focus on a comparison of the firm's present situation with that of potential suppliers with respect to the matters of design, manufacturing, and quality capabilities. Similarly, relative costs and volume requirements also need to be compared and evaluated as supplementary information to be used in conjunction with the strategic analysis in reaching a final decision.

This, then, is the approach used at the strategic level of analysis to determine whether a firm should make an item or outsource it. These are the crucial decisions that to a great extent shape the destiny of the firm.

Let us turn now to make-or-buy decisions that are made at the operating level.

---

[6]Bjorn Axelsson, Ph.D., Finn Wynstra, Ph.D., and Arjan van Weele, Ph.D., "Purchasing Involvement in Product Development: A framework," *European Journal of Purchasing and Supply Management* 5, nos. 3/4 (September/December 1999), pp.129–141.

Deal First with Subsystems of the Product:

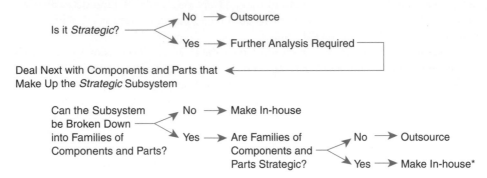

Figure 14.2 | Analyzing Strategic Outsource Decisions

* In some cases, in the short run it is not possible to make such an item in-house. This may be due to budget constraints, capability problems, capacity limitations, and so on. In these cases, until the problem is resolved, the item must be outsourced under a carefully crafted and managed contract.

Tactical Decisions

After the strategic make-or-outsource decisions are finalized, and as operations progress, a number of situations inevitably arise that require additional make-or-buy analyses at something less than a strategic level. Unsatisfactory supplier performance in the case of some outsourced items, cost considerations, changing sales demands, restricted manufacturing capacity, and the modification of an existing product are just a few of the operating factors that generate these needs. As a general rule, from a "make" perspective these tactical make-or-buy situations involve items for which the firm already possesses most of the necessary production resources. Small investments in tooling, minor equipment, or a few additional personnel usually are all that would be needed to do the job in-house. Consequently, these investigations tend to be driven by operating considerations of efficiency, control of quality and reliability, cost, capacity utilization, and so on.

In any case, the make-or-buy possibility requiring only a modest expenditure of funds in the event of a make decision is the type most commonly encountered by supply managers. A decision of this type usually does affect a firm's resource allocation plans; however, its effect on the firm's future is minimal compared with a decision requiring a major capital investment. Although the decision requiring a nominal expenditure of funds does not require direct top-management participation, it does require coordinated study by several operating departments—perhaps using a team approach. Top management's responsibility is to develop an operating procedure which provides for the pooling and analysis of information from all departments affected by the decision. In other words, management should ensure that the decision is made only after all relevant inputs have been evaluated.

Factors Influencing Make-Or-Buy Decisions

Two factors stand out above all others when considering the make-or-buy question at the tactical level: total cost of ownership and availability of production capacity. A good make-or-buy decision, nevertheless, requires the evaluation of many less tangible factors, in addition to the two basic factors. The following considerations influence firms to make or to buy the items used in their finished products or their operations.

Considerations Which Favor Making

1. Cost considerations (less expensive to make the part).
2. Desire to integrate plant operations.
3. Productive use of excess plant capacity to help absorb fixed overhead.
4. Need to exert direct control over production and/or quality.
5. Design secrecy required.
6. Unreliable suppliers.
7. Desire to maintain a stable work force (in periods of declining sales).

Considerations Which Favor Buying

1. Limited production facilities.
2. Cost considerations (less expensive to buy the part).
3. Small volume requirements.
4. Suppliers' research and specialized know-how.
5. Desire to maintain a stable work force (in periods of rising sales).
6. Desire to maintain a multiple-source policy.
7. Indirect managerial control considerations.
8. Procurement and inventory considerations.

Cost Considerations

In some cases cost considerations indicate that a part should be made in-house; in others, they dictate that it should be purchased externally. Cost is obviously important, yet no other factor is subject to more varied interpretation and to greater misunderstanding. A make-or-buy cost analysis involves a determination of the cost to make an item—and a comparison of this cost with the cost to buy it. The following checklist provides a summary of the major elements which should be included in a make-or-buy cost estimate.

To Make

1. Delivered purchased material costs.
2. Direct labor costs.[7]
3. Any follow-on costs stemming from quality and related problems.
4. Incremental inventory carrying costs.
5. Incremental factory overhead costs.
6. Incremental managerial costs.
7. Incremental purchasing costs.
8. Incremental costs of capital.

---

[7]It is assumed that all inspection costs associated with the "make" operation are included in the direct labor costs.

To Buy

1. Purchase price of the part.
2. Transportation costs.
3. Receiving and inspection costs.
4. Incremental purchasing costs.
5. Any follow-on costs related to quality or service.

To see the comparative cost picture clearly, the analyst must carefully evaluate these costs, considering the effects of time and capacity utilization in the user's plant.

The Time Factor   Costs can be computed on either a short-term or a long-term basis. Short-term calculations tend to focus on direct measurable costs. As such, they frequently understate tooling costs and overlook such indirect materials costs as those incurred in storage, purchasing, inspection, and similar activities. Moreover, a short-term cost analysis fails to consider the probable future changes in the relative costs of labor, materials, transportation, and so on. It thus becomes clear that in comparing the costs to make and to buy, the long-term view is the correct one. Cost figures must include all relevant costs, direct and indirect, and they must reflect the effect of anticipated cost changes.

Since it is difficult to predict future cost levels, estimated average cost figures for the total time period in question are generally used. Even though an estimate of future costs cannot be completely accurate, the following example illustrates its value.

Suppose the user of a particular stamped part develops permanent excess capacity in its general-purpose press department. The firm subsequently decides to make the stamped part that had previously been purchased from a specialized metalworking firm. Because this enables the firm to reactivate several unused presses, the additional cost to make the item is less than the cost to buy it. However, the user finds that the labor segment of its total cost is much higher than the labor segment of the automated supplier's cost. Should labor costs continue to rise more rapidly than the other costs of production, the user's cost advantage in making the part may soon disappear. Thus, an estimate of future cost behavior can prevent a make decision that might well prove unprofitable in the future.

Another factor that should be considered is the need for time-based competition. Many companies, especially high-tech firms, compete by reducing the amount of time necessary to produce or complete activities. The ability to reduce cycle time is a key strategy for gaining competitive advantage. Time is a critical issue when developing new products and bringing them to market. Making the decision to outsource research and development, the manufacturing, or distribution of a product will affect the time required to bring new technology to market. Make-or-buy decisions have a strong impact on reducing cycle time in all aspects of a business.

The Capacity Factor   When the cost to make a part is computed, the determination of relevant overhead costs poses a difficult problem. The root of the problem lies in the user's capacity utilization factor. As is true in most managerial cost analyses, the costs relevant to a make-or-buy decision are the incremental costs. In this case, incremental costs are those costs which would not be incurred if the part were purchased outside. The overhead problem centers on the fact that the incremental overhead costs vary from time to time, depending on the extent to which production facilities are utilized by existing products.

For example, assume that an automobile engine manufacturer currently buys its piston pins from a distant machine shop. For various reasons, the engine producer now decides that it wants to make the piston pins in its own shop. Investigation reveals that the machine shop is loaded to capacity with existing work and will remain in that condition throughout the foreseeable future. If the firm decides to make its own piston pins, it will have to either purchase additional machining equipment or free up existing equipment by subcontracting to an outside supplier a part currently made in-house. In this situation, the incremental factory overhead cost figure should include the variable overhead caused by the production of piston pins, plus the full portion of fixed overhead allocable to the piston pin operation.[8]

Now assume that the same engine manufacturer wants to make its own piston pins and that it has enough excess capacity to make the pins in its machine shop with existing equipment. Investigation shows that the excess capacity will exist for at least the next two or three years. What are its incremental overhead costs to make the pins in this situation? Only the variable overhead caused by production of the piston pins! In this case, fixed overhead represents sunk costs which continue to accumulate whether piston pins are produced or not. The total machine shop building continues to generate depreciation charges. Heat, light, and janitorial service are still furnished to the total machine shop area. Also, property taxes for the machine shop remain the same regardless of the number of machines productively employed. The firm incurs these same fixed costs regardless of the make-or-buy action it decides on. Such costs, under conditions of idle capacity, are not incremental costs and, for purposes of the make-or-buy decision, must be omitted from computation of the cost to make a new part.

The concept can also be observed from a slightly different point of view in the graphic representation of Figure 14.3. Note that a 12½ percent increase in production volume (an increase from 80 to 90 percent of capacity) can be achieved by a total cost increase of only 10 percent. This favorable situation results simply because the 12½ percent increase in production is accomplished by activating unused capacity. Fixed overhead costs are incurred irrespective of the decision to make piston pins by utilizing unused capacity.

Finally, consider a third common situation in which the same engine manufacturer wants to make its own piston pins. Investigation in this case reveals that enough excess capacity currently exists in the machine shop to permit production of the piston pins. However, management expects a gradual increase in business during the next several years, which will eliminate all excess capacity by the end of the second year. How should the make-or-buy decision be approached in this particular case?

---

[8]In the event that piston pin production replaces production of another part, the piston pin operation should carry the same absolute amount of fixed overhead that was carried by the part replaced. In the case where new equipment is purchased to produce piston pins, the piston pin operation should be charged with the additional fixed overhead arising from acquisition of the new equipment.

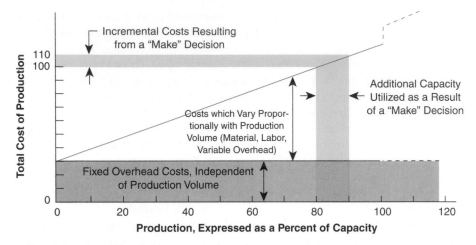

Figure 14.3 | A Representative Case Illustrating the Incremental Costs Resulting from a "Make" Decision when Operating at 80 Percent of Production Capacity

As always, the starting point of the analysis is an estimate of the costs to make versus the costs to buy. For the first one to two years, the cost to make piston pins will not include fixed overhead because excess capacity exists. Beyond two years, however, the cost to make must include fixed overhead; if piston pins are not made, increased production of some other part will, in the normal course of business, carry its full share of fixed overhead. One alternative is to consider the make-or-buy decision separately for each of the two time periods. While the analysis may indicate that it is profitable to make the pins in both cases, it will probably reveal that it is profitable to make the pins only for the first two years and to buy them beyond that date. In this case, several qualitative factors must be investigated to determine the practical feasibility of a split course of action. If the split course of action does not appear feasible, a second alternative is to compute a weighted average cost to make the pins during both time periods. The cost data can then be used in considering the total make-or-buy question.

In practice, an infinite number of situations exist between the two extremes of excess capacity and full capacity. There is no simple, absolutely accurate solution to any of these problems. Each situation must be analyzed in its own dynamic context.

In summary, an analyst should be guided by several basic ideas. First, incremental costs are virtually always the costs germane to the managerial decision-making process. Second, the determination of a realistic cost to make an item requires a realistic estimate of the future conditions of capacity. When capacity can be utilized by existing business or by alternative new projects, incremental overhead costs to make a new item must reflect total overhead costs. During any period when this condition does not exist, the incremental overhead to "make" consists only of variable overhead. When conditions of capacity normally oscillate frequently between partial load and full load, it is likely that the make-or-buy decision for a new project of substantial duration will turn largely on considerations other than comparative cost.

Precautions in Developing Costs   If a firm decides to buy a part that it has made in the past, it must exercise particular care in interpreting the quotations it receives from potential suppliers. Some suppliers may prepare the quotation carelessly, with the mistaken idea that the user does not really intend to buy the part. Other suppliers may bid unrealistically low in an attempt to induce the user to discontinue making the part in favor of buying it. Once the user has discontinued its make operation, resumption of the operation in the future may be costly. Thus, the user may be at the mercy of the supplier in case the supplier later chooses to increase the price.[9] It is essential that the supply management professional carefully evaluate the reliability of all quotations in his or her attempt to determine a realistic estimate of the total cost to buy the part.

In estimating the cost to make a part, an analyst must ensure that the firm possesses adequate equipment and technical know-how to do the job. Moreover, in an industry in which technological change occurs rapidly, a firm can find its equipment and know-how competitively outmoded in a few short years. Thus, the factor of obsolescence should also be given adequate consideration in determining the ultimate costs of equipment and personnel training.

The proper equipment to make an item sometimes may be easier to acquire than the properly skilled manpower. Large-volume requirements, complex skill requirements, or unique geographic locations can precipitate shortages of adequately skilled manpower. In preparing cost-to-make estimates, the local manpower situation must be evaluated. Should it be necessary to import adequately skilled personnel, total labor costs can substantially exceed initial estimates.

In the case of a make decision, it is equally important to investigate the availability and price stability of required raw materials. Large users of particular materials generally find the availability and price structure of these materials much more favorable than do small unspecialized users. Wise analysts ensure that their estimates for raw material are realistic.

Finally, in estimating the cost to make a part for the first time, the analyst must also investigate several practical production matters. The first deals with the cost of unacceptable production work. What is the expected rate of rejected and spoiled parts? Equally important, what learning curve can the production department reasonably expect to apply? Answers to these questions may vary substantially, depending upon the complexity of the job and the type of workers and equipment available. The resulting influence on the make-buy cost comparison can be considerable, however, and realistic answers should be sought.

Control of Production or Quality

Consider now some of the factors other than costs that influence make-or-buy decisions. Two conditions weigh heavily in some firms' decisions to make a particular part—control of production and control of quality.

---

[9]A partnering arrangement or a long-term requirements contract may be used to help control such price increases.

Production Requirements   The need for close control of production operations is particularly acute in some firms. A company whose sales demand is subject to extreme short-run fluctuations finds that its production department must operate on unusually tight time schedules. This kind of company often produces a small inventory of those parts used in several different products. However, it produces to individual customer order the parts unique to a particular product or customer specification. Sales fluctuations for products using unique parts therefore influence the planning and scheduling of numerous assembly and subassembly operations, as well as single-part production operations. Efficient conduct of assembly operations thus depends on the firm's ability to obtain the unique unstocked parts on short notice.

Most suppliers serving a number of customers normally cannot tool up and fit an order for a unique part into existing schedules on a moment's notice unless they operate under some type of JIT or partnering arrangement. If a user cannot tolerate suppliers' lead-time requirements, its only other major alternative is to control the part production operations itself. Thus, by making the item, the user acquires the needed control. It is possible to quickly revise job priorities, reassign operators and machines to specific jobs, and require overtime work as conditions demand.

Some firms also choose to make certain critical parts to assure continuity of supply of these parts to succeeding production operations. This type of integration guards against production shutdowns caused by supplier labor problems, local transportation strikes, and miscellaneous supplier service problems. These are particularly important considerations when dealing with parts that feed an automated production operation whose downtime is tremendously expensive. If such action reduces the risk of a production stoppage, it may well justify the incurrence of extra materials costs.

Quality Requirements   Unique quality requirements frequently represent a second condition requiring control of part production operations. Certain parts in technical products are occasionally quite difficult to manufacture. Compounding this difficulty, at times, is an unusually exacting quality specification the part must meet. In certain technological fields or in particular geographical areas, a user may find that the uniqueness of the task results in unsatisfactory performance by an outside supplier. Some companies find that their own firm is in a better position to do an acceptable production job than are external suppliers.

A user normally understands more completely than an outside supplier the operational intricacies connected with usage of the part. Therefore, if the using firm makes the part itself, there can be greater coordination between the assembly operation and the part production operation. Conducting both operations under one roof likewise eliminates many communications problems which can arise between a supply management professional and supplier whose operations are geographically separated. Finally, large users often possess technological resources superior to those of smaller suppliers. Such resources may be needed in solving new technical problems in production.

For example, one producer of hydraulic systems makes a practice of subcontracting production of some of the valves used in its systems. The production of one particular subcontracted valve involved difficult interior machining operations as well as tight quality requirements. Of the supplier's first four shipments, the systems manufacturer rejected 80 percent of the valves for failure to meet quality specifications. During the ensuing months, the systems manufacturer worked closely with the subcontractor in an attempt to solve the quality problem. With the passage of time, however, it became clear that the systems manufacturer was contributing considerably more to solution of the problem than was the supplier. Eventually, the systems firm decided to make the valve. Although production of the valve still remained a difficult task, the systems manufacturer was able to develop the techniques necessary to produce a valve of acceptable quality, with a greatly reduced reject percentage.

Business Process Outsourcing

As outsourcing has gained popularity, the opportunity to outsource business processes has greatly increased. Lisa Ellram and Arnold Maltz have described business process outsourcing as "the transfer of responsibility to a third party of activities which used to be performed internally."[10] Many consulting firms are competing to be external providers of these services (because of the "commodization" of generic services). Companies that formerly only outsourced IT now outsource many business processes that are not core competencies. Advertising, maintenance, auditing, travel, and human resources are all types of functional services commonly outsourced. In addition, companies are beginning to outsource major business systems including logistics, real estate, and software systems development. Companies are realizing more than cost reduction by outsourcing these activities. They are able to take advantage of innovative, specialized suppliers. James Brian Quinn has stated, "Proper outsourcing of entire business processes can speed and amplify major innovative changes."[11]

The success experienced by outsourcing business processes has encouraged many firms to outsource entire operational functions. Firms have been outsourcing supply management without receiving much improvement in cost reduction or innovation. Often internal purchasing has proven to be more effective than using a third-party supplier for supply management. Firms using programs such as JIT or VMI (vendor managed inventory) have the most success outsourcing the activities associated with those programs. MRO purchasing is another activity that is often outsourced successfully.

The high-tech industry may benefit the most by outsourcing supply chain management activities. The need for faster cycle times and flexibility was the reason for Toshiba's recent decision to combine operations with a supply management provider. Toshiba outsourced responsibility for supplier management, logistics, manufacturing, testing, and order processing. Yasuo Morimoto, president and CEO of Toshiba Semiconductor Co., explained, "To be successful in this extremely competitive environment, it is absolutely essential to have the most efficient and flexible method to service the customer, wherever the customer need arises."[12] The business model Cisco Systems established relies on the outsourcing of many supply management activities to strategic partners.

While the outsourcing of some supply activities is beneficial, the need to perform critical sourcing activities internally has become apparent. Loss of control over performance or cost is important to consider when deciding on outsourcing supply management activities.

---

[10]Ellram and Maltz, "Outsourcing Supply Management."

[11]James Brian Quinn, Ph.D., "Outsourcing Innovation: The New Engine of Growth," *Sloan Management Review,* July 1, 2000, pp. 13–28.

[12]"Toshiba and Kingston Establish New Supply Chain Management Model," *Business Wire,* February 29, 2000.

A third party may not be aggressive in seeking improvements. Ellram and Maltz have stated, "Supply management skills are strategic, hard to duplicate, lead to success in multiple business units, and can lead to dominance over competitors."[13]

Design Secrecy Required   Although their number is small, a few firms make particular parts primarily because they want to keep secret certain aspects of the part's design or manufacture. The secrecy justification for making an item can be found in highly competitive industries in which style and cost play unusually important roles. Also, a firm is more likely to make a key part for which patent protection does not provide effective protection against commercial emulation.

If design secrecy is really important, however, a firm may have nearly as much difficulty maintaining secrecy when it makes a part as it would when a supplier makes it. In either case, a large number of individuals must be taken into the firm's confidence, and once information leaks to a competitor, very little can be done about it. Nevertheless, a firm can usually control security measures more easily and directly in its own plant. In either case, however, the element of trust is extremely important. World-class firms work hard to create an atmosphere of trust surrounding both internal and external activities.

Technology Risk and Maturity

Technology life cycles are an important factor in the make-or-buy decision. Technology that is continually changing indicates that it is not mature and has short life cycles. Parts produced using this type of technology may be too risky to make internally. The investment in capital equipment would not be reasonable. Outsourcing technology that is changing rapidly will place the risk on the supplier. It is less risky to invest in production of a part that uses mature technology. The life cycle of mature technology is reasonably stable and long term. Supply management professionals closely survey expected changes in technology. It is important to continually obtain insight into technology life cycles of potential materials and processes.

Outsourcing is not a viable option for products with specifications that are fluctuating because of continually developing technology or technology that is truly new. For example, Cisco Systems has decided to make many of the products in the demanding industry of optical networks. Cisco Systems is forced to integrate and perform product development internally in order to be competitive in this industry. Fiber optic technology is still in a fluctuating stage, which makes it difficult to define the specifications required to successfully outsource development and manufacturing.[14] Technology life cycles are a function of customer demand and technological advancements.

Unreliable Suppliers

Some firms decide to make specific parts because their experience has shown that the reliability record of available suppliers falls below the required level. The likelihood of encountering such a situation 30 years ago was infinitely greater than it is now. Today,

---

[13]Ellram and Maltz, "Outsourcing Supply Management."

[14]Clayton M. Christensen, Ph.D., "Limits of the New Corporation," *Business Week,* August 28, 2000, pp. 180–81.

competition in most industries is so keen that grossly unreliable performers do not survive the competitive struggle. With one major exception, unreliable delivery or unpredictable service is confined largely to isolated cases in new, highly specialized lines of business where competition has not yet become established. Such businesses are usually characterized by low sales volumes, the requirement of highly specialized production equipment, or the unique possession of new technological capabilities.

The one major exception mentioned above is the case of the firm that purchases only an insignificant fraction of a specific supplier's total volume of business. Even the most reputable suppliers are forced, at times, to shortchange very small accounts in order to give significant attention to their major accounts. Regardless of the reasonableness of the cause, however, consistently unreliable performance by a supplier is sufficient grounds for shifting suppliers or possibly reconsidering the original make-buy decision.

Suppliers' Specialized Knowledge and Research

A primary reason underlying most decisions to buy a part rather than make it is the user's desire to take advantage of the specialized abilities and/or research efforts of various suppliers.

Lest the preceding discussion of "make" decisions distort the total procurement picture, bear in mind that the typical American manufacturing firm spends more than 50 percent of its sales dollar for purchases from external suppliers. Modern industry is highly specialized. No ordinary firm, regardless of size, can hope to possess adequate facilities and technical know-how to make a majority of its production part requirements efficiently. Large corporations spend millions of dollars on product and process research each year. The fruits of this research and the ensuing technical know-how are available to customers in the form of highly developed and refined parts and component products. The firm that considers forgoing these benefits in favor of making an item should, before making its final decision, assess carefully the long-range values that accrue from industrial specialization.

Small Volume Requirements

When a firm uses only a small quantity of a particular item, it usually decides to buy the item. The typical firm strives to concentrate its production efforts in areas in which it is most efficient and in areas it finds most profitable. The work of designing, tooling, planning, and setting up for the production of a new part is time-consuming and costly. These fixed costs are recovered more easily from long production runs than from short ones. Consequently, more often than not, the small-volume user searches for a potential supplier who specializes in production of the given part and can economically produce it in large quantities. Such specialty suppliers can sell to a large number of users in almost any desired quantity at relatively low prices.

Small-volume production of unique, nonstandard parts may likewise be unattractive to external suppliers. Every supplier is obligated to concentrate first on its high-volume, high-profit accounts. Thus, cases may develop in which a user is virtually forced to make a highly nonstandard part it uses in small quantities. Generally speaking, however, as the part tends toward a more common and finally a standard configuration, the tendency to buy increases proportionally.

Limited Facilities

Another reason for buying rather than making certain parts is the physical limitation imposed by the user's production facilities. A firm with limited facilities typically attempts to utilize them as fully as possible on its most profitable production work. It then depends on external suppliers for the balance of its requirements. Thus, during peak periods a firm may purchase a substantial portion of its total requirements because of loaded production facilities, and during slack periods, as internal production capacity opens up, its purchases may decrease markedly.

Workforce Stability

Closely related to the matter of facilities is the factor of workforce stability. A fluctuating production level compels a firm to face the continual problem of contracting and expanding its workforce to keep in step with production demands. Significant continuing fluctuation, moreover, adversely affects the quality of workers such a firm is able to employ. The less stable an operation is, the more difficult it becomes to retain a competent workforce.

At the time when a firm sizes the various segments of its production operation, many make-buy decisions are made. One factor which often bears heavily on the decision is the firm's desire to develop an interested, responsible group of workers with a high degree of company loyalty. Awareness that stable employment facilitates the attainment of this objective sometimes prompts a firm to undersize its production facility by a slight margin. Its plan is to maintain as stable an internal production operation as possible and to buy requirements in excess of its capacity from external suppliers. This policy is most effective in firms whose products require a considerable amount of general-purpose equipment in the manufacturing operation. Equipment, as well as personnel, that can perform a variety of different jobs provides the internal flexibility required to consolidate or split work among various production areas as business fluctuates. This capability is necessary for the successful implementation of such a policy. As business increases, it is not feasible to place small orders for a large number of different parts with outside suppliers. It is much more profitable to farm out large orders for a small number of parts.

Firms that successfully solve their workforce problems in this way frequently create problems in the purchasing area. External suppliers are, in effect, used as buffers to absorb the shocks of production fluctuations. This action transfers many of the problems associated with production fluctuations from the user to the supplier. The supplier's ability to absorb these production shocks is therefore an important consideration. In some instances it may be able to absorb them reasonably well; in others, it may not.[15] In all

---

[15] Two factors largely determine a supplier's ability to absorb fluctuating order requirements from a user.

  1. The similarity of the work involved in producing a particular user's requirement and in producing other customers' orders. The more similar the requirements are, the less is the expense of special planning setup work for a particular user.
  2. The extent to which other customers' orders offset the peaks and valleys in the supplier's production operation. The more stable the supplier's total production operation is, the less disturbing is the effect of an occasional fluctuating account.

cases, however, the supplier prefers, as does the user, to maintain a stable production operation. Consequently, many suppliers are not interested in the user who buys only its peak requirements. The question naturally arises, "Will a supplier ever be motivated to perform well for a purchaser who uses the supplier only for surplus work?" This question should be considered carefully before a "buy" decision of this type is made.

A third choice is available for maintaining a stable workforce. A company may choose leased labor to alleviate the need to maintain a steady number of employees during fluctuations in production. External temporary manpower support is utilized instead of permanent employees or completely outsourcing the task or function. Leased labor can run the gauntlet from clerical to highly skilled professionals. Quality is maintained by selecting leased employees who are competent in the areas required. The supply management professional must be aware of all aspects of the leased-labor business. Agencies providing leased labor should be analyzed and selected with great care. Payment terms, temporary to permanent employment options, and functional variations should be determined prior to implementing a plan to use leased labor.

Multiple-Source Policy

Some firms occasionally make and buy the same nonstandard part. This policy is followed for the explicit purpose of having available a reliable and experienced second source of supply. Firms adopting a make-and-buy policy recognize that they may not always be able to meet their internal production schedules for certain parts. In case of an emergency, an experienced outside source is usually willing to increase its delivery of the part in question on a temporary basis until the situation is under control.

Managerial Control Considerations

Companies occasionally buy and make the same part for the purpose of developing managerial control data. Some firms use outside suppliers' cost and quality performance as a check on their own internal production efficiency. If internal costs for a particular part rise above a supplier's cost, the user knows that somewhere in its own production system some element of cost is probably out of line. An investigation frequently uncovers one or more problems, some of which often extend to other production areas. These consequent improvements may exhibit a compounding effect as they reach into other operations where inefficiencies might otherwise have gone undetected.

Procurement and Inventory Considerations

A "buy" decision produces several significant benefits in the management of supply and inventory activities. For supply management, a buy decision typically means that it has fewer items to buy and fewer suppliers to deal with. Usually, though not always, when a component is made in-house a number of different materials or parts must be purchased outside to support the "make" operation. A corresponding buy decision usually involves only one or two suppliers and a relative reduction in the associated buying, paperwork, and follow-up activities. The same relative reduction in workload occurs in receiving, inspection, stores, and inventory management groups. Typically, inventory investment is also reduced.

Netsourcing

The Internet has enabled companies to manage supply more efficiently and effectively. The supply management professional can now locate and research new suppliers by accessing information on the Internet. The Internet has become an open market for electronic business transactions. Many tactical supply management activities can be replaced by using electronic forms and direct connections with suppliers. Intranets have become a way to provide services to personnel by connecting employees directly with preferred providers. The Web offers an aggregation of common business tools allowing more efficient management of many business processes. The Internet can replace many different services and functions including human resources, accounts payable and receivable, and document storage systems. The online business revolution requires companies to develop infrastructures and websites quickly.

Many companies are outsourcing infrastructure development and maintenance to what the Yankee Group has termed "Netsourcers." Chris Selland, Yankee Group analyst, has defined this term as suppliers of a "highly available, scalable, high-performance platform for hosted business applications."[16] Many companies are not readily staffed with personnel who can manage the complex infrastructure and websites necessary to keep a company competitive in the e-business marketplace. Outsourcing network infrastructure development and maintenance has become popular since it allows a company to achieve high performance and a strong presence online quickly with the flexibility to make changes. "Netsourcing" is viewed as adding significant value by providing sustained performance and operational support. Many companies prefer to outsource these activities in order to eliminate the need to train or hire specialized personnel.

The Volatile Nature of the Make-or-Buy Decision

Although make-or-buy investigations usually begin with a cost analysis, various qualitative factors frequently portend more far-reaching consequences than does the cost analysis. Therefore, a correctly approached make-or-buy decision considers the probable *composite effect* of all factors on the firm's total operation.

A thorough investigation is complicated considerably by the dynamics and uncertainties of business activity. Certain factors can hold quite different implications for a make-or-buy decision at different points in time and under different operating conditions. As pointed out, changing costs can turn a good decision into a bad one in a very short time. In addition, future costs, complicated by numerous demand and capacity interrelationships, are influenced substantially by such variable factors as technological innovation and customer demand. The availability of expansion capital also influences make-or-buy decisions. An "easy money" policy, a liberal depreciation policy, or liberal government taxing policies tend to encourage "make" decisions. Contrary policies promote "buy" decisions. These federal policies fluctuate with economic and political conditions.

---

[16]Leigh Buchanan, "Do Your Own Thing," *Inc.*, March 1, 1999.

The tendency toward favoring "make" decisions in order to stabilize production and workforce fluctuation is usually greater in small firms than it is in large ones. In some small shops the loss of just a few orders results in the temporary layoff of a sizable percentage of the workforce until additional orders can be obtained. Generally speaking, larger organizations do not have such severe problems because their fluctuations in production volume relative to total capacity are smaller. As large firms adopt compensation plans that move toward a guaranteed wage structure, however, they too will feel a similar pressure to favor "make" decisions.

Finally, the labor-relations climate within a firm can influence its make-or-buy decisions. A hostile union may seize the opportunity to irritate management as a result of the decision to buy an item previously made in-house. An amicable labor-management climate may evoke a very different reaction.

To summarize: beware of rigid formulas and rules of thumb that claim to produce easy make-or-buy decisions. The make-or-buy question is influenced by a multitude of diverse factors that are in a constant state of change. Under such conditions, few easy decisions turn out well in both the short and the long run. Moreover, the relevant factors vary immensely from one firm to another. For these reasons, every company should periodically evaluate the effectiveness of its past decisions in order to gain information helpful in guiding future courses of make-buy decision making.

Insourcing

Core competencies change. Thus, periodic reevaluation of outsourcing decisions is a strategic necessity. Although it is often expensive and difficult to bring an activity back in-house, changes in core activities, technology, or strategy may require a company to reverse a make-or-buy decision. Continued involvement is always necessary when a "buy" decision has been implemented. Managing the supplier relationship for an outsourced activity will allow a company to make adjustments when problems arise. Change management has been recognized as a needed skill for handling the transition of such activities. Implementing the decision to outsource or bring an activity back in-house involves a formal transition process that affects the organizations of both the firm and the supplier.

Dangers of Outsourcing

Loss of Control   Entrusting an entire process to an external provider may cause loss of control and of skills, resulting in overdependency. A firm may lose key information resources without continuous and active management of the outsourcing contract. Information that is required to manage the business and future growth effectively will not be communicated. Inadequate involvement is often the cause of this problem. Supply professionals must be good at supplier management for an outsourcing program to work.

Loss of Client Focus   The goals and objectives of the selected external provider may differ from the firm's goals. Eventually the provider will lose touch with the firm's business plan and strategy. A conflict of interest may be triggered if the provider performs similar outsourced functions for other organizations. Key resources from one firm may be used to support other clients. These activities affect the timely and successful performance of the outsourced function.

Lack of Clarity   Failure to clearly articulate the responsibilities of the selected external provider is a major concern. A formal service level agreement (SLA) contract must be developed prior to commencing outsourced services. Without a clear and agreed-upon contract, the outsource provider can cause costly and disruptive disputes with claims of "out of scope" work. A formal agreement avoids the extra charges for every change or request that such providers can assess. The agreement should specify how changes and requests would be processed with a mechanism or formula for pricing such changes.

Lack of Cost Control   Many outsourcing decisions are made in an effort to lower overall costs. Changes in company objectives and rising prices can take costs beyond estimates made for the initial analysis. If the outsourcing contract does not include long-term pricing with appropriate incentives, then the outsource provider will not be motivated to control costs or maintain quality. This problem is impacted by an inflexible contract. The buying company should specify in the outsourcing contract the degree to which it desires to manage costs and the appropriate mechanics. It can be very difficult to disengage from a poorly structured outsourcing contract. Inflexible conditions limit the ability to support changing business strategies and objectives. If a company is unable to manage an outsourcing contract appropriately, it may need to in-source in order to regain control of those activities. Bringing a function or service back in-house is expensive and the organization usually lacks employees with the required skill sets.

Ineffective Management   The selected external provider may not perform the outsourced function better than the client organization. Many companies have outsourced a function without carefully prequalifying the provider on efficiency, effectiveness, and total capabilities. Careless outsourcing ultimately costs more than keeping a function in-house. Without proper analysis and consideration, a function may be outsourced for the wrong reasons. Managers may decide to outsource because of a problem they are experiencing with a function in-house only to find that the selected provider cannot solve the problem. For example, management may believe that the internal IT department is not sensitive to the needs of the users. An external provider is not necessarily going to be more sensitive to user needs. This type of problem can be avoided by developing a precise statement of work, carefully researching and prequalifying providers, and utilizing a clear service-level agreement.

Loss of Confidentiality   Outsourcing often means off-loading sensitive functions involving proprietary corporate data. Concerns about loss of control of these functions and the protection of the underlying information are valid, particularly in an environment where hacking is a blood sport. This raises several issues:

■   Is the outsourcing service provider's system secure against external and internal threats?

■   What kind of security monitoring is in place?

■   How will the service provider prevent intentional and unintentional disclosure of private data?

■ What may the service provider do with data it has received from your company?

■ How will your company know if sensitive data has leaked from the service provider's system?

Service providers must answer all these questions satisfactorily, and executives charged with outsourcing IT functions should validate all claims before retaining any service provider.[17]

Double Outsourcing   The practice of double outsourcing is essentially the subcontracting of an outsourcing contract. This type of arrangement can backfire if the client does not manage the agreements with both companies. Double outsourcing is common with functions that are often outsourced, such as information technology (IT). The external provider may not have the necessary technical skills to perform all of the outsourced work and will subcontract to fulfill the contract requirements. If the selected external provider is considering the use of a third party, then the supply manager should select and manage the subcontractor. Problems occur when the provider utilizes a subcontractor without involving the client. This leaves the client firm with little control over problems caused by the outsource provider's subcontractor.[18]

Administration of Make-or-Buy Activities

It is not difficult to find otherwise well-managed firms in which many tactical make-or-buy decisions are inadvertently delegated to an operating person in inventory control or production control. It should now be apparent that this is a poor practice. In the first place, such a person usually does not have adequate information with which to make an intelligent decision from a companywide point of view. Second, even if adequate information were available, this type of person typically lacks the breadth of experience to evaluate fully the significance of the information and the resultant decision.

Chief Resource Officer

Strategic outsourcing is an emerging trend in the business world. A new management role is being developed as a result of this trend: the Chief Resource Officer.[19] The CRO manages and initiates outsourcing for direct support to the company's bottom line. Outsourcing deals are becoming an increasingly large amount of corporate expenditures. Both the overall risks and rewards are becoming greater with increased outsourcing activity. The need for active management and skilled leadership is increasing. The CRO, essentially the director of external resources, is responsible for all outsourcing relationships and ensuring they live up to expectations. Companies that are embracing strategic outsourcing are beginning to realize the need for a dedicated team of individuals to oversee

---

[17]Scott J. Nathan, "Reducing the Risk of Outsourcing," *Supply Strategy,* May/June 2001, p. 20.

[18]"Getting into Outsourcing," *NAPM InfoEdge,* January 1998, pp. 1–16.

[19]Frank Casale, "The Rise of The Chief Resource Officer," *Business Briefing: European Purchasing and Logistics Strategies,* July 1999, pp. 81–82.

outsourcing activities. John Chiazza, chief information officer at Kodak, advocates establishing relationship management groups to "research potential outsourcers, negotiate terms, and address other matters of policy . . . individual relationship managers interact with the outsourcing providers on a day-to-day basis."[20] These outsourcing professionals possess three essential skills: negotiation, communication, and project management skills.

Framework for Outsourcing

Many frameworks have been developed for successful outsourcing. All of them involve information gathering, developing a strategic roadmap, and creating a decision flowchart.[21] Developing a "transition back" plan is an important step that is often ignored. It is less costly to have a plan in place in the event that the outsourced function needs to be brought back in-house. It will be easier to transfer the function back in-house or to another provider if such a contingency was planned for initially. In addition to providing an operational framework within which make-or-buy alternatives are investigated, a review system is necessary. The system should provide procedures for three important additional activities: (1) the entry of projects into the study system, (2) the maintenance of essential records, and (3) a periodic audit of important decisions.

Procedures should be established as part of a firm's product development program, compelling high-value and strategically oriented parts in new products to enter the make-or-buy analysis process. In some cases, this analysis can be effectively integrated with preproduction value engineering investigations. Similarly, existing production parts should be subjected to a systematic review which searches for borderline make-or-buy items warranting careful study.

Regardless of the source of entry, all make-or-buy investigations should be classified as "major" or "minor," based on the value and strategic nature of the part. In one firm, all items involving expenditures under $25,000 are classed as minor. Subsequent studies of minor items involve personnel from production, supply management, quality control, and occasionally design engineering. Major items entail expenditures over $25,000, and additionally involve personnel from finance, marketing, and other production areas.

Summary records are essential to full utilization of the data developed in make-or-buy investigations. The record should be designed to serve as a useful future reference. A brief discussion of all factors pertinent to the decision that was made should be included, as well as the primary reasons for the decision. Assumptions about future conditions should be stated. An accurate summary of cost data should always be included. Records of this type provide the information required when a firm is forced to make quick decisions about subcontracting work under peak operating conditions or about bringing work back into the shop when business slumps. Accurate records can mean the difference be-

---

[20]Scott Leibs, "Special Report on Outsourcing: How You Slice It," *CFO Magazine,* February 2001, pp. 81–86.

[21]For more information, see Eric Sislian and Ahmet Satir, "Strategic Sourcing: A Framework and a Case Study," *Journal of Supply Chain Management,* Summer 2000.

tween a profitable decision based on facts and a hopeful decision based on intuition and hunches. Finally, investigation records provide the basic data for post-decision audits.

Executive-Level Involvement

In most cases, make-or-buy decisions should be made, or at least reviewed, at the executive level. The decision maker must be able to view such decisions with a broad companywide perspective. Many progressive firms use a team or committee approach to analyze make-or-buy alternatives. The important point to keep in mind is that all departments that can contribute to the decision, or that are affected by it, should have some voice in making it. A team or committee accomplishes this directly. In other cases, a formal mechanism must be established which facilitates, and perhaps requires, all interested departments to submit relevant data and suggestions to the decision maker. Moreover, to ensure thoroughness and consistency, the system must detail the cost computation procedures to be used and assign cost investigations to specific operating groups.

Concluding Remarks

If one takes a broad view of the American industrial scene over the past several decades, three characteristics stand out clearly: (1) Firms are becoming more aware of the strategic dimension of the make-or-buy decision; management is more proactive in identifying and exploiting the firm's core competencies as organizations adopt lean manufacturing strategies; (2) most manufacturing firms have become much more specialized as technology has advanced—in the words of researchers Peters and Waterman, they "stick to their knitting";[22] and (3) the cost of materials, expressed as a percentage of total product cost, has continued to increase in many industries. These three factors lead to the inevitable conclusion that, in the aggregate, American firms are buying more and making less. Planned or unplanned, the trend continues to develop.

Yet, at the managerial level, many successful firms have not handled the recurring make-or-buy issue in a well-organized, systematic manner. Instead, many have elected to deal with specific cases on an ad hoc basis as they arise.

This situation is understandable, yet ironic. In earlier years when the cost-price squeeze was less severe for many firms, poor decisions in this area did not affect earnings dramatically. Yet, in the aggregate, make-or-buy decisions do significantly affect a firm's ability to utilize its resources in an optimal manner. Past practices are changing. Three forces will continue to stimulate this change:

1. *Pressures on profit margins* are severe, and will continue to increase. Resources must be utilized more effectively.

2. *Firms continue to become more highly specialized* in products and production technology, producing greater cost differentials between making and buying for many users.

---

[22]T. J. Peters and R. H. Waterman, *In Search of Excellence*, (New York: Harper & Row, 1982), pp. 292–305.

3. *Computer modeling capability* is becoming commonplace; make-or-buy evaluation and control systems can be developed and handled quasi-automatically with this capability.

Just as materials management organizations, MRP systems, and JIT systems have developed over the past several decades, so will implementation systems for recurring make-or-buy analysis. Interaction of the three factors noted above will produce refined make-or-buy operating systems in many firms in future years.[23]

Endnote

Jeffrey Dyer points out that the make/buy decision actually has three dimensions: firms must know what to do in-house, what to outsource to alliance partners, and what to outsource to arms-length (transactional) suppliers.[24]

---

[23]Readers interested in a detailed examination of the make-or-buy issue should review the classical study conducted some years ago by J. W. Culliton, *Make or Buy?* Research Study 27, Boston: Graduate School of Business Administration, Harvard University, 1942 (4th reprint, 1956).

[24]Dyer, p. 13. Jeffrey H. Dyer, *Collaborative Advantage: Winning Through Extended Supplier Networks,* Oxford University Press, Oxford, England, Nov. 2000

15

Sourcing

World Class Supply Management^{SM} requires supply management to develop a strategic sourcing plan that details how supply management will discover, evaluate, select, develop, and manage a viable supplier base.

KEY CONCEPTS

Supply Management and Strategy

In a recent Certificate in Purchasing Management (CPM) seminar attended by 29 supply managers from Silicon Valley area firms, the instructor asked several strategic supply management questions. The first was on the topic of the seminar, "How many of you are involved in developing the materials budget?" Having recently graduated with a Ph.D. and little real-world experience, the instructor expected about half of the hands to rise. Only two did. Surprised, he then asked, "How many of you are involved in the design process for your products and services?" The same two hands went up. Clearly rattled by the low responses, he asked, "How many of you are involved in any strategic activities?" Now half of the hands went up, but still not as many as he had expected given the general nature of the question. No wonder the economy downturn of 2001 resulted in so many high-tech corporations having problems with bloated inventories, unreliable "hard-times" suppliers, and massive layoffs.

Unfortunately, strategic planning in supply management has not been a high enough priority for either supply management or upper management who must provide support to pursue strategic activities when supply management is willing. Regardless of the reasons, almost all supply managers will tell you that they firmly believe in strategic planning. Among the most critical of these plans is the strategic sourcing plan.

The Strategic Sourcing Plan

Development of a strategic sourcing plan is driven by the recognition that tactical sourcing will not succeed in developing a supply base that will yield the benefits[1] of collaborative relationships and alliances. Development of collaborative relationships and eventually World Class Supply Management^{SM} requires concerted strategic planning. This chapter presents a generic road map that details how supply management can develop a strategic sourcing plan that will enable supply management to discover, evaluate, select, develop and manage a viable supplier base. The "road map" is presented in Figure 15.1.

Before pursuing the development of a supplier base for any material or service, the buying firm must first determine whether the material or service should be outsourced at all. The "make or buy" chapter given earlier in the book addresses this issue in detail. World Class Supply Management^{SM} firms conduct a strategic analysis of what their core

---

[1] The benefits of collaborative relationships and alliances are presented in Chapter 5.

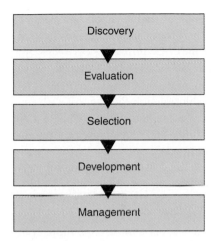

Figure 15.1 I Strategic Sourcing Plan Stages

competencies are through analyzing the skills and processes which form the basis of their success and competitive advantage. As Prahalad and Hamel say, "Core competencies are the wellspring of new business development."[2] If an item or service represents a core competency or supports or interfaces with such a competency, then the source of supply should be the firm itself.

Also prior to the development of a strategic sourcing plan, companywide support and financial backing must be given by the chief executive officer. The strategic sourcing plan is doomed to failure without companywide support from the various departments and financial backing to allow supply management time to be spent on planning activities.

Discovering Potential Suppliers

Prior to the information age and globalization of markets, the discovery process for potential suppliers was greatly limited. Today, suppliers throughout the globe can be found by simply typing several key words into a worldwide Web search engine or letting suppliers find your company through a variety of posting methods. While the opportunities to source via the Web are amazing, supply managers should not ignore other sources of information and the maintenance of existing information in soft and hard copy media. The following information sources should prove helpful to a supply manager in establishing a robust list of potential suppliers.

■ **Supplier Web Sites** Today, most suppliers have websites that provide detailed information about their products and services. The sites usually are registered with search

---

[2] For more insight into this important strategic issue, see C. K. Prahalad and Gary Hamel, "The Core Competence of the Corporation," *Harvard Business Review,* May–June 1990, pp. 79–91.

engine providers such as Lycos or Yahoo! Search engines enable supply managers to type in key words such as "third party logistics" and receive a "hit list" of sites that contain the key words. The worldwide Web has become one of the primary ways to discover sources of supply.

■ **Supplier Information Files** Supply management departments should keep supplier information files on past and present suppliers which include the name of each supplier, a list of materials available from each supplier, the supplier's delivery history, the supplier's quality record, the supplier's overall desirability, and general information concerning the supplier's plant and management. In addition to a departmental file, supply managers usually maintain a personal supplier file for their own use. Supplier information files are important because many supply management operations are repetitive; hence, it would be poor management indeed if supply managers spent time repeatedly recapturing information which was once available to them but had been needlessly lost. Web-enabled centralized databases make maintenance and dissemination of supplier information files a relatively easy task compared to the hardcopy alternative.

■ **Supplier Catalogs** Because catalogs are a commonly used source of supplier information, many supply management departments maintain a hardcopy catalog library. The alternative gaining in popularity is the use of electronic catalogs. Regardless of the storage medium, users may examine the catalogs to locate the materials they need. The firm's supply managers also use catalogs to determine potential sources of supply and, on occasion, to estimate prices and total cost of ownership.

■ **Trade Registers and Directories** *Thomas' Register of American Manufacturers* is typical of several widely known trade registers and directories. These registers are available in book and searchable compact disk and website formats. They contain information on the addresses, number of branches, and affiliations of all leading manufacturers. Financial standings of firms are also frequently given. The registers are indexed by commodity, manufacturer, and trade name or trademark description of the item. Kompass Publications in Europe provides similar information for European firms.[3]

■ **Trade Journals** Trade journals are another excellent source for obtaining information about possible suppliers. Advertisements in trade journals are often a supply manager's first contact with potential suppliers and their products. For example, a supply manager in the aircraft industry would routinely read *Aviation Week*. Many journals have moved or are moving to the worldwide Web and compact disk where archived editions are easily searched for specific sourcing needs.

■ **Phone Directories** Prior to the 1990s this source of information was of limited value to industrial supply managers because local telephone books list only local companies and searching through volumes of telephone books was a cumbersome activity. Today, phone directories are available online and on searchable compact disks that are available for purchase in computer retail stores. Phone directories can serve as a useful starting point if other sources have proved fruitless or if local sources are desired.

---

[3] Kompass Publications, Ltd., Windson Court, East Grimstead House, East Grimstead, Sussex, RH19-IXD, England.

■ **Filing of Mailing Pieces** Many mail advertisements are worth saving. These should be given a file number, dated, and indexed by the name and number of each publication. When supply managers seek a new source, they can then refer to the index and review the appropriate brochures and booklets. Some supply management departments ask prospective suppliers to complete a simple form giving basic information about themselves and their products. This information, which includes company name, address, officers, local representatives, and principal products, is kept in a set of loose-leaf notebooks or preferably in a searchable database or spreadsheet. By referring to these standardized data, a supply manager can obtain immediate, current information about potential new sources.

■ **Sales Personnel** Sales personnel are excellent sources for information about suppliers and materials. Not only are they usually well informed about the capabilities and features of their own products, but they are also familiar with similar and competitive products as well. By the very nature of their specialized knowledge, salespeople can often suggest new applications for their products which will eliminate the search for new suppliers. From their contacts with many companies, salespeople learn much about many products and services, and all this information is available to the alert, receptive supply manager. This is a key reason why sales personnel should always be treated courteously and given ample time to make their sales presentations. To deny them this opportunity is to risk the loss of valuable information, including information concerning new and reliable sources of supply.

■ **Trade Shows** Regional and national trade shows are still another way by which supply managers learn about possible sources of supply. Trade shows provide an excellent opportunity for supply managers to see various new products and modifications of old products. They also offer supply managers an opportunity to compare concurrently similar products of different manufacturers. Regional trade shows are sponsored periodically by many manufacturers, distributors, and trade organizations. Information about trade shows is usually sent to all interested supply management and technical personnel in the area. If not, then a quick search of the worldwide Web will usually yield information about upcoming shows.

■ **Company Personnel** Personnel from other departments in a supply manager's firm often can provide supply management with helpful information about prospective suppliers. Through their associations in professional organizations, civic associations, and social groups, these employees often learn about outstanding suppliers. Scientific, technical, and research personnel who use sophisticated materials or services always have many valuable suggestions to make regarding possible sources of supply. From their attendance at conventions and trade exhibits, and from their discussions with associates, these personnel are particularly well informed regarding new products, new methods, and new manufacturers.

■ **Other Supply Management Departments** Supply management departments in other firms can be helpful sources of information regarding suppliers. Information exchanged among individuals from these departments can be mutually beneficial for all participating companies; therefore, this source of information should be actively developed.

■   **Professional Organizations**   Local supply management associations, such as the local affiliates of the Institute for Supply Management (formerly NAPM), the Purchasing Management Association of Canada, the National Institute of Governmental Purchasing, and the National Association of Educational Buyers, publish a list of their members. One of the basic objectives of a supply management association is that its members help each other in every possible way. Accordingly, members usually will do everything possible to help fellow members locate and evaluate new sources of supply.

The previous list for discovering new potential suppliers leaves out the possibility that an existing supplier could be developed as a new potential supplier. Jim Wehrman, assistant vice president of purchasing at Honda America Manufacturing, points out, ". . . a top-level supply chain management effort must focus heavily on the development of current suppliers, and must devote significant resources to strengthening current suppliers and improving their capabilities." [4] An existing supplier may have the capability to fulfill new sourcing needs, which, if selected, strengthens the existing relationship.

Evaluating Potential Suppliers

After developing a comprehensive list of potential suppliers, the supply manager's next step is to evaluate each prospective supplier individually. The type of evaluation required to determine supplier capability varies with the nature, criticality, complexity, and dollar value of the purchase to be made. The evaluation also varies with the supply manager's or sourcing team's knowledge of the firms being considered for the order.

In some cases, an evaluation is unnecessary. For many uncomplicated, low-dollar-value purchases, an examination of basic information readily available, such as a mailing or website, is sufficient. For complex, high-dollar-value, and perhaps critical, purchases, additional evaluation steps are necessary. Marc Ensign, director of Strategic Sourcing for Honeywell IAC, provides the following guidelines for whether an assessment is necessary.

■   Is the supplier strategically important? If the supplier provides a product, or access to a future product, that is critical to the buying firm's success, take the time.

■   Is the product or service being procured considered strategic? If yes, then take the time to perform the evaluation.

■   Are there other short-term alternatives available? If supply management can modify the request to allow another product, service, or supplier to be quickly substituted, then they can reduce the thoroughness of the evaluation. [5]

Steps for complex, high-dollar-value, and perhaps critical, purchases can include surveys, financial condition analysis, third-party evaluators, evaluation conferences, plant visits, and selected capability analyses. Usually surveys and an analysis of the financial condition come first. Companies that have positive survey results and good

---

[4] Roberta J. Duffy, "The Future of Purchasing and Supply: Supply Chain Partner Selection and Contribution," *Purchasing Today,* November 1999.

[5] M. Ensign, "Breaking Down Financial Barriers," *Purchasing Today,* July 2000.

financial standing may require facility visits. As necessary, visits are followed by even more detailed analyses of the most promising suppliers' management, quality, capacity, service, just-in-time, and information technology capabilities. All of the approaches and analyses given here are by no means an exhaustive list, but they do provide a starting point for supply managers in evaluating potential suppliers. The approaches and analyses are discussed in greater detail below.

■ **Supplier Surveys** A survey should provide sufficient knowledge of the supplier to make a decision to include or exclude the firm from further consideration. A survey is based on a series of questions which often cover the following areas: principal officers and titles, bank references, credit references, annual history of sales and profit for the past five years, a referral list of customers, number of employees, space currently occupied, expansion plans (including sources of funds), an indication of the use of Design of Experiments (DOE), current production defect rate for similar products, number of inspectors used, quality methods adopted, and a list of all equipment and tools which would be used to manufacture, test, and inspect the purchase in question. Appendix A at the end of this chapter provides an example supplier survey that can be used to develop other surveys.

■ **Financial Condition Analysis** Preliminary investigation of a potential supplier's financial condition often can avoid the expense of further study. A qualified supply manager or professional from the finance department conducts these investigations. A review of financial statements and credit ratings can reveal whether a supplier is clearly *incapable* of performing satisfactorily. Financial stability is essential for suppliers to assure continuity of supply and reliability of product quality. Imagine the difficulty of getting (1) a financially weak supplier to maintain quality, (2) a supplier who does not have sufficient working capital to settle an expensive claim, or (3) a financially unsound supplier to work overtime to meet a promised delivery date. For additional information on financial ratio calculations, refer to Appendix B at the end of the chapter.

■ **Third Party Evaluators** Independent third-party firms can be hired to conduct many of the analyses given in this section. For example, a Dun and Bradstreet Information Services supplier evaluation typically contains sections describing the company's address, size, organizational structure, officers, financial condition, bankruptcies, suits, liens, newsworthy events, performance versus industry competitors, operations, facilities, subsidiaries, corporate relations, minority ownership, payments, and other public record information. As the databases, accumulation procedures, and query procedures of third-party evaluators improves over time, the use of this source of information in evaluating suppliers will continue to grow.

■ **Evaluation Conference** For an extremely critical purchase, a supplier evaluation conference is frequently held at the supply manager's plant to discuss the purchase. From such a discussion, it is usually easy to differentiate among those suppliers who understand the complexities of the purchase and those who do not. By eliminating those who do not, the search for the right supplier is further narrowed.

■ **Facility Visits** By visiting a supplier's facility, the sourcing team can obtain first-hand information concerning the adequacy of the firm's technological capabilities, manufacturing or distribution capabilities, and its management's technical know-how and orientation. Depending on the importance of the visit, the company may send representatives from only supply management and engineering; or it may also include some combination of representation from these functions and finance, operations, quality assurance, marketing, and industrial relations. For example, engineering's task may be to review and assess the technological capability of the potential supplier.[6] Occasionally, top management may also participate in the visit and the evaluation. When the concurrent approach to the design of new products is utilized, appropriate members of the cross-functional team conduct the visit and evaluation.

■ **Quality Capability Analysis**   The firm's quality capability is a critical factor to examine. If the prospective supplier's process capability is less than the buying firm's incoming quality requirements, the supplier typically is not worthy of further investigation. An obvious exception is the case in which no supplier possesses the required process capability. In this case, the two firms will have to work together to improve the supplier's process capability. An analysis of the quality capability should also include investigating upper management's philosophy toward quality, the quality department (if one is present), and the firm's abilities with quality assurance techniques and Design of Experiments (DOE). These critical issues are discussed in detail in the chapter in this book on quality. According to Forker, Ruch, and Hershauer, "Managers in customer firms should not underestimate the importance of a supplier's top management and its quality department in shaping and implementing quality improvement efforts. Top management support has been shown repeatedly to be paramount to the success of a quality improvement program."[7]

■ **Capacity Capability Analysis**   Ensuring continuity of supply is one of the most fundamental objectives of supply management. A supply manager is rarely noticed if materials arrive on time; but if materials are late such that expensive operations grind to a halt, the supply manager can become infamous and perhaps unemployed. Unscrupulous suppliers will often promise that they can meet future demands when in fact they do not have the capacity. Some suppliers' salespeople do not have a solid understanding of their own manufacturing capacity and the demands on that finite capacity. In 2000, one large telecommunications company did not investigate its second-largest supplier's capacity prior to entering into a "partnership length and quantity" contract for the critical components in DSL kits. The supplier did not have the capacity to meet the buying firm's demand. The buying firm's parts and components from other suppliers arrived, but the parts could not be kitted since all parts were not available.

■ **Management Capability Analysis**   Evaluating an organization's management style and compatibility usually requires several visits to the potential supplier's facilities. A quick way to draw conclusions that will often hold true is to evaluate the management capability of the firm by evaluating the sales representative, facility grounds, and even the parking lot.[8] A properly trained sales representative knows his or her product thoroughly,

---

[6] IOMA's *Report on Managing Design Engineering,* January 2000.

[7] L. Forker, W. Ruch, and J. Hershauer, "Examining Supplier Improvement Efforts from Both Sides," *Journal of Supply Chain Management,* Summer 1999, pp. 40–50.

[8] Ensign, "Breaking Down Financial Barriers."

understands the buying firm's requirements, gives useful suggestions to the supply manager and appropriate members of the buying team, commits the company to specific delivery promises, and follows through on all orders placed. This type of sales representative indicates that the supplier's firm is directed and managed by responsible and enterprising executives. Even a parking lot analysis can yield information about the management. Few cars, poorly maintained landscaping, poor quality of structures, and irregular condition of pavement can be indicators of problems. A well-maintained and managed firm seldom experiences the instability that results from continual labor problems and always strives to reduce its cost. Such a company can be a good supplier.

■ **Service Capability Analysis** "Service" is a term that varies in meaning depending on the nature of the product being purchased. Specifically, good service always means delivering on time, treating special orders specially, filling back orders promptly, settling disputes quickly and fairly, and informing supply managers in advance of impending price changes or developing shortages. In some situations, it means exceptional post-sale service. Service also can include actions such as stocking spare parts for immediate delivery, extending suitable credit arrangements, or warranting the purchased item's quality and performance to a degree beyond that normally required. In the aggregate, good service means that a supplier will take every reasonable action to ensure the smooth flow of purchased materials between the supplying and buying firms.

■ **Flexibility Capability Analysis** One issue that emerged from the stock market declines of 2001 was the importance of supplier flexibility to adjust production volumes with short notice and to remove inventory out of the chain. Flexibility is achieved through methods encapsulated in the just-in-time philosophy, also known as lean strategy. According to a 10-year forecast for the 2000s, "Lean supply chains will be a competitive strategy."[9] When properly implemented, a just-in-time (JIT) system results in the following *supply chain* benefits: reduced inventory, increased quality, reduced lead time, reduced scrap and rework, and reduced equipment downtime.[10] JIT requires a high degree of integration of the customer's and supplier's operations. The inevitable changes in a customer's production plans and schedules affect the supplier's schedules. Experience has demonstrated that dependable, single-source collaborative relationships are virtually essential if the required level of integration is to result. A firm that is considering the adoption of JIT manufacturing must focus on its suppliers' abilities and willingness to meet the stringent quality and schedule demands imposed by the system. The sourcing team must carefully investigate a potential supplier's capability as a JIT manufacturer.

■ **Information Technology Capability Analysis** Information sharing is a key enabler of effective supply chain management. Information sharing does not require technology, but technology is increasingly being used as the "vehicle of use." As reported in the *European Journal of Purchasing and Supply Management,* "Without a doubt, competitive advantage accrues to those who effectively adapt information technology

---

[9] P. L. Carter, J. R. Carter, R. M. Monczka, T. H. Slaight, and A. J. Swan, "The Future of Purchasing and Supply: A Ten-Year Forecast," *Journal of Supply Chain Management,* Winter 2000, pp. 14–26.

[10] Caron H. St. John and Kirk C. Heriot, "Small Suppliers and JIT Purchasing," *International Journal of Purchasing and Materials Management,* Winter 1993, p. 12.

to better disseminate information within the supply chains. In a number of industries, the ability to link electronically has become a right of entry and a prerequisite just to be considered as a potential supply chain partner."[11] What type of analysis is required depends greatly on the buying firm's technology capability. The critical issue of information technology is discussed in detail in the chapter in this book on e-Commerce II.

The analyses given above should not necessarily be limited to potential first-tier suppliers. Today's supply chains have multiple tiers which may be critical to analyze. In the 10-year forecast on the future of supply management referred to above, several noted academicians stated, "Determination of first-, second-, and possibly third-tier suppliers will become more critical to supply chain dominant companies in the future."[12]

A common approach to summarizing the analyses given above or to conduct them on an individual basis is a weighted-factor analysis. The analysis requires the development of a spreadsheet and calls for two activities: (1) the development of factors (selection criteria) and weights and (2) the assignment of ratings. The first step, identification of the key factors to be considered in the selection decision, along with their respective weights, typically is accomplished by a committee of individuals involved in evaluating the suppliers. Step 2 requires the assignment of numerical ratings for each of the competing firms. These assessments are based on the collective judgments of the evaluators after studying all the data and information provided by the potential suppliers, as well as that obtained in field investigations.

Selecting Suppliers

After one or more potential suppliers have passed the evaluation process, the selection process must begin. The supply manager or the sourcing team will now invite potential suppliers to submit bids or proposals. A decision must be made as to whether to use competitive bidding or negotiation (or a combination of the two) as the basis for source selection.

Bidding versus Negotiation

When competitive bidding is used by private industry, requests for bids are traditionally sent to three to eight potential suppliers depending on the dollar size and complexity of the purchase. Requests for bids ask suppliers to quote the price at which they will perform in accordance with the terms and conditions of the contract, should they be the successful bidder. The traditional bidding process is usually one iteration. In contrast, reverse auctions, discussed in the eCommerce II chapter, use the Internet for online "real-time" interaction in which the iterations of bids submitted are limited primarily by the time provided by the buyer for the process. In addition, the number of bidders in reverse auctions can be very large. Discussions with managers in industry on the subject of online reverse auctions urge caution in opening the bidding process to unqualified

---

[11] R. E. Spekman, J. Kamauff, J. Spear, "Towards More Effective Sourcing and Supplier Management," *European Journal of Purchasing and Supply Management* 5 (1999), p. 105.

[12] Carter et al., "The Future of Purchasing and Supply."

suppliers.[13] A two-step bidding process is recommended. Please refer to the eCommerce II chapter for more details. Government supply managers generally are not able to restrict the number of bidders to only eight. Rather, all suppliers desiring to bid are permitted to do so (for large purchases, the numbers are literally in the hundreds). Under competitive bidding, industrial supply managers generally, *but not always,* award the order to the lowest bidder. By law, government supply managers are routinely required to award the order to the lowest bidder, provided the lowest bidder is deemed qualified to perform the contract.

Prerequisites to Bidding   The proper use of competitive bidding is dictated by five criteria. When all five criteria prevail, competitive bidding is an efficient method of source selection and pricing. The criteria are:

1.   The dollar value of the specific purchase must be large enough to justify the expense, to both buying and selling firms, that accompanies this method of source selection and pricing.
2.   The specifications of the item or service to be purchased must be explicitly clear to both the buying and selling firms. In addition, the seller must know from actual previous experience, or be able to estimate accurately from similar past experience, the cost of producing the item or rendering the service.
3.   The market must consist of an adequate number of sellers.
4.   The sellers that make up the market must be technically qualified and *actively want* the contract—and, therefore, be willing to price competitively to get it.
5.   The time available must be sufficient for using this method of pricing—suppliers competing for large contracts must be allowed time to obtain and evaluate bids from their subcontractors before they can calculate their best price. Thirty days is not an uncommon time; however, the increasing use of online bidding using the worldwide Web is forcing compression of bid preparation time.

Conditions Demanding Negotiation   In addition to satisfying the preceding five prerequisites, four other conditions should *not* be present when employing competitive bidding as the means of source selection:

1.   Situations in which it is impossible to estimate costs with a high degree of certainty. Such situations frequently are present with high-technology requirements, with items requiring a long time to develop and produce, and under conditions of economic uncertainty.
2.   Situations in which price is not the only important variable. For example, quality, schedule, and service may well be negotiable variables of equal importance.
3.   Situations in which the buying firm anticipates a need to make changes in the specification or some other aspect of the purchase contract.
4.   Situations in which special tooling or setup costs are major factors. The allocation of such costs and title to the special tooling are issues best resolved through negotiation.

---

[13]Supply Chain Management Forum: Focus on Supply Management, The University of San Diego, 2001.

If these nine conditions are satisfied, then competitive bidding usually will result in the lowest price and is the most efficient method of source selection. To ensure that the lowest prices are obtained, the competing firms must be assured that the firm submitting the low bid will receive the award. If the buying firm gains a reputation for negotiating with the lowest bidders *after* bids are opened, then future bidders will tend *not* to offer their best prices initially, believing that they may do better in any subsequent negotiations. They will adopt a strategy of submitting a bid low enough to allow them to be included in any negotiations. But their initial bid will not be as low as when they are confident that the award will be made to the low bidder without further negotiation.[14] When any of the prerequisites to the use of competitive bidding are not satisfied, the *negotiation process* should be employed to select sources and to arrive at a price.

In his now famous lectures in Japan, W. E. Deming extolled that organizations should "end the practice of awarding business on the basis of price tag alone."[15] Several progressive supply management professionals offer two additional arguments that favor the use of negotiation over competitive bidding for critical procurements:

1.   The negotiation process is far more likely to lead to a complete understanding of all issues of the procurement. This improved understanding greatly reduces subsequent quality and schedule problems.

2.   Competitive bidding tends to put great pressure on suppliers to reduce their costs in order to be able to bid a low price. This cost pressure may result in sacrifices in product quality, development efforts, and other vital services.

When all the prerequisite criteria prevail, the competitive bidding system itself usually evaluates quite accurately the many pricing factors bearing on the purchase being made. These factors include determinants such as supplier production efficiency, willingness of the seller to price this particular contract at a low profit level, the financial effect on the seller of shortages of capital or excesses of inventories, errors in the seller's sales forecast, and competitive conditions in general.

Two-Step Bidding/Negotiation

On occasion, large, technically oriented firms and the federal government use a modified type of competitive bidding called "two-step bidding." This method of source selection and pricing is used in situations in which *inadequate specifications* preclude the initial use of traditional competitive bidding. In the first step, bids are requested only for technical proposals, without any prices. Bidders are requested to set forth in their proposals the technical details describing how they would produce the required materials, products, or services. After these technical bids are evaluated and it is determined which proposals are technically satisfactory, the second step follows.

---

[14] On occasion, a supply manager may intend to use the initial proposal solicitation process to identify firms with which he or she plans to conduct follow-on negotiations. In this case, professional ethics as well as good business judgment dictate that the initial solicitation state clearly that follow-on negotiations will be conducted.

[15] Larry Weinstein, "Single-Source Successes and Snafus," *Purchasing Today,* April 2000.

In the second step, requests for bids are sent only to those sellers who submitted acceptable technical proposals in the first step. These sellers now compete for the business on a price basis, as they would in any routine, competitive-bidding situation. The price is determined in either of two ways: (1) award may be based solely on the lowest price received from those competing, or (2) the price proposals for the accepted technical approaches may be used as the beginning point for *negotiations*. It is important that the supply manager specify *at the outset* which of the two procedures will be used.

The Solicitation

Once a decision has been made as to whether to use competitive bidding or negotiation as the means of selecting the source, an *invitation for bids (IFB)* or a *request for proposal (RFP)* is prepared. The IFB or RFP normally consists of a purchase description of the item or service required, information on quantities, required delivery schedules, special terms and conditions, and standard terms and conditions. The legal implications of these documents and processes are discussed in the chapter on legal issues in this book.

When an RFP is used in anticipation of cost negotiations with one or more suppliers, the supply manager should request appropriate cost data in support of the price proposal. The supply manager must also obtain the right of access to the supplier's cost records that are required to support the reasonableness of the proposal. *The cost data and the right of access must be established during the RFP phase of the procurement, at a time potential suppliers believe that there is active competition for the job.* See the chapter on negotiation for more detail.

Responsibility for Source Selection

While supply management has the ultimate responsibility for selecting the "right" source, the process is handled in many ways. Procedurally, the simplest approach is when a single *supply manager* conducts the analysis and makes the selection. A second common approach calls for the use of a *cross-functional team* consisting of representatives of supply management, design engineering, operations, quality, and finance. See the chapter on cross-functional teams for more detail. The third common approach is the use of a commodity team.

Commodity teams are created to source and manage a group of similar components. Commodity teams frequently consist of supply managers, materials engineers, and production planners. Larger commodity teams include a commodity manager (normally from supply management) and representatives of materials, design and manufacturing engineering, quality, and finance. Commodity teams are essentially a type of cross-functional team. The principle difference between them is that commodity teams tend to be fairly permanent, while cross-functional teams tend to be one-time assignments.

Developing Suppliers

Not all suppliers need development, but to reach the lofty status of a world-class collaborative relationship, development is needed. Even suppliers recognized as the "best of the best" require investment on the part of the buying firm to realize the full benefit of the collaborative relationship. For example, Solectron is a two-time winner of the Malcolm Baldrige Award, the top award in the United States for quality. Solectron supplies high-technology parts, subassemblies, and finished goods to original equipment manufacturers (OEMs). Since Solectron is not an OEM, it is relatively unknown to the general public. For Solectron to accomplish its supply chain role properly, it will foster many of the strategic activities presented throughout this book.

At Sun Microsystems, located in Silicon Valley near Solectron, management treats development of suppliers as a two-way effort. In the late 1990s, Sun started having suppliers measure their performance using scorecards modified from the ones Sun used to evaluate their suppliers. The benefits to Sun were numerous. Suppliers felt as if Sun finally started to listen to their ideas instead of trying to push the Sun way of doing business on them. Suppliers could then contribute to developing Sun and improving the collaborative relationship to find "win-win" opportunities. The proactive efforts of Sun present the issue that the term "development" is actually a misnomer that implies a one-way interaction in which the buying firm "develops" the supplying firm. The process of development should also include the development of the buyer in collaborative relationships.

In many instances, the buying firm may be unable to identify a world-class supplier that is willing (or able) to meet its needs. If the requirement is sufficiently important, the buying firm will select the most attractive supplier(s) and then develop the supplier into one capable of meeting its present and future needs. Training in project management, teamwork, quality, production processes, and supply management may prove to be a worthy investment. Such training has been provided by several leading customer firms for well over a decade.

Managing Suppliers

The challenging issue of managing suppliers is dealt with in several chapters in this book. At this point, however, it is essential to recognize that the supply manager has many responsibilities associated with the management of his or her suppliers. Satisfying these responsibilities should ensure that suppliers perform as required or that appropriate corrective action is taken to upgrade or eliminate them from the firm's supplier base.

In addition, supply management must, on a periodic basis, analyze its suppliers' abilities to meet the firm's long-term needs. Areas that deserve particular attention include the supplier's general growth plans, future design capability in relevant areas, the role of supply management in the supplier's strategic planning, potential for future production capacity, and financial ability to support such growth.

If present suppliers appear to be unlikely to be able to meet future requirements, the firm has three options: (1) It may assist the appropriate supplier(s) with financing and technological assistance, (2) it may develop new sources having the desired growth potential, or (3) it may have to develop the required capability internally.

Additional Strategic Issues

The buying firm must consider many factors in selecting sources of supply. This section presents several areas of concern. Since all of the decisions in this section have impacts beyond the supply management department, other departments must be involved in the decision making and approval of the strategic outcomes should be sought from management above the functional areas impacted.

Early Supplier Involvement

As presented in the chapters on new product development and specifications and standardization, early supplier involvement (ESI) is an approach in supply management to bring the expertise and collaborative synergy of suppliers into the design process. ESI seeks to find "win-win" opportunities in developing alternatives and improvements to materials, services, technology, specifications and tolerances, standards, order quantities and lead time, processes, packaging, transportation, redesigns, assembly changes, design cycle time, and inventory reductions. Today, early supplier involvement (ESI) is an accepted way of life at many proactive firms and a requirement for World Class Supply Management[SM]. ESI helps in developing trust and communication between suppliers and the buying firm. ESI normally, but not always, results in the selection of a single source of supply. At most progressive companies, this selection process is the result of intensive competition between two or three carefully prequalified potential suppliers. The company selected becomes the single or primary source of supply for the life of the item using its material. The results of ESI translate into tangible cost savings. According to Dave Nelson (currently VP, Global Purchasing, Delphi Automotive Systems, former senior vice president of Purchasing and Corporate Affairs for Honda of America, and former V.P. Worldwide Supply Management, Deere & Company), suppliers helped design the 1998 Accord and, as a result, saved over 20 percent of the cost of producing the car.[16]

Supply Base Reduction

One of the interesting transitions taking place in supply management is the shift from enlarging the firm's supply base to downsizing the base. Reduction of the supply base is usually achieved through both reducing the variety of items procured and consolidating items previously procured from different suppliers into one supplier.

Examples of supply base reduction success stories are abundant. For example, Xerox reduced its supply base by 92 percent in the early 1980s—from 5,000 to 400 suppliers. Chrysler winnowed its supplier base from a mass of 2,500 in the late 1980s to a lean, long-term nucleus of 300. During the 1990s, suppliers loved working for Chrysler, and for obvious reasons: The company's production volume was growing rapidly. Chrysler included suppliers in development activities from day one and listened eagerly to their suggestions for design improvements and cost reductions. Chrysler had replaced its adversarial bidding system with one in which the company designated suppliers for a component and then used target pricing (discussed in the Total Cost of Ownership chapter) to determine with suppliers the component prices and how to achieve them. Most parts were sourced from one supplier for the life of the product.[17]

---

[16] Spekman et al., "Towards More Effective Sourcing."

[17] James P. Womack and Daniel T. Jones, "From Lean Production to the Lean Enterprise," *Harvard Business Review,* March–April 1994, p. 97.

Applied Materials reduced its supply base from 1,200 suppliers in the early 1990s to 400 by 2001.[*] Applied Materials states that the reduction has resulted in significant cost reductions in manufacturing and supply chain operations. Applied Materials develops and works with preferred suppliers that pass a series of qualification criteria. The reduced risk of being a preferred supplier empowers the company to invest in long-term strategies, such as early supplier involvement in design, materials research, process value analysis, and workforce education.

Similar supply base reductions have occurred at other major corporations. IBM uses 50 suppliers for 85 percent of its production requirements. Sun Microsystems uses 40 suppliers for 90 percent of its production material needs.[18] Such accomplishments generally require significant research and development expenditures and/or capital investment.

Two benefits of supply base reduction cited by Deere & Company are increased leverage with suppliers and better focus and supplier integration in product development. According to Deere, the increased leverage primarily results from the increased volume of business with the supplier.[19] However, as observers of Deere over the last several years, the authors of this book can safely state that the increased leverage is also due to the increased involvement with the suppliers which builds goodwill and trust.

Single versus Multiple Sourcing

Few strategic sourcing issues ignite more debate in corporate boardrooms across the world than the single versus multiple source issue. Such decisions are larger than the supply management department, the commodity team, or the cross-functional team responsible for source selection. These decisions may affect the success—or even the survival—of the firm.

The major argument for placing all of a firm's business with *one supplier* is that in times of shortage, this supplier will give priority to the needs of a special customer. Additionally, single sources may be justified when:

- Lower total cost results from a much higher volume (economies of scale).
- Quality considerations dictate.[20]
- The buying firm obtains more influence—clout—with the supplier.
- Lower costs are incurred to source, process, expedite, and inspect.
- The quality, control, and coordination required with just-in-time manufacturing require a single source.
- Significantly lower freight costs may result.
- Special tooling is required, and the use of more than one supplier is impractical or excessively costly.

---

[*] Based on presentation by Applied Materials Management at the 2001 Silicon Valley Tech Tour sponsored by the University of San Diego.

[18] James Carbone, "Evaluation Programs Determine Top Suppliers," *Purchasing,* November 18, 1999.

[19] Bill Butterfield, "Supplier Development at John Deere," presentation at The 16th Annual Supply Chain Management Forum, San Diego, CA, November 2001.

[20] James Dairs, manager of Transportation Programs at G.E.'s Plastics Group, Pittsfield, MA, quoted in Somerby Dowst, "The Winning Edge," *Purchasing,* March 12, 1987, p. 57.

- Total system inventory will be reduced.
- An improved commitment on the supplier's part results.
- Improved interdependency and risk sharing result.
- More reliable, shorter lead times are required.[21]
- Time to market is critical.[22]

A common approach to multiple sourcing that can still yield many of the benefits of single sourcing is the "70-30" approach. Through the award of 70 percent of the volume to one supplier and 30 percent to a second supplier, economies of scale are obtained from the "big supplier" while the "little supplier" provides competition. Using the "70-30" strategy, when the 70 percent supplier "misbehaves," its volume is reduced to 30 percent and the smaller supplier is awarded an increase to 70 percent. (An interesting approach to discipline!)

Although the "70-30" strategy is reported to have started in Japan in the 1970s with just-in-time firms, the strategy is firmly established in many world-class companies. For example, visits in 2001 by one of the authors of this book verified that Solectron, Applied Materials, and Cisco Systems all cognitively use the "70-30" approach in sourcing selected materials. Dual or multiple sourcing may be appropriate:

- To protect the buying firm during times of shortages, strikes, and other emergencies.
- To maintain competition and provide a backup source. To meet local content requirements for international manufacturing locations.
- To meet customers' volume requirements.
- To avoid lethargy or complacency on the part of a single-source supplier.
- When the customer is a small player in the market for a specific item.
- When the technology path is uncertain.
- In areas where suppliers tend to leapfrog each other technologically.[23]

Note that the term "collaborative relationship" implies neither the presence nor the absence of a single-source relationship. That is, the buying firm may have one, two, or three "partners" for the same item, although the trend is toward single sourcing.

Share of Supplier's Capacity

Many highly regarded firms try not to exceed 15 to 25 percent of any one supplier's capacity. The percentage refers to the company's entire capacity and not one individual product or service. For example, Palm might contract for 15 percent of Flextronics production capacity, but purchase 100 percent of a specific product from Flextronics. Palm

---

[21] Interview with Ron Reese of Haliburton Energy Services, in Weinstein, "Single-Source Successes and Snafus."

[22] Bob Bretz, former director of Corporate Purchasing for Pitney Bowes and 1994 Shipman Medalist, indicates that "'single sourcing' is much simpler. There's less effort on the part of the seller and it's easier to resolve issues." Patrick Robert Bretz, quoted in Patrick Flanagen, "The Rules of Purchasing Are Changing," *Management Review,* March 1994, p. 30.

[23] Several large corporations use a dual or multiple approach to sourcing items with dynamic technology. See "Buyers Beef Up Supplier Management Skills," *Purchasing,* October 21, 1993, p. 28.

might reason that if its purchases represent too large a share of the supplier's business and they discontinue a product or purchase an item from another supplier, they could put Flextronics in a very difficult financial situation.

This issue became all too real in the early 2000s with the economy downturn. Many companies cancelled orders that had long supplier lead times, which resulted in suppliers being caught with, in some cases, hundreds of millions of dollars of work-in-process. Cisco Systems, for example, had outstanding orders that totalled nearly 2 billion dollars! Unlike many companies during the early 2000s, Cisco paid for almost all of its orders and maintained its reputation as a good business partner. If Cisco had not paid its suppliers, the financial ruin that would have spread would have been even more staggering. Still, Cisco's suppliers had to contend with few, if any, follow-on orders since demand for Cisco's products had greatly diminished.

Local, National, and International Sourcing

Prior to the discovery process for building a supply base, the company must consider the issues of local versus national versus international sourcing. Local sourcing implies that the firm's headquarters and all facilities are located in the city or region (such as northern California) where the materials or services will be used. Local sources are usually relatively small in contrast to national and international sources. National sourcing implies that the source is headquartered within the country and has facilities in multiple regions throughout the country. National sources are also larger companies as defined by the buying firm. For example, a national firm might be defined by a company as having a presence in at least two regions other than the one of the buying firm and having at least 2,000 employees and annual revenues in excess of 100 million U.S. dollars. The delineation between what constitutes a national source and an international source also should be defined by the buying firm. The common definition is that an international source is headquartered outside the buying firm's country, but this does not define where the company has its operations. For example, Flextronics is headquartered in Singapore, but has virtually no manufacturing in Singapore.[24] The lines between local, national, and international sourcing have become blurred in the last 30 years.

Buying Locally   Most supply managers prefer to patronize local sources whenever prudent. A Stanford University research study found that approximately three-fourths of 152 supply managers surveyed indicated a preference to buy from local sources whenever possible. Many of them were willing to pay slightly higher prices to gain the advantage of better service and immediate availability of materials offered by some local suppliers, lowering total cost.

Just-in-time manufacturing requires dependable sources of defect-free materials which arrive within a very tight time frame. Suppliers to JIT customers are meeting their requirements in three ways: (1) They are locating close to their customers;[25] (2) suppli-

---

[24] The tax benefits of headquartering in Singapore make Singapore a popular location choice.

[25] For example, Chrysler builds additional buildings on-site and leases them to its suppliers. Robert M. Faltra, "How Chrysler Buyers Make Quality a Standard Feature," *Electronics Purchasing* 101 (July 10, 1986), p. 62A15.

ers are implementing responsive manufacturing systems; and (3) they are taking aggressive action to control the transportation of their materials to their customers.

In summary, local buying has the following advantages:

1. Closer cooperation between buying and selling firms is possible because of close geographical proximity. JIT deliveries are thus facilitated.
2. Delivery dates are more certain since transportation is only a minor factor in delivery.
3. Lower total costs can result from consolidated transportation and insurance charges. A local supplier, in effect, brings in many local buying firms' orders in the same shipment.
4. Shorter lead times frequently can permit reductions or the elimination of inventory. In effect, the seller produces just-in-time.
5. Rush orders are likely to be filled faster.
6. Disputes usually are more easily resolved.
7. Implied social responsibilities to the community are fulfilled.

Buying Nationally National buying has the following advantages:

1. National sources, as a result of economies of scale, can in some situations be more efficient than local suppliers and offer higher quality or better service at a lower price.
2. National companies often can provide superior technical assistance.
3. Large national companies have greater production capacity and therefore greater production flexibility to handle fluctuating demands.
4. Shortages are less likely with national companies because of their broader markets.

Buying Internationally This important sourcing consideration is discussed in detail in the chapter on global supply management. It is mentioned here only to note that it is an important factor in supplier selection.

Manufacturer or Distributor?

In deciding whether to buy from a manufacturer or distributor, a supply manager's considerations should focus largely on the distributor's capabilities and services, not on its location. In the steel industry, for example, distributors pay the same prices for steel as other buying firms. Distributors, however, buy in carload lots and sell in smaller quantities to users whose operations do not justify carload lot purchases. The distributors realize a profit because large lots sell at lower unit prices than small lots. If a buying firm wishes to purchase steel directly from the mill and bypass the distributor, it is perfectly free to do so; however, when it does, it usually forgoes certain special services that a competent distributor is equipped to offer. Distributors, for example, have cutting and shaping tools and skilled personnel to operate them. They maintain large, diverse inventories. They are also able to perform numerous customer services.

When the materials ordered from a distributor are shipped directly to the user by the manufacturer (a *drop shipment*), an additional buying decision becomes necessary. In this situation, the distributor does not handle the materials physically; it acts only as a broker.[26] Under such circumstances, a supply manager is strongly motivated to buy directly from the manufacturer—if the manufacturer will sell to his or her firm.

Supply managers should be aware that distributors stock many manufacturers' products. Hence, ordering from a distributor can significantly reduce the total number of orders a supply manager must place to fill some of his or her materials requirements. If there were no distributors, orders for production as well as maintenance, repair, and operating (MRO) requirements would all have to be placed directly with many different manufacturers. This obviously would increase direct supply management costs. Furthermore, for every additional purchase order placed, an additional receiving, inspection, and accounts payable operation is created.

In the final analysis, the manufacturer–distributor decision centers on one critical fact: The functions of distribution cannot be eliminated. The supply manager needs most of these functions; therefore, the supply manager should pay for them once—but he or she should not pay for them twice. Either the distributor or the manufacturer must perform the essential distribution functions of carrying the inventory, giving technical advice, rendering service, extending credit, and so on. The supply manager must decide for each individual buying situation how to best purchase the functions needed. The supply manager must answer the question: Is it my company, the distributor, or the manufacturer that can perform the required distribution services satisfactorily at the lowest cost?

"Green" Supply Management

Environmentally sensitive supply management can make good business sense. Many of us have heard the story of young Henry Ford. It seems that Mr. Ford was very explicit in the dimensions and quality of the lumber used in constructing the packing crates his suppliers used to ship parts to Ford. One day, one of the suppliers asked a Ford employee why a throwaway packing crate had to be made to such explicit specifications. The answer was "because we use the wood to build the floorboards of our Model T." Was Mr. Ford an environmentalist or a good businessman? Quite obviously, he was both!

Environmentally sensitive supply management has two components: (1) the purchase of materials and items which are recyclable and (2) the environmental and liability issues associated with the use and discharge of hazardous materials—anywhere in the supply chain. Green Supply Management is discussed in greater detail in the chapter on supply management's social responsibilities.

Environmental and Liability Issues   Supply management, the firm's environmental engineer (or environmental consultant), and the firm's attorney should study the firm's value chain to identify the possible uses and disposal methods for environmentally hazardous substances and materials. It is entirely possible, for example, that a supplier who disposes of hazardous waste in an environmentally unsafe manner, while producing a product for the buying firm, may subject the buying firm to financial liability, should the

---

[26]Manufacturers' representatives, who usually deal only in technical items, also effect deliveries by drop shipments, and they act as brokers. Manufacturers' reps also aid a supply manager by being able to furnish numerous product lines from a single source.

supplier have limited financial resources. Current statutes cover present and previous operators and owners.

Additionally, supply management has a responsibility to ensure that a supplier's salvage and disposal contractors meet OSHA standards both prior to award and during performance under the contracts. One way of dealing with this challenging issue is to require the supplier to post adequate performance and liability bonds.

Minority- and Women-Owned Business Enterprises

As discussed in Chapter 4, many forces motivate a buying firm to develop and implement programs designed to ensure that minority- and/or women-owned businesses receive a share of the firm's business. These motivators include federal and state legislation, set-aside quotas in government appropriations, the actions of regulatory bodies such as the state public utilities commission, chambers of commerce, civil rights activists, and a firm's "corporate social consciousness." Perhaps one of the most significant motivators is the recognition by a firm's management that *its customer base* includes minority- and women-owned business enterprises and their employees. Companies that can demonstrate minority supplier content in their products are more likely to receive business from minority customers.[27] In addition to a sense of social responsibility, MWBE should be focused on bottom-line profitability and good business sense.[28] For more information on this issue refer to Chapter 4 on supply management's social responsibilities.

Ethical Considerations

Supply managers must be aware of potential conflicts of interest when selecting suppliers. A conflict of interest exists when supply managers must divide their loyalty between the firm which employs them and another firm. In supply management, this situation usually occurs when a supply manager is a substantial stockholder in a supplier's firm or when he or she makes purchases from close friends and relatives. Conflicts of interest are discussed more fully in Chapter 23. The subject is introduced here solely to remind the reader that such conflicts always should be avoided in all source selection decisions.

Supply managers should keep themselves as free as possible from unethical influences in their choice of suppliers. It is very difficult to maintain complete objectivity in this matter, for it is only human to want to favor one's friends. On occasion, friends can make unusually good suppliers. They will normally respond to emergency needs more readily than suppliers without a strong tie of personal friendship. On the other hand, supply managers tend not to discipline friends who perform poorly to the same degree that they do other suppliers.

---

[27] Ginger Conrad, John F. Robinson, and Forrest Walker, Jr., "Conquering the M/WBE Challenge," *Purchasing Today,* April 2000.

[28] Debbie Newman, Patricia Richards, and Linda Butler, "Shared Commitment to MWBE Development," *NAPM Conference Proceedings,* Tempe, AZ, 1994, p. 300.

Reciprocity

When supply managers give preference to suppliers that are also customers, they are engaging in a practice known as *reciprocity*.[29] The practice can be illegal, and the line between legal and illegal reciprocal practices frequently is very thin. It is entirely legal to buy from one's customers at fair market prices, without economic threat, and without the intent of restricting competition. A key criterion used by the courts in determining illegality is the degree to which reciprocal activity tends to restrict competition and trade. Hence, those who engage in reciprocal practices must do so with care and legal consultation.

Most supply managers disapprove of the practice of reciprocity, even when legal, because it restricts their ability to achieve competition among potential suppliers. However, the proponents of reciprocity contend that it is simply good business. They believe that if a supply manager buys from a friend, both the supply manager and the friend will profit in the long run. They maintain that service is better from suppliers who are also customers. They argue that reciprocity is a legitimate way to expand a company's markets. Consequently, some U.S. firms proclaim a reciprocity policy similar to this one: "When important factors such as quality, service, and price are equal, we prefer to buy from our customers."[30]

In the final analysis, reciprocity is neither a marketing problem nor a supply management problem; rather, it is a management problem. If management believes that it can expand its markets permanently and add to the firm's profit *legally* through reciprocity, then this is the decision management should make. Conversely, if management believes buying without the constraints of reciprocity will increase profit, then that is the policy management should adopt. Although reciprocity can benefit a firm, no economist would argue that it benefits a nation's total economy.

Concluding Remarks

The supply manager's first responsibility in source selection is to develop and manage a viable supply base. Prior to development of the supply base, many strategic issues need to be addressed, such as supply base size, single versus multiple sourcing, supplier involvement in design, negotiation versus bidding, share of supplier's capacity, whether to internationally source, manufacturer or distributor, whether to pursue "green" supply management, and policies related to diversity, ethics and reciprocity. These issues should be addressed in the strategic sourcing plan where relevant. In the plan, details about how suppliers will be identified, evaluated, selected, developed, and managed should be committed to paper.

Clearly, the activity of developing a strategic sourcing plan impacts many functional areas as well as supply chain members. As such, the strategic sourcing plan should not

---

[29] Reciprocity becomes more insidious when it involves more than one tier of suppliers. For example, A is asked to buy from B, not because B is A's customer, but because B is C's customer, and C is A's customer, and B wants to sell to A. Obviously, it is possible for reciprocal relationships to extend to four or more tiers.

[30] Some firms use vague phrases such as "Buy from customers when doing so will contribute to the greatest economic good of the firm."

be developed in a supply management vacuum. The plan should be developed in a collaborative environment that includes all relevant functional area representatives and supply chain members.

Selection of the right source is more important today than ever before, since more firms are entering into long-term collaborative relationships with a single source of supply. The benefits of such collaborative relationships are many, but the risks are great. Careful selection of suppliers and the professional management of the relationships are essential.

Appendix A: Illustrative Plant Survey

After conducting preliminary surveys of potential suppliers of critical materials, equipment, or services, it is frequently desirable to conduct a plant visit to one or two of the most attractive candidates. The purpose of such visits is to gain firsthand knowledge of the supplier's facilities, personnel, and operations. Such a visit normally is conducted by a team from the buying firm. Each member will study his or her area of expertise at the potential supplier's operation.

The plant survey shown in the following figure is used by one high-tech manufacturer. The evaluation form calls for yes or no answers to specific questions and evaluation ratings for all questions, asking the team member to evaluate how well the supplier is doing in a given area. The evaluation ratings are described below.

Rating	Description
10	The provisions or conditions are extensive and function is excellent.
9	The provisions or conditions are moderately extensive and function is excellent.
8	The provisions or conditions are extensive and are functioning well.
6/7	The provisions or conditions are moderately extensive and are functioning well.
4/5	The provisions or conditions are limited in extent but are functioning well.
2/3	The provisions or conditions are moderately extensive but are functioning poorly.
1	The provisions or conditions are limited in extent and are functioning poorly.
0	The provisions or conditions are missing but needed.

Assume that the buying firm's quality manager is rating a potential supplier on the sections entitled quality management and quality information. When these phases of the study are complete, the quality manager is in a position to assign an average or overall rating for quality management on the first sheet of the survey.

Such an evaluation is used in at least two ways: (1) It is now possible to compare competitors' operations, with major emphasis on quality, and (2) actual or potential problem areas for an otherwise attractive supplier may be identified. The buying firm then may require that the area of concern be corrected or upgraded before award, or as a condition of award.

Design Information

Control of design and manufacturing information is essential for the control of product. Such control consists of making sure that operating personnel are furnished with complete technical instructions for the manufacture and inspection of the product. This information includes drawings, specifications, special purchase order requirements, engineering change information, inspection instructions, processing instructions, and other special information. A positive recall system is usually considered necessary to ensure against use of superseded or obsolete information.

1. (　) How well do procedures cover the release, change, and recall of design and manufacturing information, including correlation of customer specifications, and how well are procedures followed?
2. (　) How well do records reflect the incorporation of changes?
3. (　) How well does quality control verify that changes are incorporated at the effective points?
4. (　) Is the design of experiments employed to ensure robust designs prior to the release of designs to manufacturing and supply management?
5. (　) How well is the control of design and manufacturing information applied to the procurement activity?
6. (Y/N) Is there a formal deviation procedure, and how well is it followed?
7. (Y/N) Does your company have a written system for incorporating customer changes into shop drawings?
8. (Y/N) Does your company have a reliability department?
9. (Y/N) Are reliability data used in developing new designs?
10. (Y/N) Is quality history fed back to engineering for improvements in current or future designs? Does quality management review new designs?
11. (Y/N) Does your company have a sample or prototype department?
12. (Y/N) Does Q.A. review sample prototypes?
13. (Y/N) Is this information used in developing shop inspection instructions?
14. (Y/N) Are customer specifications interpreted into shop specifications?
15. (Y/N) Do drawings and specifications accompany purchase orders to suppliers?
16. (Y/N) Are these reviewed by quality management?
17. (Y/N) Are characteristics classified on the engineering documents as to importance?
18. (Y/N) Does Q.A. review new drawings with the intent of designing gauging fixtures?

Procurement-Control of Purchased Material

It is essential for the assurance of quality that outside suppliers meet the standards for quality imposed on the firm's own operations department. Sources should be under continuous control or surveillance. Incoming material should be inspected to the extent necessary to assure that the requirements have been met.

19. (　) How well are potential suppliers evaluated and monitored?
20. (　) How well are quality requirements specified?
21. (　) How well are inspection procedures specified, and how well are they followed?
22. (　) How adequate are inspection facilities and equipment?

23. (   ) Have you certified (approved) key suppliers' design manufacturing and quality processes so that their shipments to you do not require inspection and testing?
24. (   ) How adequate are "certifications" which are used in lieu of inspection?
25. (   ) How well are certifications evaluated by independent checking?
26. (   ) How well are inspection results used for corrective action?
27. (Y/N) Do you have an incoming inspection department? (If yes, list personnel) Inspectors _____ Supervisors _____ Quality Engineers _____
28. (Y/N) Are purchase orders made available to incoming inspection?
29. (Y/N) Is there a system for keeping shop drawings up to date?
30. (Y/N) Are written inspection instructions available?
31. (Y/N) Is sample inspection used?
32. (Y/N) Is gauging equipment calibrated periodically?
33. (Y/N) Is gauging equipment correlated with suppliers' equipment?
34. (Y/N) Are suppliers' test records used for acceptance?
35. (Y/N) Are commercial test records used for acceptance?
36. (Y/N) Is material identified to physical and chemical test reports?
37. (Y/N) Are records kept to show acceptance and rejection of incoming material?
38. (Y/N) Does your company have a supplier rating system?
39. (Y/N) Is it made available to the supply management department?
40. (Y/N) Is the supplier notified of nonconforming material?
41. (Y/N) Does your company have an approved supplier list?
42. (Y/N) Does your company survey supplier facilities?
43. (Y/N) Does the incoming inspection department have adequate storage space to hold material until it is inspected?
44. (Y/N) Is nonconforming material identified as such?
45. (Y/N) Is nonconforming material held in a specific area until disposition can be made? Who is responsible for making disposition of nonconforming material? _____

Material Control

Control of the identity and quality status of material in-stores and in-process is essential. It is not enough that the right materials be procured and verified; they must be identified and controlled in a manner that will assure they are also properly used. The entire quality program may be compromised if adequate controls are not maintained throughout procurement, storage, manufacturing, and inspection.

46. (   ) How adequate are procedures for storage, release, and movement of material, and how well are they followed?
47. (   ) How well are incoming materials quarantined while under test?
48. (   ) How well are materials in-stores identified and controlled?
49. (   ) How well are in-process materials identified and controlled?
50. (   ) How well are materials in inspection identified and controlled?
51. (   ) How adequate are storage areas and facilities?
52. (   ) How well is access to material controlled?

53. (   ) How well do procedures cover the prevention of corrosion, deterioration, or damage of material and finished goods?
54. (   ) How well are they followed?
55. (   ) How well are nonconforming items identified, isolated, and controlled?

Manufacturing Control

In-process inspection, utilizing the techniques of quality control, is one of the most satisfactory methods yet devised for attaining quality of product during manufacture. Because many quality characteristics cannot be evaluated in the end product, it is imperative that they be achieved and verified during the production process.

56. (   ) How well are process capabilities established and maintained?
57. (   ) How well is in-process inspection specified?
58. (   ) How effectively is it performed?
59. (   ) How adequate are inspection facilities and equipment?
60. (   ) How well are the results of in-process inspection used in the promotion of effective corrective action?
61. (   ) How adequate are equipment and facilities maintained?
62. (   ) How adequate are housekeeping procedures, and how well are they followed?
63. (   ) Does your company have a process inspection function? (If yes, list on a separate sheet inspectors, supervisory and quality engineering personnel.) To whom does process inspection report? _____
64. (Y/N) Are inspection stations located in the production area?
65. (Y/N) Are shop drawings and specifications available to inspection?
66. (Y/N) Is there a system for keeping the documents up to date?
67. (Y/N) Are written inspection instructions available?
68. (Y/N) Is there a system for reviewing and updating inspection instructions?
69. (Y/N) Is sample inspection used?
70. (Y/N) Do production workers inspect their own work?
71. (Y/N) Are inspection records kept on file?
72. (Y/N) Is inspection equipment calibrated periodically?
73. (Y/N) Is all material identified (route tags, etc.)?
74. (Y/N) Is defective material identified as such?
75. (Y/N) Is defective material segregated from good material until disposition is made?
76. (Y/N) Are first production parts inspected before a job can be run?
77. (Y/N) Is corrective action taken to prevent the recurrence of defective material?
78. (Y/N) Who is responsible for making disposition of nonconforming material?
79. (Y/N) Does your company use x-bar and R charts?
80. (Y/N) Does your company use process capability studies?
81. (Y/N) Are standards calibrated by an outside source that certifies traceability to NBS?
82. (Y/N) Are standards calibrated directly by NBS?
83. (Y/N) Are packaged goods checked for proper packaging?

Quality Management

The key to the management of quality lies in philosophy, objectives, and organization structure. The philosophy forms the primary policy and should include the broad principles common to good-quality programs. The objectives should be clearly stated in specific terms and should provide operating policies which guide the activity of the quality program. The organizational structure should clearly define lines of authority and responsibility for quality from top management down to the operating levels.

84. (   ) Does the potential supplier embrace total quality management?
85. (   ) How adequate is the quality philosophy, and how well is it explained in operating policies and procedures?
86. (   ) How adequate is the technical competence in the quality discipline of those responsible for assuring quality?
87. (   ) How well does the organizational structure define quality responsibility and authority?
88. (   ) How well does the organizational structure provide access to top management?
89. (   ) How adequate is the documentation and dissemination of quality control procedures?
90. (   ) How adequate is the training program, including employee records?

Does the quality department have:

91. (Y/N) Written quality policy and procedures manual?
92. (Y/N) Written inspection instructions?
93. (Y/N) A quality engineering department?
94. (Y/N) Person or persons who perform vendor surveys?
95. (Y/N) Incoming inspection department?
96. (Y/N) In-process inspection department?
97. (Y/N) Final inspection department? To whom does the inspection department report? _____
98. (Y/N) A quality audit function?
99. (Y/N) A gauge control program?
100. (Y/N) A gauge control laboratory?
101. (Y/N) Other quality laboratories? (If yes, specify type) _____
102. (Y/N) A quality cost program?
103. (Y/N) A reliability department?
104. (Y/N) Does the quality department use statistical tools (control charts, sampling plans, etc.)? Explain _____
105. (Y/N) Is government source inspection available to your plant? Resident _____ Itinerant _____ No _____

Quality Information

Records should be maintained of all inspections performed, and the data should be periodically analyzed and used as a basis for action. Quality data should always be used, whether it be to improve the quality control operation by increasing or decreasing the amount of inspection, to improve the quality of product by the initiation of corrective action on processes or suppliers, to document certifications of product quality furnished to customers, or to report quality results and trends to management. Unused or unusual data are evidence of poor management.

106. (   ) How well are records of inspections maintained?
107. (   ) How adequate is the record and sample retention program?
108. (   ) How well are quality data used as a basis for action?
109. (   ) How well are quality data used in supporting certification of quality furnished to customers? How well is customer and field information used for corrective action?
110. (   ) How well is it reported to management?

Calibration—Inspection and Testing

Periodic inspection and calibration of certain tools, gauges, tests, and some items of process control equipment are necessary for the control and verification of product quality. Controlled standards, periodically checked or referenced against national standards, will assure the compatibility of vendor and vendee measurements. Inaccurate gauges and testers can compromise the entire quality control program and may result in either rejection of good material or acceptance of defective material.

111. (   ) How well do internal standards conform to national standards or customer standards?
112. (   ) How well are periodic inspections and calibrations specified?
113. (   ) How adequate are calibration facilities and equipment?
114. (   ) If external calibration sources are utilized, how adequate is the program and how well is it executed?
115. (Y/N) Does your company have a gauge control function?
116. (Y/N) Does your company have written instructions for operating inspection and test instruments?
117. (Y/N) Are all inspection instruments calibrated at periodic intervals?
118. (Y/N) Are records of calibration kept on file?
119. (Y/N) Is there a system to recall inspection instruments when they are due for calibration?
120. (Y/N) Are the inspection instruments used by production calibrated?
121. (Y/N) If so, are these instruments removed from use until they can be repaired or recalibrated?
122. (Y/N) Are shop masters calibrated at periodic intervals to secondary standards traceable to NBS?

Inspection of Completed Material

123. (Y/N) Does your company have a final inspection function? If yes, list inspection, supervisory, and quality engineers on a separate sheet. To whom does the final inspection department report? _____
124. (Y/N) Are shop drawings and specifications available to inspection?
125. (Y/N) Is there a system for keeping the documents up to date?
126. (Y/N) Are written inspection instructions available?

127. (Y/N) Is there a system for reviewing and updating inspection instructions?
128. (Y/N) Is sample inspection used?
129. (Y/N) Are inspection records kept on file?
130. (Y/N) Are records of inspection results used for corrective-action purposes?
131. (Y/N) Is inspection equipment calibrated periodically?
132. (Y/N) Is all material identified (route tags, etc.)?
133. (Y/N) Is defective material identified as such?
134. (Y/N) Is defective material segregated from good material until disposition is made?
135. (Y/N) Who is responsible for making disposition of nonconforming material? _____
136. (Y/N) Is reworked material submitted for reinspection?

Final Acceptance

Final inspection, testing, and packing are critical operations necessary to assure the acceptability of material. The specifications must form the basis for these activities. And to the extent that certifications or in-process inspections are used, in lieu of final inspection, records of those activities should be reviewed to verify conformance.

137. (   ) How well are specifications used in determining the acceptability of material?
138. (   ) How well are certifications and in-process inspection records used in the final acceptance decisions?
139. (   ) How adequate are inspection procedures? How well are they followed?
140. (   ) How adequate are inspection facilities and equipment?
141. (   ) How well are inspection results used for corrective action?
142. (   ) How adequate are packing and order-checking procedures?
143. (   ) How well are they followed?

Appendix B: Financial Statement Analysis[31]

The following information is useful during preliminary sourcing. These ratios and measures are useful for analyzing company-specific trends and for making comparisons among competing suppliers. Comparative data for specific industries may be obtained from Dun and Bradstreet or Robert Morris Associates.

Liquidity Measures. Liquidity refers to a company's ability to pay its bills when they are due and to provide for unanticipated cash requirements. In general, poor liquidity measures imply short-run credit problems. From a supply-management perspective, short-run credit problems could signal possible decreases in quality or difficulties in meeting scheduled deliveries. Three common liquidity measures are:

1. **Working capital** = Current assets − Current liabilities

   Working capital measures the amount of current assets that would remain if all current liabilities were paid.

---

[31]This Appendix was prepared by Donn W. Vickrey of the University of San Diego.

2. **Current ratio** = Current assets/Current liabilities

    The current ratio is a standardized measure of liquidity. In general, the higher the ratio the more protection a company has against liquidity problems. However, the ratio can be distorted by seasonal influences and abnormal payments on accounts payable made at the end of the period.

3. **Quick ratio** = Quick assets/Current liabilities

    The quick ratio is a standardized measure of liquidity in which only assets that can be converted to cash quickly (e.g., cash, accounts receivable, and marketable securities) are included in the calculation.

    Funds Management Ratios. The financial position of a company depends on how it manages key assets such as accounts receivable, inventory, and fixed assets. As a business grows, the associated expansion of these items can lead to significant cash shortages—even for companies that maintain profitable operations. As implied previously, short-term cash problems may signal future decreases in quality or delays in scheduled deliveries. Six frequently used measures of funds management are:

1. **Receivables to sales** = Accounts receivable/Sales

    In the absence of detailed credit information, the receivables-to-sales ratio can be used to analyze trends in a company's credit policy.

2. **Average collection period** = (Accounts receivable/Sales) $\times$ 365

    The average collection period is used to assess the quality of a company's receivables. The average collection period may be assessed in relation to the company's own credit terms or to the typical credit terms of firms in its industry.

3. **Average accounts payable period** = (Accounts payable/Purchases) $\times$ 365

    The average accounts payable period is used to assess how well a firm manages its payables. If the average days payable is increasing, or large in relation to the credit terms offered by the company's suppliers, it may signal that trade credit is being used as a source of funds.

4. **Inventory turnover** = Cost of goods sold/Average inventory

    The inventory-turnover ratio indicates how fast inventory items move through a business.

5. **Average days in inventory** = 365/Inventory turnover

    The average days in inventory is a simple conversion of the turnover ratio to a more intuitive measure of inventory management.

6. **Fixed asset turnover** = Sales/Average fixed assets

    The fixed asset turnover provides a crude measure of how well a firm's investment in plant and equipment is managed relative to the sales volume it supports.

Unfortunately, interpreting the fixed asset turnover ratio is not always a straightforward proposition. For example, a decrease in the firm's turnover ratio could result from poor management of fixed assets *or* from an investment in new technology (e.g., computer integrated manufacturing).

Profitability Measures. Profitability refers to the ability of a firm to earn positive cash flows and to generate a satisfactory return on shareholders' investments. Profitability measures provide an indication of a firm's long-term viability. Profitability measures may be used to infer quality in the sense that, to generate a satisfactory return, a firm must ensure that it provides quality products from year to year. Profitability measures may also be used, to some extent, to infer a company's pricing policies. Thus, they may be useful for negotiating contract prices and, in particular, the profit portion of such prices.

1. **Profit margin** = Net income/Sales

   The profit margin percentage measures the amount of net income earned on a dollar of sales.

2. **Gross profit margin** = Gross margin/Sales

   The gross margin percentage measures the gross profit earned on each dollar of sales. Thus, this ratio may be used to infer the typical markup percentage used by a supplier.

3. **Return on assets** = Net income/Average total assets

   Return on investment measures how efficiently assets are used to produce income.

4. **Return on equity** = Net income/Average stockholders' equity

   Return on equity measures the percentage return on the stockholders' average investment.

Measures of Long-Term Financial Strength. The ability to deliver quality products over time is contingent on the long-term financial strength of the supplier. Difficulties meeting long-term obligations may also signal insolvency. The disruptions caused by insolvency can cause major delays in shipments, decreases in quality, or complete inability to perform.

1. **Debt to equity** = Total liabilities/Stockholders' equity

   Since debt requires periodic interest payments and eventual repayment, it is inherently more risky than equity. The debt-to-equity ratio measures the proportion of the company that is financed by creditors relative to the proportion financed by stockholders.

2. **Times interest earned** = Operating profit before interest/Interest on long-term debt

   The times-interest-earned ratio measures the extent to which a company's operating profits cover its interest payments. A low times-interest-earned ratio may signal difficulties in meeting long-term financial obligations.

Appendix C: Planning a Facility Visit

In planning facility or plant visits, only a few outstanding potential suppliers' plants should be chosen for observation because of the time and costs involved. In addition to observing production equipment and operations, there are other compelling reasons for plant visits. It is vital, for example, to determine a supplier's managerial capabilities and motivation to meet contractual obligations. The buying firm wants suppliers whose management is committed to excellence. To make such a determination properly requires an overall appraisal.

Among the factors to be addressed are:

- Attitude and stability of the top- and middle-management teams.
- R&D capability.
- Appropriateness of equipment.
- Effectiveness of the production control, quality assurance, and cost control systems.
- Competence of the technical and managerial staffs.

Other important factors include:

- Morale of personnel at all levels.
- Industrial relations.
- Willingness of the potential supplier to work with the buying firm.
- Quantity of back orders.
- Effectiveness of supply management and materials management operations.

And past performance:

- Past major customers.
- General reputation.
- Letters of reference.

The plant visit should be planned carefully to provide the required level of knowledge and insight into the potential supplier's operations, capacity, and orientation. The efficiency with which the plant visit is planned and conducted reflects on the buying organization. To provide the reader with a sense of the detail in which some plant visits are conducted, one firm's evaluation form is reproduced in Appendix A of this chapter. This evaluative instrument is used by a high-tech firm that utilizes a number of single-source collaborative relationship arrangements.

Although it varies with the firm's size and organizational structure, the *initial orientation meeting* typically is attended by the sourcing team members and their management counterparts from the potential supplier's organization. In smaller firms, the president often leads the supplier group. In this session, the sourcing team provides general information and explains the interests of its company: its kind of business, a brief history, kinds of products, the importance of the item(s) to be purchased, and volume, quality, and delivery requirements.

The prospective supplier usually is requested to provide additional information on the company's history, current customers, sales volume, and financial stability. If classified or confidential data might be involved during design and production operations, the sourcing team must review the supplier's security control system.

In the quality area, the supply manager and his or her sourcing teammates should attempt to understand the *supplier's attitude* toward quality by asking questions such as: How do you feel about zero defects and total quality management? Are you ISO 9000:2000 certified? Do you employ the Design of Experiments during new product development? Do you employ statistical process control? Have you adopted a total quality commitment plan? How do you measure customer satisfaction? Show us how you've implemented these concepts. Do you have a quality manual? Copies of the manual and the policy should be reviewed by the buying team's quality representative. The potential supplier should also be asked to describe *its own* supplier quality control program. The more technical aspects of supplier quality are addressed in Chapter 7.

An increasing number of firms, including Motorola and many other leading-edge manufacturers, require that potential suppliers be registered under the appropriate ISO 9000:2000 quality standard(s).[32]

If the sourcing team is satisfied with the results of the introductory meeting, a tour of the facilities typically is made. Prior to the tour, the sourcing team should get permission to talk freely with various individuals working in the operation, not just handpicked managers.

The potential supplier's management often assumes that satisfactory operating controls are in place. In reality, however, experience frequently shows that some of these controls may not have been implemented, or that they may have been discontinued. When management describes these things, the sourcing team should respond, "That sounds excellent, we'd like to see them." The team should also check controls by asking such questions as, "How do you ensure that the most current drawing is in use?" "How do you segregate rejected materials?"[33]

As a cross-check on specific information obtained in the initial meeting, perceptive team members often ask shop and staff personnel similar types of questions. When the potential supplier's managers are not present, operating personnel should be asked about *their* understanding of the firm's quality systems, schedules, cost control efforts, and related requirements. Workers can also be asked about working conditions and turnover, about the firm's commitment to quality, about quality tools, and about training.

When observing plant equipment, the sourcing team should determine whether the equipment is modern, whether it is in good operating condition, whether tolerances can be held consistently, and what the output rates are. The sourcing team also should look for special modifications or adaptations of equipment; these things often provide clues to the ingenuity of operating management personnel.

The first impression of a supplier's operation is generally obtained through observing the housekeeping of the plant itself. Is it clean and well organized? Are the machines clean? Are the tools, equipment, and benches kept orderly and accessible? Good housekeeping tends to be an indication of efficiency. Many sourcing team members responsible for source selection believe it is reasonable to expect that a firm displaying pride in its facilities and equipment will also take pride in the workmanship that goes into its products.

---

[32]"Does the ISO 9000 Need Fixing?" Industry Forum Supplement to the June 1994 issue of *Management Review.*

[33]Warren E. Norquist, director of Worldwide Purchasing and Materials Management, Polaroid Corporation, personal interview, October 1987.

During the visit, responsible sourcing team members should investigate production methods and efficiencies. Is a just-in-time system utilized to a significant extent? Is material moving freely from storage to production areas? Are there any production bottlenecks? Is the production scheduling and control function organized and functioning well? Is reserve production capacity available? Is it available on a regular or an overtime basis? Does the potential supplier have a competent maintenance crew? And, finally, the sourcing team should determine whether inventory levels for both production materials and finished goods are adequate for the company's needs.

Employee attitudes are extremely important. In the long run, production results often depend more on people than on the physical plant. Do the employees seem to work harmoniously with one another and with their supervisors? Are they interested in quality and in improving the products they make? Is enthusiasm at a reasonable level? In short, do the people take pride in their jobs and in the firm—or do they view it as an eight-to-five, clock-punching operation?

16

CHAPTER

Global Supply Management

I am neither an Athenian nor a Greek, but a Citizen of the world
Socrates

Operating in an increasingly interconnected world, leading companies perceive competition as global and are moving to implement an integrated strategy worldwide. Global competitors are learning to develop and manufacture products that can be introduced and marketed simultaneously in many countries. In doing so, they are sourcing technology, materials, and components from sites and suppliers located throughout the world.
Carl R. Frear, Lynn E. Metcalf, and Mary S. Alguire[1]

Supply Managers who strive for World Class Supply Management^{SM} have chosen to pursue a global supply philosophy that unifies rather than divides humanity. As such, a world class supply manager chooses to pursue global supplier relationships that are based on fairness, honesty and trust, which result in lower total costs without exploitation.

KEY CONCEPTS

---

[1]C. R. Frear, L. E. Metcalf, and M. S. Alguire, "Offshore Sourcing: Its Nature and Scope," *International Journal of Purchasing and Materials Management,* Summer 1992, p. 2.

Case

Sopraffino Goes Global

Pam grimly looked over her spreadsheet analysis for her first year's profits. Her business, Sopraffino, which means *super-fine* or *first-class* in Italian, was started in 1998 in Danville, California, with about $10,000. The original idea was to sell gallery items, beautiful gifts, and furniture. Pam hoped that the Italian name coupled with her artistic background, Italian heritage, and imported dried flowers and gifts would give Sopraffino a niche in Danville's heavily saturated retail market. But after six months of business, Pam discovered that the gallery items did not sell very well. In fact, Sopraffino had a net income of only $4,000 in the first year of business because of high costs and low sales.

Although she kept the name, the store shifted over to selling mostly dried floral arrangements, along with soaps, lotions, containers, cards, and similar items. The growth for sales of dried floral arrangements appeared to have a 71 percent annual rate if extrapolated over the following year. Customers loved the dried floral arrangements that could be customized to each customer's home using a raw material inventory of about 30 varieties of dried flowers.

Like all products sold in the store, Pam purchased the dried floral materials in San Francisco through wholesalers. When she had first opened the store she had been unable to research more direct sources of supply, so using wholesalers as intermediaries made economic and managerial sense. The manufacturers that supplied wholesalers were clearly labeled on the boxes of dried flowers. In every case, the suppliers were overseas, primarily Israel and Holland. Once a week, Pam would awake at 4:00 A.M. to drive to San Francisco to purchase and transport dried flowers into her Suzuki Sidekick 4-door. Sometimes, she would have to make two or more trips in a week if she could not fit all of the flowers into her Suzuki or if the wholesalers were out of stock for a specific flower. After unloading the flowers at her store, she would use them throughout the week to make arrangements for custom orders and stock for the store. The traveling created a strain on her marriage and made for difficult 16-hour workdays, but the thrill of making products customers were excited about and readily bought made the sacrifice worthwhile.

Using spreadsheet data from the first year, she forecast expected profits for the next year. She discovered that sales would have to nearly double from $88,000 to $160,000 for her to start making any significant profit. The prospects for doubling sales seemed grim. She did not want to close the business. Was increasing sales the only answer?

She remembered a discussion she had once had on global supply management with a professor of supply chain management at California State University, Hayward. He had said that when intermediaries, such as wholesalers, outlived their usefulness one could move to direct buying. She had dismissed the comment at the time in the belief that manufacturers would not sell directly to her because wholesalers had exclusive rights to the northern California region. Surely that was the case, she thought. After all, why would the wholesalers sell her boxes with the manufacturers' names on them! Now, however, was the time to check out this assumption.

First, she typed the names of the manufacturers into a search engine and visited their websites. Next, she contacted them and quickly discovered that not only could she buy directly from them at about 40 percent less, but also they would deliver the boxes to her door. The issues she had thought might exist with global sourcing were virtually nonexistent. In the short span of one hour, she had found the profit she needed to keep her business open without unrealistic increases in sales. In addition, she would no longer need to take these early morning trips. She wondered how many other companies used intermediaries after their usefulness no longer existed. It was time now to research her other products.

Global Management Perspective

The supply management profession operates in an environment characterized by: (1) the general issues and concerns of a truly mutually interdependent "global economy"; (2) a supplier selection and development process that seeks collaborative and collaborative-based relationships with the very best suppliers worldwide; (3) supply management strategies which reflect forward-looking, long-term global supplier relationships; and (4) the supply chain management (SCM) orientation that extends supplier selection and relationship management issues well beyond the traditional business perspective of "buyer-seller" to those of a multi-tiered, highly interdependent worldwide system.

Future of Global Supply Management

In an ambitious consideration of what the future holds for the supply management profession, the Center for Advanced Purchasing Studies (CAPS) concluded:

> Largely driven by political and technological change, world financial markets are closely linked through 24-hour trading. A drop in one nation's economic fortunes can directly affect financial markets worldwide. Organizations such as the International Monetary Fund and the World Bank are increasingly involved in stabilizing and localizing negative economic effects. Also, international business is no longer limited to large multinational corporations. Small-to medium-sized enterprises increasingly source from or operate in foreign countries. Finally, there are fewer marketplace differences both in terms of consumer preferences and industrial capabilities. For example, although often viewed negatively as supplanting local customs and values, the "Westernization" of global consumer markets is occurring at a rapid rate. Further, manufacturing firms in "developing" countries that were originally used solely to access low labor costs have improved their capabilities to the point that they provide innovative product and process technologies that create competitive advantages for a corporation. Productivity and quality are dramatically improving worldwide.[2]

The CAPS study supports the following conclusions:

- Regional and global sourcing strategies will become a critically important source of competitive advantage.
- The number of key suppliers to firms will be reduced to maximize leverage on a global basis. Suppliers' regional and global capability expectations will increase.
- Strategic and tactical sourcing work will be further separated.
- Executive management expectations of supply management will increase on account of the cross-functional, cross-boundary emphasis and focus on alliances with both suppliers and customers.
- Supply management will be increasingly integrated with the strategic plans of the firm to maximize companywide leverage.
- Supply management performance measures will become further aligned with companywide measurements.
- Information systems/technology will be key to globalization and sourcing strategies enterprisewide.
- New, more complex skills and focus will be required in supply management to operate in a globally complex and uncertain world.
- More flexibility and external customer focus will be required in supply management activities to maximize supplier contributions.[3]

Procuring products and services of foreign origin can be extraordinarily challenging. On the one hand, virtually all of the practices and procedures described in this book are applicable. On the other hand, many new issues must be addressed if a supply team

---

[2]Philip L. Carter, Joseph R. Carter, Robert M. Monczka, Thomas H. Slaight, and Andrew J. Swan, "The Future of Purchasing and Supply: A Five and Ten-Year Forecast," Center for Advanced Purchasing Studies (CAPS) Focus Study, 1998, p. 16.

[3]Ibid.

is to ensure that its organization receives the right quality, in the right quantity, on time, with the right services, at the right cost. In recent years, the term "foreign sourcing" has largely been replaced with "international sourcing": the process of purchasing from suppliers outside the firm's country of manufacture. As with other areas in purchasing and supply chain management, the process of worldwide sourcing is going through evolutionary change.

Stages to Global Supply Management

At a number of leading firms, international sourcing is being replaced by a broader philosophy of "global supply management."[4] Joseph Carter suggests three stages of worldwide sourcing as follows:[5]

- *Stage One*: International Purchasing—Organizations focus on leveraging volumes, minimizing prices, and managing inventory costs. These areas are characteristic of an organization first entering the global purchasing arena.

- *Stage Two*: Global Sourcing—Organizations focused on global opportunities will put more emphasis on supplier capability, supporting production strategies, and servicing customer markets. Of those that have sourced offshore for some time, most are at this stage.

- *Stage Three*: Global Supply Management—Here, organizations optimize supply networks through effective logistics and capacity management. These organizations have effectively minimized risks in offshore sourcing and have sourced worldwide for technology leadership.

Transnational Corporation Christopher A. Bartlett and Sumantra Ghoshal suggest that another stage exists that they term the transnational corporation. The transnational corporation is the next stage in the evolution of global supply management. The transnational corporation is one that has evolved in response to a changing global environment, characterized by such features as:

- Instantaneous electronic communications capabilities.
- Instantaneous electronic funds transfer.
- Distributed and highly autonomous local operations.
- The global real-time flow of intellectual property among members of product- and service-focused supply and value chains.
- Products which are highly differentiated for specific customer needs in tightly defined markets.
- An environment in which there is a worldwide flow of raw materials and finished goods, highly insensitive to both national and corporate boundaries.[6]

---

[4]Robert M. Monczka and Robert J. Trent, "Global Sourcing: A Development Approach," *International Journal of Purchasing and Materials Management,* Spring 1991, p. 3.

[5]Joseph R. Carter, Ph.D., "The Global Evolution," *Purchasing Today,* July 1997, p. 33.

[6]Christopher A. Bartlett and Sumantra Ghoshal, *Managing Across Borders: The Transnational Solution,* 2d. ed. (Boston: Harvard Business School Press, 1998), pp. 65–81.

Transnational firms tend to operate with matrix-type structures in which both product divisions and areas have significant influence. Creativity and product innovation are dispersed throughout the entire scope of the transnational enterprise. There emerges the critical need to coordinate global activities, rather than direct them from "headquarters." Core competencies of the enterprise are freely transferred from one global location to another, while simultaneously coordinating key strategies with centralized staff functions. Examples of transnational corporations are IBM, Toyota Motors, Honda, ABB, and Boeing.

Rick James, president of Boeing Europe, noted (prior to the terrorist attacks of September 11, 2001):[7]

> Looking 20 years out, we forecast that seven out of every 10 commercial airplanes we deliver will go to non-U.S. customers. And our defense and space products also are in service worldwide with governments and military alliances such as NATO. Our supplier base is just as international. We currently have nearly 1,000 suppliers outside the U.S. We invest more than $5 billion annually with them, and that supports more than 150,000 jobs each year. Boeing is equally at home in Europe, where nearly half of our international suppliers are located. Our involvement with European industry spans more than a quarter of a century and some of our relationships, such as the one we have with Shorts Brothers in Northern Ireland, goes back almost as far. We currently work with nearly 500 firms in 21 countries. In this region alone, we expect to spend more than $14 billion over the next five years. And that means about 90,000 jobs annually.

Reasons for Global Sourcing

Global sourcing requires additional efforts when compared with domestic sourcing, but can yield large rewards. One of the complexities of buying goods and services of foreign origin is the wide variability among the producing countries in characteristics such as quality, service, and dependability. Quality, for example, may be very high in products from one country but inconsistent or unacceptably low in products from a neighboring land. With this caveat in mind, let us look at six common reasons for purchasing goods and services from international sources.

- **Superior quality.** A key reason for global supply management is to obtain the required level of quality. Although this factor is declining in significance, supply managers in a variety of industries still look to global sources to fulfill their most critical quality requirements. Please refer to the chapter on quality for more details.

- **Better timeliness.** A second major reason for global sourcing is to improve the certainty of the supplier in meeting schedule requirements. Order lead-time lengths and variability in the lead-time estimations may be better than those provided by domestic sources. A U.S. manufacturer of board games formerly owned by one of the authors of this book discovered that parts and components for games could be manufactured in Taiwan with equal quality, lower price, smaller lot sizes

---

[7]Rick James, president, Boeing Europe, "Economic Value through Global Relationships," presentation at the Farnborough International Air Show (England), September 9, 1998.

and shorter lead time than from suppliers in the United States.[8] As with quality, the timeliness capability of suppliers around the globe has steadily improved. Once initial difficulties of the new business relationship have been overcome, many international sources have proved to be remarkably dependable in meeting time schedules.

■ **Lower cost.** International sourcing generates expenses beyond those normally encountered when sourcing domestically. For example, additional communications and transportation expenses, import duties, and greater costs when investigating the potential supplier's capabilities all add to the buying firm's total costs. To illustrate the point, one major computer manufacturer uses a rule of thumb that a foreign material's price must be at least 20 percent lower than the comparable domestic price to compensate for these additional costs. Nonetheless, after all of the additional costs of "buying international" are considered, in the case of many materials it frequently is possible to reduce the firm's *total cost* of the material through global sourcing.

■ **More advanced technology.** No country holds a monopoly on advanced and new product and process technology. Global sources in some industries are more advanced technologically than their domestic counterparts. Not to take advantage of such product or process technologies can result in a manufacturer's losing its competitive position to manufacturers that incorporate the more advanced technologies.

■ **Broader supply base.** Sourcing globally increases the number of possible suppliers from which the buying firm can select. Increased competition for the buying firm's business will then better enable the firm to develop reliable, low-cost suppliers. Broadening the supply base does not mean increasing the number of suppliers. Broadening the supply base actually increases the opportunity to find better suppliers, thereby enabling the buying firm to decrease the number of contracted suppliers and pursue collaborative or alliance relationships when appropriate.

■ **Expanded customer base.** Sourcing globally can create opportunities to sell in countries where the buying firm's suppliers are based. Where trade restrictions are minimal, the interaction itself may yield some of the sales opportunities. However, in some countries, trade restrictions are in place requiring nondomestic suppliers to procure materials in the buying country as part of the sales transaction. These arrangements commonly are called *barter, offsets,* or *countertrade.* The tying of *sales into a country* with *the purchase of goods from that country* makes both marketing and supply management far more challenging than when pure monetary transactions are involved. For a firm to compete and make sales in many countries, increasingly it is necessary to enter into agreements to purchase items made in those countries. Countertrade is discussed in detail later in this chapter.

---

[8]The game company was started by Stephen Starling at the age of nineteen and is one of the reasons the author became enamored with the impact that well-managed supply management can have on the supply chain. Stephen closed the company to pursue higher education, but the "real world" lessons learned are still vivid.

Potential Problems

■ **Cultural issues.** Cultural issues can be a problem in global sourcing on account of the wide variety of approaches to conducting business in different regions of the world. One of the authors of the book recently stayed in a hotel in Hong Kong that did not have a fourth floor. The floor was there, but it was completely empty, with no walls! The number four has a variety of connotations depending upon whom you speak to in Asia. The explanation given by management at the hotel was that four means "death" and as such it would be bad luck to have a fourth floor. Imagine entering into a negotiation with the owner of the building that you want to set for 4:00 P.M. Cultural issues are very real and should not be ignored in global sourcing. Cultural issues are discussed later in this chapter.

■ **Long lead times.** Variable shipping schedules, unpredictable time requirements for customs activities, the need for greater coordination in global supply management, strikes by unions, and storms at sea (which can cause both delays and damage) usually result in longer lead times. Airfreight may be used to offset some of the problems of variable shipping schedules, but at a significant increase in cost.

■ **Additional inventories.** The quantity of additional inventory needed when purchasing from foreign sources can be difficult to determine. Quite often, however, the additional inventories are not as large as one might expect. Nevertheless, inventory-carrying costs must be added to the purchase price, the freight costs, and the administrative costs to determine the true total cost of buying from global sources. Occasionally, when a domestic industry is producing at full capacity, it is possible to get both faster delivery and lower prices from global sources. Routinely, however, additional lead times, which traditionally exceed 30 days, must be considered in planning foreign purchases when surface transportation is involved. It should be noted that some supply managers do *not* add buffer stocks, relying on airfreight in case of emergencies.

■ **Lower quality.** As previously mentioned, global suppliers frequently are utilized because many of them can provide a consistently high level of quality. But problems do exist. For example, the United States is the only major nonmetric country in a metric world. This frequently leads to manufacturing *tolerance problems* for buyers of U.S. products and U.S. buyers of products from metric countries. Additionally, nondomestic suppliers tend to be less responsive to necessary design changes than do their domestic counterparts. In many cases, there is the risk that production outside of the domestic firm's control can result in "off-spec" incoming materials. Potential rework or scrap costs could add substantially to the total cost of doing business with global suppliers.

■ **Social and labor problems.** In Europe and the United States, unions and some politicians are pushing for retaliatory measures against exporting countries where workers lack clout and labor laws are either weak or routinely flouted. Retailers such as Levi, Nordstrom, Wal-Mart, and Reebok discern a greater tendency by some customers to shun production from "sweatshops." Documentaries by the news media of working conditions in some international plants have made U.S. retailers sensitive to working conditions in those plants. It seems highly likely that manufacturers will soon have similar concerns with their global suppliers.

■ **Higher costs of doing business.** The need for translators, communications problems, the distances involved in making site visits, and so on all add to the cost of doing business with global suppliers. Port-order services are more complicated because of currency fluctuations, methods of payment, customs issues, and the utilization of import brokers and international carriers. Inadequate local (international) logistical support functions such as communication systems (telephones, fax machines, Internet), transportation systems, financial institutions, and so forth can complicate communications and product distribution.

■ **High opacity.** Investors, chief financial officers, bankers, equity analysts, and supply managers involved in global activities have long been aware that the risk of conducting business in different countries varies. Recently, a risk factor called the "Opacity Index" has been developed to address the risk costs associated with conducting business in a specific country.[9] The Global Opacity Index addresses the following areas: (1) corruption in government bureaucracy; (2) laws governing contracts or property rights; (3) economic policies (fiscal, monetary, and tax-related); (4) accounting standards; and (5) business regulations. China, for example, has high opacity in comparison to the United States. The United States has less bureaucracy, fewer government-imposed restrictions, less monetary transaction constraints, and very little corruption.

Questions before Going Global

Several years ago, Raul Casillas, of the Alps Manufacturing organization, suggested that to help in determining if a part, product, or process is a candidate for global sourcing, ask the following six questions:[10]

1. Does it qualify as high volume in your industry?
2. Does it have a long life (two to three years)?
3. Does it lend itself to repetitive manufacturing or assembly?
4. Is demand for the product fairly stable?
5. Are specifications and drawings clear and well defined?
6. Is technology not available domestically at a competitive price and quality?

If the answer to all six questions is yes, then the supply manager may want to evaluate the support network within his or her firm, asking the following questions:

■ Does sufficient engineering support exist to efficiently facilitate engineering change orders (ECOs) when they occur?

■ Will the buyer be able to allow sufficient time to phase out existing "in the pipeline" inventory?

---

[9]"The Opacity Index: Launching a New Measure of the Effects of Opacity on the Cost and Availability of Capital in Countries World-Wide (Executive Summary)," Price Waterhouse Coopers, London, January 2001, pp. 1–13. http://www.opacityindex.com/.

[10]Raul Casillas, "Foreign Sourcing: Is It for You?" *Pacific Purchaser,* November–December 1988, p. 9. Also, for a more recent analysis, see Robi Bendorf, C.P.M., "The Global Sourcing Process—On the Road to World-Class," 86th Annual International Purchasing Conference Proceedings, May 2001, Orlando, Florida.

■ Will the supply manager's firm take the responsibility for providing the necessary education and training for those that will have to interact with and support foreign suppliers?

■ Is the firm prepared to make a financial commitment for expensive trips to the supplier?

■ Is management willing to change the approach, in some cases even the policy of how business and related transactions are conducted?

■ Is the buyer aware of the environment, including current and forecasted exchange rates, general impact of tariff schedules, available technologies, and products from other countries, as well as their political climates, and leading economic indicators both domestically and abroad?

If the answers to both sets of questions are all positive, global sourcing may be a realistic possibility. A significant number of negative responses indicates the potential for real problems if a global sourcing arrangement is developed. Before a positive decision is made, however, the buyer needs to explore several issues with top management. First, do the required procedural and policy changes mesh satisfactorily with the firm's existing mode of operation? More important, is the global sourcing concept, and its underlying rationale, compatible with the firm's long-term plans? It is important that the program contribute positively to achievement of the firm's long-range goals—and that the commitment is made as something more than a short-term-strategy decision.

Supply Channels

The next step after deciding to source globally is to decide what supply channels to use. The lowest-price method for procuring goods globally usually is to procure them directly. Direct procurement requires the buying firm to deal with all of the issues associated with getting the goods to facilities. Although direct procurement may result in a low price, total costs may be prohibitive. In addition, limited resources in supply management may make direct procurement infeasible. The simplest way to source globally is through the use of an intermediary. The value of using intermediaries dissipates over time as learning by the buying firm increases.

Global Trade Intermediaries

Selection of the appropriate intermediary is a function of availability and of the services required. The use of such intermediaries typically adds a significant cost to the overall cost of the transaction but in most cases avoids many unforeseen problems.[11] The supply manager who is venturing into global sourcing is well advised to solicit the advice of colleagues from the local supply management association.

Some typical intermediaries are described below:[12]

■ *Import merchants* buy goods for their own account and sell through their own outlets. Since they assume all the risks of clearing goods through customs and performing all the intermediate activity, their customers are relieved of import problems and, in effect, can treat such transactions as domestic purchases.

---

[11]Dick Locke, "Get the Purchasing Channel You Want," *Electronics Components,* October 1993, p. U-12.

[12]N. A. DiOrio, "International Procurement," *Guide to Purchasing,* National Association of Purchasing Management, Tempe, AZ, 1987, p. 7.

■ *Commission houses* usually act for exporters abroad, selling in the United States and receiving a commission from the foreign exporter. Such houses generally do not have goods billed to them, although they handle many of the shipping and customs details.

■ *Agents* or *representatives* are firms or individuals representing sellers. Since the seller pays their commission, their primary interests are those of the exporter. They generally handle all shipping and customs clearance details, although they assume no financial responsibility of the principals.

■ *Import brokers* act as "marriage brokers" between buyers and sellers from different nations. Their commissions are paid by sellers for locating buyers and by buyers for finding sources of supply, but they are *not* involved in shipment or clearance of an order through customs. They also may act as special purchasing agents for designated commodities on a commission basis. Like agents, import brokers do not assume any of the seller's fiscal responsibility.

■ *Trading companies* are large companies that generally perform all the functions performed individually by the types of agencies previously listed. The worldwide operations and know-how of such firms offer significant advantages and convenience. Standard directories and trade publications list such firms, their capabilities, and areas of service.

■ *Subsidiaries* are established by multinational corporations in countries where a physical presence is needed to improve competitive capability and/or meet host government restrictions. For example, Hitachi, a Japanese company, created a Hitachi Americas subsidiary to serve North American markets. Subsidiaries can increase sales and lower costs through employing a workforce with unique training and education and through reduced transport distances and tariffs. Subsidiaries usually start with a large percentage of expatriate managers competent in the local language, which lessens over time as qualified managers from the host country are developed. Subsidiaries serve to buffer the supply manager from both language and time-zone problems. They offer to set prices in local currency and deliver material to buyers with all duties paid. Unfortunately, they are often remote from manufacturing and marketing decision makers and can be blockers in the flow of technical information. One experienced global sourcing authority finds that subsidiaries add 5 to 35 percent for their services.[13]

International Procurement Offices

When an organization's purchases in a foreign country or region warrant it, consideration should be given to establishing an international procurement office (IPO), also called an international purchasing office.[14] An IPO is an office in a foreign country that is owned and/or operated by the parent company in order to facilitate business interactions in the foreign country and surrounding region.

---

[13]Locke, "Get the Purchasing Channel You Want." Mr. Locke formerly was a director of international sourcing at Hewlett-Packard and is founder of the San Francisco–based Global Procurement Group.

[14]Prior to publishing this book, the authors debated as to whether to use another term for IPO, since IPO is popularly known as "initial public offering." The decision to keep the acronym IPO is based on its entrenchment in supply management literature and the lack of a better term. We considered the obvious, GPO (global procurement office), but quickly realized that GPO already means group purchasing organization.

Supply management professionals at an IPO quickly become familiar with qualified sources, thereby expanding the buying firm's potential supplier base. IPO personnel can physically and personally evaluate suppliers, negotiate for price and other terms, and monitor quality and job progress through direct site visits. IPO personnel are in a position to develop and maintain better information on local conditions such as materials shortages, labor issues, and governmental actions than are domestically based supply managers. The IPO facilitates payments to suppliers, provides on-site support at the supplier's site if problems arise, and provides logistical support.

Expatriates who have worked for the domestic manufacturer, usually in a technical role, normally staff IPOs; however, this generalization is changing as the percentage of locals staffing IPOs is increasing. IPOs normally are established as cost centers, charging a percentage markup (typically 2 percent) for their services. Competition from other channels (foreign trade intermediaries and direct relations) tends to keep IPOs efficient. The one weakness of IPOs that has been observed is their tendency to represent the local supplier's interests over those of the parent company.

Deere & Company has undertaken an aggressive globalization program under the direction of Dave Nelson, vice president of Worldwide Supply Management. Deere's International Supply Management Services has established IPOs around the world. According to a Deere & Company newsletter, the International Supply Management Services "group's mission has evolved into leveraging opportunities around the world for strategic sourcing teams and for all of Deere's 75 factories."[15] Three of the group's key responsibilities are (1) "maintaining cross-cultural relationships and training sourcing team members in global supply management," (2) "serving as the main link between supply management activities and the Deere & Company functions that global trade requires: customs, law, finance, and others that deal with such murky issues as quotas and duties, world economic forecasts, business development, risk management, currency and taxes," and (3) establishing and facilitating International Purchasing Offices. According to Dave Nelson, "These offices will link local manufacturing to common enterprise processes, work to improve supplier capability by accessing and applying proven Deere & Company programs (such as Achieving Excellence and Supplier Development), and facilitate understanding of in-country trade and regulatory requirements, as well as cultures."[16]

Direct Suppliers

Dealing directly with the supplier usually will result in the lowest *purchase price* (including transportation and import duties). It eliminates the markups of global trade intermediaries. But it requires an investment in travel, communications, logistics, and interpretation of costs. Direct relations with the supplier should be undertaken only after carefully conducting a cost/benefit analysis. It is important to note that conditions in developing countries are often problematic. Buyers should anticipate problems. For example, China, India, South America, and Eastern Europe have relatively

---

[15]"Global Surge," *Supply Management Linkages: A Newsletter from John Deere,* Summer 2000.
[16]Ibid.

poor transportation infrastructure systems in comparison to North America, Western Europe, and the Pacific Rim.

Eliminating Intermediaries

After the buying firm has gained confidence in the quality of the imported materials, and volume increases, the firm typically attempts to discontinue the use of global trade intermediaries for major procurements. Its major motivation is to avoid the intermediary's markup. The supply manager should inform its supplier of this new policy and then visit each of the manufacturers, *without the intermediaries,* to negotiate new contracts. While cost and the desire for direct dealings on technical issues may motivate the buying firm to deal directly with the supplier, the final decision will be made at the supplier's headquarters. The supply manager should anticipate resistance by both the intermediaries and their manufacturers. But this resistance normally can be overcome. In some cases, new suppliers may have to be developed because of the tight ties the global trade intermediaries may have with the existing supplier. Before taking such action, the supply manager must ensure that his or her company is set up to handle items such as traffic, customs clearance, and international payments.[17]

Direct procurement requires the involvement of the company in all aspects of the transaction; when properly conducted, it eliminates the added profit of the middleman. Outside agencies may be engaged to perform specialized services. For example, *customs brokers* can be used to handle entry requirements, *export brokers* to handle foreign clearances, and *freight forwarders* to arrange for transport. Such agents do not take title to the goods. Most direct purchasers whose scale of activities does not warrant such in-house capability use outside agencies.

Definitions of terms which the supply manager may encounter when dealing globally may be obtained by visiting the following websites:

CISG—Table of Contracting States **http://www.cisg.law.pace.edu/cisg/ countries/cntries.html**

Dictionary of International Trade Terms **http://www.itds.treas.gov/ glossaryfrm.html**

International Chamber of Commerce **http://www.iccwbo.org/**

International Trade Administration of the U.S. Department of Commerce OANDA—The Currency Site **http://www.oanda.com/**

The International Monetary Fund (IMF) **http://www.imf.org/**

The U.S. Central Intelligence Agency's World Factbook **http://www.odci.gov/cia/publications/factbook/**

The World Trade Organization (WTO) **http://www.wto.org/index.htm**

Understanding Incoterms **http://www.iccwbo.org/incoterms/ understanding.asp**

---

[17]Richard G. Novotny, "Global Search," *Electronic Buyers' News,* December 19, 1988, p. 34.

Identifying Direct Suppliers

Global trade intermediaries also are an excellent source of information. Unfortunately, these organizations have a vested interest in maintaining their position in the supply channel. The best way to prepare to bypass the intermediary is to develop direct contacts with key players at the division performing the design, manufacture, and marketing of the item or commodity class. The supply manager should provide performance feedback *directly* to the supplier. The supply manager should tell the intermediary that he or she wants to visit with the supplier's key personnel the next time they are in the country or the next time the key personnel are in the buyer's country. Dick Locke recommends meeting the supplier's key personnel and presents other tips summarized in the following list:[18]

- Use the meeting to provide performance feedback and to explain your company's purchasing goals and values. Take care not to appear to be an unreasonable company to work with, even if you must deliver a critical message. Work to make foreign visitors to your company feel as welcome as possible.

- As part of the strategy, consider the timing of your request. The ideal time is when you are considering a change in suppliers or are selecting a supplier for a new project. The possibility of a major increase in business will give you more leverage.

- If you're dealing with a new supplier, state your intention to deal directly right from the start. Once a subsidiary or representative has started to handle your business, they are difficult to dislodge. It's easier to change your mind and start dealing through reps than the other way around.

- Once your company has established a relationship with the business and technical staff of the supplier, make the request to deal more directly. You might be requesting to deal through an IPO (referred to as GPO in this book), or you might be asking to deal directly. This request should go to the supplier's sales management, and specifically to an individual whom you already know.

- Be prepared to give reasons. These might be that you need a lower cost and believe that both parties can benefit by removing intermediaries. Another might be that the representative or subsidiary doesn't add enough value to the transaction to justify the markups it must be charging.

Potential direct global suppliers can be located through a wide variety of sources. The chapter on sourcing presents a detailed section on discovering sources of supply. In the chapter on sourcing, the increasing use of the Internet in identifying sources is discussed. The use of the Internet is particularly advantageous in discovering global sources.

Qualifying Direct Suppliers

Prior to investing additional energy in dealing with a global supplier, two issues should be addressed: *country and regional stability* and the *potential supplier's financial condition.*

---

[18]Locke, "Get the Purchasing Channel You Want," p. U-11.

For approximately $750, Dun & Bradstreet will prepare a Country Analysis Report for its clients, including some 70 pages of in-depth research, information on both the current and historical economy and government, import and export practices, trading partners, and monetary policies.

Most experts recommend a survey of a region as well as the company and country because such factors as political and monetary stability, currency transfer laws, and trade and product liability policies may be crucial to doing business there. According to Heidi Jacobs and Barbara Ettorre,

> The client should also ask what is needed to engage in commerce in a particular country. Credit professionals cite such factors as: required documentation for transactions, the transportation and distribution infrastructure, religious customs, quality standards and existing regulations that may restrict sale of the client's product or service. Will there be overseas agents to facilitate a deal? How reliable and experienced are they? Many a deal has been derailed by such cross-border questions as whether the desired country prohibits sales of products whose *components* originated in a certain country.[19]

The supply manager or buying team is cautioned not to judge the creditworthiness of the potential supplier by the ability of its key personnel to speak fluent English. A careful financial analysis (as discussed in Chapter 15) must be conducted. Jacobs and Ettorre list the following sources of information for such analyses: Dun & Bradstreet, Gradon America, Owens On Line, Justitia International Inc., and Piguet International.[20] International credit specialists representing U.S. firms also caution their clients to familiarize themselves with the Foreign Corrupt Practices Act, which bars United States companies from engaging in bribery and other practices when doing business overseas.[21]

Preparing for Direct Relations

Preparation for direct relations includes all the issues raised in the source selection chapter, as well as intercultural preparation, the hiring of a competent translator, and an exhaustive technical and commercial analysis.

Cultural Preparation Virtually all supply relationships with global suppliers are the result of negotiations. The success of each of these negotiations is influenced, in part, by the negotiator's ability to understand the needs, and ways of thinking and acting, of representatives of global firms. What is considered ethical in one culture may not be ethical in another. The intention of filling commitments, the implications of gift giving, and even the legal systems differ widely.

---

[19]Heidi Jacobs and Barbara Ettorre, "Evaluating Potential Foreign Partners." Cited by permission of publisher. From *Management Review,* October 1993, p. 60. American Management Association, New York. All rights reserved.

[20]Ibid., p. 61. For more information, the following numbers are provided to the reader: Dun & Bradstreet (800-234-3867), Gradon America (800-466-3163), Owens On Line (800-745-4656), Justitia International Inc. (203-589-1698), and Piguet International (203-584-8088). Please refer to the company websites if the numbers are no longer valid.

[21]Ibid., p. 60.

In addition to the conventional preparation for any negotiation, it is essential to conduct an extensive study of the culture(s). It is important to emphasize that this study should focus on the culture, not the language. The ability to understand a supplier's cultural background is of great practical advantage for several reasons. Negotiators perform more effectively if they understand the cultural and business heritage of their counterparts and the effect of this heritage on their counterparts' negotiation strategies and tactics. Also, it puts the supplier off his or her guard. Talk with others who have experienced living or working in the culture. Learn what the holidays are, what the units of measure are, what the currency exchange is, what topics are taboo, and so on.

Another aspect of cultural preparation becomes important in cases in which there is a strong likelihood of continuing relations (i.e., one or more transactions that would require a year or more for completion). Under such circumstances, the supplier's representatives (accompanied by their spouses) frequently visit the domestic firm. The buying firm's hosts should go to considerable lengths to become acquainted with their counterparts (and their spouses) on a social basis. Americans, for example, should entertain the visitors in their homes (a rarity in Europe and the Far East). This will give the Americans and their spouses an opportunity to develop good relations with their counterparts. This bank of goodwill, while not a means of co-opting the foreign supplier, projects a desire and willingness to understand, which frequently proves to be invaluable during subsequent transactions.

One other aspect of cultural preparation needs to be emphasized: It takes much longer to negotiate with foreign suppliers. This is especially true if the supplier has not had extensive exposure to the buying firm's business practices and specifications. The time required varies based on the mode of operation. In the case of European firms, it usually takes at least twice as much time as with U.S. firms, and up to six times as long is often required for Far East firms. As a result, U.S. negotiators must be aware of the requirement for additional time and plan accordingly.

Cultural preparation is specific to the country in which a supply professional is planning to conduct business. As a result, a detailed discussion is beyond the scope of this book. Several excellent resources are provided in the footnote below to aid the reader in his or her efforts.[22]

Interpreters   Language frequently poses a significant barrier to successful global business relations. Bilingual business discussions usually require a third-party interpreter even when both of the principal parties are fluent in one of the two languages. Differences in culture, language, dialects, or terminology may result in miscommunication and cause problems. Both parties may think they know what the other party has said, but true

---

[22]Four sound investments to help prepare for cultural issues are: Dick Locke, *Global Supply Management: A Guide to International Purchasing* (Burr Ridge, IL: Irwin Professional Publishing, 1996).

Fons Trompenaars and Charles Hampden-Turner, *Building Cross Cultural Competence: How to Create Wealth from Conflicting Values* (New York: McGraw-Hill, 2000).

Fons Trompenaars and Charles Hampden-Turner, *Riding the Waves of Culture: Understanding Diversity in Global Business,* 2d ed. (London: McGraw-Hill, 1998).

Edward and Mildred Hall's *Understanding Cultural Differences* (Intercultural Press, 1990).

agreement and understanding often may be missing. Think, for instance, of the confusion the simple word "ton" can create. Is it a short ton (2,000 lb), a long ton (2,240 lb), or a metric ton (2,204.62 lb)? The use of textbook English raises innumerable interesting problems. For example, in the Far East, the word "plant" is interpreted to mean only a living organism, not a physical facility.

When there are language differences between cultural groups, many busy executives believe that a competent interpreter is all that is necessary to overcome these differences. While a good interpreter can speed negotiations, an ineffective interpreter, or one ineptly used, can convert even simple matters into interminable wrangles. Complex discussions may simply grind to a halt amid a haze of miscommunication. The inexperienced supply manager risks wasting inordinate amounts of time for very little gain while acquiring the necessary communication skills. According to Hal Porter, a specialist with interpreters, "One or two words with a double meaning can certainly change the entire content of a statement." Executives experienced in international trade usually have learned these lessons, if only by trial and error. The use of interpreters, while allowing communication to take place, does not obviate the need for an understanding of the supplier's culture. Even when one overcomes the natural barriers of language difference, it is still possible to fail to understand and be understood.[23]

Technical and Commercial Analysis   Technical and commercial analysis is discussed in greater detail in the chapter on source selection in this book. *Before* dealing with identified global candidate suppliers, the supply management team should:

- Prepare and review specifications and drawings.
- Pack samples or photos of required materials if they would help in communicating requirements.
- Clearly prepare the quality requirements.
- Identify specific scheduling requirements.
- Determine (as a group) what percentage of the annual requirements for the item can be placed offshore.
- Determine requirements for special packaging.
- Identify likely lead times.
- Develop a clear idea of the price objective.
- Prepare a briefing on your (the buying) firm. Frequently, much effort will be expended selling the potential suppliers on doing business with the buying firm. The briefing should include:
    Information on the relevant product line and related lines.
    Actual and forecasted sales volume.
    Customers.
    Market share.

---

[23]Hal Porter, "Interpreters: What They'll Do for You," *Across the Board,* October 1993, p. 14.

Unclassified corporate strategy information.

Annual reports.

An indication of why the buying firm is soliciting the potential global supplier's interest (quality? price?).

The Initial Meeting

Adequate preparation as detailed in the previous section will increase the probability of a smooth, efficient, and successful initial meeting. At the initial meeting it is good to conduct a facility tour or visit of the potential supplier's facilities and meet with critical personnel. Plant visits are discussed in detail in the chapter on source selection. For large procurements with complex specifications, the buying firm's technical people clearly must be part of the visiting team. The potential supplier will be judging the buying firm just as much as the buyer will be judging the potential supplying firm. Experience has shown that the controller of the target supplier usually occupies a very influential position. To gain his or her support, the supply manager or buying firm's team should describe how and when the supplier's firm would get paid! Currency and payment issues are discussed in the next section.

Currency and Payment Issues

From the buying firm's point of view, the preferred method of payment is after receipt and inspection of the goods. However, it is customary in many countries for advance payments to be made prior to commencing work. Such a provision ties up the purchaser's capital. Letters of credit also are common in global commerce. Again, the purchaser's funds may be committed for a longer period of time than if a domestic source were involved, and a cost is incurred in obtaining the letter of credit.

Exchange Rates

The absence of fixed exchange rates can be a problem; it creates at least four potential situations, as described below.

Case 1 A contract calls for *payment in a foreign currency.* The exchange rate moves against the U.S. dollar during performance of the contract. For example assume that a contract was awarded to a supplier in Germany for 1 million euros. Assume further that the rate of exchange was U.S. $1.00 = Eu 1.5; that is, one U.S. dollar purchased 1.5 Eu at the time the contract was awarded. Ignoring all other costs, the dollar cost to the U.S. buyer would be

$$\frac{\text{Eu } 1,000,000}{\text{Eu } 1.5/\$} = \$666,666.66$$

Assume that the U.S. dollar weakens to the point that $1.00 buys only Eu 1. The cost in dollars then becomes

$$\frac{\text{Eu } 1,000,000}{\text{Eu } 1.0/\$} = \$1,000,000$$

This is an increase of $333,333.33, or a 50 percent increase in the cost of the item in U.S. dollars. Note that the German supplier is no better off, since it receives only Eu 1 million, while the U.S. purchaser has suffered the 50 percent increase in the cost of the item in *U.S. dollars.*

Case 2 A contract calls for *payment in a foreign currency* (Eu), and the exchange rate improves for the U.S. dollar so that $1 now buys Eu 2. The cost of the item in U.S. dollars now is

$$\frac{\text{Eu } 1,000,000}{\text{Eu } 2/\$} = \$500,000$$

The U.S. buyer has reduced its costs from the initial likely amount of $666,666.66 to $500,000.00, a 25 percent saving.

Case 3 The contract is with a global supplier, *with payment in U.S. dollars,* and the dollar weakens. Assume that when the contract was awarded, the rate of exchange was U.S. $1 = Eu 1.5; the cost of the item was Eu 1 million, or $666,666.66. Were there no change in the rate of exchange, the supplier would convert the $666,666.66 received into Eu 1 million. Unfortunately for the supplier, the dollar has weakened so that $1 will buy only Eu 1. Now, when the supplier receives its $666,666.66 and has this converted to euros, it receives only Eu 666,666.66, a 33 percent reduction from what it expected under the former exchange rate. Quite obviously, the supplier will be very unhappy and may translate this either to nonperformance or to a demand for a price increase.

Case 4 The contract is with a global supplier *with payment in U.S. dollars.* The dollar strengthens. As with case 3, the contract called for a payment of $666,666.66. Assume that the rate of exchange changes so that $1 U.S. purchases Eu 2. When the supplier receives its $666,666.66 and has it converted to euros at the current rate, it will receive 666,666.66 × 2 = Eu 1,333,333.32, a windfall gain of Eu 333,333.33. While the German supplier may be delighted, the U.S. buyer should be less enthusiastic.

The issue of currency risk is examined in greater detail in the Appendix to this chapter.

Payments

Payments to a global supplier are simplified when a trade intermediary or an IPO is involved. When payment is to be made directly by the buying firm to the supplier, a letter of credit frequently is used.

Letters of Credit As part of the negotiations, many global suppliers will request that the buying firm obtain a letter of credit from its bank. A letter of credit is an instrument issued by a bank at the request of a buyer. It promises to pay a specified amount of money upon presentation of documents stipulated in the letter. The letter of credit is not a means of payment, but merely a promise to pay. Actual payment is accomplished through a draft, which is similar to a personal check. It is an order by one party to pay another party. Documents commonly stipulated in the letter of credit include the bill of lading, a consular invoice, and a description of goods. In effect, if the purchaser defaults, then the bank has to foot the bill. Thus, any risk of nonpayment is transferred to the bank. Frequently, the global supplier will use the purchase order (contract) together with the letter of credit as security when obtaining a loan for working capital for the required labor and materials.

Letters of credit are classified three ways:

■ *Irrevocable versus revocable.* An irrevocable letter of credit can be neither canceled nor modified without the consent of the beneficiary.

■ *Confirmed versus unconfirmed.* A bank that confirms the letter of credit assumes the risk. The best method of payment for an exporter in most cases is a confirmed, irrevocable letter of credit. Some banks may not assume the risk, preferring to take an advisory role. Such banks and their correspondents believe that they are better able to judge the credibility of the issuing bank than the exporter.

■ *Revolving versus nonrevolving.* Nonrevolving letters of credit are valid for one transaction only. When relationships are established, a revolving letter of credit may be issued.

Obtaining a letter of credit may take three to five business days. A detailed application must be completed. Since a letter of credit is an extension of credit from the bank, it is processed much as a loan is processed. If no line of credit has been previously established with the bank, the applicant must prepay the specified amount. Typical charges involved include an application fee—0.008 percent on a $125 minimum—plus a negotiation charge—0.0025 percent on a $110 minimum. In case of cancellation, a charge of $100 is common.

Countertrade

The term *countertrade* refers to any transaction in which payment is made partially or fully with goods instead of money. Countertrade links two normally unrelated transactions: the sale of a product into a foreign country and the sale of goods out of that country. Foreign governments normally impose countertrade requirements in an effort to gain foreign exchange or foreign technology.[24] Countertrade has several distinct definitions:

■ **Barter.** This form of transaction preceded the use of money. Goods are exchanged for other goods with no money involved. This is the simplest form of countertrade. If goods are bartered to save on transportation costs, the arrangement is called a swap.

■ **Offset.** Under this form of transaction, some, all, or even more than 100 percent of the value of the sale is *offset* by the purchase (or facilitation of purchases by others) of items produced in the buying country. Offsets are categorized as direct and indirect. A *direct offset* involves close technological ties between the items sold and purchased. For example, when the government of Australia purchased helicopters made by Boe-

---

[24]The interested reader is encouraged to read *Creative Countertrade: A Guide to Doing Business Worldwide* by Kenton W. Elderkin and Warren E. Norquist (Cambridge, MA: Ballinger, 1987); and the more recent study by Laura Forker, "Countertrade: Purchasing's Perceptions and Involvement," Center for Advanced Purchasing Studies/National Association of Purchasing Management, Inc., Tempe, AZ 1991. Single copies are available gratis by written request to the Center for Advanced Purchasing Studies, P.O. Box 22160, Tempe, AZ 85285-2160.

ing, Boeing agreed to buy ailerons for the 727 from an Australian supplier. An *indirect offset* involves the purchase or facilitation of sales of commodities unrelated to the purchasing country. When the Swiss purchased F-5 aircraft, the manufacturer (Northrop) facilitated sales of Swiss elevators and other nonaircraft products in North America.

■ **Counterpurchase.** With this type of transaction, unrelated goods are exchanged. The U.S. manufacturer purchases goods in the foreign country from a supplier who is paid in local currency by the buyer of the manufacturer's goods. Counterpurchase normally involves two separate, but linked, contracts: one for purchase and one for counterpurchase.

■ **Buy-back/compensation.** Buy-back (or compensation) is an agreement by the seller of turnkey plants, machinery, or other capital equipment to accept as partial or full payment products produced in the plants and/or on the capital equipment.

Laura Forker, in her 1991 report on countertrade, identifies the following advantages and disadvantages:

Countertrade's Advantages Companies involved in countertrade frequently have enjoyed a variety of marketing, financial, and manufacturing advantages that have resulted in increased sales, increased employment, and enhanced company competitiveness. By accepting goods or services as payment instead of cash, countertrade participants have been effective in (1) avoiding exchange controls; (2) selling to countries with inconvertible currencies; (3) marketing products in less-developed, cash-strapped countries (with centrally planned economies) that could not make such purchases otherwise; and (4) reducing some of the risks associated with unstable currency values. In overcoming these financial obstacles, countertrading firms have been able to enter new or formerly closed markets, expand business contacts and sales volume, and dampen the impact of foreign protectionism on overseas business.

Countertrade has also engendered goodwill with foreign governments concerned about their trade balances and hard currency accounts. Finally, Western participants in countertrade have enjoyed fuller use of plant capacity, larger production runs, and reduced per-unit expenses because of the greater sales volume. Their expanded sales contacts abroad have sometimes led to new sources of attractive components and, at other times, to valuable outlets for the disposal of declining products. Countertrade has opened up many new opportunities for American firms willing to become involved in it.

Countertrade's Disadvantages Experienced companies have encountered a number of problems unique to or exacerbated by countertrade. Countertrade negotiations tend to be lengthier and more complex than conventional sales negotiations and, at times, must be conducted with powerful government supply agencies that enjoy negotiating strength. Additional expenses in the form of brokerage fees, additional transaction costs, higher supply management involvement, and transactions in goods problems reduce the profitability of countertrade deals. For example, countertrade contracts that use goods as payback often result in difficulties with the quality, availability, and disposal of the goods. Countertrade also introduces pricing problems associated with the assignment of values to products and/or commodities received in exchange. Commodity prices can vary widely over the lengthy negotiation and delivery periods, and trading partners may differ as to the worth of particular products. All of these drawbacks result in higher risk and greater uncertainty about the profitability of a countertrade deal.

Offsets entail further concerns in the form of technology transfer requirements, local procurement conditions that favor local suppliers, and rigidities that offsets introduce into the buying process. The result for Western firms is often increased competition. Offset customers can become competitors later on. And some offset requirements divert a Western firm's resources to less-than-optimal suppliers. These additional costs must be considered when a proposed deal is being evaluated.[25]

Supply Management's Role

Historically, the firm's marketing people who are intent on making a sale have coerced reluctant supply managers to engage in a countertrade transaction. One of the authors was involved in such transactions during the 1970s. Little thought was given to the domestic seller's countertrade obligations until the purchasing government brought economic and political pressure to bear. At this point, the domestic firm's supply managers frantically began to see what could be purchased in the foreign country. As a result, a very uncomfortable relationship developed between the customer country and the seller.

Both marketing and supply managers must recognize that they need to work as a team if countertrade is to operate to the firm's benefit. When countertrade is used to facilitate sales, supply management should be involved *up front*. Supply managers should review the items their company requires. Similar requirements must be levied on the firm's suppliers so that they are in a position to assist the manufacturer in meeting its present or potential obligations.

Creative Countertrade

Elderkin and Norquist define traditional countertrade as focusing "on existing goods to be brought out of the host country and sold in existing world markets. Traditional countertrade must deal with the limitations of fitting what already exists into unresponsive markets."

"Creative countertrade," on the other hand, with its focus on creating future goods for *new market niches,* has greater flexibility and wider possibilities. Creative countertrade is broader than traditional countertrade. It includes not only traditional countertrade, but also international investment and joint venture activities. It carefully analyzes the needs of all the major parties, including the potential development of new global suppliers, and creatively applies existing business tools to answer these needs.

Traditional countertrade provides quick-fix solutions to ongoing trade problems. But it lacks the depth and longer time horizons of creative countertrade. It seems likely that progressive firms will embrace creative countertrade as a means of both increasing sales and developing new dependable sources of supply.[26]

---

[25]Forker, "Countertrade," pp. 11–12.

[26]Elderkin and Norquist, *Creative Countertrade,* pp. 122–123.

Political and Economic Alliances

Global political and economic changes are constant issues for supply managers to identify and address. Countries in various regions of the world have restructured trade laws and developed compromise based agreements in efforts to stabilize trade, open markets, and create a body for addressing trade issues. These new laws and agreements have had and will continue to have an impact on global supply management. Among the more prominent economic alliances are The European Union (EU), North American Free Trade Agreement (NAFTA), MERCOSUR, South American Free Trade Area (SAFTA), Association of Southeast Asian Nations (ASEAN), and Asia Pacific Economic Cooperation (APEC).[27] Most of the discussion in this section is on the European Union since it is the most recent economic alliance.

European Union[28]

The European Union is based on a treaty that calls for "common foreign, security and, eventually, defense policies, and a common central bank and single currency."[29] The inspiration for the EU is thought by many to have come from the example of the United States. Others argue that the EU had its roots in the 1958 Treaty of Rome, and was first envisioned as a "Common Market of Western Europe." Regardless of how the EU has come into being, the impact of the EU is profound on the field of supply management, creating opportunities as well as new challenges. William L. Richardson, former director of Commercial Services for British Steel, Inc., in London, made the following comments in 1993 that still hold true today:

> For the American purchaser, the European Single Market offers considerable opportunities and it makes purchasing easier. . . . First, it will strengthen or create new effective alternatives to existing large manufacturers, be they in the U.S.A., Japan, or elsewhere. Second, it makes purchasing easier by virtue of the creation of European standards where as many as 12 different national standards can exist. This is a huge aid to the cost of reducing and simplifying the quality and performance comparisons purchasers have to make when evaluating the advantages of different supply sources.
>
> If the U.S.A. fears the European Single Market, it is a misplaced fear. In a sense Europe has looked at the U.S.A., seen how America has created a giant manufacturing base and said to itself, what is it that prevents us Europeans from achieving similar growth and prosperity? The European answer is, first, to tear down its own internal barriers and then to open up its market to world trade fairly conducted within international law.[30]

---

[27]Current maps of the countries included in the alliances listed above are readily available at a variety of websites, such as cnn.com as of August 2001. We have chosen to not include maps because of frequent changes in the alliance countries.

[28]The European Community, now called the European Union, consists of the following countries (as of November 2001): Austria, Belgium, Britain, Denmark, Finland, France, Germany, Greece, Holland, Ireland, Italy, Luxembourg, Norway, Portugal, Spain, and Sweden.

[29]Sally Jacobsen, "Europe Finally to Be United, but Federation Is a Loose One," *The Arizona Republic,* October 13, 1993, p. A10.

[30]Quoted in Richard L. Pinkerton, "Voices from Europe," *NAPM Insights,* July 1993, p. 27.

Richard L. Pinkerton, in the conclusion to his article reporting on the history and evolution of the European Community (EC) and the implications for purchasing managers, writes:

> Supply managers should be prepared to join their firm's EC strategy/tactics team. Each supply management professional must investigate the specific EC technical directives and the implications of the ISO 9000 standards as they apply to his or her firm. Subsequently, the development of implementation plans should be undertaken as an integral part of the firm's overall EC strategy and plan.
>
> In many respects, the standardization directives and programs of EC 92 will facilitate trade with Europe by reducing a number of different codes into a single code. Not only does this "harmonization" reduce the need for 12 different sets of paperwork, including border documents, and for a variety of rules and regulations, it should also reduce the costs of products bought and sold. Additionally, a more efficient and uniform European transportation system is expected to develop. Although some product variation will always be present as a result of differing styles, tastes, languages, and other cultural nuances among the member nations, it is very clear that Europe is moving toward essentially the same type of free market that currently exists in the United States. Sourcing should be accomplished more quickly, with fewer suppliers, as customers in all 12 countries utilize a common set of standards and procedures, coupled with the growth of mass distribution centers.[31]

The words of Richardson and Pinkerton have not yet been proven wrong, but the advancement of the EU's objectives has been slow.

The Euro   The European Monetary Unit (EMU) called the Euro was launched on January 4, 1999, with eleven EU member countries voting. Initially, it was an electronic currency, which could be bought and sold on markets in which consumers could establish bank accounts and credit cards. In January 2001, the Euro (in cash and coin form) began circulating alongside national currencies for up to two months until national notes and coins were withdrawn.

Economically, the Euro is meant to complete the European single market, bolstering cross-border mergers, improving price transparency, and eliminating exchange-rate risk. Enthusiasts also hope it will be a rival to the hegemony of the U.S. dollar. But as of late 2001, the fledgling currency had lost a quarter of its value since its introduction, largely because of gloom about Europe's economic performance.

The Euro has both a political and an economic rationale, but several key European countries do not support it. Denmark rejected the Euro in a referendum, and Sweden has stayed out because of a similar cool reception at home. As of late 2001, Britain's Labour government was undecided about adoption of the Euro, saying it is waiting for five economic criteria to be met before calling a referendum. As of late 2001, there was notable widespread public opposition to the use of the Euro in Britain.

What possible consequences could the Euro and its adoption pose for supply management professionals in non-EU states? Scholar Richard L. Pinkerton studied the po-

---

[31]Richard L. Pinkerton, "The European Community—'EC 92': Implications for Purchasing Managers," *International Journal of Purchasing and Materials Management,* Spring 1993, p. 25.

tential risks as well as advantages for U.S. supply managers.[32] The potential advantages of the Euro for U.S. supply management personnel were given by Pinkerton as follows:

■ *Greatly reduced transaction costs.* The U.S. firm is now dealing with one exchange rate versus 12. This is especially significant when U.S. firms in the 12 EMU countries buy from one another, either on an intra- or extra-firm basis.

■ *Increased competition (the level playing field concept).* This should produce lower prices as firms are forced to be more productive as a result of price transparency.

■ *Reduced exchange rate risk.* U.S. firms will only have to hedge against one versus 12 countries. This also reduces transaction costs as noted previously.

■ *Increased trade and capital movement.* The Euro dollar will create a greatly increased capital bond and stock market and reduce the historical EU reliance on government and bank loans. Price stability and lower interest rates with controlled inflation should stimulate capital investment and, as a result, a sustainable economic growth rate in the 12 countries. Increasing unemployment within the EU, especially France and Germany, is a major concern.

The potential disadvantages of the Euro for U.S. supply management personnel were given as follows:

■ *The Euro could fail.* Many experts have suggested that the ECB will not be able to manage the Euro as the U.S. Federal Reserve System manages the U.S. dollar. Can the European Community Bank (ECB) effectively manage one interest rate for 12 different economies? If the national governments or people panic and pull out of the EMU, there would at least be short-term economic chaos, somewhat like the Exchange Rate Mechanism (ERM) crisis of 1992 when Britain was forced out of the ERM by currency speculators.[33]

■ *Transition period is awkward and complicated.* The transition period is supposed to end in 2002. This is a major problem for smaller firms, in particular the retail outlets in the 12 countries as they must maintain dual pricing and cash registers for a rather long period of time.

■ *"Wait and see" United Kingdom effect.* Can the United Kingdom continue to stay out of the EMU? The answer is "no," and the huge, leading financial capital of the world,

---

[32]Richard L. Pinkerton, "Implications of the Euro Dollar for U.S. Supply Management Personnel," presented at the NAPM Global Supply Management Conference, November 8–9, 1999, Phoenix, AZ, and at the Proceedings of the World Congress of the International Federation of Purchasing and Materials Management (IFPMM), London, July 1999. Note: An update was inserted in this list to reflect the addition of a twelfth member to the EU.

[33]In the 1990s, ERM attempted to bring national currencies into line based on a basket weight of all 15 EU members against an "ECU," a pre-1999 designation of the single currency. The British pound was simply pegged too high against the benchmark Deutschemark at 2.95. The erosion of national monetary sovereignty and loss of exchange rates as an adjustment mechanism for the national economy are major reasons why the United Kingdom and the other two qualifiers have not joined the EMU. In addition, conversion costs are very high—but are incurred only once, while transaction costs are saved year after year.

London, is pushing for entry as are the big U.K. multinationals. Temporary nonparticipation by the U.K. has so far not been a problem for the Euro. First, the London financial market is already dealing with the Euro, and while the public polls in the U.K. indicate 70–80 percent against joining, Prime Minister Tony Blair and the Labour party are launching a major campaign to gain popular acceptance prior to the next U.K. election, before 2002. If one wants to influence the rules of any organization, one must be a member first. The alternative is to see Germany quickly become the EU financial leader, and Frankfurt may indeed be in first place within one to two years.

■ *Skeptics predict an unstable Euro.* There are some experts who feel cyclical unemployment coupled with creeping inflation rates and infighting within the ECB over economic policies will eventually lead to conflict and an unstable Euro. Other experts state the lack of homogeneity among the 12 in terms of price and wage flexibility, labor mobility, and ease of fiscal transfers all make the Euro risky. Both the United Kingdom and the United States (and many EU experts) are very worried over the German-French policy conflict, with Germany stressing low inflation and France focusing on low unemployment that has translated to excessive government debt and high inflation results that Germany cannot tolerate.

North American Free Trade Agreement

In June 1990, the presidents of the United States and Mexico endorsed the idea of a comprehensive U.S.-Mexico Free Trade Agreement in order to guarantee that the positive effects of export growth and industrial competitiveness, which had already begun, would continue to expand. By 1991, Canada joined the talks, leading to the three-way negotiation known as the North American Free Trade Agreement, or NAFTA. This agreement was designed to create a Free Trade Area (FTA) comprising the United States, Canada, and Mexico. Consistent with World Trade Organizations (WTO) rules, all tariffs will be eliminated within the FTA over a transition period. NAFTA involves an ambitious effort to eliminate barriers to agricultural, manufacturing, and service trade; to remove investment restrictions; and to protect intellectual property rights effectively. In addition, NAFTA marks the first time in the history of U.S. trade policy that environmental concerns have been directly addressed in a comprehensive trade agreement. By accelerating the integration of the three markets, NAFTA should enable North American businesses to produce goods that are more competitive compared with goods produced in Asia and in the European Union and will allow North American consumers to benefit from a greater selection of higher-quality, lower-priced goods.[34]

Implications of NAFTA   Canada and the United States have long been sources of supply to each other. Modern-day Mexico has pockets of expertise that are world-class. Many U.S. buyers already avail themselves of Mexican sources of supply.

When a global analysis of potential suppliers reveals that it makes sense to develop a world-class supplier in Mexico, a joint venture with carefully developed plans, objectives, action plans, and milestones is the appropriate way of developing the supplier. (Obviously,

---

[34]*NAFTA, the Beginning of a New Era,* Business America (partial extract), August 24, 1992, National Trade Data Bank, March 27, 1994.

these principles apply to the development of suppliers in many parts of the world.) This approach brings together the social, political, and economic strengths of the supplier with the knowledge, technology, systems, and commercial expertise of the global buyer.

Mercosur

The Mercosur was formed in 1991 as a common market consisting of Argentina, Brazil, Paraguay, and Uruguay. The ambitious goal of the Mercosur is to create a free trade zone in Latin American countries. In 1995, Chile and Bolivia became associate members. Following the trend set by the European Union, Mercosur's role is not restricted to trade. It has also a mandate to facilitate the co-operation in many cultural and political aspects. Another role of Mercosur is to help member countries to overcome their internal problems such as those linked with public administration and the control of inflation.[35]

Association of Southeast Asian Nations

The Association of Southeast Asian Nations (ASEAN) was formed in 1967 by Indonesia, Malaysia, the Philippines, Singapore, and Thailand to promote political and economic cooperation and regional stability. The ASEAN Declaration, signed in 1976 by ASEAN leaders in Bali and considered ASEAN's foundation document, formalized the principles of peace and cooperation to which ASEAN is dedicated. Brunei joined in 1984, shortly after its independence from the United Kingdom. In the 1990s, Vietnam, Laos, Burma, and Cambodia became members of ASEAN as well.

Also in 1976, ASEAN heads of state signed the Treaty of Amity and Cooperation in Southeast Asia (TAC). The stated goal of the treaty is to foster a peaceful, cohesive region and to promote regional economic cooperation. In July 1998, ASEAN Foreign Ministers signed the Second Protocol to the TAC, which permits accession by non–Southeast Asian countries. ASEAN then invited, and has since been urging, the Dialogue Partners to accede to the treaty.

ASEAN has established ten "Dialogue Partner" relationships with other countries. The two sides meet at a Post-Ministerial Conference (PMC), which follows the annual ASEAN Ministerial Meeting (AMM). In 1994, ASEAN established the ASEAN Regional Forum, which focuses on regional security issues. This left the PMC to deal with international economic and political issues and transnational issues.

Asia Pacific Economic Cooperation

Asia-Pacific Economic Cooperation (APEC) was established in 1989 in response to the growing interdependence among Asia-Pacific economies.

Begun as an informal dialogue group, APEC has since become the primary regional vehicle for promoting open trade and practical economic cooperation. Its members define the geographic littoral of the Asia-Pacific Basin. Its goal is to advance Asia-Pacific economic dynamism and sense of community. APEC's 21 member economies had a

[35]Joaquina Pires-O'Brien, *Latin American Integration and the Formation of the Mercosur,* The Contemporary Review Company Limited, Oxford, England, June, 2000.

combined Gross Domestic Product of over US$18 trillion in 1999 and 43.85 percent of global trade.[36] This makes APEC the world's largest free trade area. Of the many issues before APEC's membership is a focus on streamlining intergovernmental procurement policies. "APEC members are now working individually and collectively (through the Government Procurement Experts Group, established in 1995 to manage APEC's work in this area) to fulfill these and other commitments articulated in the OAA. Indeed, this initiative, which aims to enhance the transparency of members' existing government procurement systems, is one of the agreed collective actions included in the OAA meant to serve the above objectives. Another is the development, completed in 1999, of a set of nonbinding principles (NBPs) on government procurement (comprising transparency; value for money, open and effective competition; fair dealing; accountability and due process; and nondiscrimination)."[37]

Concluding Remarks

A firm's approach to global supply management normally progresses from a reactive mode to a proactive one. Under reactive global sourcing, the firm reacts to opportunities in the supply marketplace. If an internationally produced good or service is the most attractive buy, then it is purchased. As the firm embraces a proactive approach to procurement and on to World Class Supply Management[SM], it develops supply strategies and supply plans for its requirements. The development of these strategies and plans calls for the analysis of all possible sources of supply, both domestic and international.

Perhaps it is the level of difficulty and the degree to which global perspectives may conflict with one another that has warned off in-depth studies of global supply management. The shift from a tactical to a strategic business focus is no less profound than the shift in perception implicit in the terms "purchasing" or "procurement" when contrasted with *supply management*. Nonetheless, it is this very complexity that requires our serious attention as we attempt to prosecute global supply management strategies successfully.

Far from merely an "inorganic" study of the various "tools" involved in the practice of global purchasing, we must seriously examine the professional competencies required in order to be effective in the global supply management environment. Supply management professionals must have the ability to (1) develop a strategic point of view with regard to global supply management; (2) deal with change and chaotic, shifting environments effectively; (3) deal with diverse cultures effectively; (4) work with and within distributed organizational structures; (5) work with others in teams and act as team leader/project manager; and (6) learn to communicate effectively with others who may hold cultural beliefs or values and exhibit behavior different from their own.

Recalling Socrates' entreaty that we are all "citizens of the world," the time has come to actively improve our understanding of world events as influenced by powerful political, economic, social, and cultural influences. Not only will we become better supply management professionals, but better human beings as well.

---

[36]APEC homepage, August 31, 2001.

[37]"Government Procurement in APEC," APEC website, August 31, 2001.

Appendix: Currency Risk

Locke and Anklesaria write:

> U.S. purchasing departments are at a disadvantage compared to their more sophisticated counterparts . . . in countries [which] deal in foreign currencies as a matter of course. . . . U.S. buyers' unfamiliarity in dealing in foreign currencies leads to higher costs in two ways. First, they attempt to put all currency risk on the supplier, which causes the supplier to include charges for hedging, or to add an extra margin for contingencies into the price. Second, in an attempt to avoid dealing in foreign currencies, buyers use suppliers' U.S. subsidiaries and representatives, who will accept payment in dollars, but who also charge high markups. . . .
>
> Buyers and finance staffs of firms should understand when to buy in foreign currencies and when to buy in U.S. dollars. They should know the measures to take to avoid major increases in dollar cost and to be flexible enough to get decreases when possible. They should understand methods of reducing short-term risk through hedging. They should have analytical tools available to help them choose between various hedging strategies.[38]

The biggest advantage comes from the choice of the best pricing currency (the currency in which prices are set). The payment currency (you may actually pay an equivalent amount of a different currency) does not make a big difference in prices. To choose a pricing currency, you must answer two questions.

First, what are you buying? Product prices can be divided into cost-driven and market-driven categories. Cost-driven prices are those for items for which the supplier can set prices based on his or her costs. Market driven prices are set on a world market, usually in U.S. dollars, and the supplier cannot sell at a higher price. Second, where is the product built? Some countries have currencies that are pegged to the U.S. dollar. Other currencies float freely. If a currency is truly pegged to the dollar, there should be no need for currency protection. Table 16.1 shows the possibilities.

Floating currency, cost-driven product. These products are typically custom or semicustom products. An example would be a printed circuit assembly from Japan or Europe. By pricing in the supplier's currency, the supplier is relieved of the currency risk. This should enable a buyer to negotiate a lower initial price than if the supplier were to take on the risk. It is better to start with the lower price, because one doesn't know if the dollar will strengthen or weaken. The buying firm can protect itself against dollar cost increases by low cost hedging.

Floating currency, market-driven product. These products are typically commodities whose price is nearly the same anywhere in the world. Examples are gold, oil, and DRAMs. For this type of product, a buyer should not hedge. The buying firm is better off negotiating one worldwide price and maintaining the price the same around the world. This works best if the firm has a purchasing presence in various regions, so that hedging does not work as it does with cost-driven parts. If the dollar strengthens, the price in another currency goes up.

---

[38]Richard Locke, Jr., and Jimmy Anklesaria, "Selection of Currency and Hedging Strategy in Global Supply Management," *Proceedings,* International Conference of Purchasing and Materials Management, Atlanta, GA, May 1994, pp. 294–99.

Table 16.1 | Best Buying Currency

	Type of Currency	
Pricing Driver	**Pegged Currency**	**Floating Currency**
Cost-based products	Dollars or supplier's currency	Supplier's product
Dollar market-based product	Dollars	Dollars

Pegged currency, cost-driven product. Countries with pegged currencies are generally smaller ones. They include Taiwan, Thailand, Hong Kong, and Korea. There is little need to hedge these currencies, because they are unlikely to move against the dollar. In addition, the foreign exchange market is thin and not well developed. Instead of hedging, a buyer should have an escape clause in the contract, because these currencies do make occasional controlled changes in value against the dollar.

Pegged currency, market-driven product. If the market is dollar based, these products need not be hedged. Similar techniques to those used for market-driven products from floating currency countries are the best choice.

Hedging

Hedging protects the dollar value of a future foreign currency cash flow. The reason to hedge is to protect against major swings in the value of a purchase. A buyer can achieve this via forward or futures contracts or via currency options. The buyer would enter into contracts to sell dollars for foreign currency at the time the supplier is paid. It's easiest to think in terms of using the foreign currency that was purchased in the hedge to pay the supplier, but this is not what happens. There is a profit or loss on a hedge contract that takes place behind the scenes. This profit or loss is applied to a material price variance that results from exchange rate changes and offsets higher or lower part costs.

Forward contracts give a fixed cost for foreign currency and therefore for foreign currency purchasing. If the interest rates in the foreign country are higher than they are in the United States, the forward rate is at a discount to the spot rate, and this reduces the dollar cost still more.

Forward contracts also have the advantage of being suitable for internal transactions. If the buying company exports to the country it is buying in, and wants to sell in local currency, purchasing in local currency reduces the company's currency exposure. The purchasing flow of funds offsets the sales office flow of funds. If an internal forward agreement is made between the two departments, only the difference between the two flows needs to be hedged at banks.

Options allow a buyer to take advantage of an increase in the value of the U.S. dollar but protect against a decrease. Unfortunately, they are expensive. A six-month option on a volatile currency typically costs about 5 percent and most people choose not to buy them. An added difficulty is that option prices for the European-style options that buyers need are not well listed in financial newspapers.

Risk of buying in dollars. Buying in dollars is not as safe a solution to global buying as many are led to believe. A dollar buyer may start off with a higher price than necessary. If the dollar weakens, the buyer is paying even more. A more sophisticated competitor would be paying less. A supplier's competitors will soon let buyers know that they are paying too much. Other channels of distribution could also open up. Finally, supplier promises of fixed dollar pricing are often broken when the value of the dollar declines.

Length of hedging. Hedging for too long a period with forward contracts can lead to the same problems as buying in dollars. If the dollar increases in value, a buyer will be paying too much. Hedging for too long with options is expensive, because the option premium increases with time. Three months of orders plus three month lead time gives six months hedging, a typical period.

Risks in hedging. Hedging does involve some risks, but they are limited and can be controlled with simple attention to the fundamentals. Risk arises from forecast inaccuracy, and can lead to unexpected price variations, either up or down. If a company overforecasts purchases and hedges with forwards, there will be larger profit or loss on the hedge than the variance on part cost. With overforecasts, there will be a loss on forward contracts if the dollar strengthens and a gain if the dollar weakens. The total unexpected gain or loss will be approximately the percent overforecasted times the percent that the dollar changed. For example, a 20 percent overforecast and a 15 percent currency strengthening will result in a 3 percent (15 percent of 20 percent) extra cost of the parts.

With underforecasts, some of the parts must be purchased at the spot rate without an offsetting hedge. If the dollar weakens, they will be more expensive and if it strengthens, they will be cheaper.

Choosing a hedging strategy. The biggest gains in currency management will come from choosing the right currency. A good negotiator should be able to get an initial price reduction of 5 percent or more against a volatile currency like the yen or the mark. The next most consequential decision is whether or not to hedge. Not hedging opens the buyer to dollar price swings that are often as much as 20 percent in six months. This uncertainty is unacceptable to most companies.

The third decision is to choose a hedging strategy![39]

In a recent article, Joseph Carter and his coauthors demonstrate the benefits of choosing a hedging strategy based on a Bayesian statistical analysis of probable outcomes. In this study, Carter shows that choosing a hedge strategy would have saved 3.6 percent compared with paying in the supplier's currency.[40]

---

[39]Ibid.

[40]Joseph R. Carter, Shawnee Vickery, and Michael P. D'Itri, "Currency Risk Management Strategies for Contracting with Japanese Suppliers," *International Journal of Purchasing and Materials Management,* Summer 1993, pp. 19–25.

PART 5

Strategic Cost Management

International Currency (*Ken Reid/FPG/Getty Images*)

To achieve World Class Supply Management^{SM}, supply professionals must become enablers at revealing synergistic opportunities while still balancing customer desires against cost.

Obtaining the *right* price is one of supply management's most important responsibilities. As described in Chapters 17 and 18, the supply professional has a wonderful and evolving arsenal of tools to help satisfy this role.

As addressed in Chapter 19, the traditional tools of price and cost analysis have been augmented with sophisticated ways of dealing with cost and technology uncertainty. Some of these compensation methods, together with the award fee, help to align buyer/supplier objectives.

Negotiation techniques, discussed in Chapter 20, have evolved to a set of principles and practices which help buyers and suppliers plan for and address all issues of the forthcoming relationship, ensure an understanding of all issues, and arrive at an agreement in which both parties reap synergistic opportunities and rewards — a truly win-win outcome. ∎

CHAPTER 17

Pricing[1]

World Class Supply Management^{SM} requires that supply managers analyze acquisition costs from multiple perspectives, including the conditions of competition, the seller's measurement system, discounts, regulations, legal implications, and perhaps most important, what is "fair and reasonable" to all parties involved in the pending transactions.

KEY CONCEPTS

---

[1]Appreciation is expressed to Ray Hummell of the University of San Diego for his assistance in updating this Chapter.

Case

A Problem of Price

Sue Jones sat at her desk reflecting on a pricing problem. Sue was a graduate of State University, where she had majored in materials management. Since joining the small manufacturing firm of Prestige Plastics in Des Moines, she had been promoted from assistant buyer to buyer. She was responsible for purchasing the chemicals used in producing the firm's plastic products.

Sue was really perplexed by a particular procurement involving the purchase of X-pane, a chemical that was formulated specifically for Prestige Plastics. Thirty-one days ago, she had forwarded a request for bids to six suppliers for Prestige's estimated annual requirement of 10,000 drums of X-pane. Yesterday morning, Sue had opened the five bids that had been received. The bids, F.O.B. Des Moines, were as follows:

	Price per Drum ($)	Total Price ($) (For Estimated Annual Requirement of 10,000 Drums)
Greater Sandusky Chemical	$312	$3,120,000
Chicago Chemical Co.	297	2,970,000
Tri-Cities Chemical	323	3,230,000
St. Louis Industries	332	3,320,000
St. Paul Plastics	340	3,400,000

The Chicago Chemical Company was low bidder for the fifth straight year. On the face of it, a decision to award the annual requirements contract to Chicago Chemical looked obvious. The day after the bid opening, the sales engineer from Greater Sandusky Chemical threw Sue a ringer. He said that no one would ever be able to beat Chicago Chemical's price. His firm estimated that setup costs associated with producing X-pane would be approximately $750,000. He went on to say that due to the uncertainties of follow-on orders, his firm would have to amortize this cost over the one-year period of the contract to preclude a loss.

Sue checked with the other unsuccessful bidders. They said substantially the same thing: $700,000 to $850,000 in setup costs were included in their prices.

Next, Sue looked at the history of past purchases of X-pane. She saw that on the initial procurement five years ago, Chicago Chemical's bid was $202 per barrel, $3 lower than the second lowest price. Since that time, bid prices had increased, reflecting cost growth in the materials required to produce X-pane. Each year, Chicago Chemical's prices were $3 to $15 per drum lower than those of the unsuccessful competitors.

Knowing that the Chicago Chemical Company should have the lowest cost, Sue decided to negotiate a more favorable price with the firm. Now she was puzzling over how to determine her objective target price.

Introduction

Obtaining materials at the right price can mean the difference between a firm's success or failure. Price, also referred to as acquisition cost, is frequently the largest component of total cost. Professional supply managers interpret the right price to mean a price that is fair and reasonable to both the buyer and the seller. Unfortunately, there is no magic formula for precisely calculating what constitutes a "fair and reasonable price." The right price for one supplier is not necessarily the right price for another supplier, either at the same time or at different points in time. To determine the right price for any specific purchase, a number of constantly changing variables and relationships must be evaluated. This chapter discusses the most important of these variables and their relationships.

General Economic Considerations

Conditions of Competition

Economists of the classical school speak of a competitive scale that includes three fundamental types of competition: pure, imperfect, and monopoly. At one end of the scale is *pure (or perfect) competition*. Under conditions of pure competition, the forces of supply and demand alone, not the individual actions of either buyers or sellers, determine prices. In this environment, producers are price takers—they have no control over the price they receive for their products.[2]

At the other end of the competitive scale is a monopoly. Under conditions of a *monopoly*, one seller controls the entire supply of a particular commodity, and thus is free to maximize its profit by regulating output and forcing a supply-demand relationship that is most favorable to the seller. In this environment, producers are price makers and exert varying degrees of control over the price they receive for their products

The competitive area between the extremes of pure competition and monopoly is called *imperfect competition*. Imperfect competition takes two forms: (1) markets characterized by few sellers and (2) those in which many sellers operate. When there are just a few sellers, an *oligopoly* is said to exist. The automobile, steel, and tobacco industries are examples of oligopolies. Generally, oligopolistic firms produce relatively few different products.

---

[2] Pure competition exists only under the following circumstances: The market contains a large number of buyers and sellers of approximately equal market power. The products traded are homogeneous (a buyer would not desire one particular seller's product over any other's). The buyers and sellers always have full knowledge of the market. The buyers always act rationally, and sellers are free to enter and to leave the market at will.

Figure 17.1 | Categories of Competition

In contrast to oligopolies, the second form of imperfect competition exists where many sellers produce many products. This form of competition is referred to as *monopolistic competition*. Most of the products sold in this market are *differentiated* (distinguished by a specific difference), although some are not. Sellers, however, spend large sums on major promotional efforts to persuade buyers that their products are different. The majority of the products made in the United States are traded in this market. These economic principles are portrayed in Figure 17.1.

In practice, the three categories of competition are not mutually exclusive; that is, they can overlap. When one considers both the buying and the selling sides of the total market, it is apparent that the number of market arrangements between individual buyers and sellers is very large.

It is frequently suggested that oligopolists conspire and act together as monopolists to thwart price competition. In fact, the U.S. Department of Justice does uncover a few conspiracies every year. The facts, however, indicate that price conspiracies among oligopolists are not the normal order of business. Any supply manager who has purchased in oligopolistic markets knows that both price and service competition can be intense. Chevrolet strives intensely to outsell Ford, and vice versa. This is not to say that oligopolistic industries do not periodically exercise monopolistic tendencies to their own advantage. They do. For example, in times of recession, it requires only a basic knowledge of economics, not a conspiracy, for oligopolies to lower production rates and thus direct a balance of the forces of supply and demand in their favor.

It should be noted that oligopolistic industries frequently hold firmly to their prices for long periods and appear noncompetitive. This appearance may be deceptive, however. Frequently, in order to gain a competitive advantage, without notice oligopolists shift their competitive efforts to other areas, such as service. Sellers may agree to perform such additional services as carrying customers' inventories, extending the payment time of their bills, or absorbing their freight charges. Such indirect price reductions often are not advertised.

Consequently, the amount of service a firm is able to obtain usually correlates directly with the perception and skills of its purchasing personnel. Foreign competitors also greatly influence the freedom of U.S. oligopolies to raise their prices above fair market prices. For example, the freedom of U.S. automobile, steel, and electronic companies to raise prices is noticeably restrained because of foreign imports. For a number of items, specialty suppliers also compete effectively with oligopolies. Consequently, the competent supply manager who learns to operate successfully within the practices of oligopolistic industries can definitely influence the firm's total cost of materials.

It is important to understand that oligopoly is not characteristic of industry as a whole. Most firms and industries operate somewhere in the area of imperfect competition. Millions of people, working in thousands of factories, produce hundreds of thousands of products substantially without governmental or any other outside direction. The firms that make up this market exercise almost complete control over their prices, and price conspiracies in this market are extremely rare. In fact, aside from utilities, transportation, and some manufacturing industries, the concentration of oligopolistic power is rare.

Most Prices Are Subject to Adjustment It is because most firms are free, within broad limits, to adjust their prices at will that competent buyers can obtain better prices in direct proportion to their ability to analyze costs, markets, and pricing methodologies. Prices can be negotiated very little with firms in the markets of pure competition or monopoly. They can be negotiated a great deal with firms operating in the markets of imperfect competition. The question then is: What proportion of the nation's total market falls within the area of imperfect competition? What percentage of a buyer's total purchases are subject to price flexibility?

Studies made at the Graduate School of Business at Stanford University show the nation's economy to be approximately 70 percent free and to exist in the area of imperfect competition. The results of similar studies by other authorities support this conclusion. Supply managers in most purchasing situations, therefore, have considerable latitude for negotiating both price and service with their suppliers. At the same time, however, every supply manager should guard against the inducement of illegal price concessions. Supply personnel must understand the operation of federal and state restraint of trade laws. (Please refer to Chapter 24 for this.)

Variable-Margin Pricing

Most industrial firms sell a line of products rather than just a single product. Very few firms attempt to earn the same profit margin on each product in the line. Most firms price their products to generate a satisfactory return on their whole line, not on each product in the line. Such a variable-margin pricing policy permits maximum competition on individual products. The profits from the most efficiently produced and "successfully priced" items are often used to offset the losses or the lower profit margins of the inefficiently produced items.

Recently, during a research project at a printed circuit manufacturer, one of the authors traced overhead for 188,000 boards consisting of about 4,000 designs. The overhead generated by the production was applied by the company to the boards on an equal basis; however, about 20 percent of the boards drove 80 percent of the overhead. As expected, the 20 percent were the low volume boards produced in small lots. Since the company based its prices on the cost estimates, the high volume boards were highly overpriced.

An understanding of the theory of variable-margin pricing is essential if supply managers are to obtain the right price. Whenever possible, sellers use average profit margins for pricing orders because it is usually advantageous to them. In some cases, this practice results in prices that sophisticated supply professionals realize are too high— particularly when low-cost, efficiently produced items are being purchased. Invariably when average margins are used, prices considerably above fair prices result for large, long-term purchases. When dealing with large, multiproduct firms which utilize this pricing approach, a supply manager must also know which of the items purchased are high-margin and which are low-margin items. Such facts are learned by noting the differences in volumes, manufacturing skills, and costs of the various producers.

The following case illustrates the practical concepts of the preceding discussion. A large, high technology research firm successfully negotiated a $2.8 million annual contract for medical and scientific supplies. At the outset, the seller proposed that the contract be priced at cost plus the firm's annual gross profit margin of 19 percent. After several hours of negotiation, the contract was priced at cost plus a 6 percent profit margin. Had the supply manager not understood the concept of variable-margin pricing, and not known which items the seller produced efficiently, this contract would have cost her company an additional $320,000.

In their search for optimum prices, competent supply managers are aided by analyzing the pricing methods of both full-line and specialty suppliers. Regrettably, only supply professionals from a few progressive firms actually make such in-depth analyses of the entire product line of the industries in which they do business. Rather, most supply managers focus their analyses on just one product at a time (the product presently being purchased). Supply professionals are rewarded by directing their efforts toward the development of savings produced by recurring long-term cost reductions, rather than focusing on savings from short-term cost reductions. In short, optimal pricing comes to professionals who understand the pricing processes for complete product lines, in all firms, in all industries from whom they buy.

In the long run, a firm must recover all of its costs or go out of business. In the long run, for any given item, the price is roughly equal to the cost of the least efficient producer who is able to remain in business. In the short run, however, prices in the free, competitive segment of the economy (roughly 70 percent of the whole) are determined primarily by competition, that is, by supply and demand, and not by costs.

Product Differentiation

Many basic differences exist between the kinds of products marketed in the various segments of the economy. Some products in the competitive segment are *undifferentiated* (not distinguished by specific differences), while others are *differentiated.* In some cases, the products are intrinsically different (differentiated); in others, manufacturers are successful at making their similar products appear different from those of their competitors. Even in those cases where a product cannot be made different in substance, producers can still get premium prices if they can persuade customers *to believe* that their products are superior. Some producers spend huge sums of money on sales personnel and advertising to accomplish such a purpose. In the jargon of the economists, "They attempt to make the demand curve for the products of their firm somewhat inelastic." If their efforts are successful, they can charge higher prices for their products. On the other hand, if their efforts are defeated by counter-efforts of competitors, as is frequently the case, price competition comparable to that in pure competition can result. Grocers, for example, are well acquainted with this economic fact.

For both differentiated and undifferentiated products, producers compete on quality and service as well as price. The consumer market is more susceptible to producers' advertising claims than the industrial market; therefore, the major portion of advertising effort is directed toward the consumer market. Nonetheless, industrial supply management professionals must be aware of advertising and sales tactics and be very careful that they determine quality from an analysis of facts, not from unsupported claims.

Six Categories of Cost

The supply professional knows that Price = Cost + Profit. He or she must understand variable, fixed, semi-variable, total, direct, and indirect costs, and how these costs influence prices. Profit is addressed in Chapter 18.

Variable Manufacturing Costs These are items of cost that *vary directly and proportionally with the production quantity* of a particular product. Variable manufacturing costs include direct labor (unless fixed by contract), direct materials (includes raw materials, subassemblies, etc.), and variable manufacturing overhead (e.g., plant utilities if they vary with machine use/output). For example, if a specific cutting tool costs $10 and lasts for 100 cuttings, each cut represents a variable cost of 10 cents. If three cuts were required in machining a specific item, the variable cost for cutting would be 30 cents. Variable costs may decrease because of economies of scale (e.g., purchase discounts on direct materials), and increase because of diseconomies of scale (e.g., too many workers in a confined workspace). Variable costs not only exist in the manufacturing environment, but also in the selling, general, and administrative areas (nonmanufacturing costs). In summary, variable costs are fixed per unit, but vary in total as the activity level changes.

Fixed Manufacturing Costs Fixed costs *do not vary with volume,* but change over time. Fixed costs are costs sellers must pay simply because they are in business. They are a function of time and are not influenced by the volume of production.[3] Fixed costs generally represent either money the seller has already spent for buildings and equipment (e.g., depreciation) or money the seller will have to spend for unavoidable expenses (e.g., rent and insurance) regardless of the plant's volume of production. For example, if the lathe that held the cutting tool in the preceding example depreciates at the rate of $250 a month, this is a fixed cost. The seller has this $250 expense every month, whether or not any turnings are made during that period. Fixed selling, general, and administrative costs may include advertising and research and development these are classified as nonmanufacturing costs. Fixed costs may be increased or decreased from one time period to another, regardless of production volume. Fixed costs are fixed in total, but vary per unit as the activity level changes (fixed costs per unit decrease as more units are produced).

Semi-Variable or Mixed Manufacturing Costs Generally, it is not possible to classify all production costs as being either completely fixed or completely variable. Many others, termed semi-variable or mixed costs, fall somewhere between these extremes. Costs such as maintenance, utilities, and postage are partly variable and partly fixed. Each is like a fixed cost, because its total cannot be tied directly to a particular unit of production. Yet, it is possible to sort out specific elements in each of these costs that are

---

[3]Fixed costs are usually "fixed" over the relevant range of production. The relevant range extends from the minimum to the maximum capacity/output of a given manufacturing facility. To increase production beyond maximum capacity requires the purchase of additional plant capacity and results in increased fixed costs.

fixed as soon as the plant begins to operate. When the fixed portion is removed, the remaining elements frequently vary closely in proportion to the production volume. For example, if a plant is producing an average of 5,000 items a month, it might have an average light bill of $700 a month. Should the number of units produced be increased to 8,000, the light bill might increase by $100 to $800. The $100 increase is not proportional to the production increase, because a certain segment of the light bill is fixed whether any production occurs or not. Above this fixed segment, however, light costs may vary in a fairly consistent relationship with production volume. Mixed selling, general, and administrative costs may include selling salary (fixed) and commission (variable), telephone service (fixed) and metered local and long distance calls (variable), and so on.

Total Production Costs The sum of the variable, fixed, and semi-variable costs comprise the total costs. As the volume of production increases, total costs increase. However, the cost to produce *each unit* of product decreases. This is because the fixed costs do not increase; rather, they are simply spread over a larger number of units of product. Suppose, for example, that a single-product firm has the following cost structure:

Variable manufacturing costs, per unit	$ 2.25
Fixed manufacturing costs, per month	$1,200.00
Mixed manufacturing costs:	
Variable portion, per unit	$ 0.30
Fixed portion, per month	$ 450.00
Variable selling, general, and administrative costs, per unit	$ 0.35
Fixed selling, general, and administrative costs, per month	$ 700.00

Under these circumstances, Table 17.1 shows how unit costs change as volume changes; this example assumes a $7 per unit selling price. A contribution format income statement used by managerial and cost accountants may help to illustrate these costs. Notice how manufacturing cost per unit and total cost per unit decrease as production increases to plant capacity. Also, notice how the income generated per unit increases as production increases. To understand the intricacies of the cost-volume-profit relationship fully it is essential to understand variable, fixed, and semi-variable costs.

Since it is difficult to allocate costs specifically as fixed, variable, and semi-variable, accountants generally classify costs in two categories—direct costs and indirect costs. These are discussed briefly below.

Direct Costs These costs are specifically traceable to or caused by a specific project or production operation. Two major direct costs are direct labor and direct materials. Although most direct costs are variable, conceptually, direct costs should not be confused with variable costs; the two terms are rooted in different concepts. The direct costs relate to *traceability* of costs to specific operations, while variable costs relate to the *behavior* of costs as volume fluctuates. The salary of a production supervisor, for example, can be directly traceable to a product even though he or she is paid a fixed salary regardless of the volume produced. Returning to the illustration of the cutting tool, if a firm pays a worker 15 cents for making the three cuts required for each item, direct labor costs are 15 cents. If the value of the piece of metal being cut is 85 cents, direct costs for the item are $1.00.

Table 17.1 | Cost, Volume, Profit Relationships

Number of units produced		500	1,000	1,500	2,000	2,500
	Per Unit					
Revenue	$7.00	$3,500.00	$7,000.00	$10,500.00	$14,000.00	$17,500.00
Variable Manufacturing Costs	2.25	1,125.00	2,250.00	3,375.00	4,500.00	5,625.00
Variable Portion of Mixed Mfg. Costs	0.30	150.00	300.00	450.00	600.00	750.00
Variable Selling, General & Administrative Costs	0.35	175.00	350.00	525.00	700.00	875.00
Total Variable Cost	2.90	1,450.00	2,900.00	4,350.00	5,800.00	7,250.00
Contribution Margin (the remainder, after deducting variable costs from revenue, to cover fixed costs and return a profit or minimize a loss)	4.10	2,050.00	4,100.00	6,150.00	8,200.00	10,250.00
Fixed Manufacturing Costs		1,200.00	1,200.00	1,200.00	1,200.00	1,200.00
Fixed Portion of Mixed Mfg. Costs		450.00	450.00	450.00	450.00	450.00
Fixed Selling, General & Administrative Costs		700.00	700.00	700.00	700.00	700.00
Total Fixed Cost		2,350.00	2,350.00	2,350.00	2,350.00	2,350.00
Operating Income		−$300.00	$1,750.00	$3,800.00	$5,850.00	$7,900.00
Total Cost Per Unit		7.60	5.25	4.47	4.08	3.84
Manufacturing Cost Per Unit		5.85	4.20	3.65	3.38	3.21
Income Generated Per Unit		−$0.60	1.75	2.53	2.93	3.16

Assumptions:
– Selling price remains constant   *—All units produced are sold*
—All Manufacturing and Non-Manufacturing Costs are included   *—Taxes are not considered*
—Variable Costs do not change with volume
—Fixed Costs do not change within the relevant range of
  production, 0-2,500 units

Indirect Costs (Overhead)   Indirect costs are associated with or caused by two or more operating activities "jointly," but are not traced to each of them individually. The nature of an indirect cost is such that it is either not possible or practical to measure directly how much of the cost is attributable to a single operating activity.[4] Indirect costs can be fixed or variable, depending on their behavior (property taxes are fixed, but the portion of energy consumption that varies with the level of production is variable). Therefore, it is important that the reader not confuse indirect costs with fixed costs.

Regulation by Competition

From a supply professional's point of view, competition is the mainspring of good pricing. As previously discussed, most producers do not have the same real costs of production. Even when their costs are the same, their competitive positions can be quite different. Hence, their prices can also be quite different. Consider the following example. Assume that a supply manager is ready to purchase 10,000 specially designed cutting tools. He sends the specifications to five companies for quotations. All five respond. For the sake of simplicity, assume that direct costs in these five companies are identical. Further, assume that each company uses the same price-estimating formula;

---

[4] Many costs treated as indirect by organizations are traceable and could become direct costs through improvements in the measurement system. The authors contend that the reasons for not tracing costs directly have diminished with information technology advances.

overhead is figured as 150 percent of direct labor, and profit is calculated as 12 percent of total cost. Each company could then lay out its figures as follows:

Cost of materials	$12,000	
Cost of direct labor	3,000	
Cost of overhead	4,500	(150 percent of direct labor)
Total cost	$19,500	
Profit	2,340	(12 percent of total cost)
Price	$21,840	

To simplify the example, assume all overhead is classified as fixed; that is, it remains constant over a given range of production.

Even with all the controlling figures fixed, the companies more than likely would not quote the same price, because *the cost of production and profit are only two of the factors a seller considers in determining asking price.* In the final analysis, it is the factors stemming from competition that determine the exact price each firm will quote. That is, when faced with the realities of competition, the price any specific firm will quote will be governed largely by *its need for business* and by *what it thinks its competitors will quote,* not by costs or profits.

Who is responsible for final determination of the price to be quoted? Generally, it is a marketing executive; in some cases, it is the president of the company. Pricing is one of the most important management decisions a firm must make. As an objective, a firm tends to seek the highest price that is compatible with its long-range goals. What is the possible price range for the order in the preceding example? The out-of-pocket (variable) costs for this order are $12,000 for materials and $3,000 for direct labor, a total of $15,000. This is the lowest price any company should accept under any circumstances. The highest price is $21,840, based on the assumption that a profit in excess of 12 percent is not in the long-range interest of the firm. (Such a profit may attract additional competition to enter this market, which in turn would erode the profitability of the market.)

What could cause one of the firms to consider a price of $17,000? Keen competition among suppliers could. On the other hand, keen competition among buyers could drive the price higher. This is why competition, as a leveler, is such a dominant factor in pricing. If the firm had been unable to obtain a satisfactory volume of other business, it would gladly take this order for a price of $17,000. As a result of the order, the $15,000 out-of-pocket costs would be covered, the experienced work force could be kept working, and a $2,000 contribution could be made to overhead. Remember that the fixed overhead would continue whether or not the firm received this order.

In the long run, a firm must recover all costs or go out of business, for in the long run, plant and machinery must be maintained, modernized, and replaced. *In the short run,* however, it is generally better for a firm to recover variable costs and some portion of overhead rather than undergo a significant decline in business. This would not be true, of course, if such additional business would affect the pricing of other orders the firm has already filled or is going to fill.

Business in good times is not ordinarily done at out-of-pocket (or variable cost) prices. A more common situation would be for each of the five firms to bid prices above the total cost figure of $19,500. How much above this figure each would bid would depend on the specific economic circumstances and expectations applicable to each firm. Those firms hungry for business would bid just slightly above the total cost figure of $19,500. Those with large backlogs and growing lists of steady customers (and therefore not in need of new business in the short run) would bid a larger profit margin (perhaps 14 percent). Sellers can be expected to evaluate competitive situations differently, depending on how much they want or need the business. Therefore, even with the simplifying assumption of identical costs, it is reasonable to expect bids in this situation to range from approximately $19,700 (1 percent profit) to $21,840 (12 percent profit). Prices close to out-of-pocket costs could be offered if the seller were attempting to obtain a desirable, prestigious account, if the supplier desired to gain experience in a situation wherein additional large orders are expected to follow, or if the supplier desired to keep its workforce employed.

Varying Profit Margins A seller must recover *all* costs from his or her total sales to make a profit. However, *each* product in the line does not have to make a profit, and not all accounts have to yield the same profit margin. Bearing these thoughts in mind, the principal cost/competition implications of pricing can be summarized as follows: *Sound pricing policy dictates that sellers, in accordance with their interpretation of the prevailing competitive forces, quote prices that are high enough to include all variable costs and make the maximum possible contribution toward fixed costs and profit.*

Similarly, sound pricing policy dictates that, for any given purchase, supply professionals should use their knowledge of products, markets, costs, and competitive conditions to estimate the price range at which sellers can reasonably be expected to do business. Finally, with this information, a knowledge of the value of the buyer's ongoing business to a seller, and an appreciation of the value of this specific order, the supply professional applies all relevant purchasing principles and techniques to purchase at prices as close as possible to the bottom of the estimated price range.

Price Analysis

Some form of price analysis is required for every purchase. The method and scope of analysis required are dictated by the dollar amount and circumstances attending each specific purchase. Price analysis is defined as the examination of a seller's price proposal (bid) by comparison with reasonable price benchmarks, without examination and evaluation of the separate elements of the cost and profit making up the price.

A supply professional has five tools which can be used to conduct a price analysis: (1) analysis of competitive price proposals; (2) comparison with regulated, catalog, or market prices; (3) use of web-based e-procurement; (4) comparison with historical prices; and (5) use of independent cost estimates.

Competitive Price Proposals

Chapter 15 describes the conditions that should be satisfied before using competitive bidding as a means of selecting the source of supply. When this approach is employed, and the following additional conditions are satisfied, then the resulting low bid normally provides a fair and reasonable price:

- At least two qualified sources have responded to the solicitation.
- The proposals are responsive to the buying firm's requirements.
- The supplier competed independently for the award.
- The supplier submitting the lowest offer does not have an unfair advantage over its competitors.
- The lowest evaluated price is reasonable.

The supply manager cannot apply this approach to pricing in a mechanical manner. He or she clearly must use common sense and ensure that the price is reasonable when compared with past prices, with independent estimates, or with realistic rules of thumb.

Regulated, Catalog, and Market Prices

Prices Set by Law or Regulation   When the price is set by law or regulation, the supplier must identify the regulating authority and specify the regulated prices. With regulated prices, some governmental body (federal, state, or local) has determined that prices of certain goods and services should be controlled directly. Normally, approval of price changes requires formal review, hearings, and an affirmative vote of the regulatory authority. No supplier may charge more or less than the approved price.

Catalog Price   An established catalog price is a price that is included in a catalog, a price list, or some other form that is regularly maintained by the supplier. The price sources must be dated and readily available for inspection by potential customers. The supply manager should request a recent sales summary demonstrating that significant quantities are sold to a significant number of customers at the indicated price before accepting a catalog price.

Market Price   A market price results from the interaction of many buyers and sellers who are willing to trade at a given (market) price. The forces of supply and demand establish the price. A market price is generally for an item or a service that is generic in nature and not particularly unique to the seller. Eggs and lumber, for example, are priced based on the market. Normally the daily market price is published in local newspapers or trade publications that are independent of the supplier.

Internet / e-Commerce II

Advanced communications using the Internet allow supply management personnel to view up-to-date pricing, as well as catalogs, specification sheets, video presentations, and other information the seller has on a material, product, or service. Since the Internet does not have geographical constraints, the information is available worldwide. Please refer to the chapter on e-Commerce II in this book for a detailed discussion of the topic. Of particular interest here are buying exchanges, reverse auctions, and the search capability of the Internet.

Buying exchanges (often referred to as B2B e-commerce) offer purchasing firms a list of pre-approved sellers offering identical and/or similar products or services, usually within a specific category, from which to choose. Normally, prices or discounts from list prices are provided.

Reverse auctions identify materials, equipment, or services required and request carefully prequalified suppliers to submit bids. Potential suppliers are able to see prices submitted by their competitors and revise their bids until the preestablished closing time for the auction. Caution must be used when employing reverse auctions since they ignore the relationship dimension of the transaction.

Tailored global searches allow expanded Internet search capabilities. Supply management professionals can investigate products or services by simultaneously scanning all *relevant* public and private websites worldwide. Obtaining the right price, quality, and delivery is becoming easier and faster as the Internet expands and more procurement-specific portals are developed.

Historical Prices

Price analysis may be performed by comparing a proposed price with historical quotes or prices for the same or similar item. It is essential to determine that the base price was fair and reasonable (as determined through price analysis) and is still a valid standard against which to measure the offered price. The fact that a historical price exists does not automatically make it a valid basis for comparison. Several issues must be considered:

- How have conditions changed?[5]
- Were there one-time engineering, setup, or tooling charges in the original price?
- What should be the effect of inflation or deflation on the price?
- Will the new procurement create a situation in which the supplier should enjoy the benefits of learning? (The concept of learning curve analysis is discussed in Chapter 18.)

Independent Cost Estimates

When other techniques of price analysis cannot be utilized, the supply manager may use an independent cost estimate as the basis for comparison. He or she must determine that the estimate is fair and reasonable.[6] If price analysis is impractical or if it does not allow the buyer to reach a conclusion that the price is fair and reasonable, then cost analysis, the subject of the next chapter, should be employed.

Purchasing Design Work

When a supply professional contracts for the design as well as the manufacture of a special component, he or she must be careful not to create a future supplier relations problem. One facet of the potential problem centers on the matter of ownership of the special design. Another facet concerns the supplier's recovery of sunk costs in design work and tooling.

---

[5] The Bureau of Labor Statistics in Washington, DC, provides thousands of different price indexes every month. Available are indexes by stage of processing, industry, and individual commodity grades. A commonly used series for these purposes is the producer price index (PPI). Also import and export price indexes broken down in the major subcategories are available. These indexes allow the price analyst to adjust historical prices by appropriate changes over time.

[6] The development and use of independent cost estimates is described in detail in D. N. Burt, W. Norquist, and J. Anklesaria, *Zero Base Pricing™: Achieving World Class Competitiveness through Reduced All-in-Cost* (Chicago: Probus, 1990), Chapter 4.

When a supplier agrees to design and manufacture a special component, or to develop a special process, who owns the resulting design—the supplier or the buyer? Who has the right to apply for a patent on the item? Further, who owns the special tooling the supplier must obtain to produce the item? The answers to these basic questions should be specified unequivocally in the purchase contract. By taking this precaution, the buying firm can avoid the uncertainties and distasteful misunderstandings that at times accompany such purchases.

The purchase price stated in the contract should reflect the decision regarding ownership of the design and tooling. From the purchaser's standpoint, the most desirable method of pricing is one that separates the supplier's charges into three categories: (1) price for design and development work, (2) price for special tooling and equipment, and (3) price for manufacturing. With this approach, both parties know precisely what the buying firm is paying for and what should be obtained in return.

If a purchasing firm can purchase design work and tooling completely apart from the manufactured components, the contract is usually clear-cut and no problems ensue. The purchasing firm can do whatever it wishes with the design or tooling without infringing on the prerogatives of the supplier. Other things being equal, this is by far the most desirable type of contract. It makes the buyer less dependent on a single supplier who chooses to operate in a short-term profit-maximizing mode in lieu of a partnership mode. It also provides more leverage that can be used in stimulating competition among additional potential suppliers.

As anyone with good business sense would suspect, some suppliers are unwilling to accept contracts for continuing business on the basis just described. A shrewd supplier may prefer to develop a proprietary product and, for a limited period of time, establish a monopolistic position. Such a situation generates supplier relations problems. Clearly, the buyer does not want to remain a captive customer of one supplier indefinitely. On the other hand, in the interest of fairness, the buying firm is obligated to see that the supplier is adequately compensated for its original design and development work. Therefore, if the supplier will not divulge design and tooling costs, the supply professional should write the purchase contract in a manner that compels the supplier to price the job to recover these costs within a reasonable period of time (usually within a year). For example, the contract might guarantee the purchase of a specified number of units, or it might state that the job will be opened for bid on an annual basis.

Although the original supplier has an inherent advantage over future bidders, it is nevertheless essential that the buying firm state at the outset the intention to open the job to competition as soon as the original supplier has recovered the sunk costs and earned a reasonable profit. This approach is in keeping with the buyer's responsibility to treat all suppliers fairly, and at the same time to seek out the efficient, low-cost producer.

Documenting a Price Analysis

A price analysis report is a written summary of the analysis for a given procurement. The report is prepared for each major procurement to summarize the basis for the supply manager's conclusion that a price is fair and reasonable. It should be included in the purchase order or contract file.

The report may be a separate document, particularly if there is to be no negotiation conference. If competitive bidding was used to select the source and the price, an abstract of the bids received will suffice. The findings of the price analysis may be incorporated in the price negotiation memorandum as part of the explanation of the prenegotiation objective and as part of the justification for the resulting price. There are strong arguments, however, for requiring a written report of price analysis before the negotiation. The discipline of writing the report requires the supply professional to sift through the data, reconstruct the process and its events, restate key issues and decisions, and state conclusions based on these findings.

The price analysis report should indicate:

- Information that was considered.
- Weight given to each piece of information and why.
- Logic supporting the determination that an offeror's price is or is not reasonable.
- Soundness of that logic.

The length of and detail in a price analysis report depend on the nature of the procurement. Similarly, the specific elements included depend on what is required to establish reasonableness and what is available.

Discounts

Discounts are frequently considered a routine, prosaic part of pricing. Perceptive supply professionals recognize that this is not always the case. As will be illustrated in the discussion to follow, discounts can sometimes succeed as a technique for reducing prices after all other techniques have failed. The four most commonly used kinds of discounts are *trade discounts, quantity discounts, seasonal discounts, and cash discounts.*

Trade Discounts

Trade discounts are reductions from list price given to various classes of buyers and distributors to compensate them for performing certain marketing functions for the original seller (usually the manufacturer) of the product. Trade discounts are frequently structured as a sequence of individual discounts (e.g., 25, 10, and 5 percent), and in such cases, they are called series discounts. Those who perform only a part of the distribution functions get only one or two of the discounts in the series. If the retail price of an item with such discounts is $100, the full discounted price is calculated as follows: 25 percent of $100 = $25; 10 percent of ($100 − $25) = $7.50; 5 percent of ($100 − $25 − $7.50) = $3.38. The manufacturer's selling price, then, is $100 − $25 − $7.50 − $3.38 = $64.12.

An industrial supply professional who purchases through distributors must, as a result of the very nature of series trade discounts, be certain that the buy is from the right distributor (i.e., the distributor obtaining the most discounts). The general guideline is to get as close to the manufacturer as is practical. For example, a large buyer normally should not purchase paper requirements from a janitorial supply house which usually does not obtain all discounts in the series for paper. If an account is sufficiently large, the buying firm should purchase from a paper distributor that normally does obtain all discounts in the series. Such a supplier can, at the same profit margin as the janitorial supply house, offer buyers lower prices. Buyers with very large accounts should purchase directly from paper manufacturers.

Quantity Discounts

These price reductions are given to a buyer for purchasing increasingly larger quantities of materials. Normally they are offered under one of three purchasing arrangements:

1. For purchasing a specific quantity of items at one time.
2. For purchasing a specified dollar total of any number of different items at one time.
3. For purchasing a specified dollar total of any number of items over an agreed-upon time period.

The third type of quantity discount noted above is called a cumulative discount. The period of accumulation can be a month, a quarter, or, more commonly, a year. For large-dollar-value, repetitive purchases, buyers should always seek this type of discount. Also, because unplanned increases in business occur with regular frequency, supply professionals should include in all quantity discount contracts a provision that if the total purchases made under the contract exceed the estimated quantities, then an additional discount will be allowed for all such excesses.

The quantity discount concept originally stemmed from the unit cost reductions inherent in large-volume manufacturing operations. In a traditional mass or batch production operation, a large production run of a single product spreads the fixed costs over the number of items produced and results in a lower production cost per item. With the continuing improvement of flexible manufacturing systems, however, the dilution of fixed setup costs becomes rather small compared with other product-specific cost elements. Consequently, if a quantity discount is based solely on the distribution of setup and order processing costs over the volume of production, there is clearly a declining incentive for such a supplier to offer this form of quantity discount.

Seasonal Discounts

Based on the seasonal nature of some products (primarily consumer products), producers commonly offer discounts for purchases made in the off-season. For example, room air conditioners usually can be purchased at a discount during the fall or winter seasons.

Cash Discounts

In many industries, sellers traditionally offer price reductions for the prompt payment of bills. When such discounts are given, they are offered as a percentage of the net invoice price. When suppliers extend credit, they cannot avoid certain attendant costs, including the cost of tied-up capital, the cost of operating a credit department, and the cost of some bad-debt losses. Most sellers can reduce these costs by dealing on a short-term payment basis. Therefore, they are willing to pass on part of the savings to buyers in the form of a cash discount.

Supply professionals should be aware of the importance of negotiating the highest possible cash discount. The most commonly used discount in practice is 2 percent 10 days, net 30 days. In industries where prompt payment is particularly important, cash discounts as high as 8 percent have been allowed. A cash discount of 2/10, net 30 means that a discount of 2 percent can be taken if the invoice is paid within 10 days, while the full amount should be remitted if payment is made between 10 and 30 days after receipt of the invoice.

A 2 percent discount, viewed casually, does not appear to represent much money. In one sense, however, it is the equivalent of a 36.5 percent annual interest rate. Because the bill must be paid in 30 days and the discount can be taken up to the tenth day, a buyer not taking the discount is paying 2 percent of the dollar amount of the invoice to use the cash involved for 20 days. In a 365-day year, there are 18.25 twenty-day periods (365/20 = 18.25). A 2/10 discount translates into an *annual* discount rate of 36.5 percent (2 percent times 18.25).[7] If a firm does not have sufficient cash on hand to take cash discounts, the possibility of borrowing the needed money should be investigated. Under normal conditions, paying 10 to 15 percent for capital that returns 36.5 percent is good business. Capable buyers understand the time value of money. In some situations, generous cash discounts can be obtained either for prepayment or for 48-hour payment.

Various other types of cash discounts are in use. One common type is the *end-of-month (EOM)* dating system. This system of cash discounting permits the buying firm to take a designated percentage discount if payment is made within a specified number of days after the end of the month in which the order is shipped. If materials are shipped on October 16 under 2/10 EOM terms, a 2 percent discount can be taken at any time until November 10.

Lower prices, in the form of higher cash discounts, are an ever-present source of price reduction that supply professionals should always explore. Frequently, sellers who will not consider reducing the prices of their products will consider allowing higher cash discounts. Such action accomplishes the identical result for the purchasing firm. For example, a major petroleum company recently was able to gain a 6 percent price reduction on the purchase of a complex testing machine—a machine the manufacturer had never before sold below its listed $92,000 selling price. The $5,520 price reduction was achieved by the supply manager's offering to pay one-half of the purchase price one week in advance of the machine's delivery to his company's testing laboratory.

Concluding Remarks

Obtaining the *right price* is one of supply management's most important responsibilities. When focusing on price, insight into the current economic environment and knowledge of the cost elements that underlie a selling price will support the most favorable procurement. In addition, the supply management professional should be aware of the various means available to locate potential suppliers, make price comparisons, and utilize competitive bidding and/or negotiation. One final note: The purchase or acquisition price should be evaluated in the context of total cost of ownership whenever possible— and whenever cost effective.

---

[7] A complete analysis of this situation must include the opportunity cost of early payment. If a firm's internal cost of capital is 15 percent/year, the net saving generated by the 2/10, net 30 discount is 36.5 percent − 15 percent, or 21.5 percent on an annualized basis.

18 CHAPTER

Cost Analysis[1]

A supply manager without an understanding of cost analysis and costing systems cannot aspire shifting his or her organization toward World Class Supply Management^{SM}. Of particular concern is the comprehension of hidden and indirect costs, as well as strategic planning using accurate cost estimates. Once understood, cost analysis becomes a cornerstone of other supply management activities, such as negotiation, pricing, forecasting, and alliance development.

KEY CONCEPTS

[1]Appreciation is expressed to Ray Hummell of the University of San Diego for his assistance in updating this chapter.

Cost Analysis

Cost analysis should be employed when price analysis is impractical or does not allow a buyer to reach the conclusion that a price is fair and reasonable. Cost analysis is generally most useful when purchasing nonstandard items and services. This chapter focuses on the application of cost analysis to the acquisition cost of materials, products, and services.

Cost Analysis Defined

We have seen that price analysis is a process of comparisons. *Cost analysis* is a review and an evaluation of actual or anticipated costs. This analysis involves the application of experience, knowledge, and judgment to data in an attempt to project reasonable estimated contract costs. Estimated costs serve as the basis for buyer-seller negotiations to arrive at mutually agreeable contract prices.

The purpose of cost analysis is to arrive at a price that is fair and reasonable to both the buying and selling firms. Estimates can be made with the help of one's engineering department or by analyzing the estimates submitted by the seller. To analyze a supplier's costs, a supply manager must understand the nature of each of the various costs a manufacturer incurs. The supply manager must compare the labor hours, material costs, and overhead costs of all competing suppliers as listed on their cost-breakdown sheets. Most important, he or she must determine the reasons for any differences, focusing on three principle elements of cost: direct, indirect (overhead), and profit. These cost elements were defined and discussed in Chapter 17.

A supply manager should always be conscious of the fact that costs vary widely among manufacturing firms. Some firms are high-cost producers; others are low-cost producers. Many factors affect the costs of specific firms, as well as the cost of individual products within any given firm. Some of the most important elements affecting costs are:

■ Capabilities of management.
■ Efficiency of labor.
■ Amount and quality of subcontracting.
■ Plant capacity and the continuity of output.

Each of these factors can change with respect to either product or time. For this reason, a specific firm can be a high-cost producer for one item and a low-cost producer for another. Similarly, the firm can be a low-cost producer one year and a high-cost producer another year. These circumstances make it extremely important for a supply manager to obtain competition among potential suppliers, when appropriate. Competition can be a supply manager's key to locating the desired low-cost producer.

Capabilities of Management

The skill with which management plans, organizes, staffs, coordinates, and controls all the personnel, capital, and equipment at its disposal determines the efficiency of the firm. Managements utilize the resources available to them with substantially different degrees of efficiency. This is one basic reason why finding the correct supplier (and price) is so profitable for astute supply management professionals.

Efficiency of Labor

Anyone who has visited a number of different firms surely has noticed the differences in attitudes and skills that exist between various labor forces. Some are cooperative, take great pride in their work, have high morale, and produce efficiently, while others do not. The skill with which management exercises its responsibilities contributes greatly to these differences between efficient and inefficient labor forces. Supply managers are well rewarded for pinpointing suppliers with efficient labor forces.

Amount and Quality of Subcontracting

When a contract has been awarded to a supplier (the *prime contractor*), the supplier frequently subcontracts some of the production work required to complete the job. The supplier's subcontracting decisions are important to the buying firm because they may involve a large percentage of prime contract money. The first decision a prime contractor must make regarding subcontracts is which items should be made and which specific items should be bought. Should the prime contractor decide to buy some of those items that can be made more efficiently, and vice versa, the buyer suffers financially. Even if the prime contractor makes the correct "make" decision, it still is responsible for selecting those subcontractors that are needed for the "buy" items.

Subcontractor prices and performance directly influence the prices the buying firm pays the prime contractor. Hence, the prime contractor's skills in both making and administering its subcontracts are of great importance to the supply manager. For this rea-

Table 18.1 I How production volume affects fixed costs, variable costs, and profit.

Production Quantity	Selling Price	Sales Revenue	Fixed Costs	Variable Costs	Total Cost	Total Profit	Profit per Unit of Added Production
0	$20	$ 0	$4,000	$ 0	$4,000	−$4,000	
							}$15
100	20	2,000	4,000	500	4,500	−2,500	
							} 15
200	20	4,000	4,000	1,000	5,000	−1,000	
							} 15
300	20	6,000	4,000	1,500	5,500	+500	
							} 15
400	20	8,000	4,000	2,000	6,000	+2,000	
							} 15
500	20	10,000	4,000	2,500	6,500	+3,500	
							} 15
600	20	12,000	4,000	3,000	7,000	+5,000	
							} 14
700	20	14,000	4,000	3,600	7,600	+6,400	
							} 12
800	20	16,000	4,000	4,400	8,400	+7,600	
							} 10
900	20	18,000	4,000	5,400	9,400	+8,600	

son, supply managers must periodically review their major suppliers to ensure that they have effective supply management and subcontracting capabilities of their own.

Plant Capacity

A plant's overhead costs are directly influenced by its size. A plant can get too large for efficient production and, as a result, lose its competitive ability. On the other hand, plants with large capital investments, or those manufacturing products on a mass production basis, can be too small to attain the most efficient production levels. The supply professional must be alert to detect firms whose operations are adversely affected by size.

Plant output is clearly one of the controlling elements in the cost/profit picture. Table 18.1 illustrates this concept numerically. Note how volume affects profit when variable costs change because of inefficient use of facilities beyond optimum plant capacity. Note also that while total profit continues to increase as production output increases, beyond a certain output profit increases at a decreasing rate. This relationship is an important one for supply professionals to keep in mind.

Sources of Cost Data

There are three primary sources of cost data: (1) from potential suppliers as a precondition of submitting proposals and bids, (2) from suppliers with whom the firm has developed preferred or strategic supplier relationships/partnerships, and (3) cost models.

Potential Suppliers

When a supply manager anticipates that cost analysis will be required, he or she should include a request for a cost breakdown with each request for quotation. This is the proper time to make such a request, *not after* negotiations have started. Suppliers cannot complain that making this breakdown is an extra burden at this time, since they must perform such an analysis to prepare their bids. A simple procedure used by a number of progressive firms for obtaining cost breakdowns is to include the following statement with their request for quotations: "We will not consider any quotation not accompanied by a cost breakdown." Not all suppliers readily provide cost-of-production information; however, the number refusing to do so for nonstandard items is declining. An example of a typical cost breakdown request form is shown in Figure 18.1.

Supply Partners

As firms develop open relationships built on trust and collaboration, the purchasing firm shares information on forecasts, schedules, the way purchased items integrate into its product or process, and so on. The supply partner shares information on its design, production, and quality processes and on its *design and production costs*.

Cost Models

On some occasions, it may not be possible to obtain cost data from the supplier. In other cases, the cost data obtained may appear unrealistic or may support prices that are unacceptable. Under these conditions, it may be necessary for the purchasing firm to develop its own cost models to estimate what the supplier's costs *should be*. The development of such models requires the application of both accounting and industrial engineering skills and is beyond the scope of the presentation in this chapter. It is sufficient at this point simply to say that this approach, though not extensively used by small and medium-sized firms, is commonly used by leading-edge firms that have the technical resources available.[2]

Direct Costs

Except in industries with heavy fixed capital investments, direct costs are normally the major portion of product or service costs and the most easily traceable. As such, they generally serve as the basis on which sellers allocate their overhead costs. The astute supply manager, therefore, must carefully investigate a seller's direct costs. *A tiny reduction here (because they are relatively large) is worth more (pricewise) to the buying firm than a major reduction in the percentage of profit* (which is relatively small). Referring to Table 18.2, a 25 percent reduction in the $8 direct labor cost of situation 1 to the $6 direct labor cost of situation 2 results in a $6.05 ($33.88 − $27.83) reduction in price. A 25 percent reduction in profit would result in only a 77 cent reduction in price (0.25 × $3.08 = $0.77).

---

[2]The interested reader is referred to D. N. Burt, W. Norquist, and J. Anklesaria, *Zero Base Pricing™: Achieving World Class Competitiveness through Reduced All-in-Cost* (Chicago: Probus, 1990), chapter 8.

COST ANALYSIS	CHECK APPROPRIATE BOX ESTIMATED COST ☐ HISTORICAL COST ☐ PERIOD COVERED:		
NAME OF SUPPLIER	INQUIRY OR PURCHASE REQUISITION NO.		
ADDRESS (Street, City, State)	QUANTITY	AT $ EACH	AMOUNT $
ARTICLE			
TERMS AND DISCOUNT	NET TOTAL OF QUOTATION $		

ANALYSIS OF COST AS OF _____ 20 ___ INDICATE WHETHER:
COST PER ITEM☐ OR TOTAL COST☐

ITEM	AMOUNT	PERCENT OF COST
1. DIRECT MATERIAL		
2. LESS SCRAP OR SALVAGE		
3. NET DIRECT MATERIAL		
4. PURCHASED PARTS - FROM SUBCONTRACTORS		
5. DIRECT PRODUCTIVE LABOR HOURS AT $		
6. DIRECT FACTORY CHARGES:		
(A) TOOLS AND DIES		
1. DIRECT WAGES HOURS AT $		
2. TOOLING BURDEN		
3. MATERIALS		
(B) SPECIAL MACHINERY		
(C) MISCELLANEOUS		
7. INDIRECT FACTORY EXPENSES (Burden), ON BASIS OF See Note*		
8. ENGINEERING AND DEVELOPMENT EXPENSES • DIRECT:		
(a) SALARIES AND WAGES HOURS AT $		
(b) BURDEN		
(c) OTHER		
TOTAL MANUFACTURING COST		
9. GENERAL AND ADMINISTRATIVE EXPENSE:		
PERCENT OF See Note*		
10. SELLING EXPENSE See Note*		
11. CONTINGENCIES See Note*		
12. OTHER EXPENSES See Note*		
13.		
14.		
15.		
16.		
17. TOTAL COST		
18. SELLING PRICE		

19. (a) Are the wage rates used in estimating the direct labor of the unit cost breakdown
       the same as those now prevailing?
    (b) If "No", explain difference and indicate approximate amount thereof.

20. (a) What operating rate has been used in calculating the above estimate?
        Hours of operation per week?
    (b) At what rate is your plant now operating?
        Hours of operation per week?

_____   _____
        (Supplier)   (Signature and title)

_____
        (Date)

a. State basis of allocation.
b. State nature of expenses included and basis of allocation.
c. State nature of expenses included and amount of advertising, if any, separately, and basis of allocation.
d. Explain in detail.
e. State nature of expenses, basis of allocation, and why related to the cost of this item.

Figure 18.1 | Cost breakdown form.

Table 18.2 | Direct costs and prices.

Cost Elements	Situation 1	Situation 2
Material	$ 8.00	$ 8.00
Direct labor	8.00	6.00
Fixed overhead at 150 percent of direct labor	12.00	9.00
Manufacturing cost	$28.00	$23.00
General and administrative overhead at 10 percent of manufacturing cost	2.80	2.30
Total cost	30.80	25.30
Profit at 10 percent of total cost	3.08	2.53
Price	$33.88	$27.83

Direct Labor

During the development and production phase of a new item, a supplier typically experiences a heavy design and production engineering push, which peaks and then decreases. As it does, tooling and setup efforts increase, peak, and decline. Machining, assembly, and test efforts then become the predominant users of labor. The supply professional should be cognizant of these factors and should analyze a supplier's estimate to ensure that it is based on proper planning, applying reasonable expectations of efficiency in this regard.

When analyzing direct manufacturing labor estimates, the supply manager should pay particular attention to the following:

■ Allowances for rework
■ Geographic variations
■ Variations in skills

Allowances for Rework   The supply manager should carefully review a bidder's estimate of rework costs. Modern production techniques now make it possible to drastically reduce scrap rates. Effective purchasing by a supplier's organization can reduce the defect rates on incoming materials by as much as 95 percent. The combined effect of reduced incoming quality problems and improved production and quality systems should reduce a supplier's requirement for rework markedly.

Geographic Variations   Wage rates vary significantly from one country to another, as well as within a country's borders. A supply manager must ensure that the wage rates proposed are, in fact, the wage rates applicable in the areas where the work is to be performed. The Bureau of Labor Statistics provides current wage rates in the United States for a variety of trades in different locations.

Variations in Skills   The supply manager, with assistance from the firm's industrial engineering or production departments, should review the types of labor skills proposed to ensure that they are relevant and necessary for accomplishing the required tasks.

Direct Materials

Direct materials are consumed or converted during the production process. Sheet metal, fasteners, electrical relays, and radios for automobiles are all examples of direct materials. In most cases, such materials are normally purchased from a wide variety of suppliers. In some cases, the materials may have been produced or partially processed in other plants or divisions of the supplier's operation. The resulting costs should be scrutinized carefully for internal transfer charges and markups.

Further analysis of proposed materials costs frequently reveals a difference between the buyer's cost estimate for a given bill of materials and the supplier's estimate for the same bill. In such cases, the supply manager should request supporting data from the supplier. In some cases, the labor component of the proposed materials costs should reflect a learning effect as more units are produced (this topic is discussed next). In any case, careful analysis and discussion should help identify the source of the variance.

Learning Curves

In many circumstances, labor and supervision become more efficient as more units are produced. The *learning curve* (sometimes called the *improvement curve*) is defined as an empirical relationship between the number of units produced and the number of labor hours required to produce them. Production managers can use this relationship in scheduling production and in determining manpower requirements for a particular product over a given period of time. Supply managers can use the relationship to analyze the effects of production and management "learning" on a supplier's unit cost of production.

Traditionally, the learning curve has been used primarily for purchases of complex equipment in the aircraft, electronics, and other highly technical industries. Recently, its use has spread to other industries. The learning curve is useful in both price and cost analysis. It is probably most useful in negotiations, as a starting point for pricing a new item. In addition to providing insurance against overcharging, the learning curve is also used effectively by government and commercial supply professionals in developing (1) target costs for new products, (2) make-or-buy information, (3) delivery schedules, and (4) progress payment schedules for suppliers.

Cumulative Curve and the Unit Curve

In practice, two basic forms of the learning curve exist. The first curve, "the cumulative average cost curve," is commonly used in price and cost analysis. This curve plots cumulative units produced against the average direct labor cost or *average labor hours required per unit for all units produced.* The second, "the unit or marginal cost curve," is also used in labor and cost-estimating work. The unit curve plots cumulative units produced against the *actual labor hours required to produce each unit.* Figure 18.2 illustrates and compares the two types of curves.

Selection of the learning curve technique to use tends to be based on an organization's past experience. Ideally, whether one should use a cumulative or a unit curve is a function of the production process itself. Some operations conform to a cumulative curve; others conform to the unit curve. The only way to know which to use is to record

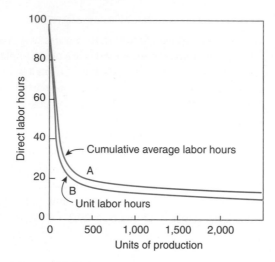

Figure 18.2 | Comparison of Cumulative average cost curve and unit or marginal cost curve.

the actual production data and then determine which type of curve fits the data the best. The relationship is strictly an *empirical* one.

Target Cost Estimation

If a new product is custom-made to unique specifications, what should be paid for the 50th item? The 500th item? Obviously, costs should decline—but by how much? Analysis of the learning curve provides an answer. Cost reductions and estimated prices can be obtained merely by reading figures from a graph.

The learning curve is a quantitative model of the commonsense observation that the unit cost of a new product decreases as more units of the product are made because of the learning process. The manufacturer, through the repetitive production process, learns how to make the product at a lower cost. For example, the more times an individual repeats a complicated operation, the more efficient he or she becomes, in both speed and skill. This, in turn, means progressively lower unit labor costs. Familiarity with an operation also results in fewer rejects and reworks, better scheduling, possible improvements in tooling, fewer engineering changes, and more efficient management systems.

Suppose a supply manager knows that it took a supplier 100 hours of labor to turn out the first unit of a new product, as indicated in Figures 18.3 and 18.4. The supplier reports that the second unit took 80 hours to make, so the average labor requirement for the two items is 180 ÷ 2 = 90 hours per unit. The production report for the first four units is summarized in Table 18.3.

Observe that the labor requirement dropped to 74 hours for the third unit and to 70 hours for the fourth unit. Column 4 shows that the average number of labor hours required for the first four units was 81 hours per unit. Investigation of the learning rate shows the following relationships:

- As production doubled from one to two units, *the average labor hours required per unit* dropped from 100 to 90, a reduction of 10 percent.

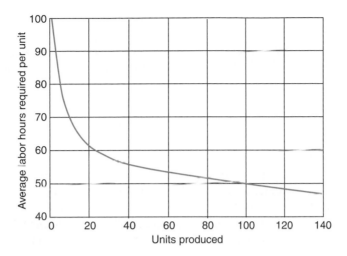

Figure 18.3 | A 90 percent cumulative average learning curve, plotted on an arithmetic grid.

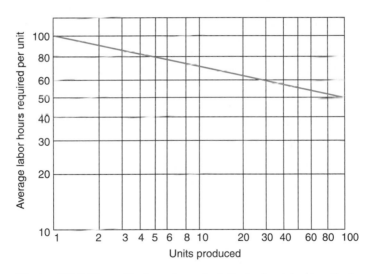

Figure 18.4 | Logarithmic scales on both the horizontal and vertical axes convert the curve of Figure 18.3 into a straight line.

■ As production doubled from two to four units, *the average labor hours required per unit* dropped from 90 to 81, a reduction of 10 percent.

Figure 18.3 indicates that the same learning rate continues as production of the new item increases. Each time production doubles, the average labor requirement for all units declines by 10 percent. Thus, the product is said to have a 90 percent learning rate, or a 90 percent learning curve. Note that this is based on the *cumulative average* learning curve phenomenon. The basic point revealed by the learning curve is that a *specific and constant percentage reduction in the average direct labor hours required per unit results*

Table 18.3 I Ninety percent cumulative learning curve data.

Unit Produced	Labor Hours Required	Cumulative Labor Hours Required	Average Labor Hours Required per Unit
1st	100	100	100.0
2nd	80	180	90.0
3rd	74	254	84.7
4th	70	324	81.0

each time the number of units produced is doubled. It is an established fact that specific learning rates occur with reasonable regularity for similar groups of products in many different industries.

Studies made in the aircraft, electronics, and small electromechanical subassembly fields indicate that learning rates of 75 to 95 percent are typical. However, learning curves can vary anywhere within the practical limits of 50 to 100 percent. As more units are produced, the effect of a constant learning rate on unit costs gradually diminishes. After several thousand units, the absolute reduction in cost from learning becomes negligible. Note in Figure 18.3 how the curve flattens out as the number of units produced increases. This is why learning curve analysis is of greatest value for new products.[3]

Most analysts prefer to plot the data for learning curves on log-log graph paper, as in Figure 18.4. The logarithmic scales on both the horizontal and vertical axes convert the curve of Figure 18.3 into a straight line (because a log-log grid plots a constant rate of change as a straight line). The straight line is easier to read, and it simplifies forecasting since a constant learning rate always appears as a straight line on log-log coordinates. To verify the fact that both graphs represent the same thing, look at the number of hours needed to produce 100 units in Figures 18.3 and 18.4; both figures indicate about 50 hours per unit.

In addition to determining the direct labor component of price, the labor hour data also have the following purchasing applications.

Direct Materials   Experience indicates the organizations "learn" how to purchase materials more efficiently as quantities increase and time progresses.

Estimating Delivery Times   Since the learning curve can be used to forecast labor time required, it is possible to estimate how many units a supplier can produce over a specified time with a given labor force. This information can be extremely helpful to a buyer in scheduling deliveries, in planning his or her firm's production, and in identifying suppliers who obviously cannot meet desired delivery schedules.

---

[3]Different types of labor generate different percentages of learning. Assembly-type labor generates the most rapid improvement and fabrication-type labor the least. Fabrication labor has a lower learning rate because the speed of jobs dependent on this type of labor is governed more by the capability of the equipment than the skill of the operator. The operator's learning in this case is confined to setup and maintenance times. In some situations, therefore, when a precise analysis is desired, a learning curve should be developed for each category of labor. Also, it should be noted that different firms within the same industry experience different rates of learning.

Supplier Progress Payments   Since the learning curve reflects changing labor costs, it provides a basis for figuring a supplier's financial commitment on any given number of units. This information is important because suppliers often operate in the red during the initial part of a production run, until learning can reduce costs below the average price. Supply managers can minimize supplier hardship by using the learning curve to break down an order into two or more production lots—each with successively lower average prices—and then set up progress payments based on the supplier's costs.

Application of Learning Curves

Before applying a learning curve to a particular item, a supply manager must be certain that learning does in fact occur at a reasonably constant rate. Many production operations do not possess such properties. Gross errors can be made if a learning curve is misapplied; therefore, buyers must be alert to the following problems.

Nonuniform Learning Rates   Learning curve analysis is predicated on the assumption that the process in question exhibits learning at a reasonably constant rate. Direct labor data from such a process should plot in a straight line on a log-log grid. If a straight line cannot be fitted to the data reasonably well, the learning rate is not uniform and the technique should not be used.

Low-Labor-Content Items   Continued learning occurs principally in the production of products entailing a high percentage of labor. The learning opportunity is particularly high in complex assembly work. On the other hand, if most work on a new item involves machine time, where output tends to be determined by machine capacity, there is little opportunity for continued learning.

Small Payoffs   Obtaining historical cost data to construct a learning curve entails much time and effort, particularly when a supplier uses a standard cost accounting system. Therefore, learning curve analysis is worthwhile only if the amount of money that can be saved is substantial.

Incorrect Learning Rates   Learning varies from industry to industry, plant to plant, product to product, and part to part. Applying one rate just because someone in the industry has used it can be misleading. Intelligent use of learning curves demands that learning rates be determined as accurately as possible from comparable past experience.

Established Items   If a supplier has previously made the item for someone else, a supply manager should not use the learning curve even if the product is nonstandard and new to the buying firm. Since most of the learning has already been done on previous work, any additional cost reduction may well be negligible.

Misleading Data   Not all cost savings stem from learning. The economies of large-scale production spread fixed costs over a larger number of output units, thus reducing the unit cost of the item. However, this phenomenon has nothing to do with the learning curve.

An Example of Learning Curve Application: The Cumulative Average Curve   The following simplified example shows a basic application of the cumulative average learning curve concept in labor cost analysis and contract pricing.

The ABC Corporation has purchased 50 pieces of a specially designed electronic component at $2,000 per unit. Of the $2,000 selling price, $1,000 represents direct labor. An audit of product costs for the first 50 units established that the operation is subject to an 80 percent cumulative average learning curve. What should ABC pay for the purchase of 350 more units?

Solution:

1. Using log-log paper, plot 50 units (on the horizontal axis) against $1,000 direct labor cost on the vertical axis (see Figure 18.5).

2. Double the number of units to 100 on the horizontal axis and plot against a labor cost of $800 (80 percent as high as the original $1,000 cost).

3. Draw a straight line through the two cost points. The line represents an 80 percent learning curve, constructed on the basis of labor cost data for the first 50 units of production.

4. Locate 400 units on the horizontal axis (the total expected production of 50 original units plus 350 new ones). Read from the curve the labor cost of approximately $510. This is the *average* expected labor cost per unit for the total production of 400 units.

5. To find the labor cost for 400 units, multiply 400 × $510, the direct labor cost per unit. The total is $204,000.

6. Subtract the labor paid in the original order to determine the labor cost of the new order of 350 units. Hence, subtract $50,000 (50 × $1,000) from $204,000. The answer is $154,000, the labor cost which should be paid for the new order of 350 units: $154,000 ÷ 350 units = $440 per unit labor cost, as compared with the original $1,000 per unit.

7. Now determine the cost for materials, overhead, and profit on the 350 units. Add this figure to the labor cost determined in step 6 to obtain the total price ABC should pay for the additional 350 units.

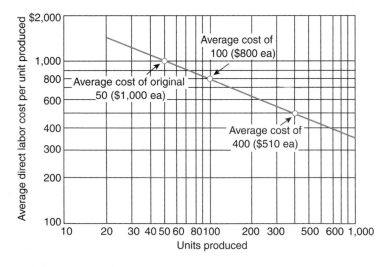

Figure 18.5 | Estimating labor cost for the new contract.

An Example of Learning Curve Application: The Unit Curve   The preceding application dealt with the use of a cumulative average learning curve. To illustrate the application of a unit learning curve, consider the following hypothetical situation.

Assume that a manufacturer receives an order to produce 515 units of a new product. After the necessary production and tooling design work is completed, the manufacturer begins production. Prior experience with moderately similar products leads the manufacturing manager to believe that a *unit* learning curve phenomenon probably will be experienced as production operations proceed.

To investigate this possibility, for the first 32 units produced, he or she records the production data shown in Table 18.4, columns 1 and 2. Then he or she makes the calculations shown in column 3. As production doubled (1 to 2, 2 to 4, 4 to 8, etc.), in each case it is clear that a significant learning effect was experienced. (The 2nd unit took 85 percent of the time required by the 1st unit, the 4th unit required 84.3 percent of the time required by the 2nd unit, and so on, as indicated in column 3.) Although the rate varies slightly, the manager concludes that a unit learning curve of approximately 85 percent is a good indicator of the manner in which the process will behave during the production of the remainder of the order (that is, that the 64th unit will require 85 percent of the time required by the 32nd unit, that the 128th unit will require 85 percent of the time required by the 64th unit, and so on).

Consequently, the supply professional constructs the curve on a log-log grid—and reads directly from the graph that the 512th unit will require approximately 13.6 direct labor hours for its production. Similar determinations for all units produced permit him to calculate the total number of labor hours for the complete job. Using this information, he can schedule production efficiently, as well as estimate the total labor cost the job will incur.

Tooling Costs

Most procurement authorities advocate that the buying firm pay for and take title to special tooling. Such an approach allows the buying firm maximum control. Analysis of production costs is easier, and the tooling can be moved if circumstances dictate.

There should be an inverse relationship between the investment in tooling and the number of hours required to produce a unit of output. The supply manager should ensure

Table 18.4 I The manufacturer's production data.

Column 1	Column 2	Column 3
Unit produced	Labor hours required to produce the corresponding unit in col. 1	Labor hours required as a percentage of those required for the preceding unit
1	60	—
2	51	85.0%
4	43	84.3
8	37	86.0
16	31	83.8
32	26	83.9

that the supplier plans to use sufficient tooling to minimize labor hours, but at the same time avoids investments that are not recovered through labor savings.

Indirect Costs

Indirect costs represent 30 to 40 percent of many suppliers' total costs of production. Five of the most common indirect cost pools are engineering overhead, materials overhead, manufacturing overhead, general and administrative expense, and selling expense.

Engineering Overhead

This is the cost of directing and supporting the engineering department and its direct labor staff. Costs include supervisory and support labor, fringe benefits, indirect supplies, and fixed charges such as depreciation.

Materials Overhead

This category of overhead usually includes the indirect costs of purchasing, transporting incoming materials, receiving, inspection, handling, and storage of materials.

Manufacturing Overhead

This category includes all production costs except direct materials, direct labor, and similar costs that can be assigned directly to the production of an item.

Manufacturing overhead includes:

■ The cost of supervision, inspection (some firms charge quality assurance or inspection as a direct cost), maintenance, custodial, and related personnel costs.

■ Fringe benefits such as Social Security and unemployment taxes, allowances for vacation pay, and group insurance.

■ Indirect supplies such as lubricating oils, grinding wheels, and janitorial supplies.

■ Fixed charges, including depreciation, rent, insurance, and property taxes.

■ Utilities.

General and Administrative

General and administrative (G&A) expenses include the company's general and executive offices, staff services, and miscellaneous activities.

Selling

Selling expenses include sales salaries, bonuses and commissions, and the normal costs of running the department.

Recovering Indirect Costs

The supplier allocates overhead costs to specific operations. Normally, this allocation is based on a product's age in terms of its life cycle. For instance, mature products generally incur lower G&A expenses than new products, which require more development and marketing effort. This allocation results in the use of an overhead rate for each indirect cost pool. The rate is determined by management personnel who select an appropriate base (or cost driver that causes the incurrence of the overhead costs) and then develop the ratio of the indirect cost pool dollars to that base. For example, the following allocation formula might be used for manufacturing overhead:

$$\frac{\text{Manufacturing overhead pool dollars}}{\text{Manufacturing direct labor hours}} = \frac{\$5,000,000}{\$1,000,000} = \begin{array}{l}\$5 \text{ per direct} \\ \text{manufacturing} \\ \text{labor hours}\end{array}$$

Overhead rates are generally established annually, typically before the start of the accounting period.

When determining the reasonableness of overhead rates, a buyer should not look only at the rate. He or she must consider the reasonableness of the indirect costs in the overhead pool and the appropriateness of the overhead allocation base. Since rates typically are established annually, the supply manager should also ensure that the allocation rate used by a supplier is applied consistently.

Activity Based Costing

Activity costing can be traced back to the late 1700s. During the intervening 200 years, management focused on labor costs, since they represented over 50 percent of total costs. The allocation of overhead costs based on the number of hours required to produce a product was relatively realistic and certainly easy.

But as direct labor costs have shrunk to 10 percent or so of total costs, they have become a less logical and realistic basis on which to allocate indirect costs. During the 1980s, a band of accounting academics, led by Professors Robert Kaplan and Robin Cooper of the Harvard Business School and Claremont McKenna College, respectively, developed what has become known as activity based costing (ABC)—a tool which more accurately identifies and allocates indirect costs to the products they support. In the 1990s, ABC evolved into activity based management (ABM). Activity based management essentially integrated ABC, continous improvement, and business process analysis.

ABC or ABM can be used to identify opportunities to reduce the supplier's indirect costs. ABC goes beyond identifying and allocating these indirect costs to products by identifying the drivers of these costs. Some examples of cost drivers are the number of orders, length of setups, specifications, engineering changes, and liaison trips required. This identification allows management to identify and implement cost savings opportunities. Quite obviously, if the supplier's management does not implement the required changes, an alert supply manager can "encourage" such action.

When analyzing a supplier's cost breakdown, it is imperative that the supply management professional understand how the supplier estimates and applies overhead to the product being purchased—it is also important to be aware of how well the supplier understands his or her own overhead cost structure. (A supply professional should develop the expertise to understand and motivate a selling firm with poor cost control to improve its system of collecting and applying costs to products.) As overhead becomes a greater proportion of product cost and as supply managers continue to seek ways to reduce acquisition cost, a small error in estimating and applying overhead can significantly affect the final cost. A note regarding accuracy: Greater accuracy may not only allow for a lower purchase price, but may also lead to a higher price because true costs are now known.

Target Costing

A number of years ago, management guru Peter F. Drucker wrote of five deadly business sins—avoidable mistakes that will (and in many cases have) harm(ed) a business.

Drucker's third deadly sin is cost-driven pricing. He argued, "The only thing that works is price-driven costing. . . . The only sound way to price is to start out with what the market is willing to pay . . . and design to that price specification."[4] Dr. Drucker's comments are as applicable to procurement today as they were then.

Some 40 years ago, the Ford Motor Company employed price-based costing in the development of its highly successful Mustang. The car was designed to retail at $1,995. This pricing objective drove design engineering to focus on cost, as well as performance and aesthetics. In turn, this drove engineers and purchasing and supply management to identify target prices for items to be purchased from suppliers. Members of these two functions then worked with their potential suppliers to develop processes and procedures to produce the required materials and components at these target prices. Curiously enough, American management largely reverted to cost-based pricing during the intervening 40 years, while its Japanese competition adopted price-based costing. Dr. Drucker points out that "cost-based pricing is the reason there is no American consumer-electronics industry anymore.[5]

It is heartening to see a growing number of organizations replace their "adversarial bidding system with one in which the company designates suppliers for a component and then uses target pricing . . . to determine with suppliers the component prices and how to achieve them."[6]

Profit

There are no precise formulas that can be used to help form a positive judgment concerning the right price, of which profit is one component (Price = Cost + Profit). There are, however, certain basic concepts of pricing on which scholars and practitioners do agree. One objective of sound purchasing is to achieve good supplier relations. This objective implies that the price must be high enough to keep the supplier in business. The price must also include a profit sufficiently high to encourage the supplier to accept the business in the first place, and, second, to motivate the firm to deliver the materials or services on time. What profit does it take to get these two desired results? On what basis should it be calculated?

If profit were calculated on a percentage-of-cost basis, the high-cost, inefficient producer would receive the higher profit (in absolute terms). To make matters even worse,

---

[4]Peter F. Drucker, "The Five Deadly Business Sins," *The Wall Street Journal,* October 21, 1993, p. 14.

[5]Ibid.

[6]James P. Womack and Daniel T. Jones, "From Lean Production to the Lean Enterprise," *Harvard Business Review,* March–April 1994, p. 97.

under the cost concept of pricing, producers who succeeded in lowering their costs by attaining greater efficiency would be "rewarded" by a reduction in total profit. For example, if an efficient producer has costs of $1,000 and a fair profit is agreed to be 10 percent of cost, its profit would be $100. If an inefficient producer has costs of $1,500, its profit on the same basis would be $150. If by better techniques the efficient producer should lower its costs to $800, the reward would be a $20 loss in profit—from $100 to $80. Obviously, the concept of determining a fair profit as a fixed percentage of cost is unrealistic.

Another concept on which profit might be determined is the relationship of capital investment required to produce the profit. Profit might be calculated as a percentage of capital investment. However, under this system, it would still be possible for the inefficient producer to receive the greater reward. For example, suppose firm A makes a capital investment of $2 million to produce product X. Firm B, on the other hand, invests only $1 million in its plant to produce product X successfully. From the buyer's point of view, there is no reason why firm A, simply because of its greater investment, should receive a higher profit on product X than firm B. Firm B, in fact, is utilizing its investment more efficiently. Thus, profit calculated as a fixed percentage of a firm's capital investment is not a satisfactory method for a buyer to use in determining a fair profit.

In a competitive economy, the major incentive for more efficient production is greater profit and repeat orders. A fair profit in our society cannot be determined as a fixed percentage figure. Rather, it is a flexible figure that should be higher for the more efficient producer than it is for the less efficient one. Low-cost producers can price lower than their competitors, while simultaneously enjoying a higher profit. Consequently, one of a buyer's greatest challenges is constantly to seek out the efficient, low-cost producer.

Considerations other than production efficiency can also rightly influence the relative size of a firm's profit. Six of the most common considerations are discussed briefly below.

1.   Profit is the basic reward for risk taking as well as the reward for efficiency; therefore, higher profits justifiably accompany extraordinary risks, whatever form they take. For example, great financial risk usually accompanies the production of new products. For this reason, a higher profit for new products is often necessary to induce a seller to take the risk of producing them.

2.   A higher dollar profit per unit of product purchased on small special orders is generally justified over that allowed on larger orders. The justification stems from the fact that the producer incurs a fixed amount of setup and administrative expense, regardless of the size of the order. Consequently, the cost of production for each unit is greater on small orders than on large orders. Since producers incur this cost at the request of the buyer, they usually demand a proportionately higher absolute profit before accepting an order that forces them to use their facilities in a less efficient manner than they might otherwise do.

3.   Rapid technological advancement creates a continuing nationwide shortage of technical talent. The cost in dollars and time of training highly technical personnel frequently makes it necessary to pay a higher profit on jobs requiring highly skilled people.

4.   In the space age, technical reliability can be a factor of overriding importance. A higher profit is generally conceded as justified for a firm that repeatedly turns out superbly reliable technical products than for one producing less reliable products. Good quality control, efficiency in controlling costs, on-time delivery, and technical assistance that has resulted in better production or design simplification all merit profit consideration.

5. On occasion, because of various temporary, unfavorable, supply-demand factors (e.g., excessive inventories, a shortage of capital, a cancellation of large orders), a firm may be forced to sell its products at a loss in order to recover a portion of its invested capital quickly or to keep its production facilities in operation.

6. A firm that manufactures a product according to the design and specifications of another firm is not entitled to the same percentage of profit as a firm that incurs the risk of manufacturing to its own design. In the first instance, the manufacturing firm is assured of a sale without marketing expense or risk of any kind, provided only that it fulfills the terms of the contract. In the second instance, the manufacturing firm is without assurance that its product can be sold profitably, if at all, in a competitive market.

In summary there is no single answer to the question: What is a fair profit? In a capitalistic society, profit generally is implied to mean the reward over costs that a firm receives for *the measure of efficiency it attains* and *the degree of risk it assumes.* From a purchasing viewpoint, profit provides two basic incentives. First, it induces the seller to take the order. Second, it induces the seller to perform as efficiently as possible, to deliver on time, and to provide all reasonable services associated with the order. Except in those temporary cases in which a firm is willing to sell at a loss, the profit is too low if it does not create these two incentives for the seller.

Concluding Remarks

Armed with an understanding of cost principles, the supply professional is now in a position to conduct an analysis of a potential supplier's proposal. Many costs are known and understood, but all companies have hidden costs that often reside in overhead. A supply professional needs an understanding of costs, cost systems, and overhead composition and allocation. Other key elements of cost analysis—labor efficiency, subcontracting, plant capacity, experience, cost modeling, and profit—should be permanent concepts in the minds of all supply management professionals. When price analysis is not possible, cost analysis becomes the basis of obtaining a *fair and reasonable* price.

CHAPTER 19

Types of Compensation

Design and development of contracts set the stage for either the success or failure of the relationship between buying and supplying firms. World-class supply professionals recognize this strategic importance and proactively analyze a variety of compensation agreements and select the type that protects the interests of both parties.

KEY CONCEPTS

Case

R&D Contract Development at PNS

Personal Network Systems (PNS) was in the process of developing a new, smart network computer for home use. The first working prototype was planned for release in seven months. The design-to-cost objective was $600 for the 5,000th unit, with a planned production run of 1 million units.

A thorough make-or-buy analysis had been conducted. One of the more costly items studied in the make-or-buy analysis was a radically new wireless networking device. The design-to-cost analysis allocated $100 per unit for the device. The make-or-buy analysis concluded that PNS should outsource the device. Based on limited experience with similar but less sophisticated devices, it was estimated that contractual development costs would be in the range of a half million dollars.

Due to staffing problems, June Oster (a newly promoted supply manager at PNS) was handling the procurement of the R&D work. She had contacted five firms that had the capability of developing the device. Two firms declined to participate in the project. The third indicated that it would be delighted to proceed with the development on a no-cost basis, provided that PNS would purchase a minimum of 500,000 devices. Production costs for these units would be based on a fixed price redeterminable contract, with the ceiling price to be negotiated on completion of the R&D portion of the work.

Ms. Oster received proposals for the R&D work from the remaining two firms. One appeared to be either a get-rich-quick proposal or a courtesy bid (she was not sure which—and really did not care) of $2 million. The other proposal was from the Tigertronix Corporation of Skunk Hollow, Arkansas. Tigertronix had been founded five years before by four engineers who had worked together at a large electronics firm in Beaverton, Oregon. The new company had expanded to 450 employees, had sales of $500 million, and enjoyed an excellent reputation in the wireless networking industry.

Ms. Oster met with Freddie Ready, vice president of marketing at Tigertronix, to discuss development of the new device. She indicated PNS's desire to pay for the development so that it would own any patents and data rights, including procurement specifications. Ms. Oster also indicated her desire to enter into an R&D contract which included a fixed price incentive option for production. PNS would retain the right to complete the production work. Obviously, the R&D supplier would have good insight into the costs and nuances of production.

On April 1, Tigertronix submitted a proposal (see Exhibit 19.1). If you were Ms. Oster, what action would you take? Why?

TIGERTRONIX CORPORATION
Skunk Hollow, Arkansas

1 April 2002

Ms. June Oster
Supply Manager
Personal Network Systems
62 Technology Drive
Sunnyvale, California 92116

Dear Ms. Oster:

We are pleased to submit our proposal for development of a smart network device. If we are able to begin work by April 15, we will be able to provide two prototype models by November 1, 2002.

We understand the confidential nature of the work and agree not to release any data to individuals not employed by your company.

We have submitted the cost breakdown data you requested. The total of our projected costs and profit is $1,242,000. We will be pleased to answer any questions you may have, while being sensitive to the time constraint under which we both are working.

In the interest of time, we are willing to enter into a cost reimbursement production option with a target cost of $100 per unit for the first 10,000 units of production. With this cost history, we then would be in a position to enter into a firm fixed unit price contract based on our production experience with these first 10,000 units.

Very sincerely,

Ron Cox
President

Attachment: Proposal

ATTACHMENT
ESTIMATED R&D COSTS

Engineering
4,000 hours @ $60/hour	$ 240,000

Supervisory
600 hours @ $100/hour	60,000
SUBTOTAL	$ 300,000
Overhead 250%	750,000
G&A 10%	30,000
SUBTOTAL	$1,080,000
Profit	162,000
TOTAL	$1,242,000

Exhibit 19.1

Introduction to Compensation Arrangements

A wide selection of contract compensation arrangements is necessary to provide the flexibility needed for the procurement of a large variety of materials and services. The compensation arrangement determines (1) the degree and timing of the cost responsibility assumed by the supplier, (2) the amount of profit or fee available to the supplier, and (3) the motivational implications of the fee portion of the compensation arrangements. The following examples are introduced in an effort to portray visually the seller's and, in turn, the buyer's problem of dealing with uncertainty.

Example 1: Low Level of Uncertainty   In this example the seller's likely cost for a project is $1,000,000. The seller is confident that the lowest possible cost will be $950,000 and the highest cost $1,050,000. This information is portrayed in Figure 19.1. One can see that the seller is virtually certain that costs will be within the range of $950,000 to $1,050,000, with the most likely outcome near $1,000,000.

   If the seller adds 10 percent for profit to the most likely cost outcome, it may be willing to agree to a firm fixed price (FFP) of $1,100,000. Note that the supplier's actual profit will be in the range of $150,000 (if actual costs are $950,000) to $50,000 (if actual costs are $1,050,000). The most likely profit is $100,000 [$1,100,000 (the price) − $1,000,000 (the most likely cost outcome)]. In this example, the use of a firm fixed price contract (as discussed below) seems appropriate.

Example 2: High Level of Uncertainty   In this example, assume that the range of likely cost outcomes is much wider—say, $500,000 to $1,500,000. (Such an extreme range of cost outcomes is highly unlikely but is used here to introduce the concept that the type of compensation agreement should be appropriate for the amount of uncertainty present.) Again, the most likely cost outcome is $1,000,000. This example is portrayed in Figure 19.2.

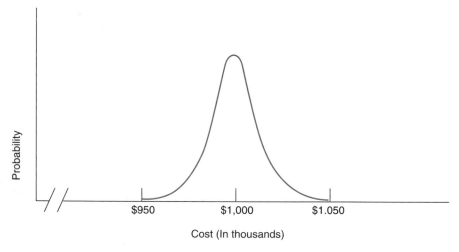

Figure 19.1 | Probability of cost outcome: low level of uncertainty

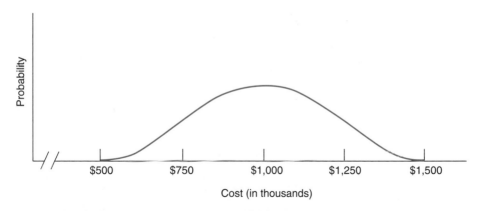

Figure 19.2 | Probability of cost outcome: high level of uncertainty

Most sellers are very risk averse: that is, they are unwilling to accept large amounts of uncertainty unless they are able to transfer the uncertainty to the buyer in the form of higher prices. In this case, the seller studies the distribution of likely cost outcomes and concludes that, 9 times out of 10, the actual cost will be $1,400,000 or less. Accordingly, if the buyer is unwise enough to insist on using a firm fixed method of compensation, the seller may demand a firm fixed price of $1,540,000 [$1,400,000 plus $140,000 (10 percent profit on this cost)].

Table 19.1 portrays the supplier's profit under various cost outcomes for this second example. It is fairly obvious that if the buyer could assume the risk inherent in this procurement, a lower price would be possible—except in the extreme case in which actual costs exceeded approximately $1,540,000.

Let us assume that the buyer and supplier agreed to a cost plus fixed fee (CPFF) contract with a target cost of $1,000,000 and a fixed fee of $50,000. Note that the fee is relatively low: 5 percent of target cost. This is so since the supplier will not incur any risk. Table 19.2 portrays the price to be paid by the buyer under different cost outcomes.

The sophisticated reader may say: "Interesting. But a fee or profit of $50,000 on a cost of $500,000 [see row 1, Table 19.2] is 10 percent. That's too high, considering that there's no cost risk! Why not apply a fixed percent fee to costs?" Such an approach is shown in Table 19-3. One does not have to be a rocket scientist to see that such an approach motivates the supplier to increase costs since the higher the cost, the higher the fee!

Table 19.1 | Supplier's Profit Using FFP under Various Cost Outcomes

Actual cost	Actual profit	Fixed price
$ 500,000	$1,040,000	$1,540,000
1,000,000	540,000	1,540,000
1,400,000	140,000	1,540,000
1,500,000	40,000	1,540,000

Table 19.2 | Buyer's Price Using CPFF at Various Actual Cost Outcomes

Actual cost	Fixed fee or profit	Price paid
$ 500,000	$50,000	$ 550,000
1,000,000	50,000	1,050,000
1,400,000	50,000	1,450,000
1,500,000	50,000	1,550,000

Table 19.3 | Fee and Price Outcomes at Various Cost Outcomes with Profit as a Fixed Percentage of Cost

Actual cost	Fee (10% of actual cost)	Price paid
$ 500,000	$ 50,000	$ 550,000
1,000,000	100,000	1,100,000
1,400,000	140,000	1,540,000
1,500,000	150,000	1,650,000

Without going into further detail at this point, it should be apparent that selection of the right type of compensation arrangement can save money. Insightful readers may be asking themselves: "What would happen if, instead of paying a fixed fee or a fixed percentage of cost, we were able to use incentives to control supplier costs?"

The supply manager has a range of compensation arrangements designed to meet the needs of a particular procurement. At one end of this range is the firm fixed price contract under which the supplier assumes all cost responsibility and, therefore, profit and loss potentials are high. At the other end of this range is the cost plus fixed fee contract under which the supplier has no cost risk and the fee (profit) is fixed, usually at a relatively low level. In between these two extremes are numerous incentive arrangements that reflect a sharing of the cost responsibility.

Contract Cost Risk Appraisal

The degree of cost responsibility a supplier reasonably can be expected to assume is determined primarily by the cost risk involved. It is to the supply manager's advantage to estimate this risk prior to negotiations. Since the majority of contracts are "forward priced," that is, priced prior to completion of the work, some cost risk is involved in each of them. The degree of cost risk involved will depend on how accurately the cost of the contract can be estimated prior to performance. The accuracy of the cost estimate and the degree of cost risk usually are a function of both technical and contract schedule risk.

A supply manager should insist on a fixed price contract unless (1) the risks will result in a contract price containing large reserves for contingencies that may not occur, or (2) the risks result in reliable suppliers refusing to agree to a fixed price contract because a significant loss might be incurred, or (3) the use of a fixed price contract could result in the supplier "cutting corners" in order to avoid taking a loss.

Technical Risk

Technical risk is associated with the nature of the item being purchased. Appraisal of technical risk includes analysis of the type and complexity of the item or service being purchased, stability of design specifications or statement of work, availability of historical pricing data, and prior production experience. Analysis of technical risk in a complex system may include appraisals by a team with members from the user group, the engineering staff, and the purchasing and supply management group. Think, for example, of the technical risk involved in the Apollo mission to put a man on the moon: leaving the earth's gravity, sustaining life in a gravityless environment, landing on an unknown surface structure of the moon's crust, and reentering the earth's stratosphere without burning up.

Technical risk is reduced as the job requirements, production methods, and pricing data become better defined and the design specifications or statement of work becomes more stable. Research and development contracts, in particular, have a rather high technical risk associated with them. This is because of the ill-defined requirements that arise from the necessity to deal beyond, or at least very near, the limits of the current technology.

Contract Schedule Risk

In addition to technical risk, schedule risk must be assessed in determining the supplier's cost risk. Preferred supply management practice calls for forward pricing of contract efforts. This practice attempts to anticipate material and labor cost increases during performance of the contract. These estimates, along with possible schedule slippage, are always subject to error. In Chapter 21, project management is discussed as a tool to reduce schedule risk.

General Types of Contract Compensation Arrangements

Compensation arrangements can be classified into three broad categories: (1) fixed price contracts, (2) incentive contracts, and (3) cost reimbursement contracts.

Fixed Price Contracts

Under a fixed price arrangement, the supplier is obligated to deliver the product or service called for by the contract for a fixed price. If, prior to completion of the product, the supplier finds that the effort is more difficult or costly than anticipated, the supplier is still obligated to deliver the product. Further, the supplier will receive no more than the previously agreed-on amount. The amount of profit the supplier receives will depend on the actual cost outcome. There is no maximum or minimum profit limitation in fixed price contracts. A fixed price arrangement is normally used in situations where specifications are well defined and cost risk is relatively low.

Incentive Contracts

Incentive contracts are employed in an effort to motivate the supplier to improve cost and possibly other stated requirements such as schedule performance. In an incentive contract, the cost responsibility is shared by the buyer and the seller. This sharing addresses two issues: (1) the desire to motivate the supplier to control cost and (2) an awareness that if the supplier assumes all or most of the risk when significant uncertainty is present, a contingency allowance will be required, thereby inflating the contract price.

Incentive contracts are of two types: (1) fixed price incentive and (2) cost plus incentive fee. With a fixed price incentive contract, the ceiling price is agreed to (or fixed) during negotiations. Under the cost plus incentive fee arrangement, the supplier is reimbursed for all allowable costs incurred, up to any prescribed ceiling. Obviously, the supplier's cost accounting system must meet commonly accepted standards and be open to the customer for review when employing incentives based on costs incurred.

Cost-Type Contracts

Under a cost-type arrangement, the buyer's obligation is to reimburse the supplier for all allowable, reasonable, and allocable costs incurred, and to pay a fixed fee. Again, the supplier's cost accounting practices must meet commonly accepted standards and be open to the customer. Most cost arrangements include a cost limitation clause that sets an administrative limitation on the reimbursement of costs. Generally, under a cost-type arrangement, the supplier is obligated only to provide its "best effort." Usually, neither performance nor delivery is guaranteed. Cost-type arrangements are normally used when:

- Procurement of research and development involves high technical risk.
- Some doubt exists that the project can be successfully completed.
- Product specifications are incomplete.
- High-dollar, highly uncertain procurements such as software development are involved.

Specific Types of Compensation Arrangements

There are a number of specific types of compensation arrangements under each of the above categories.

1. Fixed price compensation arrangements:
   - Firm fixed price
   - Fixed price with economic price adjustment
   - Fixed price redetermination
2. Incentive arrangements:
   - Fixed price incentive
   - Cost plus incentive fee
3. Cost-type arrangements:
   - Cost plus fixed fee
   - Cost plus award fee
   - Cost without fee
   - Cost sharing
   - Time and materials
   - Letter contracts

The applicability, elements, structure, and final price computation for the various compensation arrangements are discussed in the following paragraphs.

Firm Fixed Price Contracts

The most preferred contract type, if appropriate for the procurement, is the firm fixed price contract. A firm fixed price (FFP) contract is an agreement to pay a specified price when the items (services) specified by the contract have been delivered (completed) and accepted. The contracting parties establish a firm price through either competitive bidding or negotiation. Since there is no adjustment in contract price after the work is completed and actual costs are known, the cost risk to the supplier can be high.

An FFP contract is appropriate in competitive bidding if the specifications are definite, there is little schedule risk, and competition has established the existence of a fair and reasonable price. An FFP contract can also be appropriate for negotiated procurements if a review reveals adequate specifications and if price and cost analysis establishes the reasonableness of the price.

As previously stated, under an FFP contract there is no price adjustment due to the supplier's cost experience. Because the supplier has all cost responsibility, the actual outcome will show up in the form of profit or losses. Therefore, the supplier has maximum incentive to control costs under an FFP contract. If the supplier incurs expenses beyond the buyer's obligation, the seller must find the required funds elsewhere. Conversely, if the supplier reduces costs, all savings contribute to the supplier's profit. This dollar-for-dollar relationship between expenditures and profit is the greatest motivator of efficiency available. An FFP contract has only one contract compensation arrangement element: total price. Although negotiations may involve the discussion of costs and profit, the contractual document reflects only total price. This structure can be seen in Figure 19.3, which depicts an FFP contract for $20,000.

In this example, cost is shown as the independent variable (x-axis), and profit, since it is a function of cost, as the dependent variable (y-axis). The graph depicts the one-to-one relationship between costs and profit by showing that as costs increase by $1, profit decreases by $1.

Computing the final price in an FFP-type contract is a simple matter. If a $20,000 firm fixed price contract is negotiated, on contract completion the supplier will receive $20,000 whether costs were $15,000 or $25,000 or any other amount.

It should be noted that a fixed price does not always stay fixed. A supplier who is losing money *may* request and get some relief, if any of the following apply:

1. The customer in some way has contributed to the loss.
2. The customer badly needs the items and other suppliers are not willing to provide them at the established price.
3. The supplier has unique facilities and time is too short to do anything but to get the product at an increased cost from the initial supplier.
4. The customer's representatives do not employ sound supply management practices.

As previously discussed, early supplier involvement (ESI) with a decision to rely on one supplier during and after development results in many benefits based on the early matching

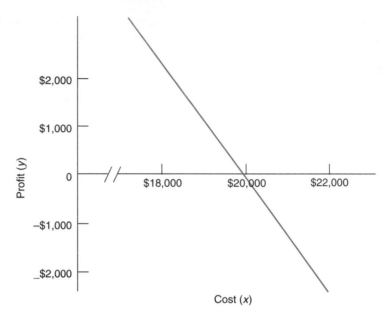

Figure 19.3 I Firm fixed price contract—$20,000

of process and product. But ESI may result in cost overruns and higher costs if the supplier can't perform at the fixed price because of unforeseen (usually technical) reasons. It should be recognized that when a supplier fails to perform under a fixed price contract and the buying firm is forced to turn the business into a cost plus type of contract, the supplier has damaged its chance for future business with the customer and other potential customers. The supply manager, on the other hand, can use the prospect of continued future business to keep the price well below what the supplier's leverage of the moment might suggest.

Variations of the FFP contract have been developed to meet special circumstances. One such variation is the FFP level-of-effort contract. This arrangement calls for a set number of labor hours to be expended over a period of time. The contract is considered complete when the hours are expended, although normally a report of findings is also required. The FFP level-of-effort contract is appropriately used when the specification is general in nature and when no specific end item (other than a report) is required. This arrangement is most frequently used for research and development efforts under $100,000 and for "get our foot in the door" consulting contracts.

Fixed Price with Economic Price Adjustment Contracts

Fixed price with economic price adjustment (FPEPA) contracts are used to recognize economic contingencies, such as unstable labor or market conditions which would prevent the establishment of a firm fixed price contract without a large contingency for possible cost increases or decreases in the unit cost of labor and/or materials. An FPEPA contract is simply an FFP contract that includes economic price adjustment clauses. Such provisions are common when purchasing items containing precious metals and construction services.

Economic price adjustments (EPA) or escalator/de-escalator clauses provide for both price increases and decreases to protect the buyer and supplier from the effects of economic changes. If such clauses were not used, suppliers would include contingency allowances in their bids or proposals to eliminate or reduce the risk of loss. With a fixed contingency allowance in the contract price, the supplier is hurt if the changes exceed its estimate, and the buyer will overpay if the input unit cost increases do not materialize.

An economic price adjustment clause may be used for fixed price–type arrangements resulting from both competitively bid and negotiated contracts. Price adjustments normally should be restricted to contingencies beyond the control of the supplier. Under an FPEPA contract, specific contingencies are left open subject to an EPA clause, and the final contract price is adjusted, depending on what happens to these contingencies. Where cost pass-through or escalator clauses cover specific materials and/or labor, the buyer should be sure that the price increase does not occur until the higher-cost material is used or until the labor contract increase takes effect.

The use of economic price adjustment clauses varies with the probability of significant price fluctuations. Their use also increases when purchasing strategy favors early supplier involvement, longer-term contracts, fewer supplies, and more single-source suppliers. An economic price adjustment clause should recognize the possibility of both inflation and deflation in determining price adjustments. Further, labor and material costs subject to economic adjustment must reflect the effects of learning on both labor and material costs. It takes considerable purchasing skill to use economic price adjustment clauses well. Decisions must be made on what items to include and which price/cost index or benchmark is best for each item.

The cost elements to adjust are high-value raw materials, specific high-value components, and direct labor. The professional supply manager generally should oppose including costs within the supplier's control such as development, depreciation, fixed expenses, other overhead items, and profit in the base subject to escalation.

In selecting indexes for price adjustment clauses, the following rules are suggested:

- Select from the appropriate Bureau of Labor Statistics category.
- Avoid broad indexes; use the lowest-level classification which includes the item.
- Develop a weighted index for materials in a product.
- Select labor rate indexes by type and location.
- Define energy indexes by fuel type and location.
- Analyze the past history of each proposed index versus the actual price change of the item being indexed.

Using a broad index can produce strange results. One executive used the producer price index (PPI) to adjust the purchase price of electronic apparatus, not recognizing that the PPI consists of about 40 percent food and fuel components with only 3 percent electronics input.

The details of the economic price adjustment clause must be thought through with various scenarios in mind. When will adjustments be made? Under what conditions can the contract be renegotiated? How will it be audited? By whom?

Fixed Price Redetermination Contracts

These contracts provide for a firm fixed price for an initial contract period with a redetermination (upward or downward) at a stated time during contract performance [FPR (prospective)] or after contract completion [FPR (retroactive)]. The FPR (prospective) is usually used only in those circumstances calling for quantity production or services where a fair and reasonable price can be negotiated for initial periods but not for subsequent periods. The FPR (retroactive) is used in those circumstances where, at the time of negotiation, a fair and reasonable price cannot be established and the amount involved is so small and the performance period so short that use of any other contract type would be impractical.

The data shown in Table 19.3 are also applicable to an FPR contract. As was observed, the supplier is motivated to increase costs, since the higher the cost, the higher the fee!

Incentive Arrangements

Firm fixed price (FFP) and cost plus fixed fee (CPFF) contracts are extremes of the range of contract compensation arrangements since in either case all of the cost responsibility falls on only one party. In between these two extremes are a number of contract arrangements where the cost responsibility is shared between the customer and the supplier. These are called incentive-type contracts.

Incentives are applied to contracts in an attempt to motivate the supplier to improve performance in cost, schedule, or other stated parameters. By far the most frequent application of incentives is in the area of cost control. However, this is not the only type of incentive. The specific type of incentive applied depends on the desired outcome. For example, if the primary interest is in developing a high-performance read head, it would be logical to reward the supplier for development and production of a read head which exceeds the minimum specifications. If the same read head were needed to meet a crash development effort, schedule may be the basis of an incentive. For the same read head, funds might be a real constraint due to budgetary limitations, and a production unit cost incentive would be appropriate. If a combination of performance and cost objectives were of concern, a multiple-incentive contract could be developed.

In this book, the discussion of incentive arrangements is limited to cost incentives. The focus will be on the two most frequently applied cost incentive compensation arrangements: the fixed price incentive (FPI) contract and the cost plus incentive fee (CPIF) contract. A general discussion of how a simplified incentive contract is structured precedes analysis of the specific elements and structure of these two compensation arrangements. The elements of a simplified incentive contract include (1) the target cost, (2) the target profit, and (3) the sharing arrangement.

Target Cost   The target cost for an incentive contract is that cost outcome which both the buyer and the supplier feel is the most likely outcome for the effort involved. The target cost should be based on costs that would result under "normal business conditions." Although the target cost is thought to be the most likely, it is recognized that the probability of the supplier's final costs being very close to the target cost is low. After all, if there were a high probability that the target cost would be close to the final cost, a firm fixed price contract would be appropriate. The target should be that cost point where both parties agree that there is an equal chance of going above or below the target.

Target Profit   In addition to a target cost, a target profit is developed. The target profit in an incentive contract is a profit amount that is considered fair and reasonable, based on all relevant facts, as discussed in Chapter 18.

Allocating Costs above or below Target   Since an incentive contract recognizes that the target most likely will *not* be met, a method of allocating cost increases above or decreases below target is necessary. The method is a sharing arrangement that reflects the sharing of the cost responsibility between the buyer and the supplier. This arrangement should reflect the cost risk involved as evidenced by the magnitude of potential increases and decreases for the specific effort. In addition, the sharing arrangement must address two questions: "What percentage of the savings below target will be required to motivate the supplier to perform as efficiently as possible?" and "What percentage of the cost overrun—cost above target—charged to the supplier (in the form of lower profit) will cause the supplier to perform as efficiently as possible?"

How is the magnitude of a potential cost increase or decrease established? It is developed through an assessment of possible cost outcomes, based on varying circumstances a supplier might face during contract performance. In addition to developing a target cost and profit outcome, the parties establish cost outcomes and associated profits for a "best case" and a "worst case" situation. The best-case cost outcome is referred to as the most optimistic cost (MOC) point, and its related profit is referred to as the most optimistic profit (MOPi) point. The worst-case cost outcome is referred to as the most pessimistic cost (MPC) point, and its profit is referred to as the most pessimistic profit (MPPr) point.

The difference between the target point and the most optimistic point provides the supply manager with the magnitude of a potential cost decrease. The difference between the target point and the most pessimistic point provides the supply manager with the magnitude of a potential cost increase. One normally would not expect these magnitudes to be equal, since the potential for things to go wrong is usually higher than the potential for things to go better than expected. Another way of looking at the magnitude of potential cost increase is that it provides an estimate of the cost risk a supplier faces if the target cost is not met. This cost risk and the supplier's assumption of this risk are reflected in the sharing arrangement.

Fixed Price Incentive Fee

Table 19.4 shows how a fixed price incentive fee contract is structured. The cost and profit outcomes shown in Table 19.4 were agreed on by the buying and the selling firms. These data are portrayed in Figure 19.4.

Computing of the final payment under an incentive arrangement is more complex than under either an FFP or CPFF contract. Under an incentive arrangement, the supplier's profit will be adjusted to reflect performance in the cost area. If the supplier has incurred costs above target, the profit will be decreased by the supplier's share of the cost above target cost up to the ceiling price. Conversely, if the supplier's costs are below target, its profit is increased. The final price outcome would be the supplier's cost plus

Table 19.4 I Fixed Price Incentive Fee

	Estimated Dollars (in thousands)	Price (in thousands)
Target cost (TC)	$1,000	
Target profit (TPr)	80	$1,080
Most optimistic cost (MOC)	800	
Most optimistic profit (MOPr)	120	920
Most pessimistic cost (MPC)	1,200	
Most pessimistic profit (MPPr)	0	1,200
Ceiling price	1,200	1,200

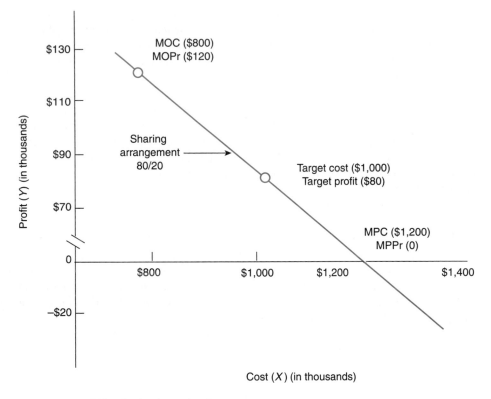

Figure 19.4 I Fixed price incentive fee

profit. The supplier's profit equals the sum of the target profit plus or minus the supplier's share of the cost savings or cost increase.

Cost Plus Incentive Fee Arrangements

CPIF contracts combine the incentive arrangement and the cost plus fixed fee arrangement. Under a CPIF arrangement, an incentive applies over part of the range of cost outcomes. The fee structure resembles a cost plus fixed fee contract at both the low-cost and

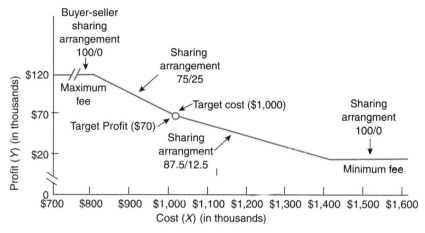

Figure 19.5 | CPIF arrangement

Table 19.5 | Cost Plus Incentive Fee

Target cost	$1,000,000
Target profit	70,000
Optimistic cost	800,000
Optimistic and maximum profit	120,000
Pessimistic cost	1,400,000
Pessimistic and minimum profit	20,000
Sharing below target (customer/supplier)	75/25
Sharing above target (customer/supplier)	87.5/12.5

high-cost ends of the range, as shown in Figure 19.5. This information is also depicted in Table 19.5. Thus, if cost were $800,000 or less, the fee would be $120,000. If cost were $1,400,000 or more, the fee would be $20,000.

A cost plus incentive fee arrangement is used in those circumstances in which the cost risk warrants a cost-type arrangement but an incentive can be established to provide the supplier with some motivation to manage costs. CPIF arrangements are most suitable for advanced development efforts and for initial production runs. In these circumstances, risk may be too high to warrant use of a fixed price arrangement or an FPI arrangement, but not high enough to require a CPFF arrangement to get a reliable supplier.

The CPIF contract is structured in a manner very similar to the FPI compensation arrangement. Cost and fee outcomes are established for target, most optimistic, and most pessimistic points. These cost and fee outcomes are used to establish the sharing arrangement for cost decrease and increase situations. The difference between the structure of the FPI and CPIF arrangements is that under the CPIF arrangement, the contract converts to a CPFF contract at both the most optimistic and the most pessimistic fee points.

The computation of the final price to be paid to the supplier on contract completion follows the same steps as in the fixed price incentive arrangement. However, in a CPIF contract a comparison is made between computed fee and minimum and maximum fees prior to the calculation of the final price. For example, using the CPIF contract structured in Figure 19.5, the supply manager would compute the final price, based on a final cost of $700,000, as follows:

> Target cost—$1,000,000
> Target profit—$70,000
> Maximum fee—$120,000
> Minimum fee—$20,000

1. Cost savings = Target cost − Final cost
   $300,000 = $1,000,000 − $700,000

2. Supplier's share of cost savings = Cost savings × Supplier share
   $75,000 = $300,000 × 0.25

3. Computed fee = Savings fee + Target fee
   $145,000 = $75,000 + $70,000

Since there is a maximum limitation on fee, a comparison is made between the computed fee and the maximum fee. In this case, the supplier receives only the maximum fee, $120,000.

4. Final price = Final cost + Maximum fee
   $820,000 = $700,000 + $120,000

The CPIF contract is an incentive arrangement that converts to a CPFF contract at both the maximum and minimum fee points. This type of contract provides the supplier some incentive to control cost outcomes in the area over which the sharing arrangements apply, called the range of incentive effectiveness.

Cost Plus Fixed Fee Arrangements

Under a CPFF contract, the buyer agrees to reimburse the supplier for all allowable, reasonable, and allocable costs that may be incurred during the performance of the contract. Moreover, the buyer agrees to pay the supplier a fixed number of dollars above the cost as the fee for doing the work. The fee changes only when the scope of work changes. Under the CPFF, the supplier has no incentive to reduce or control costs.

The contractual elements of this arrangement include an estimated cost and a fixed fee. The estimated cost represents the best estimate of the customer and the supplier for the work involved. The fixed fee is the amount of fee the supplier will receive regardless of cost outcome. Because the supplier has no cost risk under a CPFF contract, the profit potential is relatively low. Normally there is a limit on the customer's total liability.

The supply professional should remember that when employing any compensation method other than a fixed price, the final cost should be audited. Supply management departments spend hours negotiating the right to inspect the actual invoices for material and the hours worked. Many, however, do not conduct an appropriate audit. It is a good use of time to look at the details even though one might not expect to find any inappropriate charges. The knowledge gained will often prove helpful in future negotiations.

Table 19.6 I Cost Plus Fixed Fee: Sample Price Outcomes

	Possible Outcomes (in thousands)			
Final cost	$800	$900	$1,000	$1,200
Fixed fee	50	50	50	50
Price to be paid to the supplier	$850	$950	$1,050	$1,250

Computing the final payment due the supplier under a CPFF contract is simply a matter of adding the incurred costs (assuming that an audit has found them to be reasonable, allowable, and allocable) to the fixed fee. In the case of a CPFF contract with an estimated cost of $1,000,000 and a fixed fee of $50,000, some possible final contract price outcomes are shown above.

The supply manager must remember that in a cost-type contract, the limit is on the fee, not on total customer obligation. Obviously, the CPFF-type contract should be used only when one cannot get a more favorable arrangement or when the presence of great uncertainty and risk would result in inclusion of a large contingency in a firm fixed price contract. The CPFF contract also is appropriate in circumstances in which the technical and schedule risks are so high that the cost risk is too large for the supplier to assume. This type of contract is designed chiefly for use in research or exploratory development when the uncertainty of performance is so great that a firm price or an incentive arrangement cannot be set up at any time during the life of the contract. Costs normally are audited by the buyer before final payment.

Cost Plus Award Fee (CPAF)

The cost plus award fee (CPAF) was pioneered by NASA when the agency was purchasing highly complex hardware and professional services in support of the space program. The award fee is very applicable to the procurement of software developed for the buying company and for janitorial, landscaping, and similar services where the ability to reward the supplier for nonquantitative aspects of its performance on a subjective basis makes good business sense. The award fee is a pool of money established by the buyer to reward the supplier on a periodic basis for the *application of effort in meeting the buyer's stated needs*. The key difference between the award fee and other fees is that the supplier's receipt of the fee is based on the buying firm's *subjective evaluation* of how well the supplier applies its *efforts* in meeting the buyer's needs. The subjective aspect provides a flexibility to contracting situations in an uncertain environment. When properly used, the award fee benefits both the buyer and the supplier. Superior performance receives superior rewards in the form of a superior fee. The award fee also introduces an element of flexibility since the buyer can change the areas receiving supplier attention by providing advance guidance for any performance period. The award fee gives the buying firm's management a flexible tool with which to influence performance.

Cost without Fee

Nonprofit institutions, such as universities, frequently do research work for both government and industry, without the objective of making a profit. Such research is done under cost-type contracts without a fee. Because universities do much of the nation's pure research, as distinguished from applied research done by industry, a growing number of contracts of this type are being used. Naturally, the universities recover all overhead costs, which generally include facilities costs and remuneration for personnel who work on the contracts. In recent years, high-technology firms have increased their use of this contract type.

Cost Sharing

In some situations, a firm doing research under a cost type of contract stands to benefit if the product developed can be used in its own product line. Under such circumstances, the buyer and the seller agree on what they consider to be a fair basis to share the costs (most often it is 50-50). The electronics industry has found this type of contract especially useful.

Time and Materials

In certain types of contracts, such as those calling for repairs to machinery, the precise work to be done cannot be predicted in advance. For instance, it cannot be known exactly what must be done to a large malfunctioning pump aboard a ship until it is opened and examined. Perhaps only a new gasket is required to put it in good working order. On the other hand, its impeller could require a major job of balancing and realignment. The time and materials contract is one method of pricing this type of work. Under this type of contract, the parties agree on a fixed rate per labor hour that includes overhead and profit, with materials supplied at cost.

Suppose a mechanic working on the ship's pump is paid $30 per hour. Assume also that overhead is calculated as 100 percent of the labor cost and profit is set at 10 percent of total cost. A billing rate for this mechanic for one hour would be calculated as shown in Table 19.7.

If it took the mechanic two days (16 hours) to repair the pump, using $320 worth of material, the job price would be $1,376 (16 × $66 + $320).[1] Profit should be paid only on labor and overhead costs. Note that the supplier is motivated to increase the number

Table 19.7 | Time and Materials: Billing Rate

Direct labor cost, per hour	$30
Overhead at 100 percent of labor	30
Total cost	$60
Profit at 10 percent of total cost	6
Billing rate, per hour	$66

---

[1] The alert reader will observe that this is really a cost plus percentage of cost contract. If the mechanic is a good worker, he might complete the job in 10 hours ($60 profit to his employer). If he is a poor worker, he could take 20 hours, and his employer would receive $120 in profit. Obviously, supply managers must exercise close control over this type of contract to be sure that inefficient or wasteful methods are not used.

of hours for two reasons: (1) The $30 of overhead commonly is a fixed cost. Thus, every additional hour contributes $30 to an overhead which probably has been amortized. In effect, this $30 becomes a gift of $30 of additional profit. (2) The stated profit of $6 increases with each additional hour.

A variation of the time and materials type of contract is called a labor-hour contract. In this type of contract, materials are not supplied by the seller; however, other costs are agreed to as in time and materials contracts.

Letter Contracts and Letters of Intent

Letter contracts are used in those rare situations in which it is imperative that work start on a complex project immediately. Letter contracts are *preliminary contractual authorizations* under which the seller can commence work immediately. The seller can prepare drawings, obtain required materials, and start actual production. Under letter contracts, the seller is guaranteed reimbursement for costs up to a specified amount. Letter contracts should be converted to definite contracts at the earliest possible date.[2]

Considerations when Selecting Contract Types

With such a wide variety of contract types available, the supply professional must exercise considerable care in selecting the best one for a particular use. If a bid or a quoted price is reasonable, this will help the supply manager decide to use a firm fixed price contract. On the other hand, if the fairness of the price is in doubt, a fixed price contract could entail excessive expense to the buying firm and would be a poor choice. If price uncertainty stems from unstable labor or market conditions, fixed price with escalation may be a solution. If the uncertainty is due to a potential improvement in production effort, an incentive contract may be the best answer. Plainly, the many factors that affect procurement costs can themselves guide the supply professional in his or her selection of the best type of contract for a given purchasing situation.

The specific nature of the materials, equipment, or services to be purchased also can frequently point up advantages of one contract type over another. The more complex or developmental the purchased item, the greater the risks and difficulties in using a fixed price contract. Any uncertainty in design affects a seller's ability to estimate costs, as does a lack of cost experience with a new item. The details of any given purchase will themselves indicate the magnitude of the price uncertainties involved. A full understanding of these uncertainties permits supply managers to allocate the risks more equitably between their firm and the supplier's firm through the proper choice of contract type.

Timing of the procurement quite frequently is a controlling factor in selection of the contract type. Allowing potential suppliers only a short time to prepare their bids can reduce the reliability of the cost estimates and increase prices. A short delivery period usually rules out the effective use of incentive contracts. On the other hand, a long contract

---

[2] For more on this topic, see William A. Hancock, "Using Letters of Intent to Provide a Framework for Relationships with Suppliers," in *The Purchaser's Legal Adviser*, January 1994, published by Business Laws, Chesterland, OH (800-759-0920).

period allows time to generate and apply cost-reducing efficiencies, an ideal situation for an incentive contract. The facts of each procurement must be considered individually in determining which contract type the supply manager should use.

Business practices in specific industries frequently can provide additional clues as to the best choice of contract type. The construction industry, for example, traditionally accepts a wider range of competitive fixed price jobs than does the aerospace industry. The lumber industry accepts prices established by open auctions. Architects and engineers frequently will not enter into price competition with one another for architectural or engineering services; neither will some management consulting firms compete with one another on price. Business factors such as these help determine the best contract type in a great many purchasing situations.

The scope and intensity of competition definitely can influence the type of contract to use. If competition is intense and the prices bid are close, then the supply manager can justifiably feel that the prices are fair and reasonable and use a firm fixed price contract. On the other hand, if competition is not adequate and the supply manager has doubts concerning the reasonableness of prices, an incentive or cost contract may be appropriate.

In short, *the supply professional's basic preference for a firm fixed price contract is just the starting point for an analysis of alternative compensation choices.* As the supply manager considers all available compensation types, he or she must weigh the preference for fixed prices against the risks involved, the time available, the degree of competition involved, experience with the industry involved, the apparent soundness of the offered price, the technical and developmental state of the item being purchased, and all the other technical and economic information that affects the purchase transaction. Determination of the best compensation agreement for a given situation requires a careful analysis of all the factors relevant to that situation.

Concluding Remarks

A supply manager can, in most instances, enter into a firm fixed price contract even when some cost risk is present. But if risk is high, there is a likelihood of either of two equally unsatisfactory results: The contract price will include a large contingency; or the supplier could incur a loss. The possibility of a loss may result in (1) reduced quality in an effort to minimize the loss, (2) a request to renegotiate, (3) refusal to complete the work, (4) insolvency, resulting in the loss of a good supplier, or (5) a "grin and bear it" approach.

The selection of the contract compensation arrangement to be used for a specific contract is an important responsibility. The selection must be based on the cost risk involved and the circumstances surrounding the procurement. The compensation agreement selected must result in a reasonable allocation of the cost risk and should provide adequate motivation to the supplier to ensure effective performance. In addition, the compensation arrangement selected must be compatible with the supplier's accounting system. Selection of the appropriate compensation method can significantly reduce expenditures when cost risk is present.

CHAPTER 20

Negotiation

The need for world-class negotiation skills and techniques is increasing in parallel with the evolution to World Class Supply Management^{SM}.

Case

Negotiating for Gold

The Faustus Company is in the process of developing an alchemist's dream: a machine which will convert lead to gold. The team responsible for the project has developed a successful prototype. Because of the need for total secrecy, no suppliers have been involved in the new product development process. Faustus has developed specifications for the key items which must be purchased. The most critical one is a bipolar catalyst with an estimated cost of $250,000 each. Four firms which can make such catalysts have been identified. An RFP (request for proposal) has been issued. The team has selected Metals 'R' Us as the most attractive potential supplier.

Angus McFee, the project engineer (and 10 percent owner of the company) is very excited. He sees an endless stream of revenue for the firm and himself. "Let's bring Metals 'R' Us in and get a contract," says Angus. Most of his teammates concur.

Traci Hunt, a recent graduate of the University of San Diego's (USD's) supply management program, Says, "Gentlemen, We've got many hours of work preparing to meet with Metals 'R' Us. The key to a successful negotiation is in its preparation. A good rule of thumb is 10 hours of preparation for every hour of face-to-face discussions." Traci doesn't enhance her popularity, but slows the project down to allow for the necessary preparations for face-to-face negotiations with Metals 'R' Us.

Introduction

Negotiation is one of the most important as well as one of the most interesting and challenging aspects of supply management. In industry, and at most levels of government, the term "negotiation" frequently causes misunderstandings. In industry, negotiation is sometimes confused with "haggling" and "price chiseling." In government, negotiation is frequently perceived to be a nefarious means of avoiding competitive bidding and of awarding large contracts surreptitiously to favored suppliers.

Webster's dictionary defines negotiation broadly as "conferring, discussing, or bargaining to reach agreement in business transactions."[1] Herb Cohen describes negotiation as a pervasive process in which people ultimately attempt to reach a joint decision on matters of common concern in situations in which there is initial disagreement. Thus, a negotiation always requires both shared interests and issues of conflict. Obviously, without commonality there is no reason to achieve resolution.[2] To be fully effective in purchasing, negotiation must be utilized in its broadest context—as a part of a decision-making process. In this context, negotiation is a process of planning, reviewing, and analyzing used by a buyer and a seller to reach acceptable agreements or compromises. These agreements and compromises include all aspects of the business agreement, not just price.

Negotiations differ from a ball game or a war. In those activities, only one side can win; the other side must lose. In most successful business negotiations, both sides win something. Popular usage calls this approach "win-win negotiation." The "winnings," however, are seldom equally divided; invariably, one side wins more than the other. This is as it should be in business. Superior business skills merit superior rewards.

Increasingly, negotiations are conducted by cross-functional teams. These teams must be well coordinated in order to function as an integrated entity. Accordingly, we will use the term *negotiator* to refer to an individual supply management professional and also to a cross-functional negotiating team.

Objectives of Negotiation

Several objectives are common to all procurement or sales negotiations:

- To obtain the quality specified.
- To obtain a fair and reasonable price.
- To get the supplier to perform the contract on time.

In addition, the following objectives frequently must be met:

- To exert some control over the manner in which the contract is performed.
- To persuade the supplier to give maximum cooperation to the purchasing company.
- To develop a sound and continuing relationship with competent suppliers.
- To create a long-term relationship with a highly qualified supplier.

---

[1]Leigh Thompson in the second edition of her insightful book, *The Mind and Heart of the Negotiator*, provides the following definition: "an interpersonal decision-making process by which two or more people agree how to allocate scarce resources." Leah Thompson, *The Mind and Heart of the Negotiator* (Upper Saddle River, NJ: Prentice-Hall, 2001), p. 2.

[2]Herb Cohen, presentation at the Learning Annex, San Diego, CA, May 22, 2001.

Quality

In most cases, the negotiator's objectives require obtaining the quality specified by design engineering or by the user group. In some cases, however, quality itself may be a variable. For example, assume that the cost per unit for a critical item of material, with a guarantee of no more than 1000 defective parts per million incoming parts, is $5. Further, assume that the cost per unit with a guarantee of no more than 100 defective parts per million is $10. Does the higher unit price result in higher or lower *total* costs? Quite obviously, a highly advanced and accurate management information system must be available to provide the necessary data to allow the negotiator to make an optimal decision.

Fair and Reasonable Price

In many cases, the establishment of a fair and reasonable price for the desired level of quality becomes the principal focus of the negotiation process. This aspect of negotiation ranges in complexity from the use of price analysis to the more complex analysis of the potential supplier's cost elements. While the negotiator may focus on obtaining a fair price, this must be done within the context of obtaining the lowest *total* cost, as previously discussed.

On-Time Performance

Inability to meet delivery schedules for the quality and quantity specified is the single greatest supplier failure encountered in supply management operations. This results primarily from (1) failure of requisitioners to submit their purchase requests early enough to allow for necessary supply and manufacturing lead times and (2) failure of supply management personnel or the negotiating team to plan the delivery phase of negotiations properly. Because unrealistic delivery schedules reduce competition, increase prices, and jeopardize quality, it is important that supply management personnel or the negotiating team obtain realistic delivery schedules which suppliers can meet without endangering the other requirements of the purchase.

Control

Deficiencies in supplier performance can seriously affect, and in some cases completely disrupt, the operations of the buying firm. For this reason, on important contracts negotiators should obtain controls which will assure compliance with the quality, quantity, delivery, and service terms of the contract. Traditionally, controls have been found to be useful in areas such as man-hours of effort, levels of scientific talent, special test equipment requirements, the amounts and types of work to be subcontracted, and progress reports.

Cooperation

Cooperation is best obtained by rewarding those suppliers who perform well with future orders. In addition to subsequent orders, however, good suppliers also expect courtesy, pleasant working relations, timely payment, and cooperation from their customers. Cooperation begets cooperation.

Supplier Relationship Management

Negotiators should recognize that current actions usually constitute only a part of a continuing relationship. Conditions which permit the negotiator to take unfair advantage of sellers invariably, with time, change to conditions which allow sellers to "hold up" the purchasing firm. For this reason, the negotiator must realize that any advantage *not honestly won* will, in all likelihood, be recovered by the supplier at a later date—probably with interest. Thus, as a matter of self-interest, negotiators must maintain a proper balance between their concern for a supplier's immediate performance on the one hand and their interest in the supplier's long-run performance on the other. This balancing is an important aspect of supplier relationship management.

In summary, the objectives of negotiation require investigation, with the supplier, of every area of negotiable concern—considering both short-term and, normally, long-term performance. Negotiation is not only used to reach an agreement on price but is a subprocess of all interactions with the supplier throughout the procurement cycle. The negotiator's major analytical tools for negotiating prices were discussed in the preceding chapters—such things as price and cost analysis and learning curves. Additional negotiating tools, as well as the development of strategy and tactics for negotiation, are discussed throughout this chapter.

When to Negotiate

Negotiation is the appropriate method for determining the reasonableness of a price when competitive bidding or reverse auctions are impractical. Some of the most common circumstances dictating the use of negotiation are noted below:

- *When any of the five prerequisite criteria for competitive bidding are absent.* The criteria are discussed in Chapter 15.

- *When many variable factors bear not only on price but also on quality and service.* Many high-dollar-value industrial and governmental contracts fall into this category.

- *When early supplier involvement* (as described in Chapter 10) *is employed.*

- *When the business risks and costs involved cannot be accurately predetermined.* When supply management seeks competitive bids under such circumstances, excessively high prices inevitably result. For self-protection, most suppliers factor every conceivable contingency into their bids. In practice, many of these contingencies do not occur. Hence, the customer firm unnecessarily pays for something not received.

- *When a customer firm is contracting for a portion of the seller's production capacity, rather than for a product the seller has designed and manufactured.* In such cases, the customer firm has designed the product to be manufactured and, as an entrepreneur, assumes all risks concerning the product's specifications and salability. In buying production capacity, the objective is not only to attain production capability but also to acquire such control over it as may be needed to improve the product and the production process. This type of control can be achieved only by negotiation and the voluntary cooperation of the supplier.

■ *When tooling and setup costs represent a large percentage of the supplier's total costs.* For many contracts, the supplier must either make or buy many costly jigs, dies, fixtures, molds, special test equipment, gauges, and so on. Because of their special nature, these jigs and fixtures are primarily limited in use to the customer firm's contract. The division of special tooling costs between such firms and a customer is subject to negotiation. This negotiation includes a thorough analysis of future buyer or seller use of the tools, the length and dollar amount of the contract, the type of compensation appropriate, and so on.

■ *When a long period of time is required to produce the items purchased.* Under these circumstances, suitable economic price adjustment clauses must be negotiated. Also, opportunities for various improvements may develop; for example, new manufacturing methods, new packaging possibilities, substitute materials, new plant layouts, and new tools. Negotiation permits an examination and evaluation of all these potential improvements. Competitive bidding does not. What supplier, for example, would modify its plant layout to achieve increased efficiency to produce the buying firm's unique material without assurance of sufficient long-term business to cover the cost involved and assurance of a reasonable profit for the effort?

■ *When production is interrupted frequently because of numerous change orders.* This is a common situation in fields of fast-changing technology. Contracts in these fields must provide for frequent change orders; otherwise the product being purchased could become obsolete before completion of production. The ways in which expensive changes in drawings, designs, and specifications are to be handled and paid for are subjects for mutual agreement arrived at through negotiation.

■ *When a thorough analysis is required to solve a difficult make-or-buy decision.* Precisely what a seller is going to make and what it is going to subcontract should be decided by negotiation. When free to make its own decision, the seller often makes the easiest decision in terms of production scheduling. This may well be the most costly decision for the customer in terms of price.

■ *When the products of a specific supplier are desired to the exclusion of others.* This can be either a single or a sole sourcing situation. In this case, competition is minimal or totally lacking. Terms and prices, therefore, must be negotiated to minimize unreasonable dictation of such terms by the seller.

In all of these situations, negotiation is essential; and, in each case, quality and service are as important as price.

Supply Management's Role In Negotiation

Depending on the type of purchase, a supply management professional plays one of two distinct roles in negotiation. In the first role, he or she is the company's sole negotiator. In the second, the supply professional leads a cross-functional team of specialists which collectively negotiates on behalf of its company.

The Supply Management Professional Acting Alone

For low-dollar-value noncritical items, the supply management professional normally acts alone. Typically, for this type of purchase, a negotiation conference is held in the supply management professional's office with the supplier's sales manager (the seller's sole negotiator). These two persons alone negotiate all the important terms and conditions of the contract.

A supply manager's "solo negotiation" is not limited to periodic formal negotiating sessions. Rather, such negotiations continue on a daily basis with both current suppliers and visiting salespersons who wish to become suppliers. Consider several typical examples. A supplier calls on the telephone and informs the supply manager that prices are to be raised 20 percent within 60 days. The supply manager responds with the thought that production in her company's plant is slack and that a price rise as high as 20 percent could well trigger a "make" decision, in lieu of what is now a "buy" decision. The supply manager is negotiating!

A seller's value analyst discovers a substantially less expensive method of manufacturing one of the purchasing firm's products. However, there is one drawback: an expensive new machine is required for the job. The supplier's sales representative informs the supply manager of the discovery. The supply manager and an engineer study the concept and determine it is a good one. The two thank the sales representative for introducing the new idea. At the same time, the supply manager explains that his or her company is financially unable, at this particular time, to invest in the required new machine. Further, the supply manager conjectures that if the seller's company were to purchase the machine, then the supply manager could get his company to reconsider the rejected long-term contract the seller proposed last year. Informal negotiations are being conducted.

A salesperson calls, and the supply manager says, "I have been thinking about your contract with us. Under the contract, our purchases now total roughly $60,000 per year, primarily for valves. But your company also manufactures a number of fittings that we use. If these fittings were combined with the purchase of the valves, what benefits would your company be able to grant us?" Another informal negotiation is under way.

The preceding year a supply manager purchased $300,000 worth of liquid oxygen in individual cylinders from a single supplier. Because of its high dollar value, the supply manager began to analyze oxygen usage requirements thoroughly. In this analysis, an interesting fact was discovered. By installing a bulk storage tank at the purchasing firm's plant (at a cost of $160,000) and having the stores personnel deliver the required liquid oxygen to the shops, $70,000 could be saved per year. When the supplier's salesperson called, she was informed of the supply manager's study and was given the supply manager's worksheets for her review and study. Negotiations were under way, and the total cost of liquid oxygen would soon be reduced.

The Supply Management Professional as the Negotiating Team Leader

The complexity of a purchasing contract frequently correlates directly with the complexity of the item being purchased. For high-value, technically oriented contracts (such as those developed for the purchase of high-technology products, capital equipment, and research and development projects), and for the development of long-term relationships where the supplier's production flows into the buying firm's operation, the supply manager typically is no longer qualified to act as a sole negotiator. His or her role, therefore, shifts from that of sole negotiator to that of negotiating team leader. A typical team consists of two to eight members, depending on the complexity and importance of the purchase to be made. Team members are selected for their expertise in the technical or business fields needed to optimize their team's negotiating strength. Customarily, members are from fields such as design engineering, manufacturing engineering, cost analysis, estimating, finance, production, traffic, supply management, and legal affairs. Frequently, such team members have limited knowledge and skill in negotiations.

In the team approach to negotiation, the supply manager frequently serves as the leader of the team (and is called the negotiator). In this capacity, he or she functions as the coordinator of a heterogeneous group of specialists from several functional areas who can be expected to view similar matters differently. As leader of the team, the negotiator must weld the team members into an integrated whole. The team leader must draw on the specialized knowledge of each team member and combine this expertise with his or her own. To accomplish this, it is very important that an overall strategy be developed by the team and that each team member be assigned a specific role. Additionally, mock negotiations should be included as one of the final steps in team preparation. Mock negotiations usually constitute the best possible insurance against the team's committing the most costly error of negotiation—that of the members speaking out of turn and thus revealing their firm's position to the seller's team. In this way, the negotiating team develops a sound, unified approach to uncover, analyze, and resolve (from a companywide point of view) all the important issues applicable to the contract under negotiation.

The Negotiation Process

In the broadest sense, negotiation begins with the origin of a firm's requirements for specific materials or services. As discussed in Part III, the ultimate in purchasing value is possible only if design, production or operations, supply management, and marketing are able to reconcile their differing views with respect to specifications or the Statement of Work (SOW). The more open the specifications, the greater the leverage of the negotiating team. Negotiators must always think in terms of total cost and total value, not in terms of price alone.

The prelude to a negotiation characteristically begins with supply management's request for proposals from potential suppliers. The formal negotiation process consists of three major phases: (1) preparation, (2) face-to-face discussions, which result in agreement on all items and conditions of a contract, or a decision not to enter into an agreement with the potential supplier, and (3) the debriefing, during which the negotiating team members review both the preparation and face-to-face discussions for lessons learned.

Preparation

Ninety percent or more of the time involved in a successful negotiation is invested in preparation for the actual face-to-face discussions. The negotiator must (1) possess or gain a technical understanding of the item or service to be purchased, (2) analyze the relative bargaining positions of both parties, (3) have conducted a price or cost analysis (as appropriate), (4) know the seller, (5) be aware of cultural nuances, and (6) in every conceivable and practicable way, be thoroughly prepared.

Know the Item or Service   The negotiator does not need to understand all the technical ramifications of the item being purchased. But it is essential that he, she, or they have a general understanding of what is being purchased, the production or services process involved, and any other issues that will affect quality, timeliness of performance, and cost of production. The negotiator should understand the item's intended use, any limitations, and the existence of potential substitutes. The buyer should be aware of any prospective engineering problems which may arise. The negotiator should be aware of the item's procurement history and likely future requirements. Ideally, the negotiator will be familiar with any phraseology or customs relevant to the industry. A similar level of knowledge is appropriate when purchasing equipment and services.

The Seller's Bargaining Strength   The seller's bargaining strength usually depends on three basic factors: (1) how badly the seller wants the contract, (2) how certain he or she feels of getting it, and (3) how much time is available to reach agreement on suitable terms.

The negotiator should encounter no difficulty in determining how urgently a seller wants a contract. The frequency with which the salesperson calls and general market conditions are positive indicators of seller interest. The sellers' annual profit and loss statements, as well as miscellaneous reports concerning backlog, volume of operations, and trends, are valuable sources of information about individual sellers. Publications such as the Department of Commerce's "Economic Indicators," *The Federal Reserve Bulletin*, industrial trade papers, the Institute for Supply Management™ (formerly NAPM) *Report on Business*, and local newspapers provide a wealth of basic information about potential suppliers and their industries in general.

The less a seller needs or wants a contract, the more powerful its bargaining position becomes. The presence of an industry boom, for example, places it in a strong position. On the other hand, when a seller finds itself in a general recession or in an industry plagued with excess capacity, its bargaining position is decidedly weakened.

If a seller learns that its prices are lower than the competition's or learns from engineering, production, or services personnel that it is a preferred or sole source of supply, it naturally concludes that its chances of getting the contract are next to certain. In these circumstances, a supplier may become very difficult to deal with during negotiations. In extreme situations, it may be unwilling to make any concessions whatever. When this happens, the negotiator sometimes has only one alternative—to accept the supplier's terms.

When trapped by such circumstances, a negotiator can threaten delay to search for other sources. Such threats are likely to be ineffective, unless the seller knows that alternative sources are actually available and interested in the business. An alternative source of possible power which may be effective when patents are not involved is the threat to manufacture the needed item in the buyer's plant. When made realistically—when the supplier believes the buyer has the technical capability, the determination, and the capacity to make the product or service—such a threat frequently gains concessions.

A buying firm's negotiating position is always strengthened when the company has a clear policy that permits only members of its supply management department to discuss pricing, timing, and other commercial terms with sellers. Most pre-negotiation information leaks that give sellers a feeling of confidence about getting a contract occur in the technical departments of a firm. Such leaks can be extremely costly, and because they are often undetected by general management, they can be a continuing source of unnecessarily high costs.

Short lead times drastically reduce one's negotiating strength. Conversely, they significantly increase the seller's bargaining strength. Once a supplier knows that a negotiator has a tight deadline, it becomes easy for the supplier to drag its feet and then negotiate favorable terms at the last minute when the negotiator is under severe pressure to consummate the contract.

The Negotiator's Bargaining Strength   The negotiator's bargaining strength usually depends on four basic factors: the extent of competition present among potential suppliers, the adequacy of cost or price analysis, the logic and reasoning behind the challenged issue, and the thoroughness with which the supply manager and all other members of the buying team have prepared for the negotiation.

Intense supplier competition always strengthens a negotiator's position. Competition is always keenest when a number of competent sellers eagerly want an order. General economic conditions can bear heavily on the extent to which a firm really wants to compete. A firm's shop load, its inventory position, and its back-order position or demand for its services are typical factors that also bear heavily on the ever-changing competitive climate.

When necessary, a supply manager can increase competition by developing new suppliers; making items in-house rather than buying them; buying suppliers' companies; providing tools, money, and management to competent but financially weak suppliers; and, above all, hiring highly skilled supply managers.

The Adequacy of Cost or Price Analysis   A comprehensive knowledge of cost analysis and price analysis is one of the basic responsibilities of all supply managers involved in negotiations. When an initial contract is awarded for a portion of a supplier's production capacity rather than for a finished product, cost analysis becomes vital. In this situation, the negotiators are not prepared to explore with the supplier the reasonableness of its proposals until after a comprehensive analysis of all applicable costs has been completed. Cost analysis in such purchases, in a very real sense, is a substitute for direct competition. Price analysis is usually sufficient to assure that prices are reasonable for contracts for common commercial items. In the aggregate, the greater the amount of available cost, price, and financial data, the greater the chances for successful negotiation.

Caution must be exercised not to overfocus on price. If a collaborative, long-term relationship is desired, price must be placed in the proper context: It is only one aspect of the negotiation!

Know the Seller   Professional negotiators should endeavor to know and understand both the prospective supplier firm and its representatives. World-class supply managers prepare for critical negotiations by reviewing financial data and articles dealing with prospective suppliers. These supply managers and all negotiating team members know how the supplier's business is faring, know of any key personnel changes, and so on. One of the keys to successful negotiations is to put oneself in the other person's shoes. Understand their wants and needs. This level of preparation pays dividends when conducting face-to-face negotiations!

Cultural Nuances   A clear understanding of the effects and nuances of both cultural similarities and differences is an essential skill for the contemporary business manager. Effective global executives are those with the ability to develop and use global strategic skills; manage change and transition; manage cultural diversity and function within flexible organization structures; work with others and in teams; communicate; and learn and transfer knowledge in an organization. . . . Developing these skills is a lifelong activity and it is unlikely that one person can encompass all of the abilities."[3]

The Thoroughness of Preparation   Knowledge is power. The more knowledge the negotiator acquires about the theory and practice of negotiation, the seller's negotiating position, and the product or service being purchased, the stronger his or her own negotiating stance will be. A negotiator without a thorough knowledge of the product being purchased is greatly handicapped. A negotiator is similarly handicapped if he or she has not studied and analyzed every detail of the supplier's proposal. Whenever feasible, before requesting proposals, the negotiator should develop an estimate of the price and value levels for the items or services being purchased. Knowledge of current economic conditions in the market for the product or service in question is also an essential element of preparation.

Prior to the face-to-face negotiating session, all members of the negotiating team must evaluate all relevant data and carefully assess their own and their supplier's strengths and weaknesses. From this assessment, they develop not only a basic strategy of operation, but also specific negotiating tactics. Alert suppliers readily recognize negotiators who are not prepared. They gladly accept the real and psychological bargaining advantage that comes to them from lack of preparation by members of the buying firm's negotiating team.

Establishing Objectives

The outcome of contract negotiations hinges on relative buyer-seller power, information, negotiating skills, and how both perceive the logic of the impending negotiations. Each of these controlling factors can be influenced by adroit advance planning. This is why proper planning and preparation is, without question, the most important step in successful negotiations.

As part of the preparation process, the negotiating team should establish objectives. Negotiation objectives must be specific. General objectives such as "lower than previous prices," "good delivery," or "satisfactory technical assistance" are inadequate. For each term and condition to be negotiated, the negotiating team should develop three specific positions: (1) an objective position (or target), (2) a minimum position, and (3) a maximum position. Using the cost objective as an example, the minimum position is developed on the premise that every required seller action will turn out satisfactorily and with minimum cost. The maximum position is developed on the premise that a large

---

[3]Gerry Darlington, "Culture: A Theoretical Review," in *Managing Across Cultures: Issues and Perspectives,* ed. Pat Joynt and Malcom Warner (London: International Thompson Business Press, 1996). Cited in a paper by James D. Reeds, "Understanding Cultural Diversity: The Influence of National Culture in Global Purchasing," 1998 International Conference of the Australian Institute of Purchasing and Materials Management, Paramatta, New South Wales, Australia, October 19, 1998.

number of required seller actions will turn out unsatisfactorily and with maximum cost. The objective position is the best estimate of what the seller's actual costs plus a fair profit should be.

In developing concrete objectives, the team must establish desired or required dates for delivery schedules, desired or required numerical ranges for quality acceptance, and dollar levels for applicable elements of cost. The major elements of cost that tradition-ally are negotiated—and for which objective, maximum, and minimum positions should be developed—include quantity of labor, wage rates, quantity of materials, prices of ma-terials, factory overhead, engineering expense, tooling expense, general and administra-tive expense, and profit. In addition to determining a position for each major element of cost, the supply manager and the negotiating team members must estimate the objective, maximum, and minimum positions of the seller. Determining the seller's maximum po-sition is easy; it is the offer made in the seller's proposal.

In addition to costs and prices, delivery schedules, and acceptable quality levels, specific objectives should be established for all items to be discussed during the negoti-ation, including:

■   All technical aspects of the purchase.
■   Types of materials and substitutes.
■   Buyer-furnished material and equipment.
■   The mode of transportation.
■   Warranty terms and conditions.
■   Payment terms (including discount provisions).
■   Liability for claims and damage.
■   F.O.B. point.
■   General terms and conditions.
■   Details on how a service is to be performed.

Other objectives may include:

■   Progress reports.
■   Production control plans.
■   Escalation/de-escalation provisions.
■   Incentive arrangements.
■   Patents and infringement protection.
■   Packaging.
■   Title to special tools and equipment.
■   Disposition of damaged goods and off-spec (nonconforming) materials.

Simulations and role-playing negotiation exercises conducted at the University of San Diego during a 10-year period demonstrate that negotiators who establish a de-manding objective, *which is within the realm of reasonableness,* normally achieve a more favorable outcome than do those who enter the negotiation with a less demanding objective.

Identify the Desired Type of Relationship

We find it extremely desirable to determine the type of relationship which we hope to establish and/or maintain during and after the face-to-face discussions. The three primary approaches are transactional, collaborative, and alliance. These relationships were described in detail in Chapter 5. As we shall see shortly, the type of relationship desired affects the tactics employed.

Five Powerful Preparation Activities

The BATNA Perhaps the most important aspect of preparation is the development of the firm's BATNA, the acronym for the "best alternative to a negotiated agreement," a term coined years ago by Roger Fisher and Bill Ury in their book *Getting to Yes*. The firm's BATNA describes what it would do if the negotiation were unsuccessful. The BATNA may be an alternative supplier (at a most likely price), a decision to "make," or incorporation of a substitute material (at a most likely total cost of ownership).

Insight into or an accurate estimate of the supplier's BATNA on each issue is of equal importance. A Fortune 50 invests considerable resources (including the use of consulting services) developing its suppliers' BATNAs on key procurements.

The Agenda Successful negotiators spend considerable time and effort developing their agendas prior to face-to-face discussions. They place major emphasis on the sequence in which they plan to address issues during all phases of the face-to-face discussions. Experience indicates that issues which are easier to agree on should be addressed early. Seasoned professionals sprinkle "throwaways" throughout their agendas. But they know that they never "give" something for "nothing," that is, they expect something in return!

All negotiations center on specific issues. One of the difficult tasks of negotiation is to define fully the important issues which are to be included on the agenda and then to be sure that the discussion is confined to these issues. Most authorities believe that the issues should be discussed in the order of their probable ease of solution. With this priority system, an atmosphere of cooperation and momentum can develop that may facilitate solving the more difficult issues.

"Murder Boards" and Mock Negotiations Experienced negotiators frequently finalize their preparation through the use of "murder boards" and mock negotiations. A murder board consists of senior supply management, finance, manufacturing, quality, engineering, operations and general management personnel. The negotiating team presents its agenda, objectives, and tactics for the forthcoming negotiations. Members of the murder board dissect the negotiating plan in an effort to identify avoidable problems.

Mock negotiations allow the members of a negotiating team to prepare for the negotiation through a simulation of what is likely to occur during the face-to-face discussions. Other members of the organization (preferably from general management) play the roles of the supplier's negotiating team members during the simulated negotiation. Suppliers generally do a good job of preparing for critical negotiations through the use of murder boards or mock negotiations. It is essential that the buying team be equally prepared.

Murder boards and mock negotiations enhance the negotiating team's level of preparation. Further, the processes result in general management's being aware of the negotiating team's agenda, objectives, and tactics. Should the subsequent negotiations deadlock, management is in a position to step in and revitalize critical negotiations.

Crib Sheets   Experience gained through 10 years of directing negotiation courses at the University of San Diego demonstrates that the development and use of a "crib sheet" is an extraordinarily powerful preparation tool. Figure 20.1 is a representative crib sheet. The process of developing the crib sheets reinforces and upgrades the preparation process. Of equal importance, the negotiating team members function much more professionally when they have a single document to which they can refer. (Obviously, this sheet must be protected from "the other side"!)

Draft Agreements   The development of one or more "ideal" agreements also is a powerful preparation tool. The process of developing such agreements helps hone the negotiating team. And possessing such a documents has been shown to expedite closure of the face-to-face process.

Face-To-Face Discussions

Establishing trust is a key ingredient in effective negotiations. Leigh Thompson lists several activities which can facilitate the development of a reasonable level of trust: agree on a common goal or shared vision, expand the pie, use fairness criteria that everyone can buy into, capitalize on network connections, find a shared problem or shared enemy (perhaps another supply chain), focus on the future (instead of the past), and use shared procedures.[4]

Fact Finding

During the initial phase of a meeting with the potential supplier, professional negotiators limit discussions to fact finding. The vast majority of negotiators appear to be unable to control themselves during this phase and react to their opposites' proposals or positions. Such digressions from fact finding block or impede the flow of information. Any inconsistencies between the supplier's proposal and the negotiator's information are investigated. Fact finding should continue until the negotiator has a complete understanding of the supplier's proposal. Questions of a how, what, when, who, and why nature are used by the negotiator. Experience has shown that when the negotiator limits this initial phase to fact finding, a satisfactory agreement often results with a minimum of hassle and disagreement. During the fact-finding process, the negotiator should gain a better understanding of both the supplier's interests and the supplier's strengths and weaknesses.

The buying and selling representatives should disclose their interests—not their objectives. Altogether too much time is wasted in haggling over positions. Professional negotiators quickly learn their opposite's interests. It is much easier to satisfy interests than it is to move one's opposites off their positions. On completion of the fact-finding process, the negotiator should call for a recess or caucus.

---

[4]Thompson, *The Mind and Heart of the Negotiator,* p. 136.

Indian Negotiating Traits:

Always use professional titles
Government Service more important than Business
Get legal and tax advice, but don't be legalisor
It is important to appear flexible

- Delays are expected
- always present business card
- Always refuse first offer of refreshment, accept the second
- business is personal with plenty of refreshments
- **Don't say "NO", say "I'll try"**

Don't shake hands, but bow with hands folded in pray under chin

India and TDC

ISSUE	IMPORTANCE	PRESENTATION	POSITIONS	RATIONALE
Government Ownership	3		Most Favorable	Hi: 40% Indian ownership with 40% of NI Lo: 10% same terms
			Compromise	Anything over 10%, India will not pay for the share. Land, access is the Indian contribution.
Development Costs	1		Most Favorable	Hi: $22.5 B Lo:10% same terms
			Compromise	Anywhere over $2 B with good package and better rates than comp.
Construction of Pipeline			Most Favorable	TDC assumes total non-reimbursed responsibility for pipeline
			Compromise	
Environmental Concerns			Most Favorable	
			Compromise	
Social Concerns			Most Favorable	Hi: $30 M local hospital and school system Lo: $10 M for same
			Compromise	
Rates			Most Favorable	Hi: $0.05/kwh Lo: $0.065/kwh
			Compromise	Compromise in middle. TDC should lower than private sector producers
Local Spending (Workers)			Most Favorable	Hi: $200 M in local contracts and 50% local employ. Lo: $200 M and 25% local employ.
			Compromise	Something that combines above

Salient Points - TDC/India
Development cost = $2.8B for plant
Government plants charge $.03/kwh(below cost)
Private sector charges $.06/kwh
Rate structure = $.07
$.0196 plant debt service
$.0050 pipeline debt service
ROI is 22%, 80% ownership, GE 20%, India 0%
600M invested so far, $200/day loss on halt
Project one third complete
Contract for $100M to Indian firms

India - Facts and Issues
Rasharastra is unpolluted
Government has zero ownership interest
BJP has recently taken control
Most other states would build pipeline

India Notes

NOTES ON OPPOSITES
Ajay Sukdial: nationalist, anti US, wants project to go-at low $
Sanjit Basak: anti-BJP, wants this deal and future deals, will pay part of pipeline
Raja mahta: Radical, concerned for environment, wants local help-hospital, exports, education, local hires
Ashok Menezes: embarrassed by BJP, wants collaboration, electricity, LT econ growth, Rate decrease to $0.06/kwh w/o paying all capital costs w/b popular

AGENDA
Arrive late
Socialize
Concerned questioning
  Cost Models
  Ownership question
Negotiate Potential Agreement
  see chart above

Long Island Ice Tea
1/3 done but 1/9 quoted

DEAL STRUCTURE - Indian
- Ownership to Indians
- Local spending and employment
- TDC buy pipeline
- Lower pipeline costs
- Rate to 6-6.5/kwh

BATNA - India
- Have another foreign developer come in to finish the job
- Curtail growth in India by prolonging power plant development

Figure 20.1 I Sample Crib Sheet for Negotiations*

*Appreciation is expressed to Matt Miller, who introduced this concept to us.

Recess

During the recess, the negotiating team should reassess its relative strengths and weaknesses, as well as those of the supplier. It may also want to review and refine its cost estimate and any other estimates or assumptions. The team then should review and revise its objectives and their acceptable ranges. Next, the team should reorganize the agenda it desires to pursue when the two teams return to the negotiating table.

Narrowing the Differences

When the formal negotiations reconvene, the negotiator defines each issue, states the facts (and any underlying assumptions), and attempts to convince the supplier's representative(s) that the negotiator's position is reasonable. If agreement cannot be reached on an issue, the negotiator moves on to the next issue. Frequently, discussions on a subsequent issue will unblock an earlier deadlock.

During this phase of the negotiating process, problem solving and compromise are used to find creative solutions wherein both parties win. For example, the buying team's manufacturing engineers may identify a more cost-effective process than the supplier had planned to use. Small acceptable changes in packaging, schedule, or tolerances; offers by the customer to furnish a material or an item of equipment; and payment terms (including possible advance payments) can unblock negotiations to the benefit of both parties.

When several issues are on the negotiating table, a "package approach" is appropriate. Let us assume there are five issues: A, B, C, D, and E. The two parties address issue A and reach tentative agreement. They then address B. No agreement. One party then says, "Let's put B on hold." On to C—agreement. On to D—no agreement. And no agreement on E. Then, one party constructs and proposes a package addressing all five points which it feels is fair and appropriate for consideration. Further, the proposing party suggests that the package be looked at as a full bucket of water. If something flows into the bucket (e.g. a higher price, longer lead time, etc.) something flows out (improved warranty, better service, etc.). The combination of the package approach and the full bucket of water is a most attractive way of avoiding deadlocks!

In 1998, Robert Porter Lynch introduced what he calls "Co-Creative Synergistic Negotiations" Lynch's approach requires six fundamental skills:

1. Design of **Breakthroughs** (new paradigm generations)
2. **Vision** of a new Future
3. **Integrity** to keep to one's word
4. **Synergy** building to focus on $1 + 1 = 3$
5. **Trust** that enables higher performance and is reinforced by integrity
6. **Attitude & Language** that create new possibilities.

Mastery of the "Synergy of Compatible Differences" — called **Dinergy** — is essential to the implementation of any co-creative negotiations.

> **Definition: Dinergy** (from the Greek; dia=opposite and ergos=working) A dinergistic relationship between two parties requires a fundamental shift in the response mechanism from traditional ways of dealing with each other and a shift in the willingness to confront traditional paradigms.

Traditional Responses	Dinergistic Responses
Blaming and defending	Turn Breakdowns into Breakthroughs
I'm right. You're wrong.	Ask "What's Possible?"
You're Different, therefore Bad.—	Can we use differences to generate new
Diversity is scorned.	paradigms? Turn Diversity into Unity.
Emphasis on importance of Knowledge &	Emphasis on importance of Creativity and
having the right answer	asking fundamental questions.
Constant Evaluation of "Right & Wrong"	Ask "What's Missing?" and "What's Possible?"
Desire for Predictability and Control	Desire for Flexibility and Coordination

Lynch recommends the use of the following tactics:

"**Negotiations as Co-Creation:** Collaboration and Alliance Architecture is the method for shifting the energy of conflict from a Resistive, Win-Lose Battle into a Co-Creative Experience.
Resolving Conflict is rarely about who is right. It is about acknowledgment and appreciation of differences.
Fear will sap one's ability to channel an opponent's energy into a co-creative win and breaks the co-creative connection of the heart, forcing ego to conquer ego.
Discovery is the power of opening yourself to the wonderful realm of possibility.
Defense is a rigid, closed belief system, while Discovery is a flexible, open belief system.
Strategic Future: Ask Critical Questions about the future, such as: What Do You Want? What's Your Vision? What Do They Want? What's Their Vision? What's Missing? What's Possible? What Shifts in Thinking are Needed?
Chemistry & Character are essential for a successful long-term relationship. Therefore, create an environment where integrity and trust can prevail.
Breakdowns: When Synergistic Processes break down, use the Win-Win, Cooperative Style. Avoid blaming and faultfinding. Use every breakdown as an opportunity to create a breakthrough.
Integration: Use co-location and secondment to understand what the issues and concerns of the partner are."

Source: Robert Porter Lynch, "Negotiations guide." The Warren Company, Providence, RI, p. 15, 1998.

In most instances, it is possible to reach a satisfactory agreement through the use of these procedures. If a satisfactory agreement cannot be reached, the negotiating team has the choice of adjourning (an attractive alternative for the buyer if another supplier is waiting in the wings) or moving on to hard bargaining.

Hard Bargaining

Hard bargaining, the last resort, involves the use of take-it-or-leave-it tactics. Its use is limited to one-time or adversarial situations in which long-term collaborative relationships are not an objective. The negotiating team should carefully and professionally review and revise its objectives and, if absolutely necessary, give the supplier the option of accepting or rejecting its final proposal. Possession of a BATNA (best alternative to a negotiated agreement) protects the buying firm from entering into an unwise agreement. The experienced negotiator does not bluff unless willing to have the bluff called. Unless a one-time purchase of an item already produced (e.g., an automobile on a dealer's lot) is involved, the wise negotiator avoids having the seller feel that it has been abused or treated unfairly. Such feelings set the stage for future confrontations, arguments, unsatisfactory performance, and possible claims.

Techniques

Negotiation techniques (tactics) are the negotiator's working tools. The negotiator uses them to achieve his or her goals. In the hands of a skillful negotiator, these tools are powerful weapons. In the hands of a novice, they can be dangerous booby traps. Competent negotiators, therefore, spend a great deal of time studying and perfecting the use of these techniques. There are so many negotiating techniques that all cannot be discussed here. Those selected for discussion represent some of the techniques that have proved to be most important and most effective for the authors, their colleagues, and their students and working professionals entrusted to their guidance.

The objective of negotiation is agreement. Even though agreement is the fundamental goal of negotiation, sometimes negotiations end without agreement. In the short run, not reaching an agreement is better than reaching an unsatisfactory agreement. Generally speaking, however, experienced negotiators seldom let negotiations break down completely. They do not intentionally maneuver their opponents or let their opponents maneuver them into take-it-or-leave-it or walkout situations unless they are involved in a one-time or adversarial relationship.

Negotiating techniques may be divided into three categories: (1) those that are universally applicable, (2) those that are applicable to transactional (and, frequently, adversarial) dealings, and (3) those that are applicable to collaborative and alliance relationships.

Universally Applicable Techniques

These are techniques applicable to all negotiations, whether in transactional dealings or collaborative relationships.

Getting to Know You   Not only is this the title of an old hit tune, it is a powerful and effective technique! The negotiator is not dealing with abstract representatives, but rather with human beings. If possible, he or she should get to know the individuals representing the seller before the face-to-face phase of the negotiation begins. Americans tend to be too anxious to rush into negotiations without getting to know and understand the other side's representatives. We have much to learn from members of other cultures. Members of most other cultures spend a good amount of time becoming acquainted with those with whom they are to negotiate before entering into the formal face-to-face phase of negotiations. These negotiators find ways to meet the seller's representatives informally. If possible, they arrive early before the face-to-face negotiation is scheduled to begin and stay late after it ends.

Use Diversions   On the human side of negotiations, the negotiator who knows the seller personally, or has carefully studied his or her personal behavior patterns (as should be the case), has an advantage. When tempers start to flare, as they occasionally do, the experienced negotiator quickly diverts attention away from the issue at hand. At such times a joke, an anecdote, or a coffee (or tea) break can be an effective means of easing tensions. This type of diversion is usually more easily accomplished when the participants know which situations are most irritating to their opposites.

Use Questions Effectively   The wise use of questions is one of the most important techniques available in negotiation. By properly timing and phrasing questions, the negotiator can control the progress and direction of the negotiation. A perceptive question can forcefully, yet tactfully, attack the supplier's position. Similarly, the negotiator can effectively defend his or her own position by asking the seller to evaluate certain carefully chosen data the negotiator has developed.

The technique of answering questions properly sometimes is as important as the technique of asking them properly. The successful negotiator knows when to answer, when not to answer, when to answer clearly, and when to answer vaguely. Not all questions require an answer. Many questions are asked for which the seller knows there is no answer; therefore, a reply is not really expected.

The correct answer to questions in negotiation is not governed by the same criteria governing the correct answer to questions in most other situations. For negotiation questions, the correct answer is the answer that furthers either the negotiator's short-term tactics or long-range strategy. Labor leaders and politicians are experts at asking and answering questions. Their questions and their answers are made to correlate with their strategic plans (strike platforms, party platforms, and so on). To an uninformed observer, it often appears that the answers given by politicians and labor leaders do not relate to the questions that they are asked. These observations are only partially correct. When answering questions, politicians and labor leaders tell their listeners what they want them to know about their platforms, whether or not the response fully answers the questions asked.

Successful negotiators realize that negotiation sessions are not like the classroom, where precise answers earn high marks. In negotiation, the purpose of questions and answers is not to illustrate to the seller how smart the negotiator is. Rather, it is to ferret out the seller's objectives and to learn as much as possible about how the seller's representatives intend to maneuver to achieve them. For this purpose, precise answers are sometimes the wrong answers. The correct degree of precision is dictated by the particular circumstances of each negotiation.

Use Positive Statements   As with sophisticated questions, perceptively used positive statements can favorably influence the course of negotiations. For example, assume a negotiator knows that certain questions will evoke an emotional reaction from the seller. The questions are asked, and an opportunity is created for the proper use of a positive statement. A competent negotiator would say something like this: "I see your point, and I understand how you feel about this matter. Your point is well taken." Contrast the effect of this type of positive response with that of an emotional, negative response in which the negotiator tells the seller that he or she is "dead wrong." When a negotiator tells a seller that the seller's viewpoint is understood and considered reasonable, even though the negotiator does not agree with it, the seller is more likely to consider the negotiator's viewpoint objectively.

Machiavelli, in *The Prince,* gave the world some unusually sage advice concerning the use and misuse of positive statements: "I hold it to be proof of great prudence for men to abstain from threats and insulting words toward anyone, for neither . . . diminishes the strength of the enemy; but the one makes him more cautious, and the other increases his hatred of you, and makes him more persevering in his efforts to injure you."[5]

Be a Good Listener   Generally speaking, salespeople thoroughly enjoy talking. Consequently, negotiators should let them talk. While talking, they very often talk themselves into concessions that a negotiator could never gain through negotiation. Listening, per se, recognizes a basic need of a seller. Additionally, listening carefully to a seller's choice of words, phrases, and tone of voice, while at the same time observing his or her gestures and other uses of body language, can be rewarding. By observing such actions, a negotiator can gain many clues regarding a seller's negotiating position.

Be Considerate of Sellers   A small number of negotiation experts contend that negotiations are best won by negotiators who are as brutal and as arbitrary as possible. This is definitely a minority opinion. Unquestionably, there are some purchasing situations in which a merciless frontal assault can be a proper and successful negotiating technique. However, for the vast majority of firms—those that seek profitable, continuing relationships with the seller—a more considerate and reasoned technique is recommended. Professionals lose no negotiating advantages whatsoever by being fully considerate of sellers personally, by letting them save face, and by reasonably satisfying their emotional needs.

Transactional Techniques

Much negotiating literature is based on traditional, even adversarial (win-lose), approaches. Two effective books addressing such approaches are Gerald Nierenberg's *The Complete Negotiator*[6] and Herb Cohen's *You Can Negotiate Anything.*[7] Two of the traditional tactics which they give, and which deserve, special emphasis are (1) keep the initiative and (2) never give anything away.

Keep the Initiative   The negotiator should strive never to lose the initiative automatically obtained when the supplier's proposal is received and reviewed. There is a good deal of truth in the old saying that a good offense is the best defense. The negotiator should constantly "carry the game" to the supplier, keep the supplier on the defensive by confronting its representatives with point after point, making the supplier continually justify its position. For example, if the supplier states the cost of materials in dollars, the negotiator should ask the seller's representative to justify the figures with a bill of materials, appropriate scrap rates, and a full explanation of the manufacturing processes to be used. The more the negotiator bores in and the more pressure he or she maintains, the better will be his or her bargaining position. If the supplier's position seems sound, the negotiator can offer a counterproposal. In either case, the negotiator starts with the initiative, and should work hard to retain it.

---

[5]Niccolo Machiavelli, *The Prince,* Great Books of the Western World, *Encyclopaedia Britannica,* 1982, vol. 23.

[6]Gerald Nierenberg, *The Complete Negotiator* (New York: Nierenberg & Zeif, 1986).

[7]Herb Cohen, *You Can Negotiate Anything,* 2nd ed. (New York: Bantam Books, 1982).

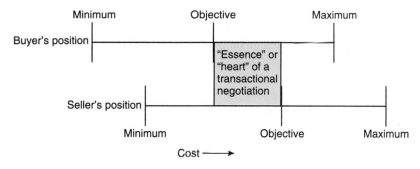

Figure 20.2 | Dynamics of Transactional Negotiation

Never Give Anything Away   As a matter of strategy, a successful negotiator periodically lets the seller maneuver him or her into accepting one of the seller's proposals. This does not mean that the negotiator gives something away. He or she never "gives anything away." The professional negotiator always expects to get a concession in exchange. On the other hand, the negotiator does not feel obligated to match every concession made by the seller. Consequently, in the exchange process, the successful negotiator makes fewer concessions than his or her less successful adversary. Through a continuation of this exchange process, a position close to the objectives of both parties is usually reached. Mutual concessions benefit both parties, and a contract so negotiated is *mutually* advantageous; but it is not *equally* advantageous.

Frame the Question   Negotiating authority Herb Cohen points out that too many of us allow "the other side" to frame the issue. In effect, we are doing business on their terms. For example, the seller says, "Do you want alternative A or B?" The professional negotiator responds, "Those certainly may be viable options, but let's develop some others."[8]

The Dynamics of a Transactional Negotiation   Typically, the two parties' positions appear as shown in Figure 20.2. The seller's positions are generally all higher than the corresponding positions of the buying firm. The closer the two objectives are initially, the easier the negotiations. As negotiations proceed, the seller tends to make concessions from its maximum position toward its objective. Simultaneously, the buying firm's negotiators reduce their demands, moving from the minimum position toward their objective.[9] Usually, little difficulty arises during this preliminary skirmish. This is not to say that this part of the negotiation process is easy or that it does not take time. Normally, vigorous testing is required to convince each party that the other is actually at his or her objective. Each party attempts to convince the other that the objective has been reached before this has, in fact, occurred. As each party approaches its objective, negotiation becomes difficult. The distance between the buying firm's objective and the supplier's objective can well be called the "essence" or "heart" of the negotiation.

---

[8]Ibid.

[9]If the negotiator believes there is a possibility of actually achieving the minimum position, he, she, or they should open with a position below this point—*provided such a position can be logically supported.*

(See Figure 20.2.) Any concession made by either party from its objective position will appear unreasonable to him or her based on the previous analysis of the facts. Changes in position, therefore, must now be the result of either logical persuasion and negotiating skills (entailing further investigation, analysis, and reassessment of the facts) or the pressure of brute economic strength.

The skillful negotiator stands out in the area of objective persuasion. He or she makes progress by uncovering new facts and additional areas of negotiation that permit the supplier to reduce its demands.

For example, an analysis of the supplier's manufacturing or services operations might reveal that if lead time were increased by only one week, the job could be done with fewer machines or human resources. This change could substantially reduce the supplier's setup and scheduling costs, thus permitting a price reduction. Additional lead time might be made available by a slight modification in the buyer's production schedule. The cost of making this change could well be much less than the seller's savings from the longer production runs. Thus both parties would profit from the change. It is this type of situation that competent negotiators constantly seek to discover and exploit in their attempt to close the gap between the seller's objective and their own. Such situations have the highly desirable effect of benefiting each party at no expense to the other party.

In some sole-source negotiations, the seller's objective is to maximize its position at the expense of the buying firm. In these situations, a continuing relationship is of secondary interest to the seller; therefore, it uses its bargaining strength to maximize price, rather than to achieve a mutually advantageous contract that will lead to continued business. The negotiator who senses such a situation should start negotiations by attacking the reasonableness of the seller's cost breakdown, using his or her own prepared cost estimates as the basis for such challenges. In the absence of competition, this is a negotiator's most logical and most effective plan of action. If the supplier refuses to divulge its cost data, the negotiator has only three available courses of action. He or she can appeal to the seller's sense of reason, pointing out the potential negative long-run implications. A second approach is to fight force with force by threatening to use substitutes, or to redesign and manufacture the product or service. A third alternative is to further develop and refine the firm's cost estimating models and utilize them more forcefully in pursuing the original course of negotiating action.

When faced with this type of problem, the negotiator must attempt to bring the supplier's price as close to the objective as possible. In the short run, the negotiator usually pays the seller's price. In the long run, the negotiator works toward the development of competing sources, substitute products, and compromises with the supplier.

If a seller's negotiation objective is to resolve issues as quickly as possible by employing logical analysis rather than economic bargaining power, it is sometimes reasonable for the negotiator to start negotiations by proposing his or her actual objective as the counteroffer to the seller's proposal. In fact, in industrial situations where continuing relationships are the rule, each successive negotiation brings the objectives of both parties ever closer together. Under these conditions, representatives of the buying and selling firms need develop only their objective positions; there is no need for maximum and minimum positions.

Collaborative and Alliance Negotiating Techniques

Getting to Yes by Roger Fisher and William Ury[10] is the most widely read book written on collaborative negotiations. The authors introduce what they call "the principled negotiation method of focusing on basic interests, mutually satisfying options, and fair standards, resulting in a wise agreement."

Fisher and Ury's method calls for the use of four powerful techniques:

- Separate the people (negotiators) from the problem (quality, price, etc.).
- Focus on interests, not positions.
- Invent options for mutual gain.
- Insist on using objective criteria.

Experience demonstrates that applying these techniques to collaborative (or win-win) negotiations will result in wise agreements and the basis of success for long-term relationships. Many of these relationships blossom into preferred partnerships and even into strategic supply alliances.

Separate the People from the Problem Successful negotiators divide the negotiation into two components: the people issue and the technical issues such as quality, time, price, etc. People issues require negotiators to understand where the other party is coming from. In effect, the negotiators must walk in the shoes of the seller's representatives. Professional negotiators work at ensuring that they understand the other party—frequently rephrasing what they have heard to ensure understanding. In addition, they frequently ask the seller's representatives to describe in their own words what the negotiator has said.

Emotions frequently get in the way of successful negotiations. Both parties to a negotiation have a right to get upset or angry and to express such emotions. Wise negotiators allow their opposites to let off steam without taking offense or allowing the negotiation to become disrupted. The perception or belief that the "other side" is stubborn or irrational is likely to manifest itself in exactly such behavior. Stop and walk in their shoes! The most constructive negotiations—the ones which well may be the basis of a beneficial long-term relationship—occur when the representatives of the buying and selling organizations work together in a search for a fair agreement in which both sides are better off than if there were no agreement.

Focus on Interests During the fact-finding phase of face-to-face negotiations, the professional negotiator learns the seller's interests while disclosing his or her own interests (but not objectives!). During the third phase (narrowing the differences), both parties work at reconciling and satisfying interests, not positions. Since both buyer and seller normally have multiple interests, it is wise to identify all of them and then work at developing a solution (agreement) which satisfies most or all of these interests. This approach calls for creativity and frequently results in increasing the size of the pie—the package of benefits to be shared by the two parties.

---

[10]Roger Fisher and William Ury, *Getting to Yes* (Boston: Houghton Mifflin, 1981; New York: Penguin Books, 1991).

James K. Sebenius of the Harvard Business School writes: ". . . interest-driven bargainers see the process primarily as a reconciliation of underlying interest: you have one set of interests, I have another and through joint problem solving we should be better able to meet both sets of interests and thus create new value."[11]

Invent Options for Mutual Gain   Fisher and Ury's third principle flows from the use of creativity to develop many options. When both parties become involved in creativity or brainstorming, they generate ingenious solutions by which both parties benefit. Two rules of thumb are (1) develop many options and (2) remain in option generation past the point of comfort. Many of the most creative ideas require time and even discomfort to develop. Only after a list including one or more truly creative ideas has been developed should the negotiators attempt to select from the list.

Use Objective Criteria   When a long-term relationship is an objective of both parties, the use of objective criteria will avoid much positional negotiation—and the possibility of disrupting or destroying the relationship. For example, if price is the issue under discussion, then possible objective criteria could include (1) the supplier's agreed-to allowable costs plus a reasonable profit, (2) development of a cost model to be used as the basis of the price, (3) a market-based pricing methodology, or (4) target (design-to-cost) pricing. (Remember, these issues were all discussed in the chapter on cost analysis.) Having identified four possible objective criteria, the issue now becomes a discussion of which criteria, or combination of them, should be applied.

Benefits Are Not Divided Equally   In some supply management circles, a common misunderstanding exists that successful negotiation means an equal distribution of the benefits. While both buyer and seller should benefit from a well-negotiated contract, the benefits are seldom divided 50-50. Based on years of observation, 60 to 70 percent of the benefits of a typical negotiated contract go to the more skillful negotiator, leaving 30 to 40 percent for the less skilled negotiator.

Lawyers

Lynch, in his pioneering work on alliances, discussed how to use lawyers effectively in synergistic negotiations:[12]

- Use lawyers only after you know what you want.
- Don't let lawyers "poison the well" with distrust that you must live with later.
- Select lawyers who understand how to operate in a collaborative environment, even when the legal system in which they practice is highly adversarial.
- Select lawyers with a high degree of integrity and who have been thoroughly trained in alliance formation and management.
- Use contracts to support and reinforce the statements of principles, understandings, and the covenant of trust.

---

[11]James K. Sebenius, "Six Habits of Merely Effective Negotiators," *Harvard Business Review,* April 2001, pp. 87–95.

[12]Lynch, op.cit., p. 66.

The Debriefing: An Incredible Learning Opportunity

Thompson points out, "Most people have little opportunity to learn how to negotiate effectively. The problem is not lack of experience but a shortage of accurate and timely feedback."[13]

Experience demonstrates that a 15-minute debriefing conducted by the negotiating team provides an incredible opportunity for learning and improvement in future negotiations. On completion of each negotiation, the negotiating teams are required to conduct a debriefing of their preparation process. They must identify both what was done well during their preparation process and lessons learned (e.g., what could/should have been done more professionally).

The team members then are required to analyze their "face-to-face" activities. They identify (reinforce) what went well. And then they identify weaknesses in their processes. (Feedback is at both an individual and team level.) Both undergraduates and graduates alike maintain that the debriefing is a marvelous tool which they plan to implement in the "real world."

Documentation

Personnel turnover and the frailties of the human memory make accurate documentation of the negotiation essential. The documentation must permit a rapid reconstruction of all significant considerations and agreements.

Documentation begins in the supply management office with the receipt of a purchase requisition and continues with the selection of potential suppliers and their proposals. Documentation of the actual negotiation must be adequate to allow someone other than the buyer to understand what was agreed to, how, and why. Burt, Norquist, and Anklesaria suggest the following format for the documentation of negotiations:[14]

Subject This is a memorandum designed for readers with many different orientations. This section, together with the introductory summary, should give the reader a complete overview of the negotiation, including information such as the supplier's name and location, the contract number, and a brief description of what is being purchased.

Introductory Summary The introductory summary describes the type of contract and the type of negotiation action involved, together with comparative figures from the supplier's proposal, the buyer's negotiation objective, and the negotiated results.

Particulars The purpose of this section is to cover the details of what is being bought and who is involved in the procurement. This should be done without duplicating information that was included in the subject section.

Procurement Situation The purpose of this section is to discuss factors in the procurement situation which affect the reasonableness of the final price.

---

[13]Thompson, *The Mind and Heart of the Negotiator,* p. 5.

[14]David N. Burt, Warren E. Norquist, and J. Anklesaria, *Zero Base Pricing^{TM}*: Achieving World Class Competitiveness through Reduced All-in-Cost (Chicago: Probus, 1990), chapter 13.

Negotiation Summary   This section shows the supplier's contract pricing proposal, the buying firm's negotiation objective, and the negotiation results, tabulated in parallel form and broken down by major elements of cost and profit. Whether these are shown as summary figures for total contract value, summary for the total price of the major item, unit price for the major items, or some other form of presentation depends on how negotiations were conducted. The general rule is to portray the negotiation as it actually took place.

Online Negotiation[15]

Studies have compared the establishment and maintenance of business relationships on the basis of forms of communication. Those founded solely on written communication tend to founder. Those that include written and telephone communication are sustainable, but the best relationships are those that go beyond other forms of communication to involve face-to-face meetings.

In face-to-face communication, one party can easily discern from facial expressions and shifts in body positioning the reaction of the other party to a stated position, or even a misinterpretation. Immediate steps can be taken to remedy any misunderstandings or to provide further explanation or support for a negotiation position. When communication takes place in written form, these remedies may not be available.

A carelessly drafted e-mail may damage a buyer-supplier relationship without the sender's even being aware of the impact on the receiver. One such situation involved a buyer who needed a prompt response to the e-mail message, so he drafted the entire message in capital letters to signify urgency. The foreign supplier interpreted the message as insulting and an attempt at intimidation, the equivalent of shouting. Needless to say, the transaction did not proceed smoothly. The list of examples is nearly endless. All of us have received e-mail messages containing spelling and grammatical errors. The unfavorable impression elicited by such messages extends not only to the sender, but to the organization as well, and may be virtually irreparable.

Examples abound of the different interpretations that a receiver may generate of communications delivered face-to-face and the same communications delivered in written form. To some extent, this can be attributed to the fact that not all of the content is contained in just the words, but is also expressed in *how* we say those words. Our tone of voice may be hard or flat, soft, cheerful, loud or strident and insistent. In response to a statement, we might say, "Oh, right," but while the words are the same in each case, if our tone signals enthusiastic agreement the message received is considerably different from the message delivered with a tone of sarcastic disagreement.

A partial remedy exists in resorting to oral communication, and we have the telephone with which to accomplish this, and do not need to resort to the Internet (except, perhaps as a means to avoid long-distance charges). Even this solution is only partial, and its inadequacy is well displayed in the frequency of business travel.

---

[15]Appreciation is expressed to Professors Lee Buddress and Alan Raedels of Portland State University and Professor Michael Smith of Western Carolina University for much of the material included in this section.

Beyond the differing expressions of our message, we also tend to convey substantially different content in what we write and what we say. For example, think about the difference between writing a letter to a friend and telling the person the same information over the phone. In written communication, there is no sense of timing, as in delivering the punch line to a joke. It is easy to sense the urgency in someone's voice, but more difficult to convey that gravity in writing. How do all of the jargon and slang words we routinely use in conversation look in print? Run-on sentences are hardly noticeable when spoken, but are painfully obvious in writing.

Further, even if we advance to videoconferencing over the Internet, many of these concerns persist. Perhaps timing and presentation will begin to approximate that of face-to-face delivery when the technology has advanced enough. However, we have not yet reached that point. Further, even with the advancement of technology to provide similar capacity, it is likely that the use of the technology will continue to change how we communicate; we have barely begun to investigate such changes and their effects on our communication.

Advantages to Online Negotiation   Experience indicates that electronic communication can separate issues from personalities. There is some evidence that groups using electronic communication tools may be freed up from inhibitions and more productive at brainstorming. Also, online communication can free the buyer and supplier from location dependency, and perhaps even the requirement to find a common time for conducting the negotiations.

An Example of a Successful Application of Negotiating Online   A recent *Wall Street Journal* article on thriving B2B software companies cites the following successful application:

> A south San Francisco–based company began marketing software this year to help automate dealings among close business partners. One of its biggest installations is Provision X, a Chicago-based meat-trading exchange unveiled this spring by five U.S. poultry, pork, and beef suppliers.
>
> Before the exchange, a buyer for a supermarket chain might call up sales managers at one or two meat suppliers and request price quotes. Those sales managers, in turn, might call up pricing managers inside their own companies who are plugged into a range of factors that shape the quantity, quality, and price of their products. Armed with data from the pricing experts, the sales staff goes back and negotiates with the buyers.
>
> Provision X transfers those processes online, creating an automated way of negotiating. Instead of trading phone and fax messages, buyers and sellers log on to create and solicit orders and price quotes, look up price lists, check sales performance against purchase contracts, and quickly generate reports summarizing the results of recent activities. Throughout these activities the relationships and hierarchies are maintained, right down to specifying the names of people who have rights to see certain data or make certain transactions.
>
> "We're not trying to take away the people-centric focus of this business," says Kevin Nemetz, Provision X's chief executive officer. "We are just trying to take those relationships online."[16]

---

[16]Don Clark, "Perception, Reality," *The Wall Street Journal,* May 21, 2001, p. R16.

Drawbacks to Online Negotiation It is far easier to say no in writing than face-to-face. The psychological separation that goes with the lack of personal contact makes it easier. On the one hand, this seems to be a distinct advantage because it curtails problems that may be associated in negotiating with people that we know and like, including reluctance to disagree for fear of damaging the relationship. On the other hand, it may make it *too* easy, leaving lingering unresolved effects.

Online negotiators are likely to feel a need to be more persuasive, more convincing. However, we must take care to avoid excessive stridency in our persuasive efforts, or our labors can easily turn counterproductive. Because of a lack of other cues, our use of language takes on particular importance, and we carefully consider the impact of each word. How might connotations or interpretations differ? Often, the same word can be taken in a number of different ways, and the limitations of online communication as currently realized make it difficult to evaluate the perception of the receiver.

Buddress, Raedels, and Smith propose the following hypotheses:

- The more important the issue, the more likely it is that it will be negotiated face-to-face.
- The more politically sensitive the issue, the more likely it is that it will be negotiated face to face.
- If either negotiator will be personally affected by the outcome, that person may want to conduct the negotiation in person.
- If the topic involves issues of firm sensitivity, such as trade secrets or core competencies, the negotiation is more likely to take place face to face.
- Buyer-supplier relationships will be perceived as more distant, the more online communication and negotiation are used.
- Less formal planning will occur prior to online negotiations than for those conducted face to face.

Negotiating for Price

Historically, price is the most difficult of all contract terms to be negotiated. Because of its high relative importance and its complexity, negotiation for price can be used as an example to illustrate what is involved in negotiating many other terms of the contract. If the reader understands what is involved in negotiating price, he or she can easily visualize what is involved in negotiating other issues.

When negotiating price, the negotiator must concurrently consider the type of contract to be used. Contract type and the negotiation of price are directly related; hence, they must be considered together. (Please see Chapter 19.)

To assure buying at favorable prices, negotiators strive to develop the greatest practical amount of competition or enter into fact-finding discussions with representatives of preferred suppliers or "partners" about their costs and cost drivers. Therefore, whenever it is possible, the initial step for a negotiator seeking successful negotiation(s) based on competition is to get an adequate number of proposals from among those potential suppliers who are genuinely interested in competing for the contract. When cost negotiations are likely, requests for proposals usually ask for not only the total price but also a complete breakdown of all supporting costs.

For every negotiated purchase, either price analysis or cost analysis, or both, is required. Which analysis is best to use and the extent of the analysis required are determined by the facts bearing on each specific purchase being negotiated. Generally speaking, price analysis is used for lower-dollar-value contracts and cost analysis for higher-dollar-value contracts. A discussion of the applicable uses of both price analysis negotiation and cost analysis negotiation follows.

Price Analysis Negotiation

Price analysis negotiation (often referred to simply as "price negotiation") is the most commonly used approach when negotiating only for price. Some proponents of cost negotiation disparage price negotiation, referring to it as "unsophisticated" and "emotional." In the many cases in which price negotiations are undertaken in an unprofessional manner, such criticism is fully justified. Banging on the table and shouting "I want lower prices" or "I can get it cheaper from another supplier" is certainly not professional price negotiation.

On the other hand, in many specific cases in which pricing data are developed and utilized with professional skill, price negotiation can be just as advantageous as cost negotiation, or more so. Compared with cost negotiation, price negotiation has three distinct advantages: (1) negotiation time is shorter, (2) support of technical specialists is seldom needed, and (3) pricing data are relatively easy to acquire.

The traditional sources from which supply management professionals get pricing data are federal government publications, purchasing trade publications, newspapers, and business journals. Competing suppliers are excellent sources of pricing data. They can provide the buyer with price lists, catalogs, numerous special pricing data, and formal price quotations. From these competing suppliers' data, the supply management professional can readily determine two very important facts: the nature of the market (competitive or noncompetitive) and the extent of supplier interest in this particular purchase. As discussed in Chapter 17, historical pricing data and engineering estimates also provide a sound basis for price analysis.

Price Comparison   The negotiator's first step in price analysis is to determine the extent of market competitiveness and supplier interest. The second step is to examine in detail the absolute and relative differences existing among the various prices quoted by the competing suppliers. From this examination, a buyer detects that differences in prices among suppliers exist but does not learn the causes of these differences. The search for causes begins in the supply management department's supplier information file.

The price proposals of the competing suppliers are compared with past prices of similar purchases from the supplier information file. The causes of all significant variations are pinpointed and analyzed. Adjustments are made for changes in factors such as specifications, quantities ordered, times of deliveries, variations which have taken place in the general levels of business activity and prices, and differences which may have resulted from learning experience. After these adjustments are made, the negotiator (sometimes with the help of an engineering estimator or a price analyst) determines whether or not the prices offered are reasonable. From this determination, the negotiator decides on the target objective to use for his or her negotiating position.

Trend Comparisons   Historical prices paid for purchases of similar quantities can be analyzed to disclose helpful price trend information. For example, if prices have been increasing, it is reasonable to expect that the seller will attempt to maintain a similar pattern of increase. Hence, by carefully analyzing the reasons for all price increases, the negotiator can structure a bargaining position on the basis of any invalidities uncovered.

Similarly, the negotiator can analyze decreasing prices to determine whether the price decrease is too little or too much. If the negotiator determines that the decrease is too large, he or she must determine whether the trend is creating, or is likely to create, quality or service problems in contract performance. If the decrease is too little, then the negotiator must determine whether the benefits of improved production processes are being proportionally reflected in lower prices.

Even a level price trend offers opportunities for price analysis. For example, the negotiator may ask whether level prices are justified, considering the many manufacturing improvements which have been made. Did the supplier charge too much initially? Has the supplier's competitive position in the industry changed? If the negotiator's analysis indicates that costs have fallen because of reductions in the supplier's cost for materials or because of improvements in the production processes, his or her negotiating position is clear. The professional negotiator obtains reductions reflecting these changes. (It must be noted that under collaborative or alliance relationships, these savings should be shared.)

Cost Analysis Negotiation

As previously stated, price analysis negotiation is more commonly used than cost analysis negotiation. In cost negotiations, each applicable cost element is negotiated individually, that is, design engineering cost, tooling cost, direct materials cost, labor hours, labor rates, subcontracting, overhead cost, other direct costs, profit, and so on. Cost analysis negotiation (commonly referred to as "cost negotiation") is steadily growing in use. It has been used successfully for decades by many large firms such as General Electric and Ford, and in recent years it has been employed increasingly by small and medium-size firms.

Colleague Bob Harrington points out that the negotiator may ask the supplier to know considerable detail about the fixed, variable, and close to marginal costs for all processes, e.g. almost activity based costing, including inventory holding costs, etc. For example, costs may vary significantly by lot size, order size, etc. Ordering in multiples of a lot size driven by manufacturing in a vat might have significant cost savings. To make really good deals, the negotiation process focuses on ways to reduce unnecessary costs such as shipping and overtime, and share these savings between the organizations or to add significant value to the supply chain and find ways to share the value equitably. The sharing is a final part of the negotiation.[17]

When sophisticated collaborative or alliance supply relationships are utilized by a firm, careful detailed analysis of the supplier's costs (both present and projected) replaces the role of competition in the marketplace. Both the buying and selling firms' representatives must see themselves as members of a supply chain competing with other supply chains for the customer's purchasing dollar. Thus, discussions about costs, cost

---

[17]Robert Harrington, various conversations during 2000 and 2001.

allocations, cost drivers, cost reductions, possible cost avoidance, and profits must be seen in context: if our supply chain becomes noncompetitive, then we will fail to attract the customer's purchase dollars and we both lose! Discussions can and often do get heated—conflict can be healthy—but the discussions should be conducted in the context of what is in the joint best interests of the two parties. In reality, they should see themselves as members of the same supply chain team.

Characteristics of a Successful Negotiator

The characteristics of successful negotiators should now be clear. These people are skillful individuals, with broad business experience. They possess a good working knowledge of all the primary functions of business, and they know how to use the tools of management—accounting, human relations, economics, business law, and quantitative analysis. They are knowledgeable about the techniques of negotiation and the products and services their firms buy. They are able to lead meetings and conferences and to integrate specialists into smoothly functioning teams. In addition to being well educated and experienced, successful negotiators excel in good judgment. It is good judgment that causes them to attach the correct degree of importance to each of the factors bearing on the major issues. Combining their skills, knowledge, and judgment, they develop superior plans. Additionally, they consider problems from the viewpoint of the firm as a whole, not from the viewpoint of a functional manager. The successful negotiator is pragmatic in use of negotiating techniques. Always searching for a collaborative or "win-win" experience, the pragmatic negotiator can adapt when the other party uses hardball or win-lose techniques. The successful negotiator has high self-esteem and is always most interested in professionalism and the best interest of the enterprise. The successful negotiator is ethical and honest and not influenced by friendship or gratuities.

Successful negotiators share four common attributes:

1. All realize that specialized training and practice are required for an individual to become an effective negotiator. Although some people have stronger verbal aptitudes than others, no one is born with negotiating knowledge and skills.
2. All habitually enter into negotiations with more demanding negotiating objectives than their counterparts, and generally they achieve them.
3. All are pragmatic and flexible in their capability to deal with different negotiation techniques from "hardball" to "collaborative."
4. All are included, or are destined to become included, among an organization's most highly valued professionals.

Concluding Remarks

Negotiation is free enterprise at its very best! When traditional negotiations (win-lose) are appropriate, negotiation matches the skills of determined buyers against those of equally determined sellers. Both explore ways to achieve objectives that tend to maximize the self-interest of their organizations. In short, in such circumstances negotiation is a powerful supply management tool which competent professionals use to achieve maximum value at minimum cost. By rewarding efficiency and penalizing inefficiency, the negotiation process not only benefits the negotiating firms, but also benefits the nation's economy as a whole.

The increasingly common collaborative approach to negotiations that is required with collaborative and alliance supply relationships substitutes a win-win approach for the more traditional, transactional one. With this approach, both parties are better off entering into the negotiated deal than were they not to reach agreement. This approach substitutes the expertise of the buying and selling firms' representatives for the forces of marketplace competition. Thus, costs must be driven to their lowest possible levels (without adversely affecting quality or service) in order to ensure the survival and success of the buyer and seller's supply chain in the marketplace.

Endnotes

One of our favorite negotiating authors is Roger Dawson. Mr. Dawson's books and tapes are both informative and entertaining.

Leigh Thompson's *The Mind and Heart of the Negotiator* provides good insight into this exciting field. (See Footnote 1 of this chapter.)

PART 6

RELATIONSHIP MANGAGMENT

Business executive meeting (*Ken Fisher/Stone/Getty Images*)

Collaborative relationships are the most essential ingredient of both successful World Class Supply Management[SM] and supply chain management. Although relationships are addressed throughout the book, this section focuses on four important relationship issues which are essential foundations of successful supply and supply chain management.

Chapter 21 addresses the balancing of relationship management and contract management. While many practitioners are tempted to focus on either relationship management *or* contract management, we believe that it is necessary to address these issues in a tightly integrated fashion. It is our observation that contract and relationship management — or what many call "post-award activities" — is the weakest of the four key phases of supply management. As a supply manager told one of us a few years ago, "If the stuff is late, we'll expedite!" We believe in and advocate a more proactive approach which ensures that "the stuff is never late!"

The competition for world-class suppliers is well under way. Since world-class suppliers are a prerequisite to and a component of WCSM, and since none may be available, frequently it is necessary to develop suppliers to world-class status. Drawing heavily on our friends at Deere & Co., Chapter 22 describes activities which supply managers can employ when helping their suppliers make such a transition. We believe that supplier development is a critical "missing link" in many corporations' supply chain strategies.

The last two chapters of this section address legal and ethical issues in supply management. While legal and ethical issues are addressed throughout the book, we believe that the importance of these issues requires chapters focusing on each. The explosive growth of the Internet and global sourcing force supply managers to address these important topics in more detail than ever. ■

CHAPTER 21

Relationship and Contract Management

World Class Supply Management^{SM} calls for contract and relationship management techniques, tools, and philosophies that enable collaboration, where appropriate. The key objectives are timely delivery, desired quality, and performance to agreed to requirements while simultaneously empowering supply professionals to foster synergistic opportunities.

KEY CONCEPTS

Case

Carol Gibbons, Hathway Technologies' expediter, is on her way to Sheffield, England, to visit CyberCirc Corporation, commonly referred to as 3C. Hathway's project manager, John Brown, has just learned that the printed circuit boards (PCBs) for his project will be eight weeks late. The delay is the result of problems 3C is having with its South Korean supplier of integrated ciruits.

This project is Hathway's first in the British market. Thus, timely completion and high quality both are essential to Hathway's future sales in the market. Hathway had awarded the PCBs to 3C based on its reputation as a quality manufacturer.

Carol's mission on this trip is to get 3C's delivery back on schedule. The delay will disrupt Hathway's ability to meet its scheduled completion date.

The resulting reputation for late completion will not help Hathway's efforts to obtain additional work in Europe. John's words are clear: "Make sure 3C understands that I will do anything in my power to ensure that they will not receive any more business if they cause problems on my project." What should Hathway have done to avoid this situation?

Need for Better Contract Management

Historically, the post-award phase of supply management has been a weak one at many organizations. Prior to the mid-1980s, large inventories were available to accommodate quality problems and late deliveries. Multiple sources of supply often allowed the buyer to live with little supplier management. But this mentality cost the buying firm dearly. Shorter production runs under a multiple-sourcing policy frequently resulted in higher prices, lower quality, and the receipt of items which were not completely identical. Late deliveries resulted in production disruptions, higher production costs, and broken delivery commitments to the firm's customers.

Today, most firms have reduced inventories as embodied in the just-in-time (JIT) philosophy. JIT creates even more need for professional post-award management. Under JIT, large inventories are no longer available to cushion the results of weak management at this stage in the process. JIT requires buyers and suppliers to work together to reduce the need for inventories. Tight schedule integration between supplier and customer must be maintained. Processes must be balanced. Waste must be reduced or eliminated. Communication must be in real-time. These requirements combine to make buyer-supplier collaboration essential. Such collaboration requires supply managers to take a proactive approach to managing both the contract and the supplier relationship. Professional supply relations management is a vital ingredient in several other settings: defense subcontracts, construction contracts, and the purchase of essential services.

The foremost prerequisite to successful contract and relationship management is a sound understanding by both parties of all aspects of the program. Early supplier involvement, as described throughout this text, greatly facilitates the development of this understanding.

This chapter discusses the many activities a supply manager must perform to ensure that the quality specified in the contract is received on time and that relations with key suppliers are managed carefully in an effort to ensure satisfaction with the supplier's performance now and in the future.

Pre-Award Conference: The Stage Has Been Set

When either the dollar magnitude, complexity, or criticality of the work to be performed dictates, professional supply managers hold a conference with the prospective supplier immediately prior to award of the contract. The supply management team—consisting of the supply manager, subcontract administrator or expediter, design engineer, manufacturing engineer, internal customer, quality engineer, and inspector(s), as appropriate—should have met with the supplier's team. The issues, presented in technical terms, will have been addressed in the request for proposal and the proposed contract. It is important that supply professionals are aware of the transformation of responsibility taking place within the supplying organization. *The supplier's employees responsible for consummating the sale normally are not responsible for performance under the contract. Thus, a new team consisting of operations, demand planning and management, quality, and the supplier's supply management assumes responsibility for performance under the terms of the contract. The pre-award conference is the vehicle the supply management professional and his or her team uses to ensure that the contract provisions are fully understood and implemented.* The following items, as appropriate, should be addressed:

- All terms and conditions.
- Delivery or operations schedule.
- Staffing and supervision.
- Site conditions, work rules, safety (if appropriate).
- Invoicing procedures and documentation (for incentive and cost contracts).
- Materials purchase procedures (for incentive, cost, and time and materials contracts).
- Background checks and security clearances.

- Insurance certificates.
- Permits.
- Possible conflicts with other work.
- Submission of time sheets (for incentive, cost, and T&M contracts).
- Buyer responsibilities. Buyer-supplied items such as customer furnished purchased materials, tools, equipment, facilities, and so on. Timeliness of buyer reviews and approvals for studies, reports, plans and specifications, and so on must be established and accepted by both parties.
- Collaboration milestones. Potential points of collaboration which improve designs, processes, communications, quality, and delivery should be identified as early as possible, rather than after award of the contract.

Major one-time projects, such as large construction or site development jobs, have their own, fairly unique, reporting requirements. These are described in Appendix A of this chapter.

Monitoring and Controlling Project Progress

Suppliers are responsible for the timely and satisfactory performance of their contracts. Unfortunately, the supply manager cannot rely entirely on the supplier to ensure that work is progressing as scheduled and that delivery will be as specified. Poor performance or late deliveries disrupt production operations and result in lost sales. Accordingly, supply management must monitor supplier progress to ensure that desired material is delivered on time. The method of monitoring depends on the lead time, complexity, and urgency of the order or contract. The level of monitoring depends upon the criticality of the supplied material or service and the demonstrated capability of the supplier in meeting the buying firm's requirements.

At the time a purchase order or contract is awarded, the supply manager should decide whether routine or special attention is appropriate. On many orders for noncritical items, simply monitoring the receipt of receiving and inspection reports may be adequate. On others, telephone confirmation that delivery will be as specified may be sufficient. But on orders for items critical to the scheduling of operations, more detailed procedures are in order.

When evaluating a supplier's progress, the supply manager is interested in *actual* progress toward completing the work. Data about progress may be obtained from a variety of sources: progress conferences over the phone or face-to-face, field visits to the supplier's facility, and periodic operations progress reports by the supplier.

Operations Progress Reports

In some instances, the supplier is required by the terms of the contract to submit a phased production schedule for review and approval. A phased operations schedule shows the time required to perform the production cycle—planning, designing, purchasing, tooling, plant rearrangements, component manufacture, subassembly, final assembly, testing, and shipping.

In many cases, the supply manager may include a requirement for production progress information in the request for proposal (RFP) and in the resulting contract. The ensuing reports frequently show the supplier's actual and forecasted deliveries, as compared with the contract schedule; delay factors, if any; and the status of incomplete preproduction work such as design and engineering, tooling, construction of prototypes, and so on. The reports also should contain narrative sections in which the supplier explains any difficulties, and action proposed or taken to overcome the difficulties. In designing the system, the supply manager should ask himself or herself, "What is really essential information?" in an effort to prevent the system from becoming a burden instead of a tool for good management.

Operations progress reports do not alleviate the requirement to conduct visits to the supplier's work site on crucial contracts. The right to conduct such visits must be established in the RFP and the resulting contract. On critical contracts, where the cost of such visits is justified, it may be desirable to establish a resident facility monitor to ensure the quality and timeliness of the work being performed at the supplier's facility.

When it is determined that an active system of monitoring the supplier's progress is appropriate, the first step in ensuring timely delivery is to evaluate the supplier's proposed delivery schedule for attainability. In their planning and control activities, most suppliers utilize a variety of graphic methods for portraying the proposed schedule and then for monitoring progress against it. These are useful management tools that also can be reviewed and evaluated by the buying team. These visual presentations are forceful and usually can be updated economically. Two progress planning and control techniques commonly used for important projects and jobs are now discussed briefly.

Gantt Charts

Gantt charts are the simplest of the charting techniques for planning and controlling major projects and the materials deliveries that flow from them. Gantt charting requires that (1) first, a project must be broken into its elements; (2) next, the time required to complete each element must be estimated and plotted on a time scale; (3) the elements then must be listed vertically in time sequence, determining which elements must be performed sequentially and which concurrently; and (4) finally, actual progress is charted against the plan on the time scale.

In addition to the detailed charts maintained by the supplier, the supply manager also can construct a master chart to use in controlling the job. In this case, the supplier is asked to submit weekly or monthly progress data that are posted to the buying firm's master chart. Figure 21.1 illustrates a typical Gantt chart of this type.

The Gantt chart, then, portrays the plan, schedule, and progress together in one easy-to-use chart. It shows the status of project elements, or activities, and identifies which are behind or ahead of schedule. Unfortunately, Gantt charts fail to provide the full impact of an activity's being behind or ahead of schedule, and they do not provide sufficient detail to detect some schedule slippages in a timely manner.

As long as the project is not too large or complex, Gantt charts work fine. As the number of *interdependent* activities increases, however, a Gantt chart fails to tell the supply manager one important fact he or she needs to know to manage the project efficiently.

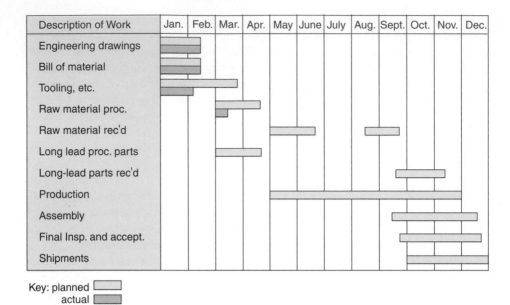

Description of Work	Jan.	Feb.	Mar.	Apr.	May	June	July	Aug.	Sept.	Oct.	Nov.	Dec.
Engineering drawings												
Bill of material												
Tooling, etc.												
Raw material proc.												
Raw material rec'd												
Long lead proc. parts												
Long-lead parts rec'd												
Production												
Assembly												
Final Insp. and accept.												
Shipments												

Key: planned
     actual

Figure 21.1 I Production Schedule and Progress Chart (Gantt Chart)

If slowdowns occur as work progresses on the various parts of the project, is the timing of some activities more critical than others? The answer is yes—and the Gantt chart does not tell which ones! For every project, at least one group of interrelated activities makes up what is called the *critical path.* If any of these activities fall behind schedule, the total project will not be completed on time. The supply manager must monitor these potential bottleneck activities very carefully. To overcome this Gantt chart deficiency, a computer-based technique called critical path scheduling has been developed to provide the required management capability.

CPM and PERT

Critical path scheduling is a tool that can be used to manage project buying activities, construction projects, and research and development projects, to name just a few. The technique can be used for these and other complex projects of a one-time nature. The project's magnitude must justify the relatively high cost of this approach to management compared with more conventional methods such as the Gantt chart. Critical path scheduling is useful for planning, monitoring, and controlling complex projects composed of a large number of *interrelated* and *interdependent* activities.

The critical path approach quantifies information about uncertainties faced by the activities responsible for meeting a predetermined time schedule. The very process of analyzing these uncertainties focuses the manager's attention on the most critical series of activities in the total project from a timing perspective—those that constitute the "critical path." The critical path activities must be accomplished sequentially, thus representing the chain of activities that require the most time from start to finish of the project. When these are pinpointed, the manager can develop an appropriate control strategy to optimize the operating results.

When used for controlling contract performance, the posting of progress data permits the supply manager to compare actual accomplishments with those planned. He or she can then determine the likely implications of slippages with respect to critical path time requirements. The supply manager then works with the supplier to correct or minimize the resulting problems.

A variety of specific techniques have been derived from the basic critical path scheduling concept. The best known of these are *critical path method* (CPM) and *program evaluation and review technique* (PERT). CPM was originally developed in 1955 by the Du Pont and Remington Rand companies for use in coping with complex plant maintenance problems. PERT emerged in 1958 through the joint efforts of the United States Navy, the Booz, Allen & Hamilton consulting firm, and the Lockheed Missile and Space Division in connection with the Polaris weapons program. With the passage of time, PERT and CPM have become very similar in concept. Currently, they differ only with respect to various details of application.

In practice, the application of CPM/PERT generally is accomplished with a computer program that uses network diagrams to show time and dependency relationships between the activities that make up the total project. The purpose of the technique is to keep all the "parts" arriving on schedule so that the total project can be completed as planned. Using CPM/PERT data outputs, the supply manager can evaluate possible trade-offs if supplier resources were reallocated in alternative ways to improve the chances of meeting the time schedule. This technique can quickly determine the results of alternative courses of action, thus making the best choice of the alternatives available.

Most important, the CPM/PERT technique is both a planning and a control tool. The fact that the individual activities of a project are structured into a network requiring time and sequence determination is critically important; it is the basis for all subsequent monitoring and control activity. Use of the technique forces the supply manager to conduct this step-by-step planning in advance and to periodically reexamine the logic of the decisions as the dynamics of the operation unfold. The mechanics of critical path scheduling are briefly described with an example in Appendix B at the end of this chapter. The evolution of CPM/PERT to the World Wide Web is discussed in the e-Commerce II chapter.

Closed Loop MRP Systems

Many manufacturers use a closed loop MRP system to schedule and control production, inventory levels, and deliveries from outside suppliers. Supplier-furnished data can be used by the individuals controlling the firm's incoming materials schedules as they monitor their system reports. Daily or weekly status reports flow from the supplier to the scheduler, who then inputs the data for the next MRP run.

A growing number of firms link their suppliers' computer-based systems into their own computer system so that real-time data are available to both parties. Systems that enable such linkage usually combine one of the three forms of EDI with other technologies described in the e-Commerce II chapter.

If supplier-furnished data indicate that the supplier's delivery dates will result in a disruption of the buying firm's schedule, the appropriate scheduler or supply manager can take action to modify the supplier's schedule or to adjust the buying firm's own production schedule, as appropriate.

Monitoring and Controlling Total Supplier Performance

The use of supplier performance evaluation systems is on the rise. A majority of major manufacturing firms, as well as an increasing number of service firms, either have established formal supplier-evaluation programs or are in the process of doing so.

Many progressive buying organizations monitor their critical suppliers' performance at both a contract and an aggregate level. This information is used to control a supplier's contract performance, and it is also used during source selection for follow-on procurements to ensure that only satisfactory performers are considered.

Supplier Performance Evaluation

After a major supplier has been selected and the buyer-supplier relationship has begun to develop, it is important to monitor and assess the supplier's overall performance. The purpose is to enhance the relationship and thereby control performance.

Many evaluation teams use a three- to six-month moving average for the aggregate evaluation of a supplier's performance. For example, with a six-month window, a supplier's rating in June is an average of all the ratings accumulated between January and June. The moving average allows suppliers to start over at some point. The suppliers' misdeeds don't haunt them forever. They're motivated to improve. The length of the window is important and should be case-specific. A shorter window may be ineffective because it lets suppliers off the hook too easily. A longer window may be punitive and self-defeating.

Three types of evaluation plans are common: the *categorical plan,* the *weighted point plan,* and the *cost ratio plan.* Each of these plans is reviewed briefly in the following pages.

Categorical Plan   Under this plan, personnel from various departments of the buying firm maintain informal evaluation records. The individuals involved traditionally include personnel from supply management, engineering, quality, accounting, and receiving. Each evaluator prepares a list of performance factors that are important to him or her for each major supplier. Each major supplier is evaluated against each evaluator's list of factors at a monthly or bimonthly meeting. After the factors are weighted for relative importance, each supplier is then assigned an overall group evaluation, usually expressed in simple categorical terms, such as "preferred," "neutral," or "unsatisfactory." Figure 21.2 portrays a typical supplier performance evaluation form used in the categorical plan. This simple qualitative plan is easy to administer and has been reported by many firms to be very effective.

The Weighted Point Plan   Under this plan, the performance factors to be evaluated (often various aspects of quality, service, and price) are given "weights." For example, in one

Supplier _____   Date: _____

Summary Evaluation, by Department	Preferred	Neutral	Unsatisfactory
Supply management	_____	_____	_____
Receiving	_____	_____	_____
Accounting	_____	_____	_____
Engineering	_____	_____	_____
Quality	_____	_____	_____

Performance Factors

	Preferred	Neutral	Unsatisfactory
Supply management			
Delivers on schedule	_____	_____	_____
Delivers at quoted prices	_____	_____	_____
Has competitive prices	_____	_____	_____
Is prompt and accurate with routine documents	_____	_____	_____
Anticipates our needs	_____	_____	_____
Helps in emergencies	_____	_____	_____
Does not unfairly exploit a single-source position	_____	_____	_____
Does not request special consideration	_____	_____	_____
Currently supplies price, catalog, and technical information	_____	_____	_____
Furnishes specially requested information promptly	_____	_____	_____
Advises us of potential troubles	_____	_____	_____
Has good labor relations	_____	_____	_____
Delivers without constant follow-up	_____	_____	_____
Replaces rejections promptly	_____	_____	_____
Accepts our terms without exception	_____	_____	_____
Keeps promises	_____	_____	_____
Has sincere desire to serve	_____	_____	_____
Receiving			
Delivers per routing instructions	_____	_____	_____
Has adequate delivery service	_____	_____	_____
Has good packaging	_____	_____	_____
Accounting			
Invoices correctly	_____	_____	_____
Issues credit memos punctually	_____	_____	_____
Does not ask for special financial consideration	_____	_____	_____
Engineering			
Has past record on reliability of products	_____	_____	_____
Has technical ability for difficult work	_____	_____	_____
Readily accepts responsibility for latent deficiencies	_____	_____	_____
Provides quick and effective action in emergencies	_____	_____	_____
Furnishes requested data promptly	_____	_____	_____
Quality			
Provides high-quality material	_____	_____	_____
Furnishes certification, affidavits, etc.	_____	_____	_____
Replies with corrective action	_____	_____	_____

Figure 21.2 | Supplier Performance Evaluation Form, Categorical Plan

circumstance, quality might be weighted 25 percent, service 25 percent, and price 50 percent. In another, quality could be raised to 50 percent, and price reduced to 25 percent. The weights selected in any specific situation represent supply manager or supply team judgments concerning the relative importance of the respective factors.

After performance factors have been selected and weighted, a specific procedure is then developed to measure actual supplier performance on each factor. Supplier performance on each factor must be expressed in quantitative terms. In order to determine a supplier's overall rating, each factor weight is multiplied by the supplier's corresponding performance number; the results (for each factor) are then totaled to get the supplier's final rating for the time period in question.

The following hypothetical case illustrates the procedure. Assume that a supply management department has decided to weight and measure the three basic performance factors as follows:

Weight	Factors	Measurement Formula
50%	Quality performance = 100% − percentage of rejects	
25%	Service performance = 100% − 7% for each failure	
25%	Price performance =	$\dfrac{\text{lowest price offered}}{\text{price actually paid}}$

Assume further that supplier A performed as follows during the past month. Five percent of its items were rejected for quality reasons; three unsatisfactory split shipments were received; and A's price was $100/unit, compared with the lowest offer of $90/unit. Table 21.1 summarizes the total performance evaluation calculation for supplier A.

This procedure can be used to evaluate any number of different suppliers whose performance is particularly important during a given operating period. The performance of competing suppliers can be compared quantitatively, and subsequent negotiating strategies developed accordingly. The user should always remember that valid performance comparisons of two or more suppliers require that the same factors, weights, and measurement formulas be used *consistently* for all suppliers.

In contrast to the categorical plan, which is largely subjective, the weighted point plan has the advantage of being somewhat more objective. The exercise of subjective judgment is constrained more tightly in the assignment of factor weights and the development of the factor measurement formulas. The plan is extremely flexible, since it can

Table 21.1 | Illustrative Application of the Weighted Point Plan

Supplier A Monthly Performance Evaluation

Factor	Weight	Actual performance	Performance evaluation
Quality	50	5% rejects	$50 \times (1.00 - 0.05) = 47.50$
Service	25	3 failures	$25 \times [1.00 - (0.07 \times 3)] = 19.75$
Price	25	$100	$25 \times \dfrac{\$90}{\$100} = 22.50$
			Overall evaluation: = 89.75

accommodate any number of evaluation factors that are important in any specific case. Also, the plan can be used in conjunction with the categorical plan if buyers wish to include important subjective matters in the final evaluation of their suppliers.

Various research studies have noted, however, that a weighted point plan must be developed with care. The estimates of factor importance must be consistent from one situation to the next, and they must be consistent with the performance measurement formulas used because of the obvious interaction between them.

Cost Ratio Plan This plan evaluates supplier performance by using the tools of *standard* cost analysis that businesspeople traditionally use to evaluate a wide variety of business operations. When using this plan, the buying firm identifies the *additional* costs it incurs when doing business with a given supplier; these are separated as costs associated with the quality, service, and price elements of supplier performance. Each of these costs is then converted to a "cost ratio" which expresses the additional cost as a percent of the buying firm's total dollar purchase from that supplier. These three individual cost ratios are then totaled, producing the supplier's overall additional cost ratio. For purposes of analysis, the supplier's price is then adjusted by applying its overall cost ratio. The adjusted price for each supplier is then compared with the adjusted price for other competitive suppliers in the final evaluation process.

For example, assume that for one supplier the quality cost ratio is 2 percent, the delivery cost ratio is 2 percent, the service cost ratio is -1 percent, and the price is $72.25. The sum of all cost ratios is 3 percent; hence, the adjusted price for this supplier is [72.25 + (0.03 × 72.25)] = $74.42. This is the price used for evaluation purposes vis-à-vis other suppliers.

Although the cost ratio plan is used by a number of large progressive firms, overall it is not widely used in industry. Operationally speaking, it is a complex plan. It requires a specially designed, companywide, computerized cost accounting system to generate the precise cost data needed for effective operation. Consequently, the majority of supply management departments employing a quantitative type of evaluation rely on the simpler but effective weighted point plan—typically, modified specifically to meet their own unique circumstances.

For these reasons, the cost ratio plan is not discussed in detail in this book. Nevertheless, it is an excellent concept that has the ability to provide the most precise evaluation data of the three plans discussed. For firms using sophisticated information systems, the cost of designing and implementing the cost ratio plan typically is repaid many times by savings resulting from more precise analysis of supplier performance.

All three of the plans discussed—categorical, weighted point, and cost ratio—involve varying degrees of subjectivity and guesswork. The mathematical treatment of data in two of the plans often tends to obscure the fact that the results are no more accurate than the assumptions on which the quantitative data are based. In the final analysis, therefore, supplier evaluation must represent a combined appraisal of facts, quantitative computations, and value judgments. It simply cannot be achieved effectively by mechanical formulas alone.

Since the late 1980s, *scorecarding* has become a trendy, but confusing, term to describe variations of these three methods. The confusion is caused by misinterpretation of the balanced scorecard, a tool developed by Kaplan and Norton that focuses on four corporate goals: financial, customer, internal business processes, and learning and growth.[1]

Cost-Based Supplier Performance Evaluation   A number of firms are experimenting with various types of cost-based evaluation plans, similar to the cost ratio plan. Such plans address the issue of how to measure overall supplier performance on a total cost basis. In addition to rationalizing lowest total cost performance suppliers, such plans demonstrate that supplier nonperformance costs can be measured. Recognizing the supplier as an integral member of the organization, competitive strategy requires the development of a system that provides supplier accountability and control while maintaining dependable, competitive suppliers. As organizations continue to secure longer-term supplier relationships, the ability to quantify performance becomes increasingly important. Companies can use the methodology as a contract monitoring tool when incorporated into long-term agreements.

Motivation

Two common approaches are used to motivate suppliers to perform satisfactorily: punishment and reward. Many progressive supply managers use a combination of both approaches.

Punishment

Quite obviously, the greatest punishment for unsatisfactory performance (if the area of litigation and punitive damages is ignored) is *not* to award contracts for future requirements. This is a powerful motivator, especially during periods when supply professionals are reducing the number of suppliers with whom they do business.

Another method is to downgrade a supplier. Applied Materials, for example, grades suppliers into categories, the highest of which is preferred. A preferred supplier will have business increased over time and be included in Applied Materials' strategic plans. A poorly performing supplier can be downgraded, thereby reducing future business opportunities.

A less drastic approach called the "bill back" is especially appropriate when dealing with a "collaborative" supplier or a defense contractor. Under the bill back, incremental costs resulting from quality problems or late deliveries are identified and then billed back to the appropriate supplier. Some progressive supply managers have increased the motivational effect of the bill back by sending the bill to the supplier's chief operating officer so that he or she is aware of problems within his or her organization.

Rewards

The biggest reward for satisfactory performance is follow-on business. As in the example above, Applied Materials rewards superior performers with follow-on business, as well as greater opportunity for future business.

---

[1]Robert S. Kaplan, David P. Norton, *Translating Strategy into Action—The Balanced Scorecard,* Harvard Business School Press, Boston, MA, 1996.

Additionally, as with raising children or dealing with "significant others," recognition also is a powerful stimulant to future successful performance. Several years ago, an Arizona supply manager divided her suppliers into three categories: outstanding, acceptable, and marginal. She wrote an appropriate letter to the CEO of each supplier firm. The results of her efforts were rewarding. The outstanding group performed even better! Most of the CEOs from the second and third groups requested meetings to discuss what they could do better to earn *an outstanding letter!*

A major appliance manufacturer publicly recognizes its most successful suppliers. Such suppliers are encouraged to share their recognition with their employees. The employees are encouraged to continue their efforts to improve quality and productivity. Many suppliers reward their outstanding employees with a trip to the buying firm to see how their products are used.

Each year, the appliance manufacturer selects its 100 "best" suppliers. This selection is based on a combination of service, responsiveness, value analysis suggestions, cost, and related factors. Each representative and CEO attends the Supplier Appreciation Group's Day. Over 50 senior managers from the buying firm also attend. Each of the 100 outstanding suppliers receives a plaque acknowledging its status and contribution. The buying firm publicizes this list in appliance and supply magazines, to the delight of those listed.

Assistance

Progressive firms have discovered that several types of assistance to suppliers pay big dividends.

Transformational Training

Many firms have learned the benefits of providing training to their suppliers in approaches such as WCSM, statistical process control (SPC), just-in-time (JIT) manufacturing, and Six Sigma. Progressive firms recognize that their ability to procure quality products and services on time requires suppliers with competence in these tools and philosophies. Transformational training sponsored by the buying firm (or jointly provided by the buyer and supplier) is discussed in Chapters 22 and 28.

Quality Audits and Supply System Reviews

As organizations realize their interdependence with their suppliers, they are becoming more proactive in assuring that their suppliers' quality systems and procurement systems operate effectively. Such assurance is often provided by quality audits and supply system reviews given by the buying firm. Such reviews should not be focused on punishment, but on identifying opportunities for improvement.

A supplier's procurement system affects its quality, cost, technology, and dependability. In theory, competition rewards suppliers who have efficient procurement systems with *survival* and *profit,* and it penalizes suppliers with inefficient systems. But such theory may take years to show results. Further, as firms move from reliance on market competition to collaborative and alliance relationships, the implications of inefficient supplier procurement systems become even more frightening. The supply system review provides a framework that a buying firm may follow when reviewing and assisting its key suppliers to upgrade their supply systems. The review is conducted in a constructive, cooperative atmosphere.

Problem Solving

Most progressive firms provide technical and managerial assistance to their suppliers when quality and related problems are encountered. Progressive supply managers have replaced the attitude "it's their contract and it's their problem" with the knowledge that the buying firm's success is dependent on its suppliers' success. Many problem-solving tools and techniques used in aiding suppliers are presented in Chapters 7 and 22, Quality Management, and Supplier Development.

Value Analysis

We continue to be amazed at how few firms take advantage of the power of value analysis (VA). Such programs enlist the supplier and his or her personnel to contribute their brain power in reducing or avoiding unnecessary costs. Well-run VA programs enjoy a return on the program's costs of 1,000 percent. The mechanics of value analysis are similar to value engineering as introduced in Chapter 10, New Product Development. An additional discussion of VE/VA is contained in Chapter 22, Supplier Development. Value analysis also can be a wonderful enabler of supplier development and is discussed in more detail in that chapter. We strongly encourage our readers to learn from the U.S. Department of Defense and from several enlightened firms who willingly share with the supplier the savings resulting from supplier-originated VA suggestions.

Supplier Surveys

Solicitation of supplier feedback is an often overlooked aspect of successful supplier relationship management. As quality guru Philip B. Crosby wrote many years ago, "You need to demonstrate your understanding and willingness to clean your own house before asking the supplier to clean his."[2] Crosby suggests soliciting answers from suppliers to the following questions:

- How knowledgeable are our supply managers?
- How accurate are our engineering specifications?
- How clearly do we state our quality requirements?
- How timely are our payments?

A major manufacturer utilizes a supplier survey at least once a year. Its supply personnel feel that the feedback obtained has played a significant role in improving supplier

---

[2]Philip Crosby, "Seven Steps for Producing a Useful Supplier Survey," *Purchasing,* September 6, 1984, p. 126.

relations and in ensuring that high-quality materials are received on time. Appendices C and D at the end of this chapter contain questionnaires designed to capture supplier input. Such surveys normally are conducted by an independent third party such as an audit firm or a supply management consultant.

In 1995, IBM surveyed its suppliers with the intent of becoming a better customer. Responses emphasized the frustrations of dealing with IBM's bureaucratic processes and long, one-sided, legalese-laden contract terms. (IBM's contracts ranged 40–80 pages.)

Suppliers also complained that IBM was unwilling to communicate openly on commercial matters such as build schedules or on technical matters. They complained that engineers, managers, and executives in procurement were inaccessible. "They basically said IBM was an unfriendly customer. We had arm's length types of relationships and didn't want to interact with suppliers other than across the negotiating table," says Javier Urioste, former Global Procurement Director of Policy Strategy and International Operations.

IBM reviewed the supplier complaints and took action. It reengineered its contract processes and documents. Old contract terms and conditions were scrapped and suppliers were invited to come up with streamlined, simple, nonlegalistic, even-handed model agreements at a series of supplier forums. The results were four- to six-page contracts rather than 40–80 page documents designed to protect IBM from every conceivable contingency.

IBM buyers and engineers also became more accessible to suppliers. The firm established a technology convergence office that reviewed suppliers' technology road maps and shared information about where IBM products were going. IBM also shared business information, sending suppliers forecasts of its build schedules. An ombudsman office was established to look into supplier complaints and issues.

"It's been a dramatic improvement. The most significant improvements were the areas of information exchange, both technical and commercial information, access to technical road maps, business plans, and product road maps themselves."[3]

Additional Approaches to Improving Supplier Relations

Riggs and Robbins, in their book *The Executive's Guide to Supply Management Strategies,* identified three strategies to help facilitate supplier development and relations.[4]

Annual Supplier Meetings

Many companies have annual supplier meetings where key suppliers are selected to come together with the buying firm. The annual supplier meeting can be used as a teaching and learning platform, as well as an opportunity to distinguish one's organization as a supply management leader. This type of meeting begins with a review of the buying

---

[3]Javier Urioste, cited in "IBM to Suppliers: How Are We Doing?" *Purchasing,* September 16, 1999.

[4]David A. Riggs and Sharon L. Robbins, *The Executive's Guide to Supply Management Strategies* (New York: Amacom, 1998), pp. 215–19.

firm's supply management performance, learning, and future goals. The centerpiece of the meeting, however, is real learning about key supply strategies that support the buyer's business. The host presents actual case studies of learning, including the before-and-after-supply-strategy approaches, which highlight benefits realized, especially the time and dollars saved. They bring experts on cutting-edge topics in to address the group. Annual supplier meetings require extensive planning and some expense, but they create a highly visible platform for leadership messages and lay the foundation for improved relationships.

Supplier Roundtables

Supplier roundtables are a more informal way to gain shared learning. The roundtable provides the opportunity to interface with seven to ten supplier representatives, ideally the chief executive, the chief operating officer, and other relevant corporate officers from marketing, research, and supply management. The roundtable discussion parallels the annual supplier meeting agenda, beginning with a review of the buying organization's progress and goals along with a description of key strategy shifts. Corporate learning also may be addressed. The supplier roundtable can work at several levels including: executive roundtables, technical roundtables, supply management roundtables—all with a shared learning agenda. This roundtable approach is informal, flexible, and can be tailored to meet the style of the business leader host. Finally, it builds a base of trust and respect, which is fundamental to a successful supplier relationship.

Supplier Workshops

Supplier workshops are aimed at creating opportunities for supply-stream innovation that will benefit all participants. This forum is composed of supplier participants who provide materials and services that are critical to the products the customer's organization brings to the marketplace. The discussion format centers on process changes necessary to provide a stretch improvement goal. Such a proactive question signals a search for real departures in approach and opens the door for a new type of collaboration. These workshop sessions also can draw upon the continual innovation process and concepts to provide the structure necessary to guide and organize discussion and work sessions.

Collaboration

Experience in recent years demonstrates that the most successful supplier management results are generated when the buyer and the supplier view their relationship as one of collaboration. Such relationships are based on mutual interdependency and respect. Collaborative relationships begin or are renewed with careful source selection during the product and/or service design and development process. At this point, the buying firm needs a dependable supplier to provide the required process, design, and technological input if a marketable, profitable product or a satisfactory service is to result. In turn, the supplier needs a responsible customer for its products and services. Supply professionals need the supplier as much as (or more than) the supplier needs them. This interdependence grows as a project moves from design into operations. Unexpected problems arise which require a

"We shall overcome" attitude by the partners. During production, the buyers and suppliers must mesh their schedules, requiring another phase of cooperation.

The *ultimate* in collaborative relationships is a virtual integration of buyer and supplier, wherein two independently owned entities integrate their energies for as long as the relationship benefits both parties. One- or two-page memoranda of agreement replace lengthy contracts, change orders, and other legalistic and defensive procedures. As discussed in Chapter 5, we reserve the term "alliances" for such relationships.

Managing the Relationship

As previously discussed, any supply management department typically will have a continuum of supplier relationships from arm's-length through collaborative to strategic alliances. The latter two types of relationships are becoming more common. Developing and managing such relationships are both challenging and fulfilling.

Several actions must be taken to ensure the success of each supply alliance relationship. (Supply managers should select and tailor appropriate actions when planning the management of collaborative relationships.) For example:

- Ideally, an interfirm cross-functional team should be established to develop and manage plans, facilitate integration, and develop and manage appropriate metrics.
- Appropriate cross-functional team members at both the buying and the selling firms should receive training in being constructive team players.
- An interfirm team composed of representatives of both firms should be formed. Members should jointly receive training in cross-functional team skills.
- The two firms must develop an integrated communication system responsive to the needs of both parties in their area of cooperation.
- Plans to increase and measure trust between the two organizations should be developed and implemented.
- Arrangements for co-location of key technical personnel and for periodic visits to each other's facilities should be developed and implemented.
- Plans should be developed and implemented for training on issues, including the designing of variance out of products and processes, quality, supply management, value analysis and engineering, strategic cost analysis, activity-based cost management, etc.
- Measurable quantifiable objectives must be established in areas, including quality, cost, time, technology, etc.
- The results of such improvement efforts must be monitored and reported to appropriate management.
- Ethics should win over expediency.
- Interfirm team members and others who are closely involved must recognize the need to change their orientation from adversarial to collaborative.
- Interfirm team members should become champions who ensure that their organizations understand and support the alliance's goals.

It is in the interest of both the buying and supplying firms for the buying firm's personnel to support the supplier's operations.

Concluding Remarks

Without question, management of supply contracts is a critical and challenging activity. Perhaps the most challenging aspect is the evolution from managing or controlling the supplier to managing the relationship. New attitudes and skills are required. Supplier relationships require the same amount of attention as a good marriage, and the many benefits of successful relationships make the efforts worthwhile.

APPENDIX A: SUPPLIER REPORTING REQUIREMENTS FOR UNIQUE MAJOR PROJECTS

During the pre-award conference, arrangements are made for the timely receipt of the following data, as appropriate:

- *A program organization chart.* For a large job, the supplier designates its program manager and shows the key members of the organization by name and function. The program manager's functional authority should be clearly defined.
- *Milestone plan.* For a complex project, this plan identifies all major milestones on a time-phased basis, including those of the supplier's major subcontractors.
- *Funds commitment plan* (incentive and cost reimbursement contracts only). This plan shows estimated commitments on a dollar versus month basis and on a cumulative dollar versus month basis.
- *Labor commitment plan.* This plan shows estimated labor loading on a labor-hour versus labor-month basis.
- *Monthly progress information.* This report should be submitted 10 days after the close of each month. The report should contain as a minimum:
- *A narrative summary of work accomplished* during the reporting period, including a technical progress update, a summary of work planned for the next reporting period, problems encountered or anticipated, corrective action taken or to be taken, and a summary of buyer-seller discussions.
  - *A list of all action items,* if any, required of the buying firm during the forthcoming performance period.
  - *An update of the milestone plan* showing actual progress against planned progress.
  - *An update of the funds commitment plan* showing actual funds committed against the planned funds by time (incentive and cost reimbursement contracts only).
  - *A report on any significant changes* in the supplier's program personnel or in the financial or general management structure, or any other factors that might affect performance.
  - *A missed milestone notification and recovery plan.* The supplier should notify the supply manager by phone, fax, or e-mail within 24 hours after discovery of

a missed major milestone or the discovery of an anticipated major milestone slip. The supplier should provide the supply manager with a missed milestone recovery plan within seven working days.

Such data can be costly to compile and should be required only when it has been determined that their cost and the cost associated with using them to manage an order will result in a net saving or the likely avoidance of a schedule slippage. The supply manager, on a case-by-case basis, must determine what level of detail is necessary.

APPENDIX B: HOW CRITICAL PATH SCHEDULING WORKS

Critical path scheduling begins with the identification and listing of all significant activities involved in the project to be planned and controlled. When the list of activities is complete, the sequential relationship between all activities is determined and shown graphically by constructing an activity network (see Figure 21.3). The network shows the time required to complete each activity, and it explicitly indicates the relationship of each activity to all other activities. Finally, it establishes the sequence in which activities should be scheduled for efficient completion of the total project. Some activities can be paralleled, allowing many different jobs to be carried on simultaneously; other activities must be placed in series to allow step-by-step completion of interrelated tasks. The complete interrelationship of all project activities is the important feature that distinguishes critical path analysis from Gantt and other bar chart planning techniques.

Construction of the network permits determination of a project's *critical path*—the sequentially linked chain (or chains) of activities requiring the most time for completion from start to finish of the project. Once the critical path is determined, the planner can identify precisely and completely the activities that require close control. He or she can also determine which activities permit the greatest latitude in scheduling and can, if necessary, most easily relinquish resources to more urgent jobs. An activity network also highlights the activities that can be expedited most effectively in case a stepped-up pace becomes necessary.

Figure 21.3 illustrates the mechanics of network development. This simplified example shows a partial network of the major subcontracted activities involved in the construction of a new laboratory. Engineering and purchasing activities prior to site preparation have been omitted for reasons of simplification. The example shows only the major activities to be completed after the site has been excavated and prepared for the concrete subcontractor.

1. Column 1 (Figure 21.4) lists the major activities to be completed.
2. Figure 21.3 shows the activities in network form. The required interdependencies and sequencing of operations have been determined and reviewed with the project engineer and the various subcontractors. Each arrow in the diagram represents an *activity* that will be conducted during a period of time. Each circle represents an *event* that will occur at a specific period of time (e.g., the start of an activity and the completion of an activity).

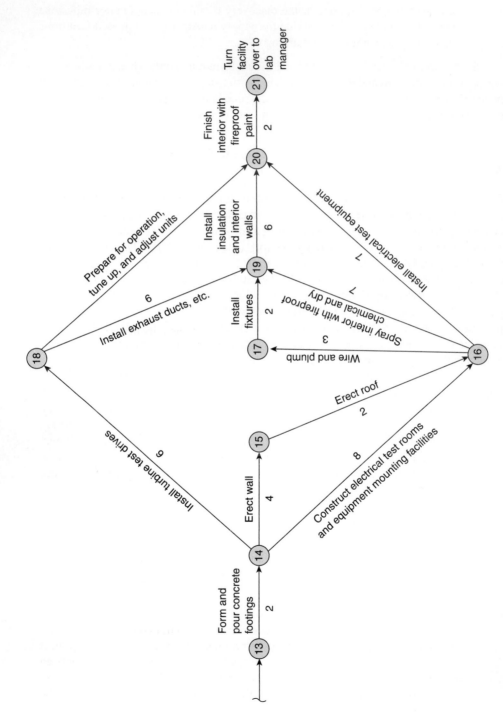

Figure 21.3 | Simplified Critical Path Network for Subcontracted Activities of a Laboratory Construction Job

Activity (1)	Earliest (2)		Latest (3)		Slack (4)
	Start	Complete	Start	Complete	
13–14 Form and pour concrete footings	0	2	0	2	0
14–16 Construct electrical test rooms and equipment mounting facilities	2	10	2	10	0
16–19 Spray interior with fireproof chemical and let dry	10	17	10	17	0
19–20 Install insulatior and interior walls	17	23	17	23	0
20–21 Finish interior with fireproof paint	23	25	23	25	0
14–15 Erect walls	2	6	4	8	2
15–16 Erect roof	6	8	8	10	2
16–17 Install electrical wiring and plumbing	10	13	12	15	2
17–19 Install fixtures	13	15	15	17	2
14–18 Install turbine test drives	2	8	5	11	3
18–19 Install exhaust ducts, etc.	8	14	11	17	3
16–20 Install electrical test equipment	10	17	16	23	6
18–20 Prepare for operation, tune up, and adjust drive units	8	16	15	23	7

Figure 21.4 I Data for Figures 21-3 and 21-5

3. Careful estimates of the time required to complete each activity have been made by the respective contractors and are noted next to the appropriate arrows.[5]

4. The critical path (longest chain of activities) consists of the activities 13-14-16-19-20-21; it will take 25 weeks to finish the project. The critical path is determined by totaling the time requirements for individual activities put together in every conceivable path from start to finish of the project. The critical path is the one requiring the longest time. Using the given time estimates, it is impossible to complete the project in less time.

5. At this point, the objective is to determine the amount of "slack time" (extra time, or leeway) existing in each of the noncritical paths. This is done by first developing the figures in column 2 (the earliest start and completion dates for each activity) and then those in column 3 (the latest possible start and completion dates for each activity) of Figure 21.4.

   The earliest start and completion date for each activity is determined by starting with the first activity and totaling the time requirements of the various paths through the network. If we say that the earliest start date for 13–14 (the concrete work) is

---

[5]The PERT technique is often used for jobs whose time requirements cannot be accurately estimated. For this reason PERT requires three time estimates for each activity: (1) t_l = longest time required under the most difficult conditions (expect once in 100 times); (2) t_s = shortest time required under the best conditions (expect once in 100 times); (3) t_m = most likely time requirement. The expected time t_e, the figure actually used on the network, is a weighted average computed as

$$t_e = \frac{t_l + t_s + 4t_m}{6}$$

today (the 0 point in time), the earliest completion date for 13–14 is the end of week 2 (0 + 2 = 2). Therefore, the earliest start date for both 14–15 and 14–16, which cannot begin before 13–14 is completed, is the end of week 2. The earliest completion date for 14–16 is the end of week 10 (2 + 8 = 10), and for 14–15 it is the end of week 6 (2 + 4 = 6). The earliest start date for 15–16 is the end of week 6, and the earliest completion date is the end of week 8 (6 + 2 = 8). What is the earliest start date for the electrical wiring and plumbing activity 16–17? Is it the end of week 8 or week 10? Clearly, it is the end of week 10, because the wiring cannot be started until the electrical test rooms and mounting facilities are completed. The analysis continues in this manner through the entire network until column 2 is complete.

The latest possible start and completion date for each activity (column 3) is determined in exactly the reverse manner. Begin with the completion date for the final activity and work backward through the network, determining the latest completion and start dates that can be used for each activity without delaying completion of the project. All activities on the critical path will have identical "earliest" and "latest" dates. This is not true, however, for the noncritical path activities.

The latest completion date for the final painting activity (20–21) is the end of week 25, and the latest start date is the end of week 23 (25 − 2 = 23). Therefore, the latest completion date for 18–20 is the end of week 23, and the latest start date is the end of week 15. Notice, however, that the latest completion date for 14–18 is not the end of week 15. Activity 14–18 must be completed by the latest start date for activity 18–19, which is the end of week 11 (23 − 6 − 6 = 11). This procedure, then, is followed back through the network to complete column 3.

5. The purpose in developing columns 2 and 3 is to determine the amount of *slack time* in each noncritical, or slack, path (column 4). The slack time existing for a particular activity is simply the difference between the earliest start date and the latest start date (or between the earliest completion date and the latest completion date). This important factor represents leeway which can be used in scheduling the slack path activity most efficiently in light of other demands for facilities and manpower.[6]

6. Figure 21.5 represents the network in Figure 21.3 drawn against a vertical slack scale. Its purpose is merely to show, at a quick glance, how much slack is available in each slack path activity. Such a chart frequently serves as a good visual planning aid.

The preceding discussion has dealt only with the rudiments of the critical path planning concept. In practice, performance is monitored, and progress data are periodically compared with the original plan. The technique is therefore an effective control device as well as an aid in making future planning decisions as changes in plans occur. The projects to which the technique is applied in practice are often made up of several thousand activities. After the initial network is constructed for such projects, a computer program such as Microsoft Project is typically used. Project management using the computer in conjunction with the World Wide Web is discussed in Chapter 9, e-Commerce II.

---

[6]Column 4 indicates that both activities 14–15 and 15–16 have two weeks' slack. Notice that this is an either-or situation. Two weeks' slack cannot be utilized in both activities; two weeks represents the total combined slack for both activities.

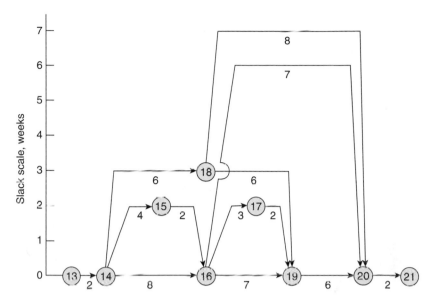

Figure 21.5 I Network of Figure 21.3 drawn against a Slack Scale

The network depicted in Figure 21.3 considers the planning and controlling activities only with respect to the factor of time. Some techniques of critical path analysis add to this the factor of cost. These techniques integrate the two important variables in a single system, permitting virtually total managerial control.

A wise manager always raises two questions about the practicality of any planning or control concept: How accurate is it? How much does it cost? Like other planning techniques, critical path analysis is no more accurate than the data it manipulates. As for cost, some companies find it profitable; others do not. Generally speaking, the greatest profit potential for such a system lies in its application to projects too complex for adequate planning with bar charts. The basic question a firm must answer is: How important is the ultimate control the system affords? When management puts a price tag on this variable, it then can determine whether or not adoption of the system is likely to be profitable.

Its current popularity indicates that a large number of users find critical path analysis profitable primarily because it forces suppliers to do more planning than they otherwise would do. Numerous governmental and industrial buyers require subcontractors to submit a critical path network (for major events, or "milestones") with their bids on subcontract and construction jobs.

APPENDIX C: SUPPLIER QUESTIONNAIRE

The Supply Management and Internal Audit Departments at _____ have developed a short questionnaire to determine weaknesses and strengths of our procurement and payable functions. To ensure creditability, all suppliers being requested to complete this form were selected by Internal Audit. We would appreciate your taking a few minutes to complete the form. While you need not identify yourself, we would appreciate a generic description of the product or service you provide—see question #7. A self-addressed postage-paid envelope is enclosed for your convenience.

1. Do you find the supply managers you interact with at ____ to possess the necessary expertise to evaluate your products or services fairly?

____ Yes ____ No

2. Are you accorded a prompt and courteous interview in the Supply Management Department?

____ Yes ____ No

3. When requested to respond to written bids, is your firm allowed sufficient time?

____ Yes ____ No

4. On a scale of 1 to 5, 5 being the highest, how would you rate the ethics (honesty, willingness to listen to both sides of an issue, impartiality, etc.) of members of the Supply Management Department?

Circle one: 1   2   3   4   5

5. Are invoices paid on time?

____ Yes ____ No

6. Do you receive a prompt response when calling regarding a delinquent payment?

____ Yes ____ No

7. Please identify the product or service you provide—examples: laboratory equipment/supplies, agricultural-related products, computer equipment/supplies, etc.

_____

_____

_____

8. Are there any additional comments you have relative to the operation of the supply management and accounts payable functions at _____?

Please return the completed questionnaire to: _____. We would appreciate a return date by _____. Your comments will be appreciated. Thank you!

APPENDIX D: INTERNAL EVALUATION

Supply Management Questionnaire for Suppliers

The following is a series of statements about supply management at _____. Please offer your perceptions of _____ supply management effort as it compares with other companies to which you sell. Simply check the appropriate box to the right of each question.

	Strongly agree	Agree somewhat	Neither agree nor disagree	Disagree somewhat	Strongly disagree
1. The supply department displays a high level of professionalism.	☐	☐	☐	☐	☐
2. The firm provides clear specifications/requirements as to what goods or services it requires.	☐	☐	☐	☐	☐
3. The supplier selection process takes longer and is more cumbersome than that of most companies.	☐	☐	☐	☐	☐
4. The firm seems to select its suppliers based on a combination of factors (price, quality, delivery reliability, etc.), rather than price alone.	☐	☐	☐	☐	☐
5. Purchase terms and conditions are more demanding than for most customers.	☐	☐	☐	☐	☐
6. The firm maintains an adversarial relationship with its suppliers.	☐	☐	☐	☐	☐
7. Supply department personnel have sufficient knowledge of the items they procure.	☐	☐	☐	☐	☐
8. The supplier selection process seems arbitrary and capricious.	☐	☐	☐	☐	☐
9. Supply personnel are demanding negotiators.	☐	☐	☐	☐	☐
10. Supply personnel are fair negotiators.	☐	☐	☐	☐	☐
11. The firm requires more paperwork to process an order than most customers.	☐	☐	☐	☐	☐
12. The percentage of rush/special orders is about the same as that of other customers.	☐	☐	☐	☐	☐
13. Once orders have been placed, the firm issues more changes to orders than most companies.	☐	☐	☐	☐	☐
14. Supply personnel check on the status of open orders more than most companies.	☐	☐	☐	☐	☐

	Strongly agree	Agree somewhat	Neither agree nor disagree	Disagree somewhat	Strongly disagree
15. Compared with most customers, the firm spends a good deal of effort controlling the quality of the goods it receives.	☐	☐	☐	☐	☐
16. Orders are placed by operating personnel (rather than supply personnel) more than most companies.	☐	☐	☐	☐	☐
17. Our sales force is likely to target operating personnel, rather than supply personnel, to promote my company's goods/services.	☐	☐	☐	☐	☐
18. The firm is timely in the payment of its purchases.	☐	☐	☐	☐	☐
19. The firm seems "bureaucratic" to deal with.	☐	☐	☐	☐	☐
20. The firm could receive better supply services by negotiating sole supplier relationships.	☐	☐	☐	☐	☐
21. Operating division personnel are more involved in the supply decision than at most companies.	☐	☐	☐	☐	☐
22. Supply makes an attempt to establish a long-term relationship with its suppliers.	☐	☐	☐	☐	☐
23. Supply and operating division personnel will often inquire independently about the same order.	☐	☐	☐	☐	☐

CHAPTER 22

Supplier Development

World Class Supply Management^{SM} requires world-class suppliers. Supplier development plays the key role in helping suppliers achieve and maintain world-class status.

KEY CONCEPTS

■   Supplier Development Enablers   525

■   Barriers to Supplier Development   534

Case

Supplier Waste at Birmingham Digital Devices

Mark Spencer, director of Supplier Development for Pendulum Scientific, sat down with five members of Birmingham Digital Devices' (BDD) upper management. Mark planned to provide an executive overview of the initial findings of his supplier development team. Pendulum is a designer, assembler, and distributor of clocks that automatically update themselves using transmissions coming from satellites. Recently, sales of satellite clocks have declined on account of the recession of 2002. Instead of focusing on the 1990s mantra of increasing sales, Pendulum has decided to focus on decreasing costs in an effort to improve its bottom line. To reduce costs, Pendulum hired Mark to focus on reducing costs in the supply chain through supplier development efforts.

John Ronchetto, the president of BDD, opened the discussion, "So Mark, what did you discover in the first discussion with our people? Did you find any opportunities for improvement?"

Mark replied, "I really wasn't sure what to expect—BDD has been a great supplier to Pendulum over the years. BDD has always met our deadlines, the quality has been terrific and dealing with BDD's sales force has always been a pleasure. I just want to say that Pendulum is delighted that BDD is working with Pendulum with the objective of improving both companies' bottom lines. I also appreciate the assignment of three of your key personnel from engineering, operations, and quality to the development team."

A little annoyed with Mark's preamble, Leslie Brown, vice president of Marketing, said, "Cut to the chase Mark. Tell us how the team is progressing."

Mark responded, "Well, we (the supplier development team) met for the first time last Wednesday to conduct a process value analysis for the Accutrack 3000. We focused strictly on process time. We selected the Accutrack 3000 because it accounts for 62 percent of Pendulum's annual purchases from BDD."

Mark pulled out a sketch of the process map to show BDD's management. "The results were no more staggering than I have experienced at some of our other suppliers. If you look at the process map, you will see the network of boxes illustrate all of the activities required to get the Accutrack 3000 to Pendulum's receiving dock. Notice the process spans across three of your suppliers. We found that considerable waste existed at two of these suppliers.

"The boxes in the sketch each have a V, N, or W within them. The V symbols represent value-added activities. The N symbols represent non-value-added but necessary activities. We used a W to denote waste, which is completely non-value-added activity from Pendulum's viewpoint. Overall, we estimated 92 percent waste, 3% non-value-added but necessary, and 5 percent value-added activity.

"For example, in the stamping process, the setup time is considered necessary, but not value-added, so it was given a symbol N. The time that the material sits waiting in work-in-process (WIP) is waste, so it received a W. The actual stamping activity is value-added, so we marked it with a V."

With a shocked look on his face, Richard Furnish, vice president of Quality said, "What? Are you nuts? How can all of this time be waste? For example, the finished goods inventory that you are calling waste is necessary to meet the delivery schedules that your company imposes on us. Doesn't that add value to Pendulum?"

Mark replied, "The answer to your last question is no. We define value-added from the perspective of our customers. Our customers want specific features and quality at a low cost. They do not care how long the clocks or their parts sit in inventory, unless they have to pay for the cost of that time in the form of a higher purchase price. If we can stop passing this cost on to our customers, BDD and Pendulum will benefit in increased sales as well as reduced costs.

"Our two companies need to work together to reduce the waste of inventory in our supply chain. We have some ideas of our own and got some from brief discussions with your people. We are working on prioritizing potential projects based on expected savings. If I had to guess, I would say the greatest opportunities exist at your suppliers' facilities. If that is the case, we will need to expand our development to including your suppliers. We should add a representative or two from your supply management group to the team."

John Ronchetto stopped Mark short of completing his explanation, "I think we get the idea Mark. The improvement team's analysis shows us we have many opportunities for collaboration between BDD, Pendulum, and other members of our supply chain. What's the next step?"

Strategic Importance of Supplier Development

As manufacturing firms outsource more materials, subassemblies, and even complete products and services to focus on their own core competencies, they increasingly expect their suppliers to deliver innovative and quality products on time and at a competitive cost. When a supplier is incapable of meeting these needs, a buyer has three alternatives: (1) bring the outsourced item in-house and produce it internally, (2) re-source with a more capable supplier, or (3) help improve the existing supplier's capabilities.[1]

The Development Decision

The strategy of choice often depends on price, volume, or the strategic nature of the procured item. For low-value-added, non-strategic commodities the cost of changing to a new supplier is low and may be the best option. At the other extreme, when a poorly

---

[1]Robert B. Handfield, Daniel R. Krause, Thomas V. Scannell, and Robert M. Monczka, "Avoid the Pitfalls in Supplier Development," *Sloan Management Review,* Winter 2000, p. 2.

performing supplier provides an innovative product or process technology that may provide a sustainable long-term advantage to the buying firm, the supply manager may wish to protect this potential advantage and bring the work in-house or acquire the supplier.

Today, however, most companies prefer to continue outsourcing in an effort to maintain flexibility in meeting changing market demands. Thus, even critical A items may be outsourced. This shift toward greater levels of outsourcing reinforces the need for strong supplier development capabilities. Supplier development increasingly is becoming the best choice for companies. Some scholars have concluded that the option of switching to another supplier should be sought only when it is "absolutely" necessary.[2]

Supplier Development Defined

Supplier development can be defined as any activity that a buying firm undertakes to improve a supplier's performance and capabilities to meet the buying firm's supply needs. Buying firms use a variety of activities to improve supplier performance including: assessing suppliers' operations, providing incentives to improve performance, instigating competition among suppliers, and working directly with suppliers, either through training or other activities.[3] Supplier development may go beyond the first tier of suppliers to the second or third tier and ultimately to "Mother Earth" if necessary.

Supplier development in world-class firms is proactive. Instead of working with suppliers for quick fixes to problems, supplier development should focus on helping suppliers retain the learning that occurs in the development process. Retained learning is critical for suppliers so that they may continuously improve their own systems. Further, a supplier who has retained its ability to improve then can work with its suppliers to help them improve. The net effect is a more capable, more competitive supply chain.

Supplier development requires that both firms commit financial, capital, and personnel resources to the work; share timely and sensitive information; and create an effective means of measuring performance and progress. Executives and employees at the buying firm must be convinced that investing company resources in a supplier is worthwhile. Executives at the supplier's firm must be convinced that their best interest lies in accepting direction and assistance from their customer. The convincing may not be congenial at first, but eventually it should evolve into collaboration based on mutual goals.

In a study of eight suppliers for the five largest American automobile manufacturers, Hartley and Choi identified that the automobile manufacturers can use supplier development programs as catalysts of process change within their suppliers.[4] Their study identified that not only does a customer provide a fresh perspective that may challenge the underlying assumptions in the supplier's organization, but also that the customer that legitimizes the need for change is generally able to overcome the supplier's organizational inertia.

---

[2]Joseph L. Cavinato, "What to Do When a Supplier Is in Trouble," *NAPM InfoEdge* 1, no. 4 (October 1995) p. 9.

[3]Handfield, Krause, Scannell, and Monczka, "Avoid the Pitfalls," p. 2.

[4]J. L. Hartley, and T. Y. Choi, "Supplier Development: Customers as a Catalyst of Process Change," *Business Horizon 39,* no. 4 (1996), pp. 37–44.

As a colleague at Honda of America Manufacturing reported a few years ago, "If a supplier has a problem that adversely affects us, we'll help it to death!" What our colleague implied was that Honda would help the supplier until it achieved and maintained world-class status.

The Supplier Performance Gap

Paraphrasing Dave Nelson and his co-authors, "There exists a 'performance gap' between what suppliers are capable of achieving and what they currently demonstrate through their cost controls, quality performance, and customer responsiveness."[5] We believe that supply management is responsible for closing this supplier performance gap.

Why has supply management not closed this gap at most suppliers? In the last two decades, many original equipment manufacturers (OEMs) such as Sony, Toyota, Solectron, and IBM have closed their internal operations gap between what they thought they were capable of achieving and their current performance. Managers of internal operations were successful at convincing upper management of the benefits of investing in a variety of management approaches such as Total Quality Management, Six Sigma, and Just-in-Time. In contrast, supply management was not very successful at convincing upper management of the benefits resulting from closing gaps between existing practices and world-class ones within its supply base. Support for developing a world-class supplier base remained a secondary priority or, at many companies, was not even a consideration. According to Nelson, Moody, and Stegner, "Drivers for improvement have rippled out laterally to what may at the time have been considered the second targets for improvement—"collateral" groups like purchasing, logistics, and order administration. We think this priority for change is flawed."[6]

Results of Supplier Development

When suppliers become proficient at new technologies, improve their quality or delivery performance, or improve their own supply management systems, they create cost savings that benefit both themselves and the end customer. The improvements also create an example for other members in the supply chain that can stimulate improvement.

The best examples of savings from supplier development in the early part of this century are coming out of Dave Nelson's former supply management operations at Deere and Company. Dave Nelson is a visionary in supply management in much the way Deming was in quality management. Dave Nelson's efforts and results in developing World Class Supply Management[SM] at Honda of America in the 1990s and, more recently, at Deere & Company are in a league of their own. On March 1, 2002, Dave refocused his legendary efforts on a new target: Delphi Automotive Systems where he is Vice President, Global Purchasing.

Dave and his Deere supplier development team expected 500 to 1,000 percent return on the dollars they invested in supplier development. Each supply manager

---

[5]Dave Nelson, Patricia E. Moody, and Jonathan Stegner, *The Purchasing Machine* (New York: Free Press, 2001).

[6]Ibid., p. 24.

involved in supplier development earned five to ten times his or her compensation. Dave employed these numbers to obtain CEO support and expand Deere's supplier support systems.[7]

As both Deere and Honda have demonstrated, rapid improvements in supply base performance do not come without an up-front investment. In the late 1990s, John Deere added 175 new strategic supply management professionals: 100 for supplier development, 50 for cost management, and 25 for Best Practices. Similarly, at Honda, purchasing employs over 400 professionals, many of whom are dedicated to supplier development initiatives.[8]

World Class Supplier Development

Before progressing further, we will outline the common best practices and characteristics of World Class Supply Management[SM] supplier development programs.

Best Practices in Supplier Development

- Create dedicated supply development teams (with no responsibilities or jobs other than supplier development).
- Teach a supplier how to develop itself after initial guidance from the supplier development team.
- Focus on underlying causes of long cycle times.
- Focus on wasteful activities in all supplier efforts.
- Involve suppliers in new product and process development at the buying firm.
- Provide training programs and training time to suppliers.
- Provide education programs offline that go beyond training.
- Provide improvement-focused seminars for suppliers.
- Provide tooling and technical assistance to suppliers.
- Provide supplier support centers.
- Loan executives, such as process engineers and quality managers.
- Drive fear out that a supplier's workforce may have toward supplier development programs.
- Set "stretch goals" to encourage radical change as well as continuous improvement.
- Improve accounting systems to enable measurement of improvements.
- Share the savings from the development improvements.
- Encourage suppliers to contribute to improving processes at the buyer's facilities.
- Provide a feedback loop for suppliers to help encourage supplier development efforts.
- Improve the supplier's supply management system.

---

[7]Ibid., p. 274.
[8]Ibid., pp. 41–42.

Developing the Supplier's Supply Management System

Experience demonstrates that a buying firm will significantly improve supply chain performance when it develops its supplier's supply management system. Improving the supplying firm's supply management system will reduce the supplier's cost and improve its quality, responsiveness, time to market, continuity, and the inflow of technology from the supplier's suppliers. In our minds, no other area offers more opportunity for impact on both firms' bottom lines! Chapter 28, "Implementing World Class Supply Management^{SM}," offers a road map to transforming a firm's supply management system to world-class status. While not every cited goal and initiative may be relevant to a specific supplier, the development team should be able to develop an appropriate action plan based on the algorithm developed in Chapter 28. The development team must be aware that the necessary transformation to world-class status is a process that may require four or more years.

Collaboration Is the Key

World-class supplier development requires a commitment to collaboration between customer and supplier. The commitment must be approached with mutual benefit in mind. Effective supplier development is more than getting cost reductions for a particular part; it means helping suppliers remove wasteful costs from their processes. The strategic intent is to create win-win opportunities wherein both the buyer and supplier gain. For collaboration in supplier development to be successful, the collaboration must have commitment, communication, measurement, and trust.

- **Collaboration Requires Commitment.** A supplier development initiative may require supply managers to spend weeks or months in the supplier's facility working with the supplying firm's management and operating personnel. Commitment may require the buying firm to provide financial assistance for needed equipment and/or training. Commitment requires that the savings from supplier development projects be shared in an equitable way. Effective supplier development looks at all of a supplier's processes with the objective of eliminating waste and gaining improvements in quality, delivery, cycle time, and costs. Such action requires: supplier involvement at the earliest stages of new product development; shared information, resources, and savings; and resources dedicated to identifying and closing performance gaps. In other words, it requires the buying firm's personnel to treat suppliers as if they were a department within the buying company.[9]

- **Collaboration Requires Communication.** According to Forker, Ruch, and Hershauer, "It is one thing to have a well-designed supplier development program; it is another thing to assure that the program is well communicated and understood by the suppliers."[10] Proactive collaboration in establishing the priorities, motives,

---

[9]Ibid., pp. 136–137.

[10]Laura B. Forker, William A. Ruch, and James C. Hershauer, "Examining Supplier Improvement Efforts from Both Sides," *Journal of Supply Chain Management,* Summer 1999, p. 45.

and methods underlying the administration of the supplier development program requires the highest levels of communication.

■ **Collaboration Requires Measurement.** World-class firms want all members of their supply chain to be strong and profitable. However, they must be sure that suppliers are charging the right fees for their purchasing, processing, and conversion work. This requires both parties to open their financial records to one another. To many supply professionals the sharing of financial records and cost data may seem like an insurmountable obstacle. If collaboration efforts are to succeed, sharing accurate costs is a policy and cultural change that must occur.

■ **Collaboration Requires Trust.** When undertaking supplier development projects, a tremendous amount of information must pass through both companies to enable the necessary improvement efforts. In many cases, this information has never been revealed outside of the company. Trust between the two organizations and the involved personnel must be present before the necessary information sharing can or will take place.

All too often, supply departments do not have accurate cost information to share. Cost management systems must allow appropriate personnel the ability to understand actual costs incurred at the supplier's facility. For example, most accounting systems apply overhead in an inaccurate or distorted manner. This can be a problem in measuring the savings from supplier development initiatives. For a more detailed discussion of costs, please refer to Chapter 8, "Total Cost of Ownership."

Despite problems in cost measurement accuracy, a simple quote form can provide the starting point for sharing cost information. A quote usually requires suppliers to provide detail describing every step and its associated cost in the processing of a part or material and/or provision of a service.[11] The quote provides the starting point for a thorough discussion of costs and measurement.

A solution to the trust problem, according to Handfield et al., is to delegate an ombudsman to overcome a supplier's reluctance to share information. Honda has supplier ombudsmen who deal with the "soft side of the business"—the human resource issues that are not associated with cost, quality, or delivery. Honda has discovered that suppliers are often more open with these ombudsmen who are not involved in the contract negotiations.[12]

12 Generic Steps

No two companies approach supplier development in exactly the same way. However, according to Nelson, Moody, and Stegner, most effective projects adhere to the following 12 steps.[13] These steps will be addressed at different points in this chapter.

1. Identify and review performance gaps.
2. Discuss specifics about how the project will be approached and implemented.
3. Work to achieve mutual agreement on project focus.

---

[11]Nelson, Moody, and Stegner, *Purchasing Machine,* pp. 122–123.

[12]Handfield, Krause, Scannell, and Monczka, "Avoid the Pitfalls," p. 8.

[13]Nelson, Moody, and Stegner, *Purchasing Machine,* p. 138.

4. Identify processes that result in waste.

5. Compare performance gaps with the desired state.

6. Establish project metrics and metrics baselines.

7. Gather and analyze data.

8. Develop improvement strategies.

9. Develop an implementation plan.

10. Calculate the return on investment.

11. Create and review a proposal with the supplier's management.

12. Execute the improvement plan.

Handfield et al. recommend that the initial supplier development project be one that is fairly simple and likely to succeed so that the "biggest quick fix" and the "greatest good" can occur.[14]

Supplier Development at John Deere

The supplier development efforts led by Dave Nelson at John Deere provide the benchmark in this aspect of supply management. Unlike many companies, John Deere has a very open policy with respect to sharing information. This openness is consistent with Deere's supplier development approach of sharing information. Deere believes that the sharing of information between all members of the supply chain is essential in order to spread best practices.

Supplier Development History   John Deere was incorporated under the name Deere & Company in 1868 in Moline, Illinois. As of April 2001, Deere was the world's leading producer of agricultural equipment and a leader in the production of equipment for construction, forestry, lawn, and turf care. The company had manufacturing facilities in Europe, Asia, and North and South America.[15] Sales and revenue for 2000 totaled $11.4 billion dollars.[16]

Deere had an annual "spend" in 2000 of about $7 billion, which was approximately 62 percent of total sales and revenue. According to Nelson, "We are aggressively pursuing our objective to run lean." In the movement toward lean production and supply management, "Deere is committed to delivering the world's finest solutions and genuine value in equipment, service, and support—on time, every time."[17]

Supply Management Philosophy   Bill Butterfield, Deere's supplier development process owner, believes that in the world of supplier development, "Things don't change unless you want them to. Part of the work of Deere's new supplier development focus is to pick the right projects that will produce the best and quickest results."[18]

---

[14]Handfield, Krause, Scannell, and Monczka, "Avoid the Pitfalls."

[15]John Deere corporate website, http://www.johndeere.com, April 2001.

[16]John Deere Factbook, 2000.

[17]John Deere corporate website.

[18]Many of the quotes attributed to Mr. Butterfield are based on his presentation at The University of San Diego's 16th Supply Chain Management Forum, November 14–16, 2001.

According to Butterfield, Deere believes that its customers deserve to buy the best products made from the best component suppliers in the world. If Deere's current suppliers are not the world's best, Deere believes that it must help them become the best. "We must view our supply chain as our customers do. Whose parts are these? They are Deere Parts! John Deere is anywhere Deere parts are being made!"

Mr. Butterfield continues, "The biggest success factor is whether the supplier wants to change or not. We have to convince them that change is required. Even suppliers of the year can find opportunities to improve."

Six Sigma   Deere knows that 70 percent of its improvement opportunities exist in its supply chains in areas such as cost, quality, responsiveness, and value. To take advantage of such opportunities, managers at Deere help a supplier achieve Six Sigma performance. (Six Sigma is presented in Chapter 7, "Quality Management.")

To reach Six Sigma goals, Deere assigns some 80 qualified personnel, called supplier development engineers and specialists, from its own facilities to assist suppliers. A key focus in Six Sigma is the assessment of supplier processes and the identification of performance gaps.

Selecting the Right Projects   Deere engineers use a spreadsheet called Decision Focus as a policy deployment tool that helps establish project priorities. The spreadsheet biases the selection process toward suppliers that represent 80 percent or more of Deere's total materials spend. Deere wants to make it clear that any improvements need to have a significant bottom-line impact. "Choke point" suppliers (ones whose products are strategic regardless of dollar volume) are also candidates. The projects must also focus on creating proactive systematic solutions to problems and issues.[19]

Start with Mapping   Process mapping is essentially sketching out the processes. The most common approach in manufacturing is to sketch out where materials flow through the enterprise and how they are moved and modified. Process mapping always results in a wealth of process detail, as well as providing insight into throughput. Terry Maruo, father of Honda's kaizen methodology, told his acolytes, "Go to the floor. The answers won't be found in the boardroom. Go to the spot."[20]

Supplier Motivation   Deere provides a "simple value proposition" of splitting the savings from improvement projects 50/50.[21] If savings are realized, they go toward increasing supplier profit and reducing John Deere's prices. If no savings are realized, no price reduction is expected as a result of the project. If implementation of the supplier development proposal requires capital investment, Deere will defer its portion of the savings until the investment is amortized through use in the production of Deere products.

Through these policies, Deere reduces financial barriers and risks for suppliers. When Deere helps with the capital expenditures, suppliers may only be responsible for covering the time and effort of their own personnel during the project. These "no risk" incentives greatly improve supplier motivation to participate.

---

[19]Nelson, Moody, and Stegner, *Purchasing Machine,* pp. 51–52.

[20]Ibid., p. 122.

[21]According to Bill Butterfield, the 50/50 split is not true of all projects, but of most.

Focus on Lead Time   According to Bill Butterfield, lead time is a key topic addressed in Deere's supplier development projects. Suppose Deere must carry 60 days' safety stock inventory because of slow response times from a supplier. The development project team focuses on improving the supplier's processes and reducing its response time. In turn, Deere can reduce its safety inventory to 10 days. This change gives 50 days of inventory disinvestments that Deere can apply to savings.

The following success story identifies the benefits to Deere of a development project with a supplier of a hydraulic integrated circuit: reduced the supplier's manufacturing lead time from 155 days to 10 days, improved on time delivery from 68 percent to 98 percent, reduced quality defects from 14,400 to 300 parts per million, and reduced work-in-process from $9.5 million to $6 million.

Deere wants to build to demand; however, the seasonal nature of the demand for products is a major challenge. Many suppliers have 40–80 days of lead time, greatly lengthening Deere's response time. If supplier lead times can be reduced to less than 10 days, then Deere can reduce its investments in materials and related inventory holding costs. The improvements enable Deere to better meet customer demands while simultaneously reducing inventories. The result? Deere's costs go down while sales go up!

Development Team Training   Before sending a team into a supplier's facility, Deere requires all team members to complete a rigorous Six Sigma training program. Team members must become certified as either a Process Pro or a Process Pro Master. The Process Pro level under Deere's Six Sigma program requires three weeks of training and six months assisting on related projects. The highest-level Six Sigma designation is Process Pro Master. This designation requires ASQ Six Sigma Blackbelt certification and a minimum of one year of experience working on relevant projects.

Some suppliers participate in the supplier development training with John Deere's supplier development teams, but most of the training for suppliers occurs during the actual supplier development projects. A goal of the training is to develop the supplier's management so that they can train their own workforce in future improvement initiatives.

Supplier Development Process

A generalized process for managing supplier development projects is presented in Figure 22.1. The process has six phases: initiate project, map and measure, process development, achieve results, control, and team recognition.[22]

Before starting the process, the following individuals should be committed to the development process: project champions, development team members, process owners, and upper management. A project champion should be designated from both the supplying and buying firms. A project champion is the key liaison to upper management. He or she must have sufficient power to provide resources and compliance by nonteam personnel as needed for the project to succeed. The development team members come

---

[22]Adapted from a presentation by Bill Butterfield of Deere & Company given at the 16th Supply Chain Management Forum at The University of San Diego. According to Mr. Butterfield, the supplier development process at John Deere is modeled after similar approaches at Allied Signal and General Electric (GE). November, 2001.

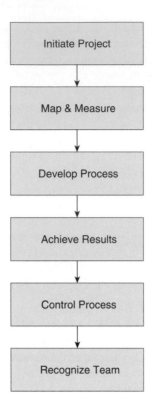

Figure 22.1 I Generalized Process for Supplier Development Projects

from both the supplying and buying firms. The primary goal of including the supplier's personnel on the development team is to create self-sufficiency in the supplier's ability to develop its own processes in the future. The process owners are the individuals that actually interact and operate the processes that are under investigation for improvement. Finally, upper management from both the firms must be committed to the project or failure is inevitable.

Initiating the Project

In the first phase, the main activities are to: develop and confirm a preliminary supplier development charter, define the supplier's processes, assess the customer's needs, and assess the business environment.

The supplier development charter is described later in the section on supplier development enablers. The supplier development charter is a firm definition of project scope and expectations for both the buying firm and the supplier. It essentially serves as an agreement on the expected deliverables. The terminology "deliverable" is used to define the outcomes of each phase of the project.

After developing the charter, the next step is to define the supplier's processes. The supplier development team narrows the project focus and further refines its understanding of related processes. In doing this, the team assesses customer needs, expectations, and requirements for the areas of project focus and translates them into project metrics. Then the team assesses the business environment surrounding the processes and analyzes how it affects the areas of project focus.

Mapping and Measuring

In this phase, the team maps the supplier's process and determines the measurement required. Deliverables from this phase include: process maps, a final project charter, and a baseline of "before" process improvement status.

- **Map/Analyze Supplier Processes.** The team maps the current and ideal processes for areas of project focus. The process maps are usually time-based visual representations of bottlenecks and capacity constraints within a process. This provides the team with information used to target project activity.
- **Identify Process Metrics.** Metrics that will be used to gauge progress toward project goals are agreed upon.
- **Collect Baseline Data.** Data defining the current process status is gathered. This data helps establish baseline metrics and further verifies process map results.
- **Analyze Baseline Data.** Gaps in the current process are identified through study of the collected data. Opportunities for improvement of manufacturing cycle time, quality, delivery, etc., are prioritized.
- **Document the Baseline.** Baseline metrics are documented to establish the before-project status.

Developing the Process

Deliverables from this phase include a project implementation plan that addresses performance gaps in current processes and drives results. The project implementation plan is usually developed using project management software. The project implementation plan should include: activities required to complete the project, expected completion time of the activities, project milestones, resources assigned to activities, and the expected completion time of the project. The plan is used to track and manage project progress, define the project's critical path(s), and detail the project's activity interdependencies.

The following critical activities occur in this phase:

- **Create Solutions.** The team brainstorms potential solutions and conducts benchmarking analyses where applicable. The output from this activity usually results in more focused process maps.
- **Select Solutions.** The solution(s) that provide the greatest potential for reducing manufacturing cycle times, improving quality and delivery, or reducing costs drives selection of solution(s). For example, a typical solution in manufacturing environments is to select reducing setup times. Setup times often result in large batch sizes and excess work-in-process.
- **Develop New Process.** Detail the new process further through study and brainstorming. The outcome of this activity is a new process.
- **Plan Implementation.** The team works with relevant personnel to develop and propose a detailed implementation plan.

Achieving Results

In this phase, the project team executes the implementation plan, conducting any necessary simulations, pilots, and releases. The deliverables from this phase are a new, lean process that has been implemented, documented, and is actually demonstrating results.

Relevant personnel, such as engineers or information technology specialists from the buying firm, are made available to assist the implementation team in keeping the project on schedule. Direction and resources are provided as required by the project champions. Project progress is communicated to upper management, champions, and process owners at designated milestones as defined by the supplier development team.

The process is documented for clarity and consistency. This documentation may include procedures, maps, flowcharts, and operational method sheets, as well as training plans, schedules, and periodic audit points. A process plan that diagrams the footprint of the process areas affected is developed showing workstations, control points, and material movements.

Controlling the Process

In this phase, plans and documentation are created to ensure consistent implementation of the process with minimized variation. Ongoing metrics are defined to allow review of the process. A closed-loop corrective action procedure system is installed to review the process, address gaps in performance, and continuously improve performance.

The deliverables from this phase are a process control plan and a corrective action plan. The control plan is used to ensure that activities in the process are executed correctly at all times and that critical elements of the process are always addressed. The corrective action plan addresses what occurs in the event of a nonconformance in the process so that the nonconformance is eliminated and recurrence is prevented, with verification that proposed corrections are effective.

Recognizing the Team

The final phase provides team recognition. Activities are organized by the project team, project champions, and process owners to promote the success of the project. In this phase, the team shares the lessons learned and best practices with the supplier's organization.

At Deere & Co., project results are published on the Deere Supplier Development Homepage to share with the rest of Deere's supply chain. If applicable, case studies are published describing the project's highlights and lessons learned. Employees and suppliers can then use the case studies to foster future learning. The cases provide yet another way to disseminate information and maintain the project's gains. Learning experiences from completed projects are shared within the suppliers' organization and Deere's Supplier Management groups. Process owners use best practices to refine key processes, such as charters, process mapping, setup reduction, cost, strategy, training, and information systems. Formal events are organized to recognize implementation team accomplishments and share the team's lessons learned.

Supplier Development Enablers

Many enablers of supplier development exist. Among the most commonly used are: developing a supplier development project charter, implementing continuous improvement techniques using the PDCA cycle, focusing on elimination of waste, conducting value analyses, and providing forums for communication.

Supplier Development Project Charter

The supplier development project charter is a dynamic document that is continually updated during the planning, execution, and completion of a supplier development project. It generally consists of the following sections: business case, situation and goals, mission or vision, project scope, and signatures.

- **Business Case.** The business case is a financial assessment of the project. In the assessment, the supplier development team documents the estimated savings from the development project along with assumptions used to create the estimate. The initial draft of the estimate will never be completely accurate, which is why the estimate must be updated as better information becomes available.

- **Situation and Goals.** In this section, a qualitative and quantitative description of the current situation and the goals for improvement are documented. Baseline data should be accumulated on the quantifiable metrics that will be used to gauge progress toward project goals. A description should be included describing how the supplier can track the improvements after implementation.

- **Mission/Vision.** The project's mission needs to be defined to be able to communicate quickly to others what the development team is trying to achieve. The mission statement should be short, concise, and to the point. The mission provides a point of reference against which team members assess activities. "Does a particular activity help to achieve the project mission?" If it does not, then there is a good chance the activity is wasteful effort or the group has strayed from its original goals.

- **Project Scope.** In this section, the development team clearly defines the project's scope. Clarifying the project scope helps to assure that the team has narrowed the project focus by refining its understanding of the activities required to complete the project.

- **Schedule and Deliverables.** A common approach in this section is to provide a printout of a PERT (Program Evaluation and Review Technique) or Gantt chart showing the relationships and deadlines of the activities required to complete the project. Completing this section of the charter reduces future misunderstandings and miscommunications.

- **Assignments and Roles.** This section simply documents who is responsible for what activities. The schedule created in the previous section provides a logical format for assigning team members responsibilities for specific activities.

- **Signatures.** Signatures are required from the upper management of all participating companies as well as key participants when establishing the charter as an official document.

PDCA Cycle

Supplier development projects usually involve continuous improvement efforts. One of the most common approaches to accomplishing continuous improvement is the use of the Plan-Do-Check-Act (PDCA) cycle, commonly referred to as the Deming Cycle. Specifics on the Deming Cycle are given in Chapter 7, "Quality Management."

The following discussion summarizes Honda's approach to supplier development using this simple, yet powerful tool. Please refer to the classic book *Powered by Honda* for a detailed description of how Honda uses supplier development to achieve World Class Supply Management^{SM} status.[23]

Phase 1: PLAN   Phase one of the selection process involves deciding specifics about the focus of the project. The highest-yield project targeting a specific process generally is selected. Metrics must be agreed to so that those involved can measure their accomplishments. The measured accomplishments create an environment of success and lay the foundation for additional projects.

In the PLAN phase, participants must recognize that no organization can attack all improvement problems in their supply chain simultaneously. The evaluation team needs to set priorities and dedicate specific resources. The focus should be on only one aspect of the supplier's need, such as housekeeping or work flow.

Honda uses what it calls a *Supplier Selection Matrix* that, through a series of four steps, is designed to remove subjectivity from the selection process. The first step is to select the precise parameters to which the development will be confined. This could include the entire supply base or a commodity group within it. The second step is the determination of selection criteria or key measurables common to all suppliers. Key measurables typically include the total volume produced by suppliers in dollars, the delivery performance or quality level as measured in parts per million rejects, and cost competitiveness as measured by quoted cost against Honda's target cost. Next, the team completes the matrix by gathering the appropriate data for each supplier that fits the chosen criteria. Finally, the team analyzes the resulting matrix and selects the best candidates.

Once the best process candidates are selected, supply management meets with top management of the selected supplier(s) to give an overview of the project and the amount and type of management commitment required.One of the objectives of this meeting is the selection of a *supplier associate* at the supplier's firm. According to Honda, every successful project requires the dedication by the supplier of at least one full-time *supplier associate.* The associate typically is a mid-level manager who has strong people and communication skills. The associate must possess and exercise strong project management skills. This individual becomes the point person for the supplier.

Another interesting aspect of Honda's approach is the development of what is called a *war room.* Effectively, the war room is set aside for planning and controlling the project. Team members and supporters need such a meeting room where they can converge regularly to post data, project findings, present ideas, and track results.

---

[23]Dave Nelson, Rick Mayo, and Patricia E. Moody, *Powered by Honda* (New York: John Wiley & Sons, 1998), pp. 170–179.

Having reached agreement on cost reduction, cost sharing, and dedicated project leadership, the team sets a project start date. The planning phase is then closed and the doing phase starts.

Phase 2: DO   The largest percentage of work is usually required in phase two. Once teams start to look for waste, some improvements become obvious. The problem with immediately "jumping in" and solving problems is that the supplier does not learn the process of the DO phase. Such an approach is reminiscent of the old wisdom, "Give a person a meal and you feed him for one meal. Teach a person to farm and that person may be able to feed himself for a lifetime." To resolve this learning problem, Honda moves suppliers through the following series of 10 steps:

- **Step 1. Training.** A six- to eight-hour training class is held for all prospective team members. All participants are familiarized with tools and techniques that will be used throughout the project.
- **Step 2. Preliminary Situation Analysis.** In this two- to three-day phase, team members develop a thorough understanding of the supplier. Honda calls this SAI, or Situation Analysis I. This project step is conducted at the facility by going to the actual process location where the parts are produced or the service is provided. The task is to gain firsthand knowledge of the supplier's operations.
- **Step 3. Suppler Orientation Meeting.** Orientation marks the first full day of the project at the supplier's facility. The meeting focuses on the philosophy, process, basic methodology, and goals of the project. Honda uses a "town meeting" format, with a 30-minute pre-shift informal gathering of all relevant employees involved in the project. The "town meeting" and follow-on team meeting clarify project goals and plans and lay the foundation for cooperation.
- **Step 4. Process Selection.** The area targeted for improvement may be a production line, a specific process, or an entire department. Whatever the target, however, it must match the scope and timing of the project.

After process selection, the team meets with associates or owners of the process. Open communication is a key aspect of this meeting. Typical employee responses range from pride in being chosen for the development activity to frustration that they are to be singled out for attention. Since so much of the project's lasting success rests on these associates, the meeting must be structured to allow feelings and attitudes to surface and be answered.

One approach to building trust with the supplier's workforce is to ask participants for their suggestions. The authors of *Powered by Honda* state that the usual response is silence. However, when team members ask if anyone has any complaints, one or two will be voiced and discussions begin. Complaints, according to Honda, are like rejects uncovered and analyzed in the production process. They are valuable gifts that will move the group to thinking actively about solutions.

- **Step 5. Baseline Data Collection.** Collect baseline data and create a snapshot of how the process is performing at the start of the project. The team must be clear on how data is calculated now and in the future. Later, the data must be calculated exactly the same way to measure project results accurately.

■ **Step 6. Second Situation Analysis.** The second situation analysis (SAII) takes the largest percentage of the project time during the DO phase. The step focuses on innovation in terms of quality and lean management techniques. Success of the step is greatly dependent on the knowledge of team members. In this step, team members investigate the process thoroughly. The team collects large quantities of data for analysis and documents its findings through charts, graphs, and sketches. The resulting analysis lays the foundation for improvement. An outcome of the SAII is that the Seven Wastes are identified (discussed later in this section).

■ **Step 7. Goal Setting.** The second situation analysis results in metrics specific to each project that can be used to measure achievement of the project's goals. Honda calls these goals SMART—**S**pecific, **M**easurable, **A**chievable, **R**ealistic, and **T**imely. Each of the goals must have objective, relevant metrics which are based on the "before" data and situation analysis results.

■ **Step 8. Develop Improvement Ideas.** Toward the end of the situation analysis, the team members individually begin to formulate some ideas for improvement. These ideas frequently emerge during brainstorming sessions.

■ **Step 9. Implementation Plan.** During this phase, engineering and maintenance personnel are brought on board. These individuals execute the implementation step and they must become aware of the time and resources they are expected to dedicate in order to achieve successful implementation.

■ **Step 10. Implementation.** After the schedule is developed, team responsibilities take on many forms, such as implementation or expediting. The team has the responsibility of implementing as many ideas on schedule as they can with their limited resources. Honda considers implementation to be the most intense time for the project. If the team has developed a detailed plan, implementation should be achieved with minimum obstacles.

Phase 3: CHECK   The next phase is to *check* the results as the actual process changes take affect. Like the DO phase, the CHECK phase at Honda has several generic steps.

■ **Step 1. Collect and Evaluate "After" Data.** After the process has stabilized for about one week, the team begins to gather data to compare with the baseline. The team calculates the "after" data for each of the goals in the same way the "before" data was collected.

■ **Step 2. Develop the Long-Term Organizational Plan.** Each project is a means of introducing continuous improvement at Honda's suppliers. It systematically teaches the techniques and tools to make that improvement a part of the supplier's organization. In order to become internalized by the supplier, the improvement philosophy must be compatible with the supplier's strategic direction.

■ **Step 3. Celebrate the Results.** The results of the team's work is presented during what Honda calls the *Celebration of Results.* This gathering is designed to celebrate the positive results achieved and to encourage future activities.

Phase 4: ACT   In the ACT phase, the lessons learned are disseminated throughout the organization and to relevant supply chain members. The goals are to use the information to document and follow up on the process to maintain and increase its yield.

Elimination of Waste

A cornerstone of continuous improvement and just-in-time philosophies is the notion of reduction and eventual elimination of waste. Recall the introductory case presented in Chapter 7, "Quality Management," where a supply manager walked through a supplier's facility and discovered many problems. This is a common approach to assessing a supplier. The traditional term for the activity when it occurs internally in one's own organization is Management by Walking Around (MBWA), but there is absolutely no reason why supply professionals should not apply the same concept when assessing suppliers. Ultimately, however, decisions regarding suppliers should be based on measurable metrics.

Tadamitsu Tsurouka, a Honda process engineer based in the Marysville, Ohio, auto plant Supplier Development Group, perfected the skill of identifying waste. After only a 20-minute plant tour, Mr. Tsurouka could write pages on the facility's weaknesses.[24] The key methodology employed by Mr. Tsurouka was the *Seven Wastes* approach. Honda defines the Seven Wastes as ones that directly affect the productivity of the manufacturing process. However, the Seven Wastes can apply to service operations as well. Further, most companies define the Seven Wastes from the viewpoint of their customers. If an activity does not add value to the customer, it is considered waste.

- **Waste #1. Overpopulation.** This waste is more commonly referred to as overproduction in manufacturing environments. The waste of overpopulation exists when a firm is producing more than is required. Overpopulation causes schedule problems and costs money by carrying excess inventories.

- **Waste #2. Idle Time.** Idle time is waste built into the production or service process. Idle time in manufacturing usually accumulates when operators watch a machine run or take too much time fixing a part while the machine remains idle.

- **Waste #3. Delivery.** Delivery is waste because it adds cost without value. Honda measures part travel distances in feet and counts the number of times a part is touched before completion as the basis of the part's delivery metric.

- **Waste #4. Work Itself.** Although most manufacturing professionals understand the need for efficient setups, the majority of manufacturers treat mold/die change as break time from production, a time when the crew can take as much time as it needs. Similar waste exists in service processes, such as purchase order processing.

- **Waste #5. Inventory.** All inventory—raw materials, work in process, and finished product—should be at an absolute minimum. The results of inventory waste include high carrying costs, transit damage, and excess materials handling systems.

- **Waste #6. Operator Movement.** Any movement in which the operator does not add value to the part or service is waste.

- **Waste #7. Rejected Parts.** One of the quickest ways to improve productivity is to eliminate rejected parts. Every reject includes not only the loss of that product but also the forgone opportunity to make a good part.

---

[24]Ibid., pp. 160–168.

Value Engineering/Value Analysis

Value engineering and value analysis are common approaches to improving products and processes. In both value engineering and value analysis, value is usually defined from the viewpoint of the customer who will use the product or process. Based upon this fundamental understanding, the common question asked in all value-based analyses is, "Does this add value to the customer?" If the answer is no, then there is high probability that whatever "this" is (cost, action, part, step, feature, tolerance), it is waste that can be reduced or eliminated.

Although the technique is applied commonly in manufacturing, value analysis has been applied to a broad range of activities and supply-related problems outside the manufacturing area. Applications range from the design of operating systems, to the development of corporate reengineering projects, to the procurement of services and transportation.

Value Engineering   As the name implies, value engineering takes place in the design process before a product is in production or a process has been implemented for the first time. Value engineering usually entails a methodical systematic study of all phases of the design of a given item or process in relation to the function (value) the finished product or process is to perform. Value engineering recognizes that the design process provides the greatest opportunity for reducing costs in a proactive manner before the costs are committed to in the actual product or process. Value engineering should play a key role in new product development. See Chapter 10 for additional insight.

Value Analysis   If value engineering (VE) is no longer a possibility, then value analysis is used. Unlike value engineering, value analysis (VA) takes place after a product has been produced or after a process has been implemented. As such, value analysis is reactive and provides less opportunity to reduce total costs over the lifetime of a design or process. However, the opportunity to reduce costs is still great in many situations, which is why value analysis remains a common approach in most industries.

VE/VA Techniques   Although different companies stress different variations of the fundamental idea, two general conceptual tools are basic to the operation of a VE/VA program: design analysis and cost analysis. Both design and cost analysis focus on the same required product, part, material, or process. However, design analysis focuses strictly on the features, functionality, and fitness for use from the perspective of the customer. Cost analysis links the design features to numerical values that can be easily compared. For example, a customer may want a wood dashboard in a car, but the cost of the wood dashboard would increase the costs of the product beyond the financial resources of the customer. Hence, design features must be coupled with costs to evaluate value.

One technique many firms use in analyzing component parts of a subassembly is to dismantle, or "explode," the unit and then mount each part adjacent to its mating part on a pegboard or a table. The idea is to demonstrate the functional relationships of the various parts visually. Each component can thus be studied as it relates to the performance of the complete unit, rather than as an isolated element. Typical questions that arise in the value analysis of a part include:

1. Can any part be eliminated without impairing the operation of the complete unit?
2. Can a part be simplified to reduce its basic cost?

3. Can a part be changed to permit the use of less costly production methods?
4. Can less expensive but equally satisfactory materials be used in the part?
5. If the item is not standard, can a standard item be used?
6. Is there a similar item in inventory that could be substituted?
7. Are closer tolerances specified than are necessary?
8. Is unnecessary machining performed on the item?
9. Are unnecessarily fine finishes specified?
10. Can the item be made less expensively in another plant?
11. Can the item be bought for less?
12. Is the item properly classified for shipping purposes to obtain lowest transportation rates?
13. Can cost of packaging be reduced?
14. Are suppliers being asked for suggestions to reduce cost?

Several examples of production parts which have been value-analyzed are shown in Figure 22.2. Small modifications to the design of a product often decrease cost while improving quality.

Process Value Analysis   Value analysis of a process is usually referred to as a process value analysis (PVA). Although value analysis does include the analysis of processes, the use of the term PVA creates better clarity. As with VA, PVA inherently assumes that the process is already in existence. Although more proactive than PVA, very rarely do companies engage in process value engineering (PVE), which provides the greatest potential for process cost reduction.

Supplier Involvement   Suppliers frequently prove to be extremely valuable assets in a firm's total value analysis effort. More than one firm has found that a majority of its value analysis savings comes directly from suggestions of suppliers who have been asked to participate in its value analysis program. Several years ago, the former Chrysler Corporation initiated a voluntary value analysis cost reduction program for its suppliers. The objective was for each supplier to value-analyze one or more of its key products sold to Chrysler and to submit the resulting value analysis suggestions for consideration. During the first two years of the program, Chrysler received more than 3,400 suggestions that materialized into projects that saved approximately $136 million.[25]

Organizing the VE/VA Process   Value analysis studies can be conducted formally by organized groups, such as supplier development teams, or informally by individuals such as supply managers, engineers, production personnel, and so forth. In either case, the elements of the study are the same. Obviously, the depth and breadth of the analysis are influenced by the size and composition of the team making the study. Figure 22.3 illustrates the process steps taken in a typical VE/VA study.

---

[25]Ernest Raia, "Advantage Chrysler: Supplier Ideas Save Automaker Millions," *Purchasing,* June 4, 1992, p. 43.

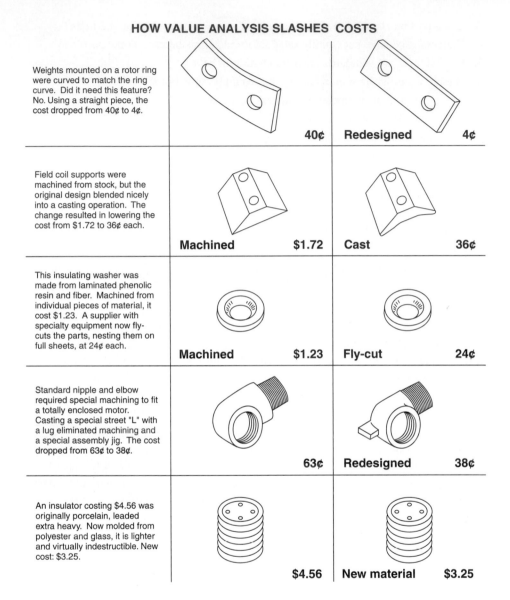

Figure 22.2 | Examples of Value Analysis Producing Spectacular Cost Reductions
Source: Reproduced with the permission *of Business Management* magazine, formerly *Management Methods* magazine.

Three basic organizational approaches are most common: (1) the specialized staff approach, (2) the cross-functional team approach, and (3) the staff training approach.

■ **Specialized Staff Approach.** The most widely used type of value analysis program among large companies is one built around a group of highly trained value analysts who function in a staff capacity. In some situations the analysts constitute a separate staff agency reporting to a general management executive; occasionally, the group re-

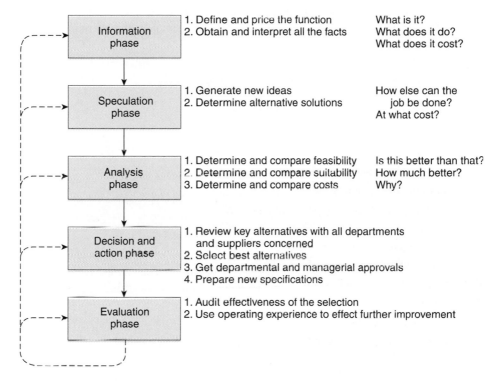

Information phase	1. Define and price the function 2. Obtain and interpret all the facts	What is it? What does it do? What does it cost?
Speculation phase	1. Generate new ideas 2. Determine alternative solutions	How else can the job be done? At what cost?
Analysis phase	1. Determine and compare feasibility 2. Determine and compare suitability 3. Determine and compare costs	Is this better than that? How much better? Why?
Decision and action phase	1. Review key alternatives with all departments and suppliers concerned 2. Select best alternatives 3. Get departmental and managerial approvals 4. Prepare new specifications	
Evaluation phase	1. Audit effectiveness of the selection 2. Use operating experience to effect further improvement	

Figure 22.3 I A Generalized Procedural Model of the Value Analysis Study

ports to a top-level engineering design manager. Most frequently, however, the value analysis staff is attached to the supply management department.[26]

- **Cross-Functional Team Approach.** A second approach used in both large and small firms today involves committee administration and team conduct of the value analysis program. This approach, or some variant of it, predominates among smaller firms. A typical value analysis committee usually is composed of four to eight people, including senior representatives from areas such as operations, engineering, supply management, marketing, and general management. The committee may be headed by a senior functional representative, frequently from supply management or general management, or by a full-time "value coordinator" assigned to the top-management staff.

- **Staff Training Approach.** Companies subscribing to the staff training approach believe that value analysis yields maximum benefits only when it is practiced by all key operating personnel. Consequently, this approach aims primarily at developing an understanding of the concept and a working knowledge of techniques among most professional and operating personnel responsible for specifying, purchasing, and using

---

[26]See the classical study by Stanley S. Miller, "How to Get the Most out of Value Analysis," *Harvard Business Review,* January–February 1955, pp. 123–132; and L. S. Miles, *Techniques of Value Analysis and Engineering,* 2nd ed. (New York: McGraw-Hill, 1972), chap. 8.

production materials. The value analysis organization in this case consists of a small staff group that reports to general management. The activities of this group focus on value analysis training.

Barriers to Supplier Development

There are many barriers to effective supplier development:[27,28]

- Poor communication and feedback.
- Complacency.
- Misguided improvement objectives.
- Credibility of customers.
- Misconceptions regarding purchasing power.
- Lack of clarity and commitment.
- Lack of a unified approach.
- Misaligned sourcing and performance metrics.
- Concealment of problems.
- Initiative fatigue.
- Resource limitations.
- "Blame the supplier" culture.
- Lack of trust.
- Confidentiality issues.
- Legal issues.
- Imbalance of power in the relationship.

The leader for the supplier development team must clearly delineate potential rewards for the supplier's organization during preliminary meetings with the supplier's top management. Otherwise, the supplier's personnel may not become fully committed to the effort and remain unconvinced that the development effort will benefit their organization. They may even agree to initial proposals but fail to implement them on account of insufficient dedication.[29]

Handfield et al. observe, "One of the biggest challenges in supplier development is cultivating mutual trust. Suppliers may be reluctant to share information on costs and processes; the need to release sensitive and confidential information may compound this hesitation. Ambiguous or intimidating legal issues and ineffective lines of communication also may inhibit the trust building necessary for a successful supplier-development effort."[30]

[27]D. M. Lascelles and B. G. Dale, "The Buyer-Supplier Relationship in Total Quality Management," *Journal of Purchasing and Materials Management,* 1989, pp. 10–21.

[28]Philip J. Southey and David Williams, "Supplier Development: Linking Performance to Capabilities at Jaguar Cars," Conference 2000, Richard Ivey School of Business, University of Western Ontario, London, May 24–27, 2000, pp. 715–718.

[29]Handfield, Krause, Scannell, and Monczka, "Avoid the Pitfalls," p. 6.

[30]Ibid., p. 8.

Concluding Remarks

Supplier development is one of the most powerful approaches that a firm can engage in on the path to World Class Supply Management^{SM}. The focus should be on developing suppliers to become self-sufficient at developing, implementing, and maintaining world-class performance. This is in contrast to what many firms call supplier development, where managers place controls on suppliers and conduct two-day "kaizen events"[31] or a few seminars that result in little retained learning.

Supplier development in the World Class Supply Management^{SM} context requires buying firms to develop full-time, dedicated resources that work hand-in-hand with the supplier's personnel. Experience at several firms close to achieving World Class Supply Management^{SM} demonstrates that the return on the investment from supplier development makes it one of the firm's best investments. The interactions also prepare the way for other strategic collaboration opportunities, such as including suppliers in the design process at the buying firm.

Lastly, a frequently overlooked supplier development approach is developing the supplying firm's supply management. Development of the supplier's supply management starts to truly enable supply chain management and refocuses the development to processes that span the chain instead of only internal functions. Supply management becomes the key to supply chain management through development efforts that go beyond the first tier of suppliers.

---

[31]A "kaizen event" is a quick, hard-hitting learning experience where a buying firm sends a team of kaizen specialists into a supplier's firm to conduct seminars and discussions of continuous improvement possibilities at the supplier. The focus tends to be on identifying waste, as presented in the PDCA discussion earlier in this chapter.

23

CHAPTER

Ethical and Professional Standards

The drive toward World Class Supply Management^{SM} has increased the need for companies to establish ethics policies and professional standards that are created through cross-functional teams. The alternative is to leave ethical decisions up to the individual manager, which may invite disaster.

■ Important Areas Requiring Amplification 546

■ Management Responsibilities 551

■ Dealing with Gray Areas 553

Case

A Question of Ethics?

Stacy Nakamura, director of Supply Management at Fremont Equipment Company (FEC), scanning his e-mail discovered an invitation from a supplier. The invitation was from Mandy Smith, sales representative of Coastal Lubricants. Every year FEC purchased approximately $1,000,000 worth of lubricants from one supplier who was selected on the basis of competitive bids each January. Coastal Lubricants was the current supplier. Stacy had been impressed by the persistent efforts of Mandy to keep her company in his thoughts and decision-making. Every month she either called him on the phone or sent an e-mail to discuss existing contracts and new products. This time the e-mail was a draft of an invitation, pending Stacy's approval, to 21 of FEC's executives and supervisors to attend a party. Those invited from FEC were:

■ The supply manager, her assistant, and three buyers.
■ The plant manager and his assistant.
■ The chief design engineer and four engineering section heads.
■ The maintenance superintendent and his three foremen.
■ The production manager and his staff assistant.
■ The controller and her assistant.
■ The sales manager.
■ The industrial relations manager.

The personnel from Coastal Lubricants who would be attending were:

- Two corporate sales managers and the district manager.
- Several sales representatives.
- A representative from the corporate research department.
- Two representatives from the corporate technical applications department.

The party was planned for a Friday evening in the private dining room of a local hotel and the e-mail included the following program:

6:30 – 7:30	Cocktail hour
7:30 – 8:30	Dinner
8:30 – 9:00	Informal discussion and a video of the supplier's technical research activities and achievements
9:00 – 9:30	Video of the Olympic Games
9:30 – 10:00	Video of "New Dimensions in Musical Entertainment"
10:00	Adjourn for continuation of the cocktail hour

Stacy looked over the draft of the invitation and wondered what he should do. He thought, "Should I accept the invitation outright? Should I place some stipulations on the party? Should I reject the invitation? Does FEC have any policies on this issue? If not, should FEC have policies on this issue? Should I really be the one to make the decision to accept the invitation?"

Ethics in the Supply Management Context

Corporate and academic interest in business ethics has blossomed in recent years. It is, however, well beyond the scope and purpose of this chapter to undertake a review of the extensive literature pertaining to business ethics. This is particularly true when one considers how ethics varies from one culture to another. Instead, most of this chapter focuses on ethical issues and guidelines frequently encountered in the supply management context.

For purposes of this chapter, our operational definition of ethics can be stated as the guidelines or rules of conduct by which we aim to live. Organizations, like individuals, have ethical standards and, frequently, ethics codes and policies. The ethical standards of an organization are judged by its actions and the actions of its employees, not by pious statements of intent put out in the company's name. The *character* of an organization is a matter of importance to its employees and managers, to those who do business with it as customers and suppliers, and to those who are considering joining it in any of these capacities.

Marks and Spencer, a highly regarded United Kingdom retailer, is an example of an organization whose character is held in high regard. Some years ago, when the British pound had declined in value, Marks and Spencer reopened a contract that it had with a United States supplier, Burlington Mills, to see whether Burlington was making an adequate profit. A Burlington official commented that this was the first time in Burlington's history that a customer had been concerned over the effect of unforeseen economic events on Burlington's ability to make a profit. Marks and Spencer's *character* undoubtedly makes it a highly desirable customer!

Whether the market rewards good corporate behavior in the context of social responsibility and in the ethical sense is open to debate. Nevertheless, a recent review of the literature shows increased social responsibility by a firm will most likely result in favorable financial performance. The review found 33 studies showing a positive relationship, 5 studies showing a negative relationship, and 14 showing no effect or inconclusive results.[1]

Procter and Gamble (P&G) understands the connection between ethical corporate behavior and financial performance. P&G takes the issue of ethics to a higher level by linking it to trust. In a recent visit at the University of San Diego, Stephen Rogers, director of Technology Purchases at P&G, presented the following:

> We believe buyers and suppliers optimize the results of the working relationship when there is a foundation of trust. By treating suppliers honestly, ethically, and fairly, we do our part in building that foundation, just as the supplier must do its part. We honor the confidentiality of proprietary supplier information regarding technology, cost, or other sensitive information unless given written permission to share it. We do this not only because we believe it to be right, but also because it makes working with P&G and supplying our requirements attractive to current and future suppliers. We strive to give a clear understanding of the "rules of the game" to suppliers before and after commercial interactions.[2]

There is little doubt that in the minds of most people, including responsible business people, ethical conduct is a more substantive and relevant issue today than it was several decades ago. Unfortunately, however, this is not a unanimous view. One of the classic dilemmas facing management at all levels of any organization is the issue of "time focus": Do we focus on the short run or the long haul? There are still a fairly significant number of individuals who are willing to "operate on the margin," or sacrifice long-term values for short-term gains acquired through unethical activities.[3] One survey of 4,035 employees at all levels across a variety of industries is quite revealing on this point:

> Ninety-seven percent of the employees surveyed said good ethics are good business. But responses to other questions indicated that many employees don't think that their companies agree. Two-thirds of the respondents said that ethical conduct isn't rewarded in American business. Eighty-two percent believe that managers generally choose bigger profits over "doing what's right." One-fourth said that their companies ignore ethics to achieve business goals. One-third reported that their superiors had pressured them to violate company rules.[4]

As the results of the foregoing survey suggest, the reasons why unethical problems occur in business are many.

---

[1]Tony McAdams with contributing authors James Freeman and Laura P. Hartman, *Law, Business, and Society,* 6th ed. (Irwin/McGraw-Hill, NY, NY., 2001), p. 95.

[2]Stephen Rogers, presentation at the University of San Diego. Reprinted with the permission of Procter and Gamble Company, November 2001.

[3]T. McAdams, *Law, Business, and Society,* p. 42.

[4]Shaun O'Malley, "Ethical Cultures—Corporate and Personal," *Ethics Journal,* Winter 1995, p. 9.

Professional Supply Management Ethics

We live and work in a highly competitive market economy with emphasis on results. There is pressure for sales, pressure to compromise, pressure to succeed in an environment of both internal and external competition, and pressure resulting from government mandates. The *pressures* that the marketplace exerts on supply management departments and on individual supply managers make it essential that top management and supply management recognize and understand both the professional and ethical standards required in the performance of their duties.

Principles and Standards of Supply Management Practice[5]

The Institute for Supply Management™, with a membership primarily consisting of U.S. supply managers, has addressed the issue of ethics since its inception over 80 years ago. ISM's *Principles and Standards of Purchasing Practice* was developed in 1992 when the Institute was still called the National Association of Purchasing Management. Since the change of name took place in 2001, new standards will probably be developed that will reflect the shift of the organization to a global emphasis and supply management focus. In lieu of publication of the new principles and standards, we present the spirit of the 1992 publication rewritten to reflect the new global supply management environment. The principles are given below exactly as they were presented in the 1992 publication.

- *Loyalty to Your Organization.*
- *Justice to Those with Whom You Deal.*
- *Faith in Your Profession.*

From these principles are derived standards of supply management practice, as presented in the following sections, with minor edits to reflect the shift to World Class Supply Management^SM.

1. Ethical Perceptions

Avoid the intent and appearance of unethical or compromising practice in relationships, actions, and communications.

    The results of a perceived impropriety may become, over time, more disruptive or damaging than an actual transgression. It is essential that any activity or involvement between a supply management professional and active or potential suppliers that in any way diminishes, or even appears to diminish, open and fair treatment of suppliers be strictly avoided. Those who do not know us will judge us on appearances. We must consider this—and act accordingly. If a situation is perceived as real, then it is in fact real in its consequences.

---

[5]Based on the content of the National Association of Purchasing Management's 1992 publication titled, *Principles and Standards of Purchasing Practice,* National Association of Purchasing Management, Tempe, AZ, January 1992.

2. Responsibilities to the Employer

Demonstrate loyalty to the employer by diligently following the lawful instructions of the employer, using reasonable care and only the authority granted.

   The supply management professional's foremost responsibility is to achieve the legitimate goals established by the employer. It is his or her duty to ensure that actions taken as an agent for the employer will benefit the best interests of the employer, *to the exclusion of personal gain.* This requires application of sound judgment and consideration of both the legal and the ethical implications of one's actions.

3. Conflict of Interest

Refrain from any private business or professional activity that would create a conflict between personal interests and the interests of the employer.

   Supply management professionals have the right to engage in activities that are of a private nature outside their employment. They must not, however, use their positions in any way to induce another person to provide any benefit to themselves, or persons with whom they have family, business, personal, or financial ties. Even though technically a conflict may not exist, supply management professionals must avoid the *appearance* of such a conflict. Whenever a potential conflict of interest arises, a supply management professional should notify his or her supervisor for guidance or resolution.

4. Gratuities

Refrain from soliciting or accepting money, loans, credits, or prejudicial discounts, and the acceptance of gifts, entertainment, favors, or services from present or potential suppliers that might influence, or appear to influence, supply management decisions.

   Gratuities include any material goods or services offered with the intent of, or providing the potential for, influencing a buying decision. Unfortunately, gratuities may, from time to time, be inappropriately offered to a buyer, or to other persons involved in supply management decisions (or members of their immediate families). Having any influence on the supply management process constitutes involvement. Those in a position to influence the supply management process must be dedicated to the best interests of their employer. It is essential to avoid any activity which may diminish, or even appear to diminish, the objectivity of the supply management decision-making process.

   Gratuities may be offered in various forms. Common examples are monies, credits, discounts, supplier contests, sales promotion items, product test samples, seasonal or personal gifts, edibles, drinks, household appliances and furnishings, clothing, loans of goods or money, tickets to sporting or other events, dinners, parties, transportation, vacations, cabins, travel and hotel expenses, and various forms of entertainment. Although it does not occur as frequently, the offering of gratuities *by a purchaser to a supplier* is as unethical as the acceptance of gratuities from a supplier. Extreme caution must be used in evaluating the acceptance of any gratuities (even if of nominal value), and the frequency of such actions, to ensure that one is abiding by the spirit of these guidelines.

The following are selected guidelines in dealing with gratuities:

Business Meals Occasionally during the course of business it may be appropriate to conduct business during meals.

- Such meals shall be for a specific business purpose.
- Frequent meals with the same supplier should be avoided.
- A supply management professional should be in a position to pay for meals as frequently as the supplier. Supply management professionals are encouraged to budget for this business activity.

Global Supply Management In some foreign cultures, *business* gifts, meals, and entertainment are considered to be part of the development of the business relationship and the buying and selling process. Acceptance of business gifts, meals, and entertainment of nominal value may be appropriate in accordance with country customs and your company's policies.

- In many foreign cultures, business is frequently conducted in the evenings and over weekends, which may be the only time key executives are available. Under these circumstances, it is understood that a supply manager would be expected to accept or provide for meals and entertainment when business matters are conducted. This is typically a more sensitive issue during the initial phase of the business relationship and may be tempered as the relationship progresses.
- Reciprocal gift giving of nominal value is often an acceptable part of the international buying and selling process. When confronted with this—when company policy does not exist—an appropriate guide would be to ensure that actions are in the best interest of your employer, *never for personal gain.*
- The definition of nominal value may be higher or lower than nominal value in your country, given custom, currency, and cost-of-living considerations, and is often guided by the duration and scope of the relationship. A supply management professional must carefully evaluate nominal value in terms of what is reasonable and customary. When in doubt, consult company managers, professional colleagues, and your conscience.

5. Confidential Information

Handle confidential or proprietary information belonging to employers or suppliers with due care and proper consideration of ethical and legal ramifications and governmental regulations.

Supply management professionals and others in positions that influence buying decisions deal with confidential or proprietary information of both the employer and the supplier. It is the responsibility of a supply management professional to ensure that such information, which includes information that may not be confidential in the strictest sense but is not generally known, is treated in a confidential manner.

Proprietary information requires protection of the name, composition, process of manufacture, or rights to unique or exclusive information that has marketable value and is upheld by patent, copyright, or nondisclosure agreement. Others in the organization may be unaware of the possible consequences of the misuse of such information. The supply management professional should therefore avoid releasing information to other parties until assured that they understand and accept the responsibility for maintaining the confidentiality of the material. Extreme care and good judgment should be used if confidential information is communicated verbally. Such information should be shared only on a need-to-know basis.

Although some of the types of information listed below must be shared with others within the supply management professional's own company, this should be done only on a need-to-know basis. Information of one supplier must never be shared with another supplier, unless laws or government regulations require that such information be disclosed. If one is unclear regarding disclosure requirements, legal counsel should be consulted. When a supply management professional is privy to cost or profit data, or other supplier information not generally known, it is his or her responsibility to maintain the confidentiality of that information.

Examples of information that may be considered confidential or proprietary are:

1. Pricing and cost data.
2. Bid or quotation information.
3. Formulas and process information.
4. Design information (drawings, blueprints, etc.).
5. Company plans, goals, strategies, etc.
6. Personal information about employees or trustees.
7. Supply sources and supplier information.
8. Customer lists and customer information.
9. Computer software programs.

6. Treatment of Suppliers

Promote positive supplier relationships through courtesy and impartiality in all phases of the supply management cycle.

It is the responsibility of a supply management professional to promote mutually acceptable business relationships with all suppliers. Affording all supplier representatives the same courtesy and impartiality in all phases of business transactions will enhance the reputation and good standing of the employer, the supply management profession, and the individual. Indications of rudeness, discourtesy, or disrespect in the treatment of a supplier will result in barriers to free and open communications between buyer and seller, and ultimately in a breakdown of the business relationship.

In addition to courtesy, a supply management professional should extend the same fairness and impartiality to all legitimate business concerns that wish to compete for orders. It is natural and even desirable to build long-term relationships with suppliers based upon a history of trust and respect. Such relationships, however, should not cause a supply management professional to ignore the potential to establish similar working relationships with new or previously untested suppliers.

7. Reciprocity

Refrain from reciprocal agreements that restrain competition.

Transactions that favor a specific customer as a supplier, or influence a supplier into becoming a customer, constitute reciprocity, as does a specific commitment to buy in exchange for a specific commitment to sell. The true test for reciprocity, however, is in the motive, since the process may be less vague than a written or formal commitment. In any such transactions the additional issue of restraint of trade places both the individual's and company's reputation for fair competitive procurement and high ethical standards under increased scrutiny. In organization structures where the supply management and marketing functions report directly to the same individual, the potential for reciprocity may be greater.

Supply management professionals must be especially careful when dealing with suppliers who are customers. Cross-dealings between suppliers and customers are not antitrust violations per se. Nevertheless, giving preference to a supplier who is also a customer should occur only when all other factors are equal. Dealing with a supplier who is also a customer may not constitute a problem if, in fact, the supplier is the best source. A company is engaging in reciprocity, however, when it deals with a supplier solely because of the customer relationship. A professional supply manager must be able to recognize reciprocity and its ethical and legal implications.

8. Governing Laws

Know and obey the letter and spirit of laws governing the supply management function, and remain alert to the legal ramifications of supply management decisions.

Supply management professionals should pursue and retain an understanding of the essential legal concepts governing our conduct as agents of our companies. For example, key laws and regulations a supply management professional should be aware of when conducting business in the United States of America are:

- Uniform Commercial Code
- The Sherman Act
- The Clayton Act
- The Robinson-Patman Act
- The Federal Trade Commission Act
- The Federal Acquisition Regulations
- The Defense Acquisition Regulations
- Patent, Copyright, and Trademark Laws
- OSHA, EPA, and EEOC Laws
- Foreign Corrupt Practices Act

9. Small, Disadvantaged, and Minority-Owned Businesses

Encourage all segments of society to participate by providing access for small, disadvantaged, and minority-owned businesses.

It is generally recognized that all business concerns, large or small, majority- or minority-owned, should be afforded an equal opportunity to compete. Within existing legal constraints, various government entities and corporations have developed specific procedures and policies designed to support and stimulate the growth of small, disadvantaged, and minority-owned businesses. Such businesses are dependent for their survival and expansion upon being given the opportunity to compete in the marketplace with larger firms.

10. Personal Purchases for Employees

Discourage supply management's involvement in employer-sponsored programs of personal purchases that are not business related.

The function of supply management is to supply the material requirements of the employer. Personal purchase programs divert organizational resources and dilute the effectiveness of the supply management function. In certain states, trade diversion laws prohibit personal purchases for employees when such materials are not manufactured by the employer or required for the health or safety of the employee. Situations in which personal purchase programs are justifiable involve items such as work-related safety gear, hand tools, and computer hardware or software for business-related work performed at home.

If management decides to establish such programs, the following are recommended guidelines in dealing with purchases for employees:

- Avoid using an employer's purchasing power to make special purchases for an individual's nonbusiness use.
- If personal purchase programs exist, the supply management professional should make certain that the arrangements are fair to suppliers, employees, and employers, and that the programs are equally available to all employees.
- Use caution to ensure that employer-sponsored programs do not force special concessions on the supplier.
- If a firm does utilize such a program, suppliers should be made aware that such purchases are not for the employer, but for the firm's employees.

11. Responsibilities to the Profession

Enhance the proficiency and stature of the supply management profession by acquiring and maintaining current technical knowledge and the highest standards of ethical behavior.

Supply management professionals have an obligation to master the basic skills of the profession, as well as keep abreast of current developments in the field.

It is equally imperative that supply management professionals reflect those same standards through their combined actions in professional groups or associations. Since the activities of groups are highly visible, attention needs to center on actions taken as a group. Each member of a group should consider it an obligation to support only those activities that uphold the high ethical standards of our profession.

12. Global Supply Management

Conduct international supply management activities in accordance with the laws, customs, and practices of foreign countries, consistent with your country's laws, your organization's policies, and these Ethical Standards and Guidelines.

Supply management professionals must be particularly cautious when operating in the international arena. Customs and culture vary from one country to another, but the differences typically are only a matter of degree rather than basic substantive differences. International business transactions dictate a need for a knowledgeable, commonsense approach, with close scrutiny to the intent of each party's actions—an attitude important in all business dealings, of course.

Important Areas Requiring Amplification

Avoid Sharp Practices

In business, the term "sharp practices" has been used for years—and it is particularly relevant for supply management professionals. One of the standards in an earlier version of ISM's *Standards of Conduct* reads, "Avoid sharp practices." Section 4.7 of the ISM *Guide to Purchasing,* authored by Dr. Robert Felch, provides a definition: "The term 'sharp practices' typically is illustrated as evasion and indirect misrepresentation, just short of actual fraud." These unscrupulous practices focus on short-term gains and ignore the long-term implications for a business relationship.

Some examples of sharp practices are:

■ A supply manager talks in terms of large quantities to encourage a price quote on that basis. The forthcoming order, however, is smaller than the amount on which the price was based. The smaller order does not legitimately deserve the low price thus developed.

■ A large number of bids are solicited in hope that the supply manager will be able to take advantage of a quotation error.

■ Bids are obtained from unqualified suppliers that the supply manager would not patronize in any case. These bids are then played against the bids of responsible suppliers in order to gain a price or other advantage. The preparation of bids is a costly undertaking that deserves sincerity in the solicitation stage.

■ A supply manager who places in competition the prices of seconds, odd lots, or distress merchandise misrepresents a market.

■ An attempt is made to influence a seller by leaving copies of bids, or other confidential correspondence, where a supplier can see them.

■ A concession may be forced by dealing only with "hungry" suppliers. The *current* philosophy is that a purchase order should create a mutual advantage with a price that is fair and reasonable.

■ Obscure contract terms of benefit to the supply manager's firm are buried in the small type of contract articles.

■ A supply manager may take advantage of a supplier who is short of cash and who may seek only to cover his/her out-of-pocket costs. Such a situation poses a dilemma, since the supplier may be saved from borrowing at a disadvantage and may look upon such an order as a blessing![6]

Acurex Corporation adds the following items to the preceding list of practices to be avoided:[7]

■ Allowing one or more suppliers to have information about their competitors' quotations and *allowing such suppliers to requote.*

---

[6]Robert I. Felch, "Proprieties and Ethics in Purchasing Management," *Guide to Purchasing* (Oradell, NJ: ISM, 1986), pp. 4.7-3 and 4.7-4.

[7]Richard E. Trevisan, "Developing a Statement of Ethics: A Case Study," *Journal of Purchasing and Materials Management,* Fall 1986, p. 13.

- Making statements to an existing supplier that exaggerate the seriousness of a problem in order to obtain better prices or other concessions.
- Giving preferential treatment to suppliers that higher levels of the firm's own management prefer to recommend.
- Canceling a purchase order for parts already in process while also seeking to avoid cancellation charges.
- Getting together with other supply professionals to take united action against another group of people or a company.
- Lying to or grossly misleading a salesperson in a negotiation.
- Allowing a supplier to become dependent on the supply management organization for most of its business.

While many of these practices were once commonplace, Dr. Felch notes that they are now replaced by a philosophy that holds that mutual confidence and integrity are far more desirable ends than the short-term gains obtained through willful misrepresentation.

Competitive Bidding[8]

Supply management professionals respect and maintain the integrity of the competitive bidding process. They:

- Invite only firms to whom they are willing to award a contract to submit bids.
- Normally award the contract to the lowest *responsive,* responsible bidder. If the supply manager anticipates the possibility of awarding to other than the low bidder, then he or she notifies prospective bidders that other factors will be considered. (Ideally, these factors will be listed.)
- Keep competitive price information confidential.
- Notify unsuccessful bidders promptly so that they may reallocate reserved production capacity.
- Treat all bidders alike. Clarifying information is given to *all* potential bidders.
- Do not accept bids after the announced bid closing date and time.
- Do not take advantage of apparent mistakes in the supplier's bid.
- Do not "shop" or conduct auctions for low prices. Although this approach is used in several industries, the unfortunate result frequently is a contract in which the supplier cuts corners in order to avoid a loss.

On the other hand, it *is* ethical for a supply manager to work with the low bidder in an effort to identify possible areas of savings. Such identified savings allow the potential supplier to reduce its *costs* and its price.

---

[8]Much of this discussion is based on material in ISM's *Guide to Purchasing,* section 4.7: "Proprieties and Ethics in Purchasing Management," by Dr. Robert I. Felch. Specific footnotes are utilized where appropriate.

Negotiation

Supply professionals maintain high ethical standards during all negotiated supply management activities.

- Competitors are informed of the factors that will be involved in source selection.
- All potential suppliers are given equal access to information and are afforded the same treatment.
- Supply professionals strive to negotiate terms that are fair to both parties. They do not take advantage of mistakes in the supplier's proposal.[9]

Samples

Many potential suppliers offer, even push, the acceptance of samples—"Just try it and see if it doesn't do a superior job for you." When a sample is accepted, supply professionals ensure that appropriate tests are conducted in a timely manner. The potential supplier then should be informed of the test results and suitability of the item in meeting the buyer's needs.

Treating Salespeople with Respect

As noted earlier, the use of courtesy and consideration by supply management personnel can influence the effectiveness of supplier relationships. The treatment of salespeople clearly produces overtones in the area of professional standards of conduct.[10]

- Salespeople should not be kept waiting for protracted periods of time; appointments should be meticulously kept. The power that is attached to the patronage position of a supply professional must not be abused so that the long-run interests of the buying company will be advanced.
- A mutually effective policy is for supply management personnel to see every salesperson on his or her first call. The appropriateness of follow-up visits should be determined by the potential strength of the buying firm's need for the supplying firm's product.

Substandard Materials and Services

When substandard materials or services are received, two proprieties should be observed:[11]

1. The supplier should be given prompt notice.
2. The appropriate supply manager should conduct negotiations for adjustments with the appropriate sales personnel in the supplier's organization.

---

[9]Ibid., pp. 4–5.

[10]Ibid., p. 7.

[11]Ibid.

Gifts and Gratuities

Nothing can undermine respect for the supply management profession more than improper action on the part of its members with regard to gifts, gratuities, favors, and so forth. People engaged in supply management should not accept from any supplier or prospective supplier any substantive gifts or favors (as defined in ISM Standard 4). All members of the supply management system must decline to accept or must return any such items offered them or members of their immediate family. The refusal of gifts and favors should be done discreetly and courteously. When the return of a gift is impractical for some reason, disposition should be made to a charitable institution, and the donor should be informed of the disposition.

Personal business transactions with suppliers or prospective suppliers should be scrupulously avoided. Offers of hospitality, business courtesies, or favors, no matter how innocent in appearance, can be a source of embarrassment to all parties concerned.

The buying firm's representatives should not allow themselves to become involved in situations in which unnecessary embarrassment results from refusal of a hospitality or a business courtesy from suppliers. Generally, the best policy is to decline any sort of favor, hospitality, or entertainment in order to *ensure that all relationships are above reproach at all times.*

Clearly, all situations require the use of common sense and good judgment. For example, acceptance of company-provided luncheons during the course of a visit to a supplier's plant located in a remote area certainly is reasonable. Likewise, the acceptance of supplier-provided automobile transportation on a temporary basis when other means are not readily available is a reasonable course of action for a supply professional to take.

Supply management personnel may ethically attend periodic meetings or dinners of trade associations, professional and technical societies, or other industrial organizations as the guest of a supplier, when the meetings are of an educational and informative nature, and when it is considered to be in the professional interest of the buyer-seller relationship. Even so, the repeated appearance of an individual at such regularly scheduled meetings, as the guest of the same company, is the type of situation that should be tactfully avoided.

The simple casual lunch or cocktail with a supplier's representative typically is merely a normal expression of a friendly business relationship, or frequently a timesaving expediency. It would be prudish to raise any serious questions on this score. The individual, himself or herself, is in the best position to judge when this point has been exceeded. Any breach of ethics can be rationalized. But members of the supply management system can avoid embarrassment or possible unethical behavior by asking, *"How would this look if reported in the company newsletter?"* It is the desire to continue to talk shop or to resolve a business issue that accounts for most buyer-supplier lunches. Because the buying firm's prestige also is involved, *there is good reason why an adequate expense account should be available to the supply professional.* This permits him or her to reciprocate in picking up the bill for lunch! It is a small price to pay for maintaining a position free from any taint of obligation.

"There's No Such Thing as a Free Lunch" Several years ago, Mike Darby of the ISM–Silicon Valley organization addressed the issue of free lunches. His comments were so appropriate that they are included below for the benefit of our readers.

The person who came up with this quote many years ago was probably a materials manager. There are many pro's and con's about buyers going to lunch with their suppliers. I don't propose to advocate one or the other, but I would like to point out some ideas that may help you to make up your own mind.

First and foremost in my mind is, *WHY* would a company want to spend some of its dollars that would normally flow directly to the bottom line to have me join them for lunch? I've asked this question of many suppliers. Some of the answers I've received include: "I have to take somebody to lunch every day, and it might as well be somebody I like"; "If I take you to lunch, then my lunch is free also"; "It will give us an opportunity to get to know each other better." These are all good answers, some of them more honest than I expected.

When I asked the same question of the buyers, the answer changed slightly. "We may need this supplier in the future, and I want to develop a close relationship with him"; "We have some serious problems to discuss"; "This will give me a good opportunity to negotiate a better deal with them."

Whatever the justification, the bottom line to me gets down to this. The supplier is willing to commit some of his profit dollars to this form of entertainment in *the belief that it will help him generate more profit in the future.* He may be in hope that the relationship he is building will help sustain him in your company through rough times, such as poor delivery performance or bad quality. He may be expecting to increase his prices, and a friend will never complain about a small change in price. He may ask you to lunch expecting that the slight social obligation he has just obtained from you may be paid back by getting another crack at a quote, first look at a new drawing, etc. Or he may join you for lunch hoping to obtain some information that will be useful to him in future negotiations.

All the above tend to add up to a one-sided deal, favoring the supplier and putting the buyer in the position of having to be very careful. Let's face it, the sales force of the supplier is being paid to perform a service to the supplier, and this is a good tool for him to use. He gets your undivided attention for a good hour or so, to use as he sees fit. Remember, it's impolite in our society to refuse to answer a question. A question as simple as "How's business?" provides the supplier with important information as to its market share within your company, business trends, and helps to set his expectations in future negotiations. It's also very difficult as a supply professional not to show a slight amount of favoritism toward the supplier that you had lunch with last Friday. Should he ask, "Where do I stand on that quote, and what do I need to do to get the job?" It gets difficult to be firm and say no to such a request.

Now before I get blasted out of the water for being one-sided, let me say that there are times when a business meal is appropriate. If you have a supplier in from out of town, and your business discussions extend through lunch or past business hours, a meal is probably appropriate. In this circumstance, I like to use the Host rule—If the meeting is in your territory, then you should be the host. If you are visiting the supplier's territory, then he can be the host. Make it fair and equitable, and the supplier loses any advantage he might have held from an obligation point of view. Remember, an obligation is in the mind of the person who received the favor. If, because of the manner in which you handle your conduct, there was no potential for a favor, then there can also be no obligation.

As a supply professional, picking up the check can quickly change a supplier's expectations, and as such is a very useful negotiation tactic. If he thought he had a contract in the bag, he suddenly begins to think that he may not be as secure as he thought. It also sends the message that you too are a professional and certainly not an easy target.[12]

Mature supply managers know that they are quickly classified among the sales fraternity by the amount of entertainment they expect or will accept. Salespeople usually speak with real respect of the supply manager who pays his or her share of entertainment expenses. The supply management expense account is the most effective answer to this ethical problem.

Traditional Sales Techniques Many supply management personnel feel that any form of gratuity constitutes a conflict with ethical standards. Others—in fact the majority, according to ISM studies—consider many of these items to be traditional sales tools. They do not, therefore, believe that such gratuities are offered with the expectation of favorable consideration.[13]

There are two common ways of controlling the acceptance of these kinds of gifts. The first is by placing a dollar limit on what can be accepted. In this case, a supply management department may have a stated policy of refusing any gratuity with a value in excess of, say, $10 or $15. Such policies provide a very simple, measurable guideline as to how a buyer should decide acceptance.

The other common policy is to forbid acceptance of any gratuity *the buying firm is not in a position to reciprocate.* Thus, if a firm's supply professionals accept sales promotion items such as pens or planning calendars, they should be in a position to reciprocate with similar items from their own firm.

Cultural Ramifications Executives of many foreign suppliers expect that supply professionals will exchange gifts with them. Such action is an accepted part of many foreign cultures. Some supply professionals encounter situations in which refusing a gift would interfere with the development of relations prerequisite to consummating a successful transaction. In such cases, supply professionals should *report* the situation to their superiors and arrive at a solution that may include acceptance *and* a reciprocal gift.[14] If a supply manager hides his or her action, he or she automatically knows that the action is unethical.

Management Responsibilities

Written Standards

Management's first responsibility is to develop a set of written ethical and professional standards applicable to all members of the organization's supply management system. Supply management supervisors, buyers, expediters, design engineers, manufacturing engineers, quality assurance personnel, maintenance supervisors, receivers, and accounts payable personnel all must accept these standards. The standards should address

---

[12]*Pacific Purchaser,* November–December 1988, p. 11.

[13]Michael H. Thomas, "Know Where You Stand on Ethics," *Purchasing World,* October 1984, p. 90.

[14]Somerby Dowst, "Taking the Mystery Out of Conflict of Interest," *Purchasing,* September 11, 1986, p. 70A1.

the topics discussed in this chapter. Research has shown clearly that *written* policies dealing with ethical issues have a strong positive influence on the behavior of a firm's supply management professionals.[15]

Ethics Training and Education

Professional supply managers, with the *assistance of top management* and their colleagues in other functional areas, must ensure that appropriate personnel receive periodic training or education with respect to the organization's ethical and professional standards. Such training cannot address all issues. It can, however, increase the sensitivity of those attending. All members of the supply management system must respect their roles as agents of their employer and must represent the best interest of their organization. Subsequent to such training, many organizations require the attendees to sign *a statement to the effect that they have taken the training and understand and will honor the standards.*

Supply managers should also ensure that their personnel receive training on current thinking and techniques in the areas of requirements planning, source selection, pricing, cost analysis, negotiation, and supplier management, as well as ethical and professional standards.

The vast majority of supply managers are dedicated and conscientious people. Accordingly, it is almost shocking to see how little high-quality training many of these individuals have received. Supply management system reviews conducted by the authors indicate that a substantial number of supply managers are being asked to perform tasks for which they have received little current training, including training in the area of ethical and professional conduct.

Departmental Environment

Department policy should make it clear that supply personnel engaging in any unethical activity do so at the risk of losing their jobs. It is a generally accepted view that a small percentage of people are dishonest, that an equally small percentage are completely honest, and that most of us are honest *or* dishonest, *depending on the circumstances.* Consequently, after the basic policy and training frameworks have been established, it appears that the surest way to encourage ethical conduct is to create a working environment in which unethical temptations seldom become realities.

The foundation for such an environment consists of the people themselves. Management will be repaid many times for the effort put into thorough, careful investigation and selection of buying personnel. Habits and attitudes are "catching" in the close working environment of a supply department. If most of the personnel are basically honest, departmental management has the major part of the ethics battle won.

One businessman once said, "The way to keep employees honest is to pay them enough to pursue a satisfying life style." There is obviously room for debate about the exact definition of a "satisfying life style," but the idea is basically sound. It makes lit-

---

[15]G. B. Turner, G. S. Taylor, and M. F. Hartley, "Ethics Policies and Gratuity Acceptance by Purchasers," *International Journal of Purchasing and Materials Management,* Summer 1994, p. 46.

tle sense to place a person who has major unfilled material needs in a position where he or she is confronted regularly with the temptation inherent in an industrial supply management job. The implication for salaries is clear.

The age-old adage "monkey see, monkey do" is certainly applicable in the matter of ethical conduct. Departmental management and supervisory people must *live* to the letter by the department's policies and ideals. Numerous studies have confirmed beyond doubt that the actions and attitudes of supervisors are the most influential single factor in determining the attitudes of a work group.

Miscellaneous Factors

Two concluding thoughts are worthy of consideration. First, some progressive organizations have established an internal or external ombudsman who can be contacted with impunity about ethical issues. Once accepted, the practice seems to work well.

Finally, the president of Seldon Associates suggests greater utilization of postpurchase audits as desirable safeguards. He writes, "When every buyer knows that his or her purchases may be audited, there is a built-in safeguard tending to assure ethical purchasing."[16]

Dealing with Gray Areas

All supply professionals have ethical obligations to three groups of people—*employers, suppliers, and colleagues*:

- *Employer.* Guidance should focus on the characteristics of loyalty, analytical objectivity, and a drive to achieve results that are in the very best interest of the employing organization.

- *Suppliers.* The essence of the guiding spirit in dealing with the supplier community is honesty and fair play.

- *Colleagues.* All individuals engaged in supply management work are regarded by outside observers as members of an emerging profession. As such, they have an obligation to protect and enhance the reputation of that body of professionals.

When supply management professionals must take action in a "gray area" not clearly covered by policy, they may find guidance by seeking answers to the following questions:

1. Is this action acceptable to everyone in my organization?
2. Is the action compatible with the firm's responsibilities to its customers, suppliers, and stockholders?
3. What would happen if *all* supply managers and salespeople behaved this way?
4. If I were in the other person's shoes, how would I feel about this action if it were directed toward me?

---

[16]Doyle Seldon, "Ethics, an Additional Look," *Purchasing Management,* December 1988, p. 41.

The Four Way Test

The businesspeople of the Rotary International organization provide a follow-up of four questions. They apply The Four Way Test to the things they think, say, or do:[17]

- Is it the TRUTH?
- Is it FAIR to all concerned?
- Will it build GOODWILL?
- Will it be BENEFICIAL to all concerned?

In making the final decision, a few moments' thought may well be devoted to the following lines, entitled "What Makes a Profession."[18]

> If there is such a thing as a profession as a concept distinct from a vocation, it must consist in the ideals that its members maintain, the dignity of character that they bring to the performance of their duties, and the austerity of the self-imposed ethical standards. To constitute a true profession, there must be ethical tradition so potent as to bring into conformity members whose personal standards of conduct are at a lower level, and to have an elevating and ennobling effect on those members. A profession cannot be created by resolution, or become such overnight. It requires many years for its development, and they must be years of self-denial, years when success by base means is scorned, years when no results bring honor except those free from the taint of unworthy methods.

Concluding Remarks

As you finish reading this chapter about ethics, consider an event that occurred at a University of San Diego career planning workshop for students who would soon be entering the job market. The workshop facilitator instructed the participants to write their own obituaries. Morbid? Maybe. Useful? Absolutely!

The purpose of the exercise was to force the students to project to the end of their lives, and then summarize how their lives had been lived. This exercise of coerced self-reflection was designed to examine each student's values. What kind of career unfolded? How did this person treat other people? Did this person touch the lives of others in such a way so as to be missed?

All of us, of course, write our own obituaries each day of our lives by the way we choose to live our lives. If your obituary discussed your ethics, what would you want it to say?

---

[17]*Manual of Procedures,* Rotary International, Evanston, IL, 1992, p. 94.

[18]*NAPM Standards of Conduct,* 1959.

CHAPTER 24

Legal Considerations[1]

World Class Supply Management^{SM} requires supply managers to possess and utilize knowledge of legal issues and considerations. Such knowledge must be coupled with the wisdom to communicate and interact with legal professionals and suppliers proactively in efforts to develop and maintain relationships between supply chain members that minimize conflict and maximize opportunities for collaborative success.

---

[1] Appreciation is expressed to Professor Craig Barkacs of the University of San Diego for his assistance in updating this chapter.

Case

Ford Firestone Fiasco

One of the longest-running partnerships in U.S. history died an ugly death in 2001 when Ford and Firestone publicly accused one another of responsibility for a string of deadly accidents involving Ford sport utility vehicles equipped with Firestone tires. Who was really at fault? Were the Firestone tires, which appeared to detread, the cause of the accidents? Or were the designs of the Ford vehicles to blame?

As this book is being written, both Ford and Firestone are in litigation with each other and the families of several victims of SUV rollovers. Time will tell who, if any one entity, is to blame. However the question arises, Could the legal issues between Ford and Firestone have been resolved in a more constructive manner without litigation?

Litigation Prevention

It may be persuasively argued that the best way to deal with legal disputes is to make sure one does one's best to avoid them in the first place! The maxim that an ounce of prevention is worth a pound of cure certainly comes to mind in this context. In professional life, supply management professionals seldom—if they're fortunate—become involved in litigation. Yet their daily activities are subject to two major areas of the law—the law of agency and the law of contracts.

A supply manager or a buyer acts as an agent for his or her firm. Legally, this relationship is defined and governed by the law of agency. When a firm buys materials and services from other firms, each purchase involves the formation of a purchase contract. Should a serious disagreement arise between the purchaser and the supplier, the conflict may then enter the realm of dispute resolution, which can be divided into four categories: (1) negotiation; (2) mediation; (3) arbitration; and (4) litigation. In any event, the dispute would be governed by the law of contracts.

A supply manager's basic responsibility is to conduct the firm's procurement business as efficiently and expeditiously as possible. Buying policies and practices are therefore predicated primarily on business requirements and business judgment, rather than on legal considerations. As Professor Dean Ammer aptly stated, "A highly legalistic approach is both unnecessary and unprofitable." From a business standpoint, contractual disputes can normally be resolved much more effectively and with less cost by negotiation. A lawsuit almost always alienates a good supplier. Additionally, the outcome of any court case is usually uncertain; otherwise, there would be little need for court action. Litigation is also costly, even in the event of a favorable decision. The total cost of legal fees, executive time diverted to the dispute, and disrupted business operations is seldom recovered from damage awards. For these reasons, when settling disputes, most business firms utilize litigation only as a last resort.

The fact that a supply management executive tries to avoid litigation, however, does not mean that he or she can overlook the legal dimensions of the job. On the contrary, a basic knowledge of relevant legal principles is essential to success. Unless a supply manager understands the legal implications of his or her job and the actions undertaken while doing it, legal entanglements are almost certain to crop up from time to time.

The purpose of this chapter is to briefly review some of the principle legal concepts as they relate to a supply management professional's responsibilities. The chapter does not attempt to provide a complete discussion of these concepts. Most supply professionals should acquire some depth in the field through selected studies in commercial law.

Dispute Resolution

Serious contract disputes are a rarity in the lives of most supply managers. But in a complex business operation, they do arise from time to time. When a dispute does arise, after doing the appropriate "homework," the first step in the resolution process is to discuss the problem with the supplier. When attempting to resolve a dispute, it pays to keep in mind six considerations: (1) time; (2) money; (3) complexity/formality of method of dispute resolution; (4) stress; (5) visibility; and (6) damage to the relationship.

Negotiation

Most disputes are best resolved through negotiation and compromise. In most cases, the executives involved want to avoid further confrontation simply because it may be too time-consuming, too costly, too messy and complicated, too stressful, and too embarrassing and damaging to the parties' relationship to do otherwise. In the event a satisfactory solution cannot be worked out by the two parties, however, three alternatives remain. They can mediate, arbitrate, or go to court.

Mediation

If negotiation fails, the disputants can consider mediation, which involves introducing a third party into the discussion. The mediator's role is to listen, sympathize, empathize, coax, cajole, and persuade. Depending on the level of trust and credibility the mediator has with the disputant, he or she may even propose, suggest, or encourage possible solutions. For that reason, the more trusted and respected a mediator is, the more likely he or she will be able to help resolve the dispute. One thing the mediator may not do, however, is decide anything. If the disputants confer decision-making authority on a third party, we are now talking about arbitration.

Arbitration

Arbitration may take many forms, but its basic feature is that the outcome of a dispute is no longer in the hands of the disputants themselves, but rather in the hands of a third party. Unlike negotiation or mediation, in which the disputants attain resolution by agreeing on the outcome, arbitration vests the decision-making authority with the arbitrator. Under such circumstances, a professional agreed-upon arbitrator will hear testimony and study evidence from both sides, then make a decision based on the facts and the law.

Litigation

Some maintain that if a commercial dispute reaches litigation, the disputants—regardless of the outcome—have already lost. Remember the six considerations of time, money, complexity/formality of method of dispute resolution, stress, visibility, and damage to the relationship? All six tend to be *maximized* at the litigation level.

So how does one best avoid ending up in litigation? As suggested at the beginning of this chapter, the best approach is avoidance and prevention of destructive legal disputes. And just how does one best avoid and prevent destructive legal disputes? This is where a fundamental understanding of certain basic legal principles can prove invaluable. One benefits most from knowing the law so as to avoid and prevent the destructive legal disputes that may ensue from ignorance of the law. After all, how many times has one heard the admonition, "ignorance of the law is no defense"?

Development of Commercial Law

Historically, in the United States each state developed its own body of statutes and common law to deal with the problems prevalent in its particular spheres of activity. Individual state development ultimately led to the creation of a series of commercial laws that varied widely from state to state—a situation that obviously produced difficulties for businesses involved in interstate commerce.

In an attempt to promote uniformity among the laws applicable to business transactions, the American Bar Association created a committee known as the National Conference of Commissioners on Uniform State Laws (NCCUSL). The assignment given to this group was to codify (i.e., set forth in writing) the laws applying to various business transactions. Its first product was the Uniform Negotiable Instruments Law, followed by the Uniform Stock Transfer Act, the Uniform Conditional Sales Act, the Uniform Bills of Lading Act, the Uniform Warehouse Receipts Act, and the Uniform Sales Act.

The work of supply management professionals has been influenced most heavily by the Uniform Sales Act, which contributed substantially to the uniformity of laws affecting sales and contracts. Unfortunately, however, in practice the act left much to be desired. The Uniform Sales Act permitted each state considerable latitude in applying its own laws of contract, and decisions on legal interpretations still varied widely among state courts. Moreover, only about three-quarters of the states adopted the Uniform Sales Act.

Recognizing the need for modernization, and noting the sporadic adoption of the act in the face of increasing interstate trade, the NCCUSL joined with the American Law Institute in the early 1940s to formulate a new uniform code. The resulting code, entitled the Uniform Commercial Code (UCC), was published in 1952; refined versions of the code followed, with the most recent published in 1991. Although the UCC covers a wide range of commercial activities, Article 2 deals specifically with the sale and purchase of goods. The UCC does not apply to the purchase of services.

A fundamental difference between the UCC and the Uniform Sales Act lies in the basic underpinnings of the acts themselves. The Uniform Sales Act determined many rights and obligations of contract parties on the basis of title; that is, such decisions depended heavily on which party had title to the material. The UCC, on the other hand, determines rights and obligations on the basis of fairness and reasonableness in the light of accepted business practice. Thus, the code is geared more closely to the needs and circumstances found in daily business operations.

Today, the UCC has been adopted by all the states except Louisiana.[2] It has effectively eliminated a majority of the important differences that existed between the commercial laws of the various states and has also provided new statutory provisions to fill many of the gaps in the prior laws. It should be noted, however, that the code is silent on some matters covered by earlier laws. Consequently, unless superseded by provisions of the UCC, earlier laws dealing with matters such as principal and agent, fraud, mistakes, coercion, and misrepresentation continue in effect and supplement the provisions of the code.

The UCC, however, was drafted prior to the advent of e-commerce. Many have argued that e-commerce has spawned the need for a new or expanded set of laws to cover cyber transactions. Accordingly, in 1995, the National Conference of Commissioners on Uniform State Laws (NCCUSL) and the American Law Institute (ALI) set about drafting a proposed Article 2B to the UCC. The purpose of 2B was to govern licences, including computer software. The completed draft, however, resulted in a split between the NCCUSL and the ALI. While the NCCUSL was satisfied with the draft, the ALI regarded many of the provisions as being too favorable to software licensors, at the expense of consumers.

Given this split of opinion, the NCCUSL unilaterally decided to make the draft its own body of law, separate and apart from the UCC. This discrete body of law then became known as the Uniform Computer Information Transactions Act (UCITA), and beginning in 1999 the NCCUSL began encouraging states to enact it. Soon thereafter, however, a majority of state attorneys general asked the NCCUSL to revise the UCITA on the basis that it undermined consumer protection by classifying consumer software as nongoods. Given the objections to the UCITA as it is currently written, its widespread adoption by the states is in doubt. As a result, the licensing of software is currently governed by UCC Articles 2 and 2A.

---

[2] Louisiana has enacted only parts of the UCC.

Topics treated throughout the rest of this chapter therefore reflect the provisions of the UCC where applicable, as well as the provisions of earlier laws not displaced by the code.

Basic Legal Considerations

Status of an Agent

In the legal sense, an agent is a person who, by express or implied agreement, is authorized to act for someone else in business dealings with a third party. Regardless of the job title, this is precisely what supply managers and buyers do. A "supply manager" is not a legal party to his or her business transactions, but rather serves as an intermediary. In this capacity, the law requires the agent to be loyal to the employer (the principal) and to perform his or her duties with diligence, dedication, and capability. Because the purchasing agent or supply manager has agreed to act for the benefit of the employer, the law permits the employer to hold its agent(s) personally liable for any secret advantages gained for himself or herself or for any aid given to competitors.

The authority under which a buyer, purchasing agent, or supply manager functions is granted by the employer. Since the law requires him or her to operate within the bounds of this authority, it behooves such individuals to know as precisely as possible the types of transactions in which he or she can and cannot legally represent the firm. In practice, the amount of authority delegated to buyers, purchasing agents, and supply managers varies significantly among companies. Hence, it is difficult for sales representatives to know the exact limits of a particular buyer's authority. Consequently, under the law, such individuals operate under two types of authority—actual authority and apparent authority. Although a salesperson may not know the buying agent's actual authority, if both act in good faith the law says that the sales representative can reasonably assume that the buyer has apparent authority comparable with that of similar agents in similar companies.

The significance of "apparent authority" becomes evident upon examination of a buyer's legal liability. For example, if an agent acts outside his or her actual authority but within what can reasonably be inferred as his or her apparent authority, the seller generally can hold the agent's firm liable for the agent's action. However, the firm, in turn, can legally bring suit against the agent for acting beyond the limit of his or her actual authority. On the other hand, if an agent exceeds the limits of both his or her actual and apparent authority, a seller usually cannot hold the firm liable, but may be able to hold the agent personally liable for the action. In both of these situations, however, if the seller knows at the time of the act that the agent is exceeding his or her authority, the seller generally has no legal recourse against the agent or the firm.

Just as supply professionals occupy the legal status of buying agents for their firms, sales representatives similarly hold the status of selling agents for their firms. Buyers, purchasing agents, and supply managers, however, usually are classified as general agents, while salespeople typically are classified as special agents, having somewhat more restricted authority. Consequently, in most cases a salesperson does not have the authority to bind a company to a sales contract or to a warranty. The courts usually hold that, unless otherwise stated, as special agents sales representatives have authority only to solicit orders. It is important that buyers recognize this fact. On important jobs, to ensure that a legally binding contract does in fact exist, a buyer should require acceptance of the order by an authorized company officer, normally one of the supplier's sales managers who customarily serves as the company's general agent for this purpose.

The Purchase Contract

Although a legalistic approach to purchasing is in most cases unnecessary, every buyer, purchasing agent, and supply manager nevertheless must protect his or her company against potential legal problems. The buyer's major responsibility in this regard is to ensure that each purchase contract is satisfactorily drawn and legally binding on both parties. To be valid and enforceable, a contract must contain four basic elements: (1) agreement ("meeting of the minds") resulting from an offer and an acceptance; (2) consideration, or mutual obligation; (3) competent parties; and (4) a lawful purpose.

Offer and Acceptance When a buyer, purchasing agent, or supply manager sends a purchase order to a supplier, this act usually constitutes a legal offer to buy materials in accordance with the terms stated in the order. Agreement does not exist, however, until the supplier accepts the offer; when this occurs, the law deems that a "meeting of the minds" exists regarding the proposed contract. In the event that a buyer requests a quotation or a bid from a supplier, the supplier's quotation usually constitutes an offer. Agreement then exists when the buyer accepts the quotations (often by subsequently sending a purchase order to the supplier).

Under the Uniform Sales Act, the law required acceptance of an offer in terms that were identical with the terms of the offer—the mirror image concept. The UCC, however, eliminates this stringent requirement. The code states that "conduct by both parties which recognizes the existence of a contract is sufficient to establish a contract or sale although the writings of the parties do not otherwise establish a contract." The code also recognizes suppliers' standard confirmation forms and acknowledgment forms as a valid acceptance, even if the terms stated thereon are different from the terms of the offer.

When the terms of an acceptance differ from the terms of the offer—the so-called battle of the forms—the terms of the acceptance will automatically be incorporated in the contract unless one of three conditions exists: (1) They materially alter the intent of the offer, (2) the offeror objects in writing, or (3) the offer explicitly states that no different terms will be accepted. What happens when an offer and an acceptance contain conflicting terms, and yet none of the preceding conditions exist? All terms except the conflicting terms become part of the contract, and the conflicting terms are simply omitted from the contract. The buyer and the supplier subsequently are expected to resolve the issues covered by the conflicting terms. This provision of the code substantially clarifies the legal position of many such purchase orders. Moreover, as a consequence, it is clear that a wise buyer should carefully review the terms contained in a supplier's acceptance.

The UCC code contains another important provision relating to the acceptance of an offer to buy. The UCC recognizes as valid the communication of an acceptance in "any manner and by any medium reasonable to the circumstances." Consequently, when a supplier receives an order for the purchase of material for immediate delivery, it can accept the offer either by prompt acknowledgment of the order or by prompt shipment of the material. The code thus permits prompt supplier performance of such proposed contracts to constitute acceptance of the offer. The contract becomes effective when the supplier ships the material.

A hitherto long-standing principle of commercial law stated that an offer could be revoked by the offeror at any time before it had been accepted, regardless of the time period stipulated in the offer. The UCC has changed this principle with respect to the purchase or sale of goods. The code states that a written offer to buy or sell material must give the offeree assurance that the offer will be held open for the time period stipulated in the offer. If no time period is stipulated, the offer can be assumed firm for a "reasonable" period of time, not to exceed three months.

This provision of the code has significant implications for industrial purchasers and their potential suppliers. Purchasers can use suppliers' quotations in making precise manufacturing cost calculations and rely on the fact that the quotations cannot be revoked before a certain date. Without the code, no such assurance existed. On the other hand, this provision prevents a buyer from canceling an order, without legal obligation, prior to acceptance. An offer to buy, like an offer to sell, must also remain firm for a stated or a reasonable period of time. To maintain firm control, it is now doubly important that the buyer state in the order the length of time for which the offer is valid (or the date by which acceptance of the order is required).

Consideration   In addition to a meeting of minds, a valid contract must also contain the element of obligation. Most purchase contracts are bilateral; that is, both parties agree to do something they would not otherwise be required to do. The buyer promises to buy from the supplier certain material at a stated price; the supplier promises to deliver the material in accordance with stated contract conditions. The important point is the mutuality of obligation. The contract must be drawn so that each party (or promisor) is bound. If both are not bound, in the eyes of the law neither is bound. Hence, no contract exists.

A buyer is confronted with the practical significance of the "mutual obligation" concept when he or she formulates the terms of purchase. The statements regarding material quantity, price, delivery, and so on must be specific enough to bind both the buyer's firm and the supplier to definable levels of performance. In writing a blanket purchase order for pipe fittings, for example, it is not sufficient to state the quantity as "all company X desires." Such a statement is too indefinite to bind company X to any specific purchase. However, if the requirement were stated as "the quantity company X uses during the month of March," most courts would consider this sufficient to define X's purchase obligation. It is also prudent to qualify such a statement by indicating approximate minimum and maximum levels of consumption.

Similar situations arise in specifying prices and delivery dates. Some companies, for example, occasionally issue unpriced purchase orders. Aside from the questionable wisdom of such a business practice, a legal question concerning the definiteness of the offer also exists. From a legal standpoint, the question which must be answered is: Under existing conditions, can the price be determined precisely enough to define the obligations of both parties? The UCC provides more latitude in answering this question than did the Uniform Sales Act. The code specifically says that a buyer and a supplier can make a binding contract without agreeing on an exact price until a later date. If at the time of shipment a price cannot be agreed on, the code includes provisions by which a fair price shall be determined. On such orders, however, a buyer should protect his or her firm by noting a precise price range or by stating how the price is to be determined.

Competent Parties   A valid contract must be made by persons having full contractual capacity. A contract made by a minor or by an insane or intoxicated person is usually entirely void or voidable at the option of the incompetent party.

Legality of Purpose   A contract whose purpose is illegal is automatically illegal and void. A contract whose primary purpose is legal, but one of whose ancillary terms is illegal, may be either void or valid, depending on the seriousness of the illegality and the extent to which the illegal part can be separated from the legal part of the contract. The latter situation may occasionally have relevance for buyers. Such would be the case, for example, if a material were purchased at a price which violated restraint of trade or price discrimination laws.

The Written and the Spoken Word   Buyers should be aware of several basic concepts concerning the construction of a contract. Contrary to common belief, a contract is not a physical thing. A contract is actually a relationship which exists between the parties making the contract. When a contract is reduced to writing, the written document is not in fact the contract; it is simply evidence of the contract. Hence, a contract may be supported by either written or oral evidence. In most cases, courts hold an oral contract to be just as binding as a written one, although it may be substantially more difficult to prove the facts on which an oral contract is based. However, the law currently requires some types of agreements to be in writing. In the case of sales transactions between qualified "merchants,"[3] for example, the UCC specifically states that when a selling price of $500 or more is involved, the contract must be reduced to writing to be enforceable.[4] As noted earlier, though, provisions of the UCC are studied on a continuing basis to detect the need for possible changes or updating. As a result of this action, it is likely that the requirement for contracts exceeding $500 to be in written form may be modified somewhat in the near future.[5] Supply professionals should stay abreast of such potential changes.

In the event an oral contract between a supplier and buyer is later confirmed in writing, the written confirmation is binding on both parties if no objection is raised within 10 days. Hence, it is important to note that when a contract is reduced to writing, the written evidence supersedes all prior oral evidence. The courts generally hold that a contract

[3] Section 2-104 of the UCC defines a "merchant" as one who deals in goods; one who holds himself out as having particular skill in the subject matter; or one who uses a person who holds himself out as having such knowledge or skill. Hence, it is generally held under this broad definition that almost every person in business, including a supply officer, is a "merchant." Even a person not in business may be classified as a "merchant" if he or she employs a supply officer or broker.

[4] Prior to enactment of the UCC, the Statute of Frauds required contracts relating to personal property, for which neither delivery nor payment had been made, to be in writing if the value of the sale exceeded a specified amount; this specified amount varied widely among states.

[5] Gaylord A. Jentz, "More on the UCC Revisions," *NAPM Insights,* November 1993, p. 18.

expressed in writing embodies all preceding oral discussion pertinent to the agreement. Generally speaking, this means that a buyer cannot legally rely on a supplier's oral statements concerning a material's performance or warranty unless the statements have been included in the written agreement. Consequently, from a legal standpoint, a buyer should carefully consider the content of his or her oral negotiations with a supplier and ensure that all relevant data to be included in the contract have been reduced to writing. The buyer should also be aware that courts have ruled that written or typed statements take precedence over printed statements on the contract form, should conflicting statements appear in the document.

Finally, in signing a written contract, a buyer or supply manager should specifically indicate on the document that he or she is acting in the capacity of an agent for his or her firm. This avoids any possible misinterpretation as to the identity of the parties making the contract. Moreover, all data to be included as part of the contract should appear above the agent's signature. Courts have ruled that data appearing below the signature are informational only and not part of the contract.

Special Legal Considerations

Inspection Rights

If a purchaser has not previously inspected the material purchased to ensure that it conforms with the terms of the contract, the law gives him or her a reasonable period of time to inspect the material after it is received. If the purchaser raises no objection to the material within a reasonable period of time, he or she is deemed to have accepted it. In court decisions on this matter, it has been largely industry practice which sets the standard for "reasonable" time.

Rights of Rejection

A purchaser has the right to reject material that does not conform with the terms of the contract. If an overshipment is received, the purchaser can either reject the complete shipment or reject the quantity in excess of the contract amount. When a buyer does not wish to accept defectively delivered material, he or she is required only to notify the supplier of this fact, describing specifically the nature of the defect or default. The buyer is not legally bound to return the rejected material. However, the buying firm is obligated to protect and care for the material in a reasonable manner. If the buyer neither returns the material nor notifies the supplier of rejection within a reasonable period of time, however, the buying firm is then obligated to pay for the material.

Title

From a legal point of view, the question of which party has title to purchased materials is normally answered by defining the F.O.B. point of purchase. In the case of an F.O.B. origin shipment, the buying firm becomes the owner when the material is loaded into the carrier's vehicle. When material is shipped F.O.B. destination, the supplier owns the material until it is off-loaded at the buyer's receiving dock.

Warranties

The UCC identifies four specific types of warranties:

1. Warranty of title.
2. Implied warranty of merchantability.
3. Implied warranty of fitness for a particular purpose.
4. Express warranty.

When a supplier agrees to sell a particular item, the firm implies that it (or its principal) has title to the item and hence has legal authority to sell it. This is the warranty of title. The supplier also implies that the item is free from defects in material and workmanship—that it is at least of "fair average quality." This means that the item meets the standards of the trade and that its quality is appropriate for ordinary use. This legal provision is the implied warranty of merchantability.

Another implied warranty a buyer may receive under certain circumstances is an implied warranty of fitness for a particular purpose. If a buyer communicates to a supplier requirements that the purchased material must satisfy, and subsequently relies on the skill or judgment of the supplier in selecting a specific material for the job, the material usually carries an implied warranty of fitness for the stated need. This assumes that the supplier is fully aware of the buyer's need and knows that the buyer is relying on guidance from the supplier's personnel. Hence, it should be amply clear why buyers, purchasing agents, and supply managers must insist that purchase orders and related material specifications be written clearly and completely.

If a supplier accepts a purchase order without qualification, descriptions of the material included on the order form—model number, size, capacity, chemical composition, technical specifications, and so on—become an express warranty. The supplier warrants that the material delivered will conform to these descriptions. Additionally, suppliers frequently make express warranties for their products in sales and technical literature. Such warranties typically refer to the material's performance characteristics, physical composition, appearance, and so on. If a buyer has no way of determining the facts of the matter and consequently relies on such warranties, the supplier is normally held liable for them. The buyer should also recognize that an express warranty nullifies an implied warranty to the extent that it conflicts with the implied warranty (with the exception of an implied warranty of fitness for a particular purpose).

Numerous variable factors influence the extent to which a buyer can rely on an implied warranty in a specific situation. The knowledge and conduct of both buyer and seller, as well as the specific conditions surrounding a transaction, are taken into consideration by the court in resolving a dispute over warranty. Generally speaking, if a buyer acts in good faith and has no knowledge of conditions contrary to an implied warranty, the law holds a supplier liable for such implied warranties, unless otherwise stated in the contract.

Recent legislation[6] has tended to increase warranty protection for buyers by strengthening and expanding the liability of manufacturers and sellers with respect to

---

[6] The Consumer Product Safety Act and the Federal Warranties Act, as well as the UCC.

warranty performance. A buyer should recognize, however, that the UCC permits a seller to exclude or modify the implied warranty for a product. A supplier can do this by including a conspicuous written statement in the sales contract. Statements commonly used to accomplish warranty exclusion are "This item is offered for sale 'as is' " or "There are no warranties which extend beyond the description on the face hereof." Interestingly, in several states such warranty disclaimers have been declared to be contrary to public policy—and, hence, invalid. As a general rule, however, a prudent supply manager adopts a caveat emptor attitude in verifying the warranty protection he or she actually has in any given purchase.

Order Cancellation and Breach of Contract

If a supplier fails to deliver an order by the delivery date agreed on in the contract, or if it fails to perform in accordance with contrct provisions, legally the supplier has breached the contract. The breach usually gives the purchaser the right to cancel the order. In addition, the purchaser can sue for damages if he or she wishes. In practice, the latter right is infrequently exercised because a more effective settlement can usually be negotiated directly with the supplier. Nevertheless, under the law, a buyer may be able to recover damages if injury is actually suffered as a result of a breach of contract. In the case of delivery failure, if the buyer subsequently purchases the material elsewhere, actual damages may be difficult to determine. In any case, the courts usually follow the general rule of attempting to place the injured party in the same financial position he or she would have been in had the contract not been breached.

When no specific delivery date is stated in a contract, the law requires the supplier to deliver within a reasonable period of time. What the buyer thinks is a reasonable period of time may or may not coincide with what the supplier or the court deems to be a reasonable period of time. Hence, in such a situation, a buyer may be on uncertain ground if he or she decides to cancel an order because of nondelivery and subsequently places the order with another supplier. The buying firm may or may not have the legal right to do so. The desirability of including a specific delivery date in the contract thus becomes amply clear.

Situations sometimes arise that compel a buyer to cancel an order before the supplier is obligated to supply the material. In making such a cancellation, the buyer breaches the purchase contract. This act is legally termed anticipatory breach, and it makes the purchaser liable for any resulting injury to the supplier. If the cancellation results in no real injury to the supplier (as is often the case with orders for standard materials), the supplier can collect no damages. On the other hand, if the cancellation leaves the supplier with partially finished goods in its shop, the firm frequently does suffer injury. In such cases, if the in-process material is salable, the purchaser is usually held liable for the difference between the prorated contract value and the market value of the in-process material. If the material is not salable, the purchaser's liability usually covers the supplier's costs prior to termination plus a reasonable profit[7] on the contract.

---

[7] A "reasonable profit" is generally calculated using the same profit margin (percentage rate) as was included in the original contract.

Liquidated Damages Provision   If it is evident at the time a major contract is drawn that breach of the contract would severely injure one or both parties and that damages would be difficult to determine, it is wise to include a termination or liquidated damages provision in the contract. Such provisions stipulate in advance the procedures to be used in determining costs and damages. In some cases, specific damage payments are stated. For example, if the contract is for the purchase of power-generating equipment to be used on a large construction project, the date of delivery may be critical for the purchaser. Perhaps installation of the equipment must precede other important phases of the construction work. If the project is delayed by late delivery of the generating equipment, the purchaser might incur heavy financial losses. Sound practice on such a contract is normally to include a liquidated damages clause that requires the supplier to pay the purchaser damages of a set amount per day for late delivery. It is essential, however, that the damage figure specified be a reasonable estimate of the probable loss to the buyer, and not be calculated simply to impose a penalty on the supplier. Courts generally refuse to enforce a penalty provision.

A termination or liquidated damages provision represents prior agreement by both parties on the ground rules to be followed in case the contract is breached. If such a breach actually occurs, the provision minimizes the possibility of misunderstandings and the generation of ill will between the two firms.

JIT Contracts

Because just-in-time purchasing and manufacturing operations are somewhat unique, they occasionally generate unexpected legal difficulties. The most common problems are reviewed briefly in the following paragraphs.

The major factor a supply manager should keep in mind is that in most cases a JIT purchasing agreement requires different levels of supplier performance than the supplier typically has been used to. Consequently, it is important that communications be clear and complete. This includes oral discussions prior to the purchase, as well as the final written documents. Requirements for quality, delivery scheduling, inventory levels, and any other key factors should be spelled out in unequivocal terms, so there is little opportunity for misunderstanding that might lead to litigation.

Consider the following illustration. Assume that a buyer and a supplier have been doing business satisfactorily for several years. During the past year, approximately one-third of the shipments from the supplier arrived a week or so late, but the buyer accepted them without serious complaints. In the eyes of the law, these acceptances by the buyer may have set a precedent which waives the buyer's rights to timely delivery on future contracts—not good for a new JIT contract. What must the buyer do to regain his or her rights? The two legal requirements are:

1. Give explicit written notice to the supplier.
2. Provide the supplier a reasonable period of time to gear up to meet the new delivery requirements.

With respect to the timing of design or configuration changes, the contract should always specify the minimal lead time, in terms of days or weeks of material usage, that the supplier will accept prior to supplying the modified material. Both parties should know what the supplier's planned inventory levels are so the firm is not likely to be left with an unusable stock built to the buyer's specifications. By the same token, the two must also agree on the minimum practical lead-time requirements for a delivery lot size increase or an accelerated delivery schedule.

The point is that JIT systems must be able to respond quickly to demand changes because of their tight scheduling and low inventory characteristics on the buyer's side. These requirements for flexibility must be built into the purchase contract to the extent possible. Although meshing the buyer's needs with the supplier's capability may be difficult, it is these issues that should be discussed ahead of time, agreed on, and stated in the contract.

Inspection and acceptance is another area that can pose problems. Many JIT shipments are delivered directly to the point of use, without first going through incoming inspection. In many cases, detection of nonconforming items does not occur until some time later, after the item has entered the production process. If no provision for this situation is made in the contract, legally the material may be considered to have been accepted when delivered. Consequently, this modified operating procedure should be detailed clearly in the contract. A satisfactory time frame for acceptance and the responsibility for subsequent rework costs should be stipulated.

In structuring JIT purchase orders and contracts, common sense tells the buyer to be conservative and to include ample detail about these unique issues in the contractual documents.

Honest Mistakes

When an honest mistake is made in drawing up a purchase contract, the conditions surrounding each specific case weigh heavily in determining whether the contract is valid or void. As a general rule, a mistake made by only one party does not render a contract void, unless the other party is aware or should be aware of the mistake. To affect a contract, a mistake usually must be made by both parties. Even then, not every mutual mistake invalidates the contract.

Assume, for example, that a supplier intends to submit a quotation with a price of $260. Through an error, the price is typed on the quotation as $250 and is so transmitted to the buyer. In such cases, courts have held that if the buyer accepts the offer, without knowledge of the error, a valid contract exists. The magnitude of the error is deemed insufficient to affect agreement materially. On the other hand, if the $260 price were incorrectly typed as $26, the court would probably hold that a competent buyer should recognize the error, and if one party knows or should know of the other's error, the contract is void.

Mutual mistakes concerning matters of opinion usually do not affect a contract. Neither is a contract affected by immaterial mutual mistakes about matters of fact. However, a mutual mistake concerning matters of fact that materially affect agreement usually renders a contract void. Assume, for example, that a buyer and a supplier agree on the sale of specific machinery. If, unknown to either, the machinery has been destroyed or for some other reason is not available for sale, the contract is void.

Generally speaking, a buyer should not assume that a mistake, however innocent, will release his or her firm from a contractual obligation. In the majority of cases, it will not do so. A prudent buyer employs all reasonable means to minimize the possibility of committing contractual mistakes.

Patent Infringement

The law gives a patent holder the exclusive right to manufacture, sell, and use the patented device for a specified number of years. A purchaser who engages in any of these activities during the period of patent protection, without permission from the patent holder, is guilty of patent infringement and can be sued for damages by the patent holder.

Supply managers frequently have no way of knowing whether their suppliers are selling patented materials with or without authorization from the patent holder. If a purchaser unknowingly buys an item from a supplier who has infringed the patent holder's rights, the purchaser is also guilty of infringement if the firm uses the item. To protect against such unintentional violations, most companies include a protective clause in their purchase orders which states that the seller will indemnify the purchaser for all expenses and damages resulting from patent infringement. Clauses of this type do not prevent the patent holder from suing the user. If properly stated, however, they can require the seller to defend the user in such legal proceedings and can give the user legal recourse to recover any resulting losses from the seller.

Infringement suits are rare in the normal course of business activities. However, one area in which most manufacturing firms frequently encounter potential infringement problems is in the maintenance of productive equipment. In some cases, a complete machine is patented, but its individual parts are not. In other cases, individual parts are patented. In cases in which the individual part is not patented, the owner of the machine usually has the right to make a replacement part or to have it made by an outside shop. When the individual part is patented, however, this cannot be done legally without permission from the patent holder.

On the other hand, if the owner of a patented machine wishes to rebuild the machine substantially, such activity is not considered within the range of normal maintenance and repair activity. To accomplish a rebuilding job, the owner must either have it done by the patent holder or obtain the patent holder's permission to do the job himself or herself.

Restraint of Trade Laws

The Robinson-Patman Act, a 1936 amendment to the Clayton Act, is designed to prevent price discrimination that reduces competition in interstate commerce. Generally speaking, the act prevents a supplier from offering the same quantity of a specific material to competing buyers at different prices, unless (1) one buyer is offered a lower price because his or her purchases entail lower manufacturing or distribution costs for the supplier, or (2) one buyer is offered a lower price in order to meet the legitimate bid of a competing supplier.[8]

---

[8]A third condition also permits the offering of a discriminatory price—namely, one in which the marketability of goods is affected. Seasonal goods or those approaching obsolescence or deterioration fall into this category.

All supply management professionals should be familiar with the detailed provisions of the act, because the act also makes it unlawful for any buyer knowingly to induce or receive a discriminatory price. Thus, if a buyer accepts a price known to be discriminatory, the buyer violates the law to the same extent as the supplier. The act does not prevent a buyer from seeking legitimate price concessions. It is imperative, however, for a buyer to ensure that any price concessions gained are in fact justifiable under the act.

In practice, the act has been enforced primarily in questionable situations involving retail industry purchases for resale to consumers. Historically, less than 5 percent of the Robinson-Patman case investigations have involved industrial materials and equipment. As a practical matter, then, while industrial purchasers clearly should operate within the provisions of the act, it is unlikely that this legislation will produce significant difficulties for them.

Nearly every state also has its own price discrimination legislation applicable to intrastate transactions. Since these laws vary widely from state to state, each buyer likewise should be familiar with the regulations in his or her state.

Product Liability

Product liability is the responsibility held by manufacturers and downstream sales organizations to pay for injuries to users (or bystanders) caused by defective or unreasonably hazardous products. During the past several decades court decisions and interpretations of legal theories have produced a marked change in the legal environment surrounding such issues. Not only are business firms now placed at greater risk—so are their supply management departments.

Two things, for the most part, have acted as catalysts to produce the sensitive situation that exists in this area today. The first was the case of *Greenbaum v. Yuba Power Products, Inc.,* handed down by the California Supreme Court in 1963. The decision concluded that "a manufacturer is strictly liable when an article he places on the market, knowing that it may be used without inspection, proves to have a defect that causes injury to a human being." The practical result of this decision was that to obtain legal redress an injured user had to prove only that the product was defective and that it caused the injury. The earlier requirement that the manufacturer be proved negligent was eliminated. Since then, a majority of the states have followed the precedent set by the California court. Additionally, over the years the strict liability concept has been extended to cover all goods, not just consumer items.

The second major occurrence was the gradual elimination of the long-standing requirement for "privity of contract" in product liability cases. Originally, if an injured user sued the manufacturer on the grounds that it had breached the product warranty, the user was required to have a purchase contract directly with the manufacturer. Since this was often not the case, the elimination of this requirement facilitated the user's access to the courts for recovery. Subsequently, court interpretations frequently extended liability to the wholesalers and retailers of the manufacturer's product. Thus, the injured party could seek redress at any point in the manufacturer-distribution chain.

For professional supply managers, the bottom line of this evolutionary pattern of events is very clear—and important. Product liability suits have skyrocketed during the past decade. Most manufacturing and distribution firms now assume a much greater potential risk than in earlier years. Whether a buyer or supply manager is purchasing a chemical compound for use within the organization or buying component parts that go into the firm's finished product, he or she often has a magnified responsibility to safeguard the interests of the firm. This requires an added emphasis on the following activities:

1. *Initial supplier investigation*—with respect to quality capability, quality control, and reliability.

2. *Purchase order or contract preparation*—with respect to clear and complete communication of specification, operating, and safety requirements, as well as test and inspection procedures.

3. *Coordination with quality control and inspection personnel*—to ensure jointly that adequate procedures are being used. Further, the buyer must ensure adequate coordination between the quality control personnel of both firms on problem issues.

4. *In the case of potentially hazardous materials*—clear communication to all users within the organization of information dealing with warnings, safety measures, usage instructions, and so on. (Material safety data sheets.)

5. *Documentation for all the preceding activities*—even though the buyer's performance may have been first-rate, it is imperative that the purchasing and quality control records show clearly what was done, and that it was done prudently and well.

In summary, from a materials point of view, supply managers assume an added responsibility to minimize the exposure of their firms to potential product liability litigation.[9]

International Considerations

When a supply manager sources outside the United States, the chances are very good that a different set of laws will govern the related purchasing transactions. If stipulated and agreed on in the contract, the governing law could be U.S. law, or it could be the law of the supplier's country. More commonly stipulated today is the United Nations' Convention on contracts for the International Sale of Goods (CISG).

In any case, in international or global procurement, it is particularly important to stipulate in the purchase order or contract which body of law is acceptable to both the buyer and the seller—and subsequently will govern the transaction. Likewise, it is also important to stipulate a mutually acceptable "choice of forum"—that is, the location at which the lawsuit will be heard, in the event a legal dispute arises.

As pointed out earlier, litigation is a time-consuming and costly way to solve domestic disputes. In the case of international disputes, litigation is even more time-consuming and more costly. Consequently, it is usually more sensible to settle such disputes by means of arbitration. Most, though not all, lawyers recommend that international contracts contain a provision for the settlement of a potential dispute through private arbitration, rather than resorting to court action.

The following sections provide an overview of two key topics for international purchasers—the CISG and the Foreign Corrupt Practices Act.

---

[9]For a thorough analysis of purchasing's responsibility in the area of product liability, see R. J. Adams and John R. Browning, "Purchasing and Product Liability," *Journal of Purchasing and Materials Management,* Summer 1989, pp. 2–9.

Contracts for the International Sale of Goods

During the early 1980s, the United Nations facilitated the development of a uniform body of law to govern contracts for the international sales of commercial goods. As noted above, the title given to this body of law is the United Nations' Convention on Contracts for the International Sale of Goods, commonly known as the CISG. The CISG's objective is much like the objective of the Uniform Commercial Code, projected to the international level. The CISG does not apply to the purchase of services or to personal purchases of consumer goods.

Generally speaking, the CISG and the UCC have more similarities than differences. However, there are five significant differences that supply professionals should know about:

- **Acceptance of an offer.** The CISG requires that an offer be accepted in identical terms—the mirror image concept. If an acceptance contains terms that conflict with those in the offer, no contract exists.

- **Contract price.** An offer must contain a firm price or a precise procedure for determining a price. Without this provision, no contract exists under the CISG. The UCC is somewhat more lenient on this issue.

- **Revocation of an offer.** The CISG permits an offer to be revoked any time before an acceptance is received. One exception is, "if it was reasonable for the offeree to rely on the offer as being irrevocable and the offeree acted in reliance on the offer," then the offer cannot be revoked. This revocation provision is less stringent than its counterpart in the UCC.

- **Formation of a contract.** Under the CISG, a contract is created at the time the acceptance is received by the offeror. Under the UCC, the contract is created when the acceptance is mailed or transmitted to the offeror.

- **Oral contracts.** The CISG recognizes oral contracts as being valid and enforceable. In contrast with the UCC, contracts exceeding $500 in value do not require written evidence.

CISG use by American purchasers is placed in focus by the following statement of an internationally known legal authority:

> The similarities between the CISG and the UCC are sufficient enough so business executives do not have to make an issue out of which set of rules applies. On the other hand, one should always be aware that there are these two sets of rules, and in specific cases one may be preferable to the other. In any event, the CISG would appear to be preferable (from the U.S. standpoint) to agreeing to (the use of) another country's law.[10]

Foreign Corrupt Practices Act[11]

In the early 1970s Congress and the American public learned about a number of questionable payments made by U.S. multinational corporations to foreign government offi-

---

[10]W. A. Hancock, "The UN Convention on the International Sale of Goods," *Executive Legal Summary,* May 1993, p. 100.004.

[11]This discussion is based on material presented by Glenn A. Pitman and James P. Sanford, "The Foreign Corrupt Practices Act Revisited: Attempting to Regulate Ethical Bribes in Global Business," *The International Journal of Purchasing and Materials Management,* Summer 1994, pp. 15–20.

cials to gain an advantage in bidding for business contracts awarded by those governments. As a result of the strong negative public reaction to these shady business dealings, appropriate federal agencies investigated the international activities of U.S. firms that appeared to involve the possibility of commercial bribery. The investigation identified several hundred major firms that had been involved in such questionable dealings with potential international customers.

As a result of these findings, in 1977 Congress passed the Foreign Corrupt Practices Act (FCPA) as an amendment to the Securities Exchange Act of 1934. The objective of the new act was to curtail U.S. corporate involvement in foreign commercial bribery activities—and more generally to enhance the image of the United States throughout the world.

The FCPA contains three major sections focusing on (1) antibribery issues, (2) record-keeping requirements, and (3) penalty provisions. The antibribery section makes it a crime for a U.S. firm to offer or to make payments or gifts of substantial value to foreign officials. The intent is to prohibit payments in any form to influence a major decision of a foreign government official.

Somewhat to the contrary, however, is the fact that the act does allow some forms of bribery—those that are considered to be minor and inconsequential in influencing important government decisions. It is permissible to make payments to operating officials with ministerial or clerical duties. Although the FCPA is vague with respect to the details of application, the Omnibus Trade Act of 1988 specifies what types of payments are acceptable and who may receive them. Such payments are termed "transaction bribes" and are intended to accelerate the performance of a routine function, such as loading and unloading cargo, processing goods through customs promptly, moving goods across country, processing papers, and so on. It is expected that these types of payments may speed up governmental actions by lower-level officials that, in time, would have occurred anyway.

All other types of bribes are considered illegal. As the law now stands, the Omnibus Trade Act holds a firm criminally liable if evidence indicates that one of its representatives had actual knowledge that an illegal payment was made to a foreign government official to secure a favorable decision on a major issue.

Clearly, the FCPA and the related Omnibus Trade Act were designed primarily to curb unacceptable international sales practices. At the same time, however, they apply to international procurement practices. Supply professionals engaged in international buying should understand the provisions of these acts, and they must know the difference between acceptable transaction bribes and bribes whose intent and motivation are illegal.

Concluding Remarks

The purpose of this chapter is to alert supply management professionals to the most basic legal considerations that relate to the supply management function. Yet there is danger in doing this. No author can briefly accomplish this objective without simplifying the issues. Such simplification may at times leave the reader with an incomplete understanding which lulls him or her into a false feeling of security.

Even though adoption of the UCC by all but one of the states creates greater uniformity among state commercial laws than ever before, it is unreasonable to assume that interpretations of the laws by the various states will not vary. Only time can reveal how significant such variations will be. Moreover, the interpretation of circumstances surrounding each specific case weighs heavily in the analysis of that particular case. These factors virtually defy a definite and unqualified analysis of a legal controversy by anyone who is not a highly skilled professional in the legal field. Heinritz, Farrell, Guinipero, and Kolchin state the matter cogently in saying that "the person who tries to be his or her own lawyer has a fool for a client."[12] Perhaps the most important function of this chapter, therefore, is to underscore that supply professionals should seek sound legal counsel whenever potential legal problems arise.

Just as a lawyer is expected to exhibit skill in extricating his or her client from legal entanglements, so a supply management executive is expected to exhibit skill in avoiding legal controversies. A supply manager must understand basic legal concepts well enough to detect potential problems before they become realities. At the same time, the most powerful tool he or she can utilize to avoid legal problems is skill in selecting sound, cooperative, and reliable suppliers. Vigilance in this area of responsibility minimizes the need for legal assistance.

---

[12]Stuart Heinritz, Paul Farrell, Larry Guinipero, and Michael Kolchin, *Purchasing Principles and Applications* (Englewood Cliffs, NJ: Prentice-Hall, 1991), p. 241.

PART 7

Institutional and Government Procurement

We have argued for years that sound procurement and, more recently, World Class Supply Management[SM] practices apply in all settings: commercial, institutional, and governmental. At the same time, we recognize that there are several nuances in institutional and government procurement which deserve to be addressed. We are extremely fortunate to have acquired the assistance of several successful practitioners in both settings who have made Chapters 25 and 26 timely and insightful.

Gears *(Nick Dolding/Stone/Getty Images)*

25 CHAPTER

Institutional Supply Management[1]

Supply Management in institutions, long thought the bastion of inefficiency and waste locked in the clerical stage of purchasing, has quietly evolved toward World Class Supply Management^{SM}.

KEY CONCEPTS

---

[1]Appreciation is expressed to Chuck Noland of the QP group, PLC, London, for his assistance in upgrading this chapter. Mr. Noland has extensive experience in institutional supply management. His expertise includes working at Lawrence Livermore National Laboratories and Kaiser Permanente where he was the vice president of Supply Chain Management.

Case

MFC Status at Kipling Health Care[2]

Sara Parker, a recently hired capital equipment supply specialist for Kipling Health Care of California, mulled over a 7 million dollar two-year contract for computer systems awarded to Ace Computer nearly two years ago. Kipling was a small player in the California health care industry in comparison to institutions such as Blue Cross/Blue Shield and Kaiser Permanente. Ace Computer was one of the largest computer manufacturers in the world. Sara had been assigned to review the "single-source" contract with Ace to determine the best course of action for Kipling after the contract expired.

Having studied internal customer surveys, Sara knew that Kipling's employees were satisfied with Ace Computer. Changing suppliers could be disruptive to Kipling in two ways. First, a new supplier could mix incompatible or difficult-to-integrate hardware and software with the systems installed by Ace. Second, Kipling would need to restart its hardware, software and supplier collaboration learning curves if a new supplier was selected. Based on the satisfactory surveys and the potential disruptions of selecting a new supplier, Sara believed it would be best to negotiate a new two-year contract with Ace that would essentially continue the successful relationship Kipling and Ace had developed over the last several years.

At a recent Institute for Supply Management conference in San Francisco, Sara had lunch with supply professionals from other health care organizations where she shared details about the contract with Ace. Through the discussion, Sara discovered that Ace was not giving Kipling the lowest prices possible, called most favored company (MFC) status. She was not alone in the discovery; several of her peers at small and medium-size institutions were also paying higher prices. Sara felt that Ace should give Kipling MFC status since Kipling was a nonprofit organization and Ace was giving MFC status to other institutions. Based on her discussions with her peers at the conference, she estimated that the discount for the computer systems with MFC status would reduce the price charged to Kipling by 1.5 percent, or $405,000 dollars if the purchases under the new contract were the same as the last contract.

Sara pondered several questions. "Was her predecessor unaware of the MFC discount? If her predecessor was unaware of the discount, then why did the supplier withhold the

---

[2]The case given is fictitious, but does present a common problem encountered in institutional supply management that is discussed later in this chapter.

information? Perhaps the supplier's salespeople did not know that Kipling was a nonprofit organization? Should she use the pricing information that she obtained from her peers at the conference in the next negotiation with Ace? Would there be a backlash by Ace Computer if Kipling pushed for MFC? Was there an approach that she had not considered?"

Introduction

The evolution of countries from agrarian to industrialized in the nineteenth century was followed by the evolution from manufacturing to services in the twentieth century. In no country has this evolution been more complete than in the United States. By spending more for *services* than for *goods,* the United States, over the last two decades, has developed into the world's largest service economy. Because the national demand for services continues to grow faster than the demand for goods, the economy is increasingly service oriented.

This chapter focuses on supply management for educational and health care institutions—two fast-growing service industries. Most of what is said, however, applies to all other types of institutions, such as penal institutions, art galleries, libraries, and similar state and local government institutions. When educational institutions are discussed, the emphasis is on colleges and universities. Because the supply operations of these institutions cover the entire spectrum of educational buying, a discussion of purchasing at this level also includes the purchasing considerations of elementary and secondary schools. Supply management differences which exist among schools are generally ones of degree, rather than substance.

Buying for institutions is big business![3] Schools and hospitals[4] are a large segment of the U.S. economy. Their economic size alone makes them important. In 1999 the cost of U.S. education at all levels exceeded $618 billion.[5] Medical services are growing at an even faster rate than education. In fact, medical services now represent the nation's fastest-growing industry. In 1998 the cost of health care was just over $1.1 trillion.[6] Health care institutions are transitioning from predominately not-for-profit to predominately for-profit institutions. The result is the health care market is becoming increasingly competitive.

Every principle of professional supply management discussed in the preceding chapters applies fully to purchases for institutions. All buying activities—whether industrial, governmental, or institutional—have one primary objective: to obtain the maximum value for each dollar spent. There is no separate group of principles for institutional supply management. In comparison with industrial supply management, however, institutional supply management places different emphasis on some of the factors of professional supply management. This chapter examines these differences.

---

[3]For institutions, the cost of materials and business services (including construction costs) averages 20 to 30 percent of total costs, rather than approximately 80 percent, as is the case for manufacturing firms. Nevertheless, the opportunity for cost savings is still important.

[4]The term "hospitals" in this discussion is used generically to include many types of medical institutions, such as clinics, convalescent homes, nursing homes, and similar health care facilities.

[5]U.S. Bureau of the Census, *Statistical Abstract of the United States, 2000,* p. 151.

[6]Ibid., p. 108.

Differences between Institutional and Industrial Supply Management

Control of Budgets

Parkinson's law on budgets states that "expenditures will always rise to exceed income." This "law" applies to many business operations; however, it is especially applicable to institutions, where the determination to control expenditures is not as strong as it is in industry. The concept of "spend it or lose it" still prevails at many institutions, and the cost savings is not accounted for in the bottom line. Until recently, it was easier for schools to raise tuition rates and hospitals to raise room and service rates than it was for industrial companies to raise the selling prices of their products. Consequently, institutions historically have not been motivated to control purchasing costs in the same way as have competitive industrial organizations. It appears, however, that this situation has changed. Governments and individual taxpayers around the world are increasingly concerned about the high cost of both education and medical care.

For example, an increasing number of health care institutions in the United States have become for-profit enterprises creating competition in the health care marketplace. This concern has been forcefully communicated to hospital and school administrators. As costs for these services continue to rise, the United States Congress is directing a larger portion of its investigatory time to these areas of expenditure. Congressional investigations, in turn, invariably result in closer control over the expenditures of government funds, which represent a significant portion of total educational and medical resources.

Savings Purchasing savings from improved Supply Management practices are as valuable to institutions as they are to industry. In industry these savings increase profits and, therefore, increase a firm's capability to survive competitively. For-profit health care institutions must be efficient and competitive to survive. In not-for-profit education and health care, purchasing savings permit a college or hospital to further pursue its goals of better education, better patient care, better physical facilities, better salaries, and so on. Because most supply savings recur year after year, such savings can be viewed much like a gift to an institution's endowment fund. For example, a major university achieved purchasing savings of approximately $2,400,000. With its endowment income generated at roughly an 8 percent earning rate, the $2,400,000 recurring saving is equivalent to an endowment gift of $30,000,000 ($2,400,000/0.08 = $30,000,000). Stated differently, each $1 saved by wise supply management has the same budgetary effect as a $12.50 gift to the institution's endowment fund. In for-profit health care institutions, the value of cost savings flows directly to the bottom line creating shareholders' equity.

Early Supply Management Involvement[7]

The gains from supply management's early involvement in the specification of requirements are especially important to institutions, because an institution buys a much

---

[7]Early supply management involvement is discussed at several points in this book. Refer to the index for exact locations.

broader spectrum of materials and services than does the average industrial firm. Unfortunately, early supply management involvement is the rare exception in many institutions. Although most teachers, researchers, and physicians are exceedingly knowledgeable about their professional specialties, they are not always equally knowledgeable about the principles of procurement for research, instructional, and medical equipment. These practitioners are commonly unaware of options and alternatives in the marketplace and also unaware of the elements of cost and price. These well-intentioned professionals typically specify their purchase requirement by brand name. Too frequently, they conduct *all* the discussions with the prospective supplier. Their focus usually is on the technical and performance aspects of the item. Few users have the orientation or requisite skills to investigate the commercial aspects of a procurement. As a result, the institution commonly pays more than if a qualified supply manager were involved early during the development of the requirement. Such early involvement allows the supply manager to assist his or her customers in selecting the most appropriate *and* nonrestrictive purchase description.

The supply manager should be involved with the user in the initial discussions with prospective suppliers of equipment, supplies, or services. The user (physician, teacher, researcher, or administrator) should focus on the performance aspects of the procurement, while the supply manager focuses on the commercial issues.

For example, assume that a chemistry professor or a medical biologist wants to acquire a complex new microscope. The supply management department can help by arranging for demonstrations of competing microscopes or scintillation machines from several major manufacturers. This is something users typically cannot accomplish by themselves, simply because they do not have the time or economic leverage to do so. The microscope supply manager learns much about many types of microscopes. He or she knows (or can learn) which models are competitive, who sells them, and which distributor has the best facilities for servicing them. Additionally, the supply manager can discuss technical and marketing changes with all manufacturer's representatives. On the other hand, even constant users of microscopes make only infrequent purchases; therefore, they normally do not keep up with the many advancements of all major manufacturers. Because the supply management department buys many things in addition to microscopes from the same distributors of scientific equipment, it usually can obtain a superior response in terms of sales effort, timing, and price.

When it comes to the acquisition of unique or seldom-purchased capital equipment, the technical competence of the customer must be relied upon heavily. The supply management staff can help by working with the user well "upstream" in planning the procurement. Supply management can help with the economic problems of capacity, prices, and obtaining favorable terms and conditions in general. A supply professional is sensitive to the importance of special terms and conditions concerning such things as warranties, responsibility for installation, responsibility for site preparation, follow-up maintenance, maintenance response times in case of problems with equipment, and acceptance testing. It is very important that these items be discussed *before* the purchase and that the understandings between the institution and the supplier be documented in writing. Such action makes the supplier's responsibilities clear and makes enforcing them much more routine when the purchase and delivery take place. Obviously, this is particularly important in the case of expensive procurements, ones which are very complex with regard to installation, calibration, and maintenance, or procurements which extend for a considerable period of time into the future. Institutions, in general, tend to be weak in documenting these requirements and tend unnecessarily to place blind faith in the good intentions of the supplier and the assurances of the sales representative, thereby placing the institution in jeopardy and having little recourse if performance is not satisfactory.

For example, in the purchase of high-speed computer memory units, a competent university purchasing specialist was able to combine his skills effectively with the technical know-how of a systems analyst and the operating experience of a professor. The professor wanted to purchase memory units that would increase the capability of his computer assisted instruction project. Among the problems included in this procurement were funding of the purchase, possible contract cancellation at no cost, deferred delivery of some units, and an option to increase the number of units at the original price approximately one year later. The purchasing specialist entered the procurement picture as soon as the requirement was known. He prepared the request for proposals, sent it to six major firms, participated in the evaluation of the proposals, negotiated with the two firms whose proposals were most favorable, and suggested in detail a possible basis for the manufacturers' financing of the sale. The contract award ultimately was made on the basis of the quality of one manufacturer's product, together with the consideration of its responsiveness to the nontechnical aspects of funding and to other desired contractual provisions. The final unit price, a high six-digit figure, was approximately 15 percent below the best quotation among the other five initial competitive proposals.

Conflicts of Interest

Conflicts of interest in institutional supply management are probably more critical than those in industry. Medical scientists and college professors control millions of research dollars flowing from the government and philanthropic foundations. These individuals, in addition to teaching and conducting research, frequently serve as consultants to industrial companies. Such companies in turn often work on projects similar, if not identical, to those the scientists work on in connection with their research grants. Additionally, some of these same people serve on boards of directors of still other companies that have similar types of research projects. Such relationships can raise many delicate questions of propriety. Consider, for example, patents and royalties. Who owns the patents to and who gets the royalties from a product developed by a consulting professor or researcher while working under a government research contract or grant? Is it the professor, the government agency, or the firm for which he or she is consulting? To confuse a situation that is already vague, various agencies of the federal government (the Departments of Energy, Defense, Health and Human Services, and Education) answer these questions differently! At the same time, some states such as California have financial conflict of interest laws.

In his book *The Closed Corporation—American University in Crisis,*[8] James Ridgeway discusses many questions of this type. Ridgeway points out that the number

---

[8]New York: Random House, 1968.

of professors involved in industry as consultants and directors is growing; an increasing number of dealings between business institutions and university officials has caused an increasing number of conflicts of interest; professors and scientists increasingly are using their prestige as scholars to advance the interest of specific firms, industries, and governmental organizations. Such situations tend to make the individuals involved biased, rather than objective, in their views. In such cases, conflicts of interest can easily follow.

To further compound matters, few institutions have developed clearly defined and effective policies concerning conflicts of interest. Many, however, now are beginning to do so. Congress historically has demanded tight controls in areas where public expenditures are high, and private foundations are now starting to examine very closely the ethical implications of their grants. An important current issue with respect to conflicts of interest is Medicare regulations. These regulations are very specific in banning any payment which may be perceived as a kickback encouraging use of a particular facility by Medicare patients. This is becoming a very touchy issue in such matters as joint ventures between hospitals and physicians for operation of freestanding facilities.

Inspection of Materials and Services

Schools and hospitals have a more difficult problem inspecting purchased items than do industrial organizations. A large university, for example, deals in nearly every field of human knowledge. This requires the purchase of practically the entire range of materials, services, and products developed by humans. The huge range of incoming materials, therefore, makes centralized inspection practically impossible. Too many different kinds of inspectors and too much expensive inspection equipment would be required to perform the function at reasonable cost.

In most universities and medical centers, therefore, receiving departments inspect only for bulk quantity and outward evidences of physical damage. The inspection for unit quantity, quality, and compliance with specifications typically is made by the individual who originated the request for the material. When desired, the receiving department can, of course, inspect for general stores-type or common-use items. Inspection is much less a problem at hospitals where there usually is a central receiving and stores function for hospital supplies.

For complex, high-value products and systems, it is very important to preestablish criteria for acceptance testing. Receiving will not perform acceptance testing; this must be completed in the laboratory, computer center, or the installation site. The purchase contract should include terms for payment only after receipt and acceptance. Acceptance test criteria must be fully documented.

Backdoor Selling

Controlling the visits of sales personnel is considerably more difficult in schools and hospitals than it is in industry. Most physicians, scientists, and professors are extremely individualistic and tend not be organization oriented, at times creating vexing problems in establishing and enforcing effective business procedures. The physical layout of most institutions compounds the problem. For example, most industrial concerns have a reception room, and visitors cannot get past this area without clearance. Such is not the case in most colleges and hospitals; here visitors are free to roam. For these reasons, and also because controls can seldom be accomplished by fiat in an academic, scientific, or medical environment, the supply management department must use the techniques of persuasion to convince its internal customers that using proper supply management procedures is to their advantage.

Naturally, there are many situations in which such individuals have a genuine need to talk with sales representatives. Indeed, as noted previously, institutions must rely on the technical competence of their physicians, academicians, and scientists to develop specifications and to recommend suppliers in those instances in which the item to be purchased is highly unique or complex. In such situations, the supply management staff should do everything possible to bring competent sales personnel (generally sales engineers) and the institution's technical personnel, together.

Controlling sales representatives properly involves scheduling them in accordance with two commonsense alternatives: (1) Those who, from an institutional point of view, can be utilized most effectively in the supply management department should be handled there; and (2) those who can be utilized most effectively by appropriate technical personnel should be assisted in establishing such relationships.

Reciprocity[9]

In theory, reciprocity should be easier to control in institutions than it is in industry; in practice, this often is not the case. Trustees, donors, and alumni on occasion bring great pressure on institutions to purchase a particular company's products or services. Generally, such pressures should be resisted. By its very nature, a school or hospital has nothing to sell back to its potential suppliers. Therefore, when a potential supplier says, "Give me your business because I gave you a donation of $10,000," he or she could in effect be saying, "I really did not want to give you $10,000, but some unstated lesser amount." If the business the donor demands for his or her firm yields a profit in excess of $10,000, then the donor is actually asking the institution to give him or her a gift.

Obviously this is a different situation from the typical scenario involving industrial reciprocity. In industry the objective of reciprocity is, in theory at least, for the buyer and the seller to reach an agreement on an exchange of business that is mutually beneficial. The preceding discussion of reciprocity is not meant to imply that donors cannot be good suppliers. They certainly can be. In fact, when they are willing to compete on the basis of quality, service, and price, they can be the very best suppliers. It is only when they are not willing to compete freely that their motives become suspect. Leading institutions deliberately separate, by policy and procedure, purchasing from any development effort involving gift giving. Supply managers are in a better position to do their job if they can say they have no knowledge of gifts—from whom received, or dollar amounts. At the same time, the development effort benefits from being able to say that it has no connection with the supply management department or any influence over purchasing decisions. In public institutions, all taxpayers are owners and must be given fair and impartial opportunity to be suppliers.

---

[9]Reciprocity is also discussed in the chapter on sourcing, as well as at several other points in this book.

Teachers and Scientists

Teachers and scientists are a valuable national resource. They have no counterparts in industry. Scholars work in industry as well as in the academic world, but when they do, they usually change their orientation. Ph.D.s or M.D.s who work at universities are usually more concerned with their own professional accomplishments than with those of the institution. If offered significantly better laboratories, teaching conditions, and assistants at another institution, frequently they will accept the offer. This is not to imply that such individuals are not loyal to their institutions. Typically, however, their loyalties are first to their professions, and second to their schools. This is the reverse of expected loyalty priorities in the business world.

During their tenure at any firm, business executives' loyalty must be first to the firm and then to their profession; otherwise, neither the executives nor the firms can be fully successful.[10] If any single basic business function in a firm (finance, supply management, personnel, production, engineering, and marketing) fails to perform satisfactorily, the firm as a whole suffers. Business managers, therefore, cannot achieve optimum individual success unless they cooperate and become team players. This is not true for academics. Scientists and teachers can be entities unto themselves. They can succeed or fail individually, without regard to the success or failure of the institutions that employ them. In addition, they are usually less motivated by material rewards than are their colleagues in industry. Typically, it is intellectual and peer recognition that inspires scientists and researchers to do their best.

Working successfully with this kind of person requires different appeals and techniques from those used in industry. Nevertheless, these professionals are concerned with getting the greatest possible mileage from their research and teaching dollars. In almost all institutions, the cost savings achieved remains in the budget and makes a direct contribution to the project. This can be a great motivation for supply professionals to participate and contribute to the project. The supply management department that proves its ability to help them achieve this goal will be welcome as a member of *their* team.

Differences between Public and Private Institutions

There can be notable differences between the supply management responsibilities of public and private institutions. Some public schools and hospitals are completely free from political supply management constraints. Such freedom, however, is not typical; rather, most public institutions are highly constrained by governmental regulations in their operations. Private institutions, on the other hand, are usually free to use their economic power in the way they deem most appropriate.

---

[10]"Loyalty" as used in this statement is not meant to imply that businesspeople would be disloyal by leaving a firm. As a matter of fact, a typical career includes employment in three or four different firms.

A primary objective of most public and private institutions is to create goodwill for the institution. Goodwill is achieved when the public feels assured that an institution treats all interested parties impartially. To satisfy such diverse institutional groups as alumni, trustees, donors, business firms, and governmental agencies, a private institution has no rational alternative but to buy without favoritism, just as public institutions are required to do by law. The difference between supply management for public and private institutions is not a matter of concept; rather, it is a matter of how the concept of buying without favoritism is implemented. Political pressures frequently cause public institutions to carry otherwise sound concepts to ridiculous extremes. For example, public institutions are often forced to use competitive bidding when negotiation would produce both lower total costs and better service.[11]

Application of Basic Principles in Institutional Supply Management

Centralization

In a large research-oriented institution, the broad scope of technical effort and the complete lack of departmental routine in many situations make it difficult to centralize supply management. To complicate matters further, universities tend to spread themselves over large physical areas. (A wit once defined a university as a "collection of colleges and schools connected more or less by inadequate plumbing.")

Coordinating widely separated organizational units is difficult under any circumstances, but in an atmosphere of academic freedom, it is especially difficult. In an academic environment, very few things can be accomplished by edict. Consequently, it is generally unwise to attempt a total centralization of the institution's supply management activities. Nevertheless, centralization benefits are as valid in an institutional setting as in a business setting. Competent institutional management, therefore, should strive to achieve centralization of the supply management function to the greatest degree practical.

Supply management authorities estimate that a well-run centralized supply management operation can achieve savings of 10 to 15 percent compared with a decentralized operation. Additionally, centralized supply management allows suppliers to give institutions better service, as well as better prices, because their expenses are reduced. Specifically, their sales representatives have fewer people to call on, fewer orders have to be serviced, fewer invoices have to be prepared, fewer shipments have to be made, fewer financial records have to be kept, and so on. The solution for many universities is a combination of both: a central supply management department for high-value/complex procurements and a decentralized approach for small-value routine items purchased directly by campus departments. The University of California, Berkeley, has delegated small-value purchasing and procurement credit cards to departments. The campus departments can directly order items up to $500. Items over $500 are processed through a department called Central Purchasing. In this large institution, 90 percent of the dollars, but only 10 percent of the trans-

---

[11]For a discussion on the criteria for using bidding, see the chapter on sourcing.

actions, are processed through Central Purchasing. By decentralizing the small-value purchasing activities, Central Purchasing is better able to focus on cost savings, service, and quality. Central Purchasing performs a leadership role in the departments' small-value purchasing activities by managing the procurement credit card system, providing approved sources, and negotiating University of California discounts.

Cooperative Purchasing

When properly guided, cooperative institutional supply management can be beneficial. Many colleges and universities have affiliated with the Educational and Institutional Cooperative Service, Inc. (E&I), an activity of the National Association of Educational Buyers, of Woodbury, New York. This national organization provides many useful services to its members. Because of the nominal cost of affiliation, a college or university cannot prudently take the financial risk of not joining E&I. Even one small purchase against any E&I contract may result in savings well in excess of the small affiliation fee.

The last decade has experienced the growth of Group Purchasing Organizations as a widespread sourcing solution for the health care industry. Group Purchasing Organizations are independent, for-profit, enterprises that provide leveraged sourcing to health care institutions. Premier, Broadlane, and Novation are GPOs competing in this marketplace. The GPOs negotiate pricing based on the combined leverage of all the member clients. The total leverage may be billions of dollars. This allows the small and medium hospitals to achieve the same discounts as a large health care organization with a billion dollar spend. The GPO earns a margin on the purchase to cover administration and profit, but still provides lower prices to the hospitals. This has proven so effective that some of the largest health care organizations are determining that the GPO is valuable. Both Kaiser Permanente and Tenet, two of the largest health care organizations, are clients of Broadlane.

Price

Until recently, many suppliers granted special prices to institutions, especially to schools and hospitals. Suppliers used to feel it was their philanthropic and patriotic duty to help these institutions financially. However, that was when the institutional market was small and financially unimportant. The health care market is transitioning to large, for-profit institutions such as Tenet and Columbia HCA. The present market has changed. Today, most suppliers view the institutional market as large, choice, highly profitable, and deserving of their best sales effort. To obtain fair prices in such a market, institutions must have supply managers and materials managers who have the knowledge and intellectual capacity to negotiate effectively with their highly competent sales counterparts.

Institutions, as a group, continue to violate one of the basic principles of good supply management—that of *not disclosing prices.* Many small institutions (especially hospitals) waste their time and money trying to improve their prices by making price comparisons with other institutions. This practice frequently penalizes the efficient institution while seldom helping the inefficient one. No rational sales representative will offer a price concession to a supply manager who he or she suspects will disclose this fact to other supply managers, who in turn would soon pressure the sales representative for the same low price. Institutions should follow the pricing practices set forth in every chapter in this book. These are the only effective practices for achieving good pricing.

Personnel

Despite their rapid growth thus far, many schools and hospitals have lagged behind industry and government in recruiting the most competent supply management personnel. Historically, institutional salary levels have been lower than industry's. As they "grew up," hospitals and schools were considered places of service that primarily attracted employees who were not materially oriented. For example, nurses are paid less than senior secretaries, and college professors' salaries usually are lower than those of some of their recent master's level graduates working in industry. The salaries for supply management personnel tend to be similarly low. Fortunately, institutional salaries are now becoming more competitive.

There is no need for institutions to deceive themselves about supply management salaries. Good supply management results primarily from professional competence. Determining the best combination of quality, service, and price is the result of actions such as effective negotiation, value analysis, supplier analysis, cost analysis, and price analysis—all actions requiring a high level of professional competence. As with other settings in industry and government, supply management makes its greatest contribution during the identification and development of requirements. Supply management must be proactively involved in this process, whether for materials, equipment, or services. The lack of highly skilled personnel in health care supply management is another reason sourcing through a GPO may be an attractive alternative.

Organization

Where a supply management department is located within an entity's organizational structure greatly influences the department's ability to function optimally and to influence the decision-making process within the entity. A significant percentage of industrial supply managers report directly to the chief executive of their companies or to a senior vice president. In government, procurement invariably reports to the chief executive officer of the unit to which the supply management department is attached. Institutions have routinely placed their supply management departments too low in the management structure. Hospitals particularly have been guilty of this error. Undoubtedly, this is another reason why some hospitals have experienced difficulty in attracting top supply management talent, and an additional reason to consider outsourcing to a GPO.

The pursuit of and the administration of government research contracts frequently entail organizational problems that also lead to ineffective procurement performance. Traditionally, one organizational unit of the university (often called "research administration") is charged with the responsibility of negotiating the university's research contracts with the government. Another organizational unit (the supply management department) is responsible for negotiating the subcontracts for all goods and services purchased from outside suppliers with funds from the government. Close coordination between these two university offices—research administration and supply management—is essential to ensure that the funds allocated under various government research contracts are (1) handled properly within the constraints of government procurement regulations, (2) expended properly in accordance with the terms of the contract, and (3) processed expeditiously to accomplish the institution's goals. In practice, such coordination frequently does not exist. Too often, the two organizational units even report to different functional heads. Consequently, many universities fail to gain the benefits which can result from an effective organization of their total government research procurement contracting effort.

Government Research Contracts

Government research contracts and grants are a major source of income for a research-oriented institution. Such contracts generally entail a highly sophisticated procurement activity. Any research effort can require complex negotiation, plus the preparation and management of complex contracts. Government research can be even more complex because it involves increasingly severe constraints. As a contractor with the United States, an institution must comply with government regulations and undergo a periodic review of its procurement system. Often, this review is made under the auspices of the Department of Defense. The Federal Acquisition Regulation (FAR) requires a review of an institution's procurement techniques when "the procurement work being done is complex and the dollar value is substantial." This audit is called a contractor procurement systems review (CPSR).

It is highly desirable for an institution to get its supply management techniques approved by the government through a regularly scheduled CPSR. Without such approval, the government will examine each subcontract involving government funds. FAR states: "Reliance upon a contractor's approved procurement system will usually obviate the need for reviewing and consenting to individual subcontracts."

Educating supply management personnel in the specifics of government procurement is extremely important. An institution can best satisfy government requirements for good supply management by hiring personnel with recognized competence in the field of government procurement. Also, as discussed earlier in this chapter, institutions can optimize their benefits from government contracts if all institutional operations regarding government contracts are coordinated and controlled by a single organizational unit.

Special Considerations

Insurance

Institutions are concerned with a large variety of activities, ranging from the operation of small electrical shops to the operation of huge linear accelerators. Also, colleges and hospitals are concerned with the physical presence of large and diverse groups of people, including faculty, staff, students, patients, and a continuous stream of visitors. For these reasons, the insurance requirements for institutions are usually more complex than those for industrial operations.

Purchasing insurance involves the application of the same principles used to purchase other services and commodities. The first procedural step—and the critical one—

is to prepare a list of exactly what categories of insurance are needed. Competent brokers or agents (the suppliers) can assist in this step. Specifically, they can caution institutions not to overlook their unusual and unique risks. For example, a college should insure against the risk of a chartered airplane crashing with its football team aboard. In the event of such a tragedy, claims far in excess of the insurance carried by the airline would result.

After an institution's insurance needs have been determined and listed, an effective broker or general agent can assist the institution in developing competition between appropriate underwriters. Competition for insurance coverage is not confined to price alone; traditionally, reliability and service are more important than price. Hence, in evaluating insurance agents and brokers, an institution must consider not only their ability to assist in selecting the correct coverage, but also their capability to help in settling claims quickly and inexpensively.

For the same reason that health care and educational institutions are concerned about their insurance coverage, it is particularly important that the supply management department ensure all suppliers have adequate insurance. When a supplier is going to deliver a product or provide a service on campus or in the hospital, supply management must receive and retain documentation that the supplier has adequate insurance coverage and designate the university or hospital as a co-insured. The risk management department generally establishes the required coverage and dollar amounts. The supply management department requires the supplier to submit a declarations sheet from its insurance carrier exhibiting the levels of insurance and naming the institution as a co-insured.

Construction and Furnishings

New construction and remodeling programs at medical and educational institutions constitute a significant part of their total expenditures. Furthermore, because construction costs are currently rising at a rate considerably above the average of other operating costs, these costs could become even more significant in the future. The interested reader is encouraged to review the section on procurement of construction in the services chapter.

Interior Furnishings   When possible, it is profitable for an institution to buy interior furnishings— such things as chalkboards, classroom and office furniture, carpets, drapes, laboratory equipment, and scientific instruments—directly from manufacturers. If such items are purchased through an architect, a general contractor, or a contract furnisher, the institution frequently pays higher prices. Prices can be as much as 40 percent above those at which the institution can purchase the items directly; typically, the middleman's markup ranges from 10 to 40 percent. Not only will the institution save on markups by purchasing directly, but since most institutions are tax-exempt, they will save a substantial amount of sales tax also.

Naturally, when an institution's supply management department contracts for the interior furnishings of a building, additional but financially rewarding work results. The methods of delivery and installation are particularly important in this context. The delivery and installation responsibilities and coordination should be very carefully spelled out in the purchase order.

Interior designers are primarily concerned about the appearance of the institution on opening day. And clearly this is important. Frequently, however, they are not very sensitive to the ongoing operational needs of the institution. For example, designers frequently specify custom fabrics primarily on the basis of style and appearance; often, however, such fabrics are very difficult to replace in case of damage or stain. Both the supply manager and the user must be sensitive to the designer's orientation, but they must also ensure that the issues of maintenance and serviceability are addressed.

One category of interior furnishings deserves special mention. Typically, as much as 90 percent of the total demand for educational office, classroom, and library furniture occurs in the summer and early fall months. Consequently, significant savings can result when orders for such furnishings are placed as far as possible in advance of desired delivery dates. Furniture manufacturers can schedule the production of long lead-time orders at times when factory workloads are light. This makes it possible for such manufacturers to price on a marginal cost basis and for institutions to receive the ultimate in good pricing. One college saved over 30 percent (over $1 million) on the cost of furniture for its new married student housing unit by placing its order eight months in advance of the date the furniture was actually needed. This saving was realized despite payment of five months' commercial storage charges.

Stores

Institutions have the same reasons as industry for carrying items in inventory—economy and service. Economy results from savings made through quantity buying with its resultant savings in paperwork, handling, and prices. Service results from having items immediately available. Stores items provide a buffer between fluctuations in demand and changes in lead time; thus they protect an institution's using department against uncertainty and delay. It is important to avoid carrying duplicated brands of the same functional item, because of the additional costs of maintaining the items in inventory and the additional cost of maintaining adequate safety stocks. This is a particularly important function in hospitals and one which ordinarily receives a good bit of attention.

In addition to economy and service, the modern university campus and some hospitals have engendered another very practical reason for having a stores system: congestion. If materials were to be delivered by suppliers as needed to each using department, most institutions would increase their traffic congestion substantially.

Hospitals must have access to immediate emergency reserves of patient care materials. Loss of life cannot be risked because of such inevitable business failures as strikes, transportation breakdowns, and fires. However, this does not mean that the hospital itself must stock all the required emergency supplies in its own storerooms. Quite the contrary, suppliers can stock many medical supplies for the hospital in their storerooms. The specific items the hospital needs to have stocked, together with their exact quantities, must, of course, be determined in advance. The materials so determined can be included as a legal requirement in the procurement contract. The supplier thus becomes legally bound not only to have these materials on hand, but also to earmark them solely for the hospital making the purchase. The supplier can own and manage the inventory on your site or theirs; this is called vendor managed inventory (VMI), or supplier managed inventory in more progressive firms. The supplier can also provide expensive items on consignment, charging for these items as used (hip and knee replacements, pacemakers, and other expensive items).

Under this concept of supply, the supplier's stores system literally becomes an extension of the hospital's stores system. Additionally, this concept usually permits the hospital to achieve its reserve supply protection at much lower warehousing costs than by using its own storerooms.

The concept just discussed clearly is not limited to medical supplies. It is equally applicable to maintenance, repair, and operating supplies items and to virtually any type of laboratory supplies. Health care and educational institutions are generally far behind the manufacturing or retail sectors in innovative solution, and need to catch up with state-of-the-art inventory management.

Auxiliary Functions

Many institutions find it organizationally desirable to group their auxiliary supply management functions—traffic, receiving, delivery, and surplus—together in what can appropriately be called the "supply services division" or the "materials management department."

Traffic   Many institutions, as contrasted with industry and government, do not have a traffic specialist. Outgoing shipments are small in number, and incoming shipments are usually consigned F.O.B. to the institution. Nonetheless, at the appropriate stage of its development, every institution should consider the advantages of having a traffic specialist. Such an individual is responsible for processing its freight bills for payment (which by law must be paid within five days) and for initiating settlement of its freight claims. In all likelihood, this individual will generate cash savings greatly exceeding his or her salary. In addition, improved traffic and damage claims service will result. For example, one institution's traffic manager, after checking the classification guide for a shipment, challenged the carrier on the classification of a $10,800 shipment. As a result of this challenge, the classification was changed from "electronics" to "radio repair parts mounted on a truck or trailer." The bill was reduced from $10,800 to $4,460, a saving of $6,340.

Receiving   Because institutions do not have production schedules to meet, they sometimes underestimate the importance of the receiving function. Poor receiving can produce costly consequences for institutions, just as it can for industry. Receiving is a critical control point in an institution's materials system. It is at the receiving dock that the paperwork directing the flow of purchased materials and the physical materials themselves meet for the first time. At this meeting, if the receiving function is performed correctly, any existing discrepancies will be uncovered. Errors are easily corrected at this time. If they are not corrected then, however, the cost to correct them later is certain to be higher. This is why the importance of the receiving function should not be underestimated.

Delivery   Many of the materials received from outside suppliers and all materials requisitioned from stores must be delivered to using departments. To the extent possible, the delivery of these two categories of materials should be combined into a single, integrated delivery system. Mail and other items to be delivered to using departments can also be included in this delivery system if such action prevents duplication of effort.

Failing to plan ahead for their materials requirements is a common shortcoming of many institutional departments. To compensate for this lack of planning, many departments frequently want immediate delivery of all materials they requisition, especially stores items. Putting all other aspects of the problem aside, institutions simply cannot afford the cost of making continuous deliveries. Schools, especially, can support only a "reasonable" delivery system, not an "express" delivery system. Each school must determine for itself what is reasonable. This is not always easy to do. Sears, JC Penney, and other similarly successful retailers have found a weekly delivery schedule to their customers to be satisfactory. Some successfully managed industrial firms now operate on a weekly delivery system, for operating supplies, from stores to various shops in their plants. At one time, all these companies thought that daily deliveries were essential for customer and production scheduling satisfaction. There appears to be no reason why institutions should not pattern their delivery systems along commercial lines.

Surplus and Salvage   In institutions, surplus and salvage sales usually are not given the importance industry accords these activities. Institutions, however, are generating larger and larger surpluses of increasing value. One university's surplus and salvage section recently returned over $940,000 in cash to the university. Nearly all of this money came from sales that formerly had not been made, or from sales of materials and equipment that formerly had been made to employees for a token payment. Without a formalized surplus and salvage program, institutions tend to sell surplus materials to employees and friends on a subjective rather than a business basis. The salvage of metals can be a source of significant revenue. Precious metals sometimes can be salvaged from old computer equipment, and such things as silver can be extracted from photographic and X-ray processes. Old film, and the extraction of silver from the chemicals used, can be especially attractive sources of revenues for some institutions.

It is often possible to use surplus items, which have relatively little value, as trade-ins for new purchases. The trade-in is really just a discount, but some suppliers would prefer to document the discount as a trade-in rather than to have a straight discount, which might create problems for them with other customers or with their suppliers.

Concluding Remarks

Most supply management savings available to industry are also available to institutions such as schools and hospitals. To attain these benefits, institutions must take five actions:

1.   Hire enough people to perform the supply management job well.
2.   Compete with industry for competent supply management personnel.
3.   Provide a stimulating environment in which the people hired will be motivated to do excellent work.
4.   Ensure adequate training and advanced education.
5.   Aggregate the purchase spend and negotiate most favored prices either independently or through a cooperative or GPO.

Education and health care institutions must understand what industry has understood for a number of years—money spent intelligently for good purchasing is not an expense, it is an investment!

CHAPTER

26

Government Procurement[1]

World Class Supply Management^{SM} applies every bit as much to government as it does in the private sector. As taxpayers and voters, we must insist on the implementation of WCSM at all levels of government.

KEY CONCEPTS

[1]Appreciation is expressed to Anthony Ratkus, Mariel D'Eustachio, Cathy Etheredge, Steven Staninger, and Larry Wood for their assistance in updating this chapter.

Introduction

The concept of the government as a sovereign power distinguishes governmental procurement from the commercial contracting processes. While many complain that the public purchasing system is bureaucratic, these laws, rules, regulations, policies and procedures exist to separate the political process from the public purchasing process, thus avoiding the perception that politicians have influence over who or what company is awarded business using public funds.

As a sovereign power, the government writes procurement rules through statutes, executive orders, regulations, and policies and procedures. In theory, the government acts in the best interest of all the people. The government can change the procurement rules to its advantage. Policies and procedures provide for equitable adjustment, but the government reserves the right of contract change. It can write and require contract clauses, sometimes extraneous to the overt objective of the contract. Size, purchasing power, and sovereignty give the skilled government acquisition or supply management official great power.

Daniel Gitterman observes, "Presidents have used their power of the purchaser to effect big, even historic changes in national policy on their own administrative or managerial authority. Chief executives since FDR have used their general power of procurement to place conditions on private-sector firms that do business with the federal government. Under the 1949 Federal Property and Administrative Services Act (FPASA), Congress delegated policy-making authority to the president, and presidents have assumed a direct and active supervisory role in procurement and exercised broad 'discretion over how best to achieve a flexible management system capable of making sophisticated judgments in the pursuit of economy and efficiency.' In practice, those wishing to do business with the federal government must meet the president's terms; others either need not enter into a contract or exit ex-post when they oppose the nature of the new provisions."[2]

Steve Kelman, a professor at the John F. Kennedy School, Harvard University, and former head of the Office of Federal Procurement Policy, writes, "contracting management must be considered a core competency of federal organizations. This is different

---

[2]Daniel P. Gitterman, "The President and the Power of the Purchaser," *California Management Review,* Fall 2000, p. 103.

from the traditional view of contracting as a subsidiary administrative function. In the 21st century, contracting management needs to become one of the central concerns of senior political and career executives, viewed the same as other core competencies."[3]

Similarities and Differences

The same fundamental principles which govern private contracts apply to government contracts. Both sets of procurement instruments are a promise or set of promises for which the law provides a remedy if breached. The legal elements of the enforceable private and government contract are also the same, namely, legal capacity of the parties, mutual assent, consideration, lawful purpose, certainty of terms, and being in a form provided by law. Similarly, both government and commercial procurement entities are concerned with buying the "right" quality, in the "right" quantity, at the "right" price and time, and from the "right" source. While the principles are the same, the process is sufficiently different to be worth examining. The following paragraphs highlight some of those differences.

Size

The first thing that catches the eye of the student of government contracting is its sheer magnitude. The numbers are overwhelming. In fiscal year 2000, nearly 10 million procurement actions resulted in an expenditure of $218 billion at the federal level.[4]

Defense and NASA expenditures account for 60 percent of the federal procurement expenditures. Few firms have the manpower, physical capacity, and technological virtuosity required to participate in the research, definition, and production cycle of major defense and space systems. As a result, there are substantial barriers to both entry into and exit from the markets for major weapon and space systems. Therefore, it should not be surprising that names such as General Dynamics, United Technologies, Lockheed Martin, Boeing, and General Electric appear year after year in the roster of firms obtaining the largest portion of Department of Defense (DOD) dollars.

While concentration of economic power is a fact of current U.S. industrial life, no other economic concentration is as great as that represented by the top defense contractors. Also, no other economic block of comparable size sells only or primarily to one customer. The economic and political power potential of this group of concentrated sellers interacting with a single buyer is one that requires constant vigilance. Former President Eisenhower highlighted the importance of this unique situation in his now-famous farewell address as president:

"Now this conjunction of an immense military establishment and a large arms industry is new in the American experience. The total influence—economic, political, and spiritual—is felt in every city, every state, every house, every office of the Federal Government. We recognize the imperative need for this development. Yet, we must not fail to comprehend its grave implications. Our toil, resources, and livelihood are all involved;

---

[3]Steve Kelman, "Contracting at the Core," Internet Message July 30, 2001.

[4]FPDS Federal Procurement Report (http://fpds.gsa.gov/fpds/FPR2000.pdf).

so is the very structure of our society."[5] At the state and local government level, similar pressures can be brought by large corporate entities skilled in political maneuvering. However, states and many localities are also sensitive to local businesses and may have preference programs that favor local establishments.

Lead Time

Lead time is another phase of procurement in which government and industry differ. Here again, the government, for other than business reasons, has added additional costs to its purchasing operation. It should be understood clearly that without restraints government procurement officials could purchase hand tools just as quickly and economically as industrial firms, and with just as few pieces of paper. Government supply managers are fully knowledgeable concerning the hand tools industry and low-cost producers in the industry, yet are mindful that they are stewards of the public trust. The advent of government purchasing cards in recent years has significantly reduced the time and cost to process orders for common commercial items of relatively low value and complexity. Correspondingly, government procurement managers do purchase supplies with the same speed as industry in *emergencies* by using *negotiation.*

Regulations

The decision-making processes of government agencies are governed by numerous regulations. The *Federal Acquisition Regulation (FAR)* is the primary regulation for use by all federal executive agencies in their acquisition of goods and services with appropriated funds. The FAR system has been developed in accordance with the requirements of the Office of Federal Procurement Policy Act. Sources of these policies (the regulation used to guide the Federal Agency in implementing the laws and policies of the United States through the procurement process) include statutes, executive orders, comptroller general decisions, attorney general opinions, agency boards of contract appeals decisions, and federal court decisions. While agencies may supplement the FAR, such additional rules are supposed to be limited to those necessary to implement the regulation's requirements within the agency[6] (and address the unique or unusual circumstances within that agency). At the state and local government level, state statutes are often implemented in "codes" of regulations. Likewise, counties, municipalities and special districts may also have ordinances and implementing regulations.

Sources of Funds

An important difference between industrial and government purchasing is the source of funds used for purchases. At all levels of government, taxes paid by citizens and businesses or debt (such as bonds) are used to purchase required goods and services. Normally, there is no profit incentive to generate funds for ongoing operations. In executing their roles as funds stewards, both the legislative and the executive arms of government

---

[5]President Dwight D. Eisenhower, farewell address, 1961.

[6]The Federal Acquisition Regulation is published under the joint auspices of the Defense Department, the General Services Administration, and the National Aeronautics and Space Administration. It is a living regulation, being frequently changed through the publication of Federal Acquisition Circulars.

promulgate procedures to carefully control funds expenditures. These procedures give government supply managers considerably less flexibility than their industrial counterparts. For example, fixed budgets often stop the government supply manager from taking advantage of quantity discounts and longer-term contracts. Similarly, the rigid requirement for competition and resulting long lead times usually keeps the government supply manager out of the quick-sale marketplace. The rules for competition frequently have been blamed for award to a low bidder who may provide an inferior-quality product. Thus, the contracting process using public funds is probably not as efficient as its commercial counterpart using funds from hard-won prior sales.

Public Review

The expenditure of public funds properly attracts the interest of taxpayers. Except for the relatively small amount of money spent in necessarily classified projects (usually in the interest of national defense), government's expenditures are open to the public. This openness is the result of federal and state constitutions, laws and statutes, and the moral obligation of government. Government contract records and files are subject to review by audit activities. The process is generally required to be conducted in full public view and all actions are a matter of public record usually with only limited exceptions. In contrast, the commercial buyer's requirements, sources, specifications, bid requirements, and prices paid are usually closely held and guarded information because of competitive considerations.

Socioeconomic Programs

The president, Congress, federal agencies, state legislatures, and local governing bodies have used and continue to use the purchasing process to accomplish social or political ends. Such laws as the Buy American Act may restrict the government supply manager from purchasing the lowest-price items that meet requirements. Rules that require purchases to be shipped on ocean-going U.S. carriers often conflict with selection of the lowest-cost carrier. Rules requiring awards to small or so-called disadvantaged businesses usually add to the price of contracts so awarded.

Conservatism

The government procurement process frequently is likened to purchasing in a goldfish bowl wherein everyone can see everything. As is true with many commercial supply management personnel, government acquisition personnel tend to be risk averse and conservative. As public officials, government personnel are subject to public censure. Thus, goldfish bowl procurement exacerbates the tendency to be ultraconservative and to "do it by the book."

Web-Based Government Procurement

The Internet has become accepted as a transaction medium. This realization has public supply professionals seeking ways to use this medium to drive broader access to public contracts and operations that are more efficient. Public institutions have goals which are similar to those of most private organizations seeking to use e-procurement systems.

- *Processes that are automated and more efficient*—Driving to a paperless process eliminates substantial costs in obtaining the goods and services required to operate the public agency.

- *Enforcement of business rules*—Automating the process eliminates deviation from established procedures creating a fairer, more uniform process for potential suppliers and the public institution alike. For example, the County of San Diego found that suppliers were more satisfied with the e-procurement system than its paper-based predecessor because the bid lists were retained electronically. This eliminated the manual system of rotating names on a bid list. By registering online, the supplier receives notification of all potential contracts in his commodity. The perception of public institution buyers showing favoritism to one supplier or another is eliminated.

- *Lower prices from broader competition*—With a simpler process of getting notices of potential contracts, more suppliers respond to online solicitations. The County of San Diego found that in the first year of posting solicitations online it received bids from as far away as Australia.

However, public institutions are also constrained by the requirement to provide equal access to opportunities where public funds are used. In the beginning of e-procurement use by public institutions, many were challenged with the reality that many small companies did not have access to computers, the Internet, or the knowledge to interface with new technology. In response to this situation in 1995, when implementing one of the first e-procurement platforms by government, the County of San Diego installed computers with Internet access in public buildings throughout the county.

Different e-Procurement Options

Most public purchasing organizations operate one of three different e-procurement models. The first and most common method involves the public purchasing organization posting solicitations electronically on the Web for potential suppliers to read only—essentially an electronic bulletin board. This model may have notification capability as well, wherein each new solicitation generates an automatic e-mail to a subset of the supplier list advising it that a new posting has been made. This type of e-procurement process can be used for all buys, from a simple request for a computer workstation to a complex purchase of construction services. The second model allows the supplier to read and respond to the solicitation. In most cases, this means inputting a proposed price back to the assigned supply manager. This model generally is used for easily defined commodity or specific manufacturer's item purchases. This model does not work well when the response to the solicitation is complex—say, for a complex service requirement. The third e-procurement model is a reverse auction. While many public agencies have not yet accepted this type of online procurement because they consider it too deviant from the generally accepted "closed- bid" process, it is still an option although legislative changes might be required to implement it. Reverse auctioning gives suppliers the ability to see what other competitors have proposed and submit a better offer. This process continues until the solicitation time expires. The contract is awarded to the lowest responsive and responsible bidder.

State and Local Government

State and local governments also have great purchasing power in the aggregate. The *Statistical Abstract of the United States* reflects some 80,000 governmental bodies that possess the power to spend.[7] That same publication goes on to indicate that state and local purchases of goods and services have grown from $119 billion in 1970 to an estimated $1 trillion in 1999.

Based on recent research conducted in the United Kingdom, Gordon Murray suggests that "local government purchasing managers could improve their contribution by adopting a more strategic approach to quality improvement and cost reduction by transferring lessons from the private sector.[8] This observation seems equally true in the United States. Like private institutions, many public organizations are challenged with performing their expected services more efficiently. While local agencies rely on public employees to perform mission critical operations such as fire and rescue services, many are reevaluating the noncore services they perform. These public managers are considering outsourcing these noncore services to outside service providers that frequently can perform the services more efficiently. These "outsourced" services can either be support functions such as vehicle maintenance or customer-facing services such as health clinic operations. These make versus buy decisions are especially difficult given that agency employee downsizing can result. For this reason, California has a constitutional provision that prohibits outsourcing any work that can be done by civil service employees. Many times, this issue is addressed by giving the displaced public agency employees an opportunity to become employed by the new service provider.

Sometimes the decision to outsource is not clear-cut. In these instances, many public managers are resorting to a process known as "Managed Competition." Managed competition is a process in which the public service employees compete with potential outside providers to retain their jobs. For example, a county vehicle maintenance garage may compete with outside garages to continue to service the county vehicle pool. The following is a typical process that frequently is followed:

1. The public agency identifies and documents the service requirements. This may entail documenting the statement of work as well as required service levels.

2. The public service organization is evaluated. If the organization is capable of accomplishing the required tasks and service levels, it will be allowed to participate in the solicitation. If it is determined that the public agency is not capable, the service is outsourced.

3. The outside service providers are given the opportunity to provide proposals based on the service requirements. Typically, this is communicated through a Request for Proposal process, based on a carefully developed statement of work. Sometimes the service providers must be prequalified before they are allowed to submit a proposal.

---

[7]U.S. Bureau of the Census, *Statistical Abstract of the United States,* 120th ed., Table No. 500, "State and Local Government Receipts and Expenditures in the National Income and Product Accounts, 1980–1999."

[8]J. Gordon Murray, "Local Government and Private Sector Purchasing Strategy," *European Journal of Purchasing and Supply Management* 7 (2001), p. 98.

4.   The public service organization independently prepares a sealed bid to perform the service.

5.   The best-value, most qualified outside service provider is evaluated.

6.   The public service organization bid is compared to that of the best outside provider.

Whichever organization has the lower bid wins the contract.

Managed competition drives efficiency and innovation. Public organization managers are required to look at their organization as a business and find and implement new and novel ideas to make it more cost effective.

Federal Government
Key Legislative Actions

The first law dealing with government procurement in the United States was passed by Congress in 1792. Under this law, the Departments of War and Treasury were given responsibility to make purchases and contracts in the name of the United States. In 1795, a purveyor of public supplies was established in the Treasury Department to act as the government's purchasing manager. In 1798 a separate Department of the Navy was established, and Congress declared that all purchases and contracts for supplies and services for the military and naval services of the United States should be made by or under the direction of the chief officers of the Departments of War and Navy, respectively.

Considering the historical interest of Congress in the profits of contractors, it is interesting to note that one of the first procurement abuses in government arose from the activities of Congressmen. They used their influence and offices to secure government contracts for their friends and for the firms with which they were associated. This situation resulted in an 1808 law which required a clause in every government contract to stipulate that no member of Congress might benefit therefrom. This clause is still required; it is now known as the "Officials Not to Benefit" clause.

In the early days of the republic, the conduct of public officials left much to be desired. Graft and favoritism in the award of government contracts were commonplace. Incoming administrations investigated the activities of the former administration. The political party out of power kept a watchful eye on the activities of the "ins." Congress soon concluded that the most effective way to prevent procurement abuses was to require that government purchases be made through the use of competitive bids. To implement this conclusion, Congress passed the Procurement Act of March 3, 1809.

This act established a general requirement that formal advertising be used in the procurement of supplies and services for the government of the United States. Over the next 50 years, a series of additional acts extended and sharpened the requirements for formal advertising and financial security from bidders. Subsequently, most state, county, and city governments adopted the same principles that are incorporated in federal government procurement legislation.

Competitive bidding, with relatively few exceptions, served the federal government effectively and adequately for well over 100 years. The increasing complexities of a rapidly evolving technology, however, combined with a dollar volume of purchases undreamed of in the past, caused the competitive bidding system to break down (almost to the point of collapse) at the beginning of World War II. As a result of this breakdown, a negotiated action frequently was substituted for competitive bidding. Local government procurement was not affected by this circumstance; states and local governments do not have the same magnitude of technical problems inherent in federal government procurement. However, in today's environment of high technology and information, many states have adopted statutes permitting negotiation or a modified process for complex transactions.

Buy American Act One of the most complex and well-established procurement processes in the award of government contracts concerns whether or not the item required is produced in the United States. Purchasing items produced within national borders provides an economic incentive for maintaining follow-on production capability. The argument proceeds that such follow-on capability may be vital in times of war, when foreign sources may be inaccessible or undependable. The Buy American Act of 1933 [updated Executive Order 10582, (1954)] was passed to foster and protect American industry, American workers, and invested American capital. State and local governments also use a similar approach to favor local business, including small business.

The Buy American Act generally requires that the federal government buy for public use only raw materials mined or produced in the United States, and only manufactured items which are made in the United States, "substantially all from" materials or items mined, produced, or manufactured in the United States. However, the act has several important exceptions: The general requirement is inapplicable if the items to be purchased are not available domestically in commercial quantities of good quality, or if the cost of the domestic items is "unreasonable," or if the head of the department otherwise determines it to be in the public interest to waive the requirement.

Post–World War II Pressures After World War II, the government faced the problem of returning to peacetime operations and peacetime procurement. To prosecute the war effectively, the rules for government purchasing had been temporarily liberalized. The question raised in 1946 was what rules should apply now that peace had been restored. In addition, the Department of War and the Department of the Navy were reorganized to form the Department of Defense. The war and the subsequent realignment of world power produced permanent changes in the mission and responsibilities of the U.S. government. The nation's armed forces were destined to remain at roughly 10 times their prewar size. These forces, spread throughout the entire world, would need vast quantities of supplies and equipment to support them. In addition to changes in size and responsibilities, constantly changing technology also complicated and enlarged the scope of postwar mission support from an acquisition perspective. Returning to the limited provisions of prewar purchasing legislation was simply out of the question. But what should the new procurement policy be?

After protracted study, Congress, in 1947, passed the Armed Services Procurement Act.[9] Later in the same year, it passed Public Law 152, which delegated to the General Services Administration the responsibility to develop, implement, and maintain the Federal Procurement Regulation (FPR), which regulated procurement in civilian agencies.

---

[9]This act, now codified as chapter 137, title 10 of the United States Code, is quite short. It is implemented within the Department of Defense by the *Federal Acquisition Regulation,* two volumes of over 3,000 pages, including appendices. In addition, the Army, the Navy, and the Air Force each have their own separate implementing regulations.

The Armed Services Procurement Act accomplished two major objectives. First, it established workable procurement policies for periods of national emergencies. Either the president or the Congress can put these policies into immediate effect when either thinks the nation is threatened. Second, the law recognized *negotiated procurement* as an authorized method of purchase in peacetime as well as in wartime.

Small Business Act: Set-Aside and Non-Set-Aside Procurement   It is the desire of Congress that small business should receive a fair share of the government's procurement dollar.[10] Procurement requirements selected as having small business application are of two types: those assigned solely to small business and those divided between big and small business.

If previous experience indicates that there are enough small firms interested in and capable of performing any given procurement, that procurement can be set aside for small business only. Theoretically, the government might pay higher prices for materials purchased in this manner, since big business could conceivably supply such materials at lower prices.

If the total quantity to be purchased is too large for small business alone but small business can handle part of it, the procurement can be divided. Divided requirements are portioned on a set-aside and non-set-aside basis. The non-set-aside portion is solicited by free and open competition wherein large businesses may compete. All small business firms wishing to be considered for the set-aside portion must bid against big business on the non-set-aside portion. When award prices for the non-set-aside portion are known, the small business concerns are given the opportunity of matching, that is, small business can have the set-aside portion of the contract at the same price paid for the non-set-aside portion. As awards to small and big business are made at identical prices, the government does not pay a premium price for materials or services purchased in this manner.

Office of Federal Procurement Policy Act   In 1972, Congress created a Commission on Government Procurement to review all facets of government procurement. The commission concluded its work by making a number of far-reaching recommendations to Congress. In 1974, Congress responded by enacting Public Law 93-400, which established the Office of Federal Procurement Policy (OFPP), under the Office of Management and Budget.

The initial mission of OFPP was to implement many of the recommendations of the Commission on Government Procurement. In 1979, to broaden the authority and responsibilities of OFPP, Congress amended Public Law 93-400 with Public Law 96-83. The combined effect of both laws is to give OFPP a mandate to develop a uniform procurement system for the federal government, giving consideration to the dissimilar program activities of the executive agencies.

---

[10] A *small business* is defined in general terms as a firm independently owned and operated, not dominant in the field in which it is bidding, and having total dollar receipts or number of employees, depending on the industry, below an amount specified by the Small Business Administration. There are special definitions tailored to the peculiarities of specific industries, e.g. construction, dredging, petroleum, and small arms. State and local governments often have different criteria for determining small business status.

One important product of the Office of Federal Procurement Policy was a 1982 proposal for a Uniform Federal Procurement System.[11] The proposal examined many of the recommendations for reform submitted by a Congressional Commission on Government Procurement, the Presidential Blue Ribbon Defense Panel, numerous General Accounting Office reports, and Congressional hearings. Specific recommendations promised a simplified and more responsive system, expanded competition, and enhanced work force professionalism. Many of the suggested improvements have been implemented and continue to affect the way the government carries out its purchasing function.

Competition in Contracting Act In 1984, the Competition in Contracting Act (CICA) was passed by Congress. This act amended the three principal statutes that prescribed authorized methods of forming government contracts (the Armed Services Procurement Act of 1947, the Federal Property and Administrative Services Act of 1949, and the Office of Federal Procurement Policy Act 1974). As amended by CICA, the basic statutes emphasize the requirements that government agencies promote the use of full and open competition in the procurement of property and services.

The law provided seven authorized exceptions to the requirement for the use of formal advertising. Extensive documentation and levels of approval were required for permission to use some of the exceptions.

Prior to enactment of CICA, the statutes were thought to have two important shortcomings: First, the statutes permitted negotiation only when one of several exceptions justified its use; second, the statutes did not adequately restrict the use of noncompetitive negotiation. Under CICA, agencies are required to use competitive procedures, whether by soliciting sealed bids or requesting competitive proposals, unless a statutory exception allows the use of noncompetitive procedures. The new statute also strengthened the requirements for justification, approval, and notice, in order to safeguard against unjustified sole-source contracts. In addition, it required the appointment of a *competition advocate* in each procuring activity to facilitate competition, enhance accountability, and further increase the emphasis on competition.

The federal government buyer may now award contracts using noncompetitive procedures under one of the following seven exceptions to competitive procurement:

1. The property or services needed by the agency are available from only one responsible source or a limited number of sources and no other type of property or service will suffice.

2. The agency's need for the property or service is of such unusual and compelling urgency that the government would be seriously injured unless the agency is permitted to limit the number of sources.

3. It is necessary to award the contract to a particular source in order to maintain an essential industrial or research capability in the United States, or to achieve national industrial mobilization.

---

[11]"Proposal for a Uniform Federal Procurement System," Executive Office of the President, Office of Management and Budget, Office of Federal Procurement Policy, Washington, DC, February 1982.

4.   The terms of an international agreement or treaty with a foreign government, or the written directions of any foreign government which reimburses the government for the cost of the property or services, have the effect of requiring the use of noncompetitive procedures.

5.   A statute expressly authorizes or requires that the procurement be made through another agency or from a specified source, or the agency's need is for a brand name commercial item for authorized resale.

6.   The unrestricted disclosure of the agency's needs would compromise the national security unless the agency is permitted to limit the number of sources from which it solicits bids or proposals.

7.   The head of the agency determines that it is in the public interest to waive the requirements for competition and notifies the Congress of this determination 30 days before award of the contract.

Before a contract is awarded without the use of competitive procedures, the contracting officer must prepare a written justification, certify it accurate and complete, and have the justification approved by higher authority. Needless to say, with such pointed motivation to compete, the percentage of competitive awards of procurement actions has increased.

As with so many fixes to complex processes, there is a negative side to the change. Some government agencies experienced increased lead times because contracting officers were taking longer to effect procurements under the new procedures. Some procurement professionals argued that the CICA legislation places a disproportionate emphasis on price, with little concern for a supplier's past performance and total cost of ownership. And many in government and the defense industry point out that the government's emphasis on competition flies in the face of the proven benefits of single-source alliances, as practiced by the commercial world.

The process of spending tax dollars to acquire supplies and services for the federal government is influenced by the legislative, executive, and judicial branches of government. The resulting procurement process needs to cope with such complexities as public perception, socioeconomic objectives, and weapon system procurement. It is now useful to examine a few of those special processes and procedures.

Some Specific Federal Governmental Procurement Practices

Historically Underutilized Business Zone (HUBZone)   The Historically Underutilized Business Zone (HUBZone) Act of 1997 (15 U.S.C. 631) created the HUBZone Program (sometimes referred to as the "HUBZone Empowerment Contracting Program") and replaced what was formerly known as the Labor Surplus Program. The HUBZone provides special consideration to firms in areas designated by the Small Business Administration (SBA). Essentially, all purchases exceeding $2,500 but less than $25,000 are reviewed to determine if portions of selected purchases can be set aside for suppliers in HUBZones. A firm that is a small business and is also located in a HUBZone gets top priority in set-aside purchases.

Value Engineering   As was discussed in Chapter 10, the concept of value engineering is a powerful way to improve product design and reduce costs. VE means to review the design of an item, review its purpose, and then explore ways to improve one or more aspects of the product to reduce costs while still accomplishing the intended purpose. The federal procurement system includes contractual tools to motivate contractors to reduce the cost of producing the items it buys through the use of value engineering. It has been found that even designs that have worked well for years can be significantly improved. The trick is to focus attention on improvement. Two approaches to harnessing the value engineering technique are described in the FAR: Contractors may (1) voluntarily suggest methods for performing more economically and share in any resultant savings or (2) be contractually required to establish a program to identify and submit to the government methods for performing more economically.

Contracting officers are instructed to include an appropriate value engineering clause in most solicitations in which the resulting contract is expected to exceed $100,000. Thus the Value Engineering Change Proposal's (VECP) potential benefit is institutionalized across the government purchasing system. It is obvious that savings are affected by the speed with which government personnel process the change proposal. Unfortunately, the technical evaluation and administrative approval processes often prevent any savings from being realized. Some contractors have been discouraged from participating further under the voluntary program because the government moved too slowly to take advantage of their good ideas.

Life Cycle Costing   In the mid-1960s, the DOD introduced the life cycle costing (LCC) approach to procurement. LCC takes into consideration the total cost of a product over its useful life, not just the purchase price. LCC is the government's version of the total cost of ownership (please see Chapter 8). Under this concept, DOD considers likely maintenance costs, as predicted by reliability and maintainability estimates, and/or test data and other costs of ownership in the award decision. For example, aircraft tires are bought on a cost per landing basis, thus motivating suppliers to build better tires. Similarly, traveling wave tubes are bought on a cost per hours of operation basis. The resulting improvements in the tubes have brought down the cost of ownership. The logic of LCC is compelling. It is simply basic, effective purchasing—the kind which many industrial firms use routinely. States sometimes do the same thing if "best value" procurement is not allowed.

Risk and the Type of Contract

As seen in Chapter 19, the concepts of risk and risk sharing are central to choosing the method of compensation for the needed goods or services. One might characterize risk as any possibility that an item would perform inadequately (*technical risk*) or cost more than planned (*cost risk*). The government usually wants the seller to assume all of the technical and cost risk. But in very complex procurements with high-risk factors, it may be necessary to share risk through some contractual arrangement other than a fixed price contract.

Research and development is a case in which fixed price contracts normally are inappropriate. New weapon systems are often at the leading edge of technology in order to provide operators an advantage over a potential enemy. Military specifications often stretch current capability in such parameters as speed, power, maneuverability, altitude, depth, and range. Accordingly, since the needed capability has never before been designed or built, the amount of effort required to accomplish the task is uncertain. The technical risk is high. It follows that when the technical risk is high, the risk of cost overrun is also high. Someone has to pay for bringing new technology to fruition.

It would be possible to use a fixed price contract to buy a new weapon system, but such an approach has drawbacks. The most obvious drawback is price. The supplier normally would have to add large contingency sums in the price to protect against possible catastrophic cost overruns associated with high-risk projects. Such contingent sums may be so high that the fixed price contractual vehicle is unaffordable. The two parties might be advised to share the risk through some type of cost reimbursement and/or incentive contract. Risk sharing would allow the supplier to lower the contingent sums needed to protect against unforeseen difficulties in completing the project.

Chapter 19 introduced the principle that as technical (and cost) risk increases, the buyer and seller should use a contractual vehicle that permits increased risk sharing. Obviously, the level of risk assessment is a subjective matter and therefore selecting the type of contract is one of the elements to be negotiated by the contracting parties. The government regularly uses the entire range of contract types discussed in Chapter 19.

The paramount advantage of firm fixed price contracts and incentive contracts is that a contractor's profit is not a predetermined amount that remains unchanged regardless of how well or how poorly it performs its contractual obligations. Rather, under these contracts, profit is an amount that varies proportionally to the contractor's efficiency or inefficiency. This method of determining profit illustrates the essence of the competitive free enterprise system: the reward of profit balanced against the risk of loss, and how profit motivates production efficiency.

The U.S. government has not solved the basic question: What is the ultimate method of compensation for large dollar value contracts involving significant risk and uncertainty? In fact, this is a problem which may never be fully solved. The primary responsibility of the nation's largest buyer is to *govern* well. To *buy* well must come second. Unfortunately, there are times when these two responsibilities are not totally compatible and, hence, are not both fully achievable.

Government Specifications and Quality

Design Specifications   As we saw in Chapter 11, a design specification provides a complete description of the item wanted. It also lists the composition of the materials to be used, their size, shape, and usually their method of fabrication. Any competent manufacturer having the specifications and the required equipment can make the item. When a purchaser develops its own design specifications, it avoids the duplication of development work by bidders. Additionally, the use of such specifications permits wide competition among firms not having the scientific or engineering staffs to do their own product development work. Further, design specifications permit formal advertising as an appropriate method of purchase because bidders can quote on exactly the same item. Where the government designs the product, the supplier is not liable for defects in design.

During a *seller's market,* buyers usually, but not always, get reasonable prices on materials purchased by design specifications. Profits are generally fair, and both efficient and inefficient producers get orders.

During a *buyer's market,* the situation usually changes. Bidding on design specifications becomes extremely keen. In order to be low bidder in such a market, few firms are able to quote prices which permit the recovery of total cost, much less include a profit. Competition sometimes forces suppliers to quote prices that cover all out-of-pocket costs and only as much overhead costs as they think they can get while obtaining the award. Economic survival forces normally uninterested firms to seek government business. Although this system of purchasing does assure the lowest possible prices to the government, it also creates problems. When faced with tight contract prices, suppliers naturally take every possible measure to minimize costs (and sometimes losses).[12] Ethical manufacturers are stimulated to operate as efficiently as possible. Less scrupulous suppliers have an incentive to cut every possible corner on quality. Industrial purchasers can avoid this latter problem of less desirable suppliers by a careful preselection of prospective suppliers. The government cannot preselect, per se, but can add an evaluation of responsibility, as part of the evaluation criterion called past performance, as a means of eliminating high-risk contractors.

The government is sometimes criticized for its use of elaborate and detailed specifications. Up to a point, such criticism is valid. However, the government is moving away from the use of these kinds of specifications and is utilizing specifications that are based on performance or existing commercial standards.

Performance Specifications   A performance specification expresses the buyer's requirements in terms such as capacity, function, or operation. Under this type of specification, the details of design, fabrication, and internal structure are left primarily to the option of the supplier. For common equipment such as automobiles, tractors, and trailers, performance specifications permit competition between manufacturers already having products available in the commercial market. Each manufacturer's equipment can differ in design specifications, yet still compete under the required performance specifications. For most standard commercial products, each manufacturer is tooled up to make equipment to its own design. The cost of changing this tooling to permit equipment to be manufactured to government design specifications would be a needless waste. It is more logical for Caterpillar, J. I. Case, and John Deere to compete on performance specifications than it is for the government to design a tractor and then pay the high prices that would attend nonstandard production.[13]

---

[12]Several years ago, the Navy gradually converted almost all its shipboard lighting from incandescent to fluorescent. A series of lighting fixtures were developed, tested, and completely described by drawings and specifications. The initial purchase price for a 4-foot fixture was $40 per unit. Unit costs were successively reduced over a six-year period (during which time raw material prices were gradually increasing) to $36, $32, $28, $24, and finally to a price of $16.75 for a quantity of 20,000. An audit of production costs on this last contract showed that tooling, direct labor, and material costs alone amounted to $17.12 per unit.

[13]A typical exception to this general rule is the purchased of military trucks. These trucks, even though purchased to detailed military specifications, are obtained at relatively low prices because of their great volume.

Performance specifications are used almost exclusively in the initial procurement of major weapon systems, since no commercial designs are available for such products. In using performance specifications for defense systems, the principal problem is to select a supplier who is technically, managerially, and financially qualified to design and manufacture the product required.

In fiscal year 2002, the government mandated that at least 20 percent of all government contracts be performance based. (This figure 20 percent is scheduled to increase in future years.) Included are service contracts for things such as base operations, technical support, computer services, and so on, that have traditionally been performed to a government-generated statement of work. Instead, the government delineates the performance outcomes and uses metrics to evaluate and monitor performance.

Quality of Government-Purchased Items   In government purchasing, it is essential that specifications be developed with great care and completeness to obtain materials of the desired quality. However, some quality characteristics are extremely difficult to define precisely. For example, how sharp is "sharp"? How free of defects is "reasonably free of defects"? Or where does a "minor defect" end and a "major defect" begin? How can such qualities be measured? These questions illustrate why writing specifications is so difficult.

In industry, suppliers normally have a strong incentive to interpret specifications in a way that is fully satisfactory to buyers. If a supplier's product turns out to be unsuitable for the purpose intended, the supplier knows the buyer is free to take its future business elsewhere. This ability motivates a rational supplier to take the initiative in clarifying questionable specifications or to make adjustments when failures do occur. For example, a household furnishings contractor recently supplied the draperies for a plush new apartment house in San Francisco. A few weeks after installations, the draperies shrank nine inches. The apartment-house owner asked the contractor for a replacement. The contractor made the same request to the textile mill that manufactured the cloth. The mill initially refused, explaining that the cloth was not preshrunk because the specifications did not call for preshrinking. The contractor admitted the mill was technically right, but implied that if the mill stood on this "technically right" position, future business relationships could be affected. The contractor contended that the mill, as a capable supplier, should have known that preshrunk cloth is a necessity for foggy areas such as San Francisco, regardless of any omission in the specifications. The mill subsequently replaced the drapery material.

The government, on the other hand, typically is not as free to take its business elsewhere as a result of such experiences. In similar situations involving the government, a contractor can, and often does, contend that its product meets the specifications and that it is a fully reliable supplier. The supplier disclaims any responsibility for its product not being serviceable, maintaining that its responsibility does not extend beyond meeting the specifications. Suppliers challenge the government to prove otherwise. The government's usual recourse to such experiences is to redraft the specifications in the hope that next time there will be no loopholes. In the absence of being able to prove clearly that the contractor has not met the specifications, the government must accept delivery of the product, and keep the supplier on the bidders' list as a qualified supplier in good standing. If the government is successful in arguing that the supplier deliberately made a substandard product, then the government has the recourse of defaulting and/or suspending the supplier from future work with the government.

Despite the difficulties in preparing foolproof design specifications, the conclusion should not be drawn that the government routinely gets cheated on quality. The government's cost of inspection to enforce compliance of quality, under a system that lets sellers choose the buyer rather than vice versa, is obviously high. On the other hand, the quality of many government specifications is attested to by the fact that private industry accepts many of these specifications as its own standard of quality. On a product-by-product basis, many GAO and DOD studies show that the prices the government pays and the quality it receives are usually satisfactory; in most cases, both compare favorably with those of private industry. Generally speaking, most industrial supply managers can learn much about the difficult art of specifications writing from their government counterparts who must truly be experts in this field.

Mechanics

Award Lead Time   Total procurement lead time includes administrative lead time. Therefore, total lead time for requisitioners can be reduced either by improving administrative scheduling or by carrying larger inventories of materials in stock.

For example, the military services must carry large inventories of many strategic items as insurance against national emergencies. No one questions the necessity for these inventories. A representative example can illustrate the lead-time problem. Suppose a government procurement manager receives a requisition for a large quantity of hand tools for delivery at 25 different locations. The specifications are clear, and bidder interest is keen. Sealed bid purchasing is therefore mandatory. The total quantity, however, cannot be solicited by an invitation for bids. A portion of the total may be set aside for later negotiation with HUBZones or small business. Two weeks are needed to develop the IFB and determine the percentage of set-asides. The bids are in the hands of all suppliers for four-and-a-half weeks. One week is needed to abstract the bids and select the tentative low bidders (multiple awards would be almost a certainty). One to two weeks are needed to check the competency of those bidders who were successful but who had not had a previous contract with the buying agency. Another week is required to prepare the contracts.

A procurement officer would be fortunate indeed if he or she could process a large advertised procurement for hand tools in less than 60 days; 90 days would not be uncommon. For cost and competitive reasons, private enterprise could not tolerate such a long lead time for the routine purchases of hand tools, or anything else. It is conservatively estimated that industry would process this purchase in minutes with the help of the Internet.

Contract Administration

Once the contract is awarded, all parties have agreed to perform in accordance with the contract terms and conditions. Too often, people in supply management or sales activities will consider the job done when the deal is closed. In recognizing this human propensity, the FAR provides for 61 different tasks to be performed as needed in administering public contracts.[14] In fact, the magnitude of the responsibility in the Department of Defense is such that a separate activity, the Defense Contract Management Command (DCMC), was formed to administer contracts let by all defense activities. The *purposes* of this action were to: (1) provide specialized assistance through field offices located at or near contractor establishments, (2) avoid or eliminate overlapping and duplication of government effort, and (3) provide more consistent treatment of contractors. In some instances, such as in small purchases or research contracts, the purchasing activity retains administration responsibility rather than assigning it to DCMC. Under the Defense Plant Cognizance Program, the service with the majority of the work in a contractor's facility retains contract administrations responsibility for all defense contracts in the plant.

Contract administration activities include such functions as inspecting or assuring quality; making transportation arrangements; monitoring delivery schedules and expediting; monitoring contractor use of government property; modifying the contract; administering payment provisions; and closing defaulted, terminated or completed contracts.[15] Many government contracts provide for inspection and acceptance of the product or service at the source, with subsequent transportation a government responsibility. Government inspectors typically examine a sample of the shipment and accept or reject the entire shipment based on the sample. The transportation people in the Contract Administration Office (CAO) will use the great purchasing power of the government to obtain most favorable rates on shipping. The goods usually are then moved on a government bill of lading. State and local government often rely on the requesting activity to perform contract administration owing to small staff. However, the supply manager often becomes involved if disputes escalate or in highly complex transactions.

Industrial specialists in the CAO monitor contractor delivery forecasts to make sure the goods will arrive when needed. Sometimes it is necessary to issue amended shipping instructions to divert products from the original destination to the point of use. Industrial specialists also are skilled at expediting partial shipments in order to obtain early delivery when needed. These contractual changes require formal contract modifications that are negotiated and executed by the administrative contracting officer (ACO).

Government contracts sometimes provide for the contractor to use government-owned materials, tools, equipment, and even factories. In these instances, property administrators from the CAO make sure the taxpayer's interest in the property is protected.

The ACO is the leader of the government contract administration team. The ACO is the only person—other than the procuring contracting officer (PCO)—who may legally commit and obligate the government to changed contract terms and conditions. The ACO carries out such functions as negotiating forward pricing rates for the benefit of all buying activities, negotiating new terms and conditions for contract changes, and certifying contractor eligibility for payment. The ACO accomplishes all contract closeout

---

[14]See Part 42 of The Federal Acquisition Regulation.

[15]Harry Robert Page expands on post-award activities in chapter 12 of his book *Public Purchasing and Materials Management* (Lexington, MA: D. C. Heath, 1980).

functions per the contract and is responsible for processing any claims, disputes, and appeals that might arise during contract performance.

Disputes

A dispute sometimes arises between the government and a contractor that the parties cannot resolve through negotiation. In that case, the disputes clause of government contracts (based on the Contract Disputes Act of 1978) provides a legal framework for resolution. The disputes process starts when a contractor files a claim with the contracting officer (CO), also known as the procuring contracting officer (PCO). The CO then has 60 days to render a decision or give a date by which a decision will be made. The CO's decision is final unless the contractor appeals or files a lawsuit. The contractor may appeal to the appropriate Board of Contract Appeals for relief from the decision within 90 days of the ruling date. Alternatively, the contractor may file a lawsuit for relief with the Claims Court within 12 months of the decision. In any event, the disputes clause of the contract requires that until a decision is rendered, both parties shall comply with the CO's decision and proceed diligently to perform the contract.

Remedies

The government also has available a number of remedies that it may apply during or even after contract performance. The contract may be terminated for default (failure to perform). This is similar to commercial breach of contract and many of the remedies available under the Uniform Commercial Code are available to government buyers. Further, the defaulted contractor may be liable for damages and/or reprocurement costs. The government also may terminate a contract for its convenience. A clause inserted in government contracts permits the CO to stop the work in whole or in part and settle with the contractor at the point of termination. Of course, in contrast to termination for default, under a termination for convenience the government expects to compensate the contractor for effort expended. Complex termination actions are usually referred to an experienced termination contracting officer (TCO) for resolution.

The government may debar, suspend, or declare ineligible an errant contractor to make sure that contracts are awarded only to responsible bidders. Firms or individuals may be excluded (debarred) from government contract awards for a defined period. A suspension of a contractor is used when immediate action is necessary to protect the government's interest pending formal proceedings such as those used in debarment. Finally, a contractor may be declared ineligible to receive contract awards for up to three years for violating a statute that provides for such action.

Statutory remedies are available if a government contractor submits a false claim such as an inflated invoice. Both civil and criminal remedies are provided.

The contract changes clause provides the government with the vehicle to amend any contract administratively. By terms of the clause, the contractor is bound to proceed with the changed terms and conditions. Subsequent equitable adjustment of the contract is prescribed by the clause.

Professor Steve Kelman[16] observes,

When government contracts for anything from technology to training, it need not know how to produce the products or services in question. But it needs to do three things well:

1. Develop a business strategy, specifying requirements for what will be bought, and choosing an appropriate contract arrangement and incentives.
2. Select the right suppliers.
3. Administer the contract once signed.

Together these activities constitute what can be called, using a slight neologism, "contracting management."

The procurement reforms of the last decade have helped government do a better job on the first two functions above, which involve activities up to the time the contract is signed. But contract administration—what happens after the contract is signed—has been the stepchild of the reform effort. And as a general matter, except for some programs and extensive audits of contractor bills, contract administration doesn't receive the emphasis it deserves. Technical or program contract overseers are often journeyman-level "doers," or at most first-line supervisors, sometimes doing contract administration along with their normal responsibilities. Many would rather be doing what they see as "real work" rather than overseeing the work of others.

Many of the tasks these people do involve low-level paperwork—reviewing contractor employee time sheets or creating meeting and phone call documentation. To feel—and show—that they are doing something, they often seek to micromanage details of how the contractor does the work, interventions that often are unhelpful.

If contracting management is to become a core competency, the first thing to realize is that it is mainly about management. A leadership job in contract administration is not a consolation prize for people who would rather be "doing"; it is a wholly different set of responsibilities. These include strategy and goal-setting; inspiring those doing the work, including contractors, with enthusiasm and public purpose; performance management; managing horizontal interfaces between the contractor and users of the contractor's services; and managing vertical interfaces with higher levels of the organization and with the external environment. The responsibilities of a contract administration leader are analogous to those of a senior executive, not a first-line supervisor or middle manager. Agencies need to do three things to make contract administration a core competency.

First, contract administration leadership jobs should be positioned as management jobs with exciting challenges and stimulation similar to that of senior executive positions. Agencies should try to attract outstanding people with a program or technical background to these jobs. Training for contract administration leaders must include training in management skills.

Second, to allow contract administration leaders to focus on management, efforts should be made to split repetitive, lower-level tasks off from more complex, and engaging, executive-type functions. (To some extent, such a division of labor already occurs in organizations with a program management structure.) Agencies should examine their internal paperwork requirements, just as many have looked at their requirements for contractor-generated reports, to see what might usefully be streamlined or eliminated. Where a contract has tangible performance measures, acceptable interim progress toward meeting goals should trigger reduced contractor reporting requirements. Organizations should assign minute-taking and generation of meeting-related paperwork to junior people, who would get an opportunity to learn about

---

[16]Taken from his Internet message on July 30, 2001.

management by sitting in on such meetings. Documentation that doesn't need to go to higher organization levels should be dictated in real time into a machine by a person's desk, to be filed as tapes and transcribed only if needed.

Third, contract administration leaders must be given responsibility for performance measurement and management of contractors. This is a key management responsibility in all organizations, but it is often difficult in a public-sector context (whether for in-house or contracted work), because financial performance measures common in the private sector don't suffice and sometimes don't even apply. Although business firms have begun to grapple with the special challenges of developing nonfinancial performance measures, advancing the art and science of such measurement is a special issue for government. The Defense Department should take the initiative to develop the discipline of nonfinancial performance measurement, just as it took the initiative in the 1960s to establish the discipline of project management to help develop large weapons systems.

It is not utopian to think that contracting management leadership jobs, properly positioned with the help of the three changes suggested above, can be attractive ones. In many technical fields that place a high value on "doing" (engineering, for example), a number of research studies have shown that it is the overwhelming rule, not the exception, that people aspire to leave technical work for managing. Contract administration leadership jobs should be "sold" to senior journeymen or first-line supervisors as an opportunity to taste responsibilities normally held by people at much more senior levels and to entry-level people as an incentive for those on a fast track.

One kind of civil servant might complain about being required to undertake executive-type responsibilities at more modest seniority levels. Another kind of civil servant—the kind the government must try to recruit— will welcome the opportunity for such challenges at an earlier career stage. These positions may indeed be especially appealing to young people seeking quick opportunities to grow and to exercise significant responsibility. Indeed, government may well be able to offer younger people holding these jobs responsibilities more significant than those they would attain in private-sector jobs.

The last decade's procurement reforms have given agencies a jump-start in making contracting management a core competency. But a lot remains to be done. And senior officials need to shepherd the effort. Contracting isn't just for weenies anymore.

The Packard Commission

This group of distinguished individuals recently reviewed the government procurement process. The following were among the commission's recommendations:

- Development of a code of business ethics and conduct addressing problems and procedures applicable to defense procurement.
- Enforcement of effective internal contractor controls to ensure compliance with the code.
- Adaptation of an internal auditing system to monitor compliance with the code.
- Oversight of the code by an independent committee.

A recent letter from the government advised defense contractors to increase the surveillance of their employees' relations with subcontractors in regard to subcontractor kickbacks. The letter stated that in the future, monitoring contractors in this area would be done by means of the Contractor Purchasing System Review (CPSR) to determine whether the contractors' internal policies include the following safeguards:

- Published standards of conduct and business ethics policy for buyers.
- Approval by higher management of purchases over $25,000 prior to procurement finalization.
- Periodic rotation of buyers' purchasing assignments.
- A management program to interview suppliers to determine if they are aware of any irregularities or questionable conduct by company buyers.
- A hot line or similar mechanism to contractor management (outside of the purchasing chain) to be used by employees and suppliers to report possible wrongdoing.
- A policy requiring the reporting of unethical conduct to the government and subsequent restitution of any resulting gain.

Code of Ethics for Government Service

Department of Defense Directive 5500.7, "Standards of Conduct," August 30, 1993, contains the following code of ethics for employees of the U.S. Government.

Any person in government service should:

1. Put loyalty to the highest moral principles and to country above loyalty to persons, party, or Government department.
2. Uphold the constitution, laws, and regulations of the United States and of all Governments therein and never be a party to their evasion.
3. Give a full day's labor for a full day's pay; giving earnest effort and best thought to the performance of duties.
4. Seek to find and employ more efficient and economical ways of getting tasks accomplished.
5. Never discriminate unfairly by the dispensing of special favors or privileges to anyone, whether for remuneration or not; and never accept for himself or herself or for family members, favors or benefits under circumstances which might be construed by reasonable persons as influencing the performance of Governmental duties.
6. Make no private promises of any kind binding upon the duties of office, since a Government employee has no private word which can be binding on public duty.
7. Engage in no business with the Government, either directly or indirectly, which is inconsistent with the conscientious performance of Governmental duties.
8. Never use any information gained confidentially in the performance of Governmental duties as a means for making private profit.
9. Expose corruption wherever discovered.
10. Uphold these principles, ever conscious that public office is a public trust.

Concluding Remarks

Government contracting is clearly bound by more rules than is commercial purchasing. The necessity to guard the public interest as well as the peculiar needs of government dictate such rules. As the process grew, Congress found it necessary to pass laws governing many aspects of government procurement. Some of these laws have social, political, and/or economic purposes, rather than just governing the purchasing function. Out of these laws, peculiar needs, and special rules grew some special procedures that guide the government contracting officer in his or her actions.

Harold Brown and James Schlesinger, both former secretaries of defense, wrote a provocative set of recommendations that appeared in the September 14, 1988, issue of the *New York Times.* The following extract from this article is nearly as timely today as when it was written.

> Project managers need to be given greater authority for day-to-day management and to be held accountable for bringing in effective programs, on time and within budget. Intervening levels of bureaucracy should be reviewed and reduced.
>
> It is particularly important to regain control of the so-called requirements process, which establishes the designs of new programs, such as weapon systems. Design specifications should be made more realistic and less detailed, permitting industry greater flexibility to solve design problems. Cost should be given higher priority in deciding among competing needs. In some cases, we gain a marginal increase in performance only at an exorbitant price of delays, reduced reliability, or higher unit cost. The government has recognized that costs are inflated by adherence to "military specifications" when commercial standards for common items of equipment would be sufficient and is now encouraging the use of commercial standards when appropriate.
>
> We should also consider integrating the acquisition system, creating a single organization staffed by civilians and military officers from each service. A radical change like this, however, should be developed, evaluated and—assuming it holds up to closer scrutiny—implemented by the government itself. The imposition of such an organization through legislation would guarantee failure.
>
> Meanwhile, Congress has been so concerned with reforming the Pentagon that it has neglected its own role in military management. We hesitate to prescribe to Congress, but the legislature must include its own procedure if any scheme of reform is to make a difference.
>
> Some in Congress already support a shift to a biennial military budget, a move that would impart far greater stability in military planning and management. But the majority resists such a change for fear of losing leverage over decisions by the executive branch. But there are ways that Congress can budget biennially without giving up any real power. One is a "Budget Adjustment Act" for the off-budget year that would cover controversial weapons but not routine military matters. Congress also should simplify its elaborate budget, authorization, and appropriation processes so as to consolidate committee jurisdictions, thus reducing the number of times that decisions are revisited.[17]

Acquisition reform has been on the forefront of the agendas of many federal government leaders in defense and civilian agencies for many years. Steps have been taken to allow the federal government to act more like industry (e.g., FAR Part 12, Acquisition of Commercial Items). However, the government has recognized that these initial attempts must be followed by a substantive look at the way industry does procurement—from strategic alliances to realistic profit objectives. The federal government is moving—albeit slowly—in the direction of industry.

---

[17]Harold Brown and James Schlesinger, "Hippocrates in the Pentagon," *New York Times,* September 14, 1988, p. A31.

PART 8

World Class Supply Chain Management

Boss with workers *(Corbis)*

We selected the title of our book, *World Class Supply Management^SM: The Key to Supply Chain Management,* with care and conviction. Relationships are the key to both successful supply management and successful supply chain management. Relationships are where companies can realize the greatest impact on their bottom line.

We observe with great concern the efforts of logisticians and quantitatively obsessed academics to hijack the term "supply chain management." The key to successful supply chain management is the relationships which are established and maintained by supply managers.

In Chapter 27, our friend and colleague James D. Reeds addresses the challenges in even agreeing on a definition of supply chain management. We have jointly adopted Stan Fawcett and Greg Magnan's definition:

> Supply Chain Management is the collaborative effort of multiple channel members to design, implement, and manage seamless value-added processes to meet the real needs of the end customer. The development and integration of people and technological resources as well as the coordinated management of materials, information, and financial flows underlie successful supply chain integration.[1]

Without question, demand management is the weakest aspect of supply chain management at most manufacturers. While we agree that forecast errors must be managed and reduced, we also recognize that perfect forecasts are extraordinarily uncommon: Good demand management must be combined with good buyer–supplier relationships in order to minimize uncertainty, risk, and waste.

Rather than summarizing in our final chapter all we have written in the first 27 chapters, we have chosen to describe a path to implementing what has now been said. We agree with our colleague Dr. Robert Kemp, who maintains that leadership is the key to successful supply management implementation. Short descriptions of three successful implementators of world-class practices demonstrate that "it can be done!" We hope that you enjoy the change from our necessarily slightly dry prescriptive writing to a more narrative style in our concluding chapter! ■

---

[1] Stanley E. Fawcett and Gregory Magnan, "Achieving World-Class Supply Chain Alignment: Benefits, Barriers, and Bridges," Center for Advanced Purchasing Studies (CAPS), July 2001, Tempe, AZ, p. 7.

CHAPTER *27*

Toward World Class Supply Chain Management[1]

The key to World Class Supply Chain Management is World Class Supply Management^{SM}.

KEY CONCEPTS

---

[1]Thanks to James D. Reeds for his assistance in developing this chapter.

- World Class Logistics Management (WCLM)   633

  Logistics Defined   634

  Integration of Logistics Planning   634

  Evolution to WCLM   635

  Implications for Supply Management   636

Case

Circus Tents for MCC Logistics

Steve Lilly, VP of Supply Chain Management for Monster Communications Corporation (MCC), watched as another large "circus style" tent was raised outside of one of the warehouses he managed. The tent was needed to handle the inventory that had accumulated over the last month due to late deliveries from Texas Digital Systems (TDS). TDS had been a reliable supplier in the past, but recent increases in orders from MCC had clearly exceeded TDS' capability and capacity.[2]

TDS supplied one specially designed rapid communications device (RCD) component that was kitted with 13 other parts at MCC's regional warehouses. Suppliers providing the other 13 components were delivering their parts on time, resulting in parts being stockpiled in the warehouses. Since demand was roughly 90,000 kits per month and TDS was about a month behind on its deliveries, MCC was storing an excess of 1,170,000 parts. This volume exceeded MCC's total warehouse space across the United States by over 770,000 parts. Tents were required to store the excesses at every regional warehouse across the United States, except Dallas, where the warehouse had large amounts of excess capacity.

At the last meeting with Steve's team of regional logistics managers, a discussion took place on TDS' responsibility for the inventory problems. Steve and his team also wanted to avoid similar future problems. The discussion quickly became heated when it was suggested that TDS send appropriate managers to address both issues.

Bob Hoskins, Logistics manager of the California region, started the barrage. "Yeah, let's invite them! We can crucify their management right on the wall over there!" Bob pointed to the largest empty wall in the room.

Janet Baker, manager of Operations in Michigan, chimed in, "I agree. TDS has caused me to exceed my budget. It is making us look bad. I say we find a new supplier—pronto!"

Steve replied, "I don't think replacing TDS is an option. We committed to them for the long term in our last contract negotiation. Let's call Procurement and resolve whether cancelling the contract is even an option." Steve called Rhonda Stevens, MCC's chief procurement officer, on the speaker phone to answer a couple of the group's questions. Steve asked the first question: "Rhonda, can we find another supplier to replace TDS?"

Rhonda replied, "Not an option Steve. It would take at least six months to bid a new contract and get the new supplier tooled and trained to produce the products."

---

[2]This case is based on a real-world scenario witnessed by one of the authors at one of the world's largest telecommunications company.

Bob chimed in, "Rhonda, how the heck did we get into a contract with a supplier that could not meet our demand?"

Rhonda replied, "Bob, TDS offered the lowest price and always delivered on time in the past, so we awarded the contract to them."

Getting a bit angry, Bob replied, "Tell me something I don't know Rhonda! Let me rephrase the question. What type of investigation of TDS did your Procurement group do to ensure that they could meet our demand? Did any of your people even visit their production facilities?"

After some hesitation Rhonda replied, "Well, no we didn't visit their facilities. We have far too many suppliers to investigate each one thoroughly. Besides, no one ever consulted Procurement about any potential issues. And—the only time we ever hear from Logistics is when a problem arises with a supplier."

The above story is essentially true, including the highly negative comments from the logistics managers. They were angry. How do companies get themselves into these expensive supply chain management problems? How can such problems be avoided in the future? The answers are probably more obvious than you might think.

The Key to Supply Chain Management

As the title of this book states, supply management is the key to supply chain management (SCM). While many functional areas lay claim to the emerging field of SCM, supply management has the strongest claim. The argument is simple. Since supply professionals are responsible for developing and managing the interrelationships between supply chain members, supply management is the critical function responsible for managing the supply chain.

The issue of how to harness the power of SCM is creating debate in upper management boardrooms and academic classrooms across the world. Firms need to come to terms with how they are going to improve their competitiveness in the future through SCM. Competition is not just firm versus firm, but chain versus chain (or network versus network.) Identification of who is in charge of SCM is the first step to moving it toward world class.

World Class Supply Chain Management (WCSCM)

What is world class supply chain management (WCSCM)?[3] In order to answer this question managers must first define SCM. A review of publications over the last several years identifies the following definitions of SCM:

■ An integrating philosophy to manage the total flow of a distribution channel from supplier to the ultimate customer.[4]

---

[3]WCSCM is defined separately from WCSM throughout this book. WCSM is a prerequisite to achieving WCSCM.

[4]Martha C. Cooper, Lisa M. Ellram, Characteristics of Supply Chain Management and the Implications for Purchasing and Logistics Strategy, The International Journal of Logistics Management, 4(2), 1993, p. 13.

■ Supply chain management is a systems approach to managing the entire flow of information, materials, and services from raw materials suppliers through factories and warehouses to the end customer.[5]

■ Supply chain management is the systematic, strategic coordination of the traditional business functions within a particular company and across businesses within the supply chain, for the purposes of improving the long-term performance of the individual companies and the supply chain as a whole.[6]

■ The supply chain encompasses all activities associated with the upstream and downstream flow and transformation of goods and information from the raw materials stage (extraction), through to the end user. Supply chain management is the integration of these activities through improved supply chain relationships, to obtain a sustainable competitive advantage.[7]

■ Supply chain management is the collaborative effort of multiple channel members to design, implement, and manage seamless value-added processes to meet the real needs of the end customer. The development and integration of people and technological resources as well as the coordinated management of materials, information, and financial flows underlie successful supply chain integration.[8]

As shown by the variation in definitions above, the definition of SCM depends on one's perspective. Reviewing these definitions, we see that disciplines of supply and logistics management are implied several times. All definitions directly or indirectly call for SCM to go beyond traditional functional silos to include cross-functional disciplines and external entities, including customers and suppliers.

The WCSCM Triangle

We believe that WCSCM consists of three critical components: World Class Supply Management[SM] (WCSM), world class logistics management (WCLM), and world class demand management (WCDM). WCSM is the focus of this book. The road to WCSM was presented in chapter 1 using the step diagram portrayed in Figure 1.1. WCLM and WCDM are presented later in this chapter. Figure 27.1 presents the WCSCM triangle.

Evolution to WCSCM

Presently, at least three stages of SCM exist: (1) SCM is the management of the internal supply chain; (2) SCM is supplier focused; and (3) SCM is the management of a network of enterprises, which includes the customer as well as suppliers. Most firms invest their resources sequentially. Generally, firms evolve from the first stage through to the last over the course of several years of effort to improve SCM. WCSCM encompasses all three stages operating in parallel.

---

[5]Michiel R. Leenders, Harold E. Fearon, Anna E. Flynn, P. Fraser Johnson, Purchasing and Supply Management, Twelfth Edition, McGraw-Hill, INc., New York, New York, 2002, p. 10.

[6]John T. Mentzer, *Supply Chain Management,* Sage Publications, Inc., Thousand Oaks, California, 2001, p. 2.

[7]Robert B. Handfield, Ernest L. Nichols, Jr., *Introduction to Supply Chain Management,* Prentice Hall, Upper Saddle River, New Jersey, 1999, p. 2.

[8]Ibid.

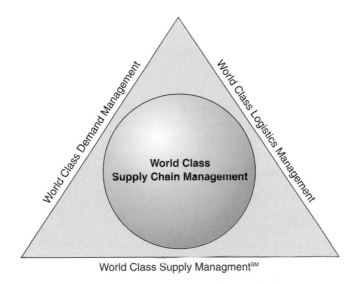

World Class Supply Managment[SM]

Figure 27.1 | The World Class Supply Chain Management Triangle

Internal Supply Chain Focus In this stage, the first priority of a business enterprise is to integrate and optimize its own operations before any attempt to extend supply chain rationalization "beyond our four walls" into the external supply chain.[9] As such, SCM may be defined as the integration of previously separate operations within a business enterprise.

Historically, initial attempts at internal functional integration followed the materials management concept. Materials management sought to integrate such activities as purchasing, inventory management, material control, stores, warehousing, material handling, inspection, receiving, and shipping. Further internal integration was achieved by linking information systems between sales order entry, production planning and control, and distribution. The focus on MRP/MRP II planning and control systems and aligning customer demand and supplier response led to further functional integration.[10] In the 1990s, Enterprise Resource Planning (ERP) Systems were developed to complete internal information system integration and automate many activities.

A majority of firms attempting to engage in SCM are still preoccupied with the internal integration of functional activities and material and information flows. For many firms, the real potential of SCM can be realized only once external integration of material, service, and information flows are attained.[11]

Supplier Focus The supplier-focused stage of SCM emphasizes the importance of fostering long-term, collaborative relationships with key suppliers. Collaboration with

---

[9]Karen L. Alber and William T. Walker, "Supply Chain Management: A Practitioner's Approach," in *Practitioner Notes* (Falls Church, VA: APICS Education and Research Foundation, October 1997), p. 68.

[10]Martin Christopher, *Logistics and Supply Chain Management: Strategies for Reducing Cost and Improving Service* (London: Financial Times–Pitman Publishing, 1998), pp. 18–19.

[11]Christine Harland, "Supply Chain Management," in *Blackwell Encyclopedic Dictionary of Operations Management,* Nigel Slack, ed. (Oxford, England: Blackwell Publishers, 1997), pp. 213–215.

suppliers has been the focus of much of the supply management and contract management literature in recent years.[12] The thrust of this thinking is based on a belief in the elimination of adversarial relations between buyer and seller and forming long-term relationships with fewer suppliers in order to gain the benefits of economy of scale, reliability, and quality. Clearly, this book supports the supplier-focused view.

Network Management Focus   The network management focus stage of SCM recognizes the complex nature of business relationships. The drivers of this perspective emphasize outsourcing of nonstrategic functions and processes. The high level of outsourcing often results in greater physical separation of operations and functional areas. In such an environment, information technology becomes critical in order to maintain communications.

Supply Networks

A network view helps one to accurately visualize the true relationships between supply chain entities. The network view aids in developing an appreciation of the range of significantly different products, processes, markets, geographical markets, and time that are concurrently present in any supply chain.[13] The network perspective properly focuses upon a reality wherein multiple supply chains exist within the same network.

A graphical representation of a three-dimensional network is given in Figure 27.2. A three-dimensional network presentation of a supply chain represents the complex nature of the relationships and flows of information, services, and materials.

World Class Demand Management (WCDM)

A major driver of the recession of 2001–2002 was the proliferation of errors in forecasts which were not identified, analyzed, and acted upon until billions of dollars worth of inventories had accumulated in some supply chains. The primary reason for the inaction on the part of supply chains that were caught with excessive inventory levels was the absence of demand management. Demand management's imperative of forecast error reconciliation with the actual order rate of an enterprise is one of the most overlooked potentials in the successful management of inventory levels, customer satisfaction, staffing strategies, and facilities expansion or contraction.

A constant truth about forecasting is that the further into the future one attempts to forecast future conditions, the greater the error. Consider the following example from a class discussion presenting the problem of extending forecasts into the future.

Error and Length of Forecast Example   You are a student in a 12-week university class in supply chain management that meets every Monday evening from 6:00 to 9:30 PM. It is the first meeting of the class, and the topic under discussion is "forecast accuracy." Your instructor asks you for a forecast with an associated probability of where you believe you will be one week into the future at exactly 6:30 PM.

---

[12]Richard Pinkerton, "The Evolution of Purchasing to Supply Chain Management," *Business Briefing: European Purchasing and Logistics Strategies* (London: World Markets Research Centre, July 1999), pp. 16–28.

[13]Harland, "Supply Chain Management."

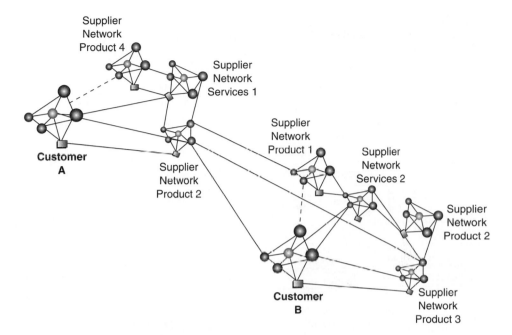

Figure 27.2 | Depiction of a Partial Supply Network
Source: James D. Reeds, "Drive Purchase Orders Out of the Supply Chain," Presentation at the South African Production and Inventory Control Society, 20th International Conference and Exhibition, Cape Town, South Africa, July 7, 1998.

You respond quickly, "I have a 98 percent degree of confidence that I will be in class for the second session of this class. The 2 percent error would consider the possibility of catching cold, or car trouble."

"Very good," responds the professor. "Now . . . could you please provide a forecast of your whereabouts on Monday evening at 6:30 PM five years hence?"

You take a deep breath, and answer, "Well—I don't know just where I'll be five years from now. I suppose that I will have graduated from the university with an under-graduate degree in Supply Management. I hope that I will work for a progressive firm in a position that is rewarding and employs my skills and learning. Maybe I will be in grad-uate school pursuing a master's degree in SCM at Michigan State University. So, I guess that my final answer is I will be sitting in a graduate class in East Lansing."

The professor asks, "Okay, but how certain are you about your answer?"

You answer, "Not very certain at all. I would give my answer a 1–2 percent chance. Too many things could happen over the next five years!"

"Exactly," replies the professor. "Now you can better understand the difficulties organ-izations face when attempting to forecast future demand for their products and services!"

Demand Management Described

Demand management seeks to estimate, control, smooth, coordinate, balance and influ-ence the demand and supply for a firm's products and services in an effort to reduce total costs for the firm and its supply chain. Demand management recognizes that

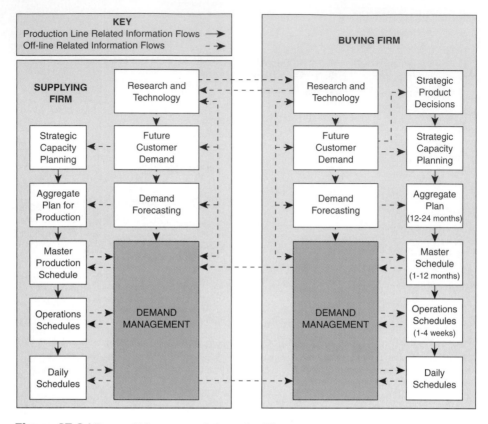

KEY
Production Line Related Information Flows →
Off-line Related Information Flows - →

BUYING FIRM

SUPPLYING FIRM

Research and Technology

Strategic Capacity Planning

Future Customer Demand

Aggregate Plan for Production

Demand Forecasting

Master Production Schedule

Operations Schedules

DEMAND MANAGEMENT

Daily Schedules

Research and Technology

Strategic Product Decisions

Future Customer Demand

Strategic Capacity Planning

Demand Forecasting

Aggregate Plan (12-24 months)

DEMAND MANAGEMENT

Master Schedule (1-12 months)

Operations Schedules (1-4 weeks)

Daily Schedules

Figure 27.3 | Demand Management Information Flows

forecasts are developed at several points throughout an organization. Demand management does not develop forecasts. Rather, it accepts forecasts from other functions and updates them based on actual, real-time demand. Demand management also works with the supply side to adjust the inflow of materials and products. Control in demand management is accomplished through the execution of effective production plans, calculation of inventory levels, setting of capacity levels, and developing customer service strategies. Demand management also is responsible for smoothing production after master production schedules have already been released to internal production and external suppliers. Smoothing requires that demand managers recognize that demand management is a process (versus a bounded business function) that requires the utmost in coordination and communication between the responsible parties. Demand can change daily, weekly and monthly. Demand managers must have contingency plans developed with supply chain members to allow modification of short-term schedules when necessary. Demand management also balances the total costs of not meeting demand against the total costs of adding additional resources required to meet demand.

Figure 27.3 shows the primary information flows required for demand management. No single figure can completely capture the full complexity of demand management activities and information flows between a single buying firm and a single supplying firm.

The complexity increases exponentially as the "real world" situation of multiple suppliers and buyers is modeled.

Figure 27.3 assumes that all firms have dedicated demand managers who are actively involved in demand decisions throughout the life cycle of the product and/or service. Demand managers are involved with product and service design teams in the early stages of design. Early involvement in design is a critical opportunity for demand management to convey the "voice of the supplier" on capacity issues and provide proactive contributions on strategic product mix decisions. Subsequent to design, demand managers must work closely with internal marketing and production managers to ensure that production planning at the strategic capacity and aggregate planning levels is communicated to and reconciled with suppliers. Demand management can provide valuable information on supplier capability and capacity at both of these planning stages.

As Figure 27.3 represents, the point of control for demand information between supplier and buyer is the linkage between the demand managers for the two organizations. Flow of demand information comes from many sources in supply chains, and such processes dilute accountability and foster distrust of forecasts. If professionals from engineering, marketing, production, supply, and other functional areas are all simultaneously communicating demand to the supplier, there will be confusion. The demand manager resolves these problems.

At the demand planning level, demand management seeks to reconcile the many problems inherent in the master schedule, which is based on the forecast and actual orders. The basic objective of demand management is to analyze the consumption of the sales forecast by the actual sales order rate on a continuous basis. Effective demand management takes tactical and operational corrective actions as required to bring forecast demand in line with actual demand from the marketplace. Tactical-level corrective actions require adjustment to the master schedule. Operational corrective actions to the weekly and daily schedules should be avoided if possible, but may be required. Time fences, discussed later, may be established to prevent operational changes in the schedule. Obviously, any changes to the tactical and operational schedules require rapid communication with suppliers.

WCDM and WCSCM

Demand management requires the inclusion of many internal functional areas and external supply chain members. World class demand management (WCDM) in a WCSCM context requires open lines of communication both internally and externally. Internally, functional areas must share information to enable improved accuracy of estimates of future demands. The demands generated through open internal communication must then be shared with external entities. A step diagram model for WCDM, similar to the one for WCSM, is presented in Figure 27.4.

The Bullwhip Effect

Failure to accurately estimate demand and share information among supply chain entities can result in bloated inventory levels due to a cumulative effect of poor information cascading up through a supply chain. Poor demand data forces the supplying firm to either carry additional inventory or increase lead times to account for the uncertainty. Either way, inventory levels in the supply chain are increased. If lead times are increased,

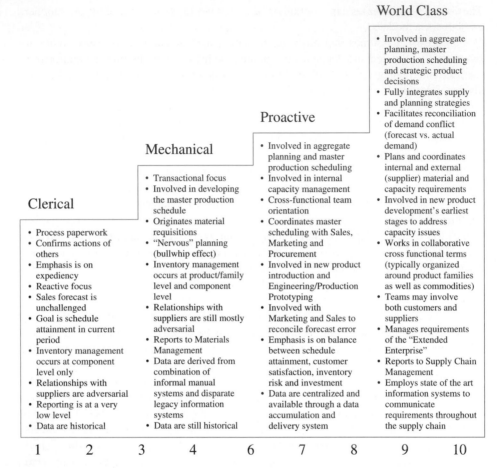

Figure 27.4 | Four-Stage Model of World Class Demand Management Characteristics

World Class

- Involved in aggregate planning, master production scheduling and strategic product decisions
- Fully integrates supply and planning strategies
- Facilitates reconciliation of demand conflict (forecast vs. actual demand)
- Plans and coordinates internal and external (supplier) material and capacity requirements
- Involved in new product development's earliest stages to address capacity issues
- Works in collaborative cross functional terms (typically organized around product families as well as commodities)
- Teams may involve both customers and suppliers
- Manages requirements of the "Extended Enterprise"
- Reports to Supply Chain Management
- Employs state of the art information systems to communicate requirements throughout the supply chain

Proactive

- Involved in aggregate planning and master production scheduling
- Involved in internal capacity management
- Cross-functional team orientation
- Coordinates master scheduling with Sales, Marketing and Procurement
- Involved in new product introduction and Engineering/Production Prototyping
- Involved with Marketing and Sales to reconcile forecast error
- Emphasis is on balance between schedule attainment, customer satisfaction, inventory risk and investment
- Data are centralized and available through a data accumulation and delivery system

Mechanical

- Transactional focus
- Involved in developing the master production schedule
- Originates material requisitions
- "Nervous" planning (bullwhip effect)
- Inventory management occurs at product/family level and component level
- Relationships with suppliers are still mostly adversarial
- Reports to Materials Management
- Data are derived from combination of informal manual systems and disparate legacy information systems
- Data are still historical

Clerical

- Process paperwork
- Confirms actions of others
- Emphasis is on expediency
- Reactive focus
- Sales forecast is unchallenged
- Goal is schedule attainment in current period
- Inventory management occurs at component level only
- Relationships with suppliers are adversarial
- Reporting is at a very low level
- Data are historical

1   2   3   4   6   7   8   9   10

then the buyer (based on conventional reorder point calculations) will increase order quantities. The supplier will interpret the increase in the order quantity as increased customer demand. The supplier will then need to take action to increase capacity to meet the fictional trend. To add greater irony to the problem, just as the supplier has added additional capacity to meet the increase in demand, demand falls off because the buying firm has excessive stock available. The supplier will then need to reduce its capacity through firing employees selling assets, or some other approach. The problem of fictional or "phantom" demand has been termed the bullwhip effect in SCM. The following example presents another way that the bullwhip effect can occur.

Bullwhip Effect Example[14]   An extreme example of this is the behavior of an individual employed as sales representative of a large tobacco firm located in Richmond,

---

[14]The problems identified with the "Bullwhip effect" and false demand were first identified as "The Phoney Backlog" by the late Oliver Wight in the late 1970s. See Oliver W. Wight, *MRP II: Unlocking America's Productivity Potential* (Williston, VT: Oliver Wight Publications, 1981), pp. 33–38.

Virginia. Every evening he would telephone 10 tobacco retailers out of several hundred to obtain reports on the day's sales of his firm's cigarettes. Each of the retailers believed that the frequency of these queries was an indication of likely increased demand for cigarette products, and, in turn, they increased their actual orders with the tobacco firm. The sales representative noted the increase in retail orders, and thus modified his own sales forecast input to the factory.

The manufacturing manager at the cigarette factory observed the upsurge in retail demand in the form of actual orders, as well as his sales representative's modification (upward) of the forecast. He planned the addition of a third shift of operation for the next month, informed supply management to order more materials, and asked human resources to hire additional workers for the next month. To meet the immediate upturn in demand, he authorized the use of overtime and expedited raw tobacco deliveries to fill the increased orders from the retailers. The cigarette firm had increased its capacity and its orders with its tobacco producers. The firm's tobacco growers concluded that the increase in orders from the factory reflected an increased market demand for cigarettes. Accordingly, they made plans to expand planting acreage for the next season and to purchase additional harvesting equipment and hire additional workers.

However, toward the middle of the following month, tobacco retailers noticed that their stocks of cigarettes were not moving from the shelves as they had expected. In fact, sales were declining as the result of ongoing antismoking campaigns and the increase in the cost of tobacco products due to increases in tobacco product taxes. Swamped with unsold inventories of cigarettes, the retailers called the sales representative and cancelled virtually all outstanding orders. They maintained that they now had many weeks of inventory on the shelves, and that they must work off the inventory before placing additional orders. The tobacco firm's sales manager reacted quickly by slashing the sales forecast. The manufacturing manager reacted to the change in the sales forecast and the cancellation of retail orders by eliminating the third and second shifts, and furloughing all of the newly hired workers, as well as eliminating all overtime. Supply management cancelled its orders for raw tobacco with the growers, who in turn cancelled their orders for new harvesters, labor, etc. Everyone involved in this scenario wondered, "What went wrong?"

Evolution to WCDM

Historically, many organizations have employed manual and/or visual systems of order replenishment. Such approaches generally fall under the category of Reorder Point replenishment techniques (ROP). Later, calculations on the effects of setup, holding, and carrying costs in addition to purchased and manufactured lot size quantities were considered and resulted in replenishment calculations known as Statistical Reorder Point techniques. With the introduction of the computer into the manufacturing and distribution environment, Material Requirements and Distribution Requirements Planning (MRP and DRP) were able to schedule orders for products against lead times and bills of materials. The resultant effect was a drastic decrease in inventory at all levels (finished goods, work-in-process, components, and raw materials) held in the production system.

Further integrative refinements (known familiarly as Manufacturing Resources Planning and Distribution Resources Planning—MRP II and DRP II) of computer-based information systems provided capabilities to manage production capacity as well as the demand for materials. These planning and information systems enabled business enterprises to effectively gauge the financial impact of various inventory–customer service–capacity decisions, and to run "what-if" simulations of various material and capacity scenarios, without the risk of inventory, labor, equipment, or facilities commitment.

Later the many influences of planning techniques, such as Just-in-Time (JIT) manufacturing and its requirements for lean operations, total quality, continuous process improvement, and the elimination of waste in all forms further defined the need for many functional disciplines to communicate and collaborate in ways never before envisioned.

Most recently, many businesses have purchased and installed enterprise information systems. The potential of such enterprise systems lies in the seamless integration of the many databases typically found in any firm. Thus equipped, the prototypical planning and control information systems applied to production and distribution have become known as the step beyond MRPII—Enterprise Resource Planning, or ERP.

While the advent of highly integrated enterprise planning systems and the application of e-Commerce, e-Procurement, and B2B capabilities have manifested themselves in recent years, by themselves they do not address the fundamental questions posed by effective demand management. For instance, thorny issues often arise when trade-off issues are considered. When the following questions arise as a firm examines the levels of customer service in terms of inventory on hand, there is often no clear solution.

- What is enough inventory?
- What is too much inventory?
- What are the cost implications?
- What are the effects on customer service levels?
- What short- and long-range capacity management decisions must be made to address demand (i.e., overtime for line workers or outsource to contract manufacturers)?

With traditional manual replenishment techniques, and later disaggregated legacy information systems, the answers to these vital questions were most often not available. There were simply not enough resources on hand (both men and machines) to answer such questions easily or quickly. With the advent of enterprise information systems and the emergence of the transparent and electronic seamless transfer of planning information between businesses, the true potential of sharing planning information throughout the supply chain may finally be realized.

Forecasting Demand

The most important output of demand management for a particular product or service is the forecast. What is a forecast? In terms of SCM, a forecast is an estimate of future demand. In other words, it is a calculated guess or estimate about the future demand for a firm's products and services under conditions of uncertainty. Forecasts fall into two categories: quantitative and qualitative.

Quantitative methods require mathematical analysis of historical data. Common mathematical approaches based on historical data are regression analysis, moving averages, and exponential smoothing. An often-favored forecasting method by managers that have little knowledge of forecasting techniques is the naïve method, where the last period's historical values become the forecast for the next period. However, historical data may not be complete or available.

Qualitative forecasts are created subjectively, using estimates from sources, such as market surveys, in-depth interviews, and experts. When historical data are available, qualitative forecasting is usually used to verify or adjust quantitative forecasting methods. In some cases, when historical data are not available, qualitative forecasting is the only alternative.

Why are forecasts necessary in SCM? The primary reason is that lead times exist for production, distribution, and services. If lead times were zero, then demand could be met as it arises. Since lead times do exist, supply chains must operate based on forecasts.

Most managers in the world today do not trust forecasts because they are fraught with error. Commonly heard comments from supply managers in industry are:

- "Forecasts are always inaccurate—why try to improve them?"
- "Forecasts are always wrong—they cannot be made right!"
- "Forecasts constantly change!"
- "Someone must be to blame for an inaccurate forecast!"
- "If only we had a good computerized forecasting software module."
- "You cannot believe the numbers!"
- "Using statistical forecasting tools takes too much time."

Planning with Time Fences

Many companies reduce uncertainty in demand by establishing time fences. A time fence reflects management decisions regarding production and supplier commitments about changes allowed to the scheduling of materials and capacity elements. Figure 27.5 presents three typical approaches to time fences: frozen, slushy, and fluid.

Typically, the demand time fence is for a short period, such as the current production month. The demand time fence establishes planning rules which, if broken, may prove very disruptive and/or costly to a firm. The most common rule is that production schedules that are within the demand time fence cannot be changed, even if the demand forecast is changed. Thus, schedules in the demand time fence are often said to be "frozen," that is, made very difficult or even impossible to change without top management approval.

Within the "slushy" time fence, many commitments for a firm's material, capacity, capital equipment, and related financial resources can be made on an advisory basis. This intermediate period is usually two to six months into the future. Some actions cannot be delayed until the frozen, immediate period. For example, long lead-time materials may need to be ordered.

"Fluid" time fences acknowledge that greater uncertainty exists as forecasts are extended farther out in the planning horizon. Commitments for materials, capacity, capital equipment, and related financial resources are highly subject to change. The chief advantage of planning during the "fluid" time fence period for materials, capacity, capital equipment, and finances is to provide as much forward visibility as possible. In SCM,

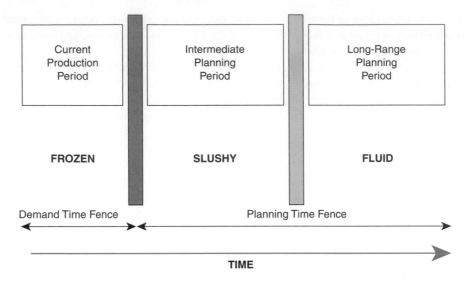

Figure 27.5 | The Concept of Time Fencing in Demand Management
Source: Thomas E. Vollmann, William L. Berry, and D. Clay Whybark, *Manufacturing Planning and Control Systems,* 4th ed. (New York: McGraw-Hill, 1997), p. 246.

such forward visibility about the changing nature of demand is of critical importance for suppliers so that they may effectively manage their own resources. Buying firms that communicate planned orders on a continuous basis with their supply chain members will achieve a distinct advantage over those firms that do not share their plans.

Implications for Supply Management

Since a primary role of demand management is in coordinating demand between the buying and supplying firm, demand management clearly fits within either supply management or supply chain management. Demand management requires open, honest, trusting, and collaborative relationships between customers and suppliers throughout the supply chain. This point underscores the critical importance of trust and relationship management in effective SCM.

The greatest potential—and challenge—for effective demand management exists in SCM. Under the imperative of SCM, the "view of the future" for the firm, as reflected in both reconciled forecast and actual demand, must be communicated to all supply chain members continuously. Who better to convey that view than a demand manager within supply chain management? Changes in demand patterns suggest that the formal planning evolutions once largely confined to processes and functions within a firm must be shared with all supply chain members.

For many supply managers, demand management requires a shift from a focus on component- and commodity-level planning to a focus on strategic product- and subassembly-level planning. If supply managers do not become involved in strategic planning, they may not be relevant in the management of the supply chain. This is especially true, for example, when an entire means of production of a particular product is outsourced to a subcontract manufacturer.

World Class Logistics Management (WCLM)

World class logistics management (WCLM) forms the third side of the WCSCM triangle. Logistics professionals play an important role in the success of supply chain management in the management of transportation, storage, and warehousing activities. Unfortunately, many companies define logistics as synonymous with the term SCM, thus ignoring the contributions and roles of supply management and demand management. A model for WCLM is presented in Figure 27.6.

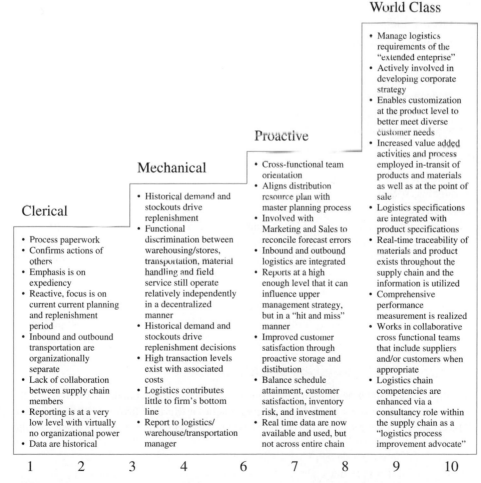

Figure 27.6 | Four-Stage Model of World Class Logistics Management

Logistics Defined

Logistics management deals with the handling, movement, and storage activities within the supply chain, beginning with suppliers and ending with the customer. One of the best selling books in logistics states: "Logistics is the part of the supply chain process that plans, implements, and controls the efficient, effective flow and storage of goods, services, and related information from point of origin to point of consumption for the purpose of conforming to customer requirements."[15] Typical logistics roles include the management of many or all of the following activities:

- Traffic and transportation
- Warehousing and storage
- Industrial packaging
- Materials handling
- Inventory control
- Order fulfilment
- Demand forecasting
- Site location analysis
- Returned goods handling
- Parts and service support
- Field service and maintenance
- Value-added services
- Salvage and scrap disposal

The list above is not exhaustive. In some organizations, supply management reports to logistics. If that is the case, then logistics is also responsible for all activities in the supply management discipline.

Storage points for goods and information, such as outside warehouses and stocking points within a firm's distribution network, are critical in meeting customer satisfaction goals. For example, transportation costs represent about 40–50 percent of the total cost of logistics and perhaps 4–10 percent of product selling prices.[16] Thus, from a total systems viewpoint, logistics becomes the means whereby the needs of customers are satisfied through the coordination of materials and information flows that extend from the marketplace, through the firm and its operations, and beyond that to suppliers.[17]

Integration of Logistics Planning

The imperative to integrate logistics planning with material and capacity planning throughout the supply chain is very real. Noted logistics scholar Martin Christopher has observed: "The concept of integration within the business and between businesses is not new, but the

---

[15]Coyle et al.

[16]Christopher, Logistics and Supply Chain Management, pp. 69–99.

[17]Ibid., p. 13.

acceptance of its validity by managers is."[18] The integration of logistics, multilevel planning, and supply management objectives makes sense when one considers the highly customer-centric business strategies that have emerged in recent years. Customer needs vary, and firms can tailor logistics systems to serve them better—and more profitably.

> Indeed, whether they know it or not, senior managers of every retail store and diversified manufacturing company compete in businesses that are distinguished by their logistics, in effect "logistically distinct businesses," organized, or potentially organized, around the delivery characteristics of logistics pipelines: the channels of transport, warehousing, handling, and control through which manufactured goods flow.[19]

As the competitive context of business continues to change, logistics activities and processes must be integrated into strategic-level thinking and planning. In addition to organizational integration, much of the focus on logistics has been on reduction of cycle times in logistics activities. Cycle-time reduction and the elimination of waste in logistics processes have had a direct correlation to the enhancement of customer satisfaction.

Evolution to WCLM

In completing the third side of the WCSCM triangle, WCLM includes the following:

- *Increased Value-Added Activities.* WCLM "tailors" products to meet customer needs. The logistics characteristics for each type of customer are incorporated into each product's specifications. This includes such features not traditionally considered as part of a product's "form, fit, and function." For example: product testing prior to delivery, applying special customer features and options prior to delivery, using packaging for a unique method of storage and/or marketing, applying special marking or labeling, employing technology to track materials throughout the supply chain, etc. The notion of "tailored logistics" implies that the product characteristics of how a product is packaged, handled, shipped, stored, and supplied becomes every bit as much a part of a product's "specifications" as its material and operating attributes.

- *Real-Time Traceability of Materials and Product throughout the Supply Chain.* WCLM organizations employ the use of paperless information technology to track inventory status and movement in real time.

- *Logistics Competencies Enhanced via Consultancy Role as "Logistics Process Improvement" Advocates.* WCLM experts are "on the road" a significant part of the time surveying supply chain members' logistics competencies. They educate supply chain members on "best practices" in a spirit of continuous improvement and the elimination of waste. The focus of logistics is "outward" toward the "extended enterprise."

- *Collaborative Cross-Functional Teams.* WCLM teams involve both customers and suppliers. The complexities of logistics environments and the ever-changing technology and world economic and political events necessitate a team-based, collaborative approach to logistics planning and execution. Teams typically are organized around product families as well as commodities.

---

[18]Ibid., p. ix.

[19]Joseph B. Fuller, James O'Connor, and Richard Rawlinson, "Tailored Logistics: The Next Advantage," *Harvard Business Review,* May–June 1993, p. 87.

Implications for Supply Management

The fact that supply management is the key to SCM does not imply that other functional areas are not important. On the contrary, each functional area serves an important role in achieving WCSCM. The difference is that professionals in logistics, operations, information technology, engineering, accounting, marketing, legal, finance, and other functional areas commonly do not have the skills and experience required to manage the interrelationships on which successful supply chains are built. The integration of these interrelationships is what separates excellent supply chains from lesser ones.

Lead- and cycle-time reduction initiatives, the elimination of waste, and the implementation of advanced, integrated information systems that have characterized supply management in recent years also are well under way in the field of logistics. Unfortunately, supply management and logistics frequently do not collaborate in many companies. The time has come for collaboration to occur. Logistics and supply management will realize their greatest gains in efficiency and effectiveness through such collaboration. Only then can both traditionally separate disciplines achieve world-class status.

Concluding Remarks

For many in the field of SCM, the future holds substantive and far-reaching changes. These changes are largely driven by the following trends:

- Institutionalization of the SCM perspective.
- Increasing emphasis on supply chain relationships.
- Increasing emphasis on the long-term view.
- Use of information technology to enhance supply chain communications.
- Use of information technology to foster rapid decision making.
- An increasing focus which looks "outward" toward the intricacies of supplier and customer relations.
- The emergence of the supply management professional as a "manager and facilitator of relationships," versus an information broker whose attention is defined by commodity knowledge.

Increasingly, supply management professionals spend a majority of their time outside the boundaries of their employers' facilities. They will often "be on the road," adding value to their enterprise by helping suppliers achieve World Class Supply Management ^{SM} status.

A thorough grasp of the continually evolving perspectives of SCM is a necessary component of the skill set of any proactive supply management professional. Such perspectives recognize the continuing need to integrate many competencies traditionally resident in other functional disciplines, in particular, demand management and logistics. Further, successful supply chain optimization depends on the coordination of cross-functional competencies in cross-enterprise teams. The supply management professional is the logical "team leader" for such initiatives.

CHAPTER 28

Epilogue: Implementing World Class Supply Chain Management

Background[1]

Two months ago, you were selected to become the new Vice President of Supply Management of Megatronics,[2] a manufacturer of test and measurement equipment with $10 billion in annual sales revenue. The position, Vice President of Supply Management, is a new one which replaces the previous position, Director of Purchasing. The Vice President of Supply Management, will report to the President. Megatronics' average pretax profit is 10 percent, or $1 billion. Megatronics' current spend is $5.25 billion. The firm has over 800 employees in supply management. The supply management departments at corporate headquarters and the four operating divisions manage a total annual operating budget of $75 million. During the negotiation leading to your employment, you and Megatronics' CEO, Frank Lazarus, agreed to the following terms:

■ Compensation: Your base salary will be $450,000 per year plus a potential $450,000 per year bonus, based on meeting target goals, which will be awarded as stock grants, and an award fee provision.[3]

■ Hiring authority: You may hire a maximum of 50 new supply management professionals. You can then decide where each will be assigned, whether to corporate supply management or one of Megatronics' four divisions.

■ Transformational training: You are authorized for a training budget of $3.25 million per year. This budget is to create and implement a program in supply chain management that focuses on collaborative opportunities. All members of Megatronics' supply management system are included in the process, not only members of the supply management departments.

■ Executive status: You will become Vice President of Supply Management and a member of the executive committee. You will represent Supply Management on the committee. You will become a member of the corporate planning group that is composed of the CEO (Frank Lazarus) and President (Curtis Cook) and the Vice Presidents of Marketing (John Gentry), Operations (Barbara Withers), Engineering (Mike Hall), and Finance (Sarah Findley).

■ Obligations: Simply stated, your obligations are in the following four areas:

1. Reduce the cost of purchased goods and services by an average of 5 percent per year, or $1.575 billion over the next six years based on this year's expenditures.

---

[1]Appreciation is expressed to long-time friend and colleague R. David Nelson and his former associates at Deere & Co. for their assistance with the development of this chapter.

[2]The name Megatronics was coined for this chapter. It is not intended to bear any similarity to an actual firm.

[3]The award fee is described in Chapter 19. In Megatronics' case, annual performance criteria are to be established at the beginning of each year, for the next year. At the completion of an award period, Megatronics' CEO, VP of Human Resources, and a leading academic in the discipline of supply management will rate the CPO's efforts to improve Megatronics' bottom line. Their consensus rating is applied to the available fee pool ($450,000 per year, in this case) to determine the period's award fee bonus.

(A detailed measurement system was agreed to.) This savings will translate to a 26 percent increase in pretax profits. The reduction assumes a steady-state of purchased goods and services over the next six years.

2. Reduce incoming material defects from a current average of 1,000 ppm[4] to 50 ppm over the next five years.

3. Improve cutting-edge technology inflow by 10 percent per year. (When Megatronics develops a new or modified design, cutting-edge technology from suppliers will be integrated where appropriate. Measurement will be based on an increase in the percent of new technology components in designs.)

4. Reduce the average product development cycle by 20 percent per year by your third year as the head of supply.

Success will be based on a combination of action plans and documented success implementing the above goals.

Leadership

Shortly after accepting this opportunity, you met with your mentor and former instructor, Professor George W. Zinke of the University of Cardiff-by-the-Sea (UCBS), to discuss the opportunities and possible dangers of this challenge. True to form, Professor Zinke could not help but profess— not the glories of supply management—but the crucial role of leadership in making the desired transformation in Megatronics' supply management system. He pointed out that your job will require you to demonstrate three critical skills, and he jumped to his white board to draw Figure 28.1.

Professor Zinke stated, "You've demonstrated excellence in the areas of knowledge and management." (You guess that he forgot about the A− he gave you in Strategic Cost Management.) "But, leadership is the key. I've watched too many of our graduates become superstar supply managers and then plateau. They appear to have the knowledge and management skills but, I suspect, not the leadership skills."

Captured by Professor Zinke's aura of excitement, you asked, "Professor, how do you define leadership?"

The good professor responded, "Let's look at what really successful leaders do. They help members of their organizations establish a vision of what they want to contribute to the larger organization, their stakeholders, and to society. The resulting vision statement must tell people what's expected of them in the broadest sense, must provide a sense of direction, must energize them, stretch them—but not to the point of breaking—and should serve as the basis of the organization's strategies.

"The leader then helps all members of the organization prepare for necessary change and helps them cope with the change as they struggle through it. He or she must motivate and facilitate necessary adaptive work by all members of the organization. Highly successful leaders energize people, maintain focus in facing adversity, listen actively, communicate clearly and convincingly, know how and when to disarm conflicts, function as empathetic mentors and process-oriented facilitators, and adapt to change quickly.

---

[4]PPM is a common term in modern-day business. It literally means defects per million.

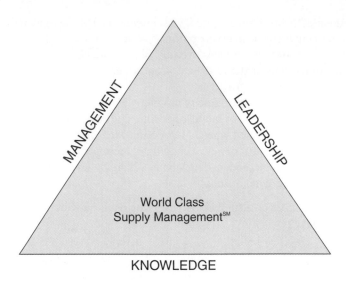

Figure 28.1 | Three Critical Skills

"One of the challenges you face is that World Class Supply Management[SM] requires more than just thinking outside of the supply management box. The old supply management box was a set of artificially imposed constraints that limited proactive, strategic, and synergistic efforts. WCSM calls for destroying the old box that was reactive and clerical and creating a new vision where these constraints are removed and the leadership capabilities and capacities are enabled and unleashed."

You responded, "I don't know, Professor Zinke, most people in our field are incapable of doing what you are saying. Must a person be born with these skills, or can they be learned?"

"Fortunately, they can be learned. One of our most successful programs at UCBS is a Master's in Executive Leadership conducted in cooperation with the Blanchard Institute. It's taught in a user-friendly, nontraditional format. I encourage you to enroll yourself and a cross-functional team of supply professionals at the earliest possible time. In the meantime, there are five literary pieces that I would encourage you to read. Relax. Three of them are only two or three pages each. I have asked several highly respected colleagues to commit to writing their observations on three of the great leaders of supply management. When I finally get around to writing my book on supply chain management, I plan to include these exhibits!" (At this juncture Professor Zinke handed you Profiles 28.1, 28.2, and 28.3.) "There is much to learn from these leaders! The fourth reading, in my mind, is a world-class article on leadership, 'The Work of Leadership,' an article which appeared in the December 2001 issue of the *Harvard Business Review,* and I also encourage you to obtain and read an outstanding book, *Becoming a Master Manager.* One additional thought: As soon as possible, it would be great if you could arrange for action-oriented training on effective leadership for all managers. As we discussed, the leader helps all members of the organization prepare for necessary change. The transformation to World Class Supply Management[SM] is an incredible shift in both thinking and action."

PROFILE 28.1 |

The Strategic Leadership Skills of R. David Nelson
by Dr. Robert Kemp*

Strategic Leadership inspires others to greatness and empowers them to reach world-class goals. Strategic *supply management* leaders involve their teams in creating a vision for excellence and a roadmap for achieving efficiencies, effectiveness, and growth, both internally and within the supply base. For more than 40 years, R. David Nelson has epitomized this kind of leader. At TRW, he rose through the ranks from a worker in the metallurgical laboratories in 1957 to director of Purchasing Worldwide in 1985. In 1987 he became Vice President–Purchasing at Honda of America Manufacturing, where he served from 1987 to 1997. During his four and one-half years at Deere & Company, Nelson created a hunger for world-class excellence and fostered the organizational cooperation required to reach it.

One of Nelson's lasting achievements at Honda of America was increased use of domestic suppliers. As Vice President–Purchasing, Nelson and his team added more than 250 domestic suppliers to the supply base. Local content in American-made products increased from 40 to 90 percent, and domestic purchases rose from $600 million to $6 billion. Under his leadership, one of Purchasing's most dramatic accomplishments was use of best practices to reduce the cost of the new model 1998 Honda Accord by more than 20 percent, compared to the previous model. In 1992, McKinsey & Co. recognized the company as a leader in procurement practices. In 1995, *Purchasing Magazine* presented Honda of America with its Medal of Excellence—purchasing's highest award. In 1996, Honda of America rewarded Nelson by naming him Senior Vice President of Purchasing and Corporate Affairs and, in 1997, naming him to the Honda of America Board of Directors. He also served on the Corporate Executive Committee and the Global Purchasing Council.

Robert A. Kemp, Ph.D., C.P.M., President, Kemp Enterprises, Professor Emeritus, Management, is a management consultant and professional trainer working in the areas of purchasing and supply management. He leads seminars for supply management professionals on a variety of topics including cost management, strategic supply management, ethics, change, EDI, procurement cards, global purchasing, current issues in supply management, and C.P.M. reviews. Prior to creating the business in 1995, he was a Professor of Management and Chair of the Management Department at Drake University. He taught in the areas of international business and world trade, business strategic management, and entrepreneurship. His research on economic issues, leadership, ethics, and global operations and his great interest in smaller businesses has led to many invitations to speak and write on contemporary issues. He has written several articles and papers on topics concerning purchasing procedures, supply management planning, and military preparedness. Dr. Kemp was the 1993–1994 President of the National Small Business Institute Directors' Association, an academic organization promoting entrepreneurship and small business. Similarly his long involvement in research and education in the purchasing profession earned him the Presidency of the National Association of Purchasing Management (NAPM) in 1997–1998. He was Chair of NAPM's Academic Planning Committee (APC) in 1993–95 and the Chair of NAPM's Volunteer Training Committee in 1995–1997. As chair he helped write three leadership manuals for NAPM's volunteer leaders. His speaking and teaching have taken him to Taiwan, Japan, Canada, and Europe. Before entering academe in 1976, Kemp earned his commission as a regular army officer in the U.S. Army Corps of Engineers and served on active duty 23 years (1950–1973) with duty in Japan, Germany, Korea (twice), and Turkey. His assignments included troop command, joint staff work, and work on the U.S. Army staff in the Pentagon in procurement and construction management for the Army's production base. A highlight of his military career was two tours of duty with the elite U.S. Army airborne divisions as a paratrooper and airborne engineer officer. He is a rated senior parachutist.

(continued)

Nelson joined Deere & Company in December 1997 as Vice President, Worldwide Supply Management. His directive: Make John Deere's supply base the most competitive in the world. With the support of top Deere leadership, Nelson established ambitious goals, recruited a strong leadership team from inside and outside the company, and married the best of his ideas with those of the divisions and factories. The result was standardized, cross-divisional supply management processes that now are paying off.

One of Nelson's first priorities was to enhance John Deere's supplier development process. John Deere immediately added 94 supplier development engineers, four of whom had Ph.D.s, and increased its involvement with key Deere suppliers. Results were profound. Deere's $7 million investment in supplier development in 2000 brought $22 million in cost savings. At the same time, Nelson worked tirelessly to bring parties with diverse divisional needs together to pursue common enterprise goals in supplier development, e-business, cost management, workforce development, and strategic sourcing. John Deere's benchmark strategic sourcing process promises long-term cost savings on Deere's $7.1 billion annual buy. Initial successes have resulted from the empowerment of sourcing teams at the factory, division, and enterprise levels and coordination and cooperation across divisions.

World-class results require the right people, and Nelson stresses careful recruiting, rotational job assignments, mentoring, involvement in annual leadership conferences, and education and development activities. Under Nelson, Deere has established close relationships with 12 college supply management programs. These relationships include scholarships, faculty support, research fellowships, and a unique online MBA program in supply management at Arizona State University for selected Deere employees worldwide.

Nelson's leadership at John Deere has not gone unnoticed by others. In 2001, John Deere won *Purchasing Magazine*'s Medal for Professional Excellence—Nelson's second such award. In March, 2002, Mr. Nelson joined Delphi Automotive as Vice President of Global Purchasing.

R. David Nelson leads through communication, dedication to purpose, vision, persistence, humility, support for associates, involvement in processes, benchmarking to world-class standards, honesty, and loyalty. This includes his relentless efforts to advance the supply management profession. He is chairman of the board and former president of the Institute of Supply Management (formerly the National Association of Purchasing Management) and serves on the Board of Trustees of CAPS Research. Dave Nelson has been a member of the University of San Diego's Supply Chain Management Institute and its predecessor since their establishment in 1984. Wherever he goes, Nelson's success in leading those around him reflects his ability to facilitate discussion, help people focus on organizational objectives, and reach a balance between competing viewpoints.

PROFILE 28.2 |

The Strategic Leadership Skills of Susanne Wagner[*]

by Dr. Emiko Banfield[†]

Strategic Sourcing at Southern California Edison (SCE) transformed the company's supply chain practice and achieved breakthrough results during the 1990s and early 2000s. Initial implementation of the strategic sourcing process in 1995 delivered $150 million in annual savings, and that amount grew to over $450 million by 2001. Cost savings were one obvious benefit, but there were others that are equally important.

Through the strong, collaborative relationships that were built with strategic suppliers, the company experienced benefits in several areas: (1) expanded field support (e.g., stocking for utility line trucks by the supplier of small tools and hardware supplies); (2) enhanced service levels (e.g., just in time delivery with reduced inventory levels); (3) product and process innovation (e.g., a new design for a barrier to protect electrical equipment from accidental contact by small animals); (4) entirely new opportunities to create shareholder value (e.g., a new revenue stream was created by leveraging in-house garage assets to maintain and fuel vehicles of contractors serving the utility). If this sounds like a lot of change, you are right. How did it all happen?

Implementing major change in organizations is difficult, complex, and hard work. There are many elements of a successful strategic sourcing initiative: a comprehensive methodology, sound analytical tools, governance structure, effective plans for project management, communications, change management, and training. These elements are all necessary, but none alone is sufficient. The single most important element in achieving successful change is leadership, which, in the SCE experience, brings us to Susanne Wagner.

Susanne Wagner is the leader of strategic sourcing at SCE. She has been a leader in strategic sourcing since its inception in 1994. Currently she is the director of Procurement and Material Management. She was a key player in the creation of the strategy and methodology that became strategic sourcing and has guided the evolution and growth of that strategy.

---

[*]Susanne Wagner has been a member of the University of San Diego's Supply Chain Management Institute since its establishment in 1999.

[†]Emiko Banfield, Ph.D., was elected vice president of Shared Services for Southern California Edison (SCE) in 1996. In this capacity, she is responsible for internal service activities including: corporate safety, procurement, warehousing and logistics, corporate security, emergency preparedness, business services, real estate, facilities, fleet management, and aircraft operations. During her tenure at SCE, Dr. Banfield has held a number of line management positions and acted as an agent for organizational change and growth. She is the author of the book, *Harnessing Value in the Supply Chain: Strategic Sourcing in Action* (John Wiley & Sons, 1999), which tells the story of the organizational transformation achieved through strategic sourcing at SCE. She currently serves on the national board of directors for Business for Social Responsibility, the executive committee of The Conference Board Executive Council of Shared Business Services, and the Advisory Board of Pantellos, an energy industry e-marketplace.

(continued)

By definition, a leader is a person who has followers—someone who inspires others to action. In an organizational setting, a leader is a person who can engage the hearts and minds of many people to act toward a common goal. There are two ways to describe a leader. One way is to talk about who a leader is. What are those personal attributes of a leader that make others want to follow? The second way of understanding leadership is to look at what a leader does. What are those actions that create a sense of shared purpose and a desire to work together to achieve a greater good? In Susanne's case, both views are relevant.

Whether they know it or not, leaders all lead by example. In organizations, people look to leaders to understand what is important, the values that govern, and how to behave. To lead by example, you must be willing to do yourself what you ask others to do. In leading others to embrace change, a critical attribute is Susanne's personal willingness to learn and change. Another element of leading change is trust. Trust is the basis of strong relationships. Susanne is able to build trust with employees, peers, and suppliers based on two attributes: openness—willingness to explain her own thinking and challenge others to do the same; and integrity in everything she does—people know that they can rely on Susanne's word. Two additional contributors to Susanne's success as a change agent are passion (commitment and excitement) and courage (organizational change is risky business).

Visible leadership is key. The design of strategic sourcing at SCE relied on cross-functional teams. This approach required employee engagement at all levels, collaborative decision-making, and teamwork. To achieve this, Susanne played several roles: (1) Visionary—first and foremost, Susanne was the keeper of the vision, the touchstone for why we were changing and what was possible; (2) Communicator—her role as communicator of this vision occasionally required missionary zeal, and communication was relentless at all levels, with all stakeholders; (3) Taskmaster—a tricky balance, this role was a mixture of driving change, keeping a results focus, and creating urgency, while displaying infinite patience for bringing people along through the change required in their thinking and behavior; (4) Cheerleader—a critical success factor in strategic sourcing was recognition and celebration. Susanne's personal attention to creating meaningful symbols and memorializing team contributions made everyone feel that they were part of something important, that they had made a difference in the company, and that their contributions were appreciated. Celebrations were an important positive reinforcement for all the change that was occurring, acknowledging that change is difficult for people and for organizations, while reassuring that the effort was worthwhile.

Leadership is a very personal thing. Whatever a leader's style, it will only be effective if it is honest, true to who the leader is. Susanne brings her unique style to her leadership of strategic sourcing at SCE. It is highly effective.

As strategic sourcing unfolds, leadership will emerge from everywhere. As people experience real participation in decision-making, problem solving, and changing the business, teams will step up to the demands for leadership. But until that happens, strategic sourcing requires strong, visible commitment from the company's leaders.

PROFILE 28.3

The Strategic Leadership Skills of Gene Richter
by Theresa Metty[*]

Gene Richter became Chief Procurement Officer at IBM in August 1994 and retired in March 2000.

Gene Richter began developing his unique leadership style when he was a junior buyer at Ford Motor Company more than 30 years ago. His solid grounding in procurement fundamentals is just one reason he earned immediate respect and credibility with any procurement team he led. Having performed nearly every job in procurement, from junior buyer to chief procurement officer, Gene can relate at all levels, on any commodity, with buyers and suppliers anywhere in the world. This makes him very "approachable," and therefore more in touch with issues and opportunities. He has always liked to get to know buyers on a personal level, and used lunch as a time to catch up on his people. Gene took chances on people. He promoted people to positions of great responsibility. He knew that they were ready even before they realized it.

Gene has always had a very participative management style. He surrounded himself with strong procurement professionals with diverse backgrounds, then engaged them in every key decision on policy, strategy, practices, structure, initiatives, objectives. He really listened to his staff, and he welcomed dissenting views. He was big on "group think," convinced that two heads are better than one, four are better than two, particularly when those "heads" come from different backgrounds with different experiences and views. With Gene decisions were made swiftly, but only after his key staff members were consulted. He also involved suppliers in "group think." He didn't just "listen" to suppliers; he actively involved them in key decisions and received invaluable input from suppliers.

Gene was amazingly consistent in his messages and his expectations. He constantly reminded everyone of procurement's core values, our mission, our goal, and our objectives. He ensured that everyone knew where we were going, how to get there, and what to expect when we got there. Gene was always very results oriented. Unmeasurable objectives (improve relationships with clients; reduce inventory; improve savings, etc.) were replaced with three or four very clear, very measurable objectives (achieve 85 percent client satisfaction; achieve 24 inventory turns; save $1.2B over the next 12 months using October as the baseline). He believed in measuring progress against our objectives, and sharing those results with all buyers every month. It was astonishing to see thousands of buyers all over the world energized to achieve a common set of consistent objectives with results better than the year before.

The accomplishments at IBM under Gene Richter's leadership were astounding:

■   Cumulative savings on direct and indirect materials exceeded $9B.

---

[*]Theresa Metty is corporate Vice President and Director of Worldwide Supply Chain Operations for Motorola's Personal Communications Sector. Theresa joined Motorola in November 2000 to lead PCS Worldwide Supply Chain Operations. Prior to Motorola, she held key supply chain management positions at IBM, most recently as Vice President of Global Procurement. She joined IBM in 1995 as Director, Global Industry Solutions Procurement, based in Charlotte, North Carolina. In 1996, she relocated to Somers, New York, to become Director, Global Customer Solutions Procurement. She was promoted to the position of Vice President, Global General and Customer Solutions Procurement, in 1998, and then to Vice President of Global Procurement. She was a key driver of change at IBM and achieved outstanding results in procurement transformation, cost reduction, and client satisfaction. A graduate of the University of Hartford, Theresa is an active member of the Manufacturers Alliance Purchasing Council. She is a frequent speaker on procurement issues and techniques, and enjoys spending time with students interested in a procurement career.

(continued)

- Gene is the only leader of a procurement organization to win the Purchasing Medal of Professional Excellence three times (IBM, H-P, and Black & Decker).
- The procurement "rulebook" went from 100 pages of brain-numbing rules to 12 pages of guidelines based on sound procurement practices.
- Supplier contracts were reduced from 40+ pages of legalese to simple six-page agreements and the contract cycle time was cut from 6–12 months to less than 30 days.
- The move to an e-procurement environment reduced Purchase Order cycle time from an average of 30 days to less than 1 day.
- He moved the procurement function from failing most business controls audits, to passing 100 percent of all audits for the second year in a row.
- Internal customer surveys showed that customer satisfaction was moved from a shocking 47 percent to consistent satisfaction ratings in excess of 80 percent. Similarly supplier surveys showed that IBM moved from dead last to first place in nearly every category.
- For the only time in history, the procurement function at IBM received the very coveted "Chairman's Award" for our leadership in e-procurement. Never before had this award been given to an internal function. CEO Lou Gerstner was so impressed by the sweeping movement within procurement to create an "e-business" within IBM, that he broke with tradition to recognize the procurement function for its leadership.

Gene Richter created a culture of constant benchmarking with other companies. IBM held benchmarking sessions monthly with dozens of other companies—learning and sharing best practices. Gene encouraged active involvement of suppliers on many occasions. We never assumed that we could adequately represent them in key decisions on policy and practices.

Gene was always very interested in knowing what was on our suppliers' minds. He created an Ombudsman office to give suppliers a penalty-free path of escalation on any issue. He hosted an annual Supplier Appreciation Day for the CEOs and presidents of our most critical suppliers and select IBM corporate officers. He hosted numerous roundtables with suppliers to hear their views on specific topics. We always learned and improved every time we involved our suppliers in "group think" on procurement policies, procedures, and practices.

Gene was also a fierce defender of procurement people and their values. There were times a buyer would be pressured to award business to a supplier without following our procurement process. Without exception, Gene defended Procurement's decision and almost always won the day. This set the tone for all buyers in IBM. They knew that Gene would defend their decision. This gave the buyers confidence and boosted morale to all-time highs.

Gene also believed in supporting the procurement profession by his direct and active involvement in professional organizations such as The Purchasing Council of Manufacturing Alliance for Productivity and Innovation (MAPI) and The Conference Board.

Gene taught us that we could always learn from others. He taught us: there is a better way—find it. After we won the Medal of Professional Excellence, he went on leading the procurement force with passion, constancy, ethics, candor, edge, vision, and a great sense of humor. What more could you want from a leader?

Gene refused to take credit for the many accomplishments; instead he gave credit to his strong procurement leadership team. This is an indication of just one more of Gene's many outstanding leadership skills, and one more reason why he is held in the highest regard by his employees, his peers, his customers, and his suppliers—all over the world.

Transformational Training

You then observed, "Professor Zinke, I've discovered the paradox of training. During boom times, firms don't have time for training. During bad times—when they should be getting ready for the next upside of the cycle—they claim that they can't afford it. But I've seen that after firms finally bite the bullet and invest in training, they all say, 'Why did we wait so long?' I'm committed to training as a vehicle of transformation. Do you have any thoughts on the subject?"

Professor Zinke responded, "I emphatically agree: you will need to develop and deliver a comprehensive training program addressing WCSM. While I encourage you to investigate a reasonable list of options and alternatives, you may want to contact Angel Mendez, senior vice president of Global Operations at Palm in San Jose, California. When Angel occupied a similar position at Gateway, he and I collaborated to develop a transformational program for all Gateway supply management personnel. Based on nearly forty years in the procurement and supply management business, I believe that all training must be transformative. Exposing people to theory and best practices may be a waste of time unless it leads to transformation. I could spend days on this idea, but I'm running late for a meeting with my dean.

"Before I leave, here's a draft list of 12 Golden Rules for World Class Supply Management[SM] my friend and colleague, David Burt, has developed. When you have an opportunity, I'd enjoy hearing your reaction."

As your meeting with Professor Zinke came to a close, he handed you a copy of the 12 Rules (see Figure 28.2). As you prepared to depart from this fountain of insight, you extracted from him a commitment that he will support you in any way that he can . . . and with the motor running!

On October 1, you joined Megatronics. You, together with your director of Supply Engineering, David Wind, and a former direct report from your previous employer, Sam Hardy, have conducted a quick evaluation of Megatronics' supply management system. For over 60 years, Megatronics operated in a decentralized mode as described

---

1. Operate Supply Management as an integrated system including customers, operations, quality, demand management, supply management, logistics, and suppliers.
2. Implement continuous improvement in all activities internally and externally.
3. Apply strategic sourcing in the selection, maintenance and development of the supply base.
4. Focus on the total cost of ownership, not purchase price.
5. Train and educate supply personnel in world-class processes, leadership, and change management.
6. Work in a cross-functional mode with internal functions and with key suppliers.
7. Recognize and reward excellence, both internally and externally.
8. Study and understand supply management's business environment.
9. Involve supply management and external suppliers in the earliest stages of new product development.
10. Develop and manage appropriate supply alliances.
11. Identify, verify, track, and control savings.
12. Foster an environment of collaboration.

Figure 28.2 I Burt's 12 Golden Rules of World Class Supply Management[SM]

in Figure 28.3. Reflecting this orientation, the corporate procurement staff you are in-heriting currently numbers only five. There are between 180 and 225 procurement per-sonnel at each of the four operating divisions. You have met with a representative sam-ple of personnel from each division to gain a better understanding of the existing organizational structure and the culture at each division. You also have visited with the chief executive officers and account managers of 10 of Megatronics' major suppliers.

The three of you agreed that Megatronics employs a combination of mechanical and proactive activities and actions. You and your colleagues agreed that Megatronics' sup-ply management system deserves an overall rating of a 4.5, on a scale of 10 on the WCSM scale. (Please see Figure 28.4.)

Strategic Planning

At this point, you thought it essential that the purchasing managers at Megatronics' four divisions be involved in the strategic planning process. Discussions with your predeces-sor, the departing Director of Purchasing, had painted a picture of a group of individu-als who preferred to maintain their autonomy. Two of the individuals resented you be-fore they met you since each felt that he or she "deserved" your position. So, you met with each of Megatronics' four divisional purchasing managers and concluded that you could work with three, but that the director of the Medical Division, John Altman, had to go. Discussions with Human Resources resulted in a retirement package that John could not refuse.

Again working with Human Resources, you brought Susan Reese on board to re-place John. You had hired Susan out of Arizona State's outstanding supply management program eight years ago. Susan was your Director of Operations at your last employer, ProAktive. Last year Susan completed her M.S. in Supply Chain Management through the University of San Diego's distance learning program. She shares your vision, could charm a lioness into giving you her cub, and is a gifted agent of change. Your plan is to have Susan lead change at her division and set the standard for her colleagues at the three other divisions.

On November 1, you scheduled an all-day, off-site planning meeting with your en-hanced team of David Wind, Sam Hardy, Professor Zinke, and the four divisional sup-ply managers. The meeting was held at the Silverado Conference Center in Napa Valley, California. Your objective was to reach consensus on a vision statement, mission state-ment, and strategic plans with measurable goals in the following areas: costs of pur-chased goods and services, incoming quality, technology inflow, product development cycle time, supplier diversity, and supplier ratings of Megatronics as a customer. You plan to input these goals and the supporting initiatives in both the corporate and supply managements' strategic plans next January.

You opened the meeting by pointing out that supply management must develop and manage the firm's supply strategy as an integrated whole instead of a series of unrelated strategies. The corporation's strategy is the key driver of the supply strat-egy. The technology, marketing, finance, and production strategies are all inputs to the supply strategy. Conversely, the supply strategy is an input to the corporation's strategies for technology, marketing, finance, and production.

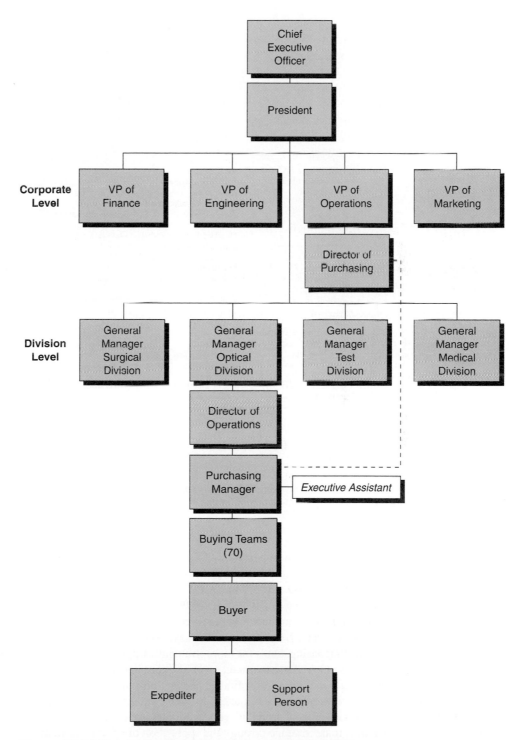

Figure 28.3 | Megatronics Corporation Organization Chart, 2002

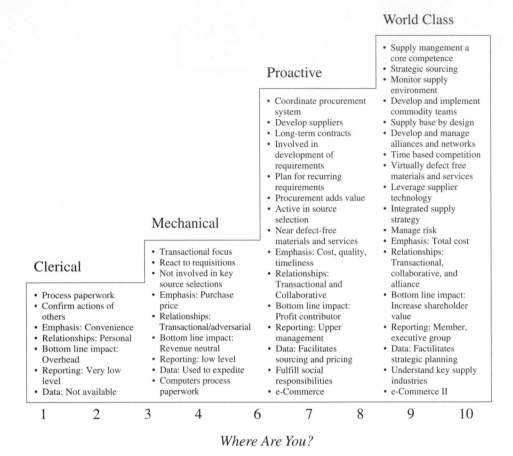

Where Are You?

Figure 28.4 I The Progression to World Class Supply Management^SM

Source: Adapted from *The American Keiretsu: A Strategic Weapon for Global Competitiveness* by David N. Burt and Michael F. Doyle (Homewood, IL: Business One Irwin, 1993).

You addressed your belief in the importance of a name or title and indicated that your title, effective January 2, is "Vice President of Supply Management." You hope to become known as Megatronics' CSO (Chief Supply Officer).

Paul Wilson, Purchasing Manager of the Surgical Division, asked, "How does the term 'supply manager' differ from 'purchasing manager'?"

You responded, "Thanks, Paul. Let's start with the term 'supply management.' Supply management involves purchasing, but is far more strategic. Supply management here at Megatronics will have as much or more impact on our bottom line than will any other function. It will contribute to increases in profitable sales by improving the quality and reliability of our products, reducing time to market, enabling the inflow of technologies which are the basis of successful new products, and providing our marketing colleagues the freedom to maximize our net revenue through the application of pricing elasticity. At

Net Income

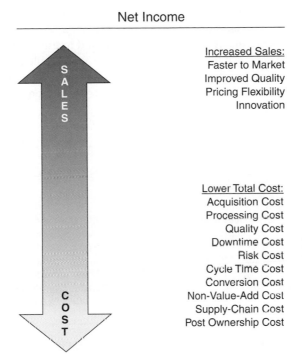

Increased Sales:
Faster to Market
Improved Quality
Pricing Flexibility
Innovation

Lower Total Cost:
Acquisition Cost
Processing Cost
Quality Cost
Downtime Cost
Risk Cost
Cycle Time Cost
Conversion Cost
Non-Value-Add Cost
Supply-Chain Cost
Post Ownership Cost

Figure 28.5 | Contributions to Net Income

the same time, our supply management activities also will focus on the total cost of ownership of the materials, equipment, supplies, and services we purchase." (See Figure 28.5.)

"You, your supply managers, and our expanded group of supply professionals at corporate will be the agents of change who will make all of this happen. Supply managers are far broader than traditional buyers. They must combine knowledge of best in class supply management processes and practices with skills in both management and leadership. Supply managers must be blessed with, or acquire, people skills. They must be proactive. They must be visionaries. They must be leaders and champions. In short, our supply managers will become recognized as the keys to Megatronics' success and survival!

"The supply manager is neither departmentally nor internally focused, but concentrates on proactively improving processes with the long-term goal of upgrading the competitive capability of our firm and its supply chain. I'm making arrangements with H.R. at each of your divisions to change your titles to *Director of Supply Management* in January. The transformational training program we are developing will help your subordinates and colleagues understand this key difference between 'purchasing' and 'supply management.' Hopefully, this transformational training will help all of our present-day buyers grow into their new roles as supply managers. If not, we will attempt to reassign them to other departments clearing the way for the hiring of 'supply managers.' "

Next at the meeting, two hours of well-invested time were spent reaching agreement on your team's vision and mission statements. (See Figure 28.6.)

You then addressed nine areas in which you desired to establish initiatives and/or stretch goals for the next year to lay the foundation for measurable accomplishments in the following years: cost, quality, technology, the new product development cycle, supplier feedback, social responsibilities, standardization, value engineering and value analysis, and organization and staffing.

The Vision Statement

"Supply management at Megatronics will perfect its worldwide process resulting in totally delighted customers and shareholders."

The Mission Statement

"We will design and implement necessary process and cultural changes to create a fully integrated customer-driven supply management system. We will integrate suppliers into our business plans and processes in an environment of respect and trust, establish full cooperation throughout the enterprise, and establish supply management as a core competency. We will improve the bottom line by facilitating increased profitable sales while minimizing the total cost of ownership of all materials, equipment, supplies, and services. We will ensure that diversity suppliers have opportunities to play vital roles in our supply base."

Figure 28.6 I Megatronics' Supply Management Vision and Mission Statements

Cost

Based on your belief that there was much low-lying fruit, you proposed an overall savings goal for the first year of 10 percent on the costs of purchased materials, equipment, supplies, and services. After half an hour of hearing why such a goal was totally out of reason, you proposed, "During the next hour, let's assume for the sake of discussion, that 10 percent *were* our goal. *What would we have to do to achieve it?*" The discussion then ranged from suggestions on supplier bashing to examining with key suppliers the drivers of cost and deciding what action must be taken jointly to drive wasteful costs out. The group accepted that, in a perfect world, it might be feasible to reduce purchase prices an average of 10 percent in the first year. The group agreed to put the cost reduction issue on hold for the moment.

You then addressed a challenging issue: total cost of ownership. The group expressed skeptical interest. An hour was spent discussing the issue. The biggest concern expressed was that employment of a TCO basis of source selection might increase the price paid in some instances. You pointed out that the TCO analysis was in the company's best interest, and you said, "I believe that we can implement a TCO approach while moderating our *price* savings objective so that we have any necessary cushion resulting from the occasional higher purchase price. Our focus must be TCO. If we pay a price premium that is offset with a reduction in the total cost of ownership, we will document our analysis. Eventually, after we've gained creditability, we may be able to transform to a TCO basis of awards. Let's hold implementation off until everyone has had the appropriate training in TCO — say Q3 next year." The group then tentatively agreed on the following:

Strategic Sourcing "During Q1 of next year, all commodity classes, equipments, and service expenditures representing a total of 80 percent of Megatronics' spend will be identified. The supply base employed to satisfy this spend will be identified. The appropriate supply manager and the division supply manager will rate each supplier on the following criteria (using a scale of 1–10):

- Cost minimization.
- Willingness to share cost data.
- Incoming quality levels (ppm, if feasible).
- Current technology status: leader/follower.
- Ability to meet Megatronics' technology needs in 3 years.
- Potential to become an alliance supplier.

"These two individuals then will categorize suppliers into one of four groups:

- World Class.
- Suppliers who are acceptable and have the potential to be developed to world-class status.
- Suppliers who are acceptable and provide products and services where a supply alliance is not needed.
- Suppliers to drop.

"Appropriate action will be taken as follows with suppliers in each group:

"Discussions will be held with world-class suppliers. We will express appreciation for their continuing support. We will ask what *we* can do to improve the relationship. We will ensure that we are in collaborative relationships and on the road to alliance relationships. We will extol them to do 'even better.' We will publicize our recognition and appreciation of a job well done in appropriate trade literature. I guarantee that the best will get even better!

"The second group (ones with potential) is more challenging. We will prioritize them by spend. Simultaneously, we will look for opportunities to rationalize our supply base. I don't want to make downsizing an initiative. But, it should be a 'guiding principle.' We probably can reduce our base by 50 percent as we match our needs with the desired supply base. By and large, I prefer a 70/30 guideline: 70 percent of an item or commodity class to our preferred supplier and 30 percent to our 'backup' supplier. When we start enjoying supply alliances, I prefer to have one alliance supplier for an item and another alliance supplier for a similar item. Ideally, each supplier will provide backup capability for the other supplier if an unforeseen situation arises. But those issues will have to be examined on a case-by-case basis.

"I understand that we do not provide supplier development assistance to our suppliers to help them learn how to become world class. We need to create supplier development teams immediately. At first, we will be able to address only the biggest dollar volume suppliers or those of critical or strategic importance. We will discuss our rating with them and ask if they desire to progress to world-class status. If the answer is "No, we will survive without you," we will consider sourcing with a more cooperative supplier. Normally, a key salvageable supplier will welcome our offer of supplier development assistance. Such suppliers are candidates for collaborative relationships and may become candidates for alliances downstream.

"I propose that we field four teams of four professionals possessing the following expertise: industrial and process engineering, cost management, supply management, and quality management. In working with the chosen supplier, we will follow the steps laid out in the chapter on supplier development in the recently published book, *World Class Supply Management*^{SM}. In parallel with this action, we will train and educate in-house resources in world-class supplier development and hire necessary additional experts on the subjects. In time, I believe that we will be able to field 12 such teams, pulling the additional resources from our existing supply departments at the divisions.

"The impact of the supplier development teams will be felt quickly. It is common to discover 70 percent of a supplier's cycle time is non-value-added wasteful activity that can be easily reduced, or better yet, eliminated. A major benefit for Megatronics will be shorter lead times for orders, which translates into smaller order quantities and lower inventories."

"Wow," observed Rosalind Hall, Director of Supply Management at the test division, "I think your cost reduction objective may be achievable!"

Susan observed, "We demonstrated that it was possible at ProAktive. Not only did we drive cost down, but we started eliminating incoming quality problems. Based on our experience, I believe that reducing our total spend by 10 percent may be possible—but it's going to be quite a reach in the first year. We may not have the resources to deploy the optimal number of supplier development teams for some time." After much discussion, the group agreed on a savings objective for the first year of 5 percent in constant year dollars, rather than your proposed 10 percent. You pointed out: "This translates to a $260 million improvement in Megatronics' bottom line, or a 26 percent increase."[5]

Quality

You continued by observing that the team had begun discussing the quality program both in the retention of Megatronics' best suppliers and in focusing on supplier development. The group agreed that it should be possible to reduce incoming defects by 10 percent the first year. But there was more. "I believe that we should have at least one quality engineer in supply management at each division. This individual will focus on the six components of a total quality management program at the division level:

- Development of clear and concise specifications by our internal customers.
- Quality considerations during sourcing.
- Development of a clear understanding with suppliers on all aspects of quality—both prior to, and subsequent to, award of a contract.

---

[5]A 5 percent reduction on a spend of $5.25 billion = $262 million. This savings will increase Megatronics' pretax profit from $1 billion to $1.260 billion.

- Identification of opportunities for supplier development.
- A comprehensive monitoring system; supplier certification.
- A motivational program addressing quality, cost, and service."

Susan asked, "What about a Six Sigma black belt program for our people? It sure helped at ProAktive." A short discussion ensued in which Susan described the program. It was agreed that such a program should be implemented after completion of the second round of training. The group agreed that the combination of these actions would lay the foundation for much more aggressive quality goals two years out.

Technology

You continued, "The biggest challenge with the existing supply base appears to be with the issue of technology. The inflow of technology is a function of two variables: the supplier's investment in advancing its technological capabilities, and the supplier's willingness to share its innovations with us. The first factor (willingness to invest) can be measured through a combination of financial analysis and an independent evaluation of the firm's technological prowess by an in-house expert or consultant. The second variable (its willingness to work with us and share appropriate technology) is a function of our relationship with the supplier. A collaborative supplier will be far more willing to share its technology than will an arm's-length one and an alliance supplier will be much more inclined to share technology than will a collaborative one.

"I believe that, over the next two years, we need an initiative to develop or hire 12 individuals capable of developing and managing strategic supply alliances. If we are going to develop supply alliances, we also will first need an initiative to identify supplier relationships that should progress to alliance status. These 12 professionals can handle both initiatives. Developing and managing alliances will improve our inflow of technology, enable continuous improvement, reduce costs, reduce defects, and compress new product development time. I doubt if we will have a measurable impact on technology inflow next year. Therefore, I recommend that we not establish a goal for next year, but that we undertake appropriate initiatives. We should start seeing benefits the following year."

The New Product Development Cycle

Jason Patel, Purchasing Manager of the Optics Division, asked, "How will these alliances reduce development time?" You answered, "Not only will these suppliers be the best of the best, but, hopefully, they will be readily accepted as contributors to our new product teams. I believe that we can take at least 50 percent out of the development cycle by involving carefully screened suppliers early in the process."

Jason responded, "What if we are developing a new product and we don't have an alliance partner?"

"Then the new product development team—which must include a supply professional with engineering knowledge—must select from two or three carefully prequalified suppliers. Under such circumstances, we must be careful about sharing any of our technology and our technology plans with a nonalliance supplier. Obviously, the sooner we develop appropriate alliances, the better.

"Early involvement of both supply management and suppliers will greatly help us in meeting our objective of reduced development time. Recently conducted research indicates that early supplier involvement (ESI) and early supply management involvement (referred to as EPI at most firms) can reduce new product development by 20–40 percent. Honda of America reduced its new product development cycle by over 60 percent one year during the 1990s! And, in the long run, such action will help Megatronics reduce new product costs and increase reliability. Professor Zinke and many supply professionals estimate that 75–85 percent of a product's costs and virtually all of its reliability are designed in during the development stage. By working with carefully prequalified suppliers, we can reduce costs, time to market, and quality problems very significantly. Thus, it's imperative that qualified supply managers and suppliers are involved in this process!"

Jason said, "Most engineers and new product development managers only talk to my people when they want them to buy something. The idea of involving my people or our suppliers in the development process is ludicrous, at best!" Jason's two long-time colleagues concurred. Susan observed, "Sounds like another initiative to me!"

You responded, "Actually, it may be two or three—or even more—initiatives. The first is to upgrade some of our trainable staff so that they bring value to the new product development process. The second may be to promote and train several Megatronics' design engineers to become supply engineers. I believe that this activity will be performed best at division level by our new supply engineers. But I want David Wind to monitor and facilitate the process at each division. David will provide any necessary help in convincing the divisional engineers that supply management has much to contribute and that supply engineers or engineering-knowledgeable supply managers must be involved early in all new product development programs. I'll talk to Human Resources about the feasibility of this one. The third initiative will be to bring some fresh talent in."

Susan said, "I recommend that with the impact early involvement of suppliers and supply management has on cost, time-to-market, and quality, we pursue all three initiatives!" All agreed.

You observed, "The other initiative is to get these valuable new resources onto appropriate new development teams. Let's start moving on these three initiatives early next year. We should be able to begin upgrading our people by the end of the second quarter. With the economy the way it is, we should be able to bring in several supply engineers by next fall. Developing supply engineers from in-house engineers is more complex and may take longer—say one and a half years. Once we have qualified resources, I have to secure engineering's acceptance of their involvement."

"Lots of luck!" said Jason.

You calmly commented, "I think I'll solicit Professor Zinke's help on this one. Doc, do you think you can convince engineering of the critical importance of such early involvement?" The professor responded, "Not a problem! I'll be happy to meet with you and the vice president of engineering as soon as you can schedule such a meeting."

Over a lunch of sand dabs, pommes frites, and Caesar salad, you raised another issue. "Let's assume that we could develop, promote, or hire a total of eight supply engineers by the end of June next year. What impact will our action have on achieving our objectives?"

David Wind, who had been a process engineer at Megatronics for seven years, responded, "I don't see much impact next year or even the following one. Considering the typical development cycle and product life cycle, it will be three years before we see much impact—in fact, it will be four years before we begin to receive major benefits."

"Ouch! Which means that we in supply management must carry the ball on cost, quality, and technology inflow for quite some time. Speaking about quality, while the largest impact we will have on quality is through early supplier and supply management involvement, we've got to get going on areas where we can have more immediate impact. We've outlined plans for driving cost down. Are there any other thoughts on cost before we address quality more fully?"

JoAnn Barber, your newly appointed Director of Measurements and Standards at the corporate level, responded, "What about Ariba or Commerce I?"

Susan commented, "These systems may save a bit of money on purchase price. But the big savings are in human resources. We implemented Ariba at ProAktive three years ago. It took over a year to implement and we were just beginning to see monetary savings after two years. It will probably take 3 or 4 years for a full payback at ProAktive, but we thought that we might save 18 MRO buyers and 12 A.P. clerks some time this year. For what it's worth, I recommend that with the number of initiatives on the table we hold this one for a year or two."

You countered, "I had a similar impression of these systems until talking with a colleague from the automotive industry earlier this year. He got payback after only four months! He indicated that much of the savings resulted from the virtual elimination of maverick spending. He estimated that 60–70 percent of MRO spending had been done outside of the formal supply management system. Based on his experience and that of another colleague in the pharmaceutical industry, I think that we should study this one before moving forward."

This recommendation received consensus almost immediately.

Susan then asked, "What about reverse auctions? I understand that they are saving 10 to 20 percent!"

Professor Zinke observed, "There are situations wherein carefully designed and professionally run reverse auctions can achieve significant savings. I recommend that when you review your commodity class as we discussed this morning, you identify commodities for reverse auctions. Remember that unless the auction is handled very professionally, you may disrupt important collaborative relationships. A client of mine employs reverse auctions as a means of rationalizing his supply base. For example, he hoped to reduce the number of injection mold suppliers from 110 to 12 worldwide. Once he had rationalized this supply base, he planned to move through collaboration to alliance status with each of the 12 suppliers. Based on my observations, you may want to apply this sourcing and pricing tool to about 20 percent of your spend. Twenty percent of a spend of $5,250,000,000—that's over $1 billion, which may lend itself to reverse auctioning. Assuming a 15 percent savings, that's $150,000,000. With a bit of luck, you're well on your way to achieving your savings goal. But remember, usually you're best off using reverse auctions only once or, at most, twice for a commodity or commodity class. Assuming that you've used the procedure correctly, you then should consider developing a collaborative relationship with the selected suppliers. Once you've developed a collaborative or alliance relationship, I recommend the use of other processes to ensure that you're paying a low, but fair, price."

You responded, "Thanks, Doc. Now let's return to the quality issue. You may remember that when we discussed supplier development this morning we talked of having a quality engineer or manager on each supplier development team. Obviously, we expect to see quality improvements with the assisted supplier. But, this will be a rather slow way of improving our overall incoming quality. Can anyone think of other initiatives which might be faster?"

Susan responded, "Yes, I can think of five:

- A Six Sigma program.
- Improve our source selection process.
- We must ensure that there is a complete understanding of all of our requirements both before and after award of a contract—before the supplier commences production.
- We should transfer the responsibility for ensuring quality from incoming inspection to the supplier whenever appropriate. This will give suppliers a greater sense of 'owning' the quality issue. Additionally, we may be able to reallocate some inspectors to higher-value-add work.
- We will work with our colleagues in quality and investigate the feasibility of certifying our major suppliers.

"And lastly, when we become aware of a problem, it's in our interest to work with the supplier to correct the root cause of the problem."

You indicated that the Six Sigma program should be a corporate initiative, not a supply management one. You planned to introduce it at the next corporate executive session. After a boisterous discussion and the promise of the afternoon break, the group reached quick agreement in support of each of Susan's other suggested initiatives. The group agreed that a 10 percent reduction from 1,000 ppm to an average of 900 was a realistic goal for year one. In succeeding years, Megatronics should gain the benefit of these initiatives and reduce incoming defects by 50 percent per year or higher indefinitely.

When the group reconvened, you observed that there were only a few remaining issues: ratings from suppliers of your competence as a responsible customer, Megatronics' social responsibilities, and the issues of standardization, value engineering, and staffing.

Supplier Feedback

David Wind, Director of Supply Engineering, volunteered, "I'd like to assume responsibility for initiating a program wherein suppliers give us semiannual ratings on how well we are doing as a customer. I have several ideas that I'd like to run past you, Professor Zinke." All agreed that this was a "done deal . . . another initiative."

Social Responsibilities

Paul Wilson, Manager of Supply for the Surgical Division, offered, "As you might suspect, supplier diversity is important to me." (Paul is an African American who has worked his way up from the factory floor to his present position. He is much respected by his colleagues and the suppliers with whom he comes in contact.) "Megatronics claims to support diversity, but I don't see it. How many women- or minority-owned businesses are even considered for anything other than MRO and services? I was reading about the programs at Agilent, Lucent, and Deere in the new book *World Class Supply Management*^{SM}. I volunteer to establish a program as good as the best!"

You then pointed out that a world-class supply chain plays a major role in protecting Mother Earth. JoAnn Barber added, "As we become a global player, we encounter some fascinating ethical, financial, and legal issues." You then asked Sam Hardy to assume responsibility for the pollution avoidance issue and JoAnn to accept responsibility for development of a program addressing ethics in the workplace for our suppliers, whether domestic or global.

Standardization

"My initial discussions with several of our people and representatives of key suppliers led me to the conclusion that a standardization program would help us in the areas of cost, quality, and compressing the development cycle. While there probably are many opportunities for standardization at the division level, I believe that standardization must be corporatewide."

During the short discussion that followed, there was agreement that standardization would provide benefits at both the division and corporate levels. You continued, "With your concurrence, I propose hiring a standards engineer to propose a standardization program to us and then to manage the program." The new hire would work directly under JoAnn Barber in the measurement and standards group. Everyone agreed.

Value Engineering and Value Analysis (VE/VA)

"I've been fascinated to see that there are no value engineering or value analysis activities or even relevant training here at Megatronics."

A short discussion involving quite a bit of defensive behavior now ensued, after which you concluded, "As we all know, VE/VA pays back an average of 10 to 30 times the investment in such programs. I propose that each division hire one or more value engineers. Based on experience, talk with your counterparts in operations and in engineering to see if they may have candidates before going outside."

Organization and Staffing

"Before taking a break, I'd like to share my vision of our evolving organization for supply management and where I see our staffing in four to six years. Many of the activities and functions we have been discussing can best be performed at corporate. Others are better at division. In time, I hope to have a direct reporting relationship with each of you who are at division level. I believe that it is best for me, best for you, and best for Megatronics.

"Staffing is a very sensitive issue. I am confident that supply management will grow larger with the many new positions we have been discussing and then will decrease to about 40 percent of our present size. As we upgrade those of our existing workforce who are upgradeable—and this includes present-day buyers, expediters, and support staff—and as we take advantage of e-Commerce II, I see us downsizing to a workforce largely consisting of supply management professionals. Collaborative and alliance relationships will virtually eliminate the need for expediters. Ariba or a similar system will eliminate the need for MRO buyers. For better or worse, most support positions will be eliminated.

"Our focus will shift from tactical to strategic. Our work will become far more challenging, stimulating, and fulfilling!"

After a boisterous break, you once more called the group to attention. "It should be apparent that we desperately need high-quality training and education. While I was at the University of San Diego's sixteenth Strategic Supply Management Forum last November, I heard an excellent presentation on a program kicked off in January, just before the recession of 2001 and 2002. The speaker described a four-tier program consisting of (1) Boot Camp (basics for supply management personnel); (2) Advance Boot Camp (more advanced training for selected personnel); (3) intermediate training and education for selected managers; and (4) a commitment to fund tuition for carefully selected personnel to pursue an M.S. in a Supply Chain Management Program. The initial boot camp was conducted in a unique format that both trained and laid the foundation for the client's transformation to a world-class player. Unfortunately, the client's financial problems resulted in the termination of the program after the completion of four basic boot camps. I propose that we adapt the program to meet our needs. Any reactions or thoughts?"

After several minutes of discussion, the group indicated that basic Boot Camp should commence next February. Selected high-potential supply management personnel will be encouraged to enroll in the next available cohort of USD's hybrid classroom/ Internet-based graduate program in supply chain management.

Sam Hardy observed that he'd heard about the use of metrics to improve supply management from his colleagues at the local chapter of the Institute for Supply Management™. He asked, "What role, if any, should metrics play in our program?"

You approvingly pointed out, "If you can't measure it, you can't manage it." You thanked Sam for raising the topic and proposed bringing Ted Ramstad (formerly with Scott Paper prior to Chainsaw Dunlap's arrival and, more recently, with The Warren Group) in to discuss metrics at your team's February meeting. Because of the meeting, Ted was retained under JoAnn Barber's leadership to facilitate the development of appropriate metrics and to conduct metrics training. Within four months, Ted had completed his mission and Megatronics' supply management personnel customized appropriate metrics for strategic and tactical issues and for appropriate contracts.

Susan then raised the issue of commodity teams. After a stimulating 20-minute discussion, it was agreed that more foundation building was required before moving on this initiative. It was tabled until next year's meeting.

"Lastly, I believe that we should invite all Megatronics' suppliers to a suppliers' day sometime in February. David, will you handle this one?"

Then Paul Wilson, director of Supply Management for the Surgical Division, offered an observation. "I believe that we are developing a set of excellent plans and initiatives. But something puzzles me. For years, I've heard about benchmarking. But there's no benchmarking on our list of initiatives."

Professor Zinke responded, "Two of my colleagues have a wonderful book out on supply management. The book addresses countless world-class practices and reduces the need for conventional benchmarking since it is possible to benchmark against the world-class processes they advocate without investing in field trips. However, there may be occasions wherein a benchmarking visit makes sense. Such benchmarking visits can provide insight on 'how-to-implement' or 'how-to-overcome' resistance to change."

It was 5 P.M. and nearly time for wine tasting at a nearby vineyard. You casually mentioned this before observing that it was essential to summarize the commitments agreed to during the day. You reminded the group that the goals, together with the supporting initiatives, would become supply management's portion of the next corporate strategic plan. You stated that there was agreement on both the vision statement and the mission statement, and you promised to provide the group with a summary list of the goals and initiatives agreed on for next year. (These are listed in Figure 28.7.)

You observed, "I had planned to establish goals on technology infusion, reduced development cycle times, diversity, and a supplier scorecard. But as we were discussing our plans, it became apparent that finite objectives in these areas probably are premature.

Goals:
- Reduce average price on incoming goods and services by 5 percent
- Reduce average incoming defects by 10 percent to 900 ppm

Initiatives:
- Implement strategic sourcing, starting Q1
- Document and obtain verification of savings, Q1
- Initiate supplier development program, starting Q2
- Implement a total cost of ownership program, Q3
- Develop and implement a training program, commencing Q1
- Initiate study of an operating resource management system, Q3
- Conduct "Supplier Day" in Q1 and annually thereafter
- Develop or hire 8 individuals capable of developing and managing supply alliances, Q4
- Identify supplier relationships which have the potential of progressing to alliance status, Q2
- Train alliance champions, Q2
- Enter into first supply alliance, Q4
- Train and upgrade all staff so that they bring value to all processes, Q2
- Promote and train several Megatronics engineers for supply engineering billets, Q2
- Hire supply engineers by Q3
- Include supply engineers on appropriate new development teams, Q4
- Initiate reverse auctions where appropriate, Q4
- Increase emphasis on quality capabilities during source selection, Q1
- Ensure understanding with all suppliers of their quality, time, and service obligations, Q1
- Document all contract files on understanding issue, Q1
- Initiate supplier certification program, Q3
- Work with suppliers to correct root causes of quality problems, Q2
- Collect and analyze feedback from suppliers on how "we" perform as a customer, Q4
- Design, develop, and implement aggressive social responsibilities program, Q2
- Hire a standards engineer to develop and manage a standardization program, Q2
- Add a value engineer to each division's staff, Q2
- Increase compensation of supply professionals to reflect the increased value they provide, Q4
- Study implications of purchasing Ariba, Q3

Figure 28.7 I Goals and Initiatives for Year One

"I plan to hire an executive assistant whose primary purpose will be to monitor these initiatives and help me utilize project management techniques to manage the processes to ensure timely action. Ladies and gentlemen: It's Wine Time!"

Rosalind Hall, director of Supply Management at the Test Division, sighed, "Oh, darn, I'd been looking forward to an eggnog latté."

Bringing the Troops Onside

It's the second Monday in January of the following year. You have decided to honor Megatronics' decentralized divisional status and have chosen to meet with all members of the supply management system, division by division. At 8 A.M., you step onto the stage of the 250-seat auditorium at the Holiday Inn, Redondo Beach, California. The room is nearly full. Elaine T., your predecessor, introduces you. You begin, "Ladies and gentlemen, I'm delighted to be here and honored to have been selected to lead you in the transformation of Megatronics purchasing to World Class Supply Management^{SM} status. We have the potential and the power to help Megatronics achieve greatness. To help you understand the road we must travel, I'm going to ask you to spend the next 10 minutes reviewing the chart describing the progression to World Class Supply Management^{SM} portrayed on page 2 of the brochure each of you received on entering the auditorium and rate our relative status on the chart. Please be honest and objective in your ratings." (See again Figure 28.4 on page 650.)

After 10 minutes, your executive assistant, Kerry Kilber, turns the projector on so that the step chart is legible to all. You continue, "Okay, let's see where we are on the road to world-class status. Any 10s? (Silence and a bit of restlessness.) Any 9s or 8s? (One timid hand.) Any 7s? (Five more hands.) Any 6s? (Twelve hands.) Any 5s? (Thirty or more hands.) Any 4s? (Perhaps 80 hands.) Okay, I'll assume that the rest of you feel that we're 3s. Now, you might ask, 'So what?' How many of you think that your job is to push papers? (A few uncomfortable titters.) How many of you think that your job is to chase parts? (Several expediters raise their hands.) How many of you spend a significant amount of your time resolving discrepancies with accounts payable? (Thirty or more hands.) How many of you think that your job is to beat your suppliers' prices down? (Twenty-five half-raised arms.) How many of you visit your suppliers other than to expedite? (Ten hands.) How many of you think that your job is to increase sales? (No hands, but many puzzled looks.)

"Again, thanks for your honesty! Now, let's turn to page 3 in your brochure. (Please see again Figure 28-5 on page 651 portraying supply management's contributions to our net income.) Ladies and gentlemen, our sole reason for existence is to improve Megatronics' bottom line. Let's look at our impact on sales. Some 75 percent of our field failures can be traced back to purchased materials. Our current incoming defect rate is over 1,000 defects per million. This is not surprising since purchased materials represent over 75 percent of all direct costs! Think of the impact on our sales of reducing this incoming defect rate to 50 ppm. Think of the cost savings to our colleagues in customer service. As we gain image as the quality leader, our share of the market will grow and our bottom line will improve significantly through additional profitable sales.

"Now, let's look at our role in bringing new technology in to our design people. When Bill and Dave laid the foundation for this firm some 60 years ago, they were pretty well self-contained, technologically speaking. Today, industry analysts indicate that our competitors attribute an average of 35 percent of their new products to technology received from their suppliers. These same analysts estimate our technology infusion at less than 20 percent. As we change our focus during sourcing from price to total cost of ownership, quality and technology, and as we build trusting relations with our key suppliers, I expect to see enormous growth in the number of successful, profitable new products based on supplier technology. As you probably know, the highest profit margins flow to the first firm to market a product meeting customer needs. We can and must become that firm!

"Next, let me turn to the issue of continuity of supply. Barbara Withers, your vice president of Operations at Corporate, has spoken of the problems, challenges, and frustrations she and her people at division face because of the late arrival of materials. Not only do late shipments result in challenges for our operations department, but they also lead to late deliveries to our customers. Dissatisfied customers soon take their business elsewhere! Better, more dependable suppliers, better-understanding suppliers, and more-trusting supplier relations are the keys to this one. Every late shipment should generate an action item identifying planned and completed corrective action. Both your department manager, Barbara, and I want to see these action items."

You had planned on discussing some of supply management's other impacts on sales, but decide that this might be overkill at this time. Maybe in six months. You next address the bottom half of Figure 28.5, the cost component of supply management's impact on the bottom line. Recognizing the danger of information overload, you say, "You'll notice that page 3 identifies 10 cost drivers, ranging from purchase price to post-ownership costs. If you don't mind, we won't go into these components of the total cost of ownership today, other than to say that we want you to start thinking and acting TCO, not purchase price, from this day on! Now, let's take a twenty minute break for a cup of coffee."

During the break, you and Susan Reese mingle and try to take the group's pulse. Comments range from "This guy's got to be smoking some of California's finest," to "Wow! This really excites me!"

After the twenty-minute break (which always takes longer), you reconvene the meeting. "Last month, the four divisional directors of supply, David Wind from my staff, Professor Zinke of UCBS, and I hammered out a vision statement of what supply management must become if Megatronics is to regain its position as number one in the industry. Let's take a look at our vision statement." (The screen comes to life and everyone reads: "Supply management at Megatronics will perfect its worldwide process resulting in totally delighted customers and shareholders.") (See again Figure 28.6 on page 652.)

"Let's take this vision to the next stage and describe our mission statement." The screen then displays:

Mission Statement: Megatronics Supply Management System

We will design and implement necessary processes and cultural changes to create a fully integrated customer driven supply management system. We will integrate suppliers into our business plans and processes in an environment of respect and trust, establish full cooperation throughout the enterprise, and establish supply management as a core competency. We will improve the bottom line by facilitating increased profitable sales while minimizing the total cost of ownership of all materials, equipment, supplies, and services. We will ensure that diversity suppliers have opportunities to play vital roles in our supply base."

You continue: "Before we go any further, let me assure you that we have developed a world-class transformational training program to be conducted by UCBS and the

Strategic Supply Management Institute, Ltd. You will be given the tools to become world-class supply managers. A considerable part of your training will focus on cross-functional teams. Whenever possible, you will be trained in a cross-functional team mode with colleagues from engineering, operations, quality, legal, and others, as appropriate. This training also will be available to key suppliers on a no-cost basis. Sign-up sheets for seven sections of the first two-day workshop are outside. There will be five additional modules, one per month. The training program is both extensive and exhaustive. On completion of the basic and then advanced training, we hope to sponsor several of you to participate in USD's two-year Master of Science in Supply Chain Management program. After another twenty minute fruit and veggie break, I'd like to describe briefly our strategic initiatives for this year."

This time, the break takes only twenty-five minutes. "Last November, our supply management executive team met to establish the vision statement and mission statements which you've seen this morning. We committed to the following goals and initiatives shown on the screen: [See again Figure 28.7 on page 661.]

"One last thing, we are attempting to develop a model 'rewards' system and sincerely solicit your thoughts. It probably will take several months to develop a refined system that HR and the corporate executive committee will bless, but we believe in recognizing and rewarding your contributions. I'm going to ask Sam Hardy to initiate a corporatewide monthly newsletter wherein we can share our success stories.

"Thank you for your attention. Now, as we move to the banquet room for a bit of sustenance, you'll realize that there truly is no such thing as a 'free lunch'!"

The following week, you repeat similar programs in Dallas, Texas; Jerome, Arizona; and Waltham, Massachusetts.

The following Monday, you meet with CEO Francis Lazarus and the executive committee. They seem to be awed by your plans and initiatives. There is unanimous support of both. You discuss the need for Six Sigma training at corporate and divisional levels. After considerable discussion, you and Barbara Withers, vice president of Operations, are charged with the responsibility of implementing appropriate training. The program is to commence in March.

In June, you begin poking around Megatronics' outsourcing process. You quickly recognize that there are both immediate and strategic icebergs floating in the sea of outsourcing. Discussions, first with the vice presidents of operations and finance, confirm both the dangers and the opportunities present. You are appointed director of Outsourcing at the next meeting of the executive committee. You immediately hire your former colleague, Lee Buddress, to develop, institute, and manage a comprehensive outsourcing program.

In November, you, your executive team, and Professor Zinke meet for a two-day retreat in Dana Point. Although final results will not be available until next January, it appears that both goals will be met or exceeded. With the dramatic improvements in the capabilities of the workforce, it is easy to "ratchet" your goals up. The group's attention then is focused on the development of statements of supply management's strategic intent and the strategic plan for next year. Based on demonstrated success, it is easy to agree in principle, but challenging to wordsmith the two statements. The promise of adjourning to the Whaler for dinner spurs things on and the group reaches agreement on the statements portrayed in Figure 28.8 and 28.9.

Our *global supply chain* will be *unequaled in performance* and one of Megatronics' *greatest competitive advantages.* Carrying out this strategic intent requires:

- An optimized, leveraged, and responsive global supplier base and an efficient supply chain between all Megatronics entities, our suppliers, and their suppliers.

- Unequaled performance as measured by A. T. Kearney and as compared to competition and best-in-class companies by 2007.

- A supply chain that creates new business opportunities for Megatronics by providing an outlet for marketing our best practices to suppliers, our sales force, and others, and by allowing us to bring suppliers' innovations to Megatronics' new markets.

Supply Management is to be a competitive advantage for current Megatronics businesses and all new growth initiatives. Our processes, employees, suppliers, and business results will demonstrate significant value for the business, for customers, and for shareholders.

Figure 28.8 | Strategic Intent

Supply Management plays a critical role in Megatronics' ability to serve its customers and thereby meet its growth and financial targets. Fulfilling its role requires that the Supply Management organization be clear about its objectives and have a strategy for achieving them in an uncertain business environment.

The business environment consists of external events and trends that affect our enterprise. These external factors have a profound effect on how we serve our customers. As we identify and understand customer needs, we will manage all resources and processes to satisfy them.

By carrying out our Strategic Plan, we will meet or exceed the corporate goal of a 12 percent return on assets (ROA) through the full business cycle. To achieve this level of performance, Supply Management will improve its business-partner and supply-chain focus and become more process driven through a Leadership Process that will allow the organization to respond rapidly to changing business conditions.

This plan is based on knowledgeable estimates of future business conditions and current conceptions of efficient processes. Change, however, is inevitable and unpredictable. The Supply Management organization, guided by the Leadership Process, will swiftly and efficiently alter these processes as needed to better meet the changing needs of our customers, the Megatronics enterprise, and our suppliers.

This plan is also based on fundamental Supply Management requirements:

- To better serve the customer, there must be a shift from a traditional functional organization to an enterprise-focused supply chain management effort that is aligned with business processes.

- To meet business partner and supply chain requirements, we must understand customer requirements and improve our business processes.

- Besides our own processes, suppliers' processes have a great impact on our ability to serve customers. We rely on our supply base to provide high-quality and low-total-cost components, assemblies, goods, and services. Supplier processes must be integrated into the product delivery and order fulfillment processes.

Figure 28.9 | Strategic Plan

More Initiatives

On Friday, the group congratulated itself on the two statements and then moved on to the development of the following goals and initiatives shown in Figure 28.10. The goals and the supporting initiatives will become supply management's strategic plan and will be input to Megatronics' corporate strategic plan.

Your group then focused on initiatives that will support your goals. You have been duly impressed with the initiatives undertaken by Megatronics' supply management personnel as a direct result of their transformational training. Over half of next year's initiatives are already being introduced at the team level by one or more teams.

Goals:
- Reduce average price of incoming goods and services by 5 percent
- Reduce average incoming defects by 50 percent to 450 ppm
- Reduce average time required to develop a new product by 10 percent
- Reduce production disruptions due to late delivery of materials by 50 percent
- Increase the number of new products based on supplier-furnished technology by 10 percent
- Decrease the supply base by 15 percent
- Increase award of production contracts to diversity suppliers to 5 percent

Initiatives:
- Develop a world-class information system, Q3
- Document, verify, and track cost savings, Q1
- Implement value engineering and value analysis programs, Q1
- Develop or hire a cadre of 8 cost engineers, Q2–3
- Develop 14 corporatewide commodity teams, Q2–3
- Expand strategic sourcing to all commodity classes, Q4
- Initiate creation of a global supplier network, Q3
- Open an Asian international procurement office, Q4
- Develop an internal Megatronics-wide education program for understanding and managing supplier diversity, Q2
- Develop a recognition program for suppliers embracing Megatronics' pollution avoidance program, Q3
- Increase supplier development efforts, ongoing
- Develop four new supplier alliances, Q4
- Increase integration of suppliers into the development process, ongoing
- Develop Web-based applications to link suppliers with Megatronics, Q1
- Analyze supply management skills systematically
- Conduct training to upgrade personnel to required levels, ongoing
- Develop leadership from within, ongoing
- Implement a college recruiting leadership program, Q1
- Recruit best candidates to fill entry-level and mid-career openings, ongoing
- Ensure clear employee performance goals, Q2
- Provide career development opportunities, ongoing
- Implement rewards and incentive plan for members of supply management system, Q2
- Ensure retention of promising employees, ongoing
- Integrate supply management, logistics, and demand management, Q3
- Increase compensation of supply professionals, Q4

Figure 28.10 | Goals and Initiatives for Year Two

The Executive Board reviewed supply management's accomplishments and updated plans at its January meeting. You felt acceptance and respect. It was time to propose a more cross-functional approach to change at Megatronics. You summarized Carlos Ghosen's 1999 and 2000 experience in turning Nissan around and the critical role played by cross-functional teams.[6] You pointed out that your supply management team was making great progress, but, all too often, progress was blocked or impeded by functional silos.[7] You proposed bringing Dr. David Lehmann, vice president of Operations, Solar (retired), in to address the topic at the next Executive Board meeting. There was agreement by all members.

The Board's next meeting focused on change and the possible role of cross-functional teams in the change process. Dr. Lehmann was retained to develop an appropriate program. He reported directly to the Chairman and President. The program was a resounding success and resulted in positive changes that went beyond your wildest dreams. Resistance to necessary change down through middle management throughout Megatronics began to dissipate.

During the first half of the year, it became apparent that the functional silo mentality of the logistics and demand management personnel was blocking your efforts to integrate these functions with supply management. Several senior level discussions resulted in supply management, logistics, and demand management being integrated into a new organization known as Supply Chain Management under your leadership. The transformation and integration of these three activities was both challenging and satisfying. The board also agreed that your de facto reporting relationship with the operating divisions be ratified: You officially have line authority over all supply management personnel. The anticipated benefits started flowing almost immediately!

Lastly, you announced to the board that the total number of employees in supply chain management now was less than one-half of the over 800 you had inherited from purchasing in 2002 plus the 80 you recently acquired from demand management and logistics. . . .

It's now November of the following year. The planning meeting is in Palm Springs. Your group has been enlarged to include a senior logistician from one of the divisions and a demand manager from another. Year-to-date results look great.

You introduce a topic about which you feel very strongly: the Toyota supplier family. "It is my belief that one of the fastest and best ways of driving Megatronics' supply management to the next level is to borrow from Toyota the idea of supplier families. These families are closely integrated networks. Best practices are shared and implemented. The impact on cost, quality, time to market, continuity of supply . . . heck, on everything, is awesome. I'd like to be personally involved in initiating this program with our first alliance partner, Diapole International."

There is enthusiastic endorsement of your idea! Knowing that the full benefits of early supplier and early supply management involvement are really kicking in, the group agrees on the goals shown in Figure 28.11. Once again, over half of next year's initiatives are a direct result of your investment in transformational training. Empowerment works!

---

[6]Carlos Ghosen, "Saving the Business without Losing the Company," *Harvard Business Review,* January 2002, pp. 37–45.

[7]The term "functional silo" is used in industry to describe how functions, such as marketing, finance and engineering, often do not work with other functional areas toward the greater good of the firm.

Goals:
- Reduce average price of incoming goods and services by 5 percent
- Reduce incoming defects by 50% to an average of 225 ppm
- Improve forecast accuracy to ±5 percent for 30 days and ±10 percent for 30–120 days

Initiatives:
- Develop 10 new supplier alliances, Q4
- Document, verify, track, and control savings, Q1
- Increase purchases from diversity suppliers to 6 percent of production materials, Q2
- Initiate one supplier family (à la Toyota) by a key first-tier supplier, Q3
- Initiate 20 quality teams, four operating groups, Q4
- Develop 16 new commodity teams, Q2
- Integrate inbound and outbound traffic, Q3
- Upgrade order and fulfillment processes, Q1
- Go global on all aspects of supply chain management, Q1
- Introduce "lean" into Megatronics' supply chain, Q2
- Optimize use of the Internet, Q3
- Increase emphasis on contract and relationship management, ongoing
- Provide ethics training to all in-house members of supply chain management system, Q2
- Focus negotiation training on synergy with suppliers, Q2
- Conduct debriefings addressing "lessons learned" on all negotiations, Q1
- Study implications of employing other than firm fixed price compensation, Q2

Figure 28.11 I Goals and Initiatives for Year Three

In November of the following year you are in Maui. Ah, the joys of success! But what a price! David Wind has taken the CSO position at H-P. Sam has moved to Cisco as CSO. Susan has become your deputy and heir-apparent, having turned down several lucrative offers. JoAnn Barber has moved to Sommers, New York, where she has become V.P., Global Supply Management (her friend and colleague, Rose Layo, has moved to Raleigh, where she has become Director of Supply Chain Management). Paul Wilson has become a full-time minister. Jason Patel has become CSO for Freightliner. Rosalind Hall is completing her Ph.D. at Claremont. Professor Zinke has retired to his wine estate in the Barossa Valley outside of Adelaide, South Australia. Fortunately, your training, education, and career progression programs have minimized the impact of the departure of these wonderful people. You have been able to fill every vacancy from your existing staff.

In preparation for this year's meeting, you have invited Professor Zinke's protege, Stephen Smith, to join the group as "academic-in-residence." After a wonderful light breakfast on the lanai, you and your new team get down to business by addressing goals for the following year. You agree on the goals shown in Figure 28.12.

After lunch, the group tees off and plays a round at Maui's finest golf course. This is pure business, since you had charged the group to come up with 15 initiatives the next day. The evening's luau is somewhat disappointing, although the mai-tai's are delightful, and the entertainment provocative.

You begin the next day's meeting by observing: "When we have completed development of a list of initiatives for next year, we're done with the formal part of our agenda."

Being highly motivated, the group agrees on the initiatives shown in Figure 28.12.

Goals:

- Reduce total cost of ownership on incoming goods and services by 5 percent
- Reduce average incoming defects by over 50 percent to an average of 110 ppm
- Develop 17 new supplier alliances
- Increase purchases from diversity suppliers to 6.5 percent of production materials
- Increase number of firms embracing Megatronics' pollution avoidance program to 53
- Globalize pollution avoidance program
- Add 2 supplier families
- Improve forecast accuracy to ±4 percent for 30 days and ±8 percent for 120 days

Initiatives:

- Champion the firm's pursuit of the Malcolm Baldrige Award by developing a three-year plan, Q2
- Develop and deploy a new metric measuring institutional trust, Q2
- Implement a program of integrated financial transaction work flows coupled with tax effective supply chain management practices, Q3
- Develop and implement supply chain scorecards, Q3
- Implement an aggressive publicity program, corporatewide Q4
- Reward 50 percent of savings documented from VA programs to suppliers, Q1
- Replace long-winded contracts with short ones whose intent is to promote teamwork, ongoing
- Experiment with allowing suppliers to construct their own contracts on our website, Q2
- Establish supply management as a recognized competency corporatewide, ongoing
- Integrate supply chain management planning tightly with other systems at all levels, ongoing
- Align Strategic Sourcing strategies across the enterprise, ongoing
- Optimize global logistics operations (inbound and outbound), ongoing
- Develop a globally integrated order fulfillment process, Q1
- Set consistent performance standards, Q2
- Communicate expectations and feedback results to suppliers, Q2
- Expand Megatronics' supplier network around the globe, ongoing
- Enable suppliers to interact seamlessly within Megatronics, ongoing
- Support strategic sourcing, supplier integration, product delivery and order fulfillment processes with timely and effective cost/financial information, Q3
- Utilize supplier development to transform the supply chain toward lean manufacturing, maximum flexibility, reduced cycle times, improved quality, and reduced overall total cost in the supply chain, ongoing
- Integrate the supply chain into the technology delivery process, ongoing
- Integrate e-Commerce II processes with all the key processes to enable better integration and strategic planning, Q3
- Develop worldwide purchase data gathering and sharing capabilities, ongoing
- Provide needed education and training, globally, across the enterprise and enable distance learning, ongoing
- Provide meaningful work, challenging assignments, and development opportunities, ongoing
- Develop individual development and succession plans, ongoing
- Identify common activities and roles where redundancies can be eliminated, ongoing
- Identify and optimize synergies across the supply chain, ongoing
- Identify and develop business marketplaces enabling supply chain leverage and synergy, ongoing

Figure 28.12 | Goals and Initiatives for Year Four

January 2006

It's January 2006, four and a half years since you were hired as Vice President of Supply Management. Megatronics' stock has increased five-fold during your tenure. You enter your new office. You get a thrill out of the sign on your new door: Office of the President and Chief Executive Officer. During a series of discussions in your first month with the V.P., Supply Chain Management, and her managers in your former organization and then with your corporate board, you have taken advantage of your honeymoon and reorganized. Susan Reese has officially been given a new title and additional responsibilities. She is the Vice President of Supply Chain Management. The new organization is depicted in Figure 28.13.

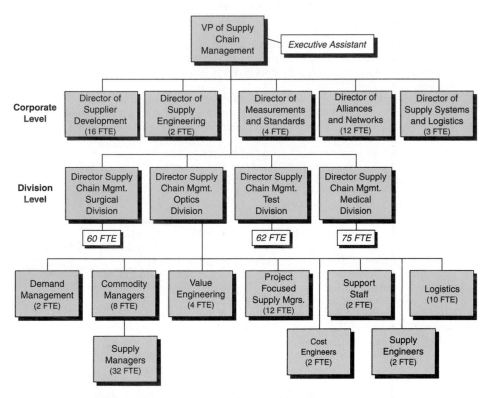

Figure 28.13 | Megatronics Corporation Representative Supply Chain Management Organization, March 2, 2006

Concluding Remarks

Implementing World Class Supply Management^SM and World Class Supply Chain Management is as much about leadership and management as it is about supply management concepts and practices. Transformational-based training and education play essential roles. The pace of change must be based on the principle: "Stretch, but don't break."

Based on its integrative, relationship, and boundary spanning nature, there is no question in our minds: "World-class supply managers have the essential skill set to become Chief Executive Officers!"

NAME INDEX

SUBJECT INDEX